CANADIAN CINEMA SINCE THE 1980s

At the Heart of the World

Award-winning author David L. Pike offers a unique focus on the crucial quarter-century in Canadian film-making when the industry became a viable force on the international stage. Pike provides a lively, personal, and accessible history of the most influential film-makers and movements of both Anglo-Canadian and Quebecois cinema, from popular movies to art film and everything in between.

Along with in-depth studies of key directors, including David Cronenberg, Patricia Rozema, Denys Arcand, Jean-Claude Lauzon, Robert Lepage, Léa Pool, Atom Egoyan, and Guy Maddin, *Canadian Cinema since the 1980s* reflects on major themes and genres and explores the regional and cultural diversity of the period. Pike positions Canadian film-making at the front lines of a profound cinematic transformation in the age of global media and presents fresh perspectives on its local and international contexts. Making a significant advance in the study of the film industry of the period, *Canadian Cinema since the 1980s* is also an ideal text for students, researchers, and Canadian film enthusiasts.

DAVID L. PIKE is a professor in the Department of Literature at American University.

DAVID L. PIKE

Canadian Cinema since the 1980s

At the Heart of the World

UNIVERSITY OF TORONTO PRESS
Toronto Buffalo London

© University of Toronto Press 2012
Toronto Buffalo London
www.utppublishing.com
Printed in Canada

ISBN 978-1-4426-4399-4 (cloth)
ISBN 978-1-4426-1240-2 (paper)

Printed on acid-free, 100% post-consumer recycled paper with vegetable-based inks.

Library and Archives Canada Cataloguing in Publication

Pike, David L. (David Lawrence), 1963–
Canadian cinema since the 1980s : at the heart of the world / David L. Pike.

Includes bibliographical references and index.
ISBN 978-1-4426-4399-4 (bound)   ISBN 978-1-4426-1240-2 (pbk.)

1. Motion pictures – Canada – History and criticism.   2. Motion picture producers
and directors – Canada.   I. Title.

PN1993.5.C3P49 2012   791.430971   C2012-902008-7

University of Toronto Press acknowledges the financial assistance to its publishing
program of the Canada Council for the Arts and the Ontario Arts Council.

 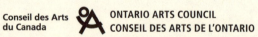

This book has been published with the help of a grant from the Canadian Federation
for the Humanities and Social Sciences, through the Awards to Scholarly Publications
Program, using funds provided by the Social Sciences and Humanities Research
Council of Canada.

University of Toronto Press acknowledges the financial support of the Government of
Canada through the Canada Book Fund for its publishing activities.

Contents

List of Illustrations   vii

Preface   ix

Acknowledgments   xv

List of Abbreviations   xvii

Introduction: What Is Canadian Cinema and What Happened to It at the End of the Twentieth Century?   3

1 Canadian Cinema 1896–1986: Invisibility and Difference   17

2 The Anxiety of Influence: David Cronenberg and the Canadian Imagination   48

3 Time Capsules: The Eighties Worlds of Denys Arcand and Patricia Rozema   79

4 Crossover Icons: The Faces of Canadian Cinema   107

5 Quebecois Auteurs: The New Internationalism of Jean-Claude Lauzon, Léa Pool, and Robert Lepage   144

6 Cronenberg's Mutant Progeny: Genre Film-making around the Turn of the Millennium   171

7 The Death of the Author? The Case of Atom Egoyan   204

8 The Canadian Mosaic: Margins and Ethnicities   227

9 Film-Making at the Heart of the World: Guy Maddin   267

Conclusion   284

Notes   289

Works Cited   317

Index   337

Illustrations

1.1 Publicity for *Back to God's Country* (1919)   21

1.2 *La petite Aurore* (1951)   25

1.3 *Neighbours* (1952)   29

1.4 The haunting freeze-frame that concludes *Mon oncle Antoine* (1971)   38

1.5 *Goin' Down the Road* (1970)   42

2.1 *Shivers* (1975)   49

2.2 The final scene of *Crash* (1996)   74

3.1 The unusual perspective of *White Room* (1990)   82

3.2 The glowing box in *I've Heard the Mermaids Singing* (1987)   86

3.3 The Université de Montréal in *Le Déclin de l'empire américain* (1986)   95

3.4 The aging ensemble cast of *Les Invasions barbares* (2003)   103

4.1 Geneviève Bujold during rehearsals for the 1971 Academy Awards   112

4.2 The ageless singer/director/actor Carole Laure at the 2006 Cannes Film Festival   115

4.3 Pascale Bussières and Roy Dupuis celebrate their wins at the 2005 Genie Awards   120

4.4 Callum Keith Rennie and Molly Parker at the premiere of their third film together, *Trigger* (2010)   127

4.5 Sandra Oh as Madame Ming in *The Red Violin* (1998)   130

4.6 Mia Kirshner, eternally the ingénue, in *The L Word*   133

4.7 Wealthy heiress Sara Stanley (Sarah Polley) in the first episode of *Road to Avonlea* (1990)   136

4.8 Sarah Polley in *Dawn of the Dead* (2004)   137

5.1 The opening shot of *Léolo* (1992)   151

5.2 Paulie (Piper Perabo) and Tori (Jessica Paré) in *Lost and Delirious* (2001)   161

5.3 The iconic concluding shot of the Quebec Bridge in *Le Confessionnal* (1995)   169

6.1 Monique Mercure in *Naked Lunch* (1991)   177

6.2 The high-concept teaser credit-sequence of *Ginger Snaps* (2000)   189

6.3 The minimalist and elegantly versatile set of *Cube* (1997)   199

7.1 Two irretrievable moments of the past in *Exotica* (1994): the pixilated video image of the lost wife and child   215

7.2 Two irretrievable moments of the past in *Exotica* (1994): the achingly beauti-
     ful green fields where Eric and Christina will soon discover a body   215
8.1 Life on the road in *Hard Core Logo* (1996)   230
8.2 Playing with the cityscape of Calgary in *waydowntown* (2000)   240
8.3 Peter-Henry Arnatsiaq, who plays the villainous Oki in *Atanarjuat: The Fast
     Runner* (2001)   255
9.1 The Winnipeg revolutionary strike in *My Winnipeg* (2007)   276

Preface

It is difficult to imagine what cinema was like in the mid-eighties if you didn't live through it. When I was a teenager in Kentucky during the late seventies, there were Lucas, Spielberg, and old movies late at night on network TV. The only alternative cinema that made it to Louisville was cult films like *Harold and Maude* and *The Magic Christian*, and Euro-film-lite like Zeffirelli's biopic of St Francis of Assisi, *Brother Sun, Sister Moon*. When I got to college, popular and art cinema were still considered to be worlds apart from one another, as were Hollywood and Europe. We studied the modernist classics of Bergman, Dreyer, and Renoir, and the only new movies we watched were German, French, and avant-garde. Narrative was acceptable only if it wasn't linear, and any form of viewing pleasure was inherently suspect. And, to be honest, Hollywood cinema was *lousy*, and it was lousy because, more than anything else, it was boring. The brat pack directors were resurrecting genre, but most of the results were enough to give genre a bad name, unless you were still a teenybopper, and I was already too old to appreciate the subtleties of John Hughes, *The Breakfast Club*, and *Sixteen Candles*.

Enter Canadian cinema. Not as a concept, and not as boosterism. I discovered Canadian cinema as a young American cinephile looking for something new, something to break the mould. It was 1986. I had just moved to New York City for graduate school, and I went with my film friends to see the new movie that had the city all abuzz, playing first run to long lines on the Upper West Side. Remember, serious cinephiles *never* went to first-run cinema back then; for us, it was all commercial tripe. But Denys Arcand's *Le Déclin de l'empire américain* simply blew our minds. It wasn't just seeing a gay man as a fully realized character allowed to interact with straights, and it wasn't just seeing the spectre of AIDS appear as a fact of life, part of the plot (and yes, this character now appears dated and stereotyped – more on that in chapter 3 – but he certainly didn't seem that way to us back then). It had a funny, literate, vicious, and ultimately, terribly sad script. It had adult dialogue full of sex and bursting with ideas. It had consummate ensemble acting. It moved like old Hollywood but it felt like new France. It was sublime.

1987. The Little Theater in Rochester, New York, the kind of cinema that showed whatever managed to squeak out of Hollywood with something resembling an adult appeal (say, an Alan Rudolph film starring Geneviève Bujold) and whatever the distributors at New Yorker Films brought over from Europe (think *Diva*).

Visiting my mother, I took her to see Patricia Rozema's *I Heard the Mermaids Singing*, released by the then-unknown distributor Miramax. It was sweet, quirky, and made me feel good without feeling guilty about it. I certainly didn't connect either Arcand's or Rozema's film with Canada at the time, but in retrospect, these films were harbingers of a tectonic shift in world cinema. Genre was very slowly being reinvented as an artistically viable concept, independent film-makers were starting to reconnect pleasure with attitude, and American directors were realizing they could mix the avant-garde with the commercial without a priori selling out. Proto-independent films such as Susan Seidelman's new wave feminist screwball comedy *Desperately Seeking Susan* (1985) and David Lynch's intensely over-the-top neo-noir *Blue Velvet* (1986) brought the margins into the mainstream while their retro attitude also made it cool to watch old movies again. Spaniard Pedro Almodóvar's first career peak brought *Matador* (1986), *Law of Desire* (1987), and *Women on the Verge of a Nervous Breakdown* (1988) with a seductive combination of melodrama, new queer cinema, and underground culture that unabashedly appropriated classic Hollywood genres to make sense of the strange new world of the eighties.

So for me, Canadian cinema was not at first *Canadian* cinema. It was part of a larger trend that meant that suddenly there were exciting movies to see in the first-run cinemas; I didn't only have to hunt them out in the museums and repertory theatres (these were, not coincidentally, in their last hurrah, soon to be killed by that still novel product, the VCR). It was only in the early nineties that something recognizably Canadian started to emerge for me from the general pack of new things. 1990: I rushed to see *Jésus de Montréal* the moment it opened, and Arcand's follow-up to *Déclin* did not disappoint. 1991: I happened to be in London when Srinivas Krishna's satirically and absurdly Canadian refraction of the still obscure Bollywood industry took the city by storm. 1992: Atom Egoyan's *The Adjuster* opened at the Lincoln Plaza Cinema, the flagship mainstream art cinema in New York (I had missed it when it played at the festival the previous year). It was a weird film, but nothing like Guy Maddin's *Careful* and Jean-Claude Lauzon's *Léolo*, which played across Broadway in Lincoln Center at the New York Film Festival the same year. I've become accustomed to Egoyan and Maddin over the years (an opportunity sadly unavailable to Lauzon, who never made another film), but when I first encountered these films, it was as if they demanded a whole new way of watching movies that I would have to learn on the fly. I will never forget Maddin himself onstage after the festival screening, wholly convincing in the persona of the mad eccentric just released from weeks locked up in an editing room in the frozen north. Nor will I forget Egoyan on the same stage two years later, fielding questions with his pregnant wife Arsinée Khanjian, consummate Toronto intellectuals, articulate and unflappable even when asked by an audience member if they could provide the address of the Exotica club in Toronto.

During this same period, David Cronenberg emerged as a force that could plausibly be connected with this group of younger film-makers. Cronenberg had hovered at the edge of my consciousness for years, ever since I had heard kids in high school back in 1981 discussing the exploding head in *Scanners* in awed tones. And *Videodrome* had a lot of cachet in the downtown art scene in the mid-eighties, partly because it remained decidedly disreputable. But exploitation was truly another world back then. I had a college friend and classmate, Steven Shareshian, who was then a film accountant (he would go on to become a successful producer; among his credits is the Chicago-set 'Canadian' indie blockbuster *My Big Fat Greek Wedding*). Steven told me confidentially that he was working on the new Jonathan Demme movie. He couldn't tell me anything about it, but it was a slasher movie. We couldn't believe it. New York hipster Demme (he had just made *Something Wild* and *Married to the Mob*) selling out? Impossible. But after *Silence of the Lambs* broke, the rules and boundaries changed pretty fast. Cronenberg hit my radar as a serious director in 1991 with *Naked Lunch*. And when *Crash* was released in 1996, I had the good fortune to be in Paris. The film was on the cover of every movie magazine, headlined at every important cinema in the city, and hit number one in the box office. It was an event.

It became easier and easier to recognize and to see Canadian movies, and there were still plenty of them worth seeing. Rozema's lesbian romance, *When Night Is Falling* (1995), cleverly niche marketed, was an art-house hit; Jeremy Podeswa's *Eclipse* (1994) played commercially the same year to similar audiences, as did his follow-up, *The Five Senses*, five years later. Film series and retrospectives began to pop up also, filling in the gaps in our knowledge and showing classics as yet unreleased on video. In a Dupont Circle multiplex in Washington, DC, I saw Deepa Mehta's *Fire* in 1997. The same year, in the same location, with great trepidation, I went to see Egoyan's *The Sweet Hereafter*. By now, I *was* a booster, and I was suspicious of non-Canuck star Ian Holm; I was suspicious of non-Canuck Russell Banks's source novel; I was suspicious of the film's multiplex anonymity. But, amazingly, Egoyan pulled it off. And when the Inuktituk epic *Atanarjuat: The Fast Runner* (2001) played for months on end at a Bethesda mall in 2002, I knew Canadian cinema had arrived, and that in arriving it had helped create a new cinematic landscape around it.

But it was not long after seeing *Atanarjuat* that I also realized that what I had come to see as Canadian cinema was no longer comfortable in the very cinematic landscape it had contributed so much to creating. Egoyan's movies after *The Sweet Hereafter* no longer did for me what they had done before; he seemed stuck in a rut. Rozema's *Mansfield Park* left me lukewarm, but nothing compared to her recent American Girl movie, *Kit Kittredge: An American Girl*. The tectonic plates had shifted again in the new millennium, or perhaps they had finally settled back into place after fifteen years of disruption. Canadian films still play in New York, of course, every few months or so, but they are once more for the most part anonymous; other key films go straight to cable – the fate of Jean-Marc Vallée's *C.R.A.Z.Y.* (2005), one of the best and most popular films made in Quebec over the past decade – or to DVD, the route taken by recent Quebecois film-makers such as Denis Villeneuve and André Turpin. There are now hundreds of Canadian films available on Internet lenders such as Netflix, but you won't find many of them indexed under 'Canada' – they are all over the map and you have to seek them out, one by one.

I include this personal history to suggest the contours of the broader reception of Canadian cinema beyond its borders, but also to identify my own paradoxically marginal/central position as an American academic approaching Canadian cinema from the outside. Throughout this book, I have taken a triple perspective towards this material: as a moviegoer (I have defined the corpus I discuss primarily in terms of distribution, by the fact that nearly all of the films mentioned were first seen by me in a commercial cinema outside Canada, or more recently, on DVD), as a film scholar who finds in Canadian cinema between 1985 and the turn of the millennium a compelling model for a narrative cinema that would be critical, aesthetically engaging, and accessible, and as teacher of Canadian cinema to primarily American students, some of whom were already fans of a particular director (primarily Egoyan and Cronenberg) but most of whom had not seen or were not aware that they had ever seen a single Canadian film. Like all subject positions, mine is a partial and compromised one, but I believe that its partialities and compromises well complement the insider's perspective characteristic of Canadian cinema studies as a field. And although I do not eschew the questions of quality that tend to dominate the latter perspective, I am particularly interested in the intersection between artistic artefacts and the marketplace since, after all, the film industry as a whole constitutes a particularly high-profile example of such an intersection.

I wrote this book because I wanted to make sense, and to help students, scholars, and fans make sense, of the arc of Canadian cinema over the past twenty-five years, of its key place in the changing landscape of world cinema during those same years, and of what it can tell us about film-making today. Canadian cinema was at the forefront of a profound transformation in the economics, the form, and indeed, the very identity of world cinema. And because of the unique position it occupied, it also produced some extraordinary films, for Canadian cinema underwent a veritable golden age in the fifteen years between the mid-eighties and the beginning of the new millennium. In 1984, Micheline Lanctôt's powerful drama *Sonatine* won the Silver Lion at the Venice Film Festival and launched the acting career of Pascale Bussières; along with Léa Pool's award-winning *La femme de l'hôtel*, *Sonatine* announced a new feminist presence in Quebecois cinema. Atom Egoyan released his first two features in 1984 and 1987. When Arcand's *Déclin* set local box office records and was nominated for an Academy Award in 1986, Rozema's *Mermaids* became a sleeper hit the following year and, along with Lauzon's scabrously brilliant *Un zoo, la nuit* (1987), stunned the folks at Cannes, a Canadian new wave was officially underway. The late 1990s marked the peak of this wave; in retrospect, they also saw a sea change in the identity of Canadian cinema. In 1997, Egoyan's *Sweet Hereafter* was feted at the Cannes Film Festival and nominated for two Academy Awards; the previous year, Cronenberg's controversial *Crash* had received a special jury prize at Cannes, and three years later he became the first Canadian to head the festival's jury. Meanwhile, the directors most prominent in the English-Canadian new wave of the late eighties were now leading Canadian cinema in a new direction, towards international co-production and broad distribution. The same phenomenon occurred in Quebec, where, in 1999, Léa Pool's Franco/Swiss co-produced homage to the French new wave, *Emporte-moi*, won awards at festivals in Berlin, Chicago, Sarajevo, Toronto, and Valladolid, Arcand shot *Stardom* (2000) in English with Anglo-Canadian Hollywood star Dan Ackroyd and French star Charles Berling in key supporting roles, and Robert Lepage (who had a key acting role in *Stardom*) filmed *Possible Worlds* in English with Brit art-film icon Tilda Swinton (2000). *Stardom*'s Canadian lead, Jessica Paré, would feature with Americans Piper Perabo and Mischa Barton in Pool's English-language debut, the lesbian boarding-school drama *Lost and Delirious* (2001). During the same years, many Canadian film-makers and actors would turn to television and other spec work to supplement or replace sputtering art-film careers. The story of Canadian cinema over these years is one of paradox: recognition as a viable and influential national cinema has gone hand in hand with a shift away from the local themes and values that had been most closely associated with that very cinema.

This book surveys the most influential film-makers and movements within Canadian cinema since the eighties, and argues that their ambiguous position between the local and the global, between the Hollywood monolith and northern obscurity, can serve as an instructive case study of the pitfalls and opportunities of personal film-making in the age of globalization. Rather than treat this period as a unique moment in the history of Canadian cinema, however, I examine it within the historical context of the institutional situation that made it possible, in the context of both Anglo-Canadian and Quebecois productions and in the context of changes within film production the world over. For what makes this period distinct from the 'pure' art films that first launched Canada into international awareness during the late sixties and early seventies is their savvy combination of commercial instincts, art-house aspirations, and no-strings financial support from Telefilm Canada and provincial funding sources. This same combination is also what made the films difficult to appreciate for hard-core supporters of avant-garde, non-commercial cinema. And while there is no question that the quality of the films of Egoyan, Rozema, and their fellow Anglo-Canadians Gary Burns, John Fawcett, Thom Fitzgerald, John Greyson, Guy Maddin, Bruce McDonald, Deepa Mehta, Mina Shum, Lynn Stopewich, Bruce Sweeney, Clement Virgo, and others, and of Quebecois Arcand, Louis Bélanger, Charles Binamé, Manon Briand, André Forcier, François Girard, Lanctôt, Lauzon, Lepage, Pool, Turpin, Villeneuve, and others is markedly superior to that of the films of the tax-shelter years (1974–83), the precise relationship of these directors to that period has not yet been fully studied. And we continue to register the changes wrought by the profound shift made by Telefilm Canada in 2000 towards 'The Math' – the requirement that government-funded films be produced with at least one eye towards box office returns – and by the equally profound shift in global film funding towards international co-production on a scale never seen before. This book asks, in other words, exactly what Canadian cinema looks like when viewed through the full spectrum of its forms and its local and global influences.

Acknowledgments

I have drawn on previously published work in the following chapters: Introduction, 'Canadian Cinema in the Age of Globalization'; chapter 4, 'Across the Great Divide: Canadian Popular Cinema in the Twenty-First Century'; chapter 7, 'The Passing of Celluloid, the Endurance of the Image: Egoyan, "Steenbeckett" and *Krapp's Last Tape*,' and 'Four Films in Search of an Author: Reflections on Egoyan since *Exotica*'; chapter 9, 'Thoroughly Modern Maddin.' My thanks to Scott Forsyth and Gary Morris, the respective editors of *CineAction* and *Bright Lights*, and to Monique Tschofen for their support of my work over the years, and to David Church, Noam Gonick, and Wyndham Wise for their generous responses to it. Several research assistants have lent their talents and critical energies to this book, including Mark Stein, Mary Sweeney, Michael Lurie, and Kelsey Blackmon, of whose timely assistance I am especially recognizant. My formal study of Canadian cinema began with a curriculum development grant from the Canadian government; the article on which part of chapter 4 is based was also supported by a research grant from the Canadian government. A research grant from the College of Arts and Sciences of American University helped defray the cost of illustrations. I am grateful for this support.

Siobhan McMenemy at the University of Toronto Press has been an ideal editor from the get-go: supportive, responsible, and always ready with thoughtful answers to my innumerable questions. Leah Connor provided thoughtful and professional copy-editing and eagle-eyed proofreading, and managing editor Frances Mundy capably shepherded the book through production. Bart Beaty gave me invaluable assistance in locating image rights, and Ron Mandelbaum at Photofest was extraordinarily efficient in clearing those rights. Erin Burke at the Canadian Film Centre, Norman Cohn at Isuma Productions, Jean du Toit at Buffalo Gal Pictures, David Fortin at the Cinémathèque Québécoise, Claude Lord at the ONF/ NFB, Vicky Mageau at Les Films Équinoxe, and Alan Virta at Boise State University Library were especially helpful in locating images and generous in granting permissions. Guy Maddin graciously bestowed his blessing on my appropriating the title of his miniature masterpiece for the subtitle of a sprawling academic monster. The two anonymous readers of the manuscript for the press had valuable suggestions for revisions and saved me some embarrassing gaffes; any that remain are my responsibility, unless I am allowed to blame my parents for the mistake of not having birthed me in, raised me in, or even ever taken me to Canada. (When they went to Montreal long ago, all I got was a lousy *Petit Larousse*. Actually, it was gorgeous. Still have it. Thanks Mom and Dad.)

I want to express my especial thanks to all of the many students in my Canadian National Cinema classes at American University for their interest, questions, insights, and critically astute impatience. I want in particular to recognize the following students: Baxter Martin, for long ago suggesting an independent study on Cronenberg at an opportune moment; Bill Schiefen, for the spirited arguments, devoted research, and engaged polemic on 'The Math' in his honours capstone essay; and Matthew Decker and Maeg Keane, for their illuminating and challenging conversations on queer theory.

This book was originally Ana's idea, but I have long since forgiven her for it.

Abbreviations

CCA	Capital Cost Allowance ('Tax Shelter')
CFDC	Canadian Film Development Corporation
CFE	*Canadian Film Encyclopedia* (http://tiff.net/canadianfilmencyclopedia/)
CJFS	*Canadian Journal of Film Studies / Revue Canadienne d'Etudes Cinémato-graphiques* (http://www.filmstudies.ca/journal/cjfs/archives/authors)
COC	Canadian Opera Company
IIPA	International Index to Performing Arts
NFB	National Film Board / Office National du Film
OFDC	Ontario Film Development Corporation
TFC	Telefilm Canada
TIFF	Toronto Festival of Festivals / Toronto International Film Festival

CANADIAN CINEMA SINCE THE 1980s

At the Heart of the World

What Is Canadian Cinema and What Happened to It at the End of the Twentieth Century?

> When I first started out, as my reaction against Canadian cinema, I thought I would never, ever mention Canada in any of my movies.
>
> Guy Maddin (2005)

The idea of a national culture has been around for as long as culture has been around, and over the millennia many different functions have been proposed for it. The earliest and most enduring role played by culture has been to define what a nation, or a particular people, is. This was the role of traditional epic, which both preserved the myths of its people and gave those myths a specifically ideological form, as when Virgil's *Aeneid* provided a definition of empire by creating a new legend about how that the empire of Rome was originally founded. Foundational myths are never without their contradictions, however; the *Aeneid*, for example, is just as much about the high human cost of founding empire as about its enduring glories. The very title of D.W. Griffith's *The Birth of a Nation* (1915) claims a national identity; its controversial account of the founding of the Ku Klux Klan is also a foundational text in the history of narrative cinema – the first epic motion picture blockbuster and the origin of the grammar of narrative film. There have been moments of fairly straightforwardly ideological national myths in Canadian cinema, particularly the Grierson-era 'voice-of-God' documentaries at the wartime National Film Board and the cinematic melodramas of post-war Quebec. There have also been the influential critical myths imported to cinema studies from literary criticism, including Northrop Frye's conceptions of 'Canadian nature with its bleak and terrifying desolation; the garrison mentality, that closely knit and beleaguered society at odds with its environment,' and the problematic of spatial identity he expressed in the question 'Where is here?'; and Margaret Atwood's claim that the 'central symbol' of Canada is the story of a person with 'no triumph or victory but the fact of his survival.'[1] The dour portrait of a Canadian character up against and frequently defeated by a hostile world was adapted by Robert Fothergill as the figure of the 'loser hero' in the documentary realist dramas of the late sixties and early seventies in probably the most influential single article in the history of Canadian cinema studies.[2] Possessing the virtue of unifying a disparate corpus of films around a single powerful (if reductive) conception, Fothergill's formulation was also plausible enough to frame debate until quite recently, to the exclusion of alternate topics and themes. But one of the complexities of Canadian identity has always been the inevitably fragmentary nature of any such mythmaking. Indeed, we could say that the transparent failure of any attempt to generate an all-encompassing national identity in Canada makes its national myths especially fertile ground for grasping the inevitable failure of even the most unified national cinema to encompass the identity of every member of its populace. The cinema of Quebec has come much closer to fulfilling the nation-building function of a national culture in Canada, with the fundamental paradox, oft-noted, that it is not a nation. Moreover, as we shall see, Quebecois cinema has always at the same time given voice to the fissures in that identity: the hybrid nature of Quebec, built out of First Nations peoples, French Canadians, Anglo-Canadians, Jews, and the many more recent immigrant populations whose presence was felt especially strongly during the roughly two-and-a-half decades since 1985 under scrutiny in this book.

Cinema is only one of many means through which to enunciate a national identity. Given that the local English-language market share persistently rests under 2 per cent, it is debatable whether it is a primary vehicle of national identity in Canada in the way, for example, that Hollywood movies continue to be for the United States, or that, say, French cinema is for its target audience. Again, the presence of a healthy popular Quebecois cinema (regularly more than 20 per cent market share since 2000) is a strong indicator of the centrality of film specifically to the culture of that province. At the same time, the way in which Quebec's cinema developed has given its film-making a different identity than in the centralized and commercialized American system or the government-supported and protected French system. In particular, the vexed relationship between popular Quebecois cinema and the art film that developed during the 1960s, hand in hand with the radical politics of the period, led to the self-conscious recourse by later film-makers such as Jean-Claude Lauzon, Robert Lepage, and Léa Pool to non-local genres, music, and other cultural markers as a way of countering what they saw as the suffocating restrictions of Quebecois cinema. During the eighties and nineties, being national in many ways meant partially or wholly repudiating what had previously been defined as being national.

The biggest bone of contention was the fact that Quebec was not a nation but part of a broader federation that was unable to define conclusively the ideal relationship between the rest of Canada and its francophone and separatist province. What anglophone Canada does share with Quebec is an oblique and parodic attitude towards the culture through which it defines itself. This attitude is born of ambivalence: in Quebec, towards the dominant culture of France, its colonial power but also its source of distinction from the rest of Canada; in anglophone Canada, towards the dominant culture of the United States, which is simultaneously part of, distinct from, and hostile to the possibility of a native cultural identity. For many Canadians, American popular culture *is* their culture, shot through as it is with Canadian actors, singers, comedians, and film-makers, even as that Canadian content is, for all intents and purposes, invisible according to traditional definitions of national identity. For all that *Saturday Night Live* is arguably a Canadian creation, in what way can that defining icon of four decades of late-night television comedy be said in any way to articulate what it means to be Canadian?[3] For all that Mike Myers and Jim Carrey may have defined American screen comedy for nearly two decades, what do the Austin Powers movies or *Dumb and Dumber* have to do with Canada? These are legitimate questions, and they cut to the heart of the issues that have given Canadian critics and scholars fits for decades now, just as they have led to much soul-searching among those film-makers who have chosen not to make the move south into the American melting pot. But it is precisely in the paradoxes and problems they pose for Canadians that these questions can also help us to articulate what is particular about Canadian cinema, what function it plays in Canadian culture, and what it can tell us more generally about the ways nations are able to define themselves in an era in which no nation bigger than a duchy is able to maintain even the pretense of being a homogeneous, unified population.

There is a moment in *Atanarjuat: The Fast Runner* (2001), the first feature-length narrative film produced by Inuits in Inuktitut, that epitomizes both the paradox and the promise of contemporary Canadian cinema. For most of its lengthy running time, *Atanarjuat* looks and feels like a mythic foundational epic. Set in a timeless period before the introduction of Western technology and belief systems, the film is based on the orally transmitted tradition of a deadly feud between rival families in an isolated and tight-knit community. Striving hard to recreate the daily life and culture of the pre-contact Inuit, *Atanarjuat* shows us the rituals and survival skills of its characters with a minimum of exposition or narrative interference. As viewers, we are drawn into a strange and hostile world that is barely explained to us. It feels alien, ancient, and marvellously strange. Then, over the final credits, the film-makers make a bold move: they show us footage of the actors on location, dressed in the dark glasses and leather jackets that are a signifier of cultural cool the world over (see figure 8.3). What is the relationship, the film-makers ask, between the extraordinary and local authenticity of the representation of Inuit culture we have been immersed in for nearly three hours and the equally authentic but global worldliness of the actors who re-enacted that culture? How is it possible, if at all, to exist in both worlds simultaneously? There is no simple answer to this question, but if we continue to ponder its paradoxes, we realize that the contradiction was there from the beginning of the film. After all, with what technology did we think the story of *Atanarjuat* was being recorded and presented to us in the first place? The self-consciousness of that concluding gesture has its own cultural context within Canadian cinema, in the innovative documentary practices of the NFB direct cinema of the 1950s and in the Quebecois direct cinema narratives of the 1960s. Moreover, the controversy of authenticity has long antecedents in Inuit culture. It dates back to one of the first feature-length documentaries, Robert Flaherty's *Nanook of the North* (1922), which famously 'staged' a number of its scenes of 'native' life, since the Inuit encountered by Flaherty in the early twentieth century with the intention of depicting as unspoiled natives had already been 'contaminated' by exposure to Western technology and culture.

For all its relevance to the vexed history of ethnographic film-making, the slyly subversive gesture that concludes *Atanarjuat* is also quintessentially Canadian in the way it pulls the rug out from under the assumptions we had been making about unified identity and authentic culture. But it is also quintessentially

Canadian in neither wholly rejecting that unified identity nor wholly embracing the ironic attitude towards that identity characteristic of the postmodernism as which it would be easy to assimilate the gesture, leather, shades, and all. Zacharias Kunuk and his collaborators thus claim the right to inhabit both attitudes simultaneously, while also acknowledging that neither attitude is wholly theirs nor by itself able to reproduce or define what they know their identity to be. It is this paradoxical position, both naive and knowing, belonging and alienated, affirmative and subversive, serious and parodic, that is characteristic of Canadian cinema of the eighties and nineties, the decades when Canadian cinema came out on the world stage for good. Moreover, if we take seriously the duplicity of *Atanarjuat*'s position, we can also find it asking us to revise conventional assessments of the Canadian cinema that preceded it, even as its clear-headed awareness of its own contradictions asks us to consider quite critically the cinematic production of the twenty-first century that followed on the unprecedented success of the position it staked out as its own. For, if the essence of Canadianness suddenly became the fallback position of global popular culture, what chance would it have of preserving the quirky and marginal Canuckness that had defined that culture to start with?

What happened during this decade and a half in which Canadian cinema burst forth as never before or since? It is difficult to overestimate the importance of the Toronto Festival of Festivals (renamed the Toronto International Film Festival in 1994), which in 1984 instituted Perspective Canada with the express purpose of promoting local film-making.[4] That year saw the premiere at TIFF of Atom Egoyan's first feature film, *Next of Kin*; over the next fifteen years, Perspective Canada would be instrumental in creating and maintaining the sense of a genuine national cinema. TIFF grew ever more important on the world festival circuit, ranking by the mid-nineties second only to Cannes and considered by some insiders to have surpassed it. Dedicated to a capacious range of moviemaking, featuring retrospectives of genres, directors, and national cinemas, TIFF not only provided a showcase for local film-makers, but affirmed their place in contemporary world cinema while giving them in return the opportunity to see the best that world cinema had to offer. Thus, when in 2001 Perspective Canada was replaced by two lower-profile programs, Canada First! (first features by Canadian film-makers) and Short Cuts Canada (Canadian short films), it signalled the end of an era. The established directors were now viewed as part of the main festival, a recognition of their international stature and of the international funding that underwrote many of their films. The shift in emphasis by Telefilm Canada (TFC) in 2000 towards commercially viable films also implied that institutionally supported cinema would be more suited to the main festival than to the local showcase, which was reoriented towards 'small films.' The consequence was another way in which the 'middle' films that had been the standard bearers of the past fifteen years of Canadian production would be squeezed out.

The changing relationship of TIFF to local film-making closely parallels shifts in government funding as well as changes in global production and distribution. The 1984 renaming of the Canadian Film Development Corporation as Telefilm Canada to reflect its funding of television was also unmistakably an act of rebranding to erase the memory of the CCA years. Two years later, the Feature Film Fund was created expressly 'to support works by Canadian filmmakers.'[5] Along with the new Ontario Film Development Corporation and other provincial bodies, these organizations enabled the emergence and flourishing of a viable and profitable Anglo-Canadian art cinema. David McIntosh pinpoints 1990 as the year in which there was the 'maximum degree of diversity as well as ... maximum funding levels' of 'state production support,' and he numbers the subsequent withdrawal of funds among the consequences of the 1989 Free Trade Agreement.[6] This withdrawal became precipitous when conservative provincial governments in Ontario and elsewhere eviscerated cultural funding in the second half of the nineties.[7] The economics mirrors the standard narrative of historians of Canadian cinema, but theirs remains a parochial narrative, for a look at the global context of independent film-making shows an almost identical trajectory: emergence as an artistic and commercial force in the mid-eighties that by the turn of the century had for all intents and purposes been swallowed up by the studios and the multinational co-production. After all, the most prominent Anglo-Canadian directors had already gone international before TFC head Richard Stursberg introduced its new Script to Screen policy, with the goal of a 5 per cent domestic box office share: Egoyan's Ireland-shot *Felicia's Journey* (1999) was produced by Mel Gibson's Icon Entertainment, and Patricia Rozema's England-based *Mansfield Park* (1999) was produced by Miramax with money from the British Council. Bruce McDonald made his last locally funded film of the period, *Hard Core Logo*, in 1996; he spent the next five years shooting television shows. Winnipegger Guy Maddin did not make a non-spec feature film between *Twilight of the Ice Nymphs* (1996) and *The Saddest Music in the World* (2003). Indeed, the film-maker whose trajectory best fits the conventional narrative is the one most frequently omitted from it: all but one of the six feature films David Cronenberg made between Hollywood productions *The Fly* (1986) and *A History of Violence* (2005) were independently produced, shot in Canada, and supported by government money and tax credits. That a director of Cronenberg's stature left behind his biggest commercial success and the support of Twentieth Century Fox to return to the friendly confines of Telefilm Canada for its most productive years before then joining New Line Cinema speaks volumes about the viability and visibility of Anglo-Canadian film during this period and its subsequent decline as a cohesive force in the new millennium.

National and provincial support for independent film-makers regardless of the bottom line performance of their films was an essential element in the rise of English-Canadian cinema at the end of the eighties. It also appears to have assisted Cronenberg in making the transition from the exploitation genre films of the tax-shelter period to his more ambitious and difficult-to-categorize products later in the century. But there is also a good deal of serendipity involved in this convergence. The worldwide success of Rozema's *Mermaids* was driven in large part by its acquisition by Harvey Weinstein's Miramax Films, which was founded in 1979 and made its name distributing some of the first financially successful independent films, including *Sex, Lies, and Videotape* (1989, United States) and *The Crying Game* (1992, UK); it would be purchased by Disney in 1993.[8] The same period was the heyday of UK-based Merchant Ivory Productions, which single-handedly invented the modern-day heritage film with its phenomenally successful adaptation of E.M. Forster's *A Room with a View* (1985), combining tastefully contemporary attitudes towards sexuality, marriage, and gender roles with sumptuous production values, location shooting, literate scripts, and accomplished acting. The same year, Stephen Frears and Hanif Kureishi's *My Beautiful Laundrette*, produced as a TV film by England's Channel Four, became a surprise theatrical hit with its matter-of-fact combination of Anglo-Indian tensions with an interracial gay relationship between Roshan Seth's Hussein and Daniel Day-Lewis's punk icon Johnny, and proved a seminal film in the new queer cinema. Robert Redford founded his Sundance Institute in 1980 to nurture independent film-makers, and the affiliated film festival, inaugurated four years later, soon became a major showplace and marketplace for independent films. By the end of the century, however, the festival had irrevocably changed: in 2001, Redford would refer to it as a 'monster … like Las Vegas.'[9] This period also saw the rise of new Black cinema with *Boyz n the Hood* (1986, John Singleton), the new respectability of the serial killer genre when Jonathan Demme's *Silence of the Lambs* swept the 1992 Academy Awards, and the phenomenal popularity of the ultra-violent genre-bending talk-cinema of Quentin Tarantino's *Reservoir Dogs* (1992) and *Pulp Fiction* (1994).

In his informative study *American Independent Cinema*, Geoff King identifies a number of factors that distinguish 'indie' films of the past twenty-five years from the non-studio productions that have been around for more than a century.[10] Earlier versions include, in particular, exploitation and low-end genre products, experimental and avant-garde cinema, and alternative narrative forms such as John Cassavetes's influential improvisational films of the 1960s. As opposed to many historians of the movement, King does not consider industrial factors to be the sole defining feature of independent cinema.[11] He divides his discussion in terms of *narrative*, or ways of telling (or not telling) events differently from classical Hollywood narrative, *form*, or ways of visually presenting events differently from Hollywood conventions of 'realism,' *genre*, or ways of mixing and complicating classical Hollywood genres, and the presentation of *social*, *political*, and *ideological* dimensions either ignored or downplayed in mainstream Hollywood features. Nevertheless, King does concede the key role played by the formation of a new distribution infrastructure in the indie movement he treats in his book.[12] And while King does not draw a firm line between truly independent production and the intermediate ones he calls 'Indiewood,' his chapter on industry clearly delineates the changing economics of independent production that identifies the years 1985–2000, like the studio 'new wave' during the late sixties and early seventies, as more than anything a period of transition, marked by the emergence of a number of small-scale distributing companies, the eighties boom in cable television, a video market that created demand for new low-cost and often niche-marketed product, and the expansion of the multiplex cinema.[13] Spearheaded by U.S.

president Ronald Reagan's deregulation of the industry, entrenchment took place over the nineties as the Hollywood studios began buying up the independent distributors, getting into indie film upfront at the production end, and ultimately locking out the majority of indie films made outside their new system.[14]

English-Canadian and Quebecois films benefitted from this movement just as they later felt the weight of the studio consolidation that began to dictate the nature of their productions, raising the financial stakes and limiting creative choices. The indie movement was far more international than most histories of Sundance and the American distributors recognize.[15] Predating *Sex, Lies, and Videotape* by several years, Arcand's *Déclin* was a formative moment in the development of sex talk as an inexpensive and marketable alternative to mainstream action-based cinema.[16] Mottram notes the influence of Egoyan's *Family Viewing* (1987) on Soderbergh's connection between video, sex, and voyeurism; one could equally cite the confessional role played by video in *I've Heard the Mermaids Singing*.[17] And the emergence of these Canadian films out of the exploitation and genre products of the tax-shelter years closely parallels developments in the United States, where most of the new independent film-makers also had roots in B-movies and grind house, either as viewers or as practitioners. The European model was equally influential on Canadian cinema, however. While TIFF was essential for creating a sense of local buzz, Cannes – where *Mermaids* made its splash, where Egoyan enjoyed a long run, and where a number of Canadians won prizes during these years – was equally essential for establishing an international reputation for 'novelty and "hipness"' and 'generating a market niche that smoothed their entry into international markets.'[18] The allure of Cannes was part of what made the model of French national cinema especially attractive, with its quota system, public-private partnerships, and explicit support of an auteur-based alternative to Hollywood genres, narratives, and forms. Although dominated by the vertically integrated giant studios Gaumont and Pathé, the French industry had long provided options for quality productions outside this system by such eminent and influential figures as Jean Renoir, Jacques Tati, Jean-Pierre Melville, Agnès Varda, and Jean-Luc Godard. Paradoxically, at the same time its past giants were providing a dominant model for aspiring American auteurs, this system during the eighties was in the process of its own transformation by a new generation of film-makers influenced by music video and advertising and a new international web of production and distribution that by the end of the century would itself be tightly interwoven with the American system of semi-independent companies. The crossover success of stylish genre-based *cinéma du look* films such as Jean-Jacques Beineix's *Diva* (1981) and Luc Besson's *Nikita* (1990, aka *La Femme Nikita*) was another determining factor in opening up markets for the American indies, even as they had to field criticism at home in France for their suspected commercialism and emptiness of meaning.[19] As opposed to the experimental and alternative U.S. and Canadian scenes in the sixties and early seventies, the majority of film-makers working in the eighties and nineties were both required and determined to be commercially viable, if only in the niche marketplaces of urban centres, splinter audiences, and cable/video. The growing Canadian film and television industry was essential in enabling this process, as also in reflecting and sometimes anticipating broader international trends. Canada arguably can boast more world-class film-makers today than any country besides the United States, and certainly as many as any country in Europe or the Commonwealth.

It is, of course, a different story if we want to find a common Canadian thread among these world-class film-makers. There is a common theme to the many attempts to distinguish what is particularly Canadian about Canadian cinema: it has always been defined negatively, in terms of its ambiguities or, as Jim Leach puts it, 'a distinctively Canadian sense of instability.'[20] This is true of the emergence of Quebecois cinema out of the Quiet Revolution and the convergence of radical film-making with decolonization around the world in the sixties; it is true of the Ontario new wave, based on a 'profound skepticism of ... the most basic principle of Hollywood cinema – the belief in the transcendent powers of individual will.'[21] It is true of the 'two solitudes' (Anglo- and Quebecois) cinema of the sixties and seventies, each partially founded on the wilful negation of the other; both ostensibly supported by the same national institutions; as it is true of the polarities that structure society (English/French, Native/non-Native, Canadian/American); and it is true of the bipolar identities attributed to the more recent ethnic and immigrant communities, simultaneously Canadian and non-Canadian. The conceptualization of Canadianness as a fractured space given cohesion only by the oppositions that fracture it is so deeply rooted that it is no surprise that the principal sign of a recognition that the landscape of oppositions was radically transformed during the nineties was the cries of warning regarding the disappearance of a critical culture and a Canadian cinema altogether.

A more current although no less deceptive version of negation takes a universalist rather than a particularist approach. Literary theorist Linda Hutcheon influentially argued that 'Canadian writers, then, may be primed for postmodernism by their history ... and also by their split sense of identity, both regional and national.'[22] That is, because their attitude to culture and to nationhood has always been unstable, profoundly ironic, and self-deflating, Canadians were postmodernist *avant la lettre*. Kieran Keohane notes a similar attitude on the level of cultural practice, singling out two primary ways in which Canadians define what is 'quintessentially Canadian': taking pleasure in enduring activities that others might find immediately pleasurable (food, driving, outdoor sports) and celebrating how they endure their essential lack of particularity as a nation.[23] This is potentially a truly empowering self-definition; after all, the Renaissance humanist Pico della Mirandola defined 'human' in just the same terms: the only animal with no distinguishing qualities except for the capacity to grasp and to adapt to any of those qualities proper to other animals. Where Keohane's definition falls short is precisely where postmodernism as a theory of society fell short in the 1980s: it ignores the continuing imaginative, affective, and material presence of bits and pieces of all of the oppositions it persuades itself it has left behind or theorized away as mere constructs.

As Hutcheon argues, Canadian postmodernism can be distinguished from its

U.S. counterpart not only in terms of its roots in local cultural practice, but also in terms of its 'ongoing engagement with the social and the historical world.'[24] Typically, postmodernist theory posited that meaning was supersaturated to the point of meaninglessness; there were only plays of signifiers, ironic quotation of the past, masks and masquerades. Proclaiming the absolute victory of capitalism and of the culture industry, it put forth ironic capitulation as the only way left to struggle against the behemoth of discourse. Hindsight shows Canadian postmodernism to have been not so much an exception to the rule as a prescient recognition that, despite appearances, the rule did not apply anywhere else either. The standard narratives of postmodernism and post-structuralism can account neither for the stubborn residue of past forms and past cultural moments, no longer symbolically unified nor exuding their intended meaning but still powerfully present, nor for the unforeseen emergence of new hybrid forms of representation, new spaces of resistance seemingly from the middle of nowhere. New conceptions of space, wrote the French sociologist Henri Lefebvre, may always strive for a perfectly controlled, perfectly closed and policed system, but new contradictions will always emerge out of the impossibility of creating such a system.[25] As John Jordan asserts about globalization, 'Transnationals are affecting democracy, work, communities, culture and the biosphere. Inadvertently, they have helped us to see the whole problem as one system, to connect every issue to every other issue, to not look at one problem in isolation.'[26] The new Canadian cinema was unmistakably a product of globalization, marking the passage from failed resistance to U.S. hegemony into an aesthetic response to the new situation of multinational hegemony, more overwhelming in its scope but more diffuse in its focus. One of its chief characteristics has been the new kind of intertextuality evident in Bruce McDonald's *Highway 61* (1991), pointed but playful, diffuse but interlocking in its representation of an emerging dialectics of Canadian culture and its many others. Arroyo has aptly described Canada as a colony of the United States, but in a peculiarly intimate relationship, more akin to 'a younger brother.'[27] The cultural anxiety attendant on such a relationship has been especially acute in the English-Canadian world, since there is no possibility of linguistic distinction. The same complaint echoes there as in England that locally made movies are deemed successful (or even released at all, as was the case with Vincenzo Natali's *Cube*, 1997) only once they have made it in the United States first. But that anxiety also brings advantages, as in Cronenberg's comment on the ability of *Crash* to mimic a Hollywood movie like a parasite, introducing something almost inimical to it while superficially faithful to it conventions. Proximity to the United States and an intimate knowledge of (and infiltration into) American popular culture have placed Canadian cinema and its practitioners in a position not simply to allegorize the colonial condition, as Fredric Jameson argued all global culture does on some level, but to allegorize a particularly skewed set of relationships to the United States, and by extension, to that globalization, the visible face of which nearly always wears American brand names.[28]

Few Canadian films of the nineties are without their allusions, however coded, to the behemoth south of Canada's border. Actors and characters frequently bear the weight of association: the presence of a well-known outsider actor among a director's regulars (even if he be English), such as Ian Holm's litigation lawyer in *The Sweet Hereafter* (1997) can give his character an added resonance. Yet the allegory works differently than in the classic formulation, for often it is the very presence of such moments that in fact signals most forcefully that the film in question is *not* quite the same as a Hollywood product. More of my (American) students have seen *The Sweet Hereafter* than perhaps any other Canadian film, but few would have identified it as Canadian or singled out anything specifically 'Canadian' about it. They were attracted more generally to the accessibility of its otherness. What a Canadian critic would identify as 'Canadian' – its oblique and understated approach to tragedy, the depressiveness and isolation of its community, the presence of Egoyan's fetish actors as townspeople versus Holm as outsider – were received by these viewers (all self-identified outsiders) as qualities of a non-nation-specific art film, full stop.

In its history, the motion picture has had two periods when advances in its technological apparatus converged with revolutionary politics – the 1920s and the 1960s. It seems unlikely that there will be a third, as cinema itself has been marginalized by digital technology just as in its heyday it marginalized the printed word. The hybrid cinema that characterized the 1990s found a new form adequate to the new role of film-making and spectatorship in a global and digital economy. In their unique geographic, economic, and cultural position, Canadian film-makers produced over the last fifteen years of the twentieth century, for better or for worse and often kicking and screaming, the first corpus of films to inhabit fully and in a formally and aesthetically cohesive fashion the global economy of the century that would follow.

This book approaches the apogee of Canadianness in popular culture through a series of chapters loosely alternating between broad surveys and detailed case studies. Its variegated methodology reflects its argument regarding the paradoxically cohesive fragmentation of Canadian cinema. Different types of film yield insight to different types of critical method. Consequently, I have adapted, borrowed, and combined theories and methods as called for by specific films, genres, film-makers, and film cultures. Where approaches collide or contradict in meaning, as in particular between the neo-formalist approach of auteurism or textual analysis of specific films and the broader sociopolitical context of genre studies, queer theory, cultural studies, or cultural geography, I have tried to signal these collisions and incorporate their results into my own argument. Since one of the characteristics of recent Canadian cinema has been its tendency to raise questions rather than resolve them, my primary goal has been to frame those questions as clearly and productively as possible rather than to strive for premature answers. One of the principal strategies I have adopted is to make connections outside the familiar interpretative paths of the critical discourse surrounding Canadian cinema, at times blithely disregarding established boundaries when they seem artificially erected and noting invisible barriers where they seem to have been ignored. Similarly, while I have attempted at least to note the major trends of Canadian cinema since the eighties, my choice of texts has been similarly motivated by local concerns rather than a universally applied template. In particular, my focus is on the narrative fiction films that primarily circulate in the global cinema market. However, because these films do not exist in a vacuum, I do touch at times on the other formative elements of Canadian national cinema – animation, documentary, and experimental film – although not in sufficient detail to do any of them justice. Again because of my peculiar subject position, I tend to follow the festival/connoisseurship/film-course organization around specific film-makers and specific films rather than the structural approach of a typical historical, economic, or sociological model, although I do have recourse to the latter at certain moments. But here, too, I have tried to match my approach to the extant criticism. Rather than repeating the well-established and uncontroversial comprehensive overview of Egoyan's early career, for example, I focus on the more difficult case of the films he has made since he achieved global 'auteur' status in the mid-nineties. Conversely, when I feel that I have significant meaning to add to the interpretation of a canonical film such as Lauzon's *Léolo* or Lepage's *Le Confessionnal*, or to the trajectory of a career like Cronenberg's, I treat them in detail. Nevertheless, when a clearly 'inferior' film raises important broader questions for the book, such as the National Lampoon–wannabe *Going the Distance* (2004, Mark Griffiths), I will treat it at a length wholly unjustified from an auteurist or connoisseurship approach. In sum, my goal has been to use my outsider's perspective not only to provide a deep yet broad look at recent Canadian cinema but also to raise questions, provoke debate, and prompt the reassessment of a number of accepted views that continue to dominate the field: documentary realism as the privileged mode of Canadian cinema; the fundamental separation between English-Canadian and Quebecois cinema, between Hollywood and Canadian cinema, and between popular genres and art cinema; and the isolation of Canadian cinema from developments elsewhere in world cinema. Rather than rejecting any of these accepted views, however, I examine them as discourses, cultural givens that reflect but also constrain the field as a whole. Constraint is simultaneously a deadening and an inspiring condition, and I choose to focus on ways in which Canadian film-makers have worked with these constraints in creative and empowering rather than solely limiting and defeating ways.

The first chapter provides a brief history of Canadian cinema up to the early eighties, focusing on the complex and usually uneven relationship with its American neighbour and considering the strategies whereby feature films came to play a significant role in the changing definitions of Canadian identity. It discusses not only landmark films in the turbulent history of Quebec in the sixties and seventies, but also such Hollywood/Canada compromises as *The Apprenticeship of Duddy Kravitz* (1974). Chapter 2 presents Canada's most successful, most studied, and least understood film-maker, David Cronenberg. In retrospect, it is evident that Cronenberg's career has managed to straddle nearly every divide in Canadian cinema: he is the only substantial film-maker to have flourished during the tax-shelter years, the only Canadian to maintain a strong artistic identity while making consistently profitable films, the only Canadian to continue to receive financing both from Canadian cultural institutions and from Hollywood and European producers, and arguably the single most important influence on Canadian film-making since the eighties. From the mid-seventies on, Cronenberg's films insinuated a disruptive force into the landscape of Canadian cinema that took recognizably intellectual form only when the film-makers around him began to catch up with his vision in the late eighties.

Chapter 3 takes a revisionist look at the seminal late eighties films of newcomer (and erstwhile Cronenberg assistant) Patricia Rozema, whose sleeper hit, *I've Heard the Mermaids Singing*, was seen by many as the first salvo of the Ontario new wave, and of veteran francophone film-maker Denys Arcand, whose duo of international hits, *Le Déclin de l'empire américain* (1986) and *Jésus de Montréal* (1989), returned Quebecois film-making to the international prominence it had briefly enjoyed during the late sixties and early seventies. The careers of both directors have been marked by inconsistency; Rozema continues to work in an internationalist framework and Arcand made the shift to English-language films before returning to his eighties heyday with the *Déclin* sequel, *Les Invasions barbares* (2003). This chapter treats both film-makers as satirists and argues that the extraordinary impact of their eighties films derived from an uncanny affinity with the times that has also caused the films to age peculiarly. My reading of these films seeks to capture their initial originality and to pinpoint the very timeliness that resonates so differently with viewers today. They provide valuable time capsules to the reasons why Canadian cinema was able to make such a radical change in direction over the space of just a few years.

Chapter 4 shifts towards the question of stars within Canadian cinema, arguing that the new Canadian cinema of the eighties and nineties was accompanied by a different sort of actor, neither invisibly Canadian in Hollywood nor confined to the northern ghetto, working simultaneously in television, Hollywood, and Canadian art film. This chapter studies the crossover icons of contemporary Canadian cinema – Montrealers Pascale Bussières and Roy Dupuis, English Canadians Mia Kirshner, Sandra Oh, Molly Parker, and Callum Keith Rennie, and multitalented actor-writer-directors Sarah Polley and Don McKellar – beginning with a comparison to a pair of Quebecois precursors, Geneviève Bujold and Carole Laure. While best known in critical circles for their art-movie personas, all of these actors either have deep roots in television (which made the careers of Bussières, Dupuis, and Polley), have since staked their claim there (the case of Kirshner, Oh, and Parker), or like McKellar and Rennie, have tried to maintain a balancing act between the two.

Chapter 5 addresses the three most prominent Quebec-based directors of the nineties: Jean-Claude Lauzon, Robert Lepage, and Léa Pool. While the backgrounds, themes, and subjects of these film-makers vary widely, they share a fascination with a cinema that is able simultaneously to represent local issues of Quebecois history and identity and to engage in a global cultural dialogue. In his brief career, Lauzon managed to combine the documentary realist tradition of Quebecois cinema with an eclectic internationalism and an immersion in French surrealism. While Pool shares an interest in the French new wave with Lauzon, her films provide a unique combination of her own Swiss heritage and a curiously diffracted portrait of issues of gender within a distinctly Canadian framework. Perhaps the most cosmopolitan of the three figures, theatre and film director Lepage constructs his films as self-conscious juxtapositions of cultures, times, and places. Again and again, the specificity of Quebec comes into contact and conflict with the global culture surrounding it.

The title of chapter 6, 'Cronenberg's Mutant Progeny,' refers to the broad range of films that emerged as genre-based moviemaking gained a new artistic and commercial currency among Canadian film-makers. Highly influenced by Cronenberg's enduring ability to raise complex emotional and intellectual questions through the disturbing imagery and familiar conventions of horror and science fiction, Canadian film-makers produced films that are nuanced in their approach to character but visceral in their imagery. Like the syndicated television shows that became something of a Canadian specialty during the nineties – among others, *Highlander: The Series* (1992–8), *Nikita* (1997–2001), *Earth: Final Conflict* (1997–2001), *Lexx* (1997–2002), and *Stargate SG-1* (1997–2007), not to mention *The X-Files* (filmed in Vancouver, 1993–8) – these films were generic in their adherence to popular conventions and elusive in their relationship to traditional definitions of cinematic Canadianness. Such genre film-making constitutes a different approach to the mixture of the traditional auteurist art film with popular traditions and conventions; this chapter analyses them both as effective examples of film-making and within the context of popular film genres, long a vexed question in Canadian cinema studies.

Probably Canada's best-known director after Cronenberg, Atom Egoyan, too was highly influenced by his compatriot, but more in terms of a fascination with technology and sexuality. In terms of genre, Egoyan remained strictly within the art-house milieu. Chapter 7 addresses the changing relationship of Egoyan to his material as his films received wider distribution. In particular, it negotiates the heady intellectual content of the films, and examines the impact on the reception of Egoyan's films of his own highly articulate discussions and writings about them. Egoyan is a model example of a contemporary film-maker quite self-consciously seeking to adjust his practices to the exigencies of present-day conditions without compromising his specific vision. Like Cronenberg, he seems to have found in the peculiar ambiguities of the Canadian industry a means of working simultaneously on the margins and in the centre of the international movie market.

Egoyan's film-making is focused on memory and identity, both of which are characteristically fragmented. Chapter 8, 'The Canadian Mosaic,' surveys a specialty of Canadian cinema: the broad range of films structured around the country's ethnic minorities and marginal communities. On the one hand, it suggests the strength and diversity of an infrastructure dedicated to funding such films; on the other, it explores the pressures and trade-offs entailed in producing a type of film predicated on representing a specific set of identities. Whereas Cronenberg's cinema established a Canadian tradition of existentialist film-making – telling stories about the irreducible singularity of individual experience and imagination – films made under the rubric of the Canadian mosaic, like the genre films treated in chapter 6, are susceptible to the pressure of meeting a fixed set of cultural assumptions. I begin with a look at the road movie as a genre whose conventions encourage reflection on cultural fragmentation before turning to the cinemas of region, ethnicity, and sexual identity. I examine the kinds of strategies employed by directors whose films will be produced and distributed in whole or in part because of their ethnic identity or marginal social status. Similarly, I look at film-makers who have come under analogous pressure working within or around the niche markets of gay, lesbian, and queer cinema.

Chapter 9 treats Guy Maddin's films as exemplary of the productive marginality of the provincial artist. Based all his life in Winnipeg, Manitoba, Maddin has successfully established a global reputation through an aesthetics of deprivation. His films are predicated on their status as marginal productions, dedicated to vanished forms, forgotten genres, and shoestring budgets. This book concludes with Maddin as a case study in the ways in which a marginal or minority status can be transformed into an epistemological and aesthetic category capable of commenting quite profoundly on the affairs of the cultural centre. As suggested by Maddin's celebrated short film from which this book draws its subtitle, Canadian cinema has managed to create a unique and significant body of globally relevant films in large part because it has come to terms with its relative insignificance on the global stage, its location, as one recent book title has it, 'north of everything.' Canada is ever more networked into the heart of the global economy while somehow irremediably distanced from it. Much of the best of Canadian cinema, I will argue, is devoted to exploring this paradox. This book is devoted to those films.

Chapter One

Canadian Cinema 1896–1986: Invisibility and Difference

> 'Canada' is possibly synonymous with our universal instinct to conform and simultaneously to resist conformity in a radical way.
>
> Karen Jaehne (1988)

The history of Canadian national cinema is a singular one. A presence from near the beginnings of the industry, it does not match the model of early success followed by periodic appearance of world-class film-makers or commercial hits observable in Scandinavia, Germany, Australia, or Britain. Existing as a national cinema only in fits and starts, it does not fit the pattern of France, India, Mexico, or Japan, which have nurtured and sustained viable home industries that sporadically gain international exposure. Its early beginnings and the important but invisible presence of its actors and technicians in Hollywood from that time onward distinguish Canadian cinema from national cinemas such as those of Africa or many Latin American countries that gathered momentum in the 1930s and 1940s, or took shape after decolonization following the Second World War. Most importantly, the enduring linguistic, industrial, and cultural distinction between Quebecois and English-Canadian cinema has no real equivalent among film-producing nations. From its inception, Canadian cinema has been predicated on the invisibility of English-Canadian cinema with respect to Hollywood and its difference with respect to Quebec, with its viable 'national' cinema under the broader umbrella of a cinema that was dysfunctional according to conventional models. Both relationships are constituted by a fraught set of components simultaneously imagined and material, but this fact has not made them any less fundamental in defining the history of Canadian national cinema.

God's Godless Country

> Canada is the essence of not being. Not English, not American. It is the mathematic of not being.
>
> Mike Myers (actor)

With very few exceptions, neither English-Canadian nor Quebecois feature films were exported or recognized as such beyond Canada before the sixties. For the first half of the century, there were sporadic English- and French-language features (fifteen of the latter, for example, were made between 1944 and 1954).[1] Neverthe-less, the only form of cinema to persist throughout the century was the signifi-cant but invisible presence of anglophone Canadians in Hollywood. Toronto-born silent actor Mary Pickford (1893–1979), 'America's Sweetheart,' and slapstick com-edy innovator Mack Sennett (1880–1960), the 'King of Comedy,' were major stars of early cinema that spent their entire careers in the United States. In two patriotic and fan-oriented books, Charles Foster has documented the substantial presence of Canadian actors, directors, and producers in Hollywood from the beginning to the end of the 'golden age,' including not only Pickford and Sennett, but also Florence Lawrence, a top star with Pickford at D.W. Griffith's Biograph Company from 1909; Norma Shearer and Marie Dressler, who won Academy Awards for Best Actress in 1930 and 1932, respectively; executives Louis B. Mayer, co-founder of Metro–Goldwyn–Mayer and founder of the Academy of Motion Picture Arts and Sciences, and Jack Warner, co-founder of Warner Brothers; leading men Glenn Ford, Lorne Greene, Raymond Massey, Leslie Nielsen, Walter Pidgeon, Christo-pher Plummer, William Shatner, and Donald Sutherland; character actors Walter Huston and Hume Cronyn; and leading ladies Yvonne De Carlo, Deanna Durbin, and Fay Wray, to name the most prominent.[2]

While many of these figures were bona fide stars at the peak of their careers, none of them, with the possible exception of Pickford, also gained the artistic reputation that is the common currency of a national cinema 'star,' and Pickford only did so as an 'American.' Americans such as James Stewart, John Wayne, and Gary Cooper attained and maintained a level of stardom that allowed them to become complex icons of American values and definitions of masculine identity in films – *Mr. Smith Goes to Washington*, *The Searchers*, *High Noon* – still regarded as masterpieces. In contrast, Quebec City native Glenn Ford had an enduring career, especially in Westerns, but his best films – the noir classics *Gilda* and *The Big Heat* – were sensationalistic B-movies whose subversive quality worked against rather than by virtue of Ford's stolid persona. Massey, best known for a number of depic-tions of Abraham Lincoln, and Pidgeon, an important figure in musicals dur-ing the thirties and in drama during the forties, accrued neither a lasting artistic presence nor any specifically Canadian identity. An unremarkable leading man in the fifties, Nielsen had a second career making straight-faced fun of his own past persona in a slew of movie parodies initiated by *Airplane!*. A younger genera-tion of actors such as Greene, Plummer, Shatner, and Sutherland produced a more diversified but frequently generic output, especially insofar as their own personas. The anonymous quality of Canadian leads continues in the present day, with the likes of Ryan Gosling, Hayden Christiansen, Ryan Reynolds, and the enigmatic Keanu Reeves, who parlayed a stoner's deadpan manner into both mainline star-dom (*Speed*, *The Matrix*) and cult credibility (Gus Van Sant's *My Own Private Idaho*) without ever being taken seriously as an 'actor.'[3] The only way that critics have distilled any essence of Canadianness out of this gallery of accomplished every-men is negatively: they are exemplary in their very lack of exceptionality.[4]

While the foreignness of several of the top actresses of the 'golden age' of Holly-

wood – Swedish-born Greta Garbo and Ingrid Bergman, Germany's Marlene Diet-
rich – was a fundamental element of their star personas, part of the success of
their Canadian counterparts appears to have been the ease with which they could
be Americanized. Or perhaps there was simply no specifically Canadian national
iconography which could be domesticated by Hollywood the way Spanish-Amer-
ican actress Margarita Carmen Cansino was able to incorporate her dancing skills
into her 'Rita Hayworth' persona or English-born actors Joan Crawford, Vivien
Leigh, Cary Grant, and Laurence Olivier could maintain an aura of old-world
sophistication even when they shed their accents in American roles. Moreover,
English actors, like their Continental counterparts, would generally leave a corpus
of national productions behind them before they made the move to Hollywood.
Because there was virtually no local film industry before the sixties, there was no
opportunity for Canadian actors to establish a national identity that could influence or modulate the personas Hollywood studios would create for them. In contrast to the iconicity of French actors such as Jean Gabin or Arletty and directors
such as Jean Renoir or Marcel Carné, conventional critical paradigms of national
cinema have no rubric for making sense of the career of a consummate studio
actor such as Norma Shearer or the equally exemplary careers of directors Norman Jewison and James Cameron in terms of their national identity. And yet the
unique position of Canada with regards to Hollywood must constitute a fundamental component of its cinema, whether we consider it as a negative influence,
a structuring absence, or a seminal force in its history. There seems little need to
contest Pierre Berton's influential argument that Canadians had at least through
the mid-1960s by and large 'accepted ... the Hollywood image of Canada ... as the
real thing'; however, there is much to debate about the degree of self-awareness,
irony, and flat-out rejection accompanying the recognition of that acceptance.[5]

Meanwhile, the history of cinema *in* Canada before the eighties can be divided
into three major phases: the highly sporadic production before the formation of
the National Film Board in 1939; the wartime and post-war dominion of the NFB
and its near-exclusive focus on documentary and animation; and the development
during the sixties and early seventies of a small but internationally reviewed and
distributed feature-film industry in both English and French.[6] The motion picture was first exhibited in Canada in 1896, on 20 June in Montreal and 21 July in
Ottawa.[7] The first Canadian films were 'agricultural subjects' filmed and taken on
tour by the Manitoban farmer James Freer beginning in 1897 to help the Canadian
Pacific railway and the Canadian government promote westward immigration.[8]
The nineteen-year-old Montreal electrician Ernest Ouimet saw his first motion picture in 1896 and opened the first large-scale cinema in North America, the 1200-
seat Ouimetoscope, eleven years later; he would eventually move to Hollywood
in 1922.[9] Meanwhile, the American-born brothers Jules and Jay Allen opened their
first theatre in Brantford, Ontario, eventually building a dominant exhibition network across the nation before selling it to Hollywood in the early twenties.[10] There
was very little Canadian production before 1914, however, although American
and French productions did record a fair number of natural sights such as Niagara
Falls, and draw on Canadian myths and icons of the wilderness and the frozen
north, such as heroic Mounties, villainous French-Canadian trappers and lum-

berjacks, and 'authentic' native peoples, including the 1903 one-reeler, *Hiawatha, the Messiah of the Ojibway*, filmed on a reservation in Ontario.[11] As Morris puts it, 'Canada's role was principally to have been used as a piece of exotic scenery,' including the first feature film made in Canada, *Evangeline* (1914), which used the natural settings of Nova Scotia as backdrop for American actors and another epic Longfellow poem.[12]

The repetitive and stereotyped representation of Canada and Canadians in these films may partially answer Morris's question as to 'why we, as Canadians, have ignored our own history; why, in the case of film, we have even assumed that there is *no* history worth considering,' but only if we assume that stereotypical representations have no place in the definition of national identity.[13] Both Melnyk and Gittings emphasize ideological critique in their accounts of Canada on film before the NFB. For Gittings, it is especially the case that 'First Nations are … figured as part of that environment whites have attained mastery over.'[14] Gittings regards this same 'white patriarchal Canadian colonial nationalism' to be present as well in Canadian-produced feature films ranging from Ernest and Nell Shipman's 'north-woods' melodrama *Back to God's Country* (1919) to the NFB-produced historical drama of the colonization of Saskatchewan from 1907 to 1938, *Drylanders* (released in 1963).[15] Melnyk is more measured but equally wary of Shipman's use of 'the American "northwoods" genre … to express a distinctly Canadian national identity … however inaccurately,' enumerating this identity as follows: 'the bilingual nature of Canada,' 'the distinctive redcoat identity of the country and its national police,' and Canada as a 'vast wilderness' and 'a northern country defined by snow and cold.'[16] Where Gittings stresses the negative impact of the stereotypical Canadian identity and its implication in oppression and discrimination, Melnyk acknowledges a more ambiguous function to these representations, an attempt at articulating local truths often at odds with the broader constraints of Hollywood generic conventions.

Kay Armatage's careful reading of Nell Shipman as female auteur argues for a different sense of *Back to God's Country* and its relation to ideology and identity.[17] Shipman's film tells the story of a young woman in the Canadian wilderness whose father is murdered and husband threatened by a sexually predatory villain who appears first disguised as a Mountie and later as the captain of a whaling ship. Shot on location near Lesser Slave Lake in Alberta, the film's enormous success in Canada and around the world was in large part due to Shipman's flamboyant persona, including a highly publicized nude bathing scene and a number of wild animal sequences (figure 1.1). Armatage sees a connection between Shipman's own 'modernist defiance of social convention' and the 'sexual spontaneity' and 'robust and artless physical informality' of her character Dolores.[18] Armatage does not deny the conventional construction of femininity in the film any more than she negates the virulent racism on display in the Inuit characterizations; however, unlike Gittings, she mobilizes feminist theory, early cinema genre criticism, and a comparison with later Hollywood versions of the same film to argue that there are meaningful gaps and contradictions in that construction.[19] Moreover, she directly attributes those gaps and contradictions to Nell Shipman's screenwriting, acting, and (uncredited) directorial contributions, supporting her argument

1.1 Publicity for *Back to God's Country* (1919): exploitation meets liberation in the Canadian backwoods. Special Collections, Boise State University Library.

with the vivid self-portrait of Shipman's autobiography.[20] We may not want to go quite so far as Armatage's assertion of her subject's 'proto-feminism, consciously articulated anti-racism, animal-rights activism, and rural Canadian chauvinism.'[21] Nevertheless, her subtle analysis elucidates what Melnyk more broadly suggests: during the open and experimental period of early cinema, popular genres such as the 'northwoods' melodrama gave ample space for the explicit and implicit articulation of a wide number of overlapping and contradictory ideological positions.

It is also clear that these positions were deeply implicated in an enduring definition of Canadianness that may have been chauvinistic and racist but was nevertheless quite different from Hollywood's triumphant narrative of westward expansion. To give one example, the brutal cold that beset the filming of *Back to God's Country*, severe enough to kill off the original (American) leading man, not only allowed the sensationalistic capitalization on Canada's wilderness reputation. It was also, as Armatage argues, a depiction of nature as irredeemably 'other,' irreducible to the constraints of civilization, just as Canada was able to figure for Hollywood a space beyond the easy domination of civilization.[22] And it was also the assertion of a faith in the ontological realism of the cinematic image that would dominate Canadian cinema through to the eighties and beyond, emblematized in the material traces of 'cold,' the frosty breath and epically snowy landscapes of so many Canadian films both rural and urban.[23]

Canada's 'Golden Age'

> We're constantly defining ourselves through difference. Our culture is owned by the Americans. You're always looking in, always pressing your face up against the glass. It's a great place to be, because it gives you a distance from which you can be critical, not just of the other but of yourself at the same time.
>
> Lynne Stopkewich (1998)

Hollywood's global hegemony originated during the First World War, but its true dominance began with the introduction of sound. The combination of ready capital, established infrastructure, executive savvy (some of it Canadian-born), and political clout helped Hollywood's studios capture the world market. They would maintain a stranglehold on that market until the fifties, when the antitrust legislation of 1948 and the rise of television began gradually but steadily to erode a streamlined production system capable of turning out great art as well as endless dreck. Canada's function within this golden age was resolutely marginal, but it was a variegated marginality. There were the Canadian executives, producers, technicians, directors, and actors who participated in the system. There was Canada's role as producer of Hollywood 'quota quickies' for the British market. There were the rare features produced in Canada about Canada and Canadians. There were the nearly twenty independent feature films made during this period in Quebec, signalling, as Melnyk argues, the existence of a provincially 'national cinema' within the confines of a nation which itself had none.[24] And, of course, there was the National Film Board, established in 1939 with the express goal of 'interpret[ing]

Canada to Canadians and the rest of the World.'[25] The result was the creation of an extensive and highly respected corpus of documentaries and animated short subjects, two minor genres in film that functioned, as Melnyk rightly phrases it, as 'the film equivalent of the nation's identity as a handmaiden of greater powers who was allowed a temporary rise in status in a specific field that did not threaten the real hegemony.'[26]

As much as Melnyk's argument persuades in historical terms, however, it underestimates the degree to which the constraints of a minor role provide real opportunities unavailable at the heart of the empire. To exist on the margins of the United States may colour every move Canadians make, and it may lead to decadence and impotence, as Quebecois director Denys Arcand pointedly argued in his signature film on the subject, *Le Déclin de l'empire américain* (1986). But it can also, as the worldwide success of Arcand's film and others of the eighties and nineties demonstrated, result in a unique and powerfully critical perspective. As the modernist German cultural critic Walter Benjamin argued during the twenties, and as theorists Gilles Deleuze and Félix Guattari echoed in a postmodern context during the seventies, 'minor' art forms are not simply pale imitations of the great masterpieces.[27] Rather, they offer qualitatively different insights and pleasures that require methodologically distinct approaches in order to grasp those insights and to enjoy those pleasures. As Scott MacKenzie dialectically redefines 'minor' cinema within the context of a global film economy: 'Multicultural minor cinemas can be most usefully understood as texts that exist at the intersection between the "global cultures" of American cinema and international "art cinema" on the one hand, and local cultures for which minor cinemas supposedly speak, on the other.'[29] Precisely because of its equivocal situation, Canadian cinema has inhabited this intersection perhaps longer than any other national cinema. And, to be sure, the history of that cinema certainly includes a history of slavish servitude to the U.S. hegemony and failed attempts to imitate the success of Hollywood, but intertwined within that servitude is something else, something unique and fascinating, albeit readily visible only at certain moments within the broader trajectory of the industry.

With a few notable exceptions, the response of the Canadian government towards questions of the cinema has been, as Gittings unequivocally puts it, 'utilitarian ... they exploit its communicative function to develop trade and commerce.'[29] This de facto policy has meant giving in and adapting to U.S. interests rather than opposing or negotiating with them, as was the practice of the French, British, and Australians, among others, when they established quotas in the late twenties in response to the overwhelming success of the first Hollywood talkies.[30] Legislation to support the development of a local film industry has been tabled at various times, in particular by several provincial governments during the thirties and again in the mid-seventies, but in both cases the federal response was instead to open up Canada to Hollywood interests.[31] In the decade between 1927 and 1938, Hollywood made twenty features in Canada aimed at evading British quotas on non-Commonwealth films. Writing in the flush of the first wave of Canadian feature film-making in the seventies, Morris came down hard on these films, dismissing them as wholly lacking in Canadian content and accusing Hollywood producers 'with the collaboration of the Canadian government' of colluding to 'circumvent the clear intent of the British quota to encourage more British and Commonwealth production.'[32]

From an artistic and an economic point of view, Morris is quite correct in his assessment of the negligible genre films and the cynical manoeuvring of the power that be. Nevertheless, Melnyk and Gittings, as well as economic historians Ted Magder and Manjunath Pendakur, are at pains to observe from a more tempered and contextualized vantage point at the end of the century that this collaboration is less an exceptional and immoral episode then a demonstrable pattern of behaviour throughout the history of Canadian cinema.[33] For better or for worse, the industrial memory of this decade of film industry in Victoria, British Columbia, certainly had an influence on the enduring relationship of that region with Hollywood. Indeed, in his popular history of cinema in Vancouver, journalist David Spaner treats the quota episode matter-of-factly as the story of England-born, Hollywood-based producer Kenneth Bishop's removal to Victoria, where he made fourteen films, a variety of action dramas in 'Canadian' settings, the lion's share, that is, of the quota films.[34] Moreover, while there is general agreement as to the poor quality and meagre economic returns of Bishop's films, it is also clear that they are not wholly lacking in 'Canadian content.'

In a detailed and uncompromising reading of Bishop's second quota film, *Secrets of Chinatown* (1934), a lurid melodrama set in Vancouver's Asian community, Gittings offers the film as 'an important cultural document of white Canada's production of a filmic imaginary community based on race.'[35] One may question the ease with which Gittings reduces the archetypal tropes of melodramatic narrative to the specific spatio-temporal situation of Vancouver's Chinatown and the history of the Chinese in western Canada. One may wish for an analysis sufficiently flexible to negotiate the mythical Hollywood type of the evil Chinaman, criminal sexuality, drugs, violence, and the underside of the modern city in terms of the local controversy aroused by that portrayal. And one might equally hope for the recognition of the limited dissemination of these representations given not only that the film was a commercial failure in British Columbia, but that it did not even meet the restrictions of the British quota law and was ruled ineligible for release in the United Kingdom.[36] For all its flaws, Gittings's analysis does conclusively establish the utility of moving beyond a criterion of quality in evaluating the historical relevance of film production within Canada.

Melnyk makes the lucid observation that Canada's support of Hollywood over the United Kingdom 'was a signal of a major geopolitical shift.'[37] Rather than blocking the development of a local film industry, such an invisible accommodation seems to have been the logical consequence of Canada's unique cultural, geographic, and economic relationship to the United States. For all the facts of a Hollywood control over distribution that Canadian critics lament as the major factor in preventing the growth of a viable local industry, it is equally true that there never was a compelling economic reason for a sustained industry to develop. Even when the government response aimed directly to counter the influence of this hegemony, as with the creation of the NFB in 1939 and the initiatives created

1.2 *La petite Aurore: L'enfant martyre* (1951): spectacular realism in historical Quebecois melodrama. Cinémathèque Québécoise. Permission of Films Équinoxe.

in the wake of the 1951 Massey Report by the Royal Commission on National Development in the Arts, Letters and Sciences, an embrace (ironic or straight) of what Berton in 1975 polemically termed 'Hollywood's Canada' remained the primary mode of most Anglo-Canadian citizens. As Dorland puts it, 'Despite its recognition that Canadians wanted commercial features, the *Report* felt that the "only truly and typically Canadian films" they should be allowed to see were those given to them by the NFB.'[38] The official definition of what Canadians 'should be allowed to see' has over the years moved ever closer to commercial features, but despite the best efforts of Anglo-Canadian film-makers over the past few decades, the embrace of Hollywood has remained the preferred mode of consumption for most Canadians. The fact of that embrace must be reckoned with; however, as we shall see below, it does not preclude the possibility of a specifically Canadian reception of Hollywood or of the existence of other, minor modes of spectatorship within a broadly hegemonic frame.

This embrace did not occur to the same degree in Quebec, which during the same period evidently did demonstrate sufficiently pressing economic and cultural reasons to develop its own partial alternative to the new hegemony of Hollywood talkies. The first reason was linguistic: the sound film made English-language Hollywood inaccessible in the short term to a francophone public. This gap was initially filled by imports from France, which during the thirties was an important player in world cinema. Three factors contributed to the production of indigenous features in Quebec in the decade following the Second World War. In 1933, the Canadian Broadcasting Corporation had created a French-language branch, Radio-Canada, which disseminated extremely popular radio (and later television) comedies and serial melodramas.[39] The German occupation of France during the Second World War put a halt to the exportation of that country's films. And the highly conservative Union Nationale came to power in 1936, led by Maurice Duplessis, who was premier from 1936 to 1939, and again from 1944 until his death in 1959. Duplessis and his party ruled the province with a repressive ideology of church, family, and rural life that had little truck even with a Hollywood newly humbled by the censorious Motion Picture Production Code.

Two production companies, Paul L'Anglais's Quebec Productions and film distributor Joseph-Alexandre DeSève's Les Productions Renaissance, made films specifically for the Quebecois market, frequently based upon popular radio serials and local novels. Two of these films seem to have been especially deeply embedded in the Quebecois imaginary: the drama of the pathologically miserly mayor Séraphin in northern Quebec of the nineteenth century and the sadomasochistic tragedy of *La petite Aurore: L'enfant martyre*. Based on a long-running radio serial (1939–62), the story of Séraphin, his martyred young wife Donalda, and her erstwhile lover Alexis, a quintessential coureur de bois, or deep woodsman, was recounted in *Un homme et son péché* (A Man and His Sin, 1949) and its sequel *Séraphin* (1950), both directed by Paul Gury. Like the radio serial and the later Radio-Canada television series (1956–70), the films were scripted by Claude-Henri Grignon from his prize-winning 1933 novel. Discussing *Séraphin: Un homme et son péché*, his 2002 remake that broke box office records in Quebec, director Charles Binamé commented, 'It's as if it's become a national duty to see it.'[40] The myth and its popular representations had deep roots in the provincial psyche. The nineteenth-century colonization of the *pays d'en haut*, or north country, of Quebec was a central concern of the powerful clergy, a solution to what it saw as the demoralizing atmosphere of the overcrowded urban centres of Montreal and Quebec City. Similar to the dust bowl homesteading of the American West, the brutal suffering encountered by the settlers became equally part of the imaginary of these histories. It certainly underpinned the theme of martyrdom and 'collective morbidity' found by Quebecois critics in their popular culture.[41]

While the character of Séraphin emerged from the realist fiction of Balzac and the frontier mythology of colonial Quebec, the story of ten-year-old Aurore Gagnon, apparently tortured to death by her father and stepmother, belonged to more recent memory, the years between 1918 and 1920 in a small village some sixty miles southwest of Quebec City. Following a sensational trial that resulted in the conviction of both parents, the events were adapted as a highly successful stage play.[42] Emile Asselin's 1951 novel became the basis for the Jean-Yves Bigras's film the same year (figure 1.2). Weinmann, Véronneau, and Lever not only relate the play's theme of innocent martyrdom to the oppressive conservatism of the Duplessis years, but as Lever puts it, see the film in retrospect to be 'in complete contradiction with the official ideology … The countryside is a site of the martyrdom of children where there is no united family, where marriage brings only unhappiness, and where religion is completely ineffective.'[43]

The very excess of the melodramatic conventions invoked in *Séraphin* and *Aurore* simultaneously affirms (patient suffering is holy) and repudiates (the authorities of state and religion are helpless to prevent, if not complicit in, misfeasance towards innocents) their overt ideology. That *Aurore*, too, was recently remade with great success (as, simply, *Aurore*, in 2005, scripted and directed by TV writer Luc Dionne), is testimony to the enduring local power of these mythic stories. Moreover, the recent success of *Séraphin* and *Aurore* testifies to the mediated nature of that power; it is through their repetition on stage, radio, film, and television that they lodged themselves in the Quebecois imaginary. Gilles Carle had similar success during the early eighties with mediated remakes of historical dramas *Les Plouffe* (1980), based on a novel (1948), radio serial (1952), and television series (1953–9) and *Maria Chapdelaine* (1983), based on a 1913 novel, and previously adapted to the screen by the French in 1934 and 1950. Consequently, although the local industry proved to be non-viable in the short term – there were no feature-length fiction films made in Quebec between 1954 and 1964 – it crystallized a particular set of cultural representations that would continue to influence the Quebecois mediascape, first negatively, in the reaction against this 'morbid' culture by the new wave film-makers of the sixties, and then more positively, as they were assimilated back into mainstream film-making during the nineties by directors such as Binamé, adept at both contemporary 'art' films and big-budget historical epics, and actors such as Pascale Bussières, Roy Dupuis, Rémy Girard, and Karine Vanasse, who could be equally persuasive in either genre (see chapter 4).

While the Quebecois imaginary created a bizarre time-bubble for itself in reflection of and reaction to the backwards-looking Duplessis ideology, English Canada found a different form of marginality with which to oppose the golden age of Hollywood: the National Film Board. Created at the instigation and under the leadership of Scottish documentarist John Grierson, the NFB was indisputably successful in creating a cinematic image for the nation of Canada abroad: by its sixtieth anniversary, the thousands of documentary and animated films it had produced had received eleven Academy Awards and been nominated for sixty-three; the NFB webpage, which streams a healthy proportion of this production free of charge online, is a testament to the success of the program's democratic goals.[44] Devised by Grierson to apply the dramatic power of fictional cinema to the ideological message of documentary, the NFB began life as a highly effective source of wartime propaganda.[45] Grierson's puritan ideology of self-sufficiency through 'strength, simplicity, energy, directness, hardness, decency, courage, duty, upstanding power' and his message of man's ability to overcome the environment were perfectly suited, as Melnyk suggests, to the myth of the Canadian frontier.[46] And although Grierson's version of this message was progressive and populist, there is no mistaking the family resemblance to the Duplessis ideology: both of them based society in the moral fibre of its citizens, and both derived the strength of that moral fibre from the assertion of a deep, emotional, and inherently optimistic connection with the land.

Just as the Duplessis years stifled change and innovation that would eventually burst forth in the flowering of film-making of the sixties, so some film-makers would come to see the NFB (albeit with less justice) as a stuffy and suffocating institution suitable primarily for producing earnest and soporific school films. Nevertheless, it is a testimony to the NFB's openness to this diversity of voices from the fifties on that the most important challenges to its own documentary model emerged from within its own organization. That openness derived from Grierson's ambition to 'cover the whole field of civic interest: what Canadians need to know and think about if they are going to do their best by Canada and by themselves.'[47] As is the way with liberal visions, however, Grierson's policies legitimated not only the NFB's gradual expansion to alternative modes of documentary film-making but also the negation of alternative voices under the guise of inclusivity. Gittings's analysis of a documentary series expressively concerned with the diversity of Canadian identity, *Peoples of Canada* (1947), makes clear the ideological limits of the Griersonian documentary in the immediate post-war period.[48] The narrative rehearses the familiar tropes and blind spots of post-war liberalism: 'Although *Peoples of Canada* legitimizes specific *ethnic* differences amongst Caucasians, its representation of *racial* differences remains conflicted and for the most part limits or elides the signification of racialized groups as peoples of Canada.'[49] In other words, while the liberal vision of Canadian identity could easily expand to include white Eastern European immigrants, as in the sensitive and unmistakably 'othered' voice of a Polish immigrant in Winnipeg in *Paul Tomkowicz, Street-railway Switchman* (1953, Roman Kroitor), its 'imagined community' was not yet able to acknowledge in the same way the presence of Asians, aboriginal peoples, and Africans. Precisely because its ideological meaning was so explicitly displayed, the Griersonian model of documentary was unable to incorporate the contradictions inherent to liberal democracy into its form. This deficiency did not go unremarked at the time, although it was expressed in the language of aesthetics and technical proficiency rather than the political criteria evoked more recently by Gittings. As D.B. Jones notes, the single critique levelled by the Massey Report against the NFB was concerned with the quality of its documentaries. Jones wrote that the NFB documentary 'typically did not probe deeply into its subject. It did not explore the reality being filmed. Instead, the Film Board documentary tended to start from certain didactic principles and then collect material useful for illustrating them,' rather than seeking 'reality' in present-day Canada.[50] While it was easily accepted that the marginal status of the documentary suited Canada's situation at the edge of the American empire, its unitary approach to meaning and identity made it increasingly ill-suited for a nation that by the sixties had become fully aware of the degree to which its identity was based instead on irreconcilable difference.

Grierson himself had taken the first step towards diversifying the NFB's film

1.3 *Neighbours*: the white picket fence transformed into the emblem of mutually assured destruction. Photofest.

production when he had hired experimental animator Norman McLaren in 1941, along with McLaren's 'open but discreet lover' Guy Glover, who would make 290 films for the NFB exhibiting, according to Thomas Waugh, a 'commitment to intercultural exchange, nonconformity, progressive causes, and especially the performing arts.'[51] Rather than explicitly divergent in their meaning, the majority of McLaren's shorts were *formally* innovative: pixelated, scratched directly on film, or using multi-imaging techniques on human figures. One of the rare times McLaren employed a straightforward narrative form suggests the as yet unrealized potential for story in incorporating ambiguity into cinematic meaning. The 1952 short film *Neighbours* combined real actors and a real location with cardboard sets and pixelated animation to create an admonitory fable about peace and cooperation (figure 1.3). When a flower appears on the open lawn between two neighbours, their initial enjoyment of its beauty and scent devolves into a battle for possession that escalates from attempts to claim it with fences to hand-to-hand fighting before ending, inevitably, in mutual destruction. In a final irony, grass-covered burial mounds rise over their bodies, the white pickets fence them in together, and one yellow flower grows atop each grave: one for each is available only in death. The visual iconography is identical to that of fifties documentary: two well-dressed middle-class Anglo-Protestant men reading the newspaper in the natural splendour of their backyard kingdoms, wives and children present but tidily out of sight and mind.

As in the excessive melodrama of the Quebecois features of the period, however, the form of *Neighbours* subverts this iconography in several ways. First, the live-action pixelation lends a highly playful and fantastic tone to the early minutes of the film reminiscent of the experimental games of Georges Méliès, as the bodies of the two men are manipulated and thrown around the backyard like toys, apparently enjoying every moment of the intoxicating effect of the flower. Second, the behaviour of the two men is the precise contrary of the responsible decorum demanded of the middle-class citizen by the Griersonian model (or the Eisenhower era in America, for that matter). The white pickets of suburban prosperity and private property are instead marked as negative signs of division before they are appropriated even more negatively as weapons of war; they conclude the film transformed into markers of death. When their conflict escalates, the two men, rather than escalate technology in the manner of the arms race, return to atavistic savagery, scratching each other's faces, ripping each other's clothes, and (in a censored scene only reinstated in 1969) killing each other's families. Rather than assuming the natural desirability of the dominant markers of race, sex, and class, the film strongly implies that they constitute a threat to civilization.

The openness of the allegorical form also works against limiting the film's meaning. Does its warning scenario about 'neighbours' refer to internal divisions within the nation of Canada, to the relationship between Canada and the United States, to the dividing lines of the Cold War, or to some universal conception of sociality? The strongest indication of a meaning beyond 'whiteness as a collective identity' is the 'moral': the series of titles that concludes the film. Again hearkening back to the days of early cinema, the first title reads, in English, 'So.' This is followed by fourteen further titles presenting the same message each in a different language, moving from the most self-evidently 'foreign' (Asian and Arab scripts) through Greek and Eastern European languages to Spanish, French, and finally, English: 'Love Your Neighbour.' While the concluding sequence in no way eliminates the problematic assumptions identified by Gittings in NFB productions in general, it is also far from taking them for granted. Zoë Druick correctly recalls the film's relation to the 'internationalism' of the period, and the function of that internationalism 'to bolster the centralizing tendencies of nationalism'; however, the film's fundamental ambiguity allows it equally to function as a critique of that very stance.[52] Just as the film proposes a choice of peaceful cohabitation or mutual destruction, so its moral figuratively interpellates all of the citizens of the world in all of their differences from one another.

The multiplicity of languages and playful homage to Méliès is if anything more strongly evident in McLaren's follow-up fable, *A Chairy Tale* (1957), co-directed with a youthful Claude Jutra, who also plays the only human role in a two-handed pixelated film relating, as Waugh phrases it, the 'hot pursuit and courtship' of 'Claude and a non-gender specific chair' in a 'struggle for an equal relationship' that concludes when 'the chair agrees to be sat on only if it's reciprocal.'[53] Waugh includes both *Neighbours* and *A Chairy Tale* in his 'queer' canon of Canadian cinema, and there is a plausible argument to be made for a specifically gay subtext both biographically (in terms of the mostly closeted sexual identities of McLaren and Jutra) and formally (in the more negative *Neighbours*, the two men eliminate each other's families as part of their struggle to the death, while in the optimistic *A Chairy Tale* they amicably resolve the dilemma of who's on top). But a more broadly queer reading could incorporate the multicultural context of both films – the inclusion by both of a global range of languages along with the background score of *A Chairy Tale* by Indian sitarist Ravi Shankar and tabla player Chatur Lai – as an expansion of the gay subtext to reflect the openness of the allegory in each film. In line with the argument I make in chapter 8, the queerness of these films would operate simultaneously to expand the range of possible identities, be they sexual, ethnic, regional, or other. Similarly, its allusion to the playful cinematic effects of Méliès, whose classic short *Le diable noir* (1905) recounts a similar (although far less amicable) encounter between a man and a magical chair, expands the range of combinations between the reality effect of live-action photography and invisible animation effects.

McLaren and the other animators were part of the NFB's Unit B, one of four units formed during the reorganization of 1950. Perceived as privileged because they were seldom required to do sponsored work and their autonomy was protected by unit head Tom Daly, the film-makers in Unit B produced, in addition to animation, 'art films (including experimental and "loners," or single items), classroom and science films, and foreign versions.'[54] In a series of stand-alone films as well as in the *Candid Eye* television films (1958–9), unit members Wolf Koenig, Colin Low, Roman Kroitor, along with voice-over author and narrator Stanley Jackson and others, invented the 'direct cinema.' Making use of newly available mobile camera and other technology permitting unobtrusive and flexible location shooting, the anglophone directors, like the closely associated Quebecois members of *l'équipe française* (including Unit B cinematographer Michel Brault and sound man Marcel Carrière) aimed to capture the 'decisive moments' of contemporary life, following the dictum of French photo-journalist Henri Cartier-Bresson.[55] While the live-action animations of McLaren challenged the transparent nature of reality from the vantage point of fiction, the direct cinema mounted a similar challenge from the vantage point of documentary. A historical documentary such as *City of Gold* (1952, Low and Koenig), although commissioned to promote Yukon tourism, used innovative animation technology to simulate movement within a collection of glass-plate negatives recording the Klondike gold rush of 1897.[56] Opening with an extended montage of present-day photographs of the near–ghost town of Dawson City, the film was bound together by the poetically autobiographical narration of Pierre Berton, son of a prospector. Kroitor and Low's ambitious and acclaimed classroom film *Universe* (1960) used realistic animation techniques to persuasively render the fabric of the cosmos from the tiny margin of earth to the distant centre of the universe, bound together again by a poetic voice-over, this time by Jackson. The creative crossover between animation and documentary produced hybrid products nevertheless profoundly invested in the 'real.'

Rather than determining the form of NFB films, the strict Griersonian model signalled an investment by the NFB in what Leach terms a 'national-realist project'

that 'was always an unstable one.'[57] Nevertheless, that investment – both ideological and financial – exerted a powerful influence on the production and reception
of Canadian cinema well into the nineties. As Melnyk suggests, the NFB was particularly well suited to the culture of Canada.[58] The various strands of the NFB
were largely responsible for the narrative form generally termed 'documentary
realism,' which, as Leach maintains, 'has played an important part in shaping how
films have been interpreted and how questions about the national cinema have
been posed.'[59] Leach goes on to argue that the tradition itself 'becomes increasingly
aware of the difficulty of adequately representing the real' and begins to produce
'investigations into the possibilities and limits of realism.'[60] Documentary realism,
that is, was simultaneously accepted as the 'typically Canadian' approach to film-
making and challenged as being inadequate for the representation of reality. Even
thus broadened, however, the concept remains insufficiently supple to incorporate a more capacious investment in the immediacy of the cinematic image that, I
argue throughout this book, distinguishes Canadian cinema even as it takes such
a varied range of forms – from the visceral impact of Cronenberg's body horror
to the psychological realism of Lauzon's surrealism to the emotional openness of
Léa Pool's late films to the psychological credibility of genre cinema such as *Ginger
Snaps* – that it is difficult to reduce it to a single national trait.

This unusually strong insistence on the bond between the cinematic image and
material reality manifests itself visually in the reality effect of so many northern
locations, the visibly and spectacularly uncontrollable traces of cold in evidence
from the wide expanses of wild nature in feature films of the silent period to the
wintry landscapes that punctuate recent features from *Away from Her* (2006, Sarah
Polley) to *Scanners 2: The New Order* (1991, Christian Duguay). Needless to say,
such traces of the real coexist uneasily with the patently unreal structures of melodramatic fiction in a film such as *Back to God's Country*, just as they are difficult to
reconcile with the fantastic qualities of Cronenberg's horror and science fiction.
And yet I think it would be a mistake not to take at face value the claim made by
posters for the *La petite Aurore* that loudly proclaimed it to be 'Extraordinaire de
réalisme!' (figure 1.2), however laughably unreal its exaggeration may seem to the
criteria of documentary realism, just as it would be a mistake to assume that the
shocking verisimilitude of the exploding head that propelled Cronenberg's sci-fi/
horror flick *Scanners* to the top of the box office in 1981 might not also somehow
relate to a Canadian enthusiasm for realist cinema not encompassed by the narrow
category of documentary realism. While the genre conventions of *Aurore* and *Scanners* have roots in popular culture dating back at least as far as nineteenth-century
spectacle, both films bring familiarly Canadian inflections to those conventions;
chief among those inflections are various forms of reality effect. An important distinction between Canadian cinema of recent decades and the canonical films of
the sixties is the way more recent films left behind a direct reaction to the perceived constraints of Griersonian documentary and the post-war social context
and began to come to terms with the more ambivalent reality effects evident in
McLaren's fantasies, the long history of Canadian genre film, and other alternative
modes of approaching the real.

While the great films of the sixties and early seventies were the product of a
rebellion against traditional NFB constraints, the very nature of that rebellion led

them to continue to work, and to be perceived to be working, broadly within the NFB framework of realism as defined by Grierson. The first true split to emerge was the call for a genuinely francophone film-making instead of the French translation of the NFB's English-language products.[61] The symbolic move of the NFB from the national capital of Ottawa to Quebec's largest city, Montreal, in 1956 was followed a year later by the appointment of Guy Roberge as its first francophone commissioner. Although a French-language production unit would not be formed until 1964, the new location facilitated the hiring of or association with film-makers such as Brault, Jutra, and Gilles Groulx, who would become central figures in Quebecois cinema.[62] A year later, the NFB began an attempt to regionalize production, recognizing that 'English Canadian film-makers at the Board emphasized the totality of a pan-Canadian cinema at the expense of the diverse "parts that made the whole meaningful."'[63] Ten years later, a similarly prescient move was made to 'provide women access to the cinematic apparatus and the production of their own images' through the creation of Studio D, 'the first publicly funded women's production unit in the world.'[64] Finally, during the nineties, the NFB began actively promoting First Nations film-making, opening Studio One in Edmonton in 1991 and initiating the decentralized Aboriginal Filmmaking Program five years later.[65] The diversification of the NFB inevitably entailed a diminished sense of its Griersonian identity and centrality to the national cinema, but its documentary roots subsist: the most frequently voiced complaint about funding continues to be the NFB prejudice against feature-length fiction.

Canada's Revolutions

> Our radio picked up Buffalo and Montreal, always together, never separate, so that the religious broadcasts always had a pleasant background of country music ... We seven children would thus recite our rosaries at a gallop, learning that in Quebec the most contradictory dreams are possible!
>
> Gilles Carle (1972)

The institutional bias against 'fiction' was equally evident in the critical community, especially during the seventies and eighties, and even within the governmental organizations developed to support the making of Canadian features. In both the Canadian Film Development Corporation (1968) and its successor, Telefilm Canada (1983), a strong tension persisted between support for Hollywood-style genre films and a suspicion of the commercial motivation of those films, along with a resistance to the intrinsic value of any feature film not exhibiting a strongly documentary and moralistic core. The standard history of the Canadian feature runs through documentary: the rise of anglophone and Quebecois direct cinema from within the NFB, the creation of landmark first features in Toronto and Montreal from within the auspices of the NFB, and the public/commercial funding of a series of internationally distributed films through the mid-seventies, all steeped in the values of documentary realism, variously inflected with, but not superseded by, the tropes of fiction.

In 1962, the NFB produced its first feature film, *Drylanders*, the historical drama

of a Montreal family colonizing Saskatchewan. Firmly in the nationally ideological tradition of its traditional documentaries, it would, after a limited theatrical
release, circulate as an educational film.[66] The creation of direct cinema within Studio B had been primarily a formal decision for Koenig and Kroitor in response
to the availability of new, lighter, more portable equipment. In contrast, *le direct*,
the analogous move by *l'équipe française*, was far more directly and more self-consciously political. Precisely because they felt misrepresented by the assumption
of objectivity and power associated with the conventional documentary format,
Brault and Groulx developed *le direct*, with the 'aim to minimize ... the mediating
work of film-maker and camera on "the real."'[67]

   Naturally, the choice of subject was as important as the way it was filmed. In *Les
Raquetteurs* (The Snowshoers, 1958), generally considered the inaugural example
of direct cinema, cinematographer Brault and editor Groulx recorded the annual
snowshoe festival in Sherbrooke, a city in southeastern Quebec. The focus of the
fourteen-minute documentary is a snowshoe race and the subsequent celebration.
There is no voice-over commentary, no linear editing, and no obvious narrative
sequencing; rather, Brault's handheld camera plunges us into the action as if we
were participants in the festival. Both formally and thematically, this is a celebration of local difference; the very subject of a snowshoe race posits an oxymoronic
quirkiness diametrically opposed to, say, the conventional celebration of athletic
grace and speed epitomized in Leni Riefenstahl's epic documentary of the 1936
Olympic Games. A similar ideology is evident in Brault and Pierre Perrault's feature-length documentary, *Pour la suite du monde* (So the World Goes On, 1962),
which records the efforts of fishermen on the St Lawrence River's Île aux Coudres
to revive (at Perrault's prompting) a tradition of beluga whale hunting abandoned
in 1924. Responding especially to the ethnographic film-making of French director
Jean Rouch, who had used Brault as cameraman in the direct cinema documentary
of Parisian life, *Chronique d'un été* (1960), Brault, Groulx, and Perrault sought a new
Quebecois identity through the cinematic equivalent of anthropological fieldwork.
If the broad ideological structures to be combated were predominantly either
Anglo-Protestant (on the federal level) or Duplessist (on the provincial level), then
they would seek the essence of the Quebecois in the local and the everyday.

   As Marshall suggests, both films raise important questions about the goals and
limitations of the direct cinema approach. First, he argues, the aim of 'recording
reality' in the present precludes the possibility of interrogating that reality and
noting, for example, the Amerindian origin of the tradition of the snowshoes in
the process of being celebrated.[68] Nevertheless, *Pour la suite du monde* does record,
without commentary, an ongoing dispute among the inhabitants of the island
over whether the practice of whale hunting was invented by 'les sauvages' or
brought over by the French. It would be a number of years before the complex
and intertwined relationship between Native peoples and French Canadians, first
broached in the stereotyped villains of the old Hollywood melodramas before
being occluded from the documentary tradition, would be reintroduced within the
context of feature film. Second, there is the question of the role of the film-makers
in the creation or recreation of tradition. By the very act of filming, as well as the
fact of encouraging the renewal of an abandoned tradition, the film-makers are

raising everyday activities to the status of myth, asserting their identity-bestowing qualities within the imagined community of the Quebecois. As Marshall puts it, 'Perrault sets up a homology between "real life," the islanders and their culture, and those aspects of "Quebec" and the "Québécois" untainted by capitalism and mass society.'[69] *Pour la suite du monde* plots an implicit narrative regarding the possibility of incorporating indigenous traditions into the modern world, with the climax of the film occurring as the islanders deliver the captured whale to the New York aquarium. However, the film's conclusion remains equivocal, recording the overall disappointment of the hunt's limited success and raising doubts that it will be anything other than a one-shot deal.

Perhaps unique among contemporary movements of decolonization and liberation, the 'Quiet Revolution' against the Duplessis years of which the *cinéma direct* was such an important element found itself subject to nearly irreconcilable contradictions. First, the Quebecois sought independence from two 'colonial' masters, the French (their cultural masters) and the English Canadians (their political and economic masters). Second, they sought liberation from their own repressive government. And, third, although seeking liberation, they were themselves a colonizing people, having displaced the First Nations. These contradictions are well articulated in Groulx's 1964 feature, *Le chat dans le sac*, which he expanded without permission from its origins as an NFB documentary. The film recounts the crumbling relationship between two young Montrealers: Barbara, who is Anglo and Jewish, and Claude, who is French Canadian. Borrowing explicitly from the French new wave cinema and the anti-colonialist theories of Martiniquan writer Frantz Fanon, Groulx filmed the feature with handheld camera, incorporating long discussions between Barbara and Claude about contemporary issues and exchanges between fictional characters and 'real' people. Montreal is characterized as a modern space full of fluid identities and jazz music. However, somewhere past the midpoint of the film, Claude moves to the countryside, where he reads, writes, and ponders his situation. Groulx marks the countryside as a fixed site of burgeoning Quebecois identity. In a key sequence, as classical music plays, Claude watches Manouche, a local girl, skating elegant circles on a frozen pond. We know that Barbara will never come to him in the country, and that Claude is stuck, unable to reconcile the fluid intellectual and aesthetic means necessary to articulate a new identity with the raw material of that identity, beautifully frozen in the ice of the little pond.

Part of what makes the Quebecois features of this period so fascinating is the different ways they choose to negotiate the complex paths towards a 'national' identity. Indeed, one could argue that, contrary to the unified veneer of Duplessis ideology, the essence of the Quiet Revolution lay in the conscious articulation of irreconcilable identities. To be sure, the embrace of contradiction also tends to lead to extremely negative endings: *Le chat dans le sac* concludes with Claude's relationship ended and his life in a dead end; Jutra's autobiographical first feature, *A tout prendre* (shot 1961–3, released 1964), ends in the protagonist's suicide; Brault's melancholy early feature *Entre la mer et l'eau douce* (*Drifting Upstream*, 1967) gives us a protagonist caught between an uncomfortable relationship with a Native woman in his home town downriver and an unconsummated relationship with a waitress in a local diner. The modernity of the city offers opportunity and intellectual and aesthetic tools, but those very tools threaten the local specificity of the identity they will be used to articulate. Naturally, the film medium itself and the urban centre of its production in Montreal further exacerbate this tension. Postcolonial artists in Latin America and Africa would more easily employ modern art forms to give visibility to indigenous cultures, but because Quebecois culture was itself colonialist and overlaid with the full weight of Duplessist ideology, that option was not so easily available. Moreover, the step forward into radical modernity taken by European film-makers meant the risk of repudiating the very 'indigenous' traditions upon which Quebecois identity seemed to be grounded.

The growth of Quebecois film-making was aided by the closely knit character of the group. As Brault put it, 'We were born in cinema together, so to speak. We worked together, learned together.'[70] Denys Arcand co-directed the first feature of the period, *Seul ou avec d'autres* (*Alone or with Others*, 1962), with Denis Héroux (who would make several films about modern-day Montreal before changing direction with *Valérie* [1967] and *L'Initiation* [1970], two enormously successful films in the soft-core cycle that became known as 'maple syrup porno'). The cinematographer of Arcand's film was Brault; its editors were Groulx and Bernard Gosselin, who collaborated with Brault on many of the key films of the period. Writers for *Entre la mer et l'eau douce* included Arcand, Jutra, and Brault. The collaboration was theoretical as well: in 1964, the left-wing journal *Parti pris* published articles by NFB film-makers arguing for a greater role for personally oriented narrative features in the formation of a Quebec national cinema by Arcand, Groulx, the writer and director Jacques Godbout, Clément Perron (who would script Jutra's masterwork *Mon oncle Antoine*), and Gilles Carle (see chapter 4). Many of them accomplished writers and critics, the Quebecois film-makers of this generation were deeply engaged in the political and intellectual life of the province. Some, like Groulx and Perrault, continued to work in various forms of documentary; others, like Jean-Pierre Lefebvre, director of intimate, carefully observed films such as *Les dernières fiançailles* (1973) and the politically astute *Le vieux pays où Rimbaud est mort* (1977), made narrative features while keeping their distance from commercial waters. Still others, like Arcand (see chapter 3), moved into commercial film-making without abandoning their previous commitments: Brault in 1974 made the landmark docudrama *Les Ordres*, a bitter but definitive account of the October Crisis, while in 1989 he directed the popular immigration comedy-drama, *Les noces de papier* (Paper Wedding); he continued to lens some of the most important films of the era, including Jutra's *Antoine* and *Kamouraska* (1973); *Mourir à tue-tête* (1979), Anne-Claire Poirier's angry feminist depiction of rape and the culture surrounding it; and *Les bons debarras* (1980), Francis Mankiewicz's brilliant portrayal of the complex relationship between a twelve-year-old girl and her marginal mother.

Perhaps the most enigmatic figure of this impressive group was Jutra, whose *À tout prendre* was the most explicitly and experimentally new wave inspired of the early features, whose second feature *Mon oncle Antoine* is still widely considered the best Canadian film ever made, and whose career took a number of odd turns before he apparently took his own life in 1986, drowning himself in the St Lawrence River after discovering that he was suffering from Alzheimer's disease. While the majority of the sixties features had focused squarely on the present day, preferring to address questions of the past in the style of the *direct*, through their function in contemporary life, *Antoine* addressed the Duplessis years head-on. Set in a 1940s mining town (it was filmed at Black Lake, Quebec, near Thetford Mines, a community that had been hit badly by asbestos poisoning), the film centres around the lives of two families: Antoine and his wife Cécile, who run the general store and serve as the town's undertakers, along with their orphaned nephew Benoît, through whose perspective most of the events in the film are narrated, and the family of Jos Poulin, a rebellious and independent mine worker who spends his winter as a logger in the north woods, and who lives in the countryside beyond the town. While the first half of the film concerns closely observed details of town life centred on the general store at Christmas time, the crux of the action concerns the nocturnal sleigh ride Benoît and his uncle take to fetch the body of the Poulin family's dead boy for burial. For young Benoît, accompanying his uncle is a wintertime adventure and a rite of passage into adulthood; for the uncle, it is a tedious chore that he accomplishes primarily through heavy drinking. When Antoine passes out on the return journey, Benoît tries the drink himself, leading to a joy ride during which the coffin drops off in the snow. Unfit to help him, Antoine breaks down in a stream of regrets to which Benoît responds unsympathetically. The next we see, Benoît is driving up the main road of the village with Antoine lying on the sled where the coffin should be, a living corpse replacing a dead one. Benoît must return to the Poulin house in a snow storm with shop manager Fernand (played by Jutra). Looking through the window, Benoît sees the family silently gathered around the boy's frozen body, evidently encountered by the father returning from the logging camp to spend Christmas at home. We watch the family with Benoît through the window, as Jutra allows the full horror of events he has chosen not to show to sink in: the father's discovery of the body abandoned in the snow of a son he didn't even know had been ill; the family's shock at the father's return with a body to which they thought they had bid farewell. The mother's withering gaze bores straight into the camera before Jutra cuts back to Benoît. The credits roll over a freeze-frame close-up of Benoît's face shot from inside the house looking out (figure 1.4), as we imagine his response to the realization of his own culpability in what has just happened.

In his book on Jutra, Leach rightly compares the shot to the celebrated conclusion of François Truffaut's new wave feature, *Les quatre cent coups* (1959), and its 'challenge to the spectator to respond to the questions that have troubled the adolescent throughout the film.'[71] Surely a pointed allusion on Jutra's part, the resemblance of the shots equally emphasizes the difference between the two films. Where the final moment of Antoine Doinel turning away from the sea he had long yearned to reach freezes us on the uncertainty of one boy's future, Jutra's shot of Benoît inserts that same future within the complex social structure the film has painstakingly established during the previous two hours. It suggests not only the realization of the practical and moral failure of his uncle as an individual and as one of the principal French-Canadian authorities in the village, but also Benoît's complicity in an act of great callousness towards a family that is his social inferior but his moral equal. The combination of dignity and accusation in the faces of the Poulin family members simply but effectively expands the political allegory

1.4 The haunting freeze-frame that concludes *Mon oncle Antoine* (1971) at a historical and an aesthetic crossroads. Photofest.

established with the opening shots of Jos Poulin at the mines and the equally cal-lous exploitation of the francophone workers by the anglophone minority.[72] As Marshall observes, Benoît's own tenuous position as an orphan and an adolescent 'challenges both the authority structure of the Duplessis era and a comfortably installed identity of self and nation. It does this not by debunking identity and community but by emphasizing their provisionality and lack of groundedness, their "lies" but also the "truths" they can offer in snatches.'[73]

Antoine was criticized at the time of its release for departing from 'pure' *cinéma direct*. This departure is especially evident in the dream sequence of the drunk and exhausted Benoît, but as Leach suggests, the very structure of the film employs 'a fluid and dreamlike time scheme' that complicates a straightforward sense of documentary reality.[74] Both Leach and Marshall note the complex way in which Jutra 'blurs' past and present, the political issues of the Quiet Revolution and the mythical past of the Duplessis era.[75] It is, of course, a logical impossibility to make a direct cinema film about the past. Documentaries such as *Les Raquetteurs* and *Pour la suite du monde* address this epistemological problem by filming the recrea-tion of past rituals in the present, the enactment of a form of history rather than history itself. But Jutra's suspicion of the verities of the present as much as of those of the past (he was a staunch separatist who was terrified by the abuses to which nationalism seemed inevitably to lead) led him to depart from the strict adherence to recording the present. The dreamlike temporality, especially evident in the first magical and then nightmarish ride through the winter woods at night, is not a repudiation of realism, however; it puts forth the argument that reality is not so fixed, so tangible, or so immutable as to be captured directly merely by the reality effect of a camera.

There were risks in this approach, in particular the loss of the local texture and familiar immediacy necessary to distinguish a film as 'Quebecois.' One of the reasons for the enduring critical reputation and popularity of *Antoine* (it is regularly screened on television to high ratings) is its ability to combine an art-film approach to narrative and cinematic time with the hallmark 'reality effect' of direct cinema. Less fortunate in his reception was the Montreal director Paul Almond, who made three haunting and highly psychological features during this period starring his then-wife Geneviève Bujold: *Isabel* (1968), *Act of the Heart* (1970), and *Journey* (1972). Although shot primarily in real locations and highly sensitive to the visual and psychological effects of the spaces in which they take place, these films, in the art-house tradition of European masters such as Ingmar Bergman, used those spaces to enact psychic and metaphysical dramas rather than raise questions of local identity. Nor is it accidental that, like *The Apprenticeship of Duddy Kravitz* (1974), Ted Kotcheff's accomplished adaptation of Mordecai Richler's novel of Montreal Jews, Almond's poorly received films took an anglophone's agnostic stance towards the issue of separatism and identity. Not that the film-makers were unaware of the issue: Bujold, of course, is French Canadian, and the Quebecois actor (and, later, acclaimed director) Micheline Lanctôt played the role of Duddy's long-suffering French-Canadian girlfriend. Moreover, a central concern of Richard Dreyfuss's frenetically ambitious Duddy is the acquisition of land, which his grandfather has assured him will guarantee him a stable identity. A stable identity is, in fact, something Yvette has always possessed, just as she offers a stable and traditional, if eventually fed up, centre for Duddy's tragicomic antics and betrayals.

Despite the local roots of Montrealers Richler and Kotcheff (they were roommates during the period in the fifties when Richler wrote the novel), *Duddy* was criticized for lacking local authenticity, especially in the casting of American actor Richard Dreyfuss in the title role (his first, and career-making, leading role). And, to be sure, the film does in many parts project a Hollywood spatio-temporal vagueness even in its use of Quebec locations. At other times, especially in the scenes with Lanctôt and in the hilarious pseudo-ethnographic 'documentary' of a bar mitzvah produced by Duddy with a washed-up and alcoholic NFB refugee (Denholm Elliot), the film most definitely captures something authentic about Montreal, albeit an aspect of it egregiously absent from Quebecois cinema of the period. This authenticity is not only the simple fact of the important Jewish presence in the history of Montreal, but also that city's underlying history of anti-Semitism, a fact against which Duddy battles for the entire film and which patently structures his stay-hungry mentality. As Melnyk aptly puts it, 'A film portraying a minority in Canada based on the writing of a novelist from that community was a breakthrough that signaled the coming age of multiculturalism.'[76] There was more to Canadian identity, in other words, than the two solitudes of Quebecois and Anglo Protestant, and there always had been. Moreover, as the film more subtly noted via Duddy's ambitions as a film producer, Canadian national cinema itself had always had a Jewish presence, and that presence operated under different rules than the ones that split anglophone and Quebecois. The Montreal film industry, like any other commercial industry, was all about the bottom line. After all, Cinépix, the production company behind maple syrup porno and also the early horror films of anglophone and Jewish Torontonian David Cronenberg, was, in the words of the latter, 'just André Link, a European Jew who spoke French, and John Dunning, who was totally WASP. For me to say they represented French-Canadian film-making is very ironic, but they did.'[77] In the world of the NFB, the critics, the direct cinema, and the Quebecois national cinema, Montreal was the capital of separatism and a single way of making movies; in the practical world of film-making and in the images of the films themselves, the reality was more fluid, more diverse, and more interesting.

The question of identity and its function in creating a national cinema was equally central to the English-Canadian feature films of the same period. Like Groulx's, Don Owen's seminal first feature, *Nobody Waved Goodbye* (1964), was cobbled together out of an NFB commission for a medium-length documentary. Owen's topic was juvenile delinquency, and the improvised scenario powerfully and self-consciously echoes the familiar tropes of Hollywood 'troubled youth' films, especially *Rebel without a Cause* (1955). Whereas director Nicholas Ray had set the tribulations of middle-class West-Coast teens James Dean, Sal Mineo, and Natalie Wood against the backdrop of gaudy widescreen Technicolor splendour, Owen employed handheld, direct cinema–style camerawork, location shooting, and the folk music ambience of sixties Toronto to create a gritty, realist context for Peter Mark's rebellion. There is little romanticism in Peter and his girlfriend Julie's dissatisfaction with the suffocating status quo; instead, like Sandy Wilson's later *My American Cousin* (1985), the film clearly identifies the James Dean persona as a borrowed and empty pose unsuited to the clear-eyed pragmatism of Canadian life. When Peter and Julie go joyriding in his car-dealer father's demo model, he gets pulled over for running a red light and jailed overnight. When he leaves home, we see him sleeping on a park bench and then seeking a job at an employment office, but relegated to work as a parking-lot attendant, where all he learns is how to short-change the customers. Despite being castigated by a French-Canadian friend for the 'American way of life' he has adopted, Peter seems unable to disentangle himself from his delinquency. Instead, he steals a car off the lot, takes the money from the cash register, and tries to skip town with his pregnant girlfriend. The film-noir fantasy of lovers on the lam is short-lived, however; upon learning of his theft, Julie gets out of the car, leaving Peter driving at night in the rain to the plangent sound of a banjo, tears in his eyes, as the screen fades to black. Owen refuses the Hollywood choice of repentance and redemption or death in a blaze of glory, but his film fails to offer the careful articulation of contradictions characteristic of the Quebecois films of the same period. For Peter, as for the English-Canadian cinema, the crisis arises not from a surfeit of conflicting sources of identity and rebellion, but from the devastating recognition that he has nothing to call his own.

The sustained sense of earnest desperation, the authenticity of the film's style, and its refusal of the narrative tropes of melodrama earned it a strong critical reception abroad and helped pave the way for further English-Canadian features. Owen made a second NFB-produced feature about an aimless, delinquent youth, *The Ernie Game* (1967), but was unable to duplicate the success of *Nobody Waved Goodbye*, and as with the careers of so many Canadian film-makers, his career failed to live up to the promise of his feature debut.[78]

In part because of its NFB origins (they would assist in the commercial release of the film by paying for the blow-up from 16 mm to 35 mm), *Nobody Waved Goodbye* was widely viewed and discussed. This was also the case with Vancouver native Allan King's controversial documentary features *Warrendale* (1967), a record of seven weeks in the lives of twelve disturbed children, and *A Married Couple* (1969), an intimate ten-week account of the disintegration of a marriage. Commissioned by the CBC, *Warrendale* ran into trouble for the explicit language used by its subjects, but was eventually broadcast and earned a number of awards.[79] Although independently produced, *A Married Couple* ran into similar trouble with the Ontario Censor Board over language and a nude swimming scene, but was nevertheless commercially released and moderately successful.[80] Unable to sustain a career with a type of documentary that 'hovers between claims to documentary authenticity and fictional artifice,' King moved into television, where he was a prolific director of drama episodes in the eighties and nineties.[81] Also from Vancouver was the independent film-maker Larry Kent, who made three innovative and locally influential feature films on a shoestring while a student at the University of British Columbia without the benefit of any local industry: *The Bitter Ash* (1963), *Sweet Substitute* (1964), and *When Tomorrow Dies* (1965).[82] Sexually frank and obscenity-laced, these semi-improvised contemporary tales of alienation employed a frenetic, new-wave-influenced style to reflect the unstable lives of their young protagonists.[83] After these films, Kent moved to Montreal, where he acted in films by Quebecois directors Carle and Lefebvre and made films regularly through the eighties, at which point he began working as a sound technician in television, while continuing sporadically to direct his own films.[84] Despite early success, neither director was able to establish a conventional film-making career.

Another Torontonian to have a career seem to go nowhere after an impressive debut was Don Shebib, whose *Goin' Down the Road* (1970) became even more of an iconic film than *Nobody Waved Goodbye* in the history of Canadian cinema. Like Owen's film, *Goin' Down the Road* used the local folk scene as a backdrop, except that the title song by Toronto singer-songwriter Bruce Cockburn was played on the soundtrack rather than appearing within the film's diegesis. Shebib's film began as a proposed television drama called 'The Maritimers,' but he turned it into a feature film when the CBC rejected it.[85] Shebib had been born and raised in Nova Scotia before moving to Toronto to study sociology, and he brought a regional sensibility to the story of Pete and Joey, two local boys who head to the big city only to be ground into submission. Cockburn's bleak ode to Cape Breton Island plays over an opening montage of images of a decaying community whose mines have been emptied and whose fishing boats 'couldn't compete with the company fleets.' The film's narrative begins and ends on the road, with Pete and Joey free and secure

1.5 *Goin' Down the Road* (1970): two hosers on the margins. Photofest.

in their masculinity in a car painted with the words, tongue in cheek, 'My Nova Scotia Home.' Once in the city, they are, of course, hopelessly out of place, inappropriate, and over-matched, to such a degree that Shebib has been accused of condescension towards his provincial characters (figure 1.5).[86] Reduced to working in a bottling depot, low-achiever Joey marries the girlfriend he has gotten pregnant, while Pete aims higher and falls lower. He is humiliated when he applies for a job above his qualifications, is played by the French-Canadian secretary he takes out, and is forced to move in with Joey and Betty when the men lose their jobs at the bottling depot. Out to get groceries for a holiday meal, they pack their cart full, try to sneak out with it, and when a grocery clerk stops them, in a panic they beat him senseless. Like Peter at the end of *Nobody Waved Goodbye*, Pete and Joey find themselves on the road, family and responsibilities left behind, and newly burdened with guilt and a sense of failure.

The primary difference – that Pete and Joey have each other while Peter is completely isolated – is also a strong indication of the social difference between the marginal Maritimers and the middle-class Torontonian. Peter is in rebellion against his own class and the generation of his parents; Pete and Joey are trapped by social forces beyond their control. As Christine Ramsay sees it, the film does not simply depict a quintessential pair of Canadian losers, but contextualizes their impotent marginalization in terms of 'Toronto's status at the centre of Canada's social and personal identity and economic prosperity.'[87] Just as *Duddy* exposes hidden seams in the conventional polarities of Montreal, so too does *Goin' Down the Road*, as Melnyk argues, reveal the 'class and regional divisions' indirectly represented by the 'loser hero' whose tradition these films were seen to have inaugurated.[88] On the road, they are forerunners of fictional hosers Bob and Doug McKenzie, created by Rick Moranis and Dave Thomas on SCTV and in the feature *Strange Brew* (1983), drinking beer and shooting the bull, trapped neither by dead-end life on the margins nor by the condescending and exploitative centre. Critics would latch onto the charismatic yet cringe-worthy duo as a paradigm of Canadian masculinity, and Anglo-Canadian cinema would chew over permutations of the road and the loser hero for decades to come.

Meanwhile, Shebib's assessment twelve years further on shows that he did no better overcoming the barriers to a fulfilling Canadian film career than many of the other Anglo-Canadian pioneers of the sixties: 'I should have left after *Goin' Down the Road*. I should have gone to California.'[89] There is a wilful irony in applying the image of the road to his own life, but the bitterness is real, for Shebib made several more excellent films that vanished nearly without a trace, including *Between Friends* (1973), the story of a botched heist at a nickel smelter in Sudbury in northern Ontario, and *Heartaches* (1981), something of a less downbeat, female version of *Goin' Down the Road*, starring Annie Potts and Margot Kidder. He has worked in television since the mid-seventies, and continues to do so. Relentlessly bleak, following the rhythms of everyday life, and naturalistically acted, Shebib's early features fit stylistically within the conventional parameters of Anglo-Canadian cinema they did so much to define. They do not, however, function as an auteurist criterion for his own body of work, nor is it possible to know for how long he would have continued in the documentary realist vein even if the option had been available. One need only observe the career trajectory of François Truffaut when the success of his achingly realistic and resolutely unsentimental debut feature allowed him to do whatever he wanted thereafter, and who chose not to make another documentary realist study of delinquency for the rest of his life, preferring genre experiments, sentimental romance, and charming comedy-dramas such as *L'Argent de poche* (*Small Change*, 1976).

France, of course, possessed the infrastructure, economic support, and local audience to give Truffaut that choice. The wayward career trajectories of the key figures in the resurgence of English-Canadian film-making give some sense of the difficulties faced by anglophone film-makers in Canada. There are a number of factors to this difficulty. First, there is the lack of a specific identity, analogous to the question of what it meant to be 'Quebecois,' around which to create a genuinely national cinema. Second, the natural desire of critics to generate such an identity led to the doctrinaire critical rubric of a documentary realist tradition unable to consider any but a handful of films as bona fide 'Canadian' films. This tendency was exacerbated by the fact that the majority of the Quebecois masterpieces from this period fit within the same rubric and by the fact that the prior history of Canadian film-making was also seen to have been based in documentary realism. Rather than a more pragmatic approach that would define English-Canadian film-making in terms of the actual production of talented directors such as Kent,

King, Owen, and Shebib, film-makers were blamed by the newly emerging field of Canadian cinema studies for not living up to a cinematic identity that had never really existed as such. As Dorland astutely puts it, 'The study of cinema in the Canadian context ... would consist in evaluating the degree of actualization by specific but changing film texts of an ideal-typical theory of a Canadian national cinema as defined by Canadian film scholars.'[90] Paradoxically, this tendency ran directly contrary to the auteurist approach that had allowed the French critics at *Cahiers du cinéma* in the fifties to re-evaluate the work of career Hollywood genre directors such as John Ford, Howard Hawks, Alfred Hitchcock, and Vincente Minnelli not solely by identifying masterworks, but by devising a critical language able to identify and interpret moments of quality or interest within otherwise mediocre or borderline unwatchable product. Moreover, holding English-Canadian directors to a fixed standard of form and content ignores the very conditions of production within which they have had to work. In the face of conflicted and fickle government support and sporadic possibilities for commercial production and distribution, the various and sometimes apparently misguided career decisions of English Canadians desiring to pursue the vocation of film-maker become far more comprehensible.

To remain wedded to the ideological and formal constraints of the NFB or to any abstract critical ideal was not ever a straightforward choice for English-Canadian or Quebecois film-makers. Not until the establishment of TFC did anything resembling a genuine option for making independent art films exist, and as we will see in later chapters, this turned out to be a window of opportunity rather than an organization able to sustain a conventional national cinema. But the understanding expressed in those later chapters has also been slanted by the critical heritage of the sixties, which for a long time precluded the recognition of other influences on the new film-makers of the eighties and nineties besides that of the documentary realist tradition. Particularly necessary is a re-evaluation of the much-maligned Capital Cost Allowance tax incentive, which between 1975 and 1981 led to an unprecedented boom in production and a frankly commercial bottom line that nevertheless somehow in its death throes gave birth to the most impressive decade of film-making since the sixties, if not ever.

Gimme Shelter

> To this day, when I mention those fabulous Canadian tax shelter flicks that were made in the late seventies and early eighties to the locals up here, people usually change the subject. They're still a little proper up here in Canada, and those films are a bit of an embarrassment to most. Not to me! I loved them. I hear our local rep house, the Cinematheque [in Winnipeg], is going to show a bunch of them soon. I'll be the first in line.
>
> David deCoteau (film-maker)

It would perhaps greatly surprise a traditional art critic to discover that contemporary Scotland-born, Canada-raised, and London-based painter Peter Doig, whose atmospheric lakeside landscapes were the subject of a 2008 retrospective at the

Tate Britain, found 'perhaps [his] single greatest quarry for images' in the slasher thriller *Friday the 13th* (1980, Sean S. Cunningham).[91] It is that same element of surprise, I expect, that downplayed recognition of the influence of David Cronenberg's early genre work on later Canadian film-makers, and that has precluded, to my knowledge, tracing the affinity of the crucial scenes of searching for the body of a murdered girl in Egoyan's art-house hit *Exotica* (1994) with a similar scene in Bob Clark's tax-shelter horror classic *Black Christmas* (1974), or the loopy narration detailing the customs of Tolzbad in Guy Maddin's cult hit *Careful* (1992) with the equally loopy barkeep narration of the lurid history of Nova Scotia's Valentine Bluffs in George Mihalka's slasher horror film *My Bloody Valentine* (1981). Influence is a devious thing, and inspiration can adapt and transform its sources in many ways beyond the simple transmission of like to like often assumed by critics and historians. So, while the most obvious, the most immediate, and the most understandable reaction to the tax-shelter debacle may have been to negate it as quickly and as completely as possible, that reaction in no way encompasses either the range of ways in which those years influenced the film-makers who lived through and came after them, nor the modes in which numerous Canadians participated in those years, nor the many different lessons they gleaned (and continue to glean) from them, especially as the quite substantial production of those years becomes ever more available for reviewing on DVD. This period has also long been regarded as the nadir of the industry, the height of its invisibility as a national cinema, and the source of a slew of films, some commercially successful, some not, with nothing whatsoever to do with Canadian cinema, notwithstanding their having been funded with government money, involved Canadian actors and crews, and been shot on Canadian locations.[92]

The tax-shelter years extended from the passage of the 1974 CCA Act legislating a 100 per cent capital cost tax deduction for any film produced with a certain percentage of Canadian funding, actors, and crew, until the deduction was reduced to 50 per cent in 1983. The period peaked in the unprecedented production of seventy Canadian films in 1979, the high-water mark, quantitatively, of the industry.[93] A revisionist look at the period has long been in order, and it has slowly started to take shape, somewhat piecemeal, in the new century, primarily under the umbrella of cultural studies, approaching the period less with regard for formal quality than in terms of theme, history, and ideology. We might begin with the Toronto International Film Festival, founded two years after the CCA Act as the Toronto Festival of Festivals. Simultaneously an art-film showcase and a commercial clearing house, TIFF premiered a number of tax-shelter films, including Richard Benner's queer cinema landmark *Outrageous!* (1977). It proved to be as variegated and hybrid as the Canadian cinema to which it is neither identical nor wholly distinct. If the youthful years of TIFF provided a context of spectatorship for the young film-makers who would emerge in the mid-eighties, the launching of Perspective Canada in 1984, aimed at promoting quality indigenous cinema, marked a clear transition from the commercial thrust of the CCA to the indie cinema of the Ontario new wave even as the endurance of the festival itself testified to the continuity of Canadian cinema culture. Also important in creating the sense of a new industry was *Cinema Canada*, the journal of record of the film and television industry from 1972 until 1989, for much of the time housed in the same building as either the CFDC or TFC.[94] Providing an opinionated but ecumenical account of all manner of film-making activity, *Cinema Canada* not only recorded the full range of the tax-shelter years, but bore witness to the opening salvos of the new Canadian cinema in the late eighties.

In addition to this institutional frame, it is important to recognize that the exploitation film and popular genres in general have a longer and more substantial history north of the border than the quality productions that generally pass for Canadian cinema. Indeed, feature film-making in Canada before 1960 was, for all intents and purposes, genre film-making and not the 'art' cinema for which the country would soon become known and as which critics would define it. We have already discussed the quota quickies of the thirties and the French-Canadian melodramas of the post-war period. In his comprehensive study of what he gleefully terms the 'paradox of the phrase "Canadian horror,"' Winnipeg native, film-maker, and historian Caelum Vatnsdal makes the long-overdue argument that a tradition of Canadian horror does in fact exist, that it is worthy of critical attention, and that there is even something 'peculiarly Canadian' about Canadian horror, although it is a quality evident only to Canadians and only then in a pointedly minor, imperfect key.[95] The horror genre gave birth to some of the first independently produced Canadian feature films, including the 3-D feature *The Mask* (1961, Julian Roffman). Production skyrocketed during the tax-shelter years before becoming a permanent fixture in the cable television and direct-to-video markets, in addition to periodically infiltrating the more hallowed realm of TFC productions. And what Vatnsdal demonstrates about Canadian horror holds equally true for a number of other popular genres, from the Quebecois staples of comedy, melodrama, and the 'maple syrup porno' that put the industry on the map commercially at the end of the sixties, to the television series and feature-length neo-noir and science-fiction vehicles that, along with horror, fuel a major portion of Canada's indigenous media industry. Peter Urquhart's work is the most thorough-going revisionism thus far, including a close reading of three 'ignored' tax-shelter films made in 1979 – *Suzanne* (1980, Robin Spry), *Yesterday* (1981, Larry Kent), and *Hot Dogs* (1980, Claude Fournier) – which, he argues, are heavily invested in a discourse of national unity in the shadow of the Quebec referendum of 1980.[96] Vatnsdal has uncovered discernibly 'Canadian' content in such tax-shelter horror films as *My Bloody Valentine* and *Deadly Eyes* (1982, Robert Clouse); indeed, he makes a convincing argument that the resolutely low-brow, mostly exploitation-based genre film-making covered in his history of 'hoser horror' constitutes a veritable branch of Canadian cinema, if a decidedly checkered one.[97] Both Urquhart and Vatnsdal call for a contextualized understanding of Canadian cinema beyond the highly subjective and historically unreliable criterion of quality.

One of the primary arguments made against the consideration of popular genre films in terms of Canadian national cinema is their lack of the spatio-temporal specificity that is the stock-in-trade of the documentary realist tradition.[98] A documentary approach to the reality of a location as an indicator of its formal or thematic significance is as limited as a documentary realist approach to narrative as the only means of articulating issues of national identity. One of the effects of the apparently rootless film-making of the tax-shelter years was to loosen the fetters of a realism defined, to use Vatnsdal's formulation, as something 'that might actually have happened.'[99] To be sure, financial incentives to disregard realism led to such unsightly circumstances as Jutra filming in English and Bob Clark making the biggest box office success in Canadian history (*Porky's*, 1981) in Florida. Still, by subordinating all ideological and aesthetic concerns to the bottom line, the tax-shelter years did have the benefit of relentlessly hybridizing Canadian cinema; it became almost impossible to make classically conceived 'art' films except, to a certain degree, in Quebec. A de facto subsidiary of Hollywood, tax-shelter Canada posed many of the same difficulties and offered many of the same rewards as the old B-movie studios in the golden age of Hollywood. Those film-makers who, like Cronenberg, found they could say what they wanted by working around and within genre conventions flourished. Those who, like Jutra, wanted to make movies as they always had did not. But those who came after, for better or for worse, had a much broader range of influences on which to draw. In other words, it was not just the essential development of federal and regional support for independent film-making that made the film-making after 1985 so good.[100] The prior bursting forth of a long submerged Canadian tradition of genre film into the open air had provided the plethora of creative models necessary to spur a new generation of film-makers. It is not accidental that, as the years move on, Cronenberg's tax-shelter-spawned shadow looms ever larger over Canadian cinema since the eighties.

Chapter Two

The Anxiety of Influence:
David Cronenberg and the Canadian Imagination

Part of my project, consciously or not, has always been to alter my own sense of aesthetics so that the things that some people find horrible I don't find horrible. I think they're beautiful.

David Cronenberg (2005)

There is a scene near the very end of David Cronenberg's first commercially released feature film that at first glance seems out of keeping with the visceral violence and raw sexuality of the rest of *Shivers* (1975) – indeed, it was not even there in his original screenplay. And yet, it provides a key insight into the ability of Cronenberg's films simultaneously to provide the requisite thrills of the genres of horror and science fiction in which he worked for so long and to transcend the constraints of those very conventions. The scene itself is a requisite station in the pessimistic variant of the zombie movie plot, the one where the hero, the last remaining person to have avoided infection, finally succumbs to the inevitable. In *Shivers*, the hero is Roger St Luc (Paul Hampton); the location is a luxury high-rise on an isolated island outside Montreal whose inhabitants have been infected by a parasite invented by a well-intentioned scientist working in the building, who first tested it on his own daughter. The effect of the parasite is to remove all inhibitions, leading to an explosion of sex and violence whose mostly repulsive effects Cronenberg realizes on screen explicitly, crudely, and as would be characteristic throughout Cronenberg's career, without aestheticizing or eroticizing them in any conventional manner.

But this last scene is different. It begins with the setting: a ground-level swimming pool enclosed by glass walls looking out onto the landscaped building grounds, the water a coolly shimmering aquamarine, refracted light dancing on its surface. The whole movie plays as oneiric, but this final dreamscape is far more ambivalent in tone than the nightmarish sequences that fill the previous eighty-five minutes. As Cronenberg noted of the zombies, 'They look very beautiful at the end of the film. They don't look diseased or awful, they're well dressed.'[1] This beauty is embodied in St Luc's love interest Nurse Forsythe (played by cult exploi-

2.1 *Shivers* (1975): the beauty of Cronenberg's horror. Photofest.

tation actress Lynn Lowry) rising out of the water to stand waist-deep in the middle of the pool, a blue-violet shirt clinging to her breasts, wet hair plastered against her narrow face, accentuating the high cheekbones and feline eyes (figure 2.1). Simply as a composition in colour, the sequence is beautiful, a shocking contrast to the often styleless photography that characterizes the rest of the film. The moment also transforms Lowry's character, a stock generic feature up to this point, into a sublime and irresistible vehicle of fate. Rather than kicking and screaming, St Luc at this crucial moment will meet his doom with a fatalistic impulsion of desire. In the autobiography included on her website, Lowry singles out this meeting as the 'favorite cinematic moment' of all her films: 'I was not supposed to be in the last scene of *Shivers* that takes place in the swimming pool. But, after they had flown me home, David decided it would be a brilliant choice to have me give Paul Hampton the parasite. When I come up out of the swimming pool, I play a beautiful, sensual, very scary nurse Forsythe. That is my favorite image of myself.'[2] It is a transformative moment in the film, as if the only way that beauty can emerge from the brutally ugly environment of modern life is through the vehicle of a deadly parasite.

And Lowry has the moment right all these years later: this is not an image of the irresistible femme fatale so dear to film noir and to vampire movies; it is a recognition, even an argument, that the sublime moment the film has achieved could only come at the price of a total loss of self. Moreover – and this is an equally fundamental tenet of Cronenberg's oeuvre – this loss of self is neither to be feared nor to be embraced: it simply *is*. At this moment, nothing exists beyond the 'beautiful, sensual, very scary' figure rising up out of the depths of a liquid no-place. Not all of Cronenberg's films contain moments exactly like this seminal, almost primal scene in his oeuvre, but I believe that their consistent appearance at some of the most extreme episodes of his long career is indicative of their crucial function in the way his films work on us as an audience. And it is this ability to work on an audience that has been responsible for Cronenberg's gradual rise from exploitation black sheep to grand old man and éminence grise of Canadian cinema.

Childhood Dreams

> My parents really invented their own version of what it is to be middle class. They also invented their own version of what it is to be Jewish.
>
> David Cronenberg (1992)

More criticism has been published on Cronenberg alone than on all other Canadian film-makers combined. This began as a testament to his cult appeal beyond the borders and expanded during the eighties into post-structuralism, feminism, and media theory, but more recently the critical literature has begun to recognize his place as something like a founding father of the contemporary Canadian film industry. Moreover, as Ernest Mathijs argues in his excellent recent monograph, Cronenberg's career was instrumental transnationally – first, in moving genre and exploitation cinema from the fringes of fandom to the mainstream of cinematic criticism and spectatorship, and second, in transforming genre formulas into tools for the articulation of a consistent and unique authorial vision.[3] Scholars such as Mathijs, William Beard, and others have made an increasingly strong case that Cronenberg is not simply a master of genre or a quirky auteur, but a central figure in the history of world cinema over the past four decades.[4] As such, he is fully deserving of the substantial if often polemical critical attention lavished on him since the release of his first commercial feature. Nevertheless, a full recognition of Cronenberg's global importance must also include a reckoning with the full weight of his stature and influence as a *Canadian* film-maker. After all, Cronenberg is the only Canadian film-maker with a long-term résumé of critical and commercial success who has also remained in any way recognizably Canadian; the only comparable figures, Hollywood directors such as Norman Jewison and James Cameron and actors such as Jim Carrey and Mike Myers, would require a different level of argument to establish a Canadian identity to their work, if it could be made.[5] Even recognizing 'the Canadianness of David Cronenberg' requires a re-evaluation of the critical paradigms that govern the discourse of Canadian cinema.[6]

Cronenberg is, first and foremost, Canadian by biography. Born and raised in a middle-class west Toronto neighbourhood where a predominantly Jewish population was gradually being replaced by more recently arriving immigrant populations of Irish Catholics, Italians, and others, Cronenberg was the child of a freelance writer and an accompanist and rehearsal pianist.[7] It was, as Cronenberg has stressed, a comfortable and non-traumatic childhood, with literate parents who encouraged the literary and artistic interests of their young son and his sister Denise (she trained as a ballet dancer and has served as costume designer for most of her brother's films) and instilled in him 'an unshakeable, totally realistic faith in my own abilities.'[8] Cronenberg would later recognize that his 'parents really invented their own version of what it is to be middle class. They also invented their own version of what it is to be Jewish.'[9] Just as he has always self-identified as Canadian, so Cronenberg continues to assert that 'I think of myself as being resolutely middle class, and yet when I see what true middle-class values are, they're not mine.'[10] This is a quintessentially Anglo-Canadian subject position vis-à-vis the hegemony of white American identity, and it is important to take it at face value rather than ironizing the statement. For part of the power of Cronenberg's film-making lies in its ability to portray an extraordinary range of behaviour, of physical appearance, of psychic processing *as* normal. We can term this effect 'rhetorical realism,' as it derives solely from the presentation of events rather than the nature of those events. This effect has distinguished Cronenberg's stylistic and thematic concerns from the beginning of his career, and marks his films as quite different from the vast majority of the genre products with which they share much of their plot devices and action.

Cronenberg's films are self-aware without being ironic and highly moral without being moralistic. Take for example, the brief opening sequence of *Dead Ringers* (1988), the closest Cronenberg has come in his oeuvre to representing the world of his childhood (the crucial family settings in *The Brood* [1979], *The Dead Zone* [1983], *A History of Violence* [2005], and *Eastern Promises* [2007] are all shot from and primarily concerned with the point of view of the adult characters). Presented as a version of the standard aetiological opening of a biopic, explicitly set in 'Toronto, 1954' (when Cronenberg himself would have been eleven), this brief scene with the ten-year-old Mantle twins has them approaching a neighbourhood girl, Raffaella, to propose sex in a bathtub in order to test their hypothesis that 'humans need to touch each other in order to achieve fertilization "because humans don't live underwater."'[11] As Cronenberg observes, 'the twins as kids [are] extremely cerebral and analytical'; when the more knowing Raffaella taunts them with their ignorance about the act they are proposing to her, they are, as Mathijs puts it, 'disappointed, but not offended' by their recognition of a fundamental difference.[12] It is an enigmatic scene, all the more so if we take seriously Cronenberg's inclusion of it among the project's initial 'touchstones … stuff that was maybe not crucial to the movie, but things that [he] needed' in order to put his mark on long-time collaborator Norman Snider's original-draft screenplay.[13]

The twins' crackpot theory that 'they [females] are so different from us, and all because we don't live underwater' plays out not only, of course, in their choice of gynaecology as a profession, in their specialization of fertility, in their fascination with unusual sexual anatomies, and in twin Beverly's consuming obsession with achieving an emotional and psychological separation from his brother through brutally physical means; it also motivates Cronenberg's stylistic choice of treating the adult twins according to the terms of their original aquatic hypothesis: 'The feeling is like an aquarium, as though these are strange exotic fish creatures. That's why I wanted their apartments to be purply and blue and sub-marine. It's very cool.'[14] Within that space, the twins' increasingly disturbed behaviour appears to them – and by extension to us – as consistently 'normal,' even as what they understand by 'normal' moves ever further from the realm of 'normal' experience. In the same way, the young twins' curiosity about sexuality and their sense of alienation faced with the greater poise and knowledge of a girl their same age are perfectly normal responses, especially among the white middle-class, semi-suburban milieu in which we see them. Just as he does with their invention of the 'Mantle Retractor' while still students at Harvard (the next sequence we see in the film, and another of Cronenberg's 'things that I needed'), the director toys with our unease regarding the recognition of abnormality and the presentation and reception of it within the film as normal. It is the precise correlative of the oft-noted disjunction between the extreme subject matter and images of Cronenberg's films and the man himself, 'accessible and gentle ... erudite, articulate, and comfortable with intellectualizing his films.'[15]

It cannot be accidental that the character of the young girl so comfortable in her own mainstream identity shares her first name with Raffaella De Laurentiis, daughter of the legendary Italian producer Dino and partner in the DEG company, which was involved in the development of *Dead Ringers* before dropping it due to financial difficulties, with the result that Cronenberg became, for the first time, his own producer. His description of the fateful meeting has an uncanny resonance with the opening sequence of the film: 'I visited Raffaella De Laurentiis. She had her hair up and back, so I knew I was in trouble ... She said, "You're going to kill me when I tell you this, but we can't do the movie. We're in trouble." ... I couldn't believe it. But I didn't go crazy, throw things around, or scream and yell. I didn't talk betrayal, because I liked them. I am Canadian; my curse is that I can see everybody's point of view.'[16] The description emphasizes both the gender separation and the complete difference in approach to film-making. Raffaella is blunt, practical, and worldly; Cronenberg is equally single-minded, but soft-spoken, impractical, and Canadian. Certainly, the coincidence of names and the resonance of 'aquatic' visuals provide paratextual reinforcement to Beard's reading of the Mantle twins as artist figures.[17] But they also insist upon a cultural context to that reading that exceeds Beard's purely formal argument. If, formally, Cronenberg translates an aesthetic argument in terms of sexual difference, he does the same thing in terms of his own identity as a Canadian. His inability to behave as expected, to 'go crazy, throw things around, or scream and yell' as any director worth his salt would be expected to do, is as much a function of his Canadianness as is the sympathetic even-handedness with which he approaches his characters. And it is an even-handedness that equally expresses itself aesthetically in his films, for the 'very cool ... purply and blue and sub-marine' lends the interiors a quality of beauty incommensurate with the horror they contain: '*Dead Ringers* is too close to home.'[18]

Adolescent Rebellion

It's a form of freedom, and you're testing your own control over a situation that has not been deemed safe. When you drive within the speed limit, it's not your own will that is keeping your life intact; it has been imposed. When you transgress that, you are reclaiming total control of a very specific situation.

David Cronenberg (1988)

Cronenberg is equally the product of a specific time and a specific place. Originally enrolled as an honours science student at the University of Toronto in 1963, he soon dropped out of the program, moved to honours English language and literatures, and made plans to become a novelist.[19] Film, as Cronenberg makes clear, was not an academic option at the time, which is why David Secter's independent feature *Winter Kept Us Warm* (1965), a key artefact in the rise of Toronto film-making, made such an impact on the young artist: 'I was stunned. Shocked. Exhilarated ... This movie, which was a very sweet film, had my friends in it as actors. And it was in Toronto, at the University, and there were scenes and places that I walked past every day. It was thrilling.'[20] And so it was that the aspiring novelist, in the best spirit of the times, aspired instead to be a local, independent, avant-garde film-maker. The four films Cronenberg made between 1966 and 1970 – the shorts *Transfer* (1966) and *From the Drain* (1967) and the short features *Stereo* (1969) and *Crimes of the Future* (1970) – were also shot in 'scenes and places that [he] walked past every day' and 'had [his] friends in [them] as actors.' But their approach to reality was not the direct cinema aesthetic of Secter's portrait of a contemporary gay-leaning relationship amid the pressures of traditional society and the changes being expressed as youthful rebellion. Cronenberg's experimental 'realism' was indebted to the Beats' attack on social hypocrisy, and especially to Williams S. Burroughs, whose fiction was both formally experimental and ground-breaking in the verisimilitude of its depiction of the fifties underworld of drug culture and homosexuality.

Like Burroughs's novels, Cronenberg's films combine a clinically detached style with a fascination for the extremes of human behaviour and a penchant for speculative scenarios bordering on the fantastic. Shot on location at two University of Toronto campuses (the brand-new, brutalist-style Scarborough campus for *Stereo* and the equally new Massey College for *Crimes*), both films create isolated scientific laboratory settings, the Sanatorium of the Academy of Erotic Inquiry in the first, and the House of Skin clinic and Institute of Neo-Venereal Disease, among others, in the second. There is a transgressive humour in Cronenberg's appropriation of the solemn halls of academe and the sober discourse of science for narratives of unfettered, telepathic sexuality and a dermatologically spread disease called Rouge's Malady. While Cronenberg may not have taken the discourse of science and academia seriously and, as he would continue to do, would make the unintended consequences of scientific experimentation the repeated cause of disease, havoc, and suffering, the films are nevertheless philosophically invested in 'this idea of a man-made, man-controlled environment short-circuiting the concept of evolution ... [T]he institutions aren't evil. They are almost noble in that they are an attempt by human beings, however crazy, to try and structure and control their own fate.'[21] Like many real-life sixties experiments with drugs, Cronenberg's scenarios combined the controlled space of the laboratory with the unforeseen and often chaotic and destructive results that occurred in those spaces.

The rhetorical realism of a distanced, observational attitude taken towards sensational events was emphasized by the decision to shoot in 35 mm without synchronized sound. Both films employ a scientistic voice-over as accessory to the generally distanced camerawork and long takes. Moreover, in *Crimes*, Cronenberg added a second soundtrack, 'made up of deep-sea creatures, dolphins, shrimp. The sound of water is very much present.' Cronenberg 'thought of it as an underwater ballet.'[22] The hermetically sealed space of the scientific laboratory is typically used to project authority, objectivity, and disinterested research; in the science fiction and horror films of the fifties, the lab-coated expert is generally either the cool and controlled hero or aide to the more impetuous real-world protagonist. Like many sixties depictions of authority, especially in the paranoid fiction of Philip K. Dick or Thomas Pynchon, Cronenberg's doctors cause more chaos than they prevent; moreover, their scientific method has generally been bent more towards heightening chaos than controlling it. The sense of both films as 'happening underwater ... of looking into an aquarium' creates both a visual otherness at odds with the geometrical familiarity of the sterile architecture and a thematic sense of controlled alienness, just as the underwater environment is simultaneously nearby and familiar but also another world in every way.

Such alienation devices are standard tropes of avant-garde film-making, especially in the sixties; their combination with a scientific setting is less common. Cronenberg would keep both the underwater, 'balletic sense of movement' and the scientific settings when he moved, five years later, into feature film-making; however, he would temper the stylistic alienation, reserving watery effects for key moments such as the slow-motion pool scene at the end of *Shivers* and the bloodsucking Rose's attack on Judy in a Jacuzzi in *Rabid* (1977). Beard relates both scenes to the slow-motion moment when Max Renn raises his head from Nicki at the end of a key sex scene in *Videodrome* (1983), suggesting that in each case we have 'a grand moment of transgressive sexual indulgence.'[23] This is a helpful formulation, since there is certainly a common theme of transgressive sexual indulgence in these scenes. But since *Shivers*, *Rabid*, and *Videodrome* are in fact riddled with scenes of transgressive sexual indulgence, it is worth looking further in order to determine what is special about these particular scenes. They are also among the most stylistically controlled and deliberate moments in each film. While elsewhere in these films, Cronenberg lets loose chaos far more spectacular and generically gratifying than in the controlled and hieratic observation of the avant-garde features, here he slows the scenes down not only to signal our need to watch them closely but also to remove them from the surrounding action, to separate them from us as in a fishbowl.

The slow motion is not simply a means of rendering spectacular events spectacularly, however; it also signifies in the underwater settings a precise means of rendering the normal appearance of a very strange place. No doubt, there is, as Beard suggests, something regressive and feminine in water imagery, but there is also something alluring and positive in those same connotations.[24] Freud's 'oceanic feeling' entails a loss of self that is both annihilating and infinitely comforting, quite similar to the all-encompassing relief of the addict's connection experienced by the vampiric Rose at the moment she is going to feed on Judy, and even more stereotypically, similar to the *petite mort* of an orgasm. What Cronenberg appears to want to capture is not the familiar resonance of these moments, but the strangeness *within* our familiarity with them. The experimental films aim to make everything in them strange; when Cronenberg incorporates these moments into the generically conventional narratives of his commercial features, he is singling out moments of transformative and beautiful strangeness from the more familiar expectations surrounding them.

Cronenberg's Canadianness was not at issue as a University of Toronto student making experimental films; he was a participating member in an underground community of like-minded Canadians. *Stereo*, for example, was first shown at Toronto's alternative Cinecity theatre before its 'official premiere' at Ottawa's National Arts Centre along with films by established avant-garde film-makers Michael Snow and Joyce Wieland, and in New York at the Museum of Modern Art and at the Film Forum, an important alternative theatre.[25] The general search for a new mode for expressing identity in sixties Canada was a common feature of the direct cinema features, the avant-garde underground, the cultural theories of Marshall McLuhan and Northrop Frye, and the Quebecois *cinéma direct*. In many ways, the early seventies marked the transformation or disappearance of all of these options, something Cronenberg seems to have recognized when he spent a year in the south of France, writing a novel and making sculptures.[26] Cronenberg traces his decision to abandon the established options to the Cannes Film Festival, where, sleeping on the couch in the CFDC offices (the CFDC had helped fund *Crimes of the Future*), he realized that he 'really wanted a broader audience. [He] really wanted to get [his] hands dirty and try.'[27] The site of this realization is significant: especially during the seventies, Cannes was the single most important commercial market for selling movies while also the single most prestigious venue for exhibiting art films. Cronenberg's relationship with the festival perfectly charts his shifting reputation as a film-maker: *Shivers*, *Rabid*, and *Fast Company* were screened there for sale to the European markets.[28] *Crash* (1996), his first film to play there in competition, signalled Cronenberg's arrival as a major auteur in the pantheon of contemporary world cinema (rather than a commercially successful maker of quality horror and sci-fi films who had already received a decent measure of critical attention), and he won a special jury award for 'originality, daring and audacity'; the film would also reach number one at the French box office. Three years later, *eXistenZ* played at Cannes while Cronenberg served as president of a Festival jury that controversially granted its top awards to the exacting realism of a pair of European art films descended from the lower-depths documentary realism of the sixties he had long eschewed in practice. In the nineties, he would be viewed from home as nothing short of a prestigious cultural ambassador, the first Canadian to preside over the jury. Back in the seventies, however, Cronenberg was still at best a nuisance and at worse anathema to everything a Canadian should be.

Although the first book on Cronenberg was published in Canada in 1983 (*The Shape of Rage*, edited by Piers Handling, later to become director and CEO of TIFF), the question of Cronenberg's Canadianness first began to be raised as worthy of critical inquiry by a substantial, though still minority, body of critics only during the nineties.[29] This was partly the result of Cronenberg's own lucid appraisal of the situation in the essential book-length interview edited by Chris Rodley in 1992. Two years later, a biography (the first) by the eminent film historian Peter Morris made clear the degree to which Cronenberg's early career was embedded in the cultural history of Canada, noted a number of Canadian motifs within the director's first ten commercial features, and argued polemically that 'in some measure, his story is also the story of thirty years of Canadian cinema.'[30] Essays by Gaile McGregor (1993), William Beard (1994), and Bart Testa (1995) for the first time placed the question of Cronenberg's Canadianness at the centre of a scholarly argument.[31] Morris's biographical approach had allowed him to sidestep the main critical barriers to considering Cronenberg as a Canadian film-maker. In contrast, Beard and Testa were almost apologetic about Cronenberg's genre-based production, treating it as a necessary obstacle towards the recognition of important thematic parallels with centrally Anglo-Canadian conventions of 'a radically indifferent Nature,' a 'powerful feeling of isolation and exclusion,' and a long tradition of passive, failed male protagonists.[32]

The sticking point of these analyses was the question of genre, for the widespread perception persists that, as Testa argued, Canadian cinema has failed to develop popular film genres of its own and has been unable to adapt imported genres with any success.[33] One of the hallmarks of recent criticism on Canadian cinema and on Cronenberg in particular has been to document the degree to which this perception, taken as critical verity for decades, was in fact only a perception. Given the furor that arose surrounding the CFDC's funding of *Shivers*, this perception is perhaps not surprising. After *Saturday Night* magazine's influential conservative film critic Robert Fulford published his front-page tirade, 'You Should Know How Bad This Film Is. After All, You Paid for It,' against the yet-to-be-released film, Cronenberg found himself at the fulcrum of a virulent debate, not so much over the validity of his films as Canadian products, which was dismissed out of hand, but over whether the Canadian government should be funding 'properly' Canadian films or repulsive sub-Hollywood dreck for the exploitation market. Things got so bad and so personal for him that his landlady, an acquaintance of Fulford, evicted him and his family from their apartment on the grounds that he was a pornographer (Cronenberg and producer Ivan Reitman had cast porn-star Marilyn Chambers, who wanted to break into 'legitimate' film, in the lead role of *Rabid*).[34]

Even Cronenberg's supporters have had a difficult time making sense of the vexed relationship of popular film genres to national cinema. Testa's thesis, for example, has been proven demonstrably wrong as scholarly work has uncovered a tradition of Canadian horror predating Cronenberg (Vatnsdal), a stronghold of

Anglo-Canadian comedy within Hollywood (Pevere), and the fact that Cronen-berg himself was centrally responsible for reshaping the sub-genre of 'body horror' (Mathijs). At the same time, the popular genres that have long dominated Quebe-cois cinema (maple syrup porno, comedy, historical melodrama) have begun to be fully, if reluctantly, incorporated into the history of that province's own 'national' cinema, and that national cinema has itself been incorporated into an account of Canada as a whole (see chapter 6). As Beard puts it, the 'element of genre' intro-duces 'loud unrepressed ("American") convulsions of feeling and explosions of violence and horror' that 'invade … the world of a nice repressed ("Canadian") protagonist.'[35] For Beard, the films would enact a dialectical allegorization of 'the relationship of Canadian and American cultures in the marketplace.'[36] Beard laud-ably attempts to capture the paradoxical position of Cronenberg at a crossroads between American market forces and Canadian cultural attitudes. His approach falls short, however; rather than a Canadianness tempered by its conflict with the alien American qualities of popular genre film-making, Cronenberg's oeuvre can in fact be seen as, and has increasingly revealed itself as, a comprehensive reckon-ing with the myriad contradictions that inhere *within* Canadian cinema.[37] To be sure, the U.S. market has exerted a profound influence on Canadian cinema since the 1890s, but it has only been as a result of Cronenberg's gradual ascension to his current status as Canadian 'culture hero' (Mathijs) that we can begin to glimpse a contradictory and multifaceted Canadian national cinema imbricated in yet independent of that market. Moreover, it is in large measure due to Cronenberg's dogged refusal to abandon Canada as his real and cinematic home or to abandon his idiosyncratic authorial practice that English Canada witnessed a resurgence of quality independent film-making and that both Anglo- and French-Canadian genre film-making flourished and matured during the nineties (see chapter 6).

Young Professional

> If it's not a horror film, you're saying that it's about these two intelligent, eccentric peo-ple who fall in love, and then the guy gets this horrible wasting disease and she kind of watches as he dies and then helps him commit suicide. That's a very tough sell. But if it's a horror, sci-fi film, it's fine. I have felt protected by the genre and I suppose that's why I was drawn to it in the first place.
>
> David Cronenberg (1999)

As Cronenberg tells it, the tale of his early years as a professional film-maker is a tale that cuts across the 'great divides' of Canadian national cinema, self-consciously straddling the fault lines between Anglo and French Canadian, between public and private funding, and between Canadian and Hollywood cinema. Speaking about the experience from the hindsight of a film-maker comfortably established in all of those milieus by the early nineties, Cronenberg could afford to downplay the anxiety and suffering that accompanied the exhilaration and creativity of those early films. Nevertheless, the key points of his argument are clear and persuasive. The first is his crossover from art to exploitation in the choice of Montreal-based

Cinépix to produce his first two commercial features. Second is his conviction that there was no fundamental incommensurability between the films he wanted to make as an artist and the commercial imperatives and genre conventions of the means he would employ to make them. Third, there was a fundamental realism embedded within the 'filmmaking of the imagination' he was striving for. And fourth, what he wanted to say in his films was eminently Canadian.

Cronenberg already knew Cinépix for the genre it had invented and made its fortune with. In Cronenberg's description, Dénis Heroux's *Valérie* (1968) becomes a film of liberation, an example of 'real movies' that showed 'stuff … you weren't allowed to see … in Toronto.'[38] At the same time, he recognized the cultural specificity in which the sex, bikes, 'great bad stuff' and 'wonderful French-Canadian melodramatic rock and roll' were embedded: 'The convent stuff in *Valerie* was no joke; it was very serious. It was very exciting to me to connect with Quebec filmmaking.'[39] Montreal was still strongly Jewish as well as French-Canadian Catholic, and the sixties child Cronenberg was clearly enticed by the unfettered culture of Montreal in comparison to the buttoned-down repression of mainstream Protestant Toronto, just as he felt more affinity to Cinépix's 'very sweet, gentle, lush softcore films with a lot of tits' than to the 'fictionalized documentaries about how hard it is to work the prairies' that he associated with the anglophone NFB.[40] Cinépix heads André Link and John Dunning also found common ground in the 'sexual sensibility' they saw in Cronenberg's otherwise recondite avant-garde features. He shot a sample sex scene for a new soft-core feature and flubbed it miserably, but ended up selling Cinépix on the script for *Shivers* instead.[41] Clear-eyed capitalists, they knew that the 'sweetness' of their local product would not export nearly as well as Cronenberg's sexual horror would.

Cinépix didn't play by the rules of nice Anglo-Canadians, either. But then, as Cronenberg also observes, the only way anybody had been able to make features in Canada up to that point had been to 'sneak' them out of the NFB. The by-any-means-necessary school of film-making immortalized by Richard Dreyfuss's Duddy Kravitz (see chapter 1) had been a consistent feature of Canadian cinema since its beginnings. The NFB had placed a cosmetic lid on the practice (although a number of fly-by-night features managed to get made during the fifties and early sixties as well), but the tax-shelter laws would soon blow the lid back off. When Cinépix could not initially persuade the CFDC to do *Shivers* since the agency had already gotten into trouble with its involvement in several of the maple syrup pornos, they decided to shop the film down south behind Cronenberg's back, offering it to a young Jonathan Demme, who was then working in Roger Corman's New World Pictures exploitation factory in Hollywood. Cronenberg discovered the betrayal at the same time as he received the news from Cinépix that the CFDC had finally agreed to contribute $75,000 of the film's $180,000 budget. In other words, Cinépix played hardball, but they were also sensible enough of their own bottom line to help Cronenberg succeed, getting him the big horror names he wanted (iconic actors Barbara Steele and Lynn Lowry) and assigning him the pragmatic and slightly more experienced Ivan Reitman as producer for the fifteen-day shoot.

As Mathijs perceptively argues, the horror genre in the early seventies offered a number of novel elements perfectly suited to the young Cronenberg. Itself undergoing a 'revolution,' it had left behind the creaky conventions of haunted houses, famous literary monsters, and heroic protagonists in favour of 'a sort of popular resistance against dictated taste,' 'a perception of independence in means of production and access to audiences,' and 'a tendency towards realism ... which claims direct cultural relevance.'[42] Horror would not become mainstream hip until the eighties; during the seventies it was still marginal, extreme, and highly subversive. It was also an enticing backdoor into the world of mainstream film-making for talented directors such as John Carpenter, Demme, Brian De Palma, Tobe Hooper, George Romero, and in Canada, Bob Clark, Reitman, and even Oliver Stone (who made his first feature, the tax-shelter horror *Seizure*, north of the border). Although their effect was not felt as quickly, these innovative and original film-makers transformed film culture at least as profoundly as the more mainstream work of the Hollywood new wave (Robert Altman, Francis Ford Coppola, Mike Nichols, Arthur Penn, Bob Rafelson, and Martin Scorsese) or the later breaking, popular-genre-attuned generation of Joe Dante, George Lucas, and Steven Spielberg. Not only could auteurs make genre exploitation, but the very fact of working or having worked in genre exploitation became something of a marker of industry authenticity, of having paid one's dues.

Especially important in Cronenberg's case was the new realism of seventies horror. This was not only a factor of the changes in film technology that made it financially possible (indeed, imperative) to shoot on location in sync sound with available light; it also went hand in hand with a new focus on the contemporary immediacy of the events being depicted in horror movies, the sense that they were happening, or could be happening, just outside the theatre in which the audience was sitting. Morris astutely comments on Cronenberg's 'visual dialectic between his characters and the space and architecture they occupy ... [Cronenberg] insists on drawing our attention to these *places*, encouraging us to see a relationship between the disjunctive characters and the deadness of the architecture in which they live and work.'[43] While I would privilege Morris's sense of a 'visual dialectic' over a sense of 'deadness,' I agree that Cronenberg's sense of place is quite distinct from the highly anonymous spaces of the nondescript houses and rural desolation that seem in a film like *Night of the Living Dead* (1968, George Romero) to have been chosen precisely for their lack of any distinguishing features. Cronenberg's settings – the Toronto campuses of *Stereo* and *Crimes of the Future*, the Nun's Island apartment complex in *Shivers*, the Montreal cityscape of *Rabid* – project the far more sinister anonymity of familiarity, just as the wintry landscapes of *Rabid*, *The Brood*, and *Dead Zone* exude a local authenticity in the Canadian context. While they have nothing of the unique texture of, say, the Dakota building in *Rosemary's Baby* (1968, Roman Polanski), these settings carry a specifically local charge to the primarily Canadian audience able to recognize them. As Don McKellar put it, remembering his first glimpse of *The Brood* as a young teenager through the window of a multiplex door in Toronto, 'It was the perfect environment in which to see a Cronenberg film from that period as there was little difference between the images on the screen and the feel of the place ... [Cronenberg] used Toronto institutional buildings – schools, police stations, hospitals – to create a sinister atmosphere.'[44] Like the 1960s Paris that Jean-Luc Godard and his cameraman Raoul Coutard managed to shoot as if it were a totalitarian future in *Alphaville* (1965), Cronenberg's Toronto and Montreal are not generically deadening so much as specifically, terrifyingly, historically so. This is pointedly the case in the depiction of a militarized city indiscriminately killing its citizens over fear of a rabies epidemic being received as a reflection of the October Crisis of 1970.[45] And the attention Cronenberg gives these settings also insists on their intrinsic meaning, shimmering between an oppressive modernity and a singular beauty characteristic of that same modernity. After all, brutalist architecture has now become a canonized aesthetic in its own right.

Although the plot devices of Cronenberg's early films are fantastic if not downright ridiculous – turd-like parasites that transform 'normal' people into sex-crazed zombies (*Shivers*); a blood-sucking, rabies-transmitting penis concealed in a young woman's armpit (*Rabid*); psychosomatically created corporal growths and monsters (*The Brood*); telepathic waves powerful enough to explode a man's head (*Scanners*, 1981) – Cronenberg's deadpan style compels viewers to react intimately to the material rather than distancing themselves from it in laughter or disgust. He has maintained this intensely observational stance throughout his career, from the driver's seat camera view of a drag race in *Fast Company* (1979) to the immersion in moments of brutal violence in *Eastern Promises*: 'You should be able to smell the guy that's attacking you; you should feel his sweat. The idea is to get really close, which is not a normal person's response.'[46] This intimacy is, if anything, even more essential in Cronenberg's 'cinema of the imagination,' where, as he said of *Shivers*, 'I have to show things because I'm showing things people could not imagine. If I had done them off-screen, they would not exist.'[47] This is simultaneously a practical and a philosophical concern for Cronenberg. As a self-identified existentialist, he would maintain, first, that nothing exists unless it is directly experienced, and second, that nothing that is directly experienced can be said not to exist. His cinema needs visualization in order to work on its audiences, and it works on its audiences precisely by persuading them that what cannot exist actually could and does.

This is where Cronenberg's concerns intersect with the generic conventions of horror, where the promised pay-off has always been the 'money shot' of the monster or the gruesome consequences of the monster's monstrosity. While the 'money shot' in old-fashioned horror was often the most disappointing (although most eagerly anticipated) moment in the film, the new prosthetic effects that paralleled and enabled the new sub-genre of body horror made it possible to realize the anticipatory imagination of the horror viewer. The pioneering special effects characteristic of Cronenberg's films through *eXistenZ* (1999) were thus born of a creative symbiosis between art and economics: he needs the effects to bring us uncomfortably close to his images and his movies need their effects to wow the genre aficionados. Rather than the duelling Canadian and American at cross purposes that Beard sees in the punctuation of bleak static pessimism with rapid-fire violence and FX, I would argue that Cronenberg's films exist in both spheres simultaneously, each feeding off the other. Cronenberg as film-maker is able simultaneously to revel in the technical and imaginative challenges of realizing his 'extreme images' in persuasively plastic terms on the screen and to immerse himself in the utter seriousness of the modernist philosophy of the duality of consciousness and nature that – here I fully agree with Beard – dominates all of his films.[48] And his films presume the audience will be able to do the same. It is not accidental, however, that his two most financially successful films, *The Fly* (1986) and *A History of Violence*, are also the two films in which the set pieces have been most fully integrated into a conventional family romance plot.

These are also, arguably, his two most self-evidently Hollywood films, even as a closer look reveals them to be as fissured as, if not more fissured than, other, more obviously extreme works. For the duality of viewing – simultaneously immersed and self-conscious – is an essentially Canadian perspective. It is not only that fabled ability, as Cronenberg likes to attribute to himself, to see an issue from every side. And it is not only the fact of inhabiting a country that, once the false post-war consensuses of a transcontinental Anglo Canada and a local Duplessist Quebec collapsed, demanded the ability to inhabit multiple viewpoints simultaneously. It is also the time-honoured Canadian ability simultaneously to enjoy Hollywood products on their own terms and to carve out a subtle difference from within those very products, either as consumers of them or as producers. Morris quotes a story told by Cronenberg to the London movie critic (and vampire novelist) Anne Billson on the 'certain tone and feel' his continued shooting in Canada bestows on his films: 'A man … called me up from Santiago [Chile], and he said: "The fact that you make your films in Canada makes them even more eerie and dreamlike, because it's like America, but it's not. The streets look American, but they're not, and the accents are American, but not quite. Everything's a little off-kilter; it's sort of like a dream image of America." There's a certain sense of rhythm that I have, and a sense of isolation, that I don't think are very American.'[49] The moments of beauty that punctuate Cronenberg's career seem to me both the sign and the epitome of this 'dream image.' Everything appears to be as anonymous, banal, and bleak as in American horror, but it's not. For all of his bleakness, Cronenberg is not nihilistic, and for all of his repudiation of the false promises of the suffocating utopia of middle-class America, he also understands the very real desires that make its siren call so effective.

We can see this difference even in his quintessential tax-shelter movie, *Fast Company*. The first movie he shot that was not based on his own script, this drag-racing story was barely released by its producers, who made it solely to receive the 100 per cent tax write-off. Nor does it appear in most accounts of Cronenberg's oeuvre, which skip from *Rabid* to *The Brood* just as they pass over the television work Cronenberg had done to support himself and learn his craft between *Crimes of the Future* and *Shivers*. Mathijs does an excellent job restoring the film to its proper place within an oeuvre he conceives more broadly than simply in terms of Cronenberg's early horror films. The tale of an aging race-car driver, his close-knit team, and their struggles with a corrupt and overbearing team manager and a nasty rival crew, the plot of *Fast Company* is pure genre formula. However, as Mathijs argues, 'the story is only a vehicle to explore [the] particular culture … of drag racing,' and the eight races depicted in the film are shot with 'a documentary presentation, a "vérité look."'[50] It is also in the context of those races that we find the only moments of true beauty in the film, in the context of the violent resolution of the film's genre justice: the climactic drag race is shot night for night and the ensuing conflagration that eliminates three villains, a car, and a private plane in a series of flames and explosions burns with stunning beauty against the dark backdrop of the night sky. Not only, as Mathijs notes, does the film continue Cronenberg's concern with the 'relationship ... between technology and humans,'[51] but this sequence in particular also places that relationship in the context of a natural setting, reinforced by the location shooting at the Edmonton Motor Speedway in Alberta.

Now, there is nothing in the film that parallels the disturbing moments that mark every other one of Cronenberg's films; rather, he appears to have gone out of his way to make a film that looks 'normal' in every way possible. But that very semblance of normality would be turned on its head by Cronenberg's subsequent car movie, *Crash*, which includes not only another night-time racing scene (the restaging of the James Dean car crash by Seagrave and Vaughan) but also the beautiful long shot of James and Catherine making love on the brilliantly green grass of the highway verge after their final car crash in the rain. Cronenberg's real-life fascination with racing culture and vintage cars has never sat well with the widespread perception of his oeuvre's thorough critique of the deleterious effects of technology (especially widespread in the aftermath of *Videodrome*). Yet this tale of a racing team's battle to maintain a non-problematically intimate relation with its machines suggests a very different sense of technology and the body. If the separation trauma of *The Brood* would proffer the most unambiguously antagonistic relationship between mind and body, human and nature (not coincidentally, in the complete absence of any advanced technology), *Fast Company* clarifies the undeniable presence of the other extreme of the dialectic within Cronenberg's oeuvre. The closest we get to perversion is a three-way involving two female hitchhikers and a can of motor oil.[52]

Although consistently dismissed in the early years of Cronenberg's career as CCA exploitation, his films were extracted one by one from that accursed appellation – all except *Fast Company*, which simply vanished. More recently, as Mathijs notes, its CCA origins have begun to be recognized as a specific indicator of the film's 'Canadianness.'[53] Moreover, for Cronenberg himself, the film marked his coming-of-age as a professional film-maker, a reputation that would soon have him regarded in Hollywood as 'something extraordinary: a critically acclaimed director who not only makes inexpensive movies but who also brings them in on time and under budget.'[54] In making *Fast Company*, Cronenberg first worked with Torontonian cinematographer Mark Irwin, who shot every one of his films until *Dead Ringers*; production designer Carol Spier and editor Ronald Sanders, who have been with him ever since; and sound engineer Bryan Day, who would work with him until 1993.[55] This 'professional family,' as Mathijs calls it, not only solidified Cronenberg's sense of himself as a film-maker, but also followed in the footsteps of the great European auteurs before him, such as Jean Renoir and Ingmar Bergman, whose repeated use of a stable group of crew and actors was an important factor in maintaining a consistently individual tone, look, and feel from film to film, characteristic of their auteurist film-making.

Finally, all of these factors were indelibly Canadian as well, not only in terms of the national origin of many of the people involved, but in that they established a professional identity for Cronenberg linked with but distinct from the unique subject matter of his films. Both Morris and Mathijs recount Cronenberg's description of his attendance of the 1979 convention of the Motion Picture Institute of Canada in Banff, where he screened *Rabid* 'as a current example of production in Canada' and was delighted to find that 'they reacted to it as *film*.'[56] Just as Cinépix had cut across the barriers established by the critical community, so was Cronenberg reassured to find in Banff that Canadian cinema was a more practical question of making films and making money, regardless of fixed criteria of identity. This is not to suggest that Cronenberg was primarily concerned with the economics of film-making; rather, a mode of film-making that concerned the bottom line as much as a specific aesthetic ideology was extremely welcome to him at that moment given the reception of his first two features by the Canadian critics. As Morris recounts, Cronenberg also encountered in Banff the film-maker Paul Almond, 'one of the few Canadian filmmakers who also worked in a nonnaturalist mode and who had equally suffered from Canadian critical attacks.'[57] Almond's subdued and impressionistic art films (see chapter 1) may have been a far cry from Cronenberg's body horror, but the two men found a common ground within an unusually capacious, ideologically neutral conception of Canadian cinema.

Family Man

> People like to talk about 'the nuclear family,' but atomic energy comes from splitting up a nucleus, and that seems to be what happens in a family when it splits up. Here is a family, a nucleus, being exploded, and the energy that's rippling out of it is going to cause great change, some mutations. Just as nuclear energy can cause radiation which can cause mutation.
>
> David Cronenberg (2001)

Maturity did not make Cronenberg less daring in his imagery or innovative in his special effects; rather, he became more adept at integrating them into his narratives. While his first two horror features unleashed the raw energy and anger over the end of an era for the film-maker and his student milieu, his next eight films were sombre meditations on family and relationships, the social structures over mature adults. In six of these films, *The Brood, Scanners, Dead Zone, The Fly, Dead Ringers*, and *M. Butterfly* (1993), we watch the violent disintegration of individuals desperately craving the simple certainties of family and children. Interspersed we find two of Cronenberg's most personal and fully developed films: the ne plus ultra of his 'philosophical project' *Videodrome* and the adaptation of idol William S. Burroughs's novels and life to the screen as *Naked Lunch* (1991). While *Videodrome* takes the question of technologically based evolution as far in a positive and a negative direction as Cronenberg would ever take it, resulting in the utter isolation of its sociopathic protagonist, *Naked Lunch* plots the fundamental incompatibility of protagonist Bill Lee's inspiration for writing, drug use, and repressed homosexuality with the married life offered by his wife, whom twice he 'accidentally' murders in the 'William Tell' game. What is fascinating about all of these films is the way Cronenberg deploys shocking moments of violence and vertiginous special effects simultaneously to estrange us from our expectations of cinematic relationships and families and to draw us intimately into their most intensely real emotions and contradictions. That he has continued to insist on tangible prosthetic effects even as cinematic representation has moved ever more into computer-generated images suggests the degree to which Cronenberg is invested in a specific kind of plastic realism. As he commented at the time of the release of *eXistenZ*, 'Because I work in a very sculptural, physical way on set, too, I'm a bit like the actors in that I like to have the real stuff there. I want to have the real clothes and the real props before I say what the shot is.'[58] While 'the first fact of human existence is the body,' it only takes on cinematic meaning from the way the space fills up around it. The feeling of solid bodies in a solid, socially comprehensible space has been a consistent effect of Cronenberg's films from his earliest experiments. However philosophically speculative and horrifically mutated, they are always grounded in the specific milieu of Toronto from which they emerged and in which Cronenberg filmed them.

Cronenberg was quite forthcoming that the bleak cinematic landscape of *The Brood* emerged directly from a bitter custody battle with his estranged wife. The closest in his oeuvre to a total repudiation of scientific experimentation, *The Brood* traces the horrific fallout of the experimental treatment of Nola Carveth (Samantha Eggar) by Doctor Raglan (Oliver Reed), founder and director of the Somafree Institute of Psychoplasmics, a combination of concrete impersonality and modern-day hunting lodge set deep in the Ontario woods. As Raglan's therapeutic technique teaches his patients to extrude their repressed anger as physically manifesting growths on their bodies, 'creatures from the unconscious, making the mental physical,' Nola's rage goes so far as to create 'the brood,' strange mutant children birthed from pustules on her abdomen who stray through the snowy landscape to wreak violent revenge on those by whom she feels wronged (e.g., her mother) and those she feels are getting too close to her estranged husband.[59] The film ends in 'classic horror' style, 'generation unto generation,' as a sore appears on the body of young daughter Candice, minutes after Frank Carveth has strangled his wife to death to put an end to the brood. The film is, famously, Cronenberg's version of Hollywood's divorce classic *Kramer versus Kramer* (1979, Robert Benton) and is, as Vatnsdal rightly observes, his 'most purely frightening horror picture.'[60] It is easily Cronenberg's most one-sided movie as well, although he partly blames that effect on the censors, who, in the movie's climactic scene, cut 'a long and loving close-up of Samantha licking the foetus ... an image that's not sexual, not violent, just gooey – gooey and disturbing. It's a bitch licking her pups.'[61] In other words, even at the moment of greatest horror and greatest villainization of Nola, Cronenberg had incorporated a scene arguing that what was happening, no matter how horrifying, was also somehow natural.

The tighter narrative structure of these films and their greater focus on family dramas heightens the impact of a central Cronenberg theme, 'There is sadness; there is separation; there is loss; there is physical decay. And if you want to say that you've embraced life fully, you have to embrace all of those things. A lot of natural processes are considered horrific or disgusting or repulsive, and I have always found that really hard to understand, even though I might have experienced it myself. You do not turn away from these things.'[62] A primary way in which Cronenberg establishes this shift in conventional metaphorical associations is through his use of space. Family in Cronenberg's films is closely associated with the external world of nature, and such settings feature in the films that are centred on the fissured nuclear family: the bleak roads and the wooded setting of Raglan's Institute; the hibernal small town of *Dead Zone*; the autumnal colours surrounding the old farmhouse just out of town in *History of Violence*. Rural, or simply exterior moments punctuate the other films also: the final scene of *Shivers*, when the libidinous zombies pile into their automobiles and move in procession from their island stronghold to take Montreal;[63] the opening sequences of *Rabid*, with Rose's wintertime motorcycle accident that leads to her experimental plastic surgery at the isolated Keloid Institute; Cameron Vale's visit to the wooded studio of scanner Benjamin Pierce (Robert Silverman), who has managed to displace the suffering of his telepathy into eerie sculptures; the desolate final scene of *Videodrome*, when Max Renn finds himself alone with a television and a gun on a deserted barge in an industrial wasteland; the lake at dawn on his Mafioso brother's vast estate where Tom Stall washes off the blood of his cathartic rampage; and the stairs down to the River Thames where, early in the film, Nikolai disposes of a frozen, identity-stripped corpse and, late in the film, prevents unstable Kirill from doing the same with the young baby of the dead prostitute Tatiana. The utter claustrophobia of the most inward-looking and family-negating of Cronenberg's films – *The Fly*, *Dead Ringers*, and *Spider* (2002) – is emphasized by the scarcity of external scenes: nearly all of *The Fly* takes place in Seth Brundle's hermetically sealed loft/laboratory, while, by Mathijs's count, there are only four exterior scenes in all of *Dead Ringers*, most of which takes place in the 'fishbowl' environs of the Mantle twins' apartment cum consulting rooms, and most of *Spider* takes place within the webs of Spider's room and his disturbed mind.[64] Similarly, Cronenberg's spatial metaphorics lead to key moments in the anonymous spaces of the contemporary city as well: the culmination of martial law in *Rabid*'s Montreal when a trigger-happy guard kills a shopping mall Santa; the concrete contours of the modernist architecture of Candy's school in *The Brood*; the shopping mall in *Scanners* where the homeless Vale lashes out against a middle-aged woman taking her tea; the tunnel in *Dead Zone* marking the border between present and future; the shopping mall in *History of Violence* where Fogarty stalks Edie and Sarah Stall as they shop for shoes.

Cronenberg's spatial metaphorics play on conventional Canadian associations with an alien, antagonistic wilderness; they equally find in Toronto's concrete modernism an apt metaphor for the benign repression of the fifties. McKellar's observation of the impact of *The Brood* is simultaneously thematic and topographical: '*The Brood* was a revelation to me – the first time I saw that Canadianness can be used to advantage, that self-loathing can be exploited, that ugliness has horrific cinematic potential.'[65] What Cronenberg refers to as the 'hyper-realism' of his films emerges from the way his spaces extrude meaning through the specific practices taking place within them, and the way external setting interacts with internal dynamics.[66] Power lurks in concrete and industrial architecture: Cronenberg's laboratories and institutes seem always to be housed in brutalist or modernist buildings. The metaphorics are not conventional or reductive, however; these spaces are simultaneously the source of repression and the abuse of power and the source of transformation and the granting of power to the impotent, such as Annabelle, Emil Hobbes's original teenage test subject for the parasite, the crash victim Rose, Nola Carveth, Cameron Vale, and Kim Obrist. The more private, less concrete, and more technologically coloured spaces of Brundle and the Mantle twins reflect the way in which they are simultaneously doctor and scientist and, by the end, test subject and empowered and condemned victim. The power that inheres in public spaces seems more specifically malevolent, repressive, and dangerous, a spatial and political conformity that projects sixties child Cronenberg's pointed critique of the Canadian establishment. While the corridors of medical and scientific power are fundamentally ambiguous, public venues such as auditoriums, shopping malls, and city streets have very little to offer Cronenberg's characters beyond suffering and death, and neither does wild nature, which suggests a passive, nearly catatonic retreat into the self. The signature moment shows sculptor-scanner Pierce seated inside his own giant sculpture of a human head, minutes before reality intrudes to kill him in a flurry of bullets, but we also see such a retreat in the drug-and-sex fuelled hallucination that occupies nearly the entirety of the wholly unstable reality of *Naked Lunch*, the equally inward-looking instability of Max Renn's Videodrome-distorted reality, and the self-deluded perceptions of René Gallimard (Jeremy Irons), unable or unwilling even to learn the sex of his lover, Song Liling (John Lone), in *M. Butterfly*.

In his argument for the relevance of *Fast Company* to the rest of Cronenberg's oeuvre, Mathijs enumerates a fascinating list of vehicles and their function. It merits citing in full:

At the end of *Shivers*, the plague/revolution spreads out of Starliner Towers via a car convoy – technology carrying the parasite further. At the beginning of Rose's infection and rage lies a motorcycle crash – technology causing the rage. A car breakdown forces Neil and Carol to knock on the door of a strange house in *The Lie Chair* [a 1975 TV movie] … [T]he final scene in *The Brood*, when Frank wrongly believes he has saved Candy, is set in a car. The car chase and crash in *Scanners* gives Cameron the opportunity to catch one of his pursuers and turn the dynamic from hunter to hunted. Likewise, *Videodrome*'s Max receives crucial information on a television in the back of a limousine. In *Dead Zone*, Johnny's coma and strange abilities to foresee the future develop after a car crash. In *The Fly*, it was Seth's car sickness that gave him the idea to experiment with teleportation … Things have shifted well beyond credibility at the end of *Naked Lunch*, but Bill nevertheless kills his wife in a car – again a car as a last location … [I]n *M. Butterfly*, Gallimard is exposed as a spy right after he has delivered documents with his vintage BMW [motorcycle]. [Mathijs here treats *Crash* and the garage scene in *eXistenZ* in greater detail.] In *A History of Violence*, it is worth noting the vehicles of Tom and Edie as indications of their desire to be all-American, and the symbolic value of Tom's night ride to Philadelphia, where he meets and kills his brother – a drive into hell. Anna's Ural motorcycle in *Eastern Promises* is not just an extension of her assertiveness and cultural roots, but also a key means through which she and Nikolai become 'attached' to each other.[67]

The first thing to note about this list is that Cronenberg's films are so generally interior-bound that cars and motorcycles are used sparingly enough to be enumerated in the space of a paragraph; indeed, the most interior-bound, and as Mathijs notes, 'the most dark (and darkly-lit)' of the films have no cars at all.[68] But the sparseness of private (and public) vehicles also redounds to Cronenberg's intimate focus on bodies in space and his desire to focus our attention completely on those bodies.

The typical function of the car, especially in American society, is as a buffer between public and private, a mobile space that insulates each monad-driver from every other. Within the cinema, the car scene is one of the most conventionally unrealistic of all stock scenes, whether the omnipresent back-projection of the studio years or the car-mounted-on-a-trailer shots more common today. Both of Cronenberg's car movies, *Fast Company* and *Crash*, resolutely break this mould. First, they approach the automobile through a sub-culture in which it has recaptured a plastic materiality and functionality, a spatiality that is open to the world around it rather than a buffer from it. Second, he shoots both films so as to emphasize that physicality and openness to the world: in *Fast Company*, the vérité-style drag races emphasize the sensual impact of the car on the driver and the space around it; in *Crash*, Cronenberg pointedly countered the Hollywood convention of aestheticized slow-motion car crashes by filming them in 'real time,' giving them, paradoxically, both an alienating novelty and a shocking hyperreality.[69] In their more limited role in the other films, cars are highly liminal spaces, exposing rather than insulating their drivers and passengers from the outside world. With its literally open design, the motorcycle heightens this effect; however, here Cronenberg amps up the sense of danger to undercut the romantically liberating image of the motorcycle in Hollywood film. As Mathijs notes in his list, car and motorcycle scenes are frequently catalytic moments within the film.[70] As such, they are both dangerous and empowering, offering a liberating sense of autonomy. In Cronenberg's words on his own fascination with racing and fast cars, 'It's a form of freedom, and you're testing your own control over a situation that has not been deemed safe. When you drive within the speed limit, it's not your own will that is keeping your life intact; it has been imposed. When you transgress that, you are reclaiming total control of a very specific situation.'[71] An individual analogy to the dangerous/liberating spaces of social power, the hospital/laboratory, Cronenberg's cars and motorcycles are often also the mode of entry of his characters into the social spaces that will transform their bodies and their lives.

Cronenberg's use of vehicles as liminal or threshold spaces resonates with the frequency with which, as Morris notes, he 'locates scenes in stairwells and corridors.'[72] Morris goes on to cite exhibition curator Louise Dompierre's classic analysis of these spaces in terms of 'a sense of duality (up and down/coming and going) … links between other architectural spaces … a sense of being "in between."'[73] For Morris, Cronenberg's spatial preference for liminality 'represents Cronenberg's own sense of being "in between" … [h]is Canadian ambivalence … the "Canadian curse" of being able to "see all sides to the story at once."'[74] There is certainly a strong sense that Cronenberg's spatial metaphorics turn American verities inside-out, introducing ambiguity where there is certainty, and exposing both the menace and the unforeseen promise in the liminal spaces which American spatial conceptions have been most concerned with rendering stable and fixed. In this sense in particular, we can see how Cronenberg destabilizes and reconstructs the nuclear family as an explosive site radiating energy and causing mutation. Whether observing the collapse of the family unit in *The Brood*, *Dead Zone*, and *The Fly*, or rendering the problematic consequences of the formation of alternate family units in *Shivers* (zombies), *Rabid* (crazies), *Fast Company* (the racing team and entourage), *The Brood* (the brood), *Scanners* (the 'good' scanners), *Videodrome* (the community of the 'new flesh'), and *Dead Ringers* (the twins), Cronenberg's films of the seventies and eighties neither reinforce the tired verities of post-war ideology nor simply upend them in straightforward rebellion. Instead, they assert their necessity while documenting their impossibility.

This contradiction is nowhere so evident or so antinomian as in the relationship of the Mantle twins in *Dead Ringers*. Moreover, in the way Cronenberg used cutting-edge camera technology and computer tracking to create a perfect illusion of a doubled Jeremy Irons, we find a symbiosis of special effects, narration, and spatial thematics characteristic of Cronenberg's oeuvre as a whole. Cronenberg's effects have always been aimed at making visible and material what would otherwise seem imaginary: if you can dream it, it exists. While this does not preclude the kind of genre appreciation characteristic of the new horror of the seventies, the trend of Cronenberg's effects has been ever more towards a seamless incorporation. Nevertheless, Cronenberg has never been afraid to use the limitations of his effects thematically. The goal of the twins is either to separate or to merge; as they believe the former strategy will result in their deaths, they choose the latter until the very end of the film. In his careful study of the formal qualities of Cronenberg's use of effects, Stefan Hantke shows how the camerawork here, rather than striving for 'self-referential irony' that would tend to 'destabilize the mimetic surface of the text,' instead tends to shift 'from an uncomfortably close proximity to a more detached panoramic point of view, invit[ing] a gaze that lingers.'[75] While this would appear to militate against the intimacy and realism I have argued are characteristic of Cronenberg's use of effects, Hantke's analysis suggests in fact that, rather than the spectacular gaze through closed fingers characteristic of classic horror, Cronenberg's films let the gaze linger in order 'to invite ambiguity.'[76] This distinct mode of filming horrific effects aims 'to visualize an affective reversal in the viewer – to see the disease from the virus's point of view.'[77] In opposition to the typical horror film's conjuring and distancing of the abject truth of death, Cronenberg's horror stresses the ambiguity of the very concept. As he puts it philosophically, 'Were human beings not in general agreement about what is living and non-living, our concepts of life and death would not exist.' For Hantke, the physical presence of the prosthetic objects on set allows 'the possibility of accidental visual discovery in contrast with the digital requirement of extensive pre- and post-production planning and an absolute separation from the world of the actors and the director. Consequently, prosthetic effects 'perform and signify mortality more honestly and poignantly than any digital effect ever could.'[78]

Rather than an exception to the prosthetic and make-up effects that Cronenberg has continued to use even as his budgets and improved technology would allow him to 'go digital,' I believe that the primarily computer-generated effects in *Dead Ringers* suggest the possibility that digital imaging, used creatively, can have a similar effect, at least in a film about conjoined twins. First of all, rather than playing against a blue screen, Jeremy Irons played opposite a stand-in on an actual set. As Steven Shaviro writes of the uncanny effect of our knowledge that the same actor is playing both characters, even as the characters are subtly differentiated so that we can nearly always distinguish between them, 'Because of their excessive physical similarity, the characters of Beverly and Elliot are more like different performances than like different selves. Neither of them is able convincingly to dislodge his interiority from its reflection in the other; neither can ever be self-sufficient or self-contained … Because their bodies are two, and separated in space, it is also impossible for them ever fully to coincide.'[79] This visual effect is reinforced by the editing. The challenge of placing Elliott and Beverly together in a single shot necessitates the frequent recourse to conventional shot/reverse-shot framing, a pattern Cronenberg otherwise has tended to avoid in favour of grouping his characters together in a single shot. This uncharacteristic stylistic conventionality perfectly reflects the periodic but impossible desire of the Mantle twins themselves to follow the typical form of individuated heteronormative subjectivity modelled, according to theories of cinema spectatorship, by the shot/reverse-shot framing.[80]

In a practice consonant with the 'money shot' convention of horror film special effects, and for both economic and thematic reasons, Cronenberg directly and visibly deploys the doubling effect quite sparingly. Shaviro notes the key moment when we watch the twins padding around their apartment in boxer shorts, one after the other: 'The precise similarity of their appearance, and the perfect correspondence of their physical gestures as they walk … are entirely singular, and yet they give the impression of being robotic or mechanized simply because they are doubled.'[81] As in Cronenberg's horror effects, the very perfection of the effect's realism calls our attention to its existence, but that attention is channelled thematically into rendering the existential dilemma of the phenomenon depicted, in this case the twins, simultaneously singular and doubled. In another three-and-a-half-minute scene, the closest the twins come to consummating the sexual tension in their relationship, both technique and form comment obliquely on the twins' relationship to heteronormative conventions. The nocturnal setting, dim lighting, and soundtrack music (the Five Satins' 1956 doo-wop ballad 'In the Still of the Night') mark the scene as Hollywood romance. Elliott, dressed in a blue silk shirt and slacks, and his lover Cary (Heidi van Palleske), wearing a slinky black dress, are slow dancing, while Beverly lies on the sofa in an off-white cable-knit sweater. The scene opens on Beverly in the foreground. Elliott and Cary slowly dance in, making out, in the background, splitting the screen horizontally. The editing then keeps the brothers in separate shots as Cary moves between them, finally persuading Beverly to dance with her. Midway through the sequence, Elliott moves into the frame with Cary and Beverly, and the three dance together, tightly entwined around Cary as in much more typically Cronenbergian framings, varying between close-ups encompassing the three heads, the midsections of all three, and a long shot. The warm familiar melody and harmonies of the pop song make a sharp contrast with the abstract and melancholy tones of Howard Shore's score else-where in the film; the lyrics, in typically Hollywood and atypically Cronenbergian fashion echo the overt bonding theme of the scene: 'Hold me again with all your might.' The threesome is simultaneously an assertion of the twins' desire for 'normal' sexuality and subjectivity and a powerful expression of their fundamental perversion of that norm. In purely spatial terms, this is the closest they come to physically merging, and Cronenberg's tight framing of the three midriffs emphasizes the clasping of the twins' hands as if trying to pull each other together across the mediation of Cary required by what remains of social conventions within their inner sanctum.

The moment breaks up as Beverly pulls away and the editing pattern reverts, jarringly, to shot/reverse shot as he stumbles in a drugged stupor onto the balcony. Within the moment of that spatial separation, he collapses onto the floor. Cary rushes out to help him, but Elliott violently tears her away, administering mouth-to-mouth resuscitation himself in what appears to be a displaced display of sexual desire. In a brief moment that foreshadows Beverly's far more violent physical intervention on Elliott later in the film, Cronenberg suggests that only in the context of a medical scenario can the twins allow themselves unmediated physical contact. While the conventional emotional cues in the sequence invite us to lose ourselves in the heat of the moment, our awareness of the technical constraints within the scene works with the essential oddness of the twins' appropriation of those cues to keep us aware that a perfect union is fundamentally impossible. Cronenberg staged the scene with a body double; only in the split-screen establishing shot do we see the brothers' faces in the same shot. This imperfect striving for a perfect union is also the closest the film approaches to a moment of Cronenbergian beauty. As opposed to the kiss in *Shivers*, however, it signifies by its failure rather than by its fruition. With its dim, atmospherically lit shades of blue echoed in Elliott's shirt and Cary's black dress, it is certainly the most underwater scene of the entire 'fishbowl' film; Beverly and his white sweater provide the jarring note that ratifies the impossibility of fusion, driving the twins towards the equally impossible and far more tragic solution of fission with which the film will conclude.

The Wisdom of Age

> There's a wonderful sense of this movie being physically and tangibly a part of my life, a part of my daily, mundane life as well as my artistic life. That's very satisfying.
>
> David Cronenberg on *Crash* (1996)

Like his younger compatriot Atom Egoyan, Cronenberg speaks so intelligently and articulately about his films that even his weaker productions sound brilliant on paper. William Beard's bravura account of Cronenberg as a modernist film-maker in *The Artist as Monster* creates a similar effect. It's an impressively holistic and inclusive reading of Cronenberg, using the various theoretical approaches that have been applied to his oeuvre as jumping-off points for Beard's own thesis of the oeuvre as charting a gradual awakening, or coming to terms, of the authorial consciousness regarding the issues it wants to express and the ramifications of those issues. For Beard, the key is the eventual focusing of desires and their consequences in a central protagonist rather than displacing them and distorting them onto other characters, especially female monsters and absent scientist figures, whose unarticulated desire is responsible for the creation of monstrosity. This process charts an allegory for the artist, so only once the creative impulse is wedded with the monstrous in the figure of the artist as central protagonist is the issue being fully articulated. The period of maturity would begin with *Videodrome* and reach its apogee with *Fly, Dead Ringers,* and especially *Naked Lunch.* Beard's account allows him to sidestep the biggest pitfall of Cronenberg criticism – the unimaginative application of post-structural theory, which is highly reductive of what is interesting about the films. And it does a nice job of plotting the development of the oeuvre. It works, for me, exactly as far as a conventionally modernist approach works, but the very fact that it can neither account for the more recent developments in Cronenberg's oeuvre nor make distinctions of quality between individual films suggests that it is limited in the very ways that conventional modernist criticism is limited: it swallows up the world around it, along with any loose ends, in a whirlpool of paradox and aporia with no apparent exit.

It is a dark reading (which makes sense in modernist terms) and as such is characteristic of conventional modernism, rather than of more recent modernist criticism. For Beard, the melancholy of the middle period masterpieces is due to the recognition of the dire consequences of creation (almost like a form of *Sprachkrise,* or loss of the power to speak or create) – there appears to be no escape from the monstrosity of the artist, and the glimpses of positive creation and of positive desire always prove illusory. This is correct, and Beard performs the reading in such depth that it is extremely satisfying. He does not ever shrink from examining possible gaps or contradictions to his reading. He has done his work so completely that he has included everything. But there is another thread of modernism, and another critical approach to it, a more fragmentary reading that would not wholly embrace the paranoid model of Burroughs. Just because the cracks and alternatives can be recuperated within the structural negativity of the modernist passion of the artist doesn't mean that we have to do so. They also can provide glimpses of alternative visions of reality not subject to the closed structure of the modern world. One could argue that this glimpse is part of what makes the Viggo Mortensen films so effective: Mortensen is persuasive simultaneously as a melancholic artist-monster *and* as a proactive, powerful, non-loser hero who takes his fate into his own hands.[82] In both *A History of Violence* and *Eastern Promises,* he is simultaneously trapped by his monstrosity and redeemed by it and through it. Moreover, he is redeemed by the social ties of those around him: his children in *A History of Violence* and Naomi Watts's Anna in *Eastern Promises.* It is no accident that these two films present the most fully realized and complex, as well as the least monstrous, female characters in Cronenberg's oeuvre. One way to chart the wisdom of age of Cronenberg's late films is through this shift in the representation of his female characters. They continue to have their problematic moments, in particular their never fully motivated attraction to the monstrous side of the protagonist, but it still feels psychologically credible, and it works to make them more human rather than simply destroying them, as happens with Claire Niveau (Geneviève Bujold) in *Dead Ringers*. The progressive deepening of female roles in Cronenberg's films began with *The Fly*, but really set in with *Crash*'s trio of strong, complex women and *eXistenZ*'s dynamic female protagonist Allegra Geller (Jennifer Jason Leigh) next to Jude Law's flat loser hero. *Spider*, a key moment in Beard's darkly modernist artist vision, is dominated by a monstrous mother and strongly recalls the destructive artist figures of the middle period films, especially *Naked Lunch*, but *History of Violence* and *Eastern Promises* are after something different.

As Mathijs's study makes subtly but unmistakably clear, Cronenberg's films generically and temperamentally exist irrefutably in a number of real-world contexts that both influence and feed off the hermetic allegories of the modernist artist they certainly also contain. It is not coincidental that the period in which the films begin to project a different order of confidence and assuredness is also the period in which Cronenberg's stature reached the level Mathijs terms 'cultural hero.' Cronenberg clearly takes great pleasure in noting that the decision to make *Crash* that directly resulted in that change in status was deemed by his then agent as the movie that would end his career.[83] Certainly the highest profile controversy of Cronenberg's career, *Crash* was distributed with the generally poisonous NC-17 rating in the United States, its release blocked by New Line Cinema executive Ted Turner, and it was banned in the UK after a virulent tabloid campaign.[84] Although its content was perhaps more extreme than any Cronenberg film since his first two features, *Crash* looked, at least on the surface, like a mainstream Hollywood feature, and it featured major stars: James Spader, Holly Hunter, Rosanna Arquette. But it also cast Canadians Deborah Kara Unger and Elias Koteas in the demanding roles of James Ballard's wife Catherine and the marginal visionary Vaughan, respectively, and it was shot on location minutes from Cronenberg's home in Toronto. The combination of apparent conformity with thoroughgoing but never explicitly articulated radicalness was as subversive as it was Canadian.

Crash appeared at the perfect moment to capture the full momentum of Cronenberg as a critical force. The early nineties had seen the emergence of a 'surge of academic publications' in just about every European language, and it was in Europe that the full force of the film was felt, especially in France.[85] The seamless synthesis of Cronenberg's thematic concerns with the look and feel of mainstream Hollywood worked especially well for continental Europeans, who had less resistance to the perversity of the film that so disturbed many in anglophone communities. But it also worked within the diegesis of the film, for its central topics – car culture and pornography – are two fundamental pillars and products of American culture and the American economy, even as Cronenberg's simultaneous embrace and deconstruction of that culture and economy was wholly alien to the American self-representation of either one. Cronenberg put the conundrum this way, 'What I wanted to do was to try and make it difficult for sexual arousal while still presenting imagery that technically should be arousing at least in terms of the psychology of such images.'[86] Similar to the tension between the technological and psychological merging of the twins in *Dead Ringers*, *Crash* created and maintained a tension between the conventional structure and expectations of sex scenes and nudity and their very different function within his film. As Cronenberg put it, 'In *Crash*, very often the sex scenes are absolutely the plot and the character development. You can't take them out. These are not twentieth-century sexual relationships or love relationships. These are something else. We're saying that a normal, upper-middleclass couple might have this as their norm in the not-so-distant future.'[87] Rather than the 'lyrical episodes' of mainstream film-making, the sex scenes have the same structural function as in pornography – they are the point of the film, and everything else is just a pretence. But rather than the extra-textual function of pornographic scenes in directly arousing and releasing the viewer's erotic impulses, the sex scenes in *Crash* have the narrative function of the non-sex scenes in a mainstream narrative movie: they develop character, advance the plot, and elaborate the movie's thematic concerns.

The 'norm in the not-so-distant future,' as articulated by Ballard regarding the 1973 novel on which Cronenberg closely based the film, is 'the car not only as a sexual image, but as a total metaphor for man's life in today's society.'[88] Cronenberg explicitly visualizes the eroticization of every aspect of life that is only implicit in contemporary Western culture, where everything is sexualized as an object of desire. The film's smooth surface, which led English writer Iain Sinclair to dismiss it as 'a film without a sense of smell,'[89] is Cronenberg's visualization of Ballard's flat, incantatory prose, itself a metaphor for the reductive homogenization of late capitalism. While Ballard's prose led many critics to view his fiction as pure simulation of the present, Cronenberg lays bare a more critical and fragmented approach to that present. First of all, while the film is resolutely and nearly seamlessly set in an anonymous, primarily nocturnal future of concrete highways, high-speed crash-oriented car racing, and high-rise apartments, it is also visibly and recognizably Toronto, just as the early films had used the modernist architecture of Toronto and Montreal as a simultaneously futuristic and close-to-home Canadian paradox. Secondly, there is only one moment when anything resembling the 'normal' world intrudes on our consciousness of this highly displaced yet eerily familiar world: when James and Gabrielle visit a Mercedes-Benz showroom. Her legs fetishistically encased in rigid metal braces over fishnet stockings and leather, Gabrielle says, 'I'd like to see if I can fit into a car designed for a normal body.' Not only is the showroom encased in glass, open to the daytime space of the city, but the dealer is played as a hypernormal young man, justifiably uneasy about the conflict before him: whether to accommodate a 'handicapped' young woman or to protect his precious merchandise. It's a nicely satirical moment, but the point is elsewhere: as Gabrielle wedges her legs with great difficulty into the driver's seat, Cronenberg graces us with tight close-ups of her nuts and bolts ripping into the leather upholstery, emphasizing the erotic potential of the moment for James and Gabrielle while also noting how the more the car is ruined the more charged with excitement it becomes for them. Moreover, like the more literally external ventures of Beverly beyond his apartment in *Dead Ringers*, this brief emergence from the otherworldly space of these characters' reality brings them up against their utter unsuitability to the contours and the rules of the 'real' world. Cronenberg's characters inhabit a parallel reality whose intersection with our own he only shows us at brief but illuminating moments.

The most illuminating of these moments, as often is the case in Cronenberg's

2.2 The horror of Cronenberg's beauty: the final scene of *Crash* (1996). Photofest

films, is the concluding scene of the film, when Catherine and James, apparently seeking the same release through death by car crash achieved first by Seagrave and then by Vaughan, survive a high-speed chase of Catherine by James in Vaughan's Lincoln, and find themselves lying, bruised and battered, on the grassy verge of a highway next to the smoking wreck of Catherine's topless Porsche (figure 2.2). It is the most strikingly beautiful scene in a film otherwise characterized by its icy cold, metallic aestheticism. That aesthetic persists in the form of the convertible corpse, but it has been newly framed by a lush green and damp muddy brown heretofore absent from the film's inorganic palette. It's not quite the underwater ending of *Shivers*, but it still feels as if the film has somehow left behind the asphalt-and-steel superhighway infrastructure that we know subliminally still lurks around the edges of the frame. Cronenberg plays with this off-screen knowledge, starting the shot, which is also the final sex scene in the film, tightly framed on Catherine and James before slowly and smoothly pulling the camera back to take in ever more of the green surroundings, cutting to the credits, presumably, at the moment when a piece of highway was about to re-enter the picture.

'Maybe the next one, darling. Maybe the next one,' intones James to his teary-eyed wife, echoing back to the first scene between the two of them in bed together, recounting their futile separate trysts with a flight instructor and a camera assistant, respectively. This time, however, as Cronenberg signals by the change of palette, something else has happened, which he has described as a form of emotional reconciliation: 'You don't realize, until the last scene, that these two people are in love with each other and that the whole effort of the film has been for them to find a way, odd though it is, to come back together.'[90] What Cronenberg leaves ambiguous is whether this breakthrough implies a rejection of the film's obsession and a return to some semblance of 'normal' life, having survived an episode of addiction, with the green and damp signalling a return to the organic, or whether they have successfully fused with technology, with the green and damp around the crashed car signalling a synthesis of organic and inorganic. As Cronenberg has said of the film, in direct contradiction of a general critical assumption as to its unremitting bleakness, 'I'm saying that if some harsh reality envelops you, rather than be crushed, destroyed or diminished by it, embrace it fully. Develop it and take it even further than it wanted to go itself. See if that's not a creative endeavour. If that is not positive.'[91] We can conclude that Cronenberg's Canadianness has gained a new wisdom as well, as the Torontonian said of the Toronto location of this provocative, disturbing vision, 'There's a wonderful sense of this movie being physically and tangibly a part of my life, a part of my daily, mundane life as well as my artistic life. That's very satisfying.'[92] He had always been able to make a creative endeavour out of the 'harsh reality' of Hollywood and America threatening to 'envelop' him, but now he was able to articulate it both within and outside his films. *Crash* was simultaneously the most American (but not the most Hollywood – that would be *The Fly* and *Dead Zone*) and the most Canadian film Cronenberg had ever made, and it set the mould for many of his subsequent films.

If *Crash* is a summation of dark American obsessions expanding to take over the world, *eXistenZ* is a strangely personal film, an assured and laid-back (for Cronenberg) review of his trademark authorial obsessions. The story of a gaming inventor who enters the virtual world of her game in order to discover the origin of a plot to murder her for assaulting 'reality,' *eXistenZ* is constructed as a series of nested worlds, one within the other. Each of those nesting worlds is inhabited, for the first time in a Cronenberg film, by familiar icons of contemporary Anglo-Canadian cinema: Don McKellar, Sarah Polley, and Callum Keith Rennie, along with old regular Robert Silverman, who hadn't appeared since *Naked Lunch*. If the futuristic *Crash* had been emptied of the IT signs of the technological present – no computers, no cell phones, no high-tech gadgets – *eXistenZ* went further: the gaming pods seem born of the same organic/inorganic fusion *Crash* had dreamed of, plugging into 'bioports' in the spines of gamers to become prosthetic extensions of their bodies. This organic technology extends to every aspect of the film, provides a great deal of its humour (especially in gaming corporation rep Ted Pikul's [Jude Law] fear of piercing), and mirrors its insistence on prosthetic and make-up effects, more gruesomely and joyously gooey and corporeal than anything since *Videodrome*.

The reminiscences of earlier Cronenberg are so strongly present as to have led some reviewers to accuse him of self-parody. But the film is less a parody than a restatement of Cronenberg's philosophy for a new millennium. He did in fact use CGI in the film, at one point invisibly, to construct a travelling shot between two geographically distant locations (the gaming pod factory and the Chinese restaurant), and at another point programmatically, to make a two-headed lizard admired by Allegra (Jennifer Jason Leigh) at the gas station where Pikul will get his diseased bioport.[93] 'A sign of the times,' Allegra smugly labels it, calling our attention to the fact that this biological impossibility is the only thing in the film represented *as if* it were actually impossible. She coos at it, and we find the first Disney moment to make it into a Cronenberg film. When next we encounter the audience-friendly creature, however, it is not as a sign of capitulation to market forces and merchandising, but of the immaterial and commodified object rendered disgustingly material: it arrives on a platter of genetically modified amphibians ordered by Pikul as the 'special' of the day in the game's 'Chinese Restaurant.' As Pikul finds himself forced by the game plot to ingest with pleasure a sign of the times he otherwise finds repulsive, *eXistenZ* begins to look more like a meditation on our desire to objectify technology as an immaterial spectacle instead of facing up to its interpenetration of our bodies and minds than a superficial pitch about virtual reality. Like the second manifestation of the lizard, the plastic effects are as stomach-churning as anything Cronenberg has done. 'Reality is consensual,' insists 'card-carrying existentialist' Cronenberg, and *eXistenZ* certainly cautions against the extremism that would maintain the pre-eminence of one form of reality above any other (the fatwa against Salman Rushdie was Cronenberg's oft-cited inspiration for the script). The final layer of reality in the film, a series of test subjects sitting in semi-circle in an isolated building that resembles a retrofitted chapel, is less futuristic, less organic, and less compelling than the one at the beginning, which we originally thought was 'reality.' It is also, interestingly, orchestrated by Merle (Polley) and designer Yevgeny Nourish (McKellar), Canadian actors as opposed to Britain's Christopher Eccleston and America's Leigh, who shared the opening scene. True, Pikul and Allegra proceed to assassinate Merle and Nourish, but I think it likely that the Canadian identity of these actors serves also to remind us of the further layer of reality that produced this game of a film, the director who has easily preserved his identity despite numerous claims to the contrary.

Both *A History of Violence* and *Eastern Promises*, Cronenberg's most ostensibly mainstream and superficially Hollywood films ever, conclude with key external and watery scenes. Both scenes explicitly deploy conventional imagery of rebirth and renewal, and both scenes posit a resolution to character-integrated formulations of Cronenberg's long-time existential concern. In *A History of Violence*, the question is whether a person can transform his personality through sheer dint of will and force of habit. In *Eastern Promises*, the question is posed from the opposite end: is it possible to preserve an ethical identity when one has totally immersed himself in the antithesis of that identity? Both questions are posed through the actor Viggo Mortensen and, specifically, through the substance of his flesh. At the end of *History*, in time-honoured film-noir tradition, Tom Stall is cleansing himself at daybreak from the dirty work of eliminating his brother and the last vestige of the hitman past he had been unable up to that point to leave behind. The scene is the first in the film not to take place within the small town where he lives with his family, or in the brother's mansion he has just left; it is the first 'natural' scene. Our familiarity with similar moments in Cronenberg's films should already suggest that it is not a simple rebirth, regardless of the baptismal heritage and the sunrise. Rather, such moments of watery beauty project an ambivalent image of escape from the closed system of Cronenberg's overt narratives. Stall has in fact succeeded in the project to which he has devoted his life from the moment, for reasons unbeknownst to us, he chose to leave behind his biological family and his former life. But he has also, as the coda to this climactic moment makes clear, failed, in that his family has been permanently altered by the knowledge its members have gained of the past of the man they thought they had known. In typical Cronenberg fashion, this core ambiguity spirals out to encompass the community itself and the American culture of violence in which Tom's narrative has situated it. There is no easier resolution to this than to any other of Cronenberg's manifestations of the 'new flesh.' Tom Stall is in many ways the direct descendant of Max Renn, who retrieved a gun from the vaginal slit that opened in his belly. The violence is internal, it is hard-wired into his body, and it is both necessary and repellent. It is not for nothing the film is entitled *A History of Violence*; like *Shivers* and its parasite, this is a film told from the point of view of the violence, not of the characters.

The central metaphor of *Eastern Promises* is writing, both the dead Tatiana's handwritten record of the torture of her body by Semyon, and Nikolai's more directly corporeal tattooed history. Bodies also write: the key to convicting crime boss disguised as restaurateur and paterfamilias Semyon is the fingerprints on a glass that will connect to a DNA test of Tatiana's baby, living evidence of his rape of the mother. We first encounter the Thames when Scotland Yard recover a body from which Nikolai has professionally erased all traces of identity; the river returns at the end as the site of Kirill's attempted murder of his baby half-brother, prevented at the last minute by Anna and Nikolai. At the river's edge, the Moses-like baby is kept from floating off in its basket of bulrushes; instead, Anna is allowed to adopt it and, perhaps, to reconstruct her own fractured family life. But the crux of the scene is Nikolai, who is placed in the plot situation of a nuclear family, while we are taunted with the typical resolution of a Hollywood narrative. But Nikolai refuses the proffered bait and the romantic conclusion, and we are left wondering exactly which motive has led him to do so. Does he feel irretrievably sullied by his criminal past and his undercover crimes (the opposite conclusion of Tom Stall in *A History of Violence*)? Has he been seduced by the possibility of taking over the Russian mafia organization Vory v Zakone for real? Is he simply acting as the consummate professional, unwilling to abandon a job until he has completed what he set out to do? Cronenberg wisely chooses to withhold the possibility of judgment.

Spider had already suggested a movement away from prominently displayed special effects, limiting them to the dual role of Spider's mother played by Miranda Richardson through the make-up effects that distinguish one from the other. But these effects were already subordinated to the narrative puzzle of Spider's past and its relationship to his present. *A History of Violence* and *Eastern Promises* go even further towards a diegetic realism. The key effects in both films emerge from Viggo Mortensen's body: the extremely violent set pieces that explode around Tom Stall in *A History of Violence* (the diner scene where he deals with the two murderous criminals, the stand-off in front of his house when he and his son eliminate Fogarty, and the climax in his brother Richie's house in Philadelphia) and the spectacle of Nikolai's tattoos, prominently displayed in the scene of his induction into

Vory v Zakone and, especially, in the bathhouse scene, where, naked and exposed, he nevertheless manages to kill the two Chechen assassins attacking him with linoleum knives. In both films, the violence is simultaneously excessive and highly realistic; we are aware that they are set pieces (indeed, some critics saw their excess simply as Cronenberg's need to be himself), but we are also aware that the visceral impact and the close-up intimacy of our view of that impact are more 'real' than the typical stylization of Hollywood violence.

The first film Cronenberg shot entirely outside Toronto, *Eastern Promises*, suggests a new breadth of scope and ambition for the film-maker.[94] Similarly, the expanded thematic range – it centrally addresses questions of ethnic identity and immigration – suggests a shift towards a more material consideration of the issues of outsiders and alienation that Cronenberg had previously addressed primarily in a metaphorical and allegorical context. Especially in relation to the four-minute short film he made for the sixtieth anniversary of the Cannes Film Festival, *At the Suicide of the Last Jew in the World at the Last Cinema in the World* (2007), Cronenberg seems to have begun circling back to the multi-ethnic milieu of West Toronto in which he grew up, and where he remembers watching ethnic Italians emerging from their own cinema in tears at the conclusion of Fellini's *La Strada* (1954) while he, on the other side of the street, had been inside the local Hollywood cinema watching a Durango Kid flick.[95] In an interview with reviewer Amy Taubin, Cronenberg suggests two contexts for the Cannes short, and also (by extension) for his recent film-making. One is local, the other global: a radical Muslim preacher on cable television calling for the annihilation of Jews and the emergence of what Cronenberg calls 'the current biggest provider of snuff pornography,' the Muslim extremist movement.[96] He would not be Cronenberg if he maintained that either phenomenon, in its media manifestation, should be censored. But he would also not be Cronenberg if he didn't register that the world and its media representation have changed dramatically since he imagined his own apolitical and atheistic snuff television in *Videodrome*.

It is not simply that the world has caught up with his imagination, but also that it has transformed that imagination. Both in Canada and globally, religion and ethnic identity have replaced sexual and political revolution as the pressing topics most requiring new modes of representation. It is curious that Atom Egoyan's recent film *Adoration* (2008) similarly addressed the role of chat rooms and blogging in working through as well as in promulgating extremism. Although his film-making may be ranging even further spatially from his Canadian base, there is no question that Cronenberg's new concerns relate, if anything, more directly than ever to that local base. At the same time, his mode of representation has approached ever more closely to the documentary realist milieu from which he originally emerged in the sixties. Finally, if we observe the moments of beauty through which he continues to express the crucial ambiguities of his films and his philosophy, we can also note that he has remained remarkably consistent in his authorial style – it is Canada that appears finally to have caught up with Cronenberg.

Chapter Three

Time Capsules: The Eighties Worlds of Denys Arcand and Patricia Rozema

Toronto's Patricia Rozema and Montreal's Denys Arcand have always had their fingers on the pulse of the moment in a way that has led to a pair of idiosyncratic cinematic oeuvres. While highly distinctive, their oeuvres do not in any obvious way follow the contours of a typical art-film auteur. This makes them quite different from those of film-makers, such as David Cronenberg or Léa Pool, who have followed their own path with a far less direct connection to what was going on in the world around them. A key factor in this difference has been the very timeliness that has caused their films to be accused of datedness very soon after their release. It is not as if they have anything else in common. Rozema and Arcand are a study in opposites: a staunch feminist and uncloseted lesbian and an unreconstructed heterosexual white male; an Anglo Canadian and a Quebecois; a small-town woman gone Hollywood and a small-town man remaining true to his roots. But there are compelling resemblances alongside those differences. Both film-makers emerged from a powerfully religious background – Rozema from a family of strict Calvinists, Arcand from a devoutly Catholic upbringing and a Jesuit education – and both, unusual in Canadian cinema, have at times used their film-making to reflect deeply on the place of religion in the modern world, Rozema in *When Night Is Falling* (1995) and Arcand in *Jésus de Montréal* (1989). Moreover, both have crossed the great divide in unusual ways: Rozema cast important Quebecois actor/director Paule Bailleargeon in *I've Heard the Mermaids Singing* and Quebecois star Pascale Bussières in *When Night Is Falling*, and contributed the short subject *Desperanto* to the omnibus 1990 film *Montréal vu par …* (including cameos in it by Arcand and Robert Lepage); Arcand has made two English-language films, *Love & Human Remains* (1993) and *Stardom* (2000), in addition to the complex engagement with American culture in *Le Déclin de l'empire américain* (1986) and, especially, *Les Invasions barbares* (2003). Simultaneously outsiders and insiders of their local film cultures, Rozema and Arcand have made careers out of simultaneously pleasing, surprising, and polarizing their core constituencies.

The Neophyte

> The biggest sin is to bore people.
>
> Patricia Rozema

Patricia Rozema claims not to have seen her first film (*The Exorcist*, 1973, William Friedkin) until she was sixteen. The late exposure that makes her path to film-making so different from those of her contemporaries seems also to have inoculated her permanently against worries about being cool. All of her films have moments where they skirt the border of tweeness – and, for some critics, pass way over to the other side. An aficionado of romance, myth, and fairy tale, Rozema has never been afraid to embrace emotion. But one can exaggerate the effect of a movie-less childhood; it is amply apparent from her films that Rozema did a lot of catching up in the fifteen-odd years between watching her first film and directing her first feature. Indeed, she recalls the profound influence of an Ingmar Bergman double feature seen while an undergraduate at Calvin College in Grand Rapids, Michigan.[1] What is clear, though, is that she inherited no youthful preconceptions from the cinema; her English major in college suggests instead the literary provenance of her favoured tropes and patterns: genre conventions from romance, myth, and fairy tale; the fairy tale happy ending, often doubled with a dark conclusion; a polarized sense of gender dynamics; and a fondness for alternative communities, or what Michel Foucault has termed 'heterotopias.'

Rozema broke out with the surprise art-house sensation, *I've Heard the Mermaids Singing* (1987), a fantasy fable widely credited with putting Anglo-Canadian cinema on the map critically for the first time in fifteen years and commercially for the first time ever. Her third film, *When Night Is Falling*, was a commercially successful entry in the burgeoning sub-genre of lesbian-themed independent movies. *Mansfield Park* (1999) was the first heritage-style adaptation to bring the submerged implications – colonialism and lesbianism – of Jane Austen's darkest novel to the surface of the images. And her 2008 feature, *Kit Kittredge: An American Girl*, for all its origins in what one reviewer called 'a feature-length advertisement for a doll,' was still widely heralded as a 'kidpic classic' with 'real girls' on the screen for a change. Rozema has proven adept over the years at making the right decision at the right moment. Her apparently irreconcilable eclecticism testifies to a willingness to go with the moment, which is also a typical trait – if also sometimes a dilemma – of the female characters that dominate her films.

Nevertheless, there are several consistent patterns of form and style even in a director able to move straight from the envelope-pushing explicit sexuality of the HBO series *Tell Me You Love Me* (2007) to the squeaky-clean traditionalism of *Kit Kittredge*. One of these traits is Rozema's refusal to intellectualize either her characters or her stories: they are always directly presented and emotionally accessible. This is clear in the changes she has made to source texts in several of her films. For her adaptation of Samuel Beckett's *Happy Days* (2000) for Channel Four television in England, Rozema was criticized for playing the final scene of the bleak drama for sentiment and reconciliation. Worried about the dead weight of a censorious and depressed Fanny Price as the heroine of Jane Austen's *Mansfield Park*, Rozema took the controversial step of updating both the subject matter (by opening out every iota of sex and violence lurking between Austen's lines) and the heroine (by merging Fanny with Austen herself and gifting her character with the wit and vivacity of the novel's narrating voice). Rozema's first feature began with its main character making an intimate confession directly at the audience, and she has never pulled back from the direct connection she made at that moment. The powerful presence of music in all of her films is an important factor in their emotional immediacy and ability to transcend, if barely, the pressures of everyday life. Equally important is an imaginative and playful visual sense that delights in providing correlatives in images of plot points and character traits. From Polly Vandersma's visions of flight, to the circus setting in *When Night Is Falling*, to the blasted but stunningly beautiful mountainous desert of Tenerife in *Happy Days*, to the elaborate tree house in *Kit Kittredge*, Rozema bypasses words to make us feel what she wants to say through the settings in which she immerses us.

Rozema's films are fundamentally optimistic, especially against the backdrop of an Anglo-Canadian tradition infamous for its dour worldview. Indeed, she has said of several films that she initially wrote them far darker than she eventually filmed them.[2] This is not to say that her films do not tackle distressing and difficult topics, but that they never leave audiences with the feeling that there is no way out. Even when her darkest film, *White Room* (1990), concluded with the suicide of its main character, Rozema seems to have felt compelled to step outside of this dead end and into the fantasy world of the young man who was its primary cause. Profoundly humiliated at a Montreal cocktail party, the Toronto housewife played by Sheila McCarthy in *Desperanto* is compensated when Denys Arcand and Geneviève Rioux (playing themselves here; Rioux had played one of the main characters in *Déclin*) take her dancing on the roof of the Olympic stadium. For all its essential sunniness as a commercial product, *Kit Kittredge* makes the audience earn its happy ending, suffering through a deeply felt plot of home foreclosures, class shame, prejudice, and deception. Consistently, Rozema's protagonists are innocents; this is the common thread that links *Kit Kittredge*, *I've Heard the Mermaids Singing*, *Happy Days*, *When Night Is Falling*, *White Room*, and *Mansfield Park*. It is not so much that Kit, Polly, Winnie, Camille, Norm and Jane, and Fanny are childlike, or asexual, or naive; it is that they are unworldly and profoundly sui generis. As Rozema said of her first feature: 'My film is really independent. It's even independent of the history of film, because I don't know the history of film. I didn't see many films, I didn't go to film school.'[3] The attempt to see the world directly with one's own eyes characterizes Rozema's descriptions of her own haphazard coming to film, but it is also an inheritance of a Calvinist past from which she has cut back all of the religious ideology but has retained the fundamental belief that the path to truth and transcendence lies through the direct and unmediated encounter of the individual with the material and spiritual world.

That Rozema translates Calvinist severity into a wide-eyed but often painful affirmation of life is one way in which her films are profoundly autobiographical in their 'sentiments,' as she puts it. And although Rozema's work has divided feminists perhaps more than any other group, these sentiments are undeniably women-centred. Only *White Room* comes remotely close to sporting a male protagonist, and only in 'Six Gestures' (1997), her hour-long film of Bach's sixth cello concerto, does she come close to creating a truly sympathetic male character. Her

3.1 From the voice in the street to a bird's-eye view of Toronto: the unusual perspective of *White Room* (1990). Photofest.

women are noticeably stronger, more fully realized, and more likeable than her men. They are autonomous, unpredictable, and wilful, although never without their own faults. To her credit, Rozema has always done just enough with men, such as Martin (Henry Czerny) in *Night Is Falling*, to prevent them from being reduced to straw men or stick figures, but only just enough.

Rozema's films conjure a powerful sense of place. She is one of the few Canadian directors to celebrate contemporary architecture unequivocally. Skyscrapers figure prominently in her films – 'I like shots directly up' she says on the commentary to the *Mermaids* DVD as Polly snaps pictures of the Royal Bank Plaza (built 1976–9), Rozema's 'favourite building.'[4] The final pre-credits shot of *Night Is Falling* cuts from Petra and Camille leaving Toronto in their circus trailer to the golden towers of the downtown skyline dominated, once again, by the Royal Bank Plaza. *Desperanto* concludes on the roof of the Olympic stadium, built for the 1976 Summer Olympics. Both *Mermaids* and *White Room* feature industrial landscapes, including giant fuel storage tanks as if in homage to the influential 'New Topographics' photographs of Bernd and Hilla Becher. And while performance artist Zelda (Sheila McCarthy) will soon reveal herself as *White Room*'s villain, her Quonset hut artist's pad and the blasted landscape, gorgeously captured in deep, rich colour by Atom Egoyan's regular cinematographer Paul Sarossy, impart a more ambivalent tone to Zelda's surroundings, just as the bravura shot where the camera slowly elevates away from the tiny green space where Zelda's news stand is situated until the shot encompasses several acres of cityscape as a beautifully abstract patchwork of colour is simultaneously soothing and chilling (figure 3.1).

Individual characters have their private lairs – Polly's isolated 'bachelorette' apartment, Zelda's hut, Norm's vintage Detroit leviathan automobile, Jane's white room, Petra's circus trailer, Camille's neo-Victorian home, Winnie's mound and handbag, Fanny's attic studio atop Mansfield Park and the bed where she and her sister sleep in Portsmouth, Kit's tree house, Will and Countee's tent in the Hobo Jungle – but the privacy of every one of these spaces is violated at some point in each film, sometimes in a positive manner, sometimes negatively, and sometimes ambivalently. Some of these spaces double as or overlap with communal spaces that reflect a set of values marginalized in the world-at-large: the forest into which Polly, Gabrielle, and Mary disappear out of her apartment at the conclusion of *Mermaids*; the Sirkus of Sorts in *Night Is Falling* and its counterpart, the religious college where Camille is teaching at the start of the film; from the initial possession of a dysfunctional family, the entirety of Mansfield Park is transformed by the end into a diverse but positive community; Kit's tree house, the Hobo Jungle, and the family house turned boarding house all play different functions as alternative communities able to resist the disintegration of values wrought by the Great Depression. In contrast, one of the most chilling aspects of *White Room* is the absence of any positive image of community; social space exists only in the terrifying apparition of the horde of rabid fans led by Zelda into besieging Jane in her sanctuary.

Rozema's first film is still widely considered her best, and it is difficult to argue with this assessment. On the strength of *Mermaids*, consistently ranked in the top ten Canadian films of all time, Rozema was perceived to be developing into an auteur of global standing. But, although *Mermaids* continues to be the object of the sort of sustained critical attention reserved for auteur films, Rozema has not yet, and may not ever, receive the legitimation of auteur status reserved for subjects of a scholarly monograph: a status restricted thus far among English-Canadian film-makers to David Cronenberg, Atom Egoyan, and Guy Maddin. In retrospect, Rozema's second feature, *White Room*, looks very much like a bid to solidify her status as auteur, and to develop further *Mermaids*' themes of new media, celebrity, duplicity, and privacy. The often brutal rejection by critics of the experimental forms of *White Room* seems to have foreclosed that ambition, and while Rozema has never abandoned the interests that drove those films, she has taken a path towards a niche commercial cinema with very little apparent investment in maintaining the type of artistic profile that would result in auteur status. Although she has generally insisted on maintaining control if not actually writing or rewriting her scripts, she has directed all of her projects on spec since *Night Is Falling*, including *Desperanto*, *Happy Days*, an episode of the TV show *The Hunger* (1997), 'Six Gestures,' *Mansfield Park*, *Tell Me You Love Me*, *Kit Kittredge*, an episode of the HBO psychotherapy drama *In Treatment* (2010), and one episode of the Ottawa-based CBC cognitive behaviour comedy *Michael: Tuesdays & Thursdays* (2011). At the same time, more evidently auteurist projects, including the long-gestating spin on Nancy Drew, *The Case of the Missing Mother*, and *Grey Gardens* (a telefilm finally made for cable in 2009 from a script by Rozema), have fallen by the wayside or been made by others.[5] The path taken by Rozema's career makes for fascinating study precisely because she has produced a strangely consistent and in fact quite accomplished body of work all the while breaking most of the rules set by the critical establishment. Perhaps partly because of the financial success of her features (all except *White Room* have turned a profit), Rozema has been able to choose her projects more sparingly and control them more closely than many of her peers. Famously, when she signed a two-picture deal with Miramax after the success of *Mansfield Park*, she was unable to agree with studio head Harvey Weinstein about a single project.

After completing *Passion – A Letter in 16 mm* (1985), a well-received, black-and-white short film about a yuppie career woman, Rozema and first-time producer and then-partner Alexandra Raffé were able to raise just enough money from the OFDC and TFC to complete *Mermaids*: $292,000.[6] Starring established theatrical actor Sheila McCarthy, *Mermaids* combines a character study of 'someone you would never talk to at a cocktail party' with a manifesto on the relativistic quality of art and an 'anti-authority message.'[7] An incompetent temp, Polly lives in an isolated 'bachelorette' apartment and spends her time watching and spying on people, snapping photos of the world around her, and having visions of herself as a woman who climbs skyscrapers, flies, walks on water, makes coherent intellectual arguments, and hears the mermaids singing. Characteristically, Rozema structures her screenplay around the sort of coincidences that drive both comedy and tragedy in the theatre: hired as a part-time secretary by pretentious gallery owner Gabrielle St Peres (Paule Baillargeon), Polly is kept on semi-permanently, evidently because the insecure Gabrielle needs someone to listen to her uncritically. Offhandedly invited to Gabrielle's birthday party, Polly is shown and then steals a glowing white painting Gabrielle says she is too shy to exhibit. When Polly shows the painting to great acclaim, it eventually emerges that the real artist is Gabrielle's lover Mary Joseph (Ann-Marie McDonald). Meanwhile, Polly has sent her own photos to Gabrielle under a pseudonym only to have them summarily dismissed. Hurt by both incidents, she semi-accidentally burns Gabrielle's face with boiling tea. When Mary Joseph and Gabrielle later seek Polly out in her apartment, everything is hastily resolved, and Polly leads them through a doorway into a woods, part of her visionary world.

Rozema steers clear of many of the pitfalls in the material, in particular the high risk of either excessive whimsy or extreme condescension that would probably have marked the film if made in an American style. The narration is entirely from Polly's point of view, ostensibly recounted in retrospect to a video camera. The film is replete with motifs of looking and seeing, from the direct address to the camera (and the audience in the camera's place) that opens the film, to Polly's eavesdropping on Gabrielle and Mary through the surveillance camera she had helped Gabrielle install in the gallery, to Rozema's processing of Polly's snapshots as black-and-white images on screen. Rozema's texturing of her film's visual qualities with different modes and types of image and her highlighting of video as an instrument of confession, observation, and surveillance doubtless hit a nerve in an eighties art world obsessed with incorporating video into gallery art and a Canadian cinema scene on which Atom Egoyan had arrived nearly simultaneously with Rozema – his *Family Viewing* was released the same year as *Mermaids* and they were often mentioned in the same breath.[8]

White Room moved even further into the dark territory Egoyan would make his own. As Robert Cagle argues, the representation of communication media is an important theme related to Canadian film-makers' self-definition in distinction to the seamless images of mainstream American cinema.[9] André Lavoie likewise identifies video imagery with the marginal position of Canadian cinema during the mid-eighties, noting its practical function of incorporating cheaply shot material into more expensive 16 mm or 35 mm footage.[10] Both critics observe the use of video's 'reality effect' against itself as a way of questioning assumptions about cinematic realism, but it also became increasingly clear that Rozema's questioning had quite a different goal than Egoyan's, her goal closer to Bruce McDonald's in his pseudo-documentary *Hard Core Logo* (1996; see chapter 8). Egoyan has made the relativism of truth and the ambivalent power of images into the cornerstone of a consistently auteurist vision while Rozema and McDonald subordinate epistemological issues to the thematic concerns of their narratives and the emotional lives of their characters.

The aesthetic quality of different visual media is strongly apparent in *White Room*, where Rozema's bigger budget allowed her to experiment with various video effects, especially in the music video of 'I Am Nobody' (end credits include 'video artist,' 'computer imaging,' and 'music video editor'). But Rozema's penchant for distinct image schemes was already apparent in the low-budget production design of *Mermaids*: the darkroom scenes are red and the visions are black and white until the end of the film; the video provides a different grain and texture than the clear colour of the default images. Mary Joseph's canvases, too (we see one frequently, and glimpse a second), play on visual texture, since the glowing white rectangle duplicates a blank movie screen. Many critics saw Rozema's choice of the painting as a clever solution to the common problem of showing art in movies that must play a plot function as 'brilliant'; it is a clever solution, but it is also a bona fide creation, with an art pedigree including Russian constructivist Kazimir Malevich, the early work of pop artist Robert Rauschenberg, and monochrome artist Robert Ryman, evincing a conceptual and ready-made aesthetic (Rozema used Scotchlite to make the painting) that simultaneously defuses their pretentiousness and lives up to their billing as transcendent.

This is especially evident in the marvellous shot that Rozema in the DVD commentary calls her favourite in the film: Polly walking down the street at night carrying the stolen painting inside a giant, glowing, paper-covered box (figure 3.2).[11] Rozema's facility with visual metaphor defines her films for both supporters and detractors, and the immediacy of her images can be somewhat disconcerting. We don't have to work to decipher what the painting means; we know intuitively and immediately. This is equally true of the eponymous white room in Rozema's second film, of the circus in *When Night Is Falling*, of the mansion of Mansfield Park, and of Kit Kittredge's elaborate tree house. The desire for transcendence Rozema inherited from her religious background brings with it a universalizing impulse, which is evident in her work on many levels.

Rozema's characters project emotion – their immediate accessibility is another factor in the popular success of her films, with the actors using gesture and expression as much as words to impart their emotions. As she defines the concept of 'Six Gestures,' her hour-long film based on Bach's sixth cello concerto, the struc-

3.2 Rozema's facility with visual metaphor: the glowing box at night in *I've Heard the Mermaids Singing* (1987). Photofest.

ture and emotion of each section of the film are defined by the gestures of the film's title, 'looking up; looking inward; hands feet working like the body working motion; hand caressing face; courtly mannered gesture; flight.'[12] The core of 'Six Gestures' is the ice-dancing of celebrated Canadian couple Torvill and Dean, choreographed to the beat and tempo of Yo Yo Ma's cello playing, and shot in backlit silhouette that recalls Polly before the glowing painting, Jane in her white room, and, especially, Petra's shadow-dancing and the scene in which Camille and Petra's lovemaking is intercut with the silhouetted twin trapeze artists at the Sirkus of Sorts. The body is simultaneously a vehicle of aesthetic pleasure and visual beauty and a means for the direct expression of self.

Body language is not only a matter of acting, however; it is equally a component of Rozema's camera set-ups, especially the direct address to the camera, which appears in one form or another in nearly every one of her films, usually shot close-up to bring us even closer to the actor speaking directly to us. In *Happy Days*, Rozema takes it to an extreme, bringing us so close to Fiona Shaw that, as one reviewer remarked, we can study every pore and blemish on Winnie's face. And while Rozema at times employs the customary angles of shot/reverse shot, she at least as frequently shoots her actors square on: 'Looking in the camera lens excites me. There's an intimacy, a directness.'[13] A leitmotif in criticism of Rozema's work is the excellent performance of the actors in spite of what is perceived as trite or clunky dialogue. Embarrassing as it can sometimes be, there is something almost *too* true to life about the banality, over-seriousness, and directness of this dialogue. It is not surprising, then, that Rozema cites 'embarrassment' as the motivation for creating Polly's character: 'It's one of the strongest human emotions, and it's physical. You can't control blushing, and that physical manifestation happens to everybody – all classes, all sexes, all types'; the starting point for *Desperanto* was the question 'What is the most embarrassing thing that can happen to somebody in public?'[14] These are all quirky and unexpected gestures towards the universal; rather than positing an alternative, outsider vision contingent on its opposition to the mainstream, Rozema's films somehow claim the mainstream *as* alternative and outsider, always winning over the audience both within and outside the film. 'Six Gestures' concludes a motif of Yo Yo Ma busking in a traffic triangle in the middle of Times Square with a scene of sustained applause by the passersby.

Spying and, especially, peeping are generally the stuff of movie deviants and criminals. Rozema does not gloss over the potentially embarrassing, invasive, and criminal consequences of surveillance – witness Polly's discovery by the necking couple she has followed into the woods of Toronto's High Park, or Norm's passive participation in a brutal rape and murder in *White Room* – but the thrust of these scenes appears to be the need to make everything public and accessible, to bring it out in the open no matter the cost. Deception never succeeds in Rozema's films, and however dubious the means employed by characters to discover deception, they are never condemned outright, not even hapless Norm in *White Room*. *Mermaids* has the potential to be a mean-spirited and devastatingly sad film, and Rozema lets us see the full force of the disappointment, rejection, and fury in Sheila McCarthy's face when Polly's idol falls to earth. But the reconciliation at Polly's apartment redeems Gabrielle as much as it does the protagonist, for Rozema has shown us Gabrielle's reasons too, shallow as they may possibly be. At the same time, the double ending makes it clear that we are in a world of fiction rather than real life, and that in real life the result could just as easily have been tragic. The first 'ending' of the film comes when Polly finishes her confession, 'Anyways, there it is. That's what happened,' abruptly cueing the end credits. The 'real' ending of the film, the happy one, unfolds slowly thereafter, interspersed with the credits, meaning that the audience that leaves impatiently will miss it completely.

Rozema's penchant for making formal patterns with surface images is closely related to her penchant for allegory, a rhetorical mode similarly characterized by the self-evident quality of its trappings. In *Mermaids*, the lesbian couple's names set them up as some form of the Father and the Holy Ghost, with Polly as a Christ figure, even as her surname, Vandersma, as explained by Rozema, combines a prefix and a suffix, with nothing in between. Given that Gabrielle's gallery is called 'The Church Gallery' and housed in a former chapel, the religious overtones are unmistakable. In addition to a time-worn mode of medieval and early-modern Christian narrative such as *Pilgrim's Progress*, allegory has a strong presence in postmodern literature and art. In the latter, however, its hallmark is uncertainty as to its ultimate meaning. As in *Mermaids*, many critics have noted the obvious presence of the allegory, but few have pinpointed its meaning or noted how Rozema has twisted the conventions in unusual ways, not only by making her Holy Trinity female and at least two-thirds lesbian, but also by rooting its meaning in the function of art in contemporary society.

The second allegorical thread signalled by Rozema and duly noted by the critics is the identification of Polly with a Canadian everyperson. Rozema is on record as having emphasized Polly's non-threatening or non-existent sexuality as a way of making it easier for male viewers to identify with her; she has also repeatedly related Polly's personality traits to typical qualities identified with Canadians in contrast to their brasher, more self-confident southern neighbours.[15] That Polly's gender functions at least in part as an allegory for Canada's feminization does not preclude the equally plausible feminist reading of the film in a non-Canadian context. Both identities especially come into play during Polly's first vision early in the film, where her fall from a Toronto skyscraper wearing a maple-leaf-embroidered toque transforms into ecstatic flight after she tosses the toque away to allow her hair to blow free. Readings of the film split down the middle, with George Godwin making a pro-feminist argument based on Rozema's reversal of a male-centred gaze and Teresa de Lauretis and Marion Harrison both derisively dismissing the film as 'trite' and 'offensive' pseudo-feminism. In hindsight, *Mermaids* was made at the moment of a decisive shift in feminism and gender studies in which the hard-line post-structuralist models invoked by de Lauretis and Harrison were being questioned by a more personal, ad hoc, and situational feminism perhaps best realized on film by the ambiguous neo-Victorian characterization of Holly Hunter's Ada in Jane Campion's *The Piano* (1992).[16]

Rather than applying a global theoretical framework or sustaining a consistent intellectual discourse on gender, Campion's and Rozema's films are character based and event driven, striving to evoke strong and contradictory emotions and ideas. As Rozema has commented, 'Gender is a category that doesn't interest me. I think we're much more affected by our educational or geographical origins than by whether we're male or female.'[17] Given the central role played by women and their identities *as* women in so many of Rozema's films, the operative word in this quote would appear to be 'category' rather than gender per se. Just as she refuses to self-identify as a lesbian despite the fact that she openly lives with a female partner, Rozema refuses to define and thereby limit her films according to any single abstract category. As Parpart writes, 'Rozema ... has resisted becoming closely identified with any group other than her fellow directors in the Ontario new wave, and has defined her film practice as neutrally as possible.'[18] Hyperconscious of her reception by critics and other film-makers, and highly capable of forging strong personal alliances and inspiring strong loyalties, Rozema appears to have chosen a quintessentially Canadian mode of being a film-maker – an irreducible mosaic of genres and modes of production united by a consistently situational and immediate approach to whatever project is in front of her. Because she is Rozema, her films somehow resemble each other, but they could never otherwise be defined as having anything in common if not for Rozema.

The Jaded Veteran

My life is always the next film, the next project.

Denys Arcand

Rozema's short film *Desperanto* begins with Sheila McCarthy's character sitting in a Montreal hotel watching *Déclin* on the television. For a generation of English Canadians (and Americans), Arcand's film was their introduction to the Quebecois and their culture. For the Quebecois locals, however, he had been on the scene for more than twenty years, a veteran of the direct cinema documentary movement and the Quebec new wave of narrative film-making in the late sixties and early seventies. But after the critical ambivalence that greeted his ambitious genre melange *Gina* (1975), Arcand did not make another feature film until *Déclin*, more than a decade later.[19] Finding himself, as he put it, 'unemployed and without any good prospects for the future,' Arcand took the typical path of Canadian film-makers: he disappeared into the anonymity of television, scripting a popular miniseries on former premier Maurice Duplessis, writing and directing *The Crime of Ovide Plouffe* (1984), also screened in a long version on television, and directing three episodes of the English-language CBC series *Empire, Inc.* (1985).[20] The difference between his pre- and post-television features is striking; as Arcand put it, 'I learned how to write dialogue.'[21] *La Maudite Galette* (*Dirty Money*, 1971), *Réjeanne Padovani* (1973), and *Gina* are scathing political satire cast in the form of experiments with popular genre cinema: film noir in the first two and rape-revenge drama in the latter; *Déclin, Jésus de Montréal*, and *Barbarian Invasions* mute radical critique in favour of sparkling entertainment with a serious underbelly. The early features are resolutely local in ambition and audience; the later ones aim globally.

While similar to Rozema's path in its excellent timing, Arcand's much longer career trajectory has been marked by a different order of controversy. His breakthrough 1970 documentary about the textile industry *On est au Coton* was shelved for six years by the NFB for being too inflammatory in the most heated years of the separatist movement. It was eventually released in a censored version shorn of material involving Dominion Textile president Edward King. His global hits *Déclin* and *Jésus de Montréal* skewered eighties materialism with such consummate skill that my tender-hearted undergraduates find them hard to watch – too mean-spirited, they complain. Arcand's return to the characters of *Déclin* and to global recognition nearly twenty years down the road in *Invasions* took up this multi-generational spin on the previous obsessions, showing the eighties characters stuck in Arcand's past and the new generation negotiating a very different and equally frightening future. In some ways, Arcand has never left behind the aesthetic of his documentary days: capturing events as they are occurring and reserving final judgment for some indeterminate future date. According to Arcand, the past has no intrinsic value; rather, the historian's task is to use the past to understand the present.[22] Consequently, the past is the key to understanding the present, but neither presents a fixed or stable vantage point from which to pass judgment or establish any more than a contingent understanding of reality.

This approach to the past is highly effective in Arcand's three feature-length documentaries, although it is also highly pessimistic. In *On est au coton*, Arcand makes a strongly critical argument through contrasting and parallel editing, especially (in the uncensored version) when he juxtaposes the words of the company president and the town mayor with the workers' descriptions of their ruined lives and the long history of the textile industry and labour struggle in Quebec. However, what emerges is not a call for revolution, but an indictment of capitalist and anglophone exploitation, on the one hand, and resignation by francophone Quebecois workers on the other. In *Québec: Duplessis et après ...* (1972), Arcand, commissioned by the NFB to make a historical documentary about the conservative provincial leader Maurice Duplessis, instead made a film about the continuing and baleful influence of Duplessis's spectre over the election of 1970, the first in which the separatist Parti Québécois was standing for election. In *Le Confort et l'indifférence* (1981), Arcand moved further from the aesthetic of direct cinema, interspersing an actor playing Niccolo Machiavelli, seated high in a tower of the brand-new Complexe Desjardins in downtown Montreal as he pronounces excerpts from realpolitik handbook *The Prince*, with interviews and documentary footage from the referendum of 1980. The juxtaposition clearly argues that Quebecois voters rejected the possibility of sovereignty for fear of losing the comforts of a successful Canada and out of indifference. Although Arcand includes highly affecting footage of disillusioned and despairing Quebecois, the lofty and distanced disinvoltura of Machiavelli sets the tone of the film, and is difficult to separate from his evident voicing of Arcand's own assessment of the situation: the end of the Quiet Revolution.

Arcand's first two fiction features are similarly straightforward in their sympathy, even while they are, as all his films, 'framed in the collective.'[23] Among the first auteurist Quebecois films to introduce genre tropes to the dominant aesthetic of documentary realism, *Maudite galette* and *Réjeanne Padovani* work because of the extraordinary underplaying of their actors: none of the players appear shocked, worried, surprised, upset, or in a hurry, even as, in the latter film, construction developer Padovani has his wife murdered while he is entertaining the most powerful men in Montreal, and her corpse is buried in the concrete foundations of his new highway. Rather than the overheated melodrama of much traditional American noir from the forties and fifties, *Réjeanne Padovani* plays more like the cool gangster films of post-war France, except that the coolness is used to transmit political invective rather than existentialist helplessness. The pointed allusions to Jean Renoir's classic dissection of pre-war class cynicism in *La règle du jeu* (1939) – like interloping aviator André Jussieu, Padovani's estranged wife Réjeanne is shot by a minion in a glass-walled hothouse – only serve to highlight the distance between Renoir's humanism and Arcand's cold gaze towards the villains of his piece. 'Everyone has his reasons,' Renoir famously said of his film; in his work of the seventies Arcand certainly demonstrated his grasp of the workings of power, but it was not until *Déclin* that he found an effective means to integrate his outrage within the workings of a plot.

In a series of conversations with Michel Coulombe in the early nineties, Arcand noted this shift in his retrospective disappointment over *Gina*. (Arcand claims to have little interest in his films once they are made, seldom revisiting them.)[24] Recalling the germ of the film in a relationship established between himself, a local stripper, and a local textile worker while making *Coton*, Arcand chides himself for the 'cowardice' he now can see in his inability to 'transpose this experience into the film,' saying, 'It was easy for me to speak of good workers and evil bosses, but more difficult to evoke my relationship with that worker and that dancer, and what happened after I left them. This is why, ten years later, I had to go further in *The Decline of the American Empire*, without of course falling into pure confession, but by being present in the four male characters of the film.'[25] Arcand groups *Gina* with *Coton*, *Duplessis*, and *Réjeanne Padovani* as 'a half-documentary half-fiction tetralogy.'[26] The diction makes it unclear whether Arcand sees all four films as hybrids, or sees them as using respectively documentary and fictional means to explore the same concerns. Certainly, *Gina* is the most hybrid of the four, staging as it does Arcand's making of *Coton* in the character of the film-maker played by his brother Gabriel, placing dialogue from *Coton* in the mouth of the female textile worker Dolorès, and intercutting her interview with Gina's striptease performed in real time. In his analysis of the film, Bill Marshall signals the uneasy analogy between the exploitation of workers, Gina's rape, and the censorship of Arcand's documentary *Coton*, and by consequence, the political views articulated through it.[27] Marshall goes on to cite a number of critiques of the film for failing fully to articulate the reflection on its own form.[28] If we return to Arcand's assessment of the film's fault, it seems clear that the shift into rape-revenge that rapidly follows on the key theoretical convergence that occurs in the striptease scene is a means of distancing the film from the consequences of the analogy Arcand has just established. Allowing Gina to take bloody revenge on her tormenters simultaneously punishes the passivity of rural Quebecois men, stages a much-desired rebellion by the oppressed that never actually occurred, and assuages the film-maker's guilt at his own inaction, even as it distances those desires through the exaggerated conventions of genre cinema.

That this argument was not fully articulated within the diegesis of the film is demonstrated by the ease with which *Gina* was re-edited by its distributor Cinépix for the U.S. drive-in market as a 'forty-minute film with nothing but strip-teases, car chases and murders.'[29] Nevertheless, it is a mistake, I think, for critics to perform the same displacement onto a dry continental dialogue about the proper political approach to film, especially for a director who has never shown any interest in orthodoxy. First, in the historical context, Arcand was clearly working through a reaction to the *films de fesses* ('butt films') that dominated the Quebec box office; these films were the commercial face of the province's cinema beyond its borders and originated with directors such as Denis Héroux and Claude Fournier who had come up in the NFB with Arcand, and the genre was taken up in an auteurist context by Gilles Carle in the years just prior to *Gina* (see chapter 4). Second, the difficulty of combining popular genre with his personal and political views has in fact been a constant in Arcand's film since *Gina* – even his television work generated a fair amount of controversy along with its popularity – and the sizeable minority who dislike his films tends to cite the obviousness of their arguments and the banality or woodenness of their dialogue – typical features of genre cinema but anathema to the auteur film. Arcand responded to a savage panning of *Jésus* by the film critic of *New York* magazine by countering with the praise he had received from a producer of the CBC series *Empire Inc.*: 'We've got ten directors like you in this country. What's important is your writing, your talent as a writer.'[30] In hindsight, *Gina* did not signal a simple retreat into the safety of genre tropes, but an early recognition of their potency as vehicles of repressed or displaced social desire, and a prescient foreshadowing of the direction independent cinema would take at the end of the century, in Quebec as elsewhere, when genre-blending and rehearsing popular tropes became legitimate strategies even in auteurist cinema. After all, what else was *Déclin* but a mature and savvy reimagining of the sex cinema of the seventies for the intellectuals of the eighties?

Arcand's migration into popular genres and advertising in the decade between *Gina* and *Déclin* was in this sense a form of research as well as a commercial necessity. In a 1987 speech, Arcand argues for advertising as a legitimate form of filmmaking and unfavourably compares the ease with which European film-makers 'go back and forth between film and advertising without batting an eye' to the puritanical American model of absolute separation.[31] He enumerates the reasons a film director such as himself should make commercials: the money, 'the pleasure of filming,' the 'chance to explore all the latest technological innovations,' the opportunity to meet actors and technicians within the context of a local media industry such as Montreal.[32] To be sure, Arcand balances his positive re-evaluation with the recognition that advertising work seldom allows him to develop his 'creative resources' or use all his 'talents' or his 'knowledge of film.'[33] Nevertheless, his clear-sighted assessment of the pros and cons of each field does acknowledge the actual state of affairs for a large number of Canadian film-makers, actors, and technicians.[34] He also anticipated the much-discussed cross-fertilization that occurred in American independent movies during the following decade in a number of directors including David Fincher and Spike Jonze. The Machiavellian dicta of *Confort* that punctuate this period refer not only to the ease with which the general public repudiated its own dreams but to Arcand's mastery of the tools he needed to sway those people. The documentary is at least as scathing about the naive politics of the 'Yes' politicians as it is about the people's submission to the demagoguery of the 'No' parties. In one movement, Arcand resolved the genre film's problematic distancing of reality – all the serious Quebecois features at the time he made *Déclin* were, he notes, period pieces – along with his own ambivalence towards his engagement with the material, retaining 'an essential affection for these characters': 'They're not insects I'm looking at, not at all. They're my friends. They're me.'[35] Indeed, casual betrayal and malicious retaliation play a structurally dramatic role in *Déclin* just as they do in *Gina*; the difference is that the drama has been transposed into words rather than deeds. As in similarly dramatic moments in Arcand's other films since *Déclin*, they are the more emotionally affecting for their primarily verbal quality.

But *Déclin* is the closest Arcand has come to emotional directness and an equal sympathy with all his characters, and even here he refuses to tie himself down to a linear narrative arc and a unified point of view, complicating his narrative with autonomous secondary characters such as Diane's macho lover Mario (*Gina*'s Gabriel Arcand, who became established as an actor through roles in his brother's early films). Arcand's later fiction films pose an unusual melange of documentary cinema with narrative that keeps his films at arm's length from conventional Hollywood and is often challenging for viewers. As Arcand puts it, they are anthropological: he chooses a subject, studies it in depth, and then records his findings. Objectivity per se is not the object; direct cinema is upfront about the presence and influence of the film-maker on his subject, a motif Arcand includes more or less explicitly in nearly all his films, most prominently in *Gina*, where he recreates the vexed production of *Coton* as a subplot, and in *Stardom*, where Robert Lepage plays an avant-garde photographer making a fly-on-the-wall documentary about the supermodel du jour who is the film's protagonist and object of scrutiny. What characterizes Arcand's films is the refusal to judge his characters, to evaluate them, or even, often, to provide us with enough information to do so ourselves. In films which also pass as classically structured narrative entertainment, this effect can be either jarring or bracingly stimulating, depending on the critical perspective. In practice, it means that his films can appear superficial because they present no easy route into deeper meaning and limited to the perspective of their often extremely limited characters, because they present no obvious or consistent authorial viewpoint.

In addition to being widely praised as one of the best Canadian films ever made, *Déclin* was the subject of virulent attack in its native province. Given its difference from the prevailing aesthetic and politics of Quebecois art cinema, this is not surprising. Rather than ground his film in the politics of sovereignty and the urban or rural milieu of the common people, Arcand chose a social elite of tenured academics at the Université de Montréal: cynical, complacent, narcissistic, and motivated by the pursuit of physical pleasure. Moreover, he readily confessed that he had chosen this demographic in part because the lack of a pronounced local accent would make the film releasable in the highly lucrative French market without subtitles. He was equally forthcoming about his decision to omit local references as much as possible so as to make his characters appear universal rather than specific to Quebec. In other words, Arcand chose explicitly to flaunt the stated objective of his co-producer, the National Film Board, to make films that would represent Canada to Canadians. As usual with Arcand, he was both stating the truth and deliberately provoking his compatriots. Part of the genius of *Déclin* is managing to be simultaneously highly specific and powerfully universal; indeed, we can say that the fundamental question raised by the film is the relation between the specifically Quebecois and the new universals of postmodern society. Characteristically, Arcand posed this question as an open-ended and dialectical inquiry rather than a defence of the former.

As historians, Arcand's characters are highly conscious of their place in the world and of their dual allegiance to the local and to the global. Their educated accents, refined dialogue, and love of wit and wordplay betray their identification in particular with the culture of France. The initial settings in which the four men and the four women meet – at a lakeside country house where the men make coulibiac, a labour-intensive gourmet Russian/French fish pie, and at a health club where the women lift weights and swim – indicate their investment in the yuppie lifestyle of the eighties as well as their disregard of certain Quebecois gender conventions. Arcand's inclusion of the openly gay Claude and the aggressively feminist Dominique and Diane emphasizes this disregard. On this level, *Déclin* plays as an up-to-the-minute snapshot of the then-novel phenomenon of the yuppie, the dramatic arc of the film plotting the moral bankruptcy of a rootless lifestyle in an application of the structuralist theory of decadence asserted by Dominique at the opening of the film as equally applicable to any advanced urban centre in the Western world: the pursuit of individual happiness at the expense of any social engagement signals the decline of an empire, *any* empire. The global viewer may read this empire as the United States, she may read it as the Christian West, or she may read it as advanced capitalism; in any case it is a broad theoretical argument driven by the very universality of its application. And it is an argument that clearly emerges from and deeply engages the mind of Denys Arcand.

The global popularity of the film derived in no small part from this broad appeal and a general assumption that its substance was constituted by a logical demonstration of the opening arguments made by its characters. But to limit the film to this superficial trajectory would be to ignore much of its content and to underestimate the subtlety and intelligence of Arcand's art. Rather than a QED of Dominique's thesis, the film acts as a carefully formulated test of its premises against the various contingencies of the actual lives and contexts of its characters. When commissioned to write and direct a Hollywood remake, Arcand concluded that the task was impossible – the particular social milieu in which he had set the film was unique to Quebec and for a number of reasons could not be duplicated in the context of American academia. Rather than exemplary representatives of a new type, these characters were in fact closely observed members of the specific community of Montreal. Moreover, Arcand signalled in various ways through the mise en scène that this community was imbricated in the social web of its community rather than simply existing in an intellectual vacuum. The bravura opening travelling shot of the credit sequence, slowly moving through the seemingly endless expanse of the athletic pavilion at the Université de Montréal may broadcast visually the spatial anonymity of the brutalist architecture of moulded concrete, but it also plots a local landmark easily recognized by inhabitants of the city (figure 3.3). The pavilion provides a strict visual analogue to the same dialectic of specific and universal exhibited by the country house that is the film's principal setting and the backdrop of its end credits. On the one hand, it stands for the generically beautiful natural setting of the weekend homes possessed by the elites of every urban conglomeration in the global north; on the other hand, it possesses the strongly local resonance of Lake Memphremagog in the Eastern Townships south of Montreal, on the border between Canada and the United States north of Plattsburgh, New York.

While heavily indebted in their structure to the conventions of French farce, the anecdotes of sexual escapades recounted by the characters are replete with local detail outlining the sexual life of 1980s Montreal. As Claude recounts his love of cruising, the film-maker shows us scenes in the Parc Mont-Royal, graphically demonstrating the transformation in spatial use of the traditional symbolic centre of the city, with the mounted policeman hinting at official resistance to that appropriation. Similarly, Rémy's tale of finding a visiting African colleague a prostitute on the rue Sainte-Catherine invokes a commonplace of Montreal's sexual geography while also subverting it – the punchline reveals the prostitute to be transvestite. Geneviève Rioux's brilliant young graduate student Danielle subtly updates the seventies tradition of 'undressing the little Quebec girl': encountered by Pierre (Pierre Curzi), putting herself through school working in a massage parlour, she can give him a hand job at the same time as she debates the fine points of medieval history (more multitasking, in fact, than he seems able to do). Similar to

3.3 The alienated no-place of urban postmodernity or a local Montreal landmark? From the opening dolly shot through the athletic pavilion of the Université de Montréal in *Le Déclin de l'empire américain* (1986). Photofest.

Jean-Luc Godard's *Two or Three Things I Know about Her* (1967), based on a newspaper article about suburban Parisian housewives selling their bodies to support their shopping habits, Arcand's film is more concerned with the changing habits of the young women of Montreal than with an ideal portrait of the world as it ought to be. The contradictions easily if perhaps troublingly embraced by Danielle are paralleled by Mario's updated coureur de bois, the opaque partner in Diane's sadomasochistic sex games. Conventional in his rejection of the imported and effeminate pretensions of the refined academics, Mario undercuts his emblematic status as an icon of 'old Quebec' through his undefined economic status and the cutting-edge shenanigans of his affair with Diane. He shows up at the house in a brand-new Jeep; he leaves her a history book as a gift – clearly he's no traditionalist. Even this character, widely interpreted as Arcand's rebuke of his rootless academics, resists a simple allegorical identification.

The opening salvo of the film – a slow fade in to a close-up of a young Vietnamese woman that opens out onto Rémy's classroom where his lecture on statistics in the study of history implies that the supremacy of numbers dooms francophone Quebec to insignificance and eventual disappearance as such – suggests Arcand's underlying local polemic. For whatever it was worth, the battle for sovereignty was inevitably lost, and both intellectuals and film-makers should instead focus their attention on what Quebec actually *is* rather than wasting their time in denial repeating old impossibilities about what it *should be*. Whether we like them or hate them, in other words, the characters and opinions in *Déclin* exist and we should come to terms with what they mean to us, figure out what good is in them and how to deal with what bad is there. After all, when we read that Arcand's quintessentially small-town riverboat pilot father was also a social snob whose best friend was a famous opera singer, it becomes eminently clear that the time-worn polarities through which Quebec has defined itself are no more stable than any such polarities ever are. What is striking in hindsight about *Déclin* – and this is where I agree with the various critics who have, albeit in an unfairly sniping manner, dismissed the film as dated – is that it makes a prescient argument about hybridity in a manner so fully rooted in its own time that we must work hard to unravel that prescience from the confines of its time-capsule perfection.

This hybridity is part of what Bill Marshall has identified as the symptoms of postmodernity in Quebec of the eighties and nineties.[36] If the rapid modernization of the Quiet Revolution during the sixties and seventies had created a secular, urbanized, and industrialized state out of Duplessis's conservative triad of church, family, and small-town values that was the driving theme of the first wave of Quebecois cinema, Arcand's *Confort* (1982), among other films, made it clear that the process, for better or worse, had stalled by the start of the decade. These trends were primarily received in terms of local concerns, especially the issue of sovereignty, and it is as a meditation on the fate of a marginal country beside a behemoth of an empire that *Déclin* was initially understood. And, indeed, given the lasting influence on Arcand of his college professor, historian Maurice Séguin, it is likely that he was thinking in terms of historical parallels rather than specific moments or shifts. For Séguin, Quebec as a small isolated francophone province was doomed to mediocrity until it finally disappeared. Much of Arcand's celebrated scepticism and the distance he kept in the main from the cinematic, artistic, and political movements in Quebec appears to stem from his belief in this theory.

What is clear in retrospect is that, like Rozema's first three films in terms of English Canada, Arcand's films between *Déclin* and *Stardom* document the effects of postmodernity on Quebec society, and that they do so by breaking out of the template generated by the film-makers of the Quiet Revolution both in their mode of production and in their form and style. One can already see traces of this break in the genre experimentation of the seventies films, but that experimentation was still conducted strictly from within traditionally Quebecois paradigms. The hybrid concerns of *Déclin* mark the shift away from those paradigms, a shift that also allowed Arcand access to a global rather than solely a local population. Whereas the wide distribution of a film such as Claude Jutra's *Mon oncle Antoine* was driven by its very status as a local and exotic document, a devastating portrait of fifties Quebec from the perspective of the Quiet Revolution, the even broader distribution of *Déclin* bespeaks its ability to address directly an audience that could recognize the film's contemporary concerns as its own. In this sense, the attacks on his film were justified: Arcand was using the specific situation of eighties Quebec to comment on a broader phenomenon of postmodernity throughout the West. The degree to which this commentary was also a highly relevant analysis of the situation of his own province was less frequently noted.

Because the local tropes of *Jésus* were more self-evidently unique to Quebec –

the St Joseph's Oratory atop Mont-Royal, the problem of Catholicism in a sec-
ularizing society, the detrimental effects of postmodernity, the disastrous state
of the provincial hospitals – its satire of postmodernity was less subject to local
attack. But when Arcand shifted to English-language production for his following two theatrical features, *Love & Human Remains* and *Stardom*, he severed pretty
much every remaining link to the Quebecois cinema of his earlier years. All three
films had originated in his own experience: an actor apologizing for the beard he
sported at his audition for *Déclin* with the words 'I'm Jesus. I'm an actor. I play
Jesus'; Arcand attending the anglophone and militantly gay Albertan playwright
Brad Fraser's *Unidentified Human Remains and the True Nature of Love* at a Montreal theatre; committing to paper his meditations on the function of beauty in the
world of today.

The three films are imbued with images of theatre, moments of theatricality, and
tropes of the mass media. In addition to the theatrical origins of its screenplay and
the search by all its characters for any kind of fixed identity, *Human Remains* features the sexual role-playing enabled by Mia Kirshner's psychic dominatrix Benita
and the video fetishization of former child-star David's (Thomas Gibson) role on
Beaverton. The formal conceit of *Stardom* is to depict nearly the entire trajectory of
the narrative as mediated through photographic technology, primarily the entertainment media but also fashion photography and the fly-on-the-wall documenta-
tion of video artist Bruce Taylor. *Jésus* adapts the Gospel according to Mark to the
terms of theatre and media. Commissioned to update the Oratory's creaky Passion
play, Daniel (Lothaire Bluteau) calls his disciples out of the everyday employment
of the Montreal mediascape: narrating documentaries, dubbing pornography,
making commercials. The place of his sermons is taken by the performances of
the Passion play that strip the veneer of organized religion down to the original
messages of the historical Jesus, staged according to the cutting-edge dicta of postmodern theatre emblematized by Lepage's presence as one of the disciples (see
chapter 5): small cast, minimal sets, shifting locations for performers and audience,
melange of documentary and dramatic narrative, onstage nudity, audience participation. Meanwhile, in the plot of the film, the temptation on the mount translates
into a lawyer high up in a skyscraper offering Daniel celebrity, fame, and fortune;
the smashing of the moneylenders' scales in the temple becomes the destruction
of photographic equipment on a commercial shoot; the passion itself occurs on a
subway platform with Daniel playing the role of a crazy busker. Fittingly, the only
moment in the allegory that exceeds the mediated framework is the resurrection,
in which we follow the trajectory of Daniel's harvested organs as they bring new
life to the ailing.

The allegory is clever but, like the anomie of *Human Remains* and the vacuous
celebrity of *Stardom*, it is not subtle, nor is it meant to be. Within postmodern discourse, theatricality is generally understood as a reaction to the capitalization of
every aspect of culture, a sense that truth-claims are no longer valid, and a retreat
into the distance of irony and alienation. *Jésus* perfectly captures this moment, but
it also resists its message. Beneath the patent surface message of cultural relativ-
ity and emptiness that greet and crucify a postmodern Jesus lies a personal and
local allegory that persists in deriving genuine meaning from that message. First,

as Arcand was quick to observe, there is the degree to which his own post-*Déclin* experience is echoed in Daniel's story. From the entire year lost to global travel supporting his film to the abortive offers from Hollywood, the story of the Passion play resonates with the recent past of Arcand's own life. But there was also the fact that, more than most of his film-making peers, former choirboy Arcand has always taken religion very seriously at the same time as he rejects the abuses of its organized forms. With this film, he recalls: 'I had wanted to recover my relationship with religion. I was raised by a mother who had been a Carmelite and a very religious father. This bathed my childhood until the age of fifteen. Thereafter, I cut all ties with any form of organized religion.'[37] Arcand's cameo appearance as a judge asking Daniel if he regrets having been born Quebecois is simultaneously an acknowledgment of this autobiographical thread and a recognition of the tension within the film between biographical facts and their broader dissemination.

The second substratum of the film, then, is the theme of historical fact and documentary research. Not only does Daniel's intensive research describe Arcand's own compositional method as a screenwriter, but the role played by documentary within the staging of the Passion play equally references the formative role of documentary in Quebecois film, even as its intellectualization of that role continues to assert Arcand's distance from the immersive tradition of direct cinema. A key moment in the film is the simultaneously facile and multilayered intervention of the African woman attending the play who takes it as real. Participating in a long-established cliché of the naive third-world spectator, this moment also invokes a refracted recognition that sub-Saharan Africa is a primary stronghold of evangelical Christianity in the contemporary world and as such constitutes a fundamental repudiation of the premise of global postmodernity. Moreover, the woman's presence at the play, while contrived in a dramatic sense, also recognizes the growing demographic presence of Africans, both francophone and anglophone, in contemporary Montreal (a presence registered more directly, although no less vexedly, in Jacques Benoit's popular comedy, *Comment faire l'amour avec un nègre sans se fatiguer* (*How to Make Love to a Negro without Getting Tired*, 1989, from the novel by Haitian-Canadian Dany Laferrière, and with an early role for well-established Ivory Coast actor Isaach de Bankolé). And, finally, it turns the question of the film's postmodernism back onto the viewer: how seriously are *we* going to take it? After all, within the diegesis of the film, the play appears to appeal only to those 'sophisticated' enough to be immune to its message.

The dramatic arc of the film suggests a third substratum, the 'Montreal' of its title. While betokening a postmodern transference from village to metropolis, and a characteristic irreverence towards its original model, the title also underlines the film's tension: is it about the contemporary world in general or is it about Montreal in particular? Certainly, the way Arcand based the film on the actual Passion play at St Joseph's Oratory suggests the very particular resonance it has within a Catholic Quebec, which for Arcand's generation had been, in the decades of their youth, little short of a theocracy. Certainly the first two-thirds of the film constitute a tour of Montreal as contemporary media capital (the only component missing, significantly, is the feature film branch of the industry); however, with the final third of the film, Arcand shifts his mise en scène out of the generically postmodern settings of the media and resolutely into the local spaces of the city. That these spaces, with the exception of Mont-Royal, remain alienated settings only strengthens the allegory. Crucified on the mountain that gave his city its name and has held a cross at its summit since the seventeenth century, Daniel's modern Jesus plays out his Passion and resurrection in the quintessentially postmodern spaces of the Montreal metro and the anonymous corridors of its hospitals. The dramatic closure may be almost too neat, but it also bespeaks Arcand's refusal to sacrifice either transcendental truth or local specificity to what he clearly sees as the inevitable encroachment of postmodernity. Nor, however, will he retreat into the jeremiad of the aging prophet; that he ironically concludes the film with the actors agreeing to establish a theatre in 'honour' of Daniel's memory reminds us that he is fully aware of the trade-offs to which he, too, will inevitably agree in order to make films and make a living.

We can view Arcand's 1996 television film *Joyeux Calvaire*, blown up from Super 16 mm for a limited big-screen release, as an extension of this aspect of *Jésus*. Although coined by novelist Réjean Ducharme (see chapter 5), the oxymoronic title aptly describes the tone of the earlier film's conclusion, simultaneously ironic and po-faced. A low-budget, street-level depiction of the lives of two homeless men on a fruitless search in the streets of Montreal, the film is simultaneously, as critic Yves Rousseau noted, the portrait of a 'decaying city.'[38] The submerged counterpart of the postmodern metropolitan settings of the other three films of this period, *Joyeux Calvaire* eschewed commentary and dramatization in favour of an episodic depiction of everyday life on the streets. Like *Human Remains*, the film was roundly criticized for Arcand's reliance on someone else's screenplay and a perceived lack of familiarity with the subject and milieu. But it also jarred many for its refusal either to entertain in the witty and irreverent manner of *Déclin* and *Jésus* or to proffer a specific message of social change or outrage in classic documentary realist fashion.

For all their gestures at theatricality, this critique was also levelled at both *Human Remains* and *Stardom*. While *Joyeux Calvaire* depicted a Quebec seldom if ever seen on screen – neither the rural hinterlands nor the glamorous metropolis – *Human Remains* and *Stardom* seem barely rooted in Montreal at all. To be sure, it is the media conglomeration of Montreal that first draws hockey-playing teenager Tina out of the hinterland of Cornwall, Ontario, setting her off on a Candide-like journey through the global network of celebrity. But most of the film (and most of its $11-million budget) is devoted to the time she spends in New York, Paris, and other hot spots of the international jet set. For *Human Remains*, Arcand transferred the original Edmonton setting of Fraser's play to Montreal and shot the film on location there.[39] But, striving to avoid the iconic settings he had used in *Jesus*, Arcand instead, as La Rochelle notes, 'transforms Montreal into a *barbarian* metropolis … a ruin among the ruins of an unrecognizable past.'[40] Whereas *Déclin* and *Jesus* preserved a visible tension between postmodernity and traditional Montreal, *Human Remains* and *Stardom* buried that tension deep within the thematics of the films. Part of what disturbed local critics was the very erosion of Quebecois culture documented by Arcand's choices of subject and producer. Both were made partly with 'Toronto' money and using English-language scripts; in addition, they were perceived to be concerned with Anglo-Canadian, or postmodern, issues. Unlike, for example, Jean-Claude Lauzon's *Night Zoo* (see chapter 5), which placed popular genre conventions, unconventional sexuality, and a nocturnal Montreal in the service of a strongly Quebecois-inflected narrative, Arcand appeared to be rejecting his own heritage.

Like David Cronenberg, who was faced with similar criticisms (see chapter 2), Arcand could simply answer that he is Quebecois, and therefore whatever film he makes reflects a Quebecois sensibility. And both films do document a demographic shift in the city: the encroachment of a universally lost and disaffected youth immersed in the English-speaking world of the global mediascape, and the dispersal of Quebecois throughout the world's metropolises. But there seems to have been a more active repudiation involved as well. As La Rochelle well documents, Arcand (like Rozema) has never had an easy time making the films he wants to make, and has had more screenplays and projects rejected than carried through to fruition. While both of these projects clearly appealed to him as a filmmaker, they were also at least partly driven by financing and the constraints of Arcand's partnerships, first with Roger Frappier and then with Robert Lantos, neither of which survived the relative failure of their respective films. *Human Remains* seems the more distanced of the two films, as if Arcand had tried to see how well suited he would be to the Toronto new wave. Borrowing Atom Egoyan's regular cinematographer Sarossy, he transformed Montreal into a deadened, sexualized, and alienated mediascape heavily indebted to the world of Egoyan's early films, in particular *Speaking Parts* (1989) and *The Adjuster* (1991). Viewed within the context of Arcand's oeuvre to this point, *Human Remains* makes little sense; viewed as an essay in Egoyanism, it finds a perfect niche, Mia Kirshner's role predating Egoyan's perfection (and deepening) of the persona a couple of years later as Christina in *Exotica*, while the characters of David and Kane (Matthew Ferguson) would be equally at home in the alienated mosaic narratives of Torontonian Jeremy Podeswa's *Eclipse* (1994, also featuring Ferguson) and *Five Senses* (2000).

In the context of Arcand's oeuvre, however, the univocality and consistent mood of *Human Remains* are strongly at odds with the dialogic context of his other films. Like Fraser, both Egoyan and Podeswa bring a dominant directorial presence to their material. While each character may have their own strand within the multi-faceted narrative, the diegetic world in which they find themselves is consistent and its unified meaning is clear to us. In Arcand's screenplays, as in Rozema's, there is never a consistent authorial viewpoint, nor is the diegetic world so uniform; Arcand's closed worlds are inevitably invaded by outside influences whose voices must also be reckoned with, like Mario in *Déclin* or the African woman in *Jésus*. *Stardom* in this sense is indisputably an Arcand screenplay, a cacophony of voices that prevents us from knowing whether we are supposed to sympathize with Tina or despise her. Compare Thomas Gibson's work in the two films. As the protagonist David in *Human Remains*, he is a piece of the puzzle, the link between the disparate strands that pulls together Fraser's portrait of contemporary youth. In his brilliant supporting turn as super-agent Renny Ohayon in *Stardom*, he brings the same soft-spoken monotone to bear on the hyperspeed world of celebrity. His refusal to be either flustered or seduced by the whirl around him becomes an acid commentary on the hard-headed financial underpinnings of the superficially giddy media circus. In *Human Remains*, we observe him unaffected; in *Stardom*, we simultaneously admire, detest, and understand him.

Where *Human Remains*, like Egoyan's early films, intimates that Canadianness, whether Anglo or Quebecois, has been fully replaced by the anodyne lineaments of postmodern culture, *Stardom* returns to the hybridity of Arcand's other films, implicitly arguing for the persistence of strange pockets of Canadianness even in the midst of the anonymously global. This is not merely a question of the hokey underpinnings of Tina's family history or the extremely funny send-up of the local media in Cornwall, Ontario, but in French actor Charles Berling's parody of the conventions of francophone machismo aesthetics, Lepage's self-parody of the postmodern artist, Canuck expat Dan Ackroyd's affecting portrait of a success-ful Montreal entrepreneur eaten alive by the sharks of a 'genuine' world city like New York, Frank Langella's vicious caricature of a suave career diplomat whose concerned pronouncements about world crises conceal a jet-setting lifestyle of hedonism, and Tina's periodic outbursts of pragmatic Canuckisms and complete refusal to submerge her jock personality to the dictates of fashion – faced with anti-fur activists at a Brooklyn photo shoot, she simply treats them as if she were in a hockey brawl. In this light, even Arcand's apparently unrealistic choice to cast amply proportioned newcomer Jessica Paré as a rail-thin supermodel reads as an understated commentary on Canadian realism versus global illusions – especially when we see the 'real' supermodel in the film, Englishwoman Camilla Ruther-ford, strung out on drugs and marketing herself as a performance artist sculpting images of her 'shit life' out of her own feces.

While neither of these films was a catastrophic failure, neither of them recouped its budget or came close to matching the acclaim that had greeted Arcand's previ-ous features. Part of the equivocal response, I think, derives from the long gesta-tion of each film, at odds with Arcand's habit of working in the moment. Because *Human Remains* originated in Fraser's 1989 play, by the time of its release, its ideas were already dated according to the way Arcand works. Perhaps less detrimental to *Human Remains* because of the closed and hieratic world in which its events take place, this effect was far more damaging to *Stardom*, whose original idea may date back as far as the late eighties, which was already written in something resembling its current form by the mid-nineties, and which was initially rejected by Alliance in 1995 before eventually being produced by Lantos at the end of the decade.[41] Had it been released five years earlier than it eventually was, the film's innovative formal structure and depiction of a wholly mediatized world would actually have antici-pated the trendy fin-de-siècle cycle of films such as *The Truman Show* (1998, Peter Weir), *The Matrix* (1999, Andy and Larry Wachowski), and Cronenberg's *eXistenZ* (1999), if not perhaps the prescient (if decidedly local) Quebecois reality-television comedy *Louis 19, le roi des ondes* (1994, Michel Poulette), remade by Hollywood as *EdTV* (1999, Ron Howard), rather than appearing as a dated copy of them from a backwards province.

While these two films in a sense were dated before they were even released, the apparently short shelf life of all of Arcand's films has been noted various times, primarily in a critical manner, as in the account discussed by Arcand and Coulombe in 1992: 'If they brilliantly bear witness to their epoch, by that same token Arcand's films age very badly. A glance at *Déclin* and *Jésus* is enough. As much as these moral tales seduced us when they came out, today they seem artificial, stiff, second-hand ... [H]is films don't gain in subtlety over the years; they lose their sheen and feel heavy.'[42] Arcand's refusal to cut his films off from the world in which he makes them is the essence of his originality and strength as a film-maker, but it was not until 2003 that he found a way to incorporate his films' susceptibility to time as a theme within them. The announcement that he was making a 'sequel' to *Déclin* was widely greeted with scepticism if not jeers, but what Arcand managed instead, in addition to winning Canada's first ever Academy Award (*as* Canada, that is, rather than invisibly in Hollywood) and making one of its most commercially successful films ever, was simultaneously to update his career peak of the late eighties and to create a profound meditation on what had changed in the seventeen years since that peak. *The Barbarian Invasions* has the crudeness and vulgarity of all of Arcand's satires, but its particular brilliance is to allow the audience to see just how much his previous satires had become dated, while making the passage of time that dated them part of his analysis of the current state of the world.

There are serious missteps, nevertheless. The use of video of the 9/11 attacks was roundly criticized as exploitative, and rightly so. Certainly, to reintroduce the callow graduate student from *Déclin* as a middle-aged talking head on television is a clever gambit, and his analysis of the unintentional hypocrisy of reactions to the bombings in relation to so many other deaths in the world is persuasive, but it would have been more so without the distraction of the actual footage. More curious is the strangely artificial effect of the acting and dialogue between the members of the *Déclin* generation. The opening scenes between Rémy and his estranged wife Louise feel especially artificial, and the sex talk feels gratuitously inserted to meet the expectations raised by the original film. In contrast, the scenes with the characters from *Jésus* seem to pick off exactly where that film left off. The bravura opening tracking shot through the 'Dante-corridor' in the hospital brilliantly recalls the opening tracking shot of *Déclin*, signalling a shift in register towards the seriousness of *Jésus*, from which Arcand imported less the satirical levity of the acting troupe than the gravity of purpose of the religious subject. What the viewer finally realizes when Rémy's son reunites the band of friends from *Déclin* is that their banter, in its very artificiality and vulgarity, functions as a sign of their own status as relics. No longer living their anecdotes, they are merely performing their past in a desperate struggle to retain some trace of the lives they had had. They are doomed to repeat the same roles over and over even as they have long since passed beyond whatever meaning those roles may have had.

It is the actors themselves, however, that provide the reality and emotion that underpin and give weight to this potentially facile insight. In the kind of gesture possible only in a closed cottage industry such as Quebec's, Arcand was actually able to reunite every member of the original ensemble. And, in a heartfelt homage to Quebec's (and his own) documentary realist tradition, Arcand films them as if it *were* a documentary, making sure that we see the often cruel marks that

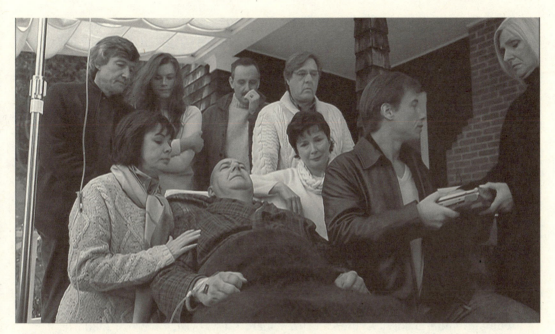

3.4 The aging ensemble cast of *Les Invasions barbares* (2003) bravely demonstrates the ravages of time. Photofest.

age has left on their faces (figure 3.4). This physical reality powerfully insinu-ates the more abstract realization that the world has irrevocably changed. The opening scramble for something as simple as a space in which to die underlines the message that however comfortable the life they led in 1986, it was unable to provide for their needs in 2003. The arrival of Rémy's son Sébastien, played by popular local comedian Stéphane Rousseau, furthers Arcand's point in a myr-iad of ways. First, Sébastien is an expatriate, and not even in Paris; he inhabits the global business centre that is anglophone London. Second, he exists at the heart of whatever form capitalism has taken along the postmodern path already skewered by Arcand back in the eighties: making millions by coldly speculating on non-existent goods, engaged in the almost incomprehensible banking prac-tices that, five years on, would nearly crash the world's financial systems. He is, then, one of the 'barbarians' of the title, indirectly responsible structurally for the very decline in standard of living that, on a personal level, he will set himself to remedy.

At the same time, the whole manner of realistic underplaying coaxed by Arcand out of Rousseau's over-the-top comic persona in itself retrospectively belies the artificial exaggerations of the original cast that in the mid-eighties had felt as much a perfectly realized depiction of the yuppie lifestyle as any image of big hair and cocaine-fuelled binges. When Arcand introduces local cinema icon Roy Dupuis in a cameo as a cynical but sympathetic policeman and rising star Marie-Josée Croze as Diane's drug-addicted daughter, the generational allegory is complete.

We certainly get the message that the parents' narcissism has bred a different kind of alienation in the new century. But we also witness a changing of the cinematic guard, and Arcand is characteristically generous in giving the plum roles in the film to Rousseau and Croze, who are allowed to change and develop in a satisfying narrative arc and an effective vote of confidence regarding the dramatic chops of the new generation. Rather than caricatures of themselves, they are allowed to play characters. After all, none of the aging actors we see ever had an impact outside Quebec (except, marginally, in Arcand's films); by contrast, both Dupuis and Croze are now well established internationally (for more on this pair, see chapter 4).

Arcand does not spare himself from the generational allegory. His cameo as the corrupt union flunky whom Sébastien must bribe in order to obtain a comfortable room for his father reads as a bitter kiss-off to his activist origins, even as it does no more than repeat the arguments of those documentaries in slightly more polarized terms. The presence of Micheline Lanctôt as the tough, tender nurse who provides the equipment for Rémy's assisted suicide at the lake house makes for a more sympathetic gesture towards the past. An established actor, including a prominent role as one of the only francophone Montrealers in *The Apprenticeship of Duddy Kravitz* (1974, Tod Kotcheff), but also an acclaimed feminist director of the seventies and eighties, Lanctôt's cameo is a more equivocal gesture of recognition of the changed climate of film-making. At the same time, there is a surprising sense of solidarity if not boosterism in Arcand's decision to cast *only* francophone Quebecois actors in his film and to make the home-movie aspect the most compelling element of the film. To be sure, this decision is reflected on the level of plot, particularly in Rémy's patriotic refusal to be moved to a facility in Baltimore.

As in all of Arcand's best films, the title metaphor is simultaneously a red-herring hook and a multifaceted metaphor with both local and global applications. There are the universally applicable bodily metaphors of cancer and drugs, the American view of outsiders, especially post 9/11, the invasion of the rest of the world by America and everything it represents. More locally, there is the original colonization of the Americas by Europeans, and in terms of the narrative, there is Sébastien and the money behind him as barbarian invaders. That his money is both feared and welcomed is an effective allegory not only of contemporary economics, but also of Arcand's attitude towards film-making, of which his film equally provides a potent allegory. That, in the end, it is all about moviemaking is made clear by the marvellous sequence of screen fantasies with which the film climaxes. From the thighs of Inès Orsini's soon-to-be-raped virgin in a fifties melodrama to the more explicitly sexual symbols of the sixties, to Chris Evert in the burgeoning celebrity culture of the seventies, Rémy's inventory of images is simultaneously critical and incantatory. Contextualized as the fantasies of an unapologetically heterosexual serial adulterer, they are also given powerful emotional force by their status as something like his final testament. At the same time, they also function to contextualize Rémy's behaviour in relation to the male heteronormative fantasies proffered by the post-war cinema. When we witness the idiosyncratic pleasure derived from them, however, it also becomes impossible to dismiss them simply as fantasies, just as, Arcand seems to be implicitly arguing, we cannot simply dismiss Rémy and we cannot simply dismiss popular cinema, not even something so execrably perverse as an Inès Orsini melodrama.

It is characteristic of Arcand that he refused to retire with a perfectly valedictory statement at the summit of his career as a film-maker. Instead, he followed the hit of *Invasions* with another miss. Moreover, because he announced his next film, *L'Age des Ténèbres* (2007), as the final instalment of a triptych including *Déclin* and *Invasions*, the minor interest of the third film somehow seemed retroactively to compromise the high ambition of the other two. As usual, Arcand was entirely lucid and persuasive in detailing his own image of the film and its goal. In practice, as with *Human Remains* and *Stardom*, it was difficult to match the intentions with the shrill and ill-judged result. Rather than connected to the previous films through character or event, it has a tenuous thematic link, the background presence of a civilization that has finally crumbled, although it insists on carrying on as if everything is normal. The main plot concerns Jean-Marc Leblanc (Marc Labrèche), a civil servant who escapes from the drudgery of his everyday life by dreaming of the trappings of celebrity, exactly the kind of celebrity, Arcand relates, that he himself has spent his life trying to avoid. Shot in the Olympic Stadium left derelict by the departing Montreal Expos, *Ténèbres* contains a submerged subtext regarding the decline of its city under the twin scourges of bureaucracy and corrupt development projects that has been a theme of Arcand's since his earliest films. Pierre Curzi makes a depressing cameo as an aged and impoverished divorcee, apparently the last stage in the decline of the once proud misanthrope of *Déclin*, while Johanne Marie Tremblay apparently reprises her earlier roles from *Jésus* and *Invasions*, now retired to the Bas-Saint-Laurent where Jean-Marc retreats when he walks away from his real as well as his fantasy life. The satire is so schematic one almost wonders if Arcand is thumbing his nose at both the problem and the facile solution, but it is likelier that *Ténèbres* represents his final repudiation of the mediated world in which he has ambivalently slaved for decades.

(Provisional) Conclusion

So what is to be learned from films that remain doggedly rooted in their moment of origin rather than deepening and maturing over time? The works of both Rozema and Arcand straddle the divide between art cinema and popular culture in an unusual way. Their datedness derives from the latter affinity, for the vast majority of popular culture is conceived as disposable, made for the primary purpose of capturing an audience in the present with no concern over what will happen to it after its initial exhibition. But their timeliness comes from the different concerns they bring to popular culture from a vantage point within art cinema. For Rozema, it is a feminist alternative perspective that imagines ideal communities and social values different from the status quo. For Arcand, it is the perspective of the sceptical historian who, by refusing to pass final judgment on the events occurring around him, is able to give voice to their multiple viewpoints. And for both, we find a consistent although highly varied concern with the spiritual values conventionally associated with religion. Moreover, Arcand and Rozema share a restlessness born from an openness to experimentation as well as the lack of consistent economic support in direct relationship to their relative inability to enter the same cinematic world each time they make a film. When they hit, we get unique and uniquely polarizing masterworks; when they miss, we get fascinating failures. Their unusual career trajectories help to delineate the false polarities that construct Canadian as they do many other national cinemas: between art and commerce, between auteur and director-for-hire, between film and other media, between English and French.

Chapter Four

Crossover Icons:
The Faces of Canadian Cinema

> I prefer living the life I want to live and I can do that far easier in Canada. I've never participated in L.A. the way one is supposed to as an actor ... Maybe there's more melancholy here, more desperation. I do believe different places make you focus differently.
>
> Callum Keith Rennie (2001)

An enduring paradox of Canadian cinema has been that the more internationally visible an actor becomes, the less Canadian he or she is perceived to be. The most globally recognizable present-day Canadian actors are seldom if ever identified as Canadian, and even north of the border their identity is mixed, at best. Nevertheless, one of the consequences of the rise of a new Canadian cinema in the late eighties was the emergence of a core of Anglo-Canadian actors who, for the first time, managed to retain their local identity while also crossing over to establish a solid presence in Hollywood: Don McKellar and Sarah Polley (as actors, writers, and directors), and Mia Kirshner, Sandra Oh, Molly Parker, and Callum Keith Rennie (as actors). As always, for Quebecois actors the situation is similar yet distinct. The Quebecois wave of the sixties produced several prominent actors, but only Geneviève Bujold and Carole Laure became international stars. Success at that level has eluded Quebecois actors of the new generation, for whom crossover visibility has generally meant the ability to work in English-Canadian features, French cinema, and local television. Pascale Bussières and Marie-Josée Croze are stars in their home province and familiar faces to English-Canadian and art-house viewers, but the closest they have come to the Hollywood mainstream has been Bussières's starring role opposite Stephen Baldwin in Allan Moyle's local sci-fi action movie *Xchange* and Croze's bit part as a femme fatale hitman in Steven Spielberg's *Munich*. Quebec's dominant male star of the turn of the millennium, Roy Dupuis, makes local blockbusters, but has never crossed over to American feature films, although he became a cult favourite for global television audiences after five years in a central role in the locally made action drama, *La Femme Nikita* (1997–2001). For all of these figures, successfully negotiating multiple identities is a complex balancing act; it is also becoming a more and more typical situation for actors and film-makers the world over.

Language and physical appearance – and deep-seated prejudice towards difference in either of these categories – have been the two primary barriers for foreign actors seeking a career in Hollywood. Women have generally had an easier time than men in this regard, due in large measure to the fact that the roles offered them have tended to deploy accent and physical variation as additional signifiers of a broader 'otherness' of gender. Foreign actresses have also found it easier to make their way in genres such as action, horror, and science fiction, where female roles tend to be subordinate and physical appearance is the bottom-line qualification. These days, moving to Hollywood almost invariably means switching identity from iconic star to run-of-the-mill player, as Spanish actress Paz Vega found when she made the jump from the internationally acclaimed art film *Lucía y el sexo* (2001, Julio Medem) to playing the Mexican housekeeper to Adam Sandler's comic lead in *Spanglish* (2004, James L. Brooks). For male actors, the situation is if anything worse, as their looks typecast them more rigidly than the gender limitations of actresses. A European megastar such as France's Gérard Depardieu can co-star as a French immigrant (*Green Card*, 1990, Peter Weir), but not play mainstream roles. Similarly, Hong Kong headliners Chow Yun-Fat and Jet Li have found themselves relegated to 'Asian' roles, genre parts, and martial-arts villains. Moreover, Hollywood's conception of local identity has always been as laughably imprecise as its blissful unconcern over geographic specificity. While accent, appearance, and a local body of work bestow highly precise ethnic and national iconicity on their home turf, once foreign actors land in Hollywood, a Hispanic actor will play anything from Mexican to Brazilian to Spanish, an Asian anything from Chinese to Japanese to Malaysian, an African any dark villain as necessary. In a typical shift, one of the most prominent Hollywood roles for Bujold (who can in fact do English accents with ease) was as Cajun rape-victim counsellor Beryl Thibodeaux, starring next to Clint Eastwood's anglophone New Orleans detective in the 1984 thriller *Tightrope*.

There is another side to the equation, of course, which is Hollywood's analogy to the American melting pot's offer of *not* being limited by one's birth identity. While we should not ignore the hegemonic levelling effect of Hollywood's disregard for local detail, we should also not underestimate the liberating possibilities of playing away from that detail – white actors, after all, have always been expected (and allowed) to play pretty much any role with disregard for their 'actual' identity. The rise of identity politics in the eighties had the dual effect within Hollywood of gradually loosening the hold on leading roles of the default anodyne whiteness long embodied by invisibly Canadian leading men and of slowly increasing the representation of local difference. Male Hispanic stars such as Mexican Gael García Bernal, Puerto Rican Benicio del Toro, and Spaniard Javier Bardem have achieved mainstream popularity despite their ethnic identities, but also because of that identity: one consequence of the economic globalization of the movie industry has been an increased and increasingly acknowledged openness to a global corps of film-makers, actors, and technicians. The ever-greater visibility of Hispanic culture and its successful resistance to the traditional melting pot of assimilation in the United States contributed to this shift, as did the gradual (if still partial) acceptance of black actors and film-makers into mainstream Hollywood at the end of the twentieth century. Canada's negotiation of these issues provides, if on a much smaller scale, an earlier model for what is now happening on an international scale within a world cinema that continues to be anchored in southern California.

In his influential work on the social significance of stars, Richard Dyer uses the concept of *discourses* to 'bring together the star seen as a set of media signs with the various ways of understanding the world which influenced how people felt about the star.'[1] The discourse of what Dyer terms the 'star phenomenon' consists of 'everything that is publicly available about stars.'[2] As Susan Hayward argues, changing stars and star discourses are an important means and measure of the articulation of national identity.[3] While Dyer emphasizes the different meanings of a particular star within different discourse communities, his work is focused on the central star system originating out of Hollywood, which defines national community primarily by assuming the universality of America. As Hayward suggests, other national cinemas define their identities both internally and in opposition to Hollywood cinema and its stars.[4] Thus, changing '"proletarian" heroes' Jean Gabin, Jean-Paul Belmondo, and Gérard Depardieu, like changing modes of eroticism in Arletty, Simone Signoret, and Brigitte Bardot, come to embody changing notions of everything that is 'French' – that is, *of the people* and *sexually liberated*, respectively.[5] Rather than fixed symbols of national identity, star discourses are one of the ways in which that identity is imagined into being and called into question. While the invisibility of Canadian stars in Hollywood may continue to apply, it is more and more of a documented rather than an unspoken invisibility, at least north of the border. In 2005, Canada's authoritative biweekly business journal, *Canadian Business*, inaugurated an annual Celebrity Power List of Canadians in Hollywood, topped by Jim Carrey, Kiefer Sutherland, Keanu Reeves, Mike Myers, and Seth Rogen, with Pamela Anderson tied for sixth with Ellen Page (on the strength of *Juno*) in 2008, the most recent list.[6] Now, just because they have made it in Hollywood doesn't mean these are 'Canadian' stars any more than their Hollywood predecessors (although Halifax native Page, at least, had worked in Canada before her big break, appearing in *Marion Bridge* [2002], McDonald's *The Tracey Fragments* [2007], and a number of television shows). On the other hand, if Mike Myers insists on incorporating Canadian allusions, or 'messages to home,' as he calls them, into his Hollywood vehicles, doesn't this suggest that popular filmgoers north of the border may indeed have a specifically Canadian relationship to their stars regardless of the superficial lack of any such context?[7]

A double stance towards Hollywood Canadians is one way the discourse of Canadian cinema and its stars both follows and diverges from the Dyer model. The ability to recognize Canadian locations, Canadian faces, and Canadian dollars masquerading within American movies and television series itself provides a common, oppositional, subversive identity that is uniquely Canadian because it is unavailable as such to any other national culture. At the same time, recognition of those same locations, faces, and money used in indigenous product provides an equally strong reassurance that something uniquely Canadian is being preserved. Consequently, like its national identity, its star discourses are multiple, contradictory, and irreducible to a single model. For instance, Bill Marshall suggests that the challenged economic structure of the Quebec industry militates against a genuine star system.[8] And yet, as his analysis of Quebec popular cinema demonstrates, stars as sign, in Hayward's sense, have been and remain central to the articulation of Quebecois identity, even if that identity must be articulated across and around the French and Hollywood systems that dominate the province. Both English-Canadian and Quebecois star discourses are marked by a high degree of code-switching between different discourses and identities. The awards – the Montreal-based Jutras for francophone films and the Toronto-based Genies, administered since 1979 by the Academy of Canadian Cinema – provide a local source of artistic recognition and a key enunciation of local celebrity. At the same time, the international significance of TIFF places local stars in the same stratosphere as the Hollywood and other national cinema stars at the festival – witness Molly Parker and Callum Keith Rennie at the premiere of McDonald's 2010 *Trigger*, granted the prestigious honour of inaugurating the new Bell Lightbox headquarters of the festival (see figure 4.4). The key sites of Canadian stardom reflect the multiple and sometimes contradictory character of that stardom; consequently, the stars who best exemplify the multiple and competing discourses of Canadian cinema are also the ones who best signify the problematic articulation of Canadian identity.

The French-Canadian Exceptions: Geneviève Bujold and Carole Laure

The way it is, though, you either work in L.A. or Paris. Bujold went to L.A., I came to Paris. It's just a question of where the industry is.

Carole Laure (1978)

Geneviève Bujold was born in 1942, daughter of a Montreal bus driver, and convent-educated, and her early life trajectory could easily, as Marshall suggests, fit 'a Quiet Revolution narrative ... of upward mobility' to 'world fame,' while her 'rebellious, mischievous ("espiègle") and individualistic' persona would project a particularly Quebecois form of identity.[9] Marshall goes on to reject this formulation as, evidently, too hybrid and compromised for a genuine articulation of 'Quebec identity construction.'[10] The tightly constellated television-movie community of local Quebecois personalities whose images seldom if ever escape the confines of the province provides a fitting popular counterpart to the inward-looking art cinema of the sixties and seventies, but it has less to tell us about the significance of the internationalization of Quebecois film-making in the nineties or about why the kinds of identities articulated by Bujold's star discourse seem more and more prescient of Quebecois cinema in the twenty-first century. For Bujold's persona not only encompasses a thorny and uncompromising personality, but also a myriad of contradictory yet coexisting roles: quintessential Quebecois of the people, English-Canadian actor, French art-film actor, Heritage actor, popular Hollywood leading lady, tax-shelter Anglo Canadian, and member of American indie director Alan Rudolph's informal 1980s 'stock company' of performers.

There is certainly nothing straightforward about Bujold's star persona or her Quebecois identity. Her film debut came in a hybrid disaster, the first feature fiction film effort by independent Ottawa-based documentary producer Budge Crawley. The 'story of a man and his mushroom-sprouting lawn,' *Amanita Pestilens* (1962) was shot in French and English simultaneously, directed by Quebecois René Bonnière, and a complete flop.[11] After a television appearance and some shorts, Bujold was cast in prominent roles in French art films when Alain Resnais asked her to play alongside Yves Montand in *La Guerre est finie* (*The War Is Over*, 1966) after spotting her performing in Paris with the Montreal theatre company Rideau Vert (green curtain).[12] The following year, Bujold appeared simultaneously in Michel Brault's masterpiece of documentary realism, *Entre la mer et l'eau douce* (see chapter 1), in Louis Malle's nouvelle vague *Le Voleur* (*The Thief of Paris*, opposite Jean-Paul Belmondo), and as the eponymous heroine in a Hallmark Hall of Fame production of George Bernard Shaw's *Saint Joan* (directed by George Schaefer); she also married anglophone Montrealer and CBC director Paul Almond, for whom she would make a trilogy of acclaimed but critically marginalized features (see chapter 1). Almond and Bujold were an oddity for the time, with an international profile allowing them to access Hollywood studio funding for their first films and a vision for an auteurist, art-based cinema that was closer to the French and English models (Almond had done TV and theatre work in London) than to the dominant Quebecois documentary realist mode.[13] Indeed, it is significant that the only film Almond cites in a 2003 discussion of the CFDC (his *Act of the Heart* was the first film to be financed by the organization) and 'this whole new wave of new Canadian films' is Denis Héroux's soft-core blockbuster *Valérie*.[14] Nothing like Almond and Bujold's combination of talent, savvy, and economic pragmatism would be seen in Canada for another twenty years, unless we count kindred spirit David Cronenberg (see chapter 2).

Almond and Bujold's first film together, *Isabel* (1968), opened in New York to rave reviews, landing Bujold's face on the pages of *Time* and *Life* magazines. This was Bujold's initial persona: deep-eyed, pouty-lipped, and highly sensual, but also innocent and authentic. The persona was inflected differently depending on the context. In Brault's film, she embodies a wholesome young Quebecois sexuality, secure in itself yet uncertain how to act or what to do. In de Broca's pacifist allegory *Le Roi de coeur* (*The King of Hearts*, 1966), where she played opposite Alan Bates, Bujold personified a childlike innocence. She was more mysteriously allegorical in Almond's films: darker, damaged, and full of the trauma of her past. Central to all of these performances was her ability, without words, to make us 'feel even her oddest experiences as if they were really happening to us.'[15] Her star persona made her perfectly suited for the Oscar-nominated role as innocent martyr Anne Boleyn opposite Richard Burton in *Anne of the Thousand Days* (1969, Charles Jarrott) that looked ready to fix her in that persona (figure 4.1). After so many 'beautiful, satisfying films' and a career that 'just sort of unfolded at the beginning,' Bujold was, like Almond, comfortable with the shift to Hollywood.[16] Nevertheless, her refusal to be typecast in heritage roles appears to have prevented her from reaching the heights of stardom that had been predicted for her.[17]

It was Hollywood, then, that brought out the 'fiery temper' that would characterize the next phase of Bujold's professional and on-screen persona during the peak of her career in the late seventies and the eighties.[18] That persona contrib-

4.1 Geneviève Bujold during rehearsals for the 1971 Academy Awards. Photo by Ron Galella/
WireImage. Getty Images.

uted to her acting in a number of middling Hollywood films, including *Earthquake* (1974, Mark Robson) and *Swashbuckler* (1976, James Goldstone); she also played a double role in Brian De Palma's classic *Vertigo* homage, *Obsession* (1976, with a script by Paul Schrader). Her prospects improved with a starring role in Michael Crichton's medical thriller, *Coma* (1978), a big moneymaker. Reviewers lauded the film-maker not only for writing an older, intelligent, and experienced woman into the protagonist role, but for allowing Bujold to play Susan Wheeler as a 'taut, edgy' heroine.[19] Toronto film critic Robert Martin went further, calling Bujold 'the best thing *Coma* has going for it' and marvelling at how well the film pulled off the counter-intuitive move of casting 'the tiny and delicate Bujold as the hero of an action picture.'[20] As the years deepened the lines in Bujold's otherworldly beauty, her fiercely intelligent presence became all the more commanding. As Martin put it, 'Right at the beginning of the film, Bujold is established as her own woman.'[21]

Bujold won a Genie award for Bob Clark's tax-shelter-era Sherlock Holmes meets Jack the Ripper yarn *Murder by Decree* (1979); following on *Obsession*, she also made something of a specialty of quirkily kinky suspense roles, especially in *Tightrope* and Cronenberg's *Dead Ringers*. In both, her confident playing transformed roles that in lesser hands could just as easily have devolved into straightforward and risible exploitation. In *Tightrope*, she played a rape-victim counsellor opposite Clint Eastwood's police detective; their relationship is based on sadomasochism and bondage. In *Dead Ringers*, she was actress Claire Niveau, also into bondage, who unknowingly becomes involved with both of the Mantle twins. As Bujold plays her, Niveau manages simultaneously to be tough and even menacing, to maintain her dignity and control, to manage her own desire, to project the nervousness of a woman who has not always been able to do either, and to preserve a nurturing love for Beverly. It is a nuanced and courageous performance, fully the match for Jeremy Irons's virtuoso turn as the twin brothers (see chapter 2).[22] Bujold seems effortlessly to project the knowingness required to balance multiple points of view and conflicting desires and priorities. That openness to ambiguity served her well in the genre films she made between the mid-seventies and mid-eighties; it served her equally well in the trio of films she made with independent American film-maker Alan Rudolph: *Choose Me* (1984), *Trouble in Mind* (1985), and *The Moderns* (1988). Of working with her on *Choose Me*, Rudolph recalls her telling him, 'Gee, I really like the fact that I never know what your camera's doing and what I think might be a closeup winds up being a master.'[23] Clearly, Bujold enjoys working with uncertainty.

It was at the end of the eighties that Bujold began her transformation into a grande dame of Canadian cinema. She was probably first labelled 'mature' by Canadian film critic Martin Knelman in praising her 'marvelous' performance in Brault's low-key comedy-drama of immigration, *Paper Wedding* (1989), more than two decades after the pair had first worked together.[24] Nevertheless, Bujold has mostly steered clear of the abrupt transition from young sex object to sexless older woman typically the fate of actresses, especially within the Hollywood system. She continues to work in Europe, Hollywood, Quebec, and English Canada, ranging as always from pulp to art to everything in between, including key roles in two films by the new generation of Quebecois film-makers: Manon Briand's acclaimed metaphysical romance, *La Turbulence des fluides* (2002), and Dénis Chouinard's drama *Délivrez-moi* (2006). Don McKellar's casting of Bujold in his apocalyptic drama *Last Night* (1998) suggests a consciousness of her presence within the psyche of his generation (he was born in 1963): she's next to last on Craig's (Callum Keith Rennie) list of women he wants to sleep with before the end, the French teacher he lusted after back in high school.[25] Again, what could easily be a pitiful throwaway instead becomes a more complex study in motivation: Mrs Carlton is at least as deeply involved psychically with her former students as they are with her. In one of the final sequences of the film, the camera focuses on her face, pointedly aged but eyes intact, sitting in the sparse audience at Massey Auditorium as another of her former students plays his first public piano recital. The casting is something of a generational passing of the torch staged by McKellar to himself, as he also gives us Cronenberg, Bujold's exact contemporary, playing a gas company manager. Both of them are, as Amy Taubin put it in the *Village Voice*, 'silly, sweet, and valiant.'[26] Both receive an intertextual treatment analogous to their influence: Bujold, a scene of complex sexuality and extended, unglamorous yet movingly beautiful close-ups; Cronenberg, an encounter with death and brutal violence as he confronts a clean-cut teenager who follows him in with a shotgun, a later shot revealing the erstwhile 'Baron of Blood' awash in a pool of his own red stuff. And both, as McKellar knew full well, represent a particularly ecumenical approach to cinema more valued in film-making and in critical circles with every year that passes.

It is instructive to compare Bujold's protean career with the more strictly francophone but equally influential trajectory of her near contemporary, Carole Laure. Born in 1951 in Shawinigan, Quebec, with a Native mother whom she never knew, Laure was convent-educated like Bujold, and trained as a concert pianist. While the elder Bujold was strongly marked by the sixties era in which her career began, Laure broke into the movies in the early seventies when she made a series of films with director/lover Gilles Carle that established her indelibly as a pre-eminent sex symbol of her day. A classically beautiful brunette, Laure's image is irrevocably filtered through her physical appearance and her skilful deployment of her body, both in Quebecois cinema and in European art films. Film critic Gerald Peary memorably described her 'as the babe-of-babes, the wet dream queen, frisky, dark-eyed, luscious-lipped,' and a leitmotif of writing about Laure has been the enduring, well-nigh unchanging quality of her sexy beauty (figure 4.2).[27] As Ray Conlogue wrote in the *Globe and Mail* of her role as a stripper in husband Lewis Furey's 2000 film, *Rats and Rabbits*, 'There are not many 52-year-old women who would play a major film role in bustier and high heels, and fewer still who could do it without irony.'[28] Where Bujold's persona was based on a cosmopolitan sixties sensuality always cloaked by and expressed through the keen intelligence of her characters, and consequently aged along with the actress, Laure's liberated sexuality was expressed through her frequently and often spectacularly naked body, 'all raw emotion and basic instinct,' closely identified with a native and rural Quebecois sensibility.[29] Carle and Laure's merging of her frank sexual persona with a conventional conception of Quebecois femininity, like their merging of the popular exploitation genre of maple syrup porno with the Quebecois art film, was successful both commercially and critically, although not always with the same

4.2 The ageless singer/director/actor Carole Laure at the 2006 Cannes Film Festival for the premiere of *Over the Hedge*. Photo by Jean Baptiste Lacroix/WireImage. Getty Images.

film. Although the quality of the half-dozen films they made together was mixed, several, including *La Mort d'un bûcheron* (*The Death of a Lumberjack*, 1973), *La Tête de Normande St-Onge* (*The Head of Normande St. Onge*, 1975), and *L'Ange et la femme* (*The Angel and the Woman*, 1977), have become classics of Quebecois cinema, while also pushing the limits on the depiction of sex on film and sowing controversy for the consistent passivity of Laure's characters. As Marshall argues in reference to the pair's glossy local hit remake of the time-worn historical epic *Maria Chap-delaine* (1983): 'Her star persona was intimately linked to the cinema of Quebec modernity, and although her status as sexual and "liberated" was complicated by the highly sexualized use to which her body was put by directors like Carle in particular, these embodiments place her ... astride another historical break, that of feminism.'[30]

Carle's classic films of the end of the sixties – *Le viol d'une jeune fille douce* (1968), *Red* (1969), *Les Mâles* (1971), and *La vraie nature de Bernadette* (1972, star-ring Micheline Lânctot) – had already begun to push the playful, political, and anti-realist tropes borrowed from the late sixties films of Godard into the serv-ice of analysing Quebecois society. The first three of Carle and Laure's films, *Les Corps Célestes* (1973), *Bûcheron*, and *Normande*, extended this experimental inquiry into the tensions between documentary realism and avant-gardism to the lim-its of coherence. Laure's body becomes the fulcrum of the intersection between local issues of Quebecois identity (the Duplessist ideology of 'church, family, and closeness to the land,' the social reality of local dialect and class divisions) and the global concerns of late sixties radicalism (sexual liberation, feminism, anti-consumerism, multiculturalism).[31] Wildly and intentionally discordant in tone and subject matter, these films are held together primarily by the performance of Laure and her co-stars, especially Carle stalwart Daniel Pilon, who played oppo-site her in a good number of them, but also specific roles such as Denise Filiat-rault's astonishingly motor-mouthed turn as the former mistress of the father of Maria Chapdelaine (Laure). But in contrast to the primarily realist mode of her co-stars, Laure's acting is as unconventional as the films. Although capable of sharp verbal outbursts and in spite of various of musical numbers, her signature state is a stubborn muteness which, at times, as in the apparently dark conclusion of *Normande* or in the character of Miss Canada in Canadian/French/German co-production *Sweet Movie* (1974, Dušan Makavejev), becomes a catatonic silence. In contrast to the individualistic expressionism of Bujold's Quebecois persona, Laure's persona far more easily personified the nation of Quebec. Such hieratic figures of allegorical female beauty were common currency in European art cin-ema of the time – mocked mercilessly by Makavejev in *Sweet Movie* – but Laure's characters were just autonomous enough and far too chaotically wilful ever sim-ply to stand for something else. Hence, Carle juxtaposes *Bûcheron*'s journey into the heart of northern darkness of the logging camp, where the lumber company has had Maria's father murdered, with extended experimental dance sequences featuring a seductively gyrating and gratuitously naked Laure. The conclusion of *Normande* alternates a long, extreme close-up of the defeated protagonist's face, one blank eye staring at the camera, with a series of sexual hallucinations envi-sioning a naked Laure in fever dreams of Quebecois history and iconography:

Laure as shaman with Natives; nuns; a canoe full of blood. Laure's star discourse is external rather than internal, playing on surfaces rather than depth. Although the camera follows her obsessively, she is inscrutable, moving through a world often rendered in the style of direct cinema but without ever revealing her relationship to that world.

There is a strong charge of exploitation running through all of Carle's films – *Bûcheron* even opens with the vintage pre-credits genre teaser of a leg severed at the ankle by a chainsaw – but, like Arcand's *Gina* (see chapter 3), it is a self-reflective charge. Nevertheless, that self-reflection emerges as a refusal of resolution or cohesion. As Leach argues, 'the films dwell on the fine line between involvement and exploitation, between the erotic as a heightening of human experience and the erotic as a voyeuristic evasion of responsibility.'[32] Perhaps no other mainstream star in movie history has had her body so exposed and so highly scrutinized as Laure has by Carle's alternately probing and caressing camera; neither has any other mainstream star maintained such control and expressed such artistic autonomy in the process. While Laure's international stardom derived from this paradox of exposure and retentiveness, it expressed itself differently beyond the local context. Although made with Canadian money and filmed partially in Montreal, *Sweet Movie* pushed the indignities suffered by her character even further than Carle did – she is urinated on by the golden-penised Mr Dollars, raped by a bodybuilder, shipped inside a suitcase from Canada to Paris, tossed out with the garbage, and bathed naked in melted chocolate. The scandalous profile of the film – it was widely reported at the time that Laure was suing Makavejev and the film is apparently still banned in Ontario and in England – resulted not so much from Laure's typically sultry yet abandoned performance as from the surrounding context: scenes of paedophilia, coprophilia, and other frontal assaults on fundamental sexual and bodily taboos.[33] Laure's scenes are not substantially different from those of Carle's films, where she dances coated in bronze paint, bathes naked in blood, or stalks the stage with a dead canary in her mouth; however, rather than immersed in the Quebecois milieu and the personal imagery of Carle and Laure, *Sweet Movie* proffers a sweeping subversion of contemporary totalitarianism in all its guises, from Stalinism and Fascism to consumerist capitalism. Taking itself far less seriously, Bertrand Blier's Oscar-winning *Préparez vos mouchoirs* (1978) reads almost as a parody of the non-verbal quality of the social radicalism of Laure and Carle's films, building an entire comic narrative around her character's refusal to smile, talk, or respond in any way to her husband (Gérard Depardieu) or his new bosom pal Stefan (Patrick Dewaere). Instead, for most of the film, she mutely offers her naked body to all concerned, distracting herself by knitting obsessively, until, finally fulfilled by a thirteen-year-old genius and his paraplegic father, she happily settles into her new role as housewife of a prominent industrial family.

Laure's sex-symbol status overlapped with a burgeoning career as a pop star, which began when she and her composer-husband Lewis Furey starred in a successful cabaret show in Paris in 1977 and recorded an album the next year.[34] While Laure has proved a versatile artist, successfully transforming herself into a pop star by the end of the seventies and a writer/director in the twenty-first century, her persona remains unchanged, and her films continue to explore the same raw, emotional sexuality that was her trademark in the seventies.[35] Interestingly, the same persona that made her a far bigger star in France than Bujold ever was seems to have militated against her success in English Canada. In an interview at Cannes, where Furey's 1985 musical *Night Magic*, co-written with Leonard Cohen and co-produced with France, was screening, Laure queried Toronto critic Jay Scott on the topic, 'How come I'm not known in English Canada? Isn't that sad? I get fan letters from Germany, Italy, everywhere and anywhere. I'm starting to get into America, but Gilles' films never worked in English Canada, and they don't know me. Maybe if I become big in America I will be known in English Canada – it's an old story, this one, yes?'[36] Laure featured in a handful of English-language films during the mid-eighties, but without any mainstream success: the L.A.-based romantic drama *Heartbreakers* (1984, Bobby Roth); the Cleveland, Ohio, filmed tax-shelter thriller *The Surrogate* (1984, Don Carmody); and the Greece/U.S. co-production *Sweet Country* (1987, Mihalis Kakogiannis), a historical drama recounting in graphic detail the brutal military takeover of Chile led by General Pinochet in 1973. Despite her indigenously Quebecois persona and the primarily local appeal of her recent films *Les fils de Marie* (2002), *CQ2* (2004), and *La Capture* (2007), however, she remains a cosmopolitan figure, splitting time between Paris and Montreal. Moreover, her music is resolutely bilingual, 'What the hell, I'm a Montrealer, and Lewis is a Montrealer. He's one of the 20-per-cent born in Montreal who's English. In my life, I've sung Lewis Furey 90-per-cent of the time, and I sang a double album of Leonard Cohen lyrics. Those two guys are Montrealers that I love and I think they're great lyricists. It's my right and I don't have any complexes about it.'[37] That choice made her acceptance as a singer slower in Quebec than in the rest of the world, but a trawl through the Internet shows that she has solved that problem more recently. And as her own films receive more attention at Cannes than anywhere in the anglophone world, the consequences of the initial choices made by Laure and Bujold continue to reverberate in their opposite but complementary discourses, the only stars to break out of the local national cinema of Quebec. At the same time, the very fact of their unusual endurance as autonomous female stars in control of their own careers has also demonstrated the short-sightedness of early feminist critiques of their sexually ambivalent roles.

The New Quebecois Firmament: Pascale Bussières and Roy Dupuis

> I'm a serial killer. In English. Only in English. I'm a mother in French. I'm a typical great mother in French. And I'm a serial killer in English. And in Spanish, I would be a muchacha.
>
> Pascale Bussières (1999)

The Quiet Revolution produced two iconic female stars; there were no more breakout stars for another couple of decades, and the very different trajectories of their careers suggests something of the changed cinematic landscape during those twenty years. Neither Roy Dupuis (b. 1963), nor Pascale Bussières (b. 1968), nor Marie-Josée Croze (b. 1970) has or seems likely ever to achieve anything like the international star profile both Bujold and Laure had reached by their mid-twenties. Nevertheless, all three have received international recognition, have done signifi-cant work beyond the confines of the Quebecois industry, and have a privileged status within their home province. Rather than the crossover personas of Bujold and Laure, however, this status has brought with it a strong measure of their local identity; especially in English-Canadian films, their presence seems generally to signify in terms of their French Canadianness. This is less the case with the work of Bussières and Croze in France, especially the latter, but remains a significant com-ponent of their iconicity within Canada. Far more than in the sixties and seventies, crossover status derives from the ability, as Bussières suggests in the quote above, to project different personas for different audiences.

There are several ways in which the discourses of Dupuis and Bussières are strangely linked. Both came to prominence within the same enormously popular television miniseries, although playing father and daughter rather than lovers, as would have seemed more probable given their similar ages and profiles. Both solidified their local stardom by playing key provincial icons in blockbuster biop-ics: Dupuis as hockey great Maurice Richard in the film of the same title, released in English as *The Rocket* (2005, Charles Binamé), and Bussières as singer Alys Robi, Quebec's first internationally known media star, in *Ma vie en cinémascope* (2004, Denise Filiatrault) (figure 4.3). Both owe their international profile almost com-pletely to English-language roles: Bussières in Patricia Rozema's art-house hit *When Night Is Falling* (see chapter 3) and Dupuis in the syndicated cult television series *Nikita* (*La Femme Nikita* internationally). Moreover, as Peter Dickinson has observed, both actors have a further transnational identity as queer icons.[38] Their multiple, apparently contradictory personas testify to the complex structures underlying global cinema today.

Dupuis and Bussières both achieved local stardom thanks to writer Arlette Cousture's bestselling family saga of Quebec between 1890 and 1945, *Les Filles de Caleb. Caleb* was first adapted in 1990–1 as a twenty-episode television series for Radio-Canada by veteran director Jean Beaudin, starring Marina Orsini as young village schoolteacher Emilie Bordeleau and Dupuis as her student and lover, the coureur de bois Ovila Pronovost. Half of Quebec tuned in to the Thursday night show, making it at the time the most popular dramatic show in Canadian television history.[39] The equally popular 1993 sequel *Blanche*, directed by Charles Binamé, starred Bussières as the title character, one of the couple's eight children. Blanche first travels to Montreal to become a doctor, but faced with sexual discrimination must settle for training as a nurse. Posted to remote Abitibi, she must confront the many trials of colonial northern Quebec, not to mention a troubled relationship with her estranged father (Dupuis), who settled in Abitibi when he abandoned his family. The star personas from this series – dark, handsome, troubled loner and tough, determined proto-feminist – would in many ways stick to the two actors despite the quite different directions their careers would take.

Not that either actor has abandoned the important fan base of local television. Among other roles, Dupuis has starred as an investigative reporter in all four seasons of the critically acclaimed newspaper drama *Scoop* (1991–5), as Maurice Richard in a 1999 TV movie, and as the ultra-cool Level 5 Operative Michael Samu-

4.3 Pascale Bussières and Roy Dupuis celebrate their respective wins for Best Actress and Best Actor at the 2005 Genie Awards. They also won at that year's Jutra Awards. Canadian Press.

elle in *Nikita*. Bussières followed up her star-making turn as Blanche Pronovost with the eleven-episode New France epic *Marguerite Volant* (1996, also directed by Binamé), the soap-opera parody *Le Coeur a ses raisons* (2005–7), and the New Brunswick–set ecological drama *Belle-Baie* (2008–9). But each has seen that same popularity open out into very different kinds of roles. Bussières attributes Rozema's decision to cast her in *When Night Is Falling* to *Blanche*.[40] Moreover, she went on to make two low-budget, contemporary art films with Binamé, funded by the success of *Blanche*: *Eldorado* (1995) and *La Beauté de Pandore* (2000). Dupuis also made his mark in art cinema, starring in Binamé's first feature film, *C'était le 12 du 12 et Chili avait les blues* (1993), and as a homosexual prostitute who kills his lover in *Being at Home with Claude* (1992), directed by *Caleb's* Beaudin. Dickinson notes the international impression (both *Eldorado* and *Claude* played at Cannes) made by the 'edgy and sexy takes on contemporary Montreal's demi-mondes of sex and drugs,' although he does not meditate further on the possible disjunction between the period pieces and the contemporary images, beyond assuming that the latter is what drew international attention and the former is what maintains the image at home.[41] Dickinson is correct, however, to stress the importance of the genres of period drama and biopic in the 'national' imaginary of Quebec (as in any national cinema/mediascape) and the way in which both Bussières and Dupuis have reinforced their star status by consistent recourse to these genres.[42]

It is less common for national stars to be able simultaneously to maintain diametrically opposed images, but this is what makes the case of Dupuis and Bussières especially interesting. The situation is partly due to the porosity of the Quebec mediascape, which is often obscured by the assumption of its insularity. First of all, *Les Filles de Caleb* was not merely a local phenomenon: it sold in twenty-eight countries, and according to Beaudin, was a top-rated show in both Germany and Israel.[43] When it first showed at home, it screened on Canada's French-language channel, but was broadcast nationwide, no doubt reaching plenty of channel-surfers who tuned in to watch the telegenic Emilie and Ovila without bothering much about understanding what they were saying. Rozema's casting decision suggests as much for the anglophone audience of *Blanche* as well, and the costume choice for mythology professor Camille Baker in *When Night Is Falling* – Victorian-style lace-up boots, long skirts, and dowdy blouses – suggests nothing so much as a tongue-in-cheek, queer homage to Bussières's prim and serious Quebecois television persona. Marshall makes much of Dupuis's 'federating but problematic mixture of virility and sexual ambivalence ... power and vulnerability ... in what remains a male-dominated society.'[44] Rather than an exception or supplement to Dupuis's Quebecois persona, Marshall regards this ambivalent identity as fundamental to the role he plays within Quebec culture, 'an unresolvedness in the general construction of masculine identity and its relationship with narratives of nation and nature.'[45] Precisely because he can combine a traditionally nature- and body-based masculinity with a contemporary urban cool, Dupuis is able to express and hold in abeyance, if not actually reconcile, the rifts in identity that have defined Quebecois culture since the Quiet Revolution: the need to ground identity in a history that must be repudiated, the failed autonomy movement, the minority identity caught between an anglophone majority and a French cultural and colonial hegemony.

Bussières would appear to have played female counterpart to this identity, hence perhaps the surprising fact that the pair have never yet played directly opposite each other as love interests.

Unlike Dupuis, Bussières's feature film debut at the age of sixteen predated her television work by a number of years. Directed by Micheline Lanctôt, *Sonatine* (1984) is a stark portrait of the friendship between two upper-middle-class girls alienated from society whose suicides go unnoticed by the world around them. The film's signature image – the two girls riding the Montreal metro with a sign announcing their intention to take their lives and asking the world to prevent them from doing so – made its own iconic announcement, albeit to a smaller population than the millions of *Blanche*'s television audiences. Like *Deux Actrices* (the second film Bussières would make with Lanctôt), *Sonatine* established a pattern of roles of failed heterosexual romance and intense same-sex friendship that not only fed easily into the proto-feminism of Blanche but also allowed a double reading in terms of queer spectatorship following the similar but explicitly lesbian narrative of *When Night Is Falling*.[46] Both actors are on record as consciously resisting the call of Hollywood, but Bussières has had an active relationship with English-Canadian cinema, appearing in Guy Maddin's *Twilight of the Ice Nymphs* (1997), Bruce McDonald's music-industry television drama, *Platinum* (1997), Jeremy Podeswa's ensemble film, *Five Senses* (1999), and Allan Moyle's science-fiction actioner, *Xchange* (2000). As in *Night Is Falling*, these films play on her Quebecois persona of cool, distant sexuality, projecting a foreignness not only through accent but in a certain unfamiliarity of body language and character. This is especially evident in her sleepwalking character in *Twilight*, the confused and irrational Camille in *Night Is Falling*, and the elegant prostitute in *Five Senses*. Bussières turned quite early to 'mature' roles: playing variations of the troubled mother in Léa Pool's coming-of-age film *Emporte-moi* (1999), in English-language feature *The Blue Butterfly* (2004), and in Isabelle Coixet's French-produced *Les filles ne savent pas nager* (*Girls Can't Swim*, 2000). While her international star may have waned since the nineties, Bussières has fashioned a varied résumé while maintaining a firm grounding on her home Quebecois turf through star vehicles such as *Ma vie en cinemascope*.

Although he has worked prolifically (fifty-odd film and television roles, mostly starring, in just over twenty years) Dupuis had done very little in English before 2004 despite his facility with the language. As if to stretch himself, he then made Jeremy Peter Allen's *Manners of Dying* (2004), Paolo Barzman's *Emotional Arithmetic* (2007), and Roger Spottiswoode's *Shake Hands with the Devil* (2007), in which he played Roméo Dallaire, the Canadian leader of the United Nations troops in Rwanda in 1994 at the time of the genocide, a role for which he won another Jutra award. And although he has at times shown a desire to break out of his trademark brooding mien and celebrated mumble, sometimes with great success, as in his eccentric golf pro in the southwestern desert in *Les Etats Unis d'Albert* (2005, André Forcier), Dupuis has primarily played to type. That type has periodically been deployed for its generational iconicity, as in his cameo as a tough, hip drug squad detective in Denys Arcand's *Les Invasions barbares* (2003) or his campily exaggerated supporting role as a surly soldier who plays treacherous foil to Peter Weller's anglophone hero in Christian Duguay's science-fiction thriller *Screamers* (1995).

Like Bussières, Dupuis has had impressive staying power, since the nineties splitting the *Montreal Mirror*'s 'Best Montreal Actor' vote every year with old-timer
William Shatner – until 2009, when both were knocked off the pedestal by the
latest Canuck comic export, Judd Apatow regular Jay Baruchel.[47] As opposed to
Bussière's solid art-house reputation, Dupuis's star status has always cut across
his reputation as an actor. His nickname, 'Le Beau Roy,' plays both on the sexual
ambivalence of his persona and on the perceived incompatibility between his
camera-ready looks and real ability, similar to the quandary in which matinee idol
Leonardo DiCaprio long found himself caught in the United States; the regal pun
on Dupuis's name alludes as well to his dominance of the industry. In 2001, the
pre-eminent Quebecois film journal *24 Images* created a furor among Dupuis fans
with critical and disparaging remarks about their idol in a double issue on actors
and cinema in Quebec.[48] The tempest in a teapot suggests the divide between a
traditionally auteurist film criticism (the *24 Images* response noted testily that they
do not review television) and a star-based fandom. Curiously, Dupuis seems also
to have taken note of the aspersions cast on his acting skills and loyalty to local
film-making, expanding his range in films such as the multiple-narrative drama
Manners of Dying and the amnesiac-in-a-coma drama *Mémoires affectives* (2004). He
has not, however, caught on with the new generation of Villeneuve, Turpin, and
others; unlike Bussières, his work continues to be primarily in genre rather than
art cinema.

There are other local icons in Quebecois culture; indeed, due to his central roles
in Arcand's films, Rémy Girard (thirteen years Dupuis's senior) is perhaps better known internationally in cinephile circles. Like his compatriot Michel Côté (a
bigger star at home but barely known abroad), Girard is a skilled character actor
and non-romantic lead who seems to have featured in just about every popular
Quebecois film made. Girard anchored the immensely lucrative *Les Boys* series
of weekend-warrior hockey comedy-dramas, played costumers alongside Dupuis
and Bussières, and of course, served as Arcand's fetish actor. Girard is a quintessentially local actor, however; he has neither the looks to be a conventional leading
man nor, apparently, any interest in making a Hollywood career as a supporting
player. Nevertheless, his identification with the talk cinema of Arcand and with
commercial television seemed to have militated against roles in the art films of the
newer generation until Villeneuve found a way to use that persona in the role of
the notary Lebel in the Academy Award nominated drama *Incendies* (2010). Meanwhile, Dupuis's contemporary Patrick Huard, who debuted with le beau Roy in
Claude Fournier's gay-bashing comedy *J'en suis!* (1997), made his name with the
Boys franchise, and is Dupuis's main competition for local heart-throb, has never
made an impact beyond the province. Neither has he worked nearly as much in
television. A local boy made good, Huard has nothing of the outsider, bad-boy
reputation of Dupuis, nor has he received any of the acting accolades actually
won by the latter (in spite of his bad press). Huard's primary claim to greater
fame is the record-breaking two solitudes buddy comedy drama, *Bon Cop Bad Cop*
(2007), playing the Quebecois role (opposite Colm Feore's Anglo-Canadian cop)
that would almost certainly have gone to Dupuis if Huard hadn't guaranteed it for
himself by writing the script.

Despite her extended résumé in television and genre films, Bussières has also consistently worked with top new and established Quebecois art-film directors. Unlike Dupuis, she has maintained the reputation of a brilliant actress who, like Bujold before her, rises above the level of whatever material she is given. It's an interesting reversal of the standard gender paradigm that seems quite specific to the Quebecois context and can be attributed to the added cachet of Bussières's work with English-Canadian and French auteurs. Bussières was at the centre of the revival of the historical picture, nearly all of which treat of central female characters who suffer either through love with coureur de bois figures (frontier melodramas like *Blanche*) or from the circumstances of their own lives and choices (biopics like *Cinémascope*). The new cycle of female biopics, which also includes *Monica la mitraille* (2004, Pierre Houle, on the life of the famous Montreal bank robber, Machine Gun Molly), is clearly related to the *Laura Cadieux* series (*C't'à ton tour, Laura Cadieux* [1998], *Laura Cadieux … la suite* [1999], and the TV miniseries, *Le petit monde de Laura Cadieux* [2003], all directed by Filiatrault) with its empowered older working-class heroine (Ginette Reno), albeit in a comic mode. The biopics combine the convention of suffering virtuous women with a new sense of empowerment and accomplishment. Alys Robi, after all, was the first globally successful Quebecois of either sex, but the film stresses a battle between the church's rigid moral strictures and her love for a married man. The specifically Quebecois identity, expressed through and embodied in the desires of the central female protagonist, is inevitably at odds with outside forces, whether they be imposed authorities of church and state or the economic forces of money and colonial exploitation.

The younger Marie-Josée Croze looked set to eclipse Bussières at home when at the turn of the millennium, after a decade of middling work at best (*Battlefield Earth*!), a starring role in Villeneuve's critical hit *Maelström* (2000), a key supporting part (as the requisite French Canadian) in Egoyan's *Ararat* (2002), and a star-making turn in *Les Invasions barbares* that won her the best actress award at Cannes led to so many offers from France that she has not stopped working there since (fifteen films in eight years). Nor has she appeared in another film in Quebec, a fact that has made her a number of enemies at home but that she attributes to circumstance and the lack of steady work, 'In fifteen years in Quebec,' she asserts, 'I made three films. Is that normal?'[49] Nevertheless, the abruptness of her precipitous flight to France (Carole Laure, for example, was able to balance both worlds throughout her career) suggests something more volitional than pure circumstance – at the very least, a refusal to play the iconic role that would easily have been hers had she stayed. The brightest young star left in town, Karine Vanasse (b. 1983), appeared out of nowhere in an art film at the age of sixteen (just like Bussières, who played her mother in the film), Pool's audience-friendly coming-of-age film *Emporte-moi*. Also like Bussières, Vanasse has since solidified her local stardom in period costume, alongside the eternally youthful Dupuis as doomed lovers in Binamé's enormously popular remake of the classic Quebecois frontier melodrama, *Séraphin: Un homme et son peché* (see chapter 1). Vanasse has not yet achieved the locally iconic status of Bussières or Dupuis, nor have her English-language films been good enough to create an international profile beyond the enduring resonance of her well-distributed debut. Lasting stars are few and far between outside the star-making capital to the south, and Bussières and Dupuis have ruled the roost for long enough now to make it clear that there is more to both of them than pretty faces.

Working English Canadians

There's no star system in this country and they don't give a fuck who you are.
Callum Keith Rennie (1996)

More than even the Quebecois cinema, English-Canadian film since the eighties has focused on a tight-knit group of film-makers and actors. Because it lacks the concentration of local television and its production is in general far more diffuse, English-Canadian cinema does not have anything like the star system of its French-Canadian counterpart. Consequently, its biggest names remain film-makers rather than actors: Cronenberg, Egoyan, Maddin, McDonald, and Rozema are the closest English-Canadian cinema has to true celebrity. Nevertheless, a handful of actors have emerged from this 'family' of film-makers who, if not possessed of the local star status of Bussières or Dupuis, nevertheless have enough visibility that their presence in a film is sufficient to guarantee public money – the sine qua non of English-Canadian cinema. Two of these actors, Molly Parker (b. 1972) and Callum Keith Rennie (b. 1960), productively ply their craft in independent cinema and local and American television; two others, Mia Kirshner (b. 1975) and Sandra Oh (b. 1971), followed up breakthrough Canadian roles in the early nineties with a long period of journeyman work in the United States before finding mainstream success on American television; yet another pair, Don McKellar (b. 1963) and Sarah Polley (b. 1979), whom I will discuss in the next section, have managed to combine established drawing power as actors with the further clout that comes in English Canada from writing and directing to become major players in the global independent film-making world. Their different choices in negotiating their careers have a lot to tell us about the complex interplay between English Canada, Hollywood, and a nebulous grey zone in between.

Male actors typically debut later, and Rennie was no exception, making his first big-screen appearance at the age of thirty-four in Mike Hoolboom's experimental short, *Frank's Cock* (1994), and his first feature film, Mina Shum's *Double Happiness*, the same year. Born in England and raised in Edmonton, Alberta, Rennie backed his way into acting after an adolescence spent in the punk scene and an intense episode of alcoholic depression. His screen persona emerged from that backdrop, marked by adjectives such as 'dark,' 'tense,' and 'edgy' and a reputation as a loose cannon and perfectionist, as in his characterization of a CBC movie in which he starred as 'crap' during publicity interviews in the run-up to its television premiere.[50] The second half of the nineties was Rennie's peak as a headliner, particularly his defining role as punk guitarist Billy Tallent in McDonald's fake rock documentary, *Hard Core Logo* (1996). McDonald's narrative caught the tension within Rennie's own character between an authentically independent actor and a desire for mainstream success. The central conflict on the disastrous reunion tour of the seminal Vancouver band Hard Core Logo is Tallent's secret negotiations to join the popular L.A. band jenifur. The film is subtle enough to remain agnostic about Tallent's decision: on the one hand, he is clearly the only one in the band with the talent, ambition, and looks to make such a move; on the other hand, the move is perceived as a betrayal of his childhood friend, possible former lover, and band frontman Joe Dick and of the punk ethos. In the event, the artistic dilemma was indeed there for Rennie, but he actually began both careers simultaneously, playing independent films for the acting and interest while also, as he put it somewhat dramatically, 'try[ing] to make enough for rent and food' by taking anything that was available in the burgeoning Vancouver industry: bit roles on whatever was shooting locally, everything from syndicated shows like *The Commish* (1991–6), *Lonesome Dove* (1989), *The Outer Limits* (1995–2002), and *The X-Files* (1993–2002) to films such as the Jean-Claude Van Damme vehicle *Time Cop* (1994, Peter Hyams) and John Dahl's sci-fi thriller *Unforgettable* (1996).[51]

Early in his career, Rennie was quite blunt about the lack of 'respect' his mainstream work received on the sets of *Double Happiness* and John L'Ecuyer's addiction memoir, *Curtis's Charm* (1995).[52] At the same time, he worried about making decisions that would lock him into the former, turning down the offer of a long-term role in *The X-Files* because he thought a six-year commitment would overly limit his options, even if working on the hit show would have opened up a television career.[53] Instead, he accepted, with some trepidation, a one-year contract to play opposite Paul Gross on the successful Alliance-produced Canadian export *Due South* (1994–9).[54] As the Mountie's American partner in the comedy-drama, Rennie was able to draw a comic version of his own edgy persona, suggesting that the sense of danger in that persona had always been somehow American in distinction to the typically unthreatening Canadian male, 'My idea of Americans … is that they're sexy and dangerous, shooting first and asking questions later. It's almost the polar opposite of Paul's character.'[55] It also clarified for him the paradox of English-Canadian film: 'I can't get asses in the seats for movies. There has been more coverage of me for a television show than for any movie I've done.'[56]

There is a distinct disconnect between the local industry and the indie scene, both in terms of media coverage, in terms of snobbery, and in terms of self-identification. Consequently, even though Rennie and Parker worked together as early as 1994, co-starring in *Paris or Somewhere* (a well-received TV adaptation of *The Playboy of the Western World*, J.M. Synge's classic Irish play of village bravado, re-imagined for a Saskatchewan setting), this work does not appear in their independent feature résumés, nor did it appear in the publicity generated by their later work together in Lynne Stopkewich's long-awaited but ultimately disappointing second feature, *Suspicious River* (2000), or the recent feature in McDonald's resurgent career, *Trigger* (figure 4.4).

It's as if the need to make a living were a dirty secret. That there is not enough work in Canada to support its actors is a leitmotif in both English-Canadian and Quebecois circles, particularly among those who have left for Hollywood or France, like Kirshner, Oh, Laure, and Croze. But it is true only in terms of feature

4.4 Callum Keith Rennie and Molly Parker at the premiere of their third film together, Bruce McDonald's *Trigger* (2010), the inaugural screening of the TIFF's new Bell Lightbox theatre. Photo by Phillip Chin/Getty Images.

film work, of course; whether English Canadian or Quebecois, there is a perfectly good living to be had shuttling between television and independent, publicly funded work. But it's not particularly stable and it's not especially glamorous. As Oh puts it, 'First of all in Canada, someone like me can be a star, a leading lady. In the U.S., much more difficult. They always want to keep you in the supporting roles. It is also debatable if there is even a star system in Canada, or an indigenous film industry. Canada is still at the mercy of the U.S. film industry. In Canada, it is very difficult to make a living as an actor ... In the U.S., there is more drive towards a certain kind of broad reaching success, and with that comes much more stress and sacrifice. In Canada, even if you are very successful, you can lead a very normal and healthy life. Maybe not much glamour or wealth or world reaching success, but quite normal.'[57] Although Oh has periodically returned to Canada for feature film work, notably in her Genie-award-winning turn opposite McKellar in *Last Night* and her reunion with Mina Shum in the Asian-Canadian ensemble piece *Long Life, Happiness and Prosperity* (2001), she has remained based in Los Angeles, and it is for her work there, especially her award-winning and star-making supporting role as Cristina Yang on the hit medical drama *Grey's Anatomy* (2005–), that she has had 'world reaching success.'

In contrast, Rennie chose, as he puts it, to be 'one of the stay-at-home actors who grind it out here.'[58] This has led to a limited number of starring roles, notably as tightly wound fathers in Keith Behrman's *Flower & Garnet* (2002) and Scott Smith's Saskatchewan-produced *Falling Angels* (2003), a lot of supporting roles in west-coast television, and a large proportion of frighteningly charismatic villains, from his abusive john in *Suspicious River* to his child-molesting Saskatchewan boyfriend in Hollywood/Canadian veteran Bob Clark's *Now & Forever* (2001) to his psychopathic hitman in McDonald's catastrophic thriller *Picture Claire* (2001) to his serial 'hunter' of Native prostitutes in Vancouver's seedy Downtown Eastside in Carl Bessai's *Unnatural & Accidental* (2006), to name a few. There is no doubt that Rennie is a master at this role, capturing the ambivalent reactions elicited by this kind of evil, and in roles that allow it, powerfully evoking the tormented and conflicted inner life of these characters. But it is a role he has played so often in the well over a hundred films and television episodes of his seventeen-year career that one is left yearning for the few times he has been allowed to stretch out even as his brief but ubiquitous appearances are always a cause for rejoicing, no matter the quality of the vehicle. Certainly, the late nineties saw him branching out into the comic potential of his persona to great effect. As the convenience store clerk Newbie in McDonald and McKellar's cult television series *Twitch City* (1997, 1999), Rennie brilliantly played the speed-talking 'expert' foil to Curtis's (McKellar) deadpan television addict. In his Genie-award-winning supporting role of Craig Zwiller in *Last Night*, Rennie neatly fended off the caricature potential of a seducer determined to check off a laundry list of sexual conquests before the end of the world. Coming off as funny, vulnerable, and earnest, Rennie also defused the character's heterosexual cliché with a comically endearing (and failed) attempt to seduce his best friend, Patrick (McKellar). More recently, he won a Gemini (the English-Canadian television awards) for his starring role as a homicide detective with multiple personality disorder in CBC drama *Shattered* (2010–11), and brought nuance to the slippery role of the fast-living, amoral record producer Lew Ashby in the second season of the Showtime comedy series *Californication* (2008). Presumably chosen by producer and star David Duchovny on the strength of his work in *The X-Files*, Rennie played the silver-maned aging party animal to perfection, retaining the character's fundamentally and frighteningly narcissistic and self-indulgent core, unable to control his least desire, while grounding the behaviour within the culture of the music business and unsentimentally projecting a desperate core of emotional vulnerability. Male actors have a long shelf life, and perhaps Rennie will eventually receive the complex roles he deserves; he certainly has the fan base for them.

Rennie's early co-stars Parker and Oh hit fame younger, more quickly, and at roughly the same time in the mid-nineties, but took divergent paths to end up comfortably ensconced in long-running American television series. While still a teenager, Oh, the Ottawa-raised daughters of Korean professionals, auditioned for and won the lead role in the 1993 CBC drama *The Diary of Evelyn Lau*, based on a memoir of the brutal life of a teenage Chinese runaway turned drug addict and prostitute. Winner of a Gemini award and best actress prize at the Cannes television festival, Oh followed up with a Genie award in her feature film debut the next year opposite Rennie in *Double Happiness* as a young Chinese Canadian who wants to become an actress. Oh's extraordinarily expressive and malleable face, able to change appearance and emotion in an instant, makes her equally convincing in the highly dramatic role of Evelyn Lau as well as the more comic tones of Jade, her character in *Double Happiness*. Nevertheless, when she chose to move to Hollywood, her persona was quickly fixed as a comic actor. She landed a minor part in the Rowan Atkinson film *Bean* (1997) and a supporting role as the executive secretary to Robert Wuhl's sports agent in the cynical HBO comedy series *Arli$$* (1996–2002). Like Rennie, Oh was aware of the conflict of interest, but chose security over flexibility. The four-months of shooting a year prevented her from doing projects such as playing the (non-Asian-specific) lead role in Shum's sophomore feature *Drive, She Said* (1997), which certainly suffered from her absence.[59] The combination of envy and a sense of betrayal captured so well in the band members of *Hard Core Logo* is certainly in evidence in Oh's assertion: 'It's too easy to get lazy with a TV show, so that's why I have to fight to make sure I get the time to do plays and films.'[60] Oh's slow path to stardom has certainly cost her local visibility, but she has also made her forays count (figure 4.5).

Like Parker, Polley, and Kirshner, Oh does not possess the conventional beauty of typical Hollywood stars, and while this lack of conventionality has benefited them on the independent scene, it has militated against headlining roles. Oh has been quite outspoken about the additional fact that she carries her identity with her ('it is my face') and about the barriers that identity has raised in landing non-Asian roles.[61] Neither her role in *Arli$$* nor the part of Cristina Yang was originally written for an Asian actor.[62] As she did when questioning the relevance of Don McKellar being asked why he cast an Asian actor as the lead in *Last Night* ('You don't have to justify anyone else in *Last Night*, because they're white. Here

4.5 Sandra Oh as Madame Ming in the Montreal episode of François Girard and Don McKellar's globe-trotting epic, *The Red Violin* (1998). Photofest.

in Canada, I feel that I am not an issue, a fucking issue'), Oh argues that the scarcity of Asian and other minority characters in medical shows does not reflect the reality of the health care system.[63] The discomforting and frustrating experience of Hollywood may have made it easier for Oh to displace similar concerns about the Canadian media – after all, there is not an abundance of Asians in non-ethnic roles north of the border either. But there is no doubt that her ability to reach a broader audience through American television has made her an important role model for Asian minorities in the United States and for Koreans abroad.[64]

While Oh's career has been defined, for better or worse, by the ethnic roles with which she began it, Parker's career has been equally marked by her breakout, Genie-award-winning performance in Stopkewich's controversial first feature film, *Kissed* (1996). Playing a necrophiliac and mortuary assistant, Parker managed not only to impart to audiences a powerful understanding of her perverse character's motivation, but to create a series of scenes that are simultaneously physical, spiritual, and deeply disturbing. Parker's face is capable of both an otherworldly glow and a knowing physicality, often expressed simultaneously. Her versatility has made her the closest English Canada has to a leading lady, and she is nearly as ubiquitous as Rennie on the independent scene. Like Oh, she has been less typecast locally than abroad, where the fact that she remains best known for the kinky sexuality of *Kissed* has led to similarly sex-centred roles such as the stripper Florence in Wayne Wang's U.S.-produced *The Center of the World* (2001) and a bikini-clad suburban housewife in the CBS-television wife-swapping drama *Swingtown* (2008). Within Canada, however, Parker has ranged the gamut from the quirky Brit-style romantic comedy of Sturla Gunnarsson's *Rare Birds* (2001) to Paul Gross's deadpan sports movie parody *Men with Brooms* (2002) to the Cape Breton Island incest drama *Marion Bridge* (2002, Wiebke von Carolsfeld; Ellen Page plays Parker's daughter). Her range was especially notable in the flurry of activity that followed *Kissed*. In 1999, she had substantial roles in three very different films: a young woman whose child disappears in Podeswa's *Five Senses*; a pregnant housewife whose marriage is crumbling in Michael Winterbottom's South London drama *Wonderland*; and the Jewish wife of Ralph Fiennes's lead in Istvan Szabo's Lantos-produced historical epic *Sunshine*. Three years later, she had another trio of films screening at the Toronto International Film Festival: *Marion Bridge*, *Pure* (in which she plays a heroin addict; directed by Gilles MacKinnon), and *Max* (in which she plays a German Jewish ballerina; directed by Menno Meyjes). In between, she played a pitch perfect twenty-something with self-esteem issues (Curtis's girlfriend on *Twitch City*) and a key role in Vancouverite Bruce Sweeney's contemporary twenty-something comedy-drama *Last Wedding* (2001).

Born and raised in Vancouver, Parker had a full résumé of fairly obscure television work, all of it Canadian and nearly all of it locally based ('lots of work there,' as she laconically put it),[65] before moving to Toronto on the heels of *Kissed*. Like Rennie, she resisted mainstream Hollywood work, maintaining that she didn't 'care about' and 'wouldn't watch' most of those films: 'I'm annoyed by the clichés that they try to pass off as true sentiment.'[66] She has perhaps been less selective in her choice of Canadian roles, including clunkers like the murder mystery *The Good Shepherd* (2004, Lewis Webb), where she played a journalist opposite Christian Slater. But she didn't start appearing in Hollywood roles until after three seasons of the critical and popular HBO hit *Deadwood* (2004–6), including *The Wicker Man* (2006, Neil LaBute), *Hollywoodland* (2006, Allan Coulter), and *The Road* (2009, John Hillcoat). Nor has she left Canada, recently teaming up with Rennie for McDonald's *Trigger* and the television series *Shattered* and *The Firm* (2012) – in both of which she plays his wife. Simultaneously fragile and tough in her persona, and unafraid of challenging and unusual roles, Parker seems well on her way to becoming a natural heir to Geneviève Bujold as a multifaceted Canadian actor.

Just as Parker's career has been defined by the sexually explicit nature of her breakout role, so has Mia Kirshner's. Cast as a dominatrix in Denys Arcand's English-language debut *Love & Human Remains* when she was seventeen and as a lap dancer with a schoolgirl routine in Atom Egoyan's *Exotica* when she was eighteen (her father had to sign a waiver allowing her to appear on a set with nudity), Kirshner's persona has been associated with a dark and moody adolescent sexuality ever since. Although sex and nudity are a long-established road of entry to Hollywood, especially for female actors, their meaning within Canadian film is often quite different than south of the border. Granted, Canada has its fair share of gratuitous nudity, especially in the burgeoning straight-to-cable and DVD market of the turn of the millennium. Nevertheless, just as there was no clear line to be drawn between straightforward maple syrup porno and the more artistically ambitious but even more sexually explicit films of Gilles Carle and Carole Laure, so do films like *Exotica*, *Kissed*, and Cronenberg's *Crash* (the highest-profile moment of Vancouver native Deborah Kara Unger's career) work as highly accomplished art films while simultaneously appealing to and marketed for a broader and lower common denominator of viewer. What distinguishes the sexuality in these films both from the run-of-the-mill de rigueur sex scene and from the intentionally repellent aesthetic of much of American indie movie sex is its use of sex scenes to develop character and its ambiguous representation of sexuality normally considered perverse and transgressive (necrophilia, car fetishism, paedophilia) as simultaneously deeply disturbing, aesthetically compelling, and without an external judgment.

Within the American context, the fine line between provocative exploration of charged material and soft-core exploitation often disappears. Partly because of her age and lack of experience, partly because of a more limited acting range than Parker or Polley, Kirshner was typecast early and apparently irrevocably into a dark and edgy jailbait persona that has persisted into her highest-profile role since *Exotica*, the aspiring writer Jenny Schecter on the Showtime television lesbian drama *The L Word* (2004–9), at least a decade younger than the stars of the show and a disruptive force and (consequently) plot catalyst (figure 4.6). While she has landed a few mainstream parts (a small role in Charles Matthau's adaptation of the Tennessee Williams play *The Grass Harp* [1995]; as Kitty in *Anna Karenina* [1997, Bernard Rose]; as a naive news intern opposite veteran Dustin Hoffman in *Mad City* [1997, Costa-Gavras]), she also found herself cast as one of a pair of disturbed and murderous sisters in *Dark Summer* (2000, Gregory Marquette), as an honours student gone bad in what one critic disparagingly termed the 'T&A visuals' of co-ed mystery *New Best Friend* (2002, Zoe Clarke-Williams), and as the one-dimensional 'super hot/super deadly' lesbian mercenary Mandy in seven episodes of the Fox television actioner *24* (2001–5).[67] The clincher on Kirshner's iconic persona has to have been her casting as 'evil sister Catherine, the cruelest girl in school' in the parody *Not Another Teen Movie* (2001, Joel Gallen).[68] To her credit, Kirshner has at times turned this persona into accomplished roles, as in the Canadian films *Century Hotel* (2001, David Weaver) and the Saskatchewan-set Native melodrama *Now & Forever* (2001, Bob Clark), or in her eponymous supporting role in the Brian De Palma adaptation of the James Ellroy bestseller *The Black Dahlia* (2006). Moreover, Kirshner has never allowed herself to be swept away by the Hollywood machine, devoting much of her time and money over several years to travelling, researching, and bringing together an impressive pool of talent to call attention to the struggles of marginalized individuals in Chechnya, Myanmar, Ciudad Juarez, and Malawi through a well-received book, *I Live Here* (2008), and an accompanying charitable foundation.[69]

The degree to which Kirshner dropped off the radar between *Exotica* and *The L Word* is evident by renewed references to her as a 'rising star'; the coverage also testifies to the now thirty-something actress's enduring persona as a sexy and disturbed youth.[70] The six-season run of the landmark show made her a cult star and a lesbian icon, even as her bisexual character was the most hated of the show and

4.6 Mia Kirshner, eternally the ingénue, as Jenny in the final season of *The L Word*. Permission of Mia Kirshner and Showtime.

began the final season floating murdered in a swimming pool. It was an enduring image: Internet coverage of her role as the 'sweet but dangerous' wife of a history teacher in six episodes of *The Vampire Diaries* (2010–11) never failed to suggest her undead character had met a similar death. Like Oh (whose *Grey's Anatomy* character has also become a queer icon), Rennie, and Croze, Kirshner has permanently settled outside Canada both physically and in terms of her public persona. The same star personas that have limited the roles available to them have also brought them a transnational fan base that itself works against the retention of the strong local identity maintained thus far by Parker, McKellar, and Polley. While projects such as Oh's theatrical sorties and Kirshner's book project and foundation avail themselves of local networks and the specific celebrity of the home-town actor made good, their paths have in the end steered more closely to the time-honoured model of the invisible Hollywood Canadian. Whether this will also be the path of the much younger Ellen Page (b. 1987) remains to be seen. Having already received an Academy Award nomination for *Juno* (2007) and co-starred with Leonardo DiCaprio in Christopher Nolan's science-fiction blockbuster *Inception* (2010), she is certainly on the way to American stardom. But it is too early to know whether she will slip into invisibility or retain some visible trace of Canadian identity in her developing star discourse.

Actors/Auteurs: Don McKellar and Sarah Polley

> Maybe that's why the idea of being famous seems so vague and random to me, because I am part of a community that won't really let me get out of hand without losing their respect. It's a community of people who all help each other and support each other, and it's a total privilege to be involved in. I see none of that in L.A. L.A. is the most isolated, competitive, nasty situation I've ever seen.
>
> Sarah Polley (1999)

Toronto natives Don McKellar and Sarah Polley came together in the same milieu of the peak of the Toronto new wave in the early nineties, both appearing in Egoyan's *Exotica*. They arrived from wildly divergent but equally Canadian paths, however; McKellar happened into screenwriting and movie acting after immersing himself in the theatre scene in high school, while Polley, the youngest daughter in a local show business family, was acting since the age of five, most notably as the child star of the hit CBC series *The Road to Avonlea* (1990–6). And while the decade concluded with both figures establishing international reputations, McKellar and Polley have resolutely stayed local, carving out key roles in the ongoing transformation of English-Canadian cinema as writers, actors, and directors. In contradistinction to the workmanlike approach of their colleagues discussed in the previous section, both McKellar and Polley are multitaskers, almost frenetically active in numerous places and fields at once, and omnivorous devourers of media. Paradoxically, it may be their openness to popular culture that has allowed them to remain focused on the art-house cinema at the centre of their respective oeuvres.

If the experience gained in the former had not so clearly infused the latter, one could easily say that Polley has had two distinct acting careers. Debuting in Bob Clark's *One Magic Christmas* (1985), the eight-year-old Polley had a traumatic experience in Spain three years later for Terry Gilliam's major studio production, *The Adventures of Baron Munchausen* (1988): gruelling work hours, hypothermia, and an irregular heartbeat as the result of an explosion near her head.[71] Her second encounter with American studios came when Disney joined the CBC and Telefilm Canada as co-producer of *Road to Avonlea*, the hugely popular adaptation of L.M. Montgomery's Edwardian-era books set in a fictional village on Prince Edward Island. '"All of a sudden the scripts were about one family pitted against the other, and the competitive entrepreneurial spirit, and all these little Canadians in this little town were trying to make money," she recalls, adding that her character became "this nasty little girl."'[72] Her growing discontent with Disney, coupled with a desire to break the constraints of her squeaky clean image and immerse herself in radical protest against the conservative government of the time, led the fifteen-year-old Polley to ask out of the show.[73] She would not work again on a major studio production until *Dawn of the Dead* (2004, Zach Snyder). Yet, as the central figure of one of the most popular shows in Canadian history, Polley's plucky persona stuck with her (figures 4.7 and 4.8). Egoyan cast her in *Exotica* fully conscious of the baggage she would bring with her from *Avonlea*, knowing it would introduce even more local tension to the audience's initial ignorance of her function in the film. Polley said: 'He cast this person who was so supposed to be the sugary sweet pure thing in a role where, at the beginning of the movie, it's ambiguous as to whether or not I might be a prostitute.'[74] Similarly, we read in a feature introducing Polley discussing the simultaneous release of *Dawn* and Peter Wellington's English-Canadian hockey gambling movie *Luck* (2003), 'It's shocking to see Canada's girl from Avonlea hold her own in a brutal horror movie.'[75] Brian Johnson could make the connection partly because Polley has never dropped the moral core of her persona, even as she would adapt that core ever more towards marginal and complex characters and away from the nostalgic and chaste simplicity in which it had originated. As she tartly responded to a Hollywood interviewer's question, 'If you could shoot a celebrity who would it be?': 'I said George Bush would be No. 1. There was this huge silence. Then this pained hissing sound as she looked at me with these shark eyes.'[76]

Polley planned a hiatus from acting, expecting, like her four child-actor siblings, never to return to it, but Egoyan's offer to play the central role in *The Sweet Hereafter* would return her to the career for good, with a new persona both miles away from and an ironic maturation of Sara in *Avonlea*.[77] Polley's Nicole is the moral centre and heart of Egoyan's film, the only survivor of the bus crash that killed the rest of the children in her town. But she is also a survivor of incest who intentionally misrepresents the facts of the events in order to sabotage the lawsuit being conducted by outsider lawyer Mitchell Stevens (Ian Holm). She is simultaneously innocent and knowing, a morally pure force who nevertheless has little to do with conventional morality. She is, in other words, an icon for a progressive and morally complex Canada counter to the conservative simplicity of her *Avonlea* persona. Of course, Polley's memory neatly simplifies the issue by blaming the conservatism of *Avonlea* on the outside influence of Disney dollars. Disney was on board from the beginning, and while they certainly eliminated regional details from the original books and insisted on frequent appearances by American guest stars, the high production values permitted by their dollars were just as certainly a factor in the show's popularity at home – many Canadians, too, liked the 'uniformly conservative, sexually repressive, and morally monolithic' image they saw of their past, including, of course, the majority who voted Conservative provincial leader Mike Harris into power in 1996.[78]

Polley responded to the trauma of her past relationship to local television and to Hollywood with a populist impulse of her own; her persona has always been earnest and approachable, and her films, if often challenging, are also down to earth and engaging. *The Sweet Hereafter* brought her myriad offers, including the lead role in the big-budget Cameron Crowe feature *Almost Famous* (2000), for which she signed up, eventually backing out of the production, to be replaced by soon-to-be-star Kate Hudson. Polley said of this choice, 'You just knew when you read the script that whoever played that part was going to have a certain kind of life, and it wasn't one I was ready for.'[79] Instead she went to film school, made a couple of shorts, and stuck to the indies, mostly in Canada, including ensemble roles in *Last Night*, Cronenberg's *eXistenZ* (1999), Doug Liman's influential indie adolescent drug comedy *Go* (1999), Michael Winterbottom's BC-set Thomas Hardy adaptation *The Claim* (2000), Clement Virgo's *Love Come Down* (2000), John Greyson's *The Law of Enclosures* (2000), and lead roles in Audrey Wells's modern Pygmalion story *Guinevere* (1999) and Hal Hartley's 'monster movie' *No Such Thing* (2001), where she met Julie Christie, who would eventually star in Polley's feature directorial debut, *Away from Her* (2006). Like Kirshner, Polley looks younger than her years

4.7 Wealthy heiress Sara Stanley (Sarah Polley) arrives in her new home in the first episode of *Road to Avonlea* (1990). Photofest.

4.8 Sarah Polley in *Dawn of the Dead* (2004), her first major studio production since *Avonlea*. Cropped frame enlargement. Photofest.

and she has been wilful in using that youthful look as part of her arsenal as an actor, drawing on the long experience of her iconicity as a child actor. In *Guinevere*, for example, she begins the film as an introverted twenty-year-old college gradu- ate, cowed by her success-driven family, yet unable to decide how to rebel until seduced and taken in by aging photographer Connie Fitzpatrick (Stephen Rea). Nurtured by ideas, companionship, and unconditional acceptance, she comes out of her shell, and Polley makes the physical transformation before our eyes. It's a flawed film, overly obvious and highly predictable, but her performance cap- tures the crucial ambiguity of a relationship that is simultaneously exploitative and liberating.

It is hard not to read the film as a fable of Polley's own transformation from plucky yet docile Sara Stanley to steely yet pliable Sarah Polley, who found her way when she found her proper milieu. But Polley has not limited her work to key figures in the English-Canadian community (Cronenberg, Egoyan, Thom Fitzgerald, Greyson, McKellar, Vincenzo Natali, Virgo); she has also teamed up with a number of international auteurs: Hartley, Winterbottom, Wim Wenders, and the Catalonian director Isabel Coixet, for whom she starred in *My Life without Me* (2003) and *The Secret Life of Words* (2005) as a young mother diagnosed with cancer and a hearing-impaired factory worker nursing a burn victim on an oil rig, respectively. But she is not simply, as a writer in *Rolling Stone* put it, an 'an art-film baby'; Polley grew up with the popular industry, and once she put the bad memories of that industry behind her, she seems to have recovered a pleasure in it as well: 'Originally the choice was quite ethical – I didn't think those films were worthy. But I've had to admit to myself that I love watching those kinds of movies.'[80] She has confessed to one interviewer the 'guilty pleasure' of Adam Sandler movies; doing publicity for *Dawn*, she repeatedly asserted her long-time obsession with zombie movies. Polley has long possessed the ability to make the emotional connection required of popular cinema; her intellectual acceptance of that connection is a logical continuation of her belief in taking all classes and all behaviours at face value. As she said of her character in *My Life without Me*, 'My character lives in a trailer and has two kids and is a completely normal, unpathetic person.'[81]

That same pragmatic empathy is strongly in evidence in Polley's miraculous first feature film, which she adapted from a short story by Alice Munro that she read on the plane home from shooting *No Such Thing* in Iceland with Julie Christie. Co-executive produced by Egoyan, *Away from Her* shares her mentor's deliberate pacing and tone of quiet observation. While no less subtle in her ability to leave the most important things unsaid, Polley invests her film far more directly in the emotions of the character than even Egoyan's most emotionally direct film, *The Sweet Hereafter*. The simple yet unpredictable story of the effect on a long-married couple (Christie along with Canadian veteran Gordon Pinsent) of the wife's institutionalization because of Alzheimer's disease, *Away from Her* is subtle, assured, and beautifully simple. Polley draws much of her meaning simply by observing her characters' faces, and by contrasting the still vastness of the snow-covered Ontario of the couple's isolated cabin with sinewy tracking shots through the equally still but far more foreboding corridors of the managed-care facility where much of the second half of the film takes place. It is as if Polley had managed to capture on film the same emotional connection and calm intelligence she projects as an actress. In finding a bridge between the documentary authenticity of traditional Canadian art film and the direct connection of popular cinema, Polley suggests a way forward for English-Canadian film, having satisfied both the strictures of quality and the recent Telefilm policy of making money. As Brendan Kelly noted in *Variety*, *Away from Her* marked 'the first time an English Canuck pic has done any business in the U.S. in years' (dare we say, since *The Sweet Hereafter*?).[82]

McKellar shares with Polley a fondness for popular culture and a knack for bridging the gap between the quality of the margins and the appeal of the mainstream. Both figures bridge that gap by bringing a peculiarly Canadian sensibility to what would otherwise be hackneyed Hollywood movies of the week and big-budget disaster movies. The difference between them is that while Polley absorbed the tropes and conventions of pop culture through the body of an actor, McKellar soaked them up as a passive consumer – whence her persona of intelligent and ambiguous empathy and his persona of intelligent and ambiguous passivity. But unlike Egoyan, whose mistrust of popular culture never quite permits an un-self-conscious release into its emotionality, Polley and McKellar seem unafraid to tap into that reservoir of identification. Typically, his screenplays begin with the appearance of an ironically depicted cliché played by McKellar himself: Russel, the would-be 'first Canadian serial killer' in *Roadkill* (1989, McDonald); the nerdy, cornet-playing yokel Pokey Jones in *Highway 61* (1991, McDonald); the agoraphobic couch potato Curtis in *Twitch City* (1997, 1999, McDonald); the mourning yuppie loner Patrick in *Last Night*; and the experimental film-maker turned driver Rick in *Childstar* (2004, McKellar). Rather than establishing an ironic superiority to the characters by letting them rise above the situation by intellectual detachment, or cutting them down to size by allowing the audience to feel superior to their stilted emotionality, McKellar plays them straight, allowing them to develop as characters but without losing or redeeming the quirks that established them to start with. It is as if he embraces a stereotype, pushes it to the point of absurdity, and then rides that absurdity as if it were real until it finally breaks through into credibility.

This narrative movement is especially effective in McKellar's first feature, *Last Night*, which introduces Patrick in the context of a cringe-inducing parody of a repressed bourgeois suburban nuclear family dealing with the impending end of the world with a simulated Christmas dinner, complete with repackaged memories of their 'happy childhood.' McKellar extends the scene longer than necessary, as if wanting to milk the images for all of their banal horror. Finally, Patrick leaves to spend the end of the world alone in his apartment, while his younger sister, Jenny (an underused Sarah Polley), heads off with her loser boyfriend to party in the apocalypse. But a funny thing happens on the way to predictability: Sandra (Sandra Oh), totally and credibly devastated by her inability either to rendezvous with or contact her husband in any way, instead takes hesitant refuge in McKellar's sanctum. Sandra's raw emotional desperation gradually shifts Patrick and the film into a different register, its effect radiating outward to the other main threads, providing a powerfully genuine emotional undercurrent to the dignified death of gas company manager Duncan (Cronenberg) at the hands of a trigger-happy youngster, to the aging French teacher Mrs Carlton's (Bujold) checking in with her old students, and especially to best friend Craig's (Rennie) obsessive sexual activity. The final sequence, with Patrick and Sandra seated on a rooftop framed in extreme long shot by the achingly beautiful backdrop of a grey building wall before moving in to an intense close-up provides an affecting emotional pay-off without ever abandoning the initial constraints of ensemble character typing.

While the distanced cool of the film initially resembles the look of early Egoyan films up to *The Adjuster*, McKellar and his cinematographer Douglas Koch (they met when Koch was shooting Rozema's *When Night Is Falling*, in which McKellar had a supporting role as the co-director of the Sirkus of Sorts) in fact modelled the look of the film on the 'harshness or starkness' of urban apocalyptic science fiction of the early seventies like *The Omega Man* (1971, Boris Sagal) and the later entries in the *Planet of the Apes* series (1968–73).[83] The difference is significant, for the concluding emotionality is precisely what McKellar derives from the generic origins of his narrative. So, on the one hand, he has fashioned a quintessentially minor Canadian response to the excessive expectations of contemporary end-of-the-world scenarios, but on the other hand he has filtered that response through a pop culture tradition, neatly defusing the opposite expectations that it would be, as the *Sight & Sound* reviewer snarkily put it, 'deeply bourgeois Canadian.'[84] Rather than deadened by the superficiality of pop culture or snobbishly immune to its cheap seductions, McKellar's characters embrace it, refract it, and somehow find meaning through it – he even manages to pull off Pete Seeger singing 'Guantanamera' over the finale. McKellar unfailingly signals this hybrid attitude as quintessentially English Canadian. Essential to this hybrid attitude is claiming, however ironically, what is one's own within the self-proclaimed monolith that is American culture while meeting that culture on its own turf. Speaking about his second feature, *Childstar*, in which the eponymous young American (played, naturally, by a Canadian, Mark Rendall) comes to Canada to shoot a Hollywood action vehicle, McKellar emphasized the hardline meaning of the set-up: 'The film is a metaphor for a lot of things, sort of like a free-floating metaphor for American cultural imperialism – this kid in another country, this monstrous force, immature but very powerful.' But then he continued, adding nuance and ambiguity to that metaphor, 'It's also about creating art and compromising, about trying to find a centre and grow up artistically ... It's about how you can still express yourself personally and still reach people in a system that is very commodified.'[85] Rather than attempt to critique the system from an outside perspective that does not exist in English Canada, McKellar endeavours to find a personal voice within that system, and he has learned cleverly to deploy his own persona as vehicle for that voice.

Given McKellar's sense of popular culture, it should not come as a surprise that his most sustained and, arguably, his most successful articulation of this representational strategy should have come in a television show, the two years of the 'anti-sitcom' *Twitch City* which he and McDonald made for CBC at the tail end of the nineties. *Twitch City* is simultaneously an embrace of television culture – its hero, Curtis, is so addicted to television that he refuses to leave his apartment – and a transformation of everything it conventionally stands for. Like traditional television, *Twitch City* takes place in an alternate dimension that closely resembles our own; however, rather than the alternate dimension of an American television studio, *Twitch City* achieves its otherness by virtue of a radically hermetic space limited to a few blocks of the grungy urban neighbourhood of Kensington, Toronto: a convenience store, a gas station, and a second-floor apartment in a crumbling Victorian-era row house. Moreover, every pop culture reference, even the most self-evidently American one, has been filtered through a Canadian sensibility. This is clearest in Curtis's favourite show, a Jerry Springer–style talk fest called the Rex Reilly Show, with the eponymous host unctuously played by former Kids in the Hall comedian Bruce McCulloch. Although the show represents the very worst of what television has to offer, its effect on the community of Curtis's apartment is far more ambiguous. In addition to being the solid core of Curtis's fandom, it provides moments of genuine connection, as in the odd friendship with the Meals on Wheels lady Curtis initially cons for free food before bonding over Reilly's execrably written autobiography in the 'Klan Bake' episode. In the same episode, Curtis's collection of Reilly videocassettes is instrumental in dismantling a nascent neo-Nazi movement that has taken over his apartment when he is able to show Rex in 'Episode 115' demolishing the movement's leader in a previous incarnation as a babbling KKK member so ineffectual he is socked by a rabbi. Rather than ironically distanced consumption, it is intense immersion that breaks through the ideological surface and opens up the detritus of pop culture to unforeseeable alternative uses.

Nor can the ideological surface in any way encompass the range of possible meanings of a cultural text once it has become unmoored from its initial condition of production and consumption. Just as Egoyan could deploy Polley's *Avonlea* persona within the antithetical discourse of *Exotica* and queer fandom can appropriate the often homophobic Quebecois star discourse of Roy Dupuis, so McKellar and McDonald posit the existence of a genuinely Canadian popular culture, reducible neither to its American models nor to the straightforward local television around it. Reviewers of the show noted, either approvingly or irritatedly, that *Twitch City* eschewed conventional plotting and pacing and provided no obvious hooks or ways into its world. Rather, it rewarded obsessively close viewing – several reviewers recommend recording it and only watching it at the end of the season, straight through – that allowed the myriad pieces and threads slowly to coalesce into an impressive final pay-off. While the pleasures of the show derive from the pitch-perfect acting of McKellar, Parker, Rennie, and McCulloch in particular and its wildly imaginative accumulation of surrealistic twists on every aspect of television culture, the core of the series is the developing relationship between Curtis and Hope. Neither character redeems nor significantly changes the other and yet a deep bond grows between them, as it does in the viewer. McKellar's Curtis, which he claims to be both a portrait of his generation and a nightmare image of himself, is not initially, nor ever, an easy character to like. In addition to being addicted to bad television, he is narcissistic to a fault, manipulative, and wholly unscrupulous in getting what he wants. And yet, somehow, McKellar manages to make him also seem likeable, intelligent, and strangely accomplished. While McKellar's roles in other people's films have often tended towards self-parody, weirdness for weirdness's sake and quintessential Canadian losers, at his best, he turns that loser image on its head, succeeding, as Curtis somehow does in *Twitch City*, on his own terms, even as we are never sure exactly what has constituted that success.

One of the most entertaining running gags in the show is the succession of eccentric characters to whom he rents the room of his initial apartment mate, the irritatingly anal Nathan (somewhat overplayed by Daniel MacIvor) who lands himself in prison in the first episode and spends the rest of the series growing into his identity as 'The Cat Food Killer.' From a gang of Thai smugglers to a cat-goddess-worshipping new-age loonie (played by McKellar's wife Tracy Wright), an overly studious young Indian engineering student, and a pair of neo-Nazi youths who end up declaring their love for one another, there is one common denominator in the room: a poster on the wall from the 1993 film *Thirty Two Short Films about Glenn Gould*, co-written by McKellar with Quebecois film-maker François Girard. It's a nice shout out to one of the landmarks of Canadian cinema in the nineties, but it's also a more complex allusion to a figure who is, as Darrell Varga argues, 'the urtext of Canadian cultural nationalism' in a film that is 'arguably, even today, still the most widely known and identifiably Canadian film ever made.'[86] For Varga, what makes Gould so significant and the film so important is the demonstration of 'how a character such as Gould is formed out of a system of relations among space, place, conditions of work and exchange, and the production of value. He is both a significant icon of Canada and a text that can be read against the grain of cultural nationalism.'[87] Rather than the 'tendency of nationalist cultural criticism to naturalize specific spatial relations in the idealization of an aesthetic canon,' Varga argues that the impressionistic, episodic, and generically hybrid structure of *Thirty Two Short Films* grounds Canadian identity in the intersection between local specificity and the global circulation of goods and images.[88] It is significant in this context that *Thirty Two Short Films*, and the English-Canadian/French-Canadian collaboration initiated by the producers, Rhombus Media, produced the single English-language inclusion in the Montreal paper *La Presse*'s 2007 list of the fifty best Quebecois films.[89] The decade of the nineties not only saw Canadian cinema widely and publicly exposed internationally *as such* for the first time in its history, but it also saw its television production become a global force for the first time, as production companies like Alliance, Atlantis, Nelvana, and Cinar began churning out shows to sell to the many new cable networks.[90] The leap in production affected English-Canadian product as much as Quebecois, and in a way it realized the 'global village' prediction of Canadian cultural critic Marshall McLuhan decades earlier; it also suggested a new application of the 'non-linear and multi-layered approach to art and ideas' Varga sees as characteristic of Gould, McLuhan, and Girard and McKellar's film.[91] No longer characterized as the embodiment of a spatially based, highly localized, and unitary national identity, Canadianness, especially for the film-makers of production centre Toronto, had to be sought in the interplay between the local and the global, in particular, in the way the local could appropriate as its own the apparently reductive tropes of global, American-derived culture.

Within a global market of proliferating media forms, stardom becomes a complex negotiation quite different from the dualities of Bujold's and Laure's careers. Like most of the Ontario new wave, McKellar's career reached a certain peak by the end of the nineties. The new century's *Childstar*, although benefiting from the gorgeous cinematography of Quebecois auteur André Turpin, was a financial and artistic disappointment, the broad strokes of its comic allegory of cultural imperialism often shading into facile comedy and its viciously clever self-consciousness coming off as navel-gazing to the detriment of its many qualities. And while McKellar showed himself still capable of brilliant work, as in the Rhombus backstage comedy series *Slings and Arrows* (2003–6, Peter Wellington), he just as often fell back on one-dimensional versions of his patented persona, as in his shrill turn as a New York cellist dying of AIDS in Thom Fitzgerald's *The Event* (2003), or the nebbish who gains a dubious victory over a trio of masseuses in Soo Lyu's *Rub & Tug* (2002). McKellar was consumed for much of the first decade of the twenty-first century with the screenplay adaptation of José Saramago's novel *Blindness* (2008, Fernando Meirelles); he re-emerged in 2011 as co-creator and director of the 'offbeat' CBC therapy sitcom *Michael: Tuesdays and Thursdays*. A multinational co-production, like McKellar's second Girard collaboration, *The Red Violin* (1998), *Blindness* was also, like *Violin*, a fascinating but ultimately deadened film, full of talent and moving imagery but lacking the cohesion that had been so striking in the films of the nineties, or for that matter, in Polley's *Away from Her*. But perhaps we are looking for the wrong qualities. While *Away from Her* is a textbook example of the way a small, local film can assume international relevance without sacrificing its specificity, *The Red Violin* and *Blindness* started out as abstract allegories of international networks, and so it is only fitting that their mode of production mirrors those allegories. As Brenda Longfellow argues of *The Red Violin*, its plot can be read as a 'cautionary tale regarding the way in which artistic vision is complexly negotiated and modulated within the context of a market-driven international co-production.'[92] If the hellish and Hobbesian world of the barracks in which the blind victims of a mysterious virus are relegated by the nameless authorities suggests, especially in Brazilian director Meirelles's vision of the film, an image of unfettered global capitalism, then the select community of survivors invited into the house of the middle-aged couple at the end of the film represents a more utopian image of the way globalization can unite a like-minded collection of individuals proofed by fire. Like Kirshner's Jenny on the *L Word*, McKellar's character in *Blindness* fails the test early on; in iconic terms, his mealy role in the film is unlikely to win him more attention outside Toronto. On the other hand, the very fact of his ground-level participation in a film of this calibre and commercial profile ratifies McKellar's iconic status as English Canada's pre-eminent collaborator and enabler, now branching out into the global marketplace. It remains to be seen if he will retain his core of Kensington's Curtis, that is, if he can overcome the agoraphobia.

There are no easy answers to the question of Canada's icons. The very fact that they have become visible first *as* Canadians dooms them to the paradoxes of Canadian culture. And yet the very fact of their survival and flourishing within the multiple identities necessary to make it in Canadian entertainment, or outside it without losing some sense of home, is testimony to the unprecedented existence of some kind of Canadian identity within their personas. It is not accidental, I think, that Polley, the star who has most flourished, is the one who spent the most time languishing in television. No longer hard-core hold outs or invisible Canadians, the faces of contemporary Canadian cinema suggest that the only way out of the iron grip of American pop culture is to pass right through it, transforming it from the inside. The question is how to choose the right path, and the right mode for that transformation.

Chapter Five

Quebecois Auteurs:
The New Internationalism of Jean-Claude Lauzon, Léa Pool, and Robert Lepage

When, after a relatively dormant period during the tax-shelter years, Quebecois cinema regained momentum in the mid-eighties, it had become a far more international movement than the inward-looking decade from the mid-sixties to the mid-seventies. As Scott MacKenzie has argued, this outward shift was partly a result of 'despair' by left-wing nationalists at the failure of the 1980 referendum to embrace Quebecois sovereignty and a consequent loss of faith in the 'utopian vision' of a 'moment of collective imagination' in which cinema could be integrally and directly involved in radical social change.[1] And while that despair would mark the changing Quebecois industry in various ways, it would also open up new possibilities. Not only was one of the key new auteurs – Léa Pool – a recent immigrant from Switzerland and thus an outsider to the dramatic events of the run-up to 1980, not to mention those of the prior decades, but the economics of production had changed, with growing companies such as Alliance Communications aggressively pursuing international markets, and new laws in place that facilitated international co-production. Alliance, the largest Canadian production and distribution company, was formed in 1984 in Toronto by Uruguayan-Hungarian emigrant Robert Lantos, Quebecois film-maker and producer Denis Héroux, and others.[2] It acquired Montreal-based francophone company Viva Communications in 1990, merged with Atlantis Communications in 1998, and was itself acquired by CanWest Global Communications in 2007.[3] Similar to the earlier Cinépix (see chapter 2) in its disregard of conventional distinctions of language, genre, or quality, although with a wider range of investment reflecting the gamut of Canadian cinema since the eighties, the company epitomizes an ecumenical approach to Canadian cinema. Alliance (later Alliance Atlantis) produced French- and English-language films, cinema, and television, small-scale art films and big-budget commercial product, and ranged in appeal from family friendly to exploitation. The new internationalism was also visible in a different aesthetic. Many film-makers, especially those who had achieved visibility outside the confines of the province, moved away from the documentary realism that had been the benchmark of the previous generation and towards a more mixed style, influenced especially by the playful and experimental attitude of the French new wave, the glossy visuals of the eighties French cinéma du look, and the formal games of postmodernism. Cultural references, too, began to incorporate the global lingua franca of pop music, abandoning the common pretence that the only music listened to by Quebecois was their own. It was a set of choices dictated both by shifting industrial and economic paradigms and by individual visions, and its results were decidedly mixed, but it was certainly the defining feature of Quebecois cinema at the end of the twentieth century. Along with the resurgence of Denys Arcand (see chapter 3), three influential new figures emerged out of a more general trend during the second half of the eighties to re-establish Quebec as an internationally significant national cinema: the enfant terrible Jean-Claude Lauzon, the Swiss émigré Léa Pool, and the postmodernist dramaturge Robert Lepage.

Jean-Claude Lauzon in the Extreme

> When I make a film, I do not judge myself against what is being done here; I think of the cinema of Wenders, Godard, and Bertolucci. It is at the international level that the competition must take place. For me, every time one judges a film that aspires to a professional quality, it must be weighed against contemporary cinema, and the cinema at this time is Spike Lee and David Lynch.
>
> Jean-Claude Lauzon (1992)

Pool's film-making is predicated on her status as a socially, sexually, and stylistically liminal outsider figure; Lepage's on the globetrotting lifestyle and aesthetics of a world-class dramatist. In his brief but brilliant career in feature films, Lauzon (1953–97) established himself equally as an outsider; however, he did so by exploding the categories of Quebecois identity from within instead of from without. A hyperbolically macho amalgam of coureur de bois and rebel film-maker deeply invested in the issues of linguistic and political sovereignty, Lauzon simultaneously embraced an international film culture and the cutting-edge image-making of the publicity industry. Not surprisingly, the two features he completed in his brief career are self-consciously seamed with the contradictions of post-referendum Quebec, wildly and imaginatively melding genres and traditions to create something no one either locally or globally had ever seen before. *Un zoo la nuit* (*Night Zoo*, 1987) jarringly combined a violent postmodern policier with the sentimental tale of the reconciliation of a son with his dying father; it opened the Directors' Fortnight at Cannes and received a record thirteen Genie awards. A temperamental perfectionist, Lauzon did not make another movie for five years, when the coming-of-age film *Léolo* (1992) played in official competition at Cannes and was widely praised as one of the year's ten best films. Lauzon, for whom film-making was an ordeal as well as only one among his many interests, never made another feature, dying before the age of forty when the bush plane he was piloting with his girlfriend, television personality Marie-Soleil Tougas, crashed while returning from a hunting expedition in the north country of Quebec.

Lauzon self-identified as an outsider and outlaw throughout his life; even when his stature as a film-maker allowed him the opportunity of 'going straight,' he refused, turning down numerous offers from Hollywood, including a contract with Disney.[4] Instead, he insisted that he had 'only four or five films inside him,' had already made two of them, and while waiting until the next one became so painful that it would force its way out, he would do what he actually liked doing instead: hunting, fishing, flying, and diving.[5] The son of a working-class Montreal family with a Native grandfather, Lauzon spent his adolescence as a delinquent in the urban underworld, hanging out in the company of bank robbers and Hells Angels. But when a teacher gave NFB director André Petrowski a copy of the film sixteen-year-old Lauzon had made just before dropping out of school, the film-maker took him under his wing, for all practical purposes adopting him as his namesake André Bazin had done with the delinquent François Truffaut.[6] Fiercely intelligent and highly ambitious, the young Lauzon was no callow backwoods yokel, however; his long-time work-for-hire shooting commercials – which he claimed, half seriously and half mockingly, to prefer to the torment of making features – not only supported his lifestyle and allowed him to be choosy about his film-making decisions, but had made him technically proficient and self-confident before he made his first film: '[It] brings a foreign perspective to reassure you that your way of seeing things is worthwhile. Shooting commercials also speeded up my evolution with regard to composition … [C]ommercials have the advantage of allowing you to try certain technical things … If you know what it means to ask for such and such a shot, you can stick to it, but you can also plan your day and let technique take its place below certain important factors, like the quality of the acting, for example. In other words, advertising is a big 'plaything' for teaching how to work.'[7] Especially for a director single-mindedly obsessed with bringing a personal vision to the screen, the commercial constraints of the publicity industry permitted a technical apprenticeship relatively free of the financial pressures of novice independent film-making, especially in a global marketplace in which more and more of a premium was being placed on technical proficiency and stylistic innovation.

It is difficult to underestimate the influence of the publicity industry on feature film-making in Quebec since the eighties. While the first generation had come of age in the NFB and the ferment of the sixties, the post–Quiet Revolution film-makers grew up under the liberal rule of the Parti Québécois and a fully modernized media culture.[8] The way through commercials was paved by Arcand, although he made his ambivalence towards the economic necessity clear in the satirical sequence in *Jésus de Montréal* where Daniel 'rescues' Mireille (Catherine Wilkening) from the sexist, demeaning, and idiotic clutches of a beer commercial shoot. Even Arcand, however, conceded the technical proficiency he received from the experience (see chapter 3). For the next generation, the ambivalence was diminished, as the publicity industry, the new music-video industry, and the traditional feature film industry had become far more integrated. Pool supported herself making commercials, and key younger figures André Turpin (b. 1965) and Denis Villeneuve (b. 1967) unproblematically brought a video aesthetic and cutting-edge technology to such stylish features as Villeneuve's *Un 32 Août sur terre* (1998) and *Maelström* (2000), and Turpin's *Un crabe dans la tête* (2001); all three films were shot by Turpin, as were McKellar's *Childstar* (2004) and others. As contemporary director Erik Canuel recounts: 'My path required 200 ads, 50 videos and 30 hours of American series because, unfortunately, I did not get an opportunity here.'[9] The result of Canuel's career path was an accomplished run of locally coloured action thrillers, including the action comedy *Le Loi du cochon* (2001), the heist drama *Le dernier tunnel* (2004), the 'two solitudes' policier and box office record-breaking *Bon Cop Bad Cop* (2007), the dark comedy *Cadavres* (2009), and the award-winning Toronto-based CBS and CTV action drama *Flashpoint* (2008–) – but there is no critical profile to date.

Arcand's fable in *Jésus* of the encroachment of an international postmodernity into the just recently modernized landscape of Montreal announced the failure of local autonomy and the triumph of globalization. At the same time, the cutting-edge theatrical production of the Passion play that drives the film, itself derived from the international techniques of a new postmodern theatre, appropriating, in other words, new non-local forms as a way of articulating new local issues. By the time of Turpin and Villeneuve, the new-media culture would be firmly and unconflictedly in place; for Lauzon, as for Arcand and, as we shall see, Lepage, who made his acting debut in *Jésus*, it was precisely the interplay between tradition and postmodernity that would drive their film-making. Where Arcand and Lepage would put the play of postmodern artifice in the forefront, Lauzon internalized the new techniques as a way of processing a more personal, less openly analytical vision of Quebec. Consequently, Lauzon was 'invariably irritated' by the constant comparisons of *Zoo* with the cinéma du look of Jean-Jacques Beineix's global hit policier *Diva* (1981) and Luc Besson's portrait of underground Paris culture in *Subway* (1985), declaring flatly: 'Those movies are empty.'[10] Nevertheless, whether the comparison was positive, as when Jay Scott remarked that *Zoo* 'makes the technically awesome *Diva* seem technically flat-footed,' or condemnatory, as when an uncomprehending Vincent Canby quipped that Lauzon had 'overdosed on a double bill of *Diva* and one of those television dramas of the 1950s that ends with the line, "I love you, Pop,"' it accurately clued into Lauzon's key innovation, which was to localize the international aesthetic of the new French cinema. Lauzon took the genre-bending, slick visuals, stylized violence, and video sensibility of music as a central element and adapted them to the constraints of a quintessentially Quebecois narrative.

His films thus function simultaneously as brutal yet seductive international art films and as provocative commentaries on local identity, just as Lauzon saw himself simultaneously as a dyed-in-the-wool coureur de bois cum working-class hero and as an international auteur on the level of art-film idols such as Wenders, Bertolucci, Godard, Lee, and Lynch. So the violent and sexually explicit set pieces that punctuate both films – the homosexual rape that opens *Zoo*, the near rape of Marcel's girlfriend turned prostitute that defines their relationship, and the shooting of an elephant in a zoo that seals the reconciliation between Marcel and his dying father; the masturbation, pederasty, and zoophilia that define Léo Lozeau's sexuality in *Léolo* – are simultaneously an attention-grabbing calling card establishing Lauzon on the world stage and thematically essential to the argument of each film. Similarly, the highly disjunctive genre pairing of *Zoo* and the surrealistic subversion of the coming-of-age film in *Léolo* may have emerged from the cinematic postmodernism of the eighties, but they also commented directly on issues of Quebecois identity.

In *Zoo*, as Bill Marshall has argued, the 'gay-baiting' prison rape, a 'birthday present' sent to Marcel by a pair of (English-Canadian) crooked cops he conned in a drug deal, serves to free the final scene, where Marcel cleanses his father's naked body and then climbs naked into bed with his father, from any possible 'taint' of homosexuality.[11] For Marshall, this structuring device speaks directly to a political allegory in which 'the "feminization" of the conquered Québec is reversed so that it is the English Canadian, and the "fédéraste" pro-Canadian Québécois such as [former prime minister Pierre] Trudeau, who are tainted with (passive) homosexuality.'[12] It is a persuasive reading of the way sexual politics allegorize national identity, but certainly not the only issue at work in the film's hallucinatory structure. Marshall equally relates the film's thematics to a working-class impotence faced with globalization – Albert lost his job when a factory migrated south to the United States.[13] For Lauzon, such meanings emerge simply because of his uncensored attempt to portray a social truth, a 'reality' seldom glimpsed as such on screen, saying, 'The way the character in the movie is about women and homosexuals, well, I was making a movie about a character who lives that way. There are too many films where people are afraid of what is real.'[14] Lauzon's conception of cinematic truth is strongly indebted to the Quiet Revolution location of identity in the countryside and to its depiction of the city as a site of representational options but problematic identity. The drug plot is shot in a stylized night-time highly reminiscent, if much grittier than, the underworld Paris of *Diva*, complete with a trendy loft apartment and riverside view, termed by Scott a 'photogenic smoky expressionism.'[15] This style contrasts strongly with the scenes with Albert in Italian Montreal and in the country, shot by veteran Quebecois cinematographer Guy Dufaux 'according to the dominant Québec realist style with painterly, rich, Brault-like flourishes for the fishing sequence.'[16] In his perceptive review of the film, Scott notes the way Lauzon refuses either to reconcile one plot with the other or to assert their independence in a postmodern play of possibilities; rather, he argues, 'therein lies the true subversiveness of *Zoo*: the accepted North American wisdom that morality is founded in the family … is rejected. There is plenty wrong with Marcel's morality from society's standpoint, but there is nothing wrong with his relationship to his father.'[17] While the fishing trip rehearses a perfect nostalgia of rural Quebecois masculinity, the key scene of the film, when it renders literal what we had assumed was merely an 'urban jungle' metaphor in the title, provides a far more hybrid, and undeniably contemporary, space. Sneaking his father out of an anonymous hospital room, Marcel puts him in a wheelchair, gives him a snort of cocaine, and breaks into the local zoo so Albert can shoot a moose before he dies. Absurdly, there is no moose, so they shoot an elephant. Marcel takes Albert home, where he can boast to his friend Tony, 'I was hunting, with Marcel.' It is a brilliantly played scene, perfectly balancing queasy sentimentality, animal-lover baiting, and genuine emotional power with a sustained destabilization of the classic Quebecois binaries of wilderness/urbanism and reality/artifice. Moreover, as Jim Leach suggests, there is some question whether the entire scene has been imagined.[18] As we shall see with Pool, Lauzon skilfully wields the tropes of melodrama to localize, individualize, and render emotionally credible the cold and empty imagery of contemporary art film and the cinéma du look. Where both film-making trends consciously mimed the vacuous superficiality of contemporary media culture, Lauzon, like Pool and Lepage, placed that international artifice in a local context to argue for its effectiveness as a tool for articulating contemporary identity.

In an interview at the time of the release of *Léolo*, Lauzon repudiated the policier thread of his first film, claiming: 'All that has stayed with me from *Un zoo la nuit* is the scene where the guy washes his father. When I began to write *Léolo*, I said to myself I would like to succeed in making a film in which there would be the same lyricism and poetry without being obliged to pass through the explanatory side that there was in that film; that is to say, the dramatic plot, the villains, the good guys, the money, the crime thriller.'[19] *Léolo* integrated the international and local threads into a single seamless flow, eschewing plot in favour of imagery. Nevertheless, Lauzon still relied heavily on genre conventions, in this case the quintessentially Canadian tradition of the coming-of-age film, whose deeply familiar stages provide structure to the otherwise stream-of-consciousness form even as the substance of the events recorded subverts the meaning of those stages. *Léolo* is simultaneously an autobiographical account of the making of a Quebecois filmmaker and a powerful argument for the impossibility of the making of a filmmaker within the conventional identity formation of Quebec. It is symptomatic that most viewers and critics regard the final image of young Léo submerged in an ice bath in the same sanatorium that contains the rest of his family as an image of failure, while Lauzon insisted on regarding it as 'a liberation' of 'the power of the imagination' evident in the writings that provide the text of the film's voice-over narration.[20]

In this sense, the written and read text of an independent artist would somehow trump the visual imagery that carries the national allegory. This split is emphasized by casting two iconic figures of Quebecois identity in their feature film debuts in roles which pointedly silence their most identifiable characteristics. Lauzon persuaded the often inflammatory separatist politician Pierre Bourgault to play the 'Word Tamer,' a mainly silent figure whose primary task is to preserve and read Léo's diary.[21] He cast forty-five-year-old star chanteuse Ginette Reno as the family matriarch, but we never hear her sing a word.[22] As Melnyk puts it, 'A film in which Québec's leading separatist is silenced, a muscular brother cowers before an Anglo half his size, most of the francophones are insane, [and] the music is non-Québec ... cannot be anything else but an allegory of a national identity crisis.'[23] And the consensus is that the film is a brutal allegory of the dysfunctional Quebecois 'family,' the nurturing if suffocating mother the only stable point, the father anally obsessed, and the grandfather the murderous source of hereditary insanity. Lauzon himself rejected a straight allegorical reading, instead insisting that '*Léolo* does not have the flag draped all over it ... [Léo] has only to open his cupboard to be somewhere else.'[24] Like *Zoo*, issues of Quebecois identity are embedded within *Léolo*, but they are embedded insomuch as they are a feature of the child's reality rather than as a more explicitly allegorical reading such as we find, for example, in the figure of Benoît in *Mon oncle Antoine* (see chapter 1). Lauzon's argument is that these are not ideological but ontological issues, and the family is not so much an allegorical representation of Quebec as it is a poetic image of his own life. Similarly, there is also a very adult playfulness in Lauzon's exerting his power as a film-maker over iconic figures such as Bourgault and Reno, as if to say that he is so much in control of his craft that he can incorporate them seamlessly as actors within the diegesis of his film *without* needing to have recourse to their extra-diegetic status. In allegorical terms, if you will, he can tear them away from their accustomed meaning and insert them within the more powerful logic of his own vision. As Christine Ramsay puts it, 'Pathologizing Québec's cultural elite in this highly blown and controversial way thus gives baroque artistic expression to a very complex personal and cultural reality.'[25] Lauzon can recognize the potential for national allegory without being subject to its pull, just as he can depict the apparent failure of Léo to achieve subjecthood without feeling that his character has actually succumbed.

Marshall astutely sees in the film's trajectory a repudiation of the typically liberal coming-of-age tale, especially the *contes pour tous*, a series of feature films inaugurated in 1984 by Quebec producer Rock Demers (who was, in a nice coincidence, honoured with a special award the same night *Zoo* swept the Genies): 'The liberal (non-sexist, non-racist, multicultural, and individualistic) world of the films and the reconciliation of their narratives hinge on processes of identification, recognition, and belonging which make links between the family and friendship formations depicted and the wider society.'[26] In contrast to this narrative of successful accession to a functional and non-repressive society, *Léolo* charts its protagonist's progression almost exclusively in transgressive bodily terms: beginning with his retentive refusal to cooperate with his father's requirement of daily bowel movements, Léo moves through masturbating in a piece of raw liver, spying on his older neighbour Bianca (Giuditta del Vecchio) as she sexually services his grandfather, passively participating in the sodomizing of a cat, and 'betraying' Bianca with a local prostitute. The perversity and proactive nature of Léo's behaviour also differentiate him from what Leach has remarked as the 'familiar motif' in Quebecois cinema of 'a child viewing, and judging, the adult world.'[27] While obsessively the locus of development, the body also proves itself resistant to any fundamental change, most pitifully in the saga of Léo's older brother Fernand, tormented by an Anglo hoodlum. Fernand spends much of the film single-mindedly beefing up his body until he has transformed himself into a muscle-bound hulk (played, at this point, by bodybuilder Yves Montmarquette). In the most viscerally violent moment of the film, the bully once again beats him to a pulp. Similarly, when early in the film Léo's grandfather tries to drown the young boy after being splashed, the point of view shifts to a stunning underwater swim after treasure, and when Léo later reciprocates with a complex contraption designed to strangle his grandfather in the bathtub, he is equally unsuccessful, landing in the hospital. The physical world is a fact of life, but it is also wholly unworthy of attention as such, because only the mind is able to effect any change in identity. As George Toles suggests in a fine analysis of the film's opening shot, the camera begins by establishing the 'drab markers of poverty and confinement' that define Léo's socio-economic background in Mile End, barely registering the six-year-old in cowboy regalia, before widening out to reveal 'a space that is alive with everyday beauty,' an 'enchanted corner of the yard' that represents the 'only spot' and the 'only angle' that allows

5.1. The opening shot of *Léolo* (1992) establishes the historicity of an otherwise highly fantastic film. Photofest.

the setting to 'release its power to console.'[28] Toles suggests that the point of view of this shot is established as belonging to the memory of the older child we soon glimpse writing at his desk; what is certain is that the vision of the camera consistently maintains a vantage point that shows us the sordid reality of the family's life while simultaneously letting us see the unmoored truth that can also be glimpsed there. The movement beyond the biographical is heightened when we know that the facade with which the shot begins is that of the house in which Lauzon himself grew up (figure 5.1).

The verbal and the textual thus exist in a wholly distinct realm from the physical. As Leach observes, the film demands that the viewer be unusually 'alert to how the images relate to the music and to the different levels of narration.'[29] And, indeed, the frequency with which critics disagree about simple facts in the movie (the chronology, the status of the 'reality' of certain episodes, the ending) suggests the degree to which Lauzon successfully sabotaged a traditional narrative structure. Nevertheless, there is structure; what happens is that it enters into the film as text, physically – most notably when the Word Tamer leaves a book in Léo's unlettered household, which Léo only discovers much later in the kitchen, where it is propping up the table. The book is Réjean Ducharme's classic novel of Quiet Revolution rebellion, *L'avalée des avalés* (1967, translated as *The Swallower Swallowed*, but just as easily made to mean 'The Valley of the Vanquished').[30] Its appearance further disrupts the traditional linearity of a coming-of-age tale, whose meaning relies on our ability to trace the development of the subject. Itself the story of a girl who creates an imaginary world and language to escape from her oppressive family, *L'avalée des avalés* pulls the otherwise clearly established 1950s setting of the film into a later epoch.[31] But then, as Leach notes, the geographically and temporally eclectic selection of music equally 'works against a firm sense of historic time.'[32]

Lauzon made clear in interviews how essential his conception of the music was to the film; indeed, the music was all written into the original screenplay.[33] Not only is the selection international, but it ranges from anglophone rock (the Rolling Stones' 'You Can't Always Get What You Want' and a pair of Tom Waits songs) to the chansons of Jacques Brel to sacred song and contemporary world music.[34] Tony Simons maintains that 'each of these musical pieces has its own identity and originates in a specific cultural environment, but all of them are integrated into the film, assimilated as so many parts of a background music. Because the events depicted on the screen do not refer to them, they simply evoke a very general context of cultural or geographical alterity.'[35] Lauzon's selection is a programmatic declaration in favour of the hybrid form of 'world' music; as Simons notes of the Greek Catholic nun Marie Keyrouz – who has devoted her career to resurrecting ancient Oriental Christian chants, and whose shimmeringly gorgeous 'Halleluia' plays over the film's mental hospital scenes – song expresses cultural difference and identity while also providing a medium whereby to transcend those very differences.[36] So while nearly all of the selections made by Lauzon mix traditions and time periods – even in the case of 'You Can't Always Get What You Want,' Lauzon chose the opening chorus sung by the unaccompanied London Bach Choir – they also create what Lauzon termed a 'lyric' effect, a 'kind of aura' that would make the excess of many of the scenes seem 'more sacred instead of … vulgar.'[37] Resolutely contemporary in its eclecticism and in many of the recordings chosen, the music constitutes not simply a background, but a bona fide further layer to the narration, as if Lauzon were reproducing the atmosphere in which he wrote the script, the atmosphere within which the horrors and despair he depicts could somehow, despite all appearances, conclude in liberation. Toles has best captured the lyricism of the soundtrack as it works against the narrative drive towards catatonic withdrawal. Describing the effect of Bianca's song (performed by the actress herself) at the conclusion of the film, Toles writes that, 'All the accumulated tensions of Leo's mind and body, including the fact of his romantic longing for Bianca, are dissolved in the music, without the necessity of anything having to be denied.'[38]

It is instructive to compare Lauzon's conceptual and lyrical use of soundtrack music to the similarly reflective deployment of it by Jean-Marc Vallée in his own coming-of-age film, *C.R.A.Z.Y.* (2005). Like Lauzon, whose *Léolo* was a strong influence, Vallée wrote the music into his screenplay; however, unlike Lauzon, Vallée did not have the commercial clout to get his producer to put up the money to acquire the rights for big-ticket items such as the Stones' 'Sympathy for the Devil,' David Bowie's 'Space Oddity,' and Pink Floyd's 'Shine On You Crazy Diamond' and 'The Great Gig in the Sky.' So deeply was Vallée invested in the film's music program that he put up the $600,000 rights fee out of his own pocket. Like *Léolo* a story of generational conflict, *C.R.A.Z.Y.* is set in the seventies, at the other side of the Quiet Revolution, and the fact that the father, too, is allowed to self-identify through pop music (Patsy Cline and Charles Aznavour, in particular) suggests the gentler, if still rough-edged approach of Vallée towards his material and characters. Vallée's music is predominantly diegetic, as both father and son articulate their identities through music. Not only does the rootless modernity of rock music represent an escape from the strict categories of local Quebecois identity, but Vallée suggests that for Zachary's father as well, the countrified Cline and the Parisian Armenian Aznavour equally represent an escape from the mundane and stultifying life of lower-middle-class Montreal – his signature song is 'Emmenez-moi' (Take me away). One of the most commercially successful films in Quebecois history, *C.R.A.Z.Y.* used the global signifiers of pop music as a way of articulating both the limits to and the necessity of local identity. Although nearly as visually inventive and darkly humorous as *Léolo*, Vallée's film has a much more conventional narrative structure, casting its hero far away from his home and his conservative family before reeling him back in for a final reconciliation, comfortably settled into his gay as well as his Quebecois identity. *Léolo* is far more modernist in its approach to identity, finding solace only in art. Nevertheless, the autobiographical substrate of the film and Lauzon's intense insistence on a vision of poetic truth ensure that, physically, it never strays too far from home, even as, in imagination, it roams freely through time and space. What Jay Scott wrote after seeing *Zoo* at Cannes – '[It] is a movie of extremes; few films in the history of the cinema have wandered so successfully over so much of the emotional map' – is equally characteristic of *Léolo*. 'Extremes' is also an accurate assessment of Lauzon's impact on Canadian cinema: not as a model to be emulated so much as a figure who split wide open the narrow confines about what a Quebecois – and a contemporary Canadian – film could look like.[39]

Léa Pool between Identities

> People said that people from Montreal would never shoot like that. And I'm sure that a Swiss filmmaker wouldn't shoot Switzerland as I filmed it – It's shot from the point of view of somebody who's strange to the place.
>
> Léa Pool (1991)

Similar to her Toronto contemporary Atom Egoyan, Pool (b. 1950) first made her mark internationally during the mid-eighties with a series of carefully structured, intellectually challenging, and self-consciously representational features. Achieving limited theatrical release, these films were primarily received on the festival circuit and by critics and academics intrigued to encounter new films that seemed in sync with cutting-edge theoretical questions of mediation, sexuality, and cross-cultural identity. While neither film-maker ever wholly abandoned the concerns that dominated early critical attention towards their work, the practice of both Egoyan and Pool inexorably shifted during the nineties towards a more accessible, emotionally direct, and story-driven film-making style.[40] Also like Egoyan (born in Egypt to Armenian parents), Pool was an outsider in her adopted homeland. Raised in the town of Soglio in southeastern Switzerland near the Italian border, Pool was working as a teacher in Geneva when she was accepted to study at the

American Film Institute. The Swiss government refused to fund her career change ('In Switzerland when you have a job, you don't change: you have that job until you die'), and the twenty-five-year-old Pool decided to move to North America anyway, settling in Montreal, where she has lived ever since. Following the micro-budget hour-long black-and-white *Strass Café* (1980), Pool's first two full-length feature films, *La femme de l'hôtel* (1984) and *Anne Trister* (1986) won festival awards and quickly established Pool as a redoubtable Quebecois auteur and a force within the new feminist cinema.

The first film traces the relationship between a creatively blocked Jewish film-maker (Paule Baillargeon), a drifting photographer with whom she becomes obsessed (Louise Marleau), and the actress playing the singer undergoing a crisis in the film-maker's project (Marthe Turgeon). In the second film, a Swiss-Jewish trompe l'oeil painter, Anne (French actress Albane Guilhe), buries her father in Israel before coming to Montreal, where she becomes deeply attracted to a psychologist (Marleau) who is treating a rebellious ten-year-old girl (Lucie Laurier) whose situation mirrors Anne's. The two films broke the mould of Quebecois cinema in a number of ways. First of all, the issues of identity with which they are concerned are existential and individual rather than explicitly Quebecois, a fact emphasized by the depiction of the central characters as rootless outsiders.[41] Their focus on same-sex desire – implicit in the first film, explicit in the second – and triangular relationships diverged from the still conservative sexual politics of Quebecois society and cinema. Moreover, Pool's preference for irresolvable triangular relationships rather than the conventionally romantic dyad further questions the stability of normative definitions of sexuality and relationships. They use their settings – Pool's early films were all filmed on location in Montreal – to establish a broadly modernist sense of urban alienation rather than a local sense of familiarity.[42] Nevertheless, she does not so much repudiate the specificity of Quebecois Montreal as place its specificity firmly within an international artistic and philosophical context.

Pool's early films are classically auteurist, stylistically and thematically consistent from one to the next. Fundamental to this consistency is what Bill Marshall terms 'a radical, deterritorializing departure for Québec national cinema, so preoccupied with constructing notions of the "home."'[43] For Marshall, the Jewish identity of Pool's characters captures 'that undecidable relationship between exile and homeland, instability and stability'; he relates this thematic to the imagery of characters in flight, and of children who can embody 'that propertyless play of past and future, loss and creativity.'[44] Jennifer Gauthier similarly stresses Pool's focus on 'liminality and states of transition,' while also calling attention to her powerful sense of place and recourse to a feminist conception of 'embodied knowledge.'[45] Part of the power of Pool's films derives from the tension between their abstract, non-narrative formal structure and the emotional intensity of the characters and their relationships. Similarly, while her dialogue can be at times portentous and banal and her situations sentimental and melodramatic, she consistently draws riveting performances from her actors, almost as if underlining the importance of the physical and material over the verbal and abstract as a source of knowledge and meaning. Consequently, even Pool's early films cannot be reduced to or even mined solely for their ideas; it is only in the often inchoate interaction of character and environment that those ideas take form, as Pool combines the visual and theoretical austerity of seventies art cinema with the emotionality and relational focus of popular women's genres such as melodrama. The highly autobiographical content of many of Pool's films emphasizes the interaction between the lived and the conceived, even as the foregrounding of images of art and artifice – especially film-making and photography – works against a straightforwardly biographical reading of that content.

Melnyk places Pool firmly in a European tradition, both in terms of a philosophical and epistemological rather than a directly political and social feminism, and in terms of an 'avant-garde, aesthetic, and introspective view of sexuality, [and] a sense of existential angst pervading human life.'[46] And, certainly, there is a lot in her outsider's stance of émigré Parisian intellectuals such as the Bulgarian exile Julia Kristeva, the Algerian Jew Hélène Cixous, and Pool's collaborator, the Canadian-born novelist Nancy Huston, not to mention the Swiss-born film-maker Jean-Luc Godard, to whom Pool pays explicit homage in *Emporte-moi* (1999). We should not disregard Pool's decision to settle in Montreal, however, nor her engagement with the local culture around her. As Gauthier argues, Pool's outsider status allows her to see and to articulate local issues differently, suggesting that the French influence is also a key component of Quebec identity, albeit mixed, especially in her later films, with the influence of American pop culture.[47] Indeed, the austere, brooding melancholy has at least as much in common with Egoyan's eighties films and Lauzon's *Un zoo la nuit* as it does with the exuberantly open form of Godard's new wave films or the slick commercialism of the cinéma du look that arose in eighties France.

In her challenge to the insularity of Quebecois cinema, Pool seems to have opened it up in a variety of ways to the world around it. The interpellation of a broader audience announced, as did Arcand's *Déclin*, that Quebecois cinema should and would reflect the internationalism of the province that had been overshadowed by the Parti Québécois's exclusive focus on francophone identity. Where other Quebecois directors such as Anne Claire Poirier, Mireille Dansereau, and Micheline Lanctôt had polemically (and often brilliantly) focused on the difficult situation of women within the province and the complexities of articulating a specifically local representation of that situation, Pool's own situation and instincts led her in a different direction.[48] Starting with her third feature, *A corps perdu* (*Straight from the Heart*, 1988), Pool took advantage of a new co-production law to reconnect with her Swiss past; her next three features, *La demoiselle sauvage* (1991), *Mouvements du désir* (1994), and *Emporte-moi*, would be co-produced with Switzerland (and, for the last two, France as well). Perhaps in part because displacement and alienation are integral to her vision, Pool managed remarkably well to maintain control over the disparate exigencies of co-production: in particular, multinational actors and settings. In *A corps perdu*, she impressionistically cross-cuts between photographer Pierre Kurwenal's (Swiss actor Matthias Habich) traumatic memories of shooting in Nicaragua with a new project of recording the 'corroding city' of Montreal, the psychic dislocation mirroring the disintegration of a ménage à trois between Kurwenal, David, and Sarah (played by Montreal actors Michel Voïta and Johanne-

Marie Tremblay, respectively), for reasons we never learn. While the resolution of either the personal or the social breakdown is by no means clear, it is evident that the only articulation of what is wrong will come through connecting, rather than ignoring, the disparate parts of the puzzle.

Marshall suggests that Pool's melancholic refusal to participate in the humour and playfulness typical of eighties postmodernism is both a conventionally modernist intellectual stance and a characteristically Quebecois attitude of helplessness in the face of forces beyond one's control exacerbated by a 'post-1980 sense of loss.'[49] And, certainly, Pool's articulation of urban anomie through the conventionally modernist modes of photography and film-making seems less contemporary than Egoyan's investment in video and media technology.[50] Her films have never ceased to be backwards-looking in this sense, even as they often refuse to fill in the personal backstory details we would normally expect to receive about our characters. Unspoken or unarticulated past traumas or crises typically motivate her characters' often incomprehensible actions, so we have simultaneously a powerful being-in-the-present and a strong sense of needing to know what happened without ever being able to. It would be easy to ground this trauma autobiographically in Pool's Polish Jewish father, a writer and Holocaust survivor whose own father was its victim, and her Protestant and emotionally absent mother. Certainly, she made that connection clear in *Emporte-moi*.[51] What is slippery about Pool is the way she destabilizes that connection, so that the autobiographical becomes more a question of emotional impact than of intellectual processing.

Consequently, the Canadian filtering of Pool's European experience has become a constitutive element of her oeuvre. In *Mouvements du désir*, she uses the single but highly mobile setting of a transcontinental VIA Rail train pulling out of Montreal both as an image of the vast interconnectedness of Canada and as a liminal space in which to explore the desire between her three main characters: a single mother (France's Valérie Kaprisky) travelling with her young daughter Charlotte (Jolianne L'Allier-Matteau) to start a new life in Vancouver, and a computer programmer (Quebec's Jean-François Pichette) on his way to meet his girlfriend. The expansive landscape of Canada passes by outside the train, opening up a space simultaneously of the present and excluded from it, and simultaneously of Canada and excluded from it. As Brenda Longfellow remarks, the very historical resonance and project of 'articulating a national social subject' the film evokes with the national symbol of the cross-country railway and the many shots of identifiable Canadian landmarks outside the train windows it also denies by privileging individual desire over that vision; the views are never framed from the point of view of the characters.[52] It is equally a transnational desire, figured as it is through the Hollywood iconography of the train as site of sexuality and romance, doubly emphasized in the casting of international sex symbol Valérie Kaprisky as Catherine and the explicit sex scene that climaxes the film's growing tension.[53] Given that *Mouvements du désir* is 'probably the only post-referendum film originating in Québec filmed outside of the limits of the province,' Longfellow is perhaps overly dismissive of its poetics of nationalism.[54] Or, rather, she knows exactly what she is arguing; for Pool's refusal to concede either the autonomy of Quebec or the unity of Canada can be seen as a pointed argument for the fluidity of social identity and its inability adequately to contain or convey individuality. Hence, Pool's claim that, 'I don't feel I'm Swiss or Quebecer or Canadian or Jewish. It's not that important to me. I make films in Québec and the people who work on the films are from Québec but what I feel when I make a film is making a film. What I feel is not connected to any country.'[55] Newfoundland native William MacGillivray's 1983 feature *Stations* similarly privileges the psychological turmoil of its protagonist, a television journalist making an undesired trip from Vancouver to his home town of St John's, Newfoundland. However, we may chart the distance from Pool's equivocal identity in the fact that MacGillivray not only identifies the external shots with the journalist's camera, but incorporates them into the diegesis: his employer has assigned him to 'produce a documentary of the trip, to capture aspects of the Canadian identity from coast to coast.'[56] While MacGillivray's regional approach uses the journey to stage questions of margin/centre and varieties of national identity (see chapter 8), Pool's perspective problematizes the utility of any identity beyond the personal.

The spatio-temporal disjunction of the immigrant experience translates into a non-linear perception of experience. Speaking of *Emporte-moi*, Pool said, 'I thought that the mixture of my childhood memories with what I received from North America, having lived there for 20 years, was a good combination because it gave me a distance on the subject. I am this child that I was, but I am also this adult who looks at the child through the eye of somebody who lives in North America.'[57] Even in *La demoiselle sauvage*, set in the Swiss Alps, Pool's argument is that the film's conditions of production and her own presence within it retain a refracted form of the Canadian. The remote valley location where Pool filmed the story of a mysterious woman's passage from the apparent murder of an abusive and evidently Canadian lover to her suicide resonated with her own childhood, close to where her family spent its summers.[58] The sense of dislocation felt by the audience confronted with a mute woman (played by Quebecois Patricia Tulasne) who begins the film by crashing her car into a flowing mountain river, simultaneously beautiful, wild, and alien thus refracts the dislocation felt by Pool on returning to her natal land. At the same time, the cast and crew reflect Pool's current Montreal base as well as her international identity. The engineer/caretaker of the dam into which the river and Marianne run is played by Swiss actor Matthias Habich, star of *A corps perdu*; the rest of the cast is a mix of Swiss and Canadian. The screenplay was adapted by Pool and a pair of Quebecois collaborators from a Swiss short story; the cinematography is by French-born but Quebec-based Georges Dufaux, and the rest of the crew was predominantly Canadian. Like Cronenberg, Pool thus pushes the limits of what can be considered a Canadian film, rejecting easy identity politics while also rejecting the equally easy transnational identities offered by global capitalism. Like Cronenberg's, her characters are simultaneously rooted and alienated.

The paradox of rootedness and alienation is most sharply articulated in Pool's best film, *Emporte-moi*, which transposes a number of facts of her own biography onto the story of an adolescent girl's coming of age in the same working-class neighbourhood of Mile End in 1960s Montreal in which Lauzon set *Léolo*. Shot by veteran French cinematographer Jeanne Lapoirie, the film was sound edited and mixed at Godard's studio in Switzerland. It is immersed simultaneously in the French new wave and the Quebecois cinema of the sixties. In preparation for the shoot, Pool and Lapoirie watched a full program of new wave films, including everything by Truffaut and Godard, whose early masterpieces *Les quatre-cent coups* (1959) and *Vivre sa vie* (1962) play a key roles in *Emporte-moi*. Like Lauzon's *Léolo*, also an important influence, Pool's film combines Montreal locations with a surrealist style and an improvisational, episodic structure. But the film opens in echt Quebecois documentary realism territory, with thirteen-year-old Hanna (the remarkable debut of Karine Vanasse) visiting her Quebecois grandmother (Monique Mercure) in the countryside. After the opening image introduces an impressionistic motif of water, blood from the swimming Hanna's first period swirling among the stones, the scene moves inside, where the grandmother provides the terrified girl with a typically opaque conservative Catholic explanation for what has just happened. The stylistic debt of this sequence to Quebecois realism is emphasized by the presence of Quiet Revolution icon Mercure as well as by the documentary touch of Carl Henenbert-Faulkner as Hanna's Down's-syndrome Uncle Martin, the only one in the house with whom she is able to connect. On the one hand, Pool establishes a classically Quebecois country/city dichotomy; on the other hand, she disrupts that dichotomy in two ways: first by having Martin break the tension at the family table by turning on the radio and dancing with Hanna to pop single, 'Runaround Sue,' and then by showing Hanna hitchhiking back to the city on the back of a motorcycle, 'Mockingbird' playing over the soundtrack. For the young Hanna and for us, the international language of pop music and iconography of pop culture signify relief or escape from the alienated and repressive confinement of local tradition.

Pool goes further by making Hanna a literal hybrid: her withdrawn and suicidal mother is played by Quebecois icon Pascale Bussières, while her moody father, a failed poet and Holocaust survivor, is played by Serbian actor Miki Manojlovic, internationally known for his roles in the films of Serbian auteur Emir Kusturica. The Montreal Jewish community portrayed with fine texture by Pool resonates with the use of the same setting in Ted Kotcheff's *The Apprenticeship of Duddy Kravitz* (1974) even as it equally resonates with *Léolo*'s depiction of the Italian-Canadian community of Mile End. By casting the cosmopolitan novelist (and co-scenarist) Nancy Huston as the sympathetic teacher in Hanna's traditional Catholic school, Pool equally confuses easy categories, just as Hanna does when introducing herself to the class in terms of the indefinability of her social identity, especially as her parents are unmarried.[59] Given this context, it is not surprising that Hanna has recourse not to the revised identity of emerging Quiet Revolution Quebec but to the international mediascape as a response to her adolescent confusion. As Pool has said of herself, 'By the time I was eighteen, I was not too wild or clever, but I was already a fan of Jean-Luc Godard.'[60] So, too, is Hanna, who falls for Anna Karina's portrayal of Nana, a woman who leaves her family, eventually falls into prostitution, and defines herself in terms of existential freedom: 'Whatever I do, I am responsible.' That she is senselessly gunned down at the end of the film only makes the physically and philosophically glamorous Nana more enticing. Moreover, Hanna's teacher cultivates Anna Karina's look in the film and projects the world-wise persona of new wave icon Jeanne Moreau, easily seducing the callow Hanna into a schoolgirl crush, and near the end of the film, presenting Hanna with the movie camera that will, evidently, rescue her from the self-destructive path on which she is tending.

Confusion over national identity becomes intertwined with sexual confusion, as there is even less place in the former for sexual ambiguity and experimentation than there is for social ambiguity. Here, Pool cannily limns the limitations of the new wave model for her young female protagonist. When the untenable home life pushes her into open rebellion, Hanna attempts to put Nana's cinematic philosophy into action, passing a night of despair that includes a brutally realistic scene where she plays out her prostitution fantasy. The horror of the scene is only mitigated by the juvenile touch of the stray dog Hanna adopts and who accompanies her through her infernal ordeal. While acknowledging its radical power, Pool also acknowledges the cold and unrealistic intellectuality of Godard's creation Nana. There is a further allusion within Hanna's odyssey: to young Antoine Doinel's night away from home on the streets of Paris in Truffaut's *Les quatre-cent coups*. The Paris streets in which the pubescent Antoine (new wave icon Jean-Pierre Léaud in his debut role) briefly pursues an alluringly mysterious older woman (Jeanne Moreau) before stealing a bottle of milk and bathing at sunrise in a fountain are powerfully redolent of adult sexuality but also safe and nurturing, especially in contrast to the hostile environment Antoine encounters indoors at home and at school. While Hanna's home and school environment is problematic, the Montreal streets are hostile and dangerous, and Hanna's night walk concludes in what appears to be the contemplation of suicide, sitting on a bridge at the end of the night. Rather than the boy's easy relationship to even the most monumental aspects of urban space, the girl's glimpses of escape and safety are less fixed and more transitory; they are liminal moments in the spatio-temporality of Montreal and evoked frequently through close-ups of Vanasse's face rather than shots of her within the setting: the feeling of safety, freedom, and comfort we glimpse on her wind-blown features as she hugs a leather-clad stranger on a motorcycle ride into Montreal; the giddy moment she shares with her mother, skating on winter ice; the mysterious figure of a cyclist, riding in circles surrounded by giant shadows, an aleatory appearance amid what appears to be a fixed and tragic life's trajectory. Surprisingly, the intensely triangular relationship between Hanna's older brother (Alexandre Mérineau) and their friend and lover Laura (Charlotte Christeler) is neither a positive nor a negative force in Hanna's life; it is simply a fact within a crisis she must resolve on her own.

The film's conclusion eschews the ambiguity of the freeze-frame close-up that concludes *Les quatre-cent coups* and its Quebecois homologue of young Benoît at the end of Jutra's *Mon oncle Antoine*, both boys caught between an untenable past and an unforeseeable future. But neither does it choose the genre-homage of pointless deaths that punctuate Godard's early films. Instead, Pool has recourse to the mise-en-abyme structuring devices dear to modernism and to the melodramatic tropes of Hollywood women's movies. As Hanna travels by bus to join her mother recuperating from a nervous breakdown at the country home that opened the film, Hanna's teacher lends her a small movie camera, inviting her, so to speak, to displace her multiple identity crises into art, just as Pool's protagonists had done in her first three features. Pool borrows a motif from the new wave – the handheld caméra-stylo (camera-pen) that the novice film-makers argued would allow them to make the cinema into a mode of self-expression rather than a commercial vehicle – and adapts it to the personal strictures of a feminist cinema. The reunion of mother and daughter and the possibility of some form of reconciliation occur mediated through Hanna's camera eye. There is no fixed and stable identity to be recovered in the past or from the past; if at all, it is available only in the liminal space-time embodied in the present of the motion picture.

Despite her modernist tendencies, Pool has had consistent recourse to the direct emotionality and overt symbolism familiar to connoisseurs of popular melodrama. Early on in her career, critical recognition of this element in her work would register solely as surprise when Pool would disrupt the emotional flatness and subtle imagery traditionally associated with the intellectual art film whose conventions she otherwise followed. So, Canadian critic Jay Scott complained about *Anne Trister* that 'When the lips of the two women inevitably meet, Pool momentarily eschews her unsentimental, formalist style of filmmaking to fill the Dolby soundtrack with a romantic theme song suitable to *Desert Hearts*, a lesbian movie in which the lovers were much livelier.'[61] In other words, he wanted either consistent art film or consistent romance, but not an unfamiliar combination of the two. As her films have moved closer to mainstream narrative, the reliance on melodrama has become more pronounced. It continues to provoke unease, as Pool consistently coaxes performances out of her female actors that turn conventional situations inside out, suggesting the genuine emotional conflict that conventional melodrama distances by stylization. The intensity of Vanasse's Jutra-award-winning performance transcends the overly familiar outline of her story, the clichéd conventions commonly dismissed as movie-of-the-week or after-school-movie material. Pool's reliance on these structures in her most recent feature films, the English-language *Lost and Delirious* (2001; the tragic tale of a girls' school romance) and *The Blue Butterfly* (2004; the tale of a cancer-stricken boy's quest to capture a rare butterfly) and her return to French in the TV movie *Maman est chez le coiffeur* (*Mother Is at the Hairdresser's*, 2008; the tale of three children abandoned by their mother when she discovers their father is gay) and *La dernière fugue* (2010; co-produced with and set in Luxembourg and starring Arcand and Lepage regular Yves Jacques in a drama about the right of the elderly to choose their moment to die), suggests Pool's real affinity to potential movie-of-the-week material. While Pool directly attributes this affinity to a 'new openness' and a desire to make movies her young adopted daughter can watch, there is also enough continuity with her previous films to argue for a thematic consistency that approaches a particular middle ground from the other, popular, side, as it were, rather than the art-cinema angle.

The strengths and drawbacks of Pool's new generic affiliation are especially evident in *Lost and Delirious* (2001), her first English-language film, the first film to bring her widespread renown as an independent film-maker, and still her best-known film in the anglophone world. Pool herself has signalled her discomfort with some of the excesses of the script, refusing outright to consider the original conclusion in Susan Swan's novel *The Wives of Bath* where a totally insane Paulie glues a taxi driver's severed penis to her body in a desperate attempt to win back

5.2. Léa Pool's intense emotionality translated into English: Paulie (Piper Perabo) and Tori (Jessica Paré) in *Lost and Delirious* (2001). Photofest.

Tori's love. It is the kind of over-the-top touch a mid-career Pedro Almodóvar might have gotten away with, but Pool's version of melodrama is, wisely, less sensationalistic. She decided she could work with playwright Judith Thurman's added Shakespearean imagery and Paulie's (Piper Perabo) identification with and nurturing of a wounded hawk. 'What I liked in *Lost and Delirious*,' she has said, 'was because of Susan Swan and Judith Thompson were two women that are much more expressive in their ways of telling a story, it pushed me in a place that perhaps myself I wouldn't have gone because it's not my normal way to express things. I think it would be impossible for me to write a thing like this, but it was very interesting and challenging to work on something like this because it pushed me to limits where I wanted to go.'[62] Certainly, as some critics suggested, it is possible that Pool's lesser degree of comfort in English led her to be less sure of the tone of the language, which is overdramatic to excess; however, there is also something emotionally apt, if thereby also cringeworthy, about that over-dramatization that is perfectly suited to her subject and her modus operandi as a film-maker. The presence of three young starlets – American Piper Perabo, Quebecois Jessica Paré, and English Mischa Barton as Mouse, the narrating observer of the crash-and-burn affair of her two roommates – was already enough to guarantee the film substantial publicity. But the jarring effect of Pool's ability to push her actors, especially Perabo, into frighteningly intense performances, playing the sometimes ridiculous dialogue absolutely po-faced, along with the typically weak Canadian distribution, doomed the film at the box office, although it has attained a cult following on DVD (figure 5.2). Its dynamic is different from the stylized irony of Sirkian melodrama, meant to make us see through the alienating social conventions that cause the movies' tragedies, and different from the magic realist emotionality of Almodóvarian melodrama, where characters are able to connect with one another through the larger-than-life roles that represent their identities better than the banalities of 'normal' life. Instead, the words and symbols of Pool's melodrama openly declare their simple insufficiency while the embodied passions of her actors express an emotional truth unable to be captured in the objective categories available to us intellectually. Pool's tenacious refusal to reduce her film-making to any straightforward identification means that none of her films is as perfectly satisfying in itself as their nouvelle vague and Quebecois antecedents, but that same refusal also means that her films manage to tread a unique path among otherwise incommensurate categories, a genre-bending exercise that gives them an exceptional currency in today's multicultural internationalism.

Robert Lepage on Stage

> I spend 70 per cent of my time working in English [in theatre]. When I work in Japan, the work language is English. I've always done that. This may sound very tacky, but just remember Québec is under the reign of Celine Dion. Celine Dion is the great Québec pioneer. She proves you can have an international career by singing in English and, at the same time, she goes to [the] Rosie O'Donnell [show] and she's Québecois all over. At the same time, she still does loads of stuff in French. I think she opened the doors for a lot of Québec artists. If Denys Arcand is working on a subject that demands to be shot in English, then he does that.
>
> Robert Lepage (1999)

Like Lauzon and Pool, Robert Lepage (b. 1957) is a singular figure in Quebecois cinema. The working-class son of a Quebec City taxi driver and a homemaker who had already adopted two anglophone children, Lepage and his sister (and part-time collaborator) Lynda Lepage-Beaulieu were raised speaking French in a bilingual household. It was a sufficiently unusual situation during the fifties in the heavily francophone provincial capital, such that Lepage's father would often be assigned as a 'tour guide' to anglophone visitors.[63] Consequently, Lepage grew up with both the advantage of bilingualism and the outsider status bestowed by that advantage within the burgeoning sovereignty movement of the province during the sixties. As he recalls it, 'I would hang out with the English-speaking kids too. So my best friend was Anglophone but I was brought up in French and I went to a French school and my family were French ... Today it is the same thing, I mean the Québecois cultural milieu is very incestuous and you know I feel a bit of an outsider because I am interested in working with people from England, Australia, Italy.'[64] In a typically miserable adolescence, Lepage was further marked as different by the medical condition of alopecia, which caused all of his hair to fall out, and by the realization that he was gay, 'You want normality, whether it's sexually, or your hair, or what you smoked. And I didn't have any hair and the first joint

I smoked was spiked.'[65] The outcome of an intensely introverted period was a mature artist able to negotiate insider/outsider identities with such skill that he had become a world-class actor/writer/director before he was thirty. Rather than fully embrace either his Quebecois heritage or a cosmopolitan or a gay identity, Lepage has skilfully navigated among them as both building blocks and metaphors for his multifaceted plays and films.

Rather than the conventional linear construction of realist drama and cinema, Lepage's work is based on Californian choreographer Ann Halprin's collaborative improvisational technique known as RSVP Cycles, which he learned while working with Jacques Lessard's theatre troupe Théâtre Repère, which Lepage joined in 1982.[66] RSVP Cycles privilege the creative process, self-expression, and communication with the audience rather than a conventionally top-down, author-driven creation.[67] In Lepage's practice, they render performances that rely heavily on generative metaphors and images, a highly flexible mise en scène able to shift rapidly between multiple times and settings, and a production of meaning through formal association and spatial juxtaposition rather than cause and effect. The six-hour *Dragons' Trilogy*, for example, grew out of Lepage's Canadian tour of the 'trilingual' 1984 show *Circulations*, when he and his troupe spent a lot of time in the Chinatowns of Montreal, Toronto, and Vancouver. He would expand that initial experience and 'resource' with 'some of his own family folklore, the tale of a grand-uncle who became so indebted to Chinese gamblers that he was forced to barter his pregnant daughter. "Robert just told us this very basic concept," says actress and long-time Lepage collaborator Marie Brassard. "There were six of us coming from very different backgrounds and every person started to bring ideas, thoughts, objects, and concepts which would go from *Tintin In China* to *The Blue Lotus* to Taoist philosophy. So, by putting these things together we had a very strange melting pot. No one had been to China so we had a naive vision. But we decided to use our ignorance."'[68] *Dragons' Trilogy* made Lepage's reputation when it premiered locally in 1985 and in London in 1987. As Jennifer Harvie writes, Lepage's pieces are characterized by their 'textual openness': explicitly credited to the entire company, their form is also famously and publicly open-ended.[69] At times, work in progress has been presented at prestigious festivals, with sometimes disastrous consequences, as in the notorious opening night of the epic *Seven Streams of the River Ota* at the 1994 Edinburgh Festival, in which, as Marie Brassard recalls, 'We were improvising in front of the audience maybe a third of the whole show'; it overran by two hours.[70] However, writes theatre critic O'Mahony, 'when all the daring connections and imaginative leaps coincide,' as in *Seven Streams* after another four years of refinement, 'the effect is spellbinding' and 'proof' of the 'radical vitality' of contemporary theatre.[71]

Rather than the next step from and apogee of a vital career in theatre, opera, and multimedia events, Lepage claims to regard film as a sideline to his primary interests; as he laconically puts it, 'I do something else for a living.'[72] He has worked selectively in the medium but with a substantial impact, particularly his debut feature, *Le Confessionnal* (1995). Film-making is both an extension of Lepage's theatrical work – *Le Polygraphe* (1996), *Nô* (1998), and *La face cachée de la lune* (*The Far Side of the Moon*, 2003) were adapted from extant plays – and a challenge to his working process. Commercial cinema is based on closure both in terms of narrative and in terms of product. And while Lepage has pushed against these constraints as much as possible, both in terms of narrative (by favouring open-ended, kaleidoscopically branching storylines and ambiguous endings) and in terms of production (by improvising extensively on set and pushing post-production deadlines), he has thus far shown limited interest in the open-ended possibilities offered by DVD and Internet technology. Instead, he has innovated more in the other direction: by bringing video technology into the theatre through films, slides, and live video projection. Unlike static backdrops, these media often interact directly and physically with the actors, as in *Needles and Opium*, where the central prop was a 'a screen that pivots, functioning as floor, ceiling and an absorbent material into which Mr. Lepage's body is occasionally ensnared,' or in *The Far Side of the Moon*, where rear projection screens behind round washer and dryer doors 'allow them to be, at turns, a clock, airplane window, goldfish bowl, TV, brain scan machine, eye of a young patient, and a womb through which a baby puppet appears, complete with umbilical cord.'[73] Lepage's plays, in other words, are theatre for a generation raised on film and television, trained to split attention and to multitask visually: 'they know what a flash-forward is and a flashback, and they know how to listen to a story that is told through jump-cutting. That's an education. Theatre that does not take into account that stories can be told in different ways is a dead theatre.'[74]

As with the younger generation who began producing films along with the elder, late arriving Lepage in the mid-nineties – Villeneuve, Turpin, Briand, to name a few – the dramaturge has been accused by detractors of cold, superficial brilliance, visually spectacular and fiendishly clever, but lacking in emotional weight and creating facile associations that fail to do justice to the potential gravity of his themes: plays and films have addressed incest, suicide, drug addiction, all manner of identity crises, the Berlin Wall, the FLQ and the October Crisis, and Hiroshima. In Lepage's case, the physical immediacy of live performance generally manages to establish the emotional connection that often seems missing from his films, as from those of his contemporaries. As British critic Jonathan Romney notes of *Possible Worlds*, 'Sometimes … it has been hard to shake off the suspicion that the films were poor relations to Lepage's theatre – displaying the same dazzling tricks and transformations but missing the imaginative lift-off that came from witnessing them in real time, in a live setting.'[75] Yet, these same 'dazzling tricks and transformations' are also the foundation of Lepage's real cinematic innovation. As Romney asks rhetorically, 'Has any director been so playfully cavalier with space and time since Alain Resnais?'[76] The French new wave director's icily controlled tracking shots and associative cross-cutting between spatio-temporally distinct events have clearly been a touchstone of Lepage's work, as they have in the criticism of that work.[77] The erotic encounter between a survival of nuclear bombing and a French woman ostracized for sleeping with a German soldier during the occupation in *Hiroshima mon amour* (1959) was one of the 'starting resources' for *River Ota* and for *Nô*'s juxtaposed storylines of a farcical performance of a French farce by a Quebecois company in Hiroshima and farcical FLQ bombers in Montreal.[78] The formal and stylistic overlaying of distinct times within a single setting that Resnais used to famous effect in *L'année dernière à Marienbad* recurs in Lepage's seamless match cuts between different 'realities' in *Possible Worlds* (2000). The use of a fragmented style to depict visually the fragmentation of memory pioneered by Resnais in *Muriel: Le temps d'un retour* (1962) equally structures the interplay in *Le Confessionnal* between the obscure events of 1952 and Pierre Lamontagne's (Lothaire Bluteau) efforts in 1989 to recover their meaning. And Resnais's propensity for parallel cuts and long tracking shots that cross years at a time became a Lepage trademark, especially in *Le Confessionnal*.[79]

Lepage also shares with Resnais a fascination with the relationship between individual memory and identity and the broader sweep of history. Like Resnais, Lepage tends to subordinate the latter to the former, a hierarchy emphasized by a stylistic virtuosity that focuses attention on the artificial play of the images over any ideological substance. This is, of course, a quintessentially postmodern attitude, to privilege the play of signifiers over any conclusive meaning. And while there may be a slow-burning anger buried in the farcical play of *Nô*, it is the ironic despair of the postmodernist who sees no solution to the idiocy of politics and not the revolutionary anger of the FLQ, which it rejects as incompetent bumbling even as it appears to sympathize with the intentions of the bunglers. The attitude taken by *Nô* towards the events of 1970 seems to parallel the director's own 'lukewarm' and jaded support for Quebecois separatism: 'I've always been more yes than no … Give us an issue that we haven't been through like zillions of times.'[80] What is tricky about Lepage is that he can't resist making movies about the very issues Quebec has 'been through like zillions of times.' It may be that here, his greater years distinguish him from his equally postmodernist colleagues, whose diegetic worlds have no truck with Quebec's past or political present, but instead tend to spin visually arresting surrealist fables about the lives of beautiful young Montreal yuppies.

Lepage was not involved in the Quiet Revolution as an adult the way his friend Denys Arcand was. Arcand's main films of the period when Lepage began film-making – *Jésus de Montréal* (1989), *Love & Human Remains* (1993), and *Stardom* (2000), in the first and third of which Lepage played supporting roles – addressed postmodernity from the point of view of that revolution, providing a scathing if sympathetic critique of the emptiness of the life it had promised. Lepage's work straddles the line between the two, refusing to decide one way or the other. In his conceptually brilliant debut, Lepage used Alfred Hitchcock's local filming of the 1952 thriller *I Confess* as the starting point, the 'resource' for a meditation on the disjunctions and continuities between the old, Duplessis Quebec and the new, postmodern province; the seamless shifts in time conveniently elide the sixties in between. Consequently, they also elide the revolution in film-making that went with that decade, working instead in a fluently international art-film style while paying prominent homage to Hitchcock along the way. A Canada/UK/France co-production, *Le Confessionnal* was made on spec, from a desire to cross-fertilize Lepage's soaring international theatrical reputation with the movie business. French and British participation brought with it the rising star Kristin Scott Thomas, fresh from the independent blockbuster *Four Weddings and a Funeral* (1994, Mike Newell), along with British rock on the soundtrack and a globetrotting post-production, 'When it's a co-production you not only divide the budget, but the creative input. Because the French were more dedicated on the visual aspect, we did the editing in Paris. We're doing the sound aspect more with the English. We've got a sound technician who is British and has his own company. British rock groups have been recruited for the soundtrack.'[81] Paradoxically, however, it was *Le Confessionnal* that led Lepage back to Quebec City after years of expatriate living, and film-making that seems to have settled him there. The provincial government has worked very hard to keep 'the most famous Canadian since Glenn Gould' happy and productive, helping him to fund his own theatre company, Ex Machina, and to establish a state-of-the-art theatre lab, La Caserne Dalhousie, in a nineteenth-century firehall.[82] The result, argue Jennifer Harvie and Erin Hurley, has been a coup for the cultural identity of the province at the expense of the greater federation, but an identity limited to the closed circuit of an elite 'international commercial network.'[83] Although they are accurate in their assessment of the funding system that supports Lepage and the primary venue in which his productions are presented, Harvie and Hurley underestimate the local cultural value of the many ancillary texts that circulate around his theatre, especially television, cinema, and Internet, both at home and for Quebecois living outside of the province, just as they underestimate the multiple ways in which these texts can be received and their meaning appropriated. The economic and cultural effects of such texts are much harder to trace and to predict, but it seems premature to dismiss Lepage's local value simply because he does not conform to a particular conception of cultural production. Nor is it possible to predict in what direction his developing career will take him, or what effect his continued base in Quebec City will have on that career. Just as long-time local pariah (and local Torontonian) David Cronenberg slowly but surely made his way into the centre of the landscape of Canadian cinema, so it is likely that Lepage will only influence Quebecois culture more the longer he remains present in it.

Although not as extreme as Lauzon's affection for the north country, Lepage's choice of his home town Quebec City over the more cosmopolitan Montreal suggests that his provincial identity, too, is primarily personal rather than ideological. And although not as consistently as Lauzon and Pool, Lepage has made prominent use of his biography in his films. In *Le Confessionnal*, it is prominent primarily in the Quebec City setting and the ambience of the gay subculture; Lepage has mentioned that some of the *I Confess* actors did in fact ride in his father's cab.[84] *Le Polygraphe* and *La face cachée de la lune*, however, are deeply autobiographical. The former is based on the rape/murder of a close friend and fellow actor, France Lachapelle. Lepage discovered the body, was initially a suspect, and submitted to a polygraph test whose results were never revealed to him.[85] Quebecois genre director Yves Simoneau adapted the material as his second feature film, *Les yeux rouges* (*Red Eyes*, 1982), evidently inviting Lepage to play the role of the murderer.[86] Both the original trauma and the film about it made their way into Lepage's stage play (1987) and film, where the protagonist François Tremblay (Patrick Goyette), still obsessed with the murder, lives next door to the actress who is playing the role of Lachapelle in the film. Less sensationalistic, the one-man show *La face cachée de la lune* and the film based on the show address the relationship between two estranged brothers, an aging philosophy of science student completing a PhD dissertation on the space race and a local Quebec City weatherman, both coming to terms with the death of their mother (Lepage's mother died while he was working on the Soviet space material). Lepage played both brothers in the show (he was eventually replaced by his friend Yves Jacques); he reprised the roles in the film.

The city itself, as Nathalie Cornelius observes, is 'omnipresent' in Lepage's films both as a 'marker of French Canadian heritage' (the oldest city in North America) and for the 'historic, mysterious and photogenic qualities' that 'confer a sense of realism and vitality.'[87] Especially for a country whose landscape has so often and for so long masqueraded as somewhere else, the use of identifiable landmarks plays an important part in establishing, maintaining, and disputing a cultural identity. As Peter Clandfield quite reasonably observes, one of the most important things a national cinema can do, regardless of the kind of stories it tells, is to use 'landmark Canadian locations (and, for that matter, quite ordinary ones as well) … in ways that evoke their particular histories as well as realising their various evolving kinds of cinematic potential in a globalized marketplace.'[88] Exactly how a local cinema can depict the radical changes brought by globalization and the postmodern cityscape is an open question, but it is also a question at the heart of much of the interesting film-making at the turn of the millennium. One of the effects of the stylistic tricks of the multimedia generation is to provide a visual correlative for this change, and when we see that style reckoning with the spatial iconography of the province we can get a glimpse of how such representations might work outside the traditional confines of documentary realism: the alternative, nocturnal urban spaces of Charles Binamé's *Eldorado*, the surrealistic talking fish–narrator within the context of the local fishing industry in Villeneuve's *Maelström*, the matter-of-fact incongruity of Algerian immigrants in the Montreal winter in Dénis Chouinard's *L'Ange de goudron* (*Tar Baby*, 2001).

Its innovative use of the urban space and iconic landmarks of Quebec City is a primary reason that *Le Confessionnal* has not only attracted the lion's share of commentary on Lepage's cinema but also more academic attention than any other Quebecois film since the original new wave. Not only does the film make creatively iconic use of the touristic landmark of the Château Frontenac and the engineering landmark of the Quebec Bridge, but it uses the spaces as generative images central to the film's complex interweaving of metaphors. Lepage employs the spaces of Quebec City to meditate on the history of Quebecois identity and the ambiguous relationship between past and present, while also showing himself supremely aware of the metacinematic status of those images by placing them in the context of Hitchcock's 'colonization' of the highly conservative city as the setting for his 'Catholic' thriller. According to Lepage, Hitchcock chose Quebec City because it was the only place 'where people will believe that this Catholic priest and this Catholic church has power.'[89] Anywhere else, as Martin Lefebvre argues, it would have had to be a period film (the source story had been published in 1902).[90] As Monique Tschofen puts it, 'what is at stake in the film is modernity itself.'[91] By representing the arrival of the 'great Hollywood machine' in backwards Quebec City, Lepage visualizes the process of change that would conclude in the Quiet Revolution, thus arguing that the arrival of global media (television arrived in Quebec in the same year) was essential to, rather than subsequent to, that change. In his unmooring of space-time from linear chronology, however, Lepage also suggests that modernity and postmodernity are not consequent social phenomena but simultaneous modes of perception and operation. The chronotope of 1952 Quebec City is simultaneously the 1902 setting of the original play, which also happens to be the period in which the Quebec Bridge was under construction, already an icon of local modernity. An elaborate ceremony was held in 1900 to mark the beginning of its construction, clearly chosen to coincide with the beginning of a new millennium; it would be the world's longest cantilevered span.[92] The first permanent link with the rest of Canada and the United States, the bridge was, and remains, a prominent symbol of the city's modernity. At the same time, as Clandfield notes, that symbolism has been a fraught focal point rather than a static truism. Not only did the nearly two decades of construction result in two fatal collapses, killing between them nearly one hundred people, but discussion of the design, construction, and maintenance of the bridge has continued to mobilize familiar arguments about federalism and sovereignty.[93]

The century of history thus encompassed by the framing image of *Le Confessionnal* brackets and contextualizes the more explicit thirty-seven years between the two sets of events. Lepage's imagery asserts both the continuity of space-time – the hereditary diabetes suffered by the Lamontagne family; the hidden cuts that match the two periods within a single shot; the family portraits whose traces refuse to vanish from the walls of the house no matter how many times Pierre paints them; and the presence of Raymond Massicotte (Jean-Louis Millette) as the confessing priest in 1952 and the powerful politician and abusive lover of Marc Lamontagne (Patrick Goyette) in 1989, ensconced, naturally, in a tower of the iconic space of the Château Frontenac – and its rupture: the finite duration of Hitchcock's visit; the suicides of Pierre's Aunt Rachel in 1952 and her son Marc in 1989; the elided Quiet Revolution itself. Lepage does not decide conclusively one way or the other, and audience response and critical interpretation of the film's stance towards the past have consequently been all over the map.[94] The film's signature concluding image, which ranks with the freeze-frame of Benoît in *Mon oncle Antoine* as one of the most famous in the history of Quebec national cinema, manages to encompass both the optimism of Pierre carrying his young nephew across the bridge into the future and into the greater world and the haunted pessimism of the slow pan across the bridge's immense expanse that summons up the past disasters of the bridge and the suicide endemic to the Lamontagne family (figure 5.3).[95] Rather than the emphatically closed ambiguity of Benoît's face, the meaning of which we are acutely aware of even while the future is unknowable, the ambiguity of the conclusion of *Le Confessionnal*, as of all of Lepage's films, is open and multifaceted. This provides the intellectual satisfaction of making a myriad of connections and associations like synapses snapping together in the brain, but it precludes the emotional closure of the modernist ambiguity of *Antoine*. In this sense, if *Le Con-*

5.3. Local landmarks: the iconic concluding shot of the Quebec Bridge in *Le Confessionnal* (1995). Permission of Cinémaginaire and Ex Machina.

fessionnal opened Lepage's oeuvre by positing the inextricability of modernism and postmodernism, the open-ended ambiguity that concludes the film decides in favour of the latter, paving the way for a Quebecois cinema freed, for better and for worse, of its modernist past.

This ambiguity is a primary reason that, even more than Lauzon's visionary masterpiece *Léolo* and Pool's revisionary coming-of-age drama *Emporte-moi*, *Le Confessionnal* has become a touchstone of contemporary Canadian cinema, a bridge between the unitary identity politics of the Quiet Revolution and the 'cultural plurality' of the new internationalism.[96] For the same reason, it is far less satisfying as a moviegoing experience than the other two films, just as the new Quebecois cinema, for all of its stunningly original and high-tech imagery and its necessary meditation on the local effects of globalization, feels empty in comparison with similar film-making elsewhere in the world – Alejandro González Iñárritu's *Amores Perros* (2000), Fernando Meirelles's *City of God* (2002), or Alfonso Cuarón's *Children of Men* (2006), to name a few. Lauzon and Pool specialize in closed, visionary films reminiscent of the great auteur cinema of the post-war period. Lepage, in contrast, has defined his oeuvre in terms of openness and play;

his films are always loaded to the bursting point with ideas, metaphors, and inter-connections. This makes them a treasure trove for critics and at times a bit of a chore for audiences. Despite (and because of) their cleverness and intellectualism, Lepage's films have a provocative brilliance that places them head and shoulders above their contemporaries in Quebecois art film. While Lauzon has long since passed, and Pool has gone mainstream, Lepage continues to ply his own inter-national niche (most recently a spectacular production of Wagner's *Ring* cycle at the Metropolitan Opera in New York), even as his cinematic oeuvre testifies to the accuracy of his assessment of its subordinate place within his own artistic identity.

Chapter Six

Cronenberg's Mutant Progeny:
Genre Film-making around the Turn of the Millennium

As far as I know, there had never been a serious horror film made in Canada before *Shivers*.

David Cronenberg

It is time for genre films to be taken seriously in Quebec, whether it's comedy, romance, fantasy or historical films. For 20 years or more, we have been fed 'auteur films,' some are good, but others are morbidly boring. I think it is possible to make meaningful films that are also entertaining.

Erik Canuel

As is the case with most national cinemas, the films that receive the bulk of the critical attention are a small percentage of what actually gets produced. Ever since production jumped dramatically during the tax-shelter years, by far the greater proportion of Canadian film production has been composed of genre films, many of them sold straight to cable television or video, but many of them nonetheless supported by government money. Indeed, there is no question that more exploitation films have been made and distributed over the past two decades than during the tax-shelter years. These films don't always show up on the official lists, and there are many levels of official support and economic exploitation. Winnipeg film-maker, critic, and fan Caelum Vatnsdal has surveyed some of these films in *They Came from Within* and Paul Corupe's Canuxploitation webpage provides further evidence of the long-time existence of this deep underbelly of the Canadian film industry; both make an implicit case for its essential place within the broader narrative of the national cinema.[1] To be sure, many of these films are formally indistinguishable from their American counterparts, many of them are of little interest aesthetically but provide fascinating insights into Canadian national cinema, and a valued minority have learned from the example of Cronenberg's tax-shelter masterworks that exploitation can provide opportunities for imaginative and thought-provoking film-making at the same time as it hits the genre-defined marks required of its target audience – usually sex and violence, and often both at once. In this chapter, I survey the development of Canadian genre cinema since the beginning of the tax-shelter era as it adapted to the economics of cable television and the new cable television and video markets, both Anglo and Quebecois. I focus on three of the most successful popular genres within Canadian film-making: sex comedies, horror, and science fiction. Each of these genres created a local niche within the exploitation market while also making its own contribution to the conception of Canadian national cinema, not least by deeply influencing Canadian auteur cinema.

For most of the film critics who have given it any thought, the term 'Canadian popular cinema' remains a vexing oxymoron. In a paradox that goes a long way towards explaining the peculiarities of the subject, success in Canadian film is generally defined as failure to be popular, while popular success tends to make the 'Canadianness' of a film invisible to the canon of Canadian national cinema. To wit, eleven films on the 2010 list of the one hundred highest grossing films of all time in the United States (including numbers one and two) can be plausibly defined as Canadian: starring Canadian-born actors (Jim Carrey, Mike Myers, Dan Ackroyd, Rick Moranis, Nia Vardalos) or made by Canadian-born directors (Ivan Reitman, James Cameron).[2] Of these eleven, only *My Big Fat Greek Wedding* (2002, Joel Zwick) is usually regarded as Canadian, and then only so as to beat it with a stick for betraying the Canadian setting of Vardalos's original screenplay, the nationality of the local crew, and the Toronto locations disguised as the more 'universal' setting of Chicago. Nevertheless, box office is a standard criterion for assessing popular culture. Indeed, it is the criterion used for the Golden Reel Award, established in 1976 by the Canadian Motion Picture Distributors Association, and presented since 1980 at the Genie Awards to the 'Canadian' film with the highest domestic earnings.[3] While the list is fairly evenly split between English-Canadian and Quebecois productions since the end of the tax-shelter years (when the former had dominated), a 'quality' English-Canadian film shows up only about once a decade – most recently Paul Gross's First World War drama *Passchendaele* (2008). In general, the list of winners wreaks havoc with fine critical distinctions regarding Canadian national cinema. *The Care Bears Movie* (1986, Arna Selznick) is followed by Arcand's *Déclin de l'empire américain* (1987); Arcand's *Jésus de Montréal* (1990) gives way to the lowbrow Quebecois sketch comedy *Ding et Dong le film* (1991, Alain Chartrand); Cronenberg's cool masterpiece *Crash* (1996) is sandwiched between Disney's canine comedy *Air Bud* (1997, Charles Martin Smith) and the cyber-noir *Johnny Mnemonic* (1995, Robert Longo).

Is it possible to posit a Canadian identity capacious enough to embrace a basketball-playing canine, a dysfunctional family of sex-addicted academics, a razor-sharp but narratively incoherent cyber future, and a pair of down-and-out stand-up comics, goofy as only the Quebeckers can make them? As the favoured national metaphor of the 'Canadian mosaic' makes clear, such a capacious identity cannot at the same time address the radical incommensurability of the different tiles in the mosaic. In their encyclopedic homage to Canadian pop culture, *Mondo Canuck*, Geoff Pevere and Greig Dymond set out to demolish the invisible wall separating loyal Anglo Canadians from those who fled to Hollywood. Another divide remains intact, however; they find room in their volume for only a single entry on Quebecois film, the dubious inclusion of Jutra's *Mon oncle Antoine*, a masterpiece, but difficult to qualify as pop culture. The entry on Jutra also contains a feature on 'Canada's Coolest French Language Movies,' but that list enumerates seven art-house gems, flouting the very criterion of 'forms of pop with a national profile' that ostensibly structures the book.[4] Fair enough as criteria go, but it still raises the question of what to do with a francophone culture that is eminently popular, is shared by around a fifth of the total population of Canada, and has placed five of its own films in Quebec's top twenty-one grossing films of all time. This is to say that only *six* Hollywood films – the three instalments of *The Lord of the Rings*, *Spiderman*, the first Harry Potter movie, and *Titanic* – outperformed Erik Canuel's local hit *Bon Cop Bad Cop* (2007) on its home ground, with the historical melodrama *Séraphin* just behind, trailing only *Spiderman 2*. Moreover, note that a top film on the list prominently features the dulcet tones of Quebec's own Céline Dion (who does get her entry in *Mondo Canuck*), not to mention the expatriate talents of Mr Cameron. We can say, in other words, that how to account for the success of Canadians in Hollywood and how to account for the success of Canadians in Quebec are the two great divides that haunt the familiar refrain of Canadian cinema studies over the four decades or so since Toronto produced its first modern feature film, the refrain that ponders in despair: why is Anglo-Canadian film so unpopular? The question cannot be answered, naturally, until we do a better job of defining exactly what 'popular' and 'Canadian' mean.

Although restricted to the purview of *la belle province*, Bill Marshall's *Quebec National Cinema* remains the most sustained attempt to tackle the issue of popular cinema within the broader conception of a Canadian national cinema. While insightful and theoretically astute, Marshall's analysis tends to work around rather than moving beyond what he terms the 'two polarities [that] have tended to be sketched out for Quebec cinema: a refusal of the world economic system (and film industry), or a complicity with it, with all the risks and opportunities that entails.'[5] Marshall argues, for example, that because Quebec does not have an 'indigenous genre cinema to rework,' its adaptation of the postmodernist pastiche of genre cinema was inevitably reliant on Hollywood genres rather than, as in France, its own history of popular genres.[6] This observation more accurately assesses prevailing critical attitudes in Quebec towards genre than the specific history of the cinema itself. First, it makes a qualitative distinction between the popular genres adopted by the French cinéma du look during the eighties – science fiction, film noir, gangster films, serial thrillers – and those specific to Quebecois popular cinema – historical melodrama, maple syrup porno, and more recently, sketch comedy.[7] Second, it underestimates the ways in which France's indigenous genres were themselves generated in response to Hollywood cinema rather than emerging in isolation from it. Third, it fails to recognize the degree to the which English-Canadian and Quebecois film cultures equally, but even more deeply, have always defined themselves in opposition to and appropriation from Hollywood. Finally, Marshall's observation makes an artificial distinction between the art cinema officially designated as Quebec national cinema and the enduring popular and exploitation industry imbricated in and encompassing the production apparatus of that art cinema. As Marshall's own discussion of Yves Simoneau well demonstrates, it is difficult to draw a firm line between a quality cinema aimed solely at representing Canada to Canadians or Quebec to Quebecois and a commercial cinema raising questions of national identity through the vehicle of international genres. Hence, Simoneau's *Pouvoir intime* (1986), a heist movie with a political backdrop, starring Pierre Curzi, who had a central role in *Déclin* the same year, became a touchstone of academic debate over its representation of homosexuality and the status of that homosexuality within a discussion of post-Duplessis Quebecois identity.[8] In contrast, Simoneau's follow-up, *Dans le ventre du dragon* (1989), a *Blade Runner*–style future noir about high-tech capitalism that did not offer a thematic local hook, was criticized for 'selling out to Hollywood values.'[9] Simoneau did indeed soon make the jump to Hollywood by way of Toronto, but his productive résumé (about thirty films in thirty years) is mostly filled with television work in a variety of genres, most prominently historical dramas and thrillers, including co-productions with France and Canada. But then, as Pierre Véronneau argues, 'genre films have in fact dominated the landscape of Quebec cinema since the mid-1980s.'[10]

Since the fifties, film studies and practical criticism have assumed a static conception of auteurist art cinema defined as oppositional or at least supplementary to the commercial film industry. Whereas the latter has long been defined in terms of its recourse to genre, the art film until recently was analysed according to the criteria of unique individual artefacts without recognition of the fact that it too follows identifiable genre conventions.[11] As Thomas Elsaesser suggests, this very definition of the film-maker as free agent bears the weight of a set of conventions, 'the quintessential and clichéd [conception] of a nation's character embodied in personal or "poetic" cinema, and the defensive stance of "hand-made films against slick entertainment."'[12] This discourse of authenticity was well-suited for articulating national identity during the Quiet Revolution and at the height of the separatism movement. However, a glance at the far more hybrid art cinema of the eighties suggests the degree to which that model was no longer adequate either economically or artistically to describe what was happening. Moreover, because Hollywood by the seventies had appropriated the auteur film as part of its properly commercial arsenal, the personal cinema no longer offered even the conflicted authenticity that it had in the sixties. One of the lessons of the eighties was that popular genres offered their own subversive qualities distinct from the proper artistic channels of auteur cinema. Rather than the nouvelle vague model of incorporating Hollywood tropes into alternative film-making, film-makers such as Cronenberg, Rozema, and Arcand incorporated alternative film-making into Hollywood tropes. It is too simple merely to dismiss genre film-making for its commerciality, just as it is not tenable to regard any feature-length art film as existing independently of commercial exigencies. Recourse to popular genres has always been a devil's bargain, but the same pact that risks the incursion of Hollywood and globally capitalist production also presents the opportunity to establish a discourse about that very incursion. If art cinema offers overt articulation of local identity amid the covert influence of global capitalism, popular genres offer covert articulation of local identity amid the overt appropriation of global forms. Because genres, in Rick Altman's terms, form '"constellated" communities – groups of individuals who "cohere only through repeated acts of imagination,"' they cut across traditional conceptions of nationhood by creating alternative community identities as much as or at the same time as they coincide with those conceptions.[13]

There is no popular Hollywood genre that has not at one time or another been appropriated as a potent vehicle for the articulation of local identity: the Bollywood musical, the spaghetti western, the French film noir, the maple syrup porno. Such appropriations often have a limited duration – the Hong Kong gangster film perfected by John Woo flourished for just over a decade in the run-up to the British handover of its former colony to mainland China – before their historical impetus runs its course or the Hollywood machine hires the genre's stars and reincorporates and homogenizes their innovations. Although generally considered a feature of postmodernism, genre mixing has been a part of local appropriation since the movies began. This also means that specific genres are more fruitful for specific cinemas at specific times than others. During the nineties, English Canada, for example, produced a number of third-rate neo-noirs and a few heist thrillers – Bruce McDonald's straight-to-video fiasco, *Picture Claire* (2001), and the expensive mainstream TFC-funded flop *Foolproof* (2003, William Phillips), to name one example of each – that mostly went straight to video and were uninspiring by just about any standard; however, English Canada has had a long, vibrant, and extremely interesting relationship with the horror film and a more recent but fruitful association with science fiction.

Comedy has been a distinctive overlay on Quebecois popular genres since the late sixties, often growing directly from the lively boulevard comedy and stand-up scene in Montreal. Sex farce, comedy thrillers, Arcand's comic art films, sports comedy, even a science fiction comedy such as the *Dans une galaxie près de chez vous* franchise (TV series, 1999; film, 2004; sequel, 2008): all of them localize familiar genre discourses by articulating them in a comic mode. In contrast, the dearth of popular English-Canadian comedy has been a familiar refrain. Indeed, the migration of invisible Canadian comics to the United States in itself can be considered something of a running gag. Not only did Toronto's Second City spawn John Candy, Rick Moranis, Dave Thomas, Catherine O'Hara, Martin Short, Dan Ackroyd, Gilda Radner, and later Mike Myers (stars of comedy shows *SCTV* and *Saturday Night Live*) migrate to the States, but the two biggest movie comedy stars of the 1990s and 2000s were southern Ontario natives Carrey and Myers, both of whom began their careers as impersonators and parodists, immersed in the pre-cable culture of network television and syndicated reruns, while former Vancouver stand-up comic and current A-list actor Seth Rogen and Jewish-Irish-French Montrealer Jay Baruchel have recently joined their aging predecessors. The expert parody and deadpan gags that punctuate the lowbrow action of Ivan Reitman's wildly successful comedies from *Meatballs* (1979) and *Stripes* (1981) through *Ghostbusters* (1984) and *Ghostbusters II* (1989) arise from this source too, as do those of so many of the movies spun off of sketch characters, a film genre that *SNL* and *SCTV* brought to a new height of exploitation, including *Strange Brew* (1983), the brilliantly self-reflexive feature film by SCTV duo Bob and Doug McKenzie (Rick Moranis and Dave Thomas). *Strange Brew* is perhaps the exception that proves the rule, an extremely funny, financially successfully local comedy that combines a sustained articulation of English-Canadian identity with a fiercely intelligent parody of popular genre conventions. Still, English Canada has been best served by the more conceptual genres of science fiction and horror, while Quebec has specialized in comedy and historical melodrama. It is significant that whereas the former have been exportable to the point of losing easily identifiable national identity, the latter deploy that identity so explicitly as to be scarcely saleable abroad. But in financial and production terms, the distinctions are not nearly so fixed. The versatile Hungarian émigré George Mihalka, for example, has helmed everything from the Canuck slasher *My Bloody Valentine* (1981) to the hit Quebecois fish-out-of-water comedy *La Florida* (1993), while ecumenical Montreal-based production companies Astral and Cinépix (which later moved west to re-emerge as Lions Gate) demonstrate that exploitation and the bottom line will always trump ideology, for better and for worse.[14] While English-Canadian popular cinema straddles the divide between Canada and the United States, Quebec financing, production facilities, and talent have in fact featured prominently in the popular genres of English Canada.

Sex and Genre

It's not the women who are the subject of ridicule in *Porky's*, not at all! It's continually the men who are made to be fools, while the girls are allowed to express their sexuality.

Bob Clark (director)

Alongside film-making personnel and government funding, sex is the great common denominator between popular and art-film genres in Canada.[15] When sultry Alexandrine (Monique Mercure) struts into the general store of Black Lake in *Mon oncle Antoine*, she brings with her the actor's iconic status of her previous year's turn as one of the *Deux femmes en or* (1970, Claude Fournier), bored housewives who sleep their way unrestrainedly and unpunished through Quebecois society, their sexual freedom embodying political and social liberation. But she also gives palpable shape to the indissoluble links between the two sides of Quebecois national cinema (figure 6.1). Jutra may have been ambivalent about that link in *Antoine*, for Mercure's character is both sexually exciting to Benoît, who spies on her as she undresses and later has an erotic dream about her, and socially compromised, the lawyer's trophy wife spoiling herself with the latest from Paris while the miners struggle to stay alive. Nevertheless, he does not deny the power and validity of this contemporary figure even within the historical narrative of his film. But given that she inspires *Antoine*'s greatest divergence from the dicta of *cinéma direct*, he may also be implying her incompatibility with that tradition. In English Canada, Egoyan's *Exotica* and Stopkewich's *Kissed* are without question serious art films, but they received widespread distribution and performed well at the box office in large part because their brilliance was enwrapped in an enticingly sexual package. The first independent feature made in Canada, Nell and Ernest Shipman's *Back to God's Country* (1919), was also the first exploitation movie made in Canada, a big hit in great part because of Ernest's canny publicity of Nell's 'nude' swimming scene (see figure 1.1).[16] While sexploitation helped establish the popular Quebecois film industry and produced the biggest hits of the tax-shelter era, it also underlies a number of the most important auteur films of the end of the

6.1 Monique Mercure's iconic Quebecois sexuality turned inside out by Roy Scheider in David Cronenberg's *Naked Lunch* (1991). Photofest.

century, from *Exotica*, *Kissed*, and *Crash* to Lauzon's *Un zoo la nuit* and *Léolo*, not to mention a large proportion of the new queer cinema. Charged language and bare flesh may serve different functions in sex comedy than in sexually charged drama, but there is more generic common ground than we might suspect, or want to admit, at first glance.[17]

A key point of origin for that common ground was, naturally, Cronenberg's first commercial feature, *Shivers* (1975). Looking for an entrance into feature film, the young film-maker turned to André Link and John Dunning's Cinépix, which had recently moved into production after starting up in 1962 as a distributor of foreign soft-core and exploitation films. Cinépix had inaugurated maple syrup porno with former NFB-documentarist Denis Héroux's *Valérie* (1968), but as Link put it, 'Everybody jumped on the bandwagon. It got too competitive.'[18] Cronenberg shot a sample scene for *Loving and Laughing*, a soft-core attempt to break into the English-language market.[19] In response, they encouraged him to make a horror film; this would eventually lead to *Shivers*. Like Ivan Reitman's debut feature *Cannibal Girls* (1973), *Shivers* was Cinépix's route out of the local arena of Quebec and into the global exploitation market. There is as much continuity as change in the widening perspective, however. In addition to the carry-over of personnel – Sue Helen Petrie went from a starring role in *Loving and Laughing* to feature in *Shivers* – the consistent use of location shooting necessitated by the low budgets also resulted in a strong sense of local setting. Cinépix was keen to use the local quality of these films for publicity, staging a sexual exhibition atop the Gaspé Peninsula's famous

Percé Rock to dramatic effect.[20] Although not all maple syrup porno equated the sexual with the political as straightforwardly as *Valérie* and *Deux femmes en or*, all of the dozen or so films released in the few years before the hard-core hit *Deep Throat* (1972, Gerard Damiano) shattered the soft-core market were steeped in the rhetoric of liberation. In this sense, they tapped into the same Quebecois zeitgeist that had manifested itself in less sexually explicit form in the early films of the new wave such as Jutra's *À tout prendre*, and would be maintained by the films of Gilles Carle and Carole Laure, positioned like Cronenberg's on a fault line between art and exploitation. Maple syrup porno approached liberation in reaction to Catholic repression; Cronenberg's film was susceptible to a similar interpretation: 'French critics really saw *Shivers* as being an attack on the bourgeois life, and bourgeois ideas of morality and sexuality. They sensed the glee with which we were tearing them apart.'[21]

It was apparent to most viewers, however, that *Shivers* had a less straightforward attitude towards morality and sexuality than an overturning of Catholic repression. The characteristically English-Canadian attitude towards sexuality involves ambivalence towards the body, especially when paired with a seriousness of intent well-suited both to horror and science-fiction and to straightforward drama. Cronenberg exists at the extreme of this attitude because his films, in Steven Shaviro's words, 'display the body in its crude, primordial materiality,' collapsing the mind/body distinction and refusing 'the pacifying lures of specular idealization.'[22] But the comic mode characteristic of Quebec was less ambivalent about the body; the local terms for what *Variety* had metonymically dubbed 'maple syrup porno' could not have been more direct: 'films de fesses' (butt movies) or 'films de cul' (ass movies).[23] As André Loiselle has argued, Quebecois comedy has its own form of subversion, and it too is rooted in the 'body as a pantomimic tool of resistance against oppression, quite literally snaking its way out of impasses and achieving sexual gratification.'[24] According to Loiselle, popular Quebec cinema tends to rely on 'visual rather than verbal communication' in contrast to the issues of language that permeate its art films.[25] The primary vehicle of this communication is the spectacular body, derived from the burlesque tradition dating back to the thirties of 'subversion through laughter.'[26] Rather than the 'loser male' of the English-Canadian tradition, including the bland protagonists characteristic of Cronenberg's films, Quebecois losers such as the nerd in *Cruising Bar* (1989, Robert Ménard; sequel in 2008), the heroes of *Ding et Dong le film* (1990), and the ragtag hockey players in *Les Boys* (1997, Louis Saïa) eventually triumph in 'a subversive reversal that turns losers into winners.'[27] The reversal is acted out through their bodies. *Cruising Bar*, for example, is dominated by Michel Côté's virtuoso performance in four separate loser roles: Gérard the Bull, a philandering spare-car-parts dealer; Jean-Jacques the Peacock, a metrosexual eighties yuppie; Patrice the Lion, a mulleted cokehead; and Serge the Earthworm, a pimply geek, all out looking for (straight) sex on a Saturday night. One of the province's most enduringly popular actors, Côté has played (and won awards for) both comic and serious roles for nearly thirty years; he is equally celebrated locally for his starring role in the long-running (1979–2006) theatrical sketch comedy *Broue*. Like *Broue*, *Cruising Bar* is built around its character studies rather than a narrative; events are highly compressed, and comprehensible only in the four-way comparison driven by extensive parallel editing between optimistic preparations for seduction, comically pitiful and degrading efforts to succeed, and final solitary misery, with the single, deus ex machina exception of Serge. Gérard ends up trapped in bed with his wife at a singles hotel for middle-aged swingers; Jean-Jacques's hook-up concludes in impotent humiliation; Patrice's failure to stay clean loses him once again the girlfriend he has just won back. Serge suffers the greatest set of trials, battered in a slam-dancing new wave bar, then cornered by a very large and amorous suitor in a gay bar, before finally being gifted with a trophy girl at the film's conclusion. Côté revisited the characters twenty years later in the equally popular *Cruising Bar 2*; this time we find, in a sign of the times, all of the characters eventually rewarded in their quests, especially, once again, Serge.

It is quite fascinating to view Arcand's *Déclin*, the second biggest local hit of the eighties (see chapter 3), in the context of comedies such as *Cruising Bar*, and not only because Rémy Girard would become a prominent figure in them, starring not only in *La Florida*, but in the wildly successful weekend-warrior ice-hockey franchise, *Les Boys* (1997–2005, television series in 2007; #4, 6, 7, and 12 among Quebecois films, and #20, 23, 25, and 52 on the all-time Quebec box office list, head-to-head against Hollywood). *Cruising Bar* is patently a response to *Déclin*, its loser quartet a parodically mundane refraction of *Déclin*'s glamorously hedonistic academic males. The connection is stressed by the casting of Geneviève Rioux (who plays the grad student cum massage girl, arguably the most positive character in *Déclin*) as Patrice's beautiful ex-girlfriend in *Cruising Bar*, the sole character in the film whose physical appearance and desires are not thoroughly mocked. Arcand's men are financially and sexually successful (at least according to the terms set by the genre); they are articulate and smugly content with their lot in life. His film's women are every bit the equal of the men financially and sexually – even the exploited adjunct Diane (Louise Portal) and the grad student Danielle appear relatively comfortable with their current lot in life. While, as Loiselle suggests, *Déclin* owed its local success to 'the sexual humor and sensual imagery' that it shares with Quebecois comedy and that document the octet's 'apolitical hedonism,' it is equally important to distinguish its slick visuals, masterful dialogue, and tight narrative construction from the episodic parody, slapstick humour, and ramshackle production values that characterize most films in the genre.[28] Moreover, the presence of Yves Jacques's unapologetically gay and sexually active Claude as a member of the quartet not only raised the titillation quotient, it also marked one of the first appearances in mainstream cinema of a gay character qua character, not to mention one of the first cinematic depictions of HIV/AIDS as a mainstream fact of life rather than the scourge of a marginal subculture. Rather than the comic structure of its generic relatives, however, *Déclin* is, strictly speaking, a tragedy, with Rémy brought low by Dominique's calculated betrayal of the secrets of a serial infidelity that all concerned had, until that point, treated as comedy.

The refusal to cater to the norms of polite discourse as regards race, class, and gender is part of what constitutes popular Quebecois cinema's self-identification as other to officially multicultural Canada; like the accented speech itself nearly incomprehensible to outsiders, it is a badge of honour, a marker of the degree to which a film refuses to aspire to an audience and a relevance beyond its own province. Arcand has proven adept at straddling the divide, appealing to both audiences equally. The homophobia that motivates the humiliation of Serge in *Cruising Bar* can be read in this sense as a riposte to *Déclin*'s cosmopolitan sophistication, just as the transmutation of Claude's gay cruiser into Gérard's effete but heterosexual Don Juan reduces and contains an autonomous and comfortably alternative sexual identity within the safe codes of failed heterosexuality. We are not meant to judge *Cruising Bar*'s quartet, nor are we meant to judge bit players such as the homosexual monster who ravages Serge; we are meant to laugh at the exaggerations while enjoying their transgressive excess. As with most popular genre subversion, this victory is equally a ratification of heteronormativity, a triumph for the male who, no matter how unsavoury, is able to win over the desirable woman. The class subversion, in other words, is incommensurate with a subversion of gender roles, unless one argues that by virtue of their repudiation of 'conventional' masculinity – the quintessential stud is either non-existent or the butt of the joke in these films – the sex comedy equally subverts the conventions of heteronormativity and the power relations associated with those conventions.

For the male characters in Quebecois comedy, victory is nearly always defined in the physical terms of sexual gratification, but we see it also in the female protagonists of maple syrup porno and the related films of Carle and Laure, where liberation is equally defined in terms of the body. Just as in Cronenberg's films, female sexuality is particularly threatening, so in sex comedy, the idealized bodies of inaccessible women threaten the uneasy construction of male masculinity. The generically central act of stripping is simultaneously liberating in its refusal of social repression that makes the clothed display of the body a sign of unattainable desire and objectifying in its refusal to acknowledge the subjectivity of the body thereby exposed. In this way sex comedy participates, along with pornography and horror, in what Shaviro views, in opposition to psychoanalytic and post-structuralist theory, as an ontological presence of the image that bypasses cogitation, 'affect[ing] the viewer in a shockingly direct way.'[29] The cruder and more extreme the direct interpellation of the viewer's desire, the more likely it is that the images will exceed the conventional boundaries of mainstream narrative. As a generic device, stupidity, if we follow Loiselle, has the potential to function as a critical tool precisely because it diverges from the respectable norm, revealing the fault lines and contradictions covered over by those norms.

These films, as Shaviro writes of pornography, 'at once provide titillation and provoke boredom. They render everything visible, and they bring everything back to the visible evidence of the body.'[30] Such images, however, can just as easily, and simultaneously, be recuperated into a conventionally repressive framework. Images, especially in their capacity to shock, are highly subject to the passage of time, but while they may always eventually be assimilated to the mainstream economic exigencies from which they arose, they do not thereby cease to be available to the divergent perspective of an alternative community of viewers. If art film incorporates a skewed perspective as part of a closed, controlled system of auteur-generated meaning while equally participating in a global marketplace its closed system occludes, so popular genres also open themselves up to a skewed appropriation, while equally offering the possibility of an unproblematically mainstream reception which would simply look past the same images, set pieces, and contradictions regarded as essential by the marginal perspective of the connoisseur fan. Canadian viewers, both English-Canadian and Quebecois, have perfected marginal perspectives as part of their identity as viewers, English Canadians in their consumption of both local and especially Hollywood product, Quebecois in a comic appropriation of Hollywood genres within their own production system.

The question of display is central to the Canadian inflection of the genres with which it has been most successful, and it certainly derives from the documentary realist tradition. In chapter 2, I wrote of Cronenberg's need to show everything in both his horror and science fiction films, because otherwise the images would not be believed. Similarly, George Mihalka recalls of the innovative special effects of *My Bloody Valentine* (1981), 'What differentiated our film from *Halloween* [1978, John Carpenter], of course, is that ours had a much stronger sense of reality. In *Halloween*, it was mostly done with cuts, but we were doing really strong state-of-the-art effects in single shots, which gave it a much stronger sense of presence.'[31] The display of Michel Côté's body playing four different characters in *Cruising Bar* similarly functions at the centre of the film's meaning, a virtuoso performance at odds with the dysfunctionality of each of the characters. The generic convention of set pieces of sex and/or violence coincides with a Canadian investment in visual authenticity and the integrity of the single shot. Mihalka notes of his teen sex comedy, *Pinball Summer* (1979), 'I would have liked to go a little deeper into social issues, but it was my first film and I was just happy to be part of the team. I wasn't going to lose the opportunity to learn how to make a film, so I decided not to flirt with other issues. Of course by the time I got to *My Bloody Valentine*, I just said, "I'm sneaking this shit in!"'[32] Similarly, Bob Clark insists on the social truth that accompanies the 'over the top' quality of his raunchy sex comedy, 'It was the most outrageous film of its kind, but it was the truth ... *Porky's* was the first one to play us the way we were and I think it did it damn well.'[33] In particular, Clark, a Birmingham, Alabama, native who settled in Canada in the early seventies, insists on the fidelity of Canadian actor Art Hindle's portrayal of a racist policeman who is also a positive character: 'I said "Guys, look, I cut immediately to Billy and Tommy looking at each other, rolling their eyes. What are they going to do in 1954, jump down and preach to this cop?"'[34]

The teen-sex-comedy cycle inaugurated by Bob Clark's *Porky's* (and a specialty of 1980s English-Canadian cinema) is of course as patently *un*realistic in its genre conventions as horror, science fiction, and other popular genres.[35] Within the exaggeration, the stylization, and the patent unreality, for example, of mature actors playing eighteen-year-olds, however, there remains a realism of desire and a realism of effect. At the same time, the stylization allows for highly self-conscious readings of the conventions without thereby disrupting their effect. For Randy Thiessen, while American in its setting and its target audience, *Porky's* can nevertheless also be read as 'a very Canadian deconstruction of traditional (American) masculine ideology – an exposition, and indeed, a subversion of the values it purports to espouse.'[36] Similar to the burlesque dynamic identified by Loiselle in Quebecois comedy, *Porky's* ends not only with the unlikely victory of the teenagers of Angel Beach High School in the Florida Everglades over the corrupt adults who run the Porky's saloon, but also with loser Peewee, the runtish butt of most of the film's jokes, achieving his sole objective in life: getting laid. For Thiessen, the film's excesses subvert the genre's gender categories from within: they expose the 'myths and obsessions' of the discourse of masculinity 'that mark[s] it as being couched in fear and overlaid with anxiety' while 'the stereotypes of the dim-witted sex bomb and the castrating woman are so exaggerated that they are exposed as masculine constructions.'[37] However, Thiessen, like Clark, is well aware that the same excess that 'interrogates' also 'indulges'; popular genres are double-edged, not unified texts, and viewers were able just as easily to accept the constructions, however excessive, as to see through them.[38]

Corupe notes of many Canadian genre movies that, while hewing to the conventions of the Hollywood genres they copy, they are also 'distinctive in the way they present concepts of individuality, community, and even morality.'[39] Just as they tend stylistically towards a greater realism of the image, they also tend to be 'more story and character focused' and display 'a satirical humour that is used to maintain a distance from American popular culture.'[40] And, surprisingly, this characterization is true even of the much maligned *Porky's*. Not only, as Clark recalls, do the boys roll their eyes at the cop's racist remarks, but a key plot point of the film revolves around one of the boy's eventual rejection of his abusive father's anti-Semitism with the simultaneously offensive and subversive taunt, 'If being a man means being like you, I'd rather be queer.' While far more vulgar than former Cinépix producer Ivan Reitman's blockbuster American frat-comedy *Animal House* (1979), *Porky's* is also far less overtly subversive socially. For all their high jinks, the Angel Beach boys and girls are good and conscientious citizens, especially in comparison with the truly dangerous and downright bad folk living in the county next door. Their jokes are more accomplished, their values sounder, and, importantly, they don't take themselves too seriously. Indeed, *Porky's* is far less mean-spirited towards its principal characters than the more recent spate of American gross-out comedies. And, to Clark's mind at least, it's even fairer to women. As he puts it, 'It's not the women who are the subject of ridicule in *Porky's*, not at all! It's continually the men who are made to be fools, while the girls are allowed to express their sexuality.'[41] Indeed, the two warring counties make for a straightforward allegory of Canada and its bigger, rougher, and disorderly neighbour with guns. The Porky's saloon may possess an object of intense desire – it does things the grown-up way, after all – but the boys soon realize that everything they want and need can actually be found on their own side of the border.

Maple syrup porno and the teen sex comedies that followed in its wake project themselves as, in the end, wholesome exaggerations of normal sexuality, just as they use traditional genre conventions to frame their narratives. The art-house cinema of eighties and nineties Canada took the opposite approach, rejecting genre conventions along with sexual norms even as they drew their ideas and iconography from the exploitation films that had preceded them. Cronenberg's production, too, moved during this period away from the confines of exploitation and into the same art-house milieu. After the mainstream genre success of *The Fly* (1986), his subsequent films *Dead Ringers* (1988), *Naked Lunch* (1991, with its own

Monique Mercure cameo as a gender-busting lesbian housekeeper turned male doctor, see figure 6.1), *M. Butterfly* (1993), and *Crash* (1996) all explored alternative sexualities in the challenging style of English-Canadian auteur films of the period. The mediated sexuality of Egoyan's early films *Family Viewing*, *Speaking Parts*, and *The Adjuster* is the most directly indebted to Cronenberg's exploration of the nexus between technology, the body, and sexuality, but Rozema's *White Room* (1990) presents similar scenarios of voyeurism and sexual and social dysfunction. Resembling Cronenberg's films less in their narrative set-ups than in their use of unconventional sexuality as an expression of character and theme, Egoyan's *Exotica*, Stopkewich's *Kissed*, and Lauzon's *Léolo*, probably the most controversial Canadian films outside of Cronenberg's own, contain non-evaluative and sensitively filmed depictions of sexual practices that would not be out of place in the most extreme of exploitation movies. Nor, in their reception, did any of these films, any more than Cronenberg's did, escape from the dual nature of exploitation: the very stuff that makes them brilliant films also makes them cult fodder for niche audiences. The other factor that made sexuality a central feature in Canadian art film of the period was the rise of the new queer cinema and the new niche audiences it could reach through the video market. While not necessarily conceived or marketed for this audience, the often sexually explicit lesbian and gay content of the films of Denys Arcand (*Love & Human Remains*), Thom Fitzgerald, John Greyson, Jeremy Podeswa, Léa Pool, Patricia Rozema, and others steered them towards a reception that was focused on their approach to queer identity (see chapter 8). What marked all of these films as distinctly Canadian alternatives to a Hollywood cinema that was just coming to terms with the possibility of openly gay and lesbian characters was their deadly seriousness.[42] Even given moments of deadpan humour and self-aware parody, these films are almost universally downbeat and earnest, as if this were the only way to distance themselves from the popular genres to which their subject matter bore, in fact, such a close resemblance.

Horror and Canadian Cult Cinema

> *My Bloody Valentine* has a totally different atmosphere and feel to it; it portrayed a gritty universe that was never shown in other horror films and still isn't. We had these working class subtexts about youth having no future and unemployment.
>
> George Mihalka (director)

As exploitation genres go, horror has quite a critical pedigree. Part of this pedigree derives from the deep roots in literature and mythology of monsters such as werewolves, vampires, zombies, ghosts, devils, and Frankenstein. Another part derives from the heavy investment of Freudian psychoanalytic theory in the uncanny and in the psychic disorders that dominate the backstory of serial killers and other members of the less supernatural breed of monsters. As a genre, horror offers an attractive set of themes for the post-structuralist theory that emerged in the early seventies: a self-aware attitude towards genre conventions, a heightened sense of the dynamics of emotional identification, a complex engagement with issues of gender and sexuality, and a core concern for exploring the thresholds of human identity and experience. Naturally, all of these themes also have their correlative in exploitation terms: fan familiarity with conventions, a gruesome spectacle just distant enough to be enjoyed without the viewer feeling implicated, lots of sex and violence, and a subversive attitude towards surface conformity. As Loiselle argues, 'Horror films, even the most reactionary, always defeat their own conservative agendas by allowing the spectator to wallow in a spectacle of madness, sexual deviancy, blood and gore.'[43] Both academic theorists and cult fans participate in an alternative reception of films that seeks out and enjoys meanings distinct from the 'conservative agenda' of the often skeletal narrative structure that contains the exploitative context within a putatively moral frame (the monster is defeated; the victims in some way merit their fate; the survivors in some way merit theirs). The alternative spectatorship is matched by alternative viewing practices: seeking out grindhouse, exploitation, and drive-in theatres exhibiting such films; watching and, later, taping late-night TV screenings; hunting through remainder bins for obscure videos and DVDs; trawling the Internet for rare rips or captures to share. As Will Straw has observed in the context of popular music, such connoisseurship can be both a means of establishing an intrinsically Canadian (or other marginal) identity and a means of receiving second-hand identities filtered through capitalism in a global marketplace.[44]

We can ask, then, in what way the alternative community established by genre connoisseurship intersects with the alternative community of national identity. What, for example, does the handful of critical essays analysing gender and folklore concerns within the *Ginger Snaps* trilogy have to contribute to a discussion of the films' place within Canadian national cinema? The growing number of indigenous outlets focused on Canadian horror – both academic and fan-based – suggests that the genre does have a specific relation to issues of Canadian identity. This impression is reinforced by the fact that certain horror subgenres dominate north of the 49th parallel – body horror, slasher movies, Satanism, and the more nebulous region of cannibals, zombies, and mutant humanoid and animal features. This work is characterized by at least a pretense of realism; with a few exceptions, and for aesthetic, economic, and ideological reasons, there is not much overtly supernatural horror – even a werewolf picture like *Ginger Snaps* is careful to distance itself from the 'magical' elements of silver bullets and the influence of the full moon. Among other recent horror films, *Blood and Donuts* (1995, Holly Dale) sets its vampire tale in the mundane spaces of contemporary Toronto. The overlooked *Pin* (1988, Sandor Stern) grounds its *Psycho*-like tale of a bloodthirsty anatomical dummy and its isolated young male friend in a claustrophobic domestic drama. The Vancouver comedy *Fido* (2007, Andrew Currie) imagines a future beyond zombie apocalypse where the undead have been 'domesticated' as pets in tongue-in-cheek Canadian suburbia. And Bruce McDonald's return to form in *Pontypool* (2008) beautifully develops the close-knit texture of an isolated Ontario community from the suspenseful confines of a glass-enclosed radio studio besieged by language-activated zombies before sinking under the weight of its own conceit in the final half hour.

Part of the new attention to the genre is historical: What do we make of the fact that Julian Roffman's locally produced features, the delinquency drama *The Bloody Brood* (1959) and the internationally distributed horror flick *The Mask* (1961), notwithstanding their precedence over the canonical 'birth' of Canadian cinema in 1964, barely figure in most histories of modern Canadian cinema?[45] What does the existence of a pronounced theatricality within the predominantly realist tradition of Quebecois cinema suggest about the function of the subgenre of horror within that cinema?[46] Or, put more simply, 'What do we in Canada make our horror movies about, and why?'[47] How can we account for the career of quintessentially Canadian directors such as William Fruet or Paul Lynch, whose extensive filmographies include both realist classics such as Fruet's gruelling depiction of Albertan patriarchy, *Wedding in White* (1972), and Lynch's loser drama of an aging country-music singer on the road in small-town Ontario, *The Hard Part Begins* (1973), and Canuxploitation horror such as Fruet's *Death Weekend* (1976), *Spasms* (1983), *Killer Party* (1986), and *Blue Monkey* (1987), a giant insect movie featuring an early appearance by the young Sarah Polley, and Lynch's *Prom Night* (1980) and *Humongous* (1981), not to mention five episodes of Canadian sci-fi TV series *Robocop*? Or how can we account for the career of Bob Clark, whose Canadian productions includes not only the top-grosser *Porky's* but also the horror landmarks *Death Dream* (1974) and *Black Christmas* (1974), the original slasher movie, and the family holiday classic *A Christmas Story* (1983)? And what of the strong and strongly Canadian supporting roles played by *Goin' Down the Road* star Doug McGrath in *Black Christmas* and *Porky's* or iconic actress and auteur Jackie Burroughs in everything from *The Care Bears Movie* (1985) and *Road to Avonlea* (1990–6) to *Food of the Gods II* (1989) and *Bleeders* (1997)? To ask such questions broadens the historical scope of Canadian film production; it also clearly permits a younger generation of film-makers and critics to find some sort of common ground between the strict 'quality' criteria of Canadian realism and the movies and television they actually grew up watching.

There is both an intellectual and a more purely visceral pleasure in what Vatnsdal terms the identification of 'Canuck-O-Vision, that peculiarly Canadian quality which infects so many movies from north of the 49th,' just as there is in the 'camp value' of trash cinema.[48] As Taylor notes, the 'real subversiveness' of 'substandard cinema' lies in its offering a different set of critical values to a specific audience: '1) an unadulterated pleasure at the "low," "base," or "carnal" qualities of the films; 2) resistance to the technical slickness of filmmaking's more dominant modes; 3) a subversion of "acceptable" exhibition and viewing practices; and 4) the potential undermining of "legitimate criticism."'[49] Such a viewing position underlies much of the more 'respectable' film-making of Canada, from the homage to *Black Christmas* in Egoyan's *Exotica* and Rozema's *White Room* to Erik Canuel's citation of comics and B-movies as his primary cinematic influences, to the explicitly trash-movie aesthetic of the avant-garde film-making of Winnipeggers Noam Gonick, Guy Maddin, John Paisz, and others. Just as the critical commonplace finds 'Canadian content' in art and auteur cinema, so the Canadian genre cinema connoisseur takes pleasure in noting 'a plaid shirt, the CN tower or a stray accidental "Eh?"'[50] – signs betraying both the local origins of an apparently anonymous exploitation film and the local interests and idiosyncrasies of the film-maker, cast, and crew insinuated into the many cracks and crevices opened up by the looser production circumstances of low-budget moviemaking. As Bob Presner, producer of *My Bloody Valentine*, recalls of the local colour effectively projected by the big-city cast, 'As far as the accents go, in the Maritimes, there are certain lilts to speech that are so infectious, that some of the actors just started taking on the Nova Scotia drawl. One of the kids from Toronto all of a sudden started saying "Aye, bye" and all that, and nobody knew where he had gotten it – it was just kind of osmotic.'[51] The result of such details of script, setting, and acting, for an audience attuned to local detail as well as genre niceties, is not simply an entertaining parlour game but, as Vatnsdal rightly argues, 'at least as enlightening and realistic a portrait of Maritime economic depression as *Goin' Down the Road*, making it perhaps the single most successful synthesis of the Canadian documentary tradition with pure genre cinema.'[52]

This is less a case of special pleading than it may at first appear. While the Toronto-centred, documentary realist drama of *Goin' Down the Road* laid the film open to accusations of condescension and the glossing over of 'class and regional divisions,' the local detail of *My Bloody Valentine*, down to shooting in a recently closed coal mine in Sidney Mines, Nova Scotia, provides no external social or class perspective from which to gain perspective on the dead-end life of the youngsters.[53] Moreover, just like *Goin' Down the Road*, the backstory plays on the two choices available to the men – either leave for the West coast, like the mayor's son T.J., and return, failures, to work in the mines, or stick around as failures, like miner's son Axel – and to the women, who can either get married or not, and choose their loser, as Sarah (Lori Hallier) must, between T.J. and Axel. Rather than structure the film's theme, however, the backstory and the realism provide an effective setting for the horror pyrotechnics, so persuasively realistic and 'ugly and mean and nasty' that the MPAA insisted on numerous cuts in order to avoid an X-rating.[54] For Mihalka, as for connoisseurs of the genre, the background realism of the film, like the integral shots that showcase the effects, set the film apart from the run-of-the-mill slasher movie; furthermore, it asserted a different attitude towards its characters, 'These things [the working-class subtext] were certainly not the domain of slasher films, which basically had interchangeable Barbies and Kens running around getting drunk and being punished for having sex. And that still seems to be the format! Even the new remake of *Valentine* focuses on that more than anything else. It's like, "It's bad to have sex, someone's gonna kill you for it!"'[55] The documentary realist tradition tends to insert working-class characters into a broader social and aesthetic framework in order to demonstrate their fundamental incommensurability with and incomprehension of the capitalist system that exploits them, aestheticizing their plight. In contrast, *My Bloody Valentine* incorporates the characters' own recognition of their exploitation within a generic framework that provides a displaced articulation of the unacceptable nature of that exploitation solely from within the aesthetic and social conventions of that community. As Mihalka puts it, 'Harry Warden [the original Valentine's Day killer] wasn't born evil, he was a hardworking guy who went insane when the bosses neglected the people that worked for them, causing a disaster. I really insisted on this subtext. Okay, it's not exactly a treatise on *Das Kapital*, but at the same time, that's who the character is.'[56] Rather than suggesting we mock and pity the characters from a distance, the peculiar realism of the horror genre makes us identify with them, both the victims and the perpetrator. Rather than vitiating the social subtext, the genre context mirrors and reinforces its argument: just as the exploitation genre renders class rage through the dominant structure of the conventional Hollywood narrative, so does the local identity emerge from the cracks of the anonymous American genre. It's 'not exactly a treatise on *Das Kapital*,' but that's the point; marginalized audiences already know their plight all too well and what they want is a different way of experiencing, mastering, and even enjoying some aspect of that plight. Neither art film nor trash cinema will cause revolution, but they do complement rather than contradict one another in the ways in which they articulate social truth and envision alternatives to exploitation and oppression.

There is no single alternative viewing position from which to encompass all of Canadian horror, or of any other Canadian genre. There is a different agenda at work in arguing that *Black Christmas* and *My Bloody Valentine* encompass a Canadian viewpoint through the realist aesthetic within which they contextualize their special effects and spectacular violence than in arguing for the appreciation of exploitation cinema for its very lack of quality and realism or for its representation of marginalized viewpoints, whether regional or gender or ethnically based. Indeed, the multiplicity of possible alternative viewing positions is one of the distinctions between a genre-based view of cinema and an auteur-based view. While the latter approach grounds its arguments in a consistent and controlled generation of meaning from the standpoint of the film-maker's intentions, the former approach bases its arguments on a fragmented generation of meaning from different and often contradictory standpoints. An auteurist approach, for example, cannot encompass the reception of *Exotica* or *Kissed* by exploitation fans, just as an exploitation fan would not understand an auteurist's disgust at their skipping around the artfully constructed narrative to get to the 'good' parts, even though that viewing position is an integral component of the diegetic meaning of both films, which are keenly, if uncomfortably, aware of their participation in it.

This distinction can be seen in the changing reception of Cronenberg's oeuvre. Up through *Videodrome*, his films looked like and were received as genre exploitation; hence, the furor over CFDC funding of *Shivers* and the either vocal or silent refusal to consider his work from within the context of Canadian cinema. At the same time, Cronenberg's stature as a horror auteur gained him a cult following focused precisely on ways in which his films subverted the mainstream in the extremity of their sex and violence, their innovative prosthetic effects, and the ambiguous spectator identification they elicited. By the time of *Videodrome*, he was recognized as an important film-maker, but within a global genre context rather than a Canadian art one. This stature was solidified with the more mainstream generic fare of *The Dead Zone* and *The Fly*; it was only with *Dead Ringers*, its thematically and narratively contextualized shock effects, and the marquee performance of Jeremy Irons that Cronenberg was reluctantly admitted within the Canadian pantheon. Nevertheless, the enduring signs of his fundamental incompatibility with key tenets of Canadian realism meant that his auteur cinema remained highly controversial, a site of virulent debate rather than the more subdued critical give-

and-take characteristic of academic criticism, especially in Canada. An important component of this effect is the fact that Cronenberg is basically the only Canadian director to have remained in Canada and also to have had a fundamental and enduring impact on a particular genre, for it is his films more than any others that helped define the critical and popular genre of body horror and articulate a fundamental shift away from the external threat of monsters and towards the internal threat of disease and psychopathy. For Linda Badley, this shift in particular marks the replacement of Freudian psychoanalytic models of the monster as a form of the return of the repressed with a culture 'saturat[ed] with sexual images and options, a state of cultural hyperconsciousness, confusion, and terror': 'Horror announced the crisis in the 1970s and 1980s through its images – its bodies in pieces and organic machines, its sexual mutations and re-genderations.'[57] While the moral evaluation of the shift remains a keen subject for debate both in Cronenberg's work and in writing on horror in general, its existence is generally accepted.

The fundamental concern for realism characteristic of the most influential Canadian horror films emerges from and is itself an important vehicle for the renewed focus on the body. Because the horror emerges now from proximity rather than distance, the effective mimesis of the familiar is essential for the unfamiliar horror that grows from it. Even within films exhibiting the cheapest production values, the extradiegetic recognition of locations, actors, and other traces of everyday life heightens rather than diminishes the power of the monstrous images, regardless of how much it violates the dictates of Hollywood 'realism.' As Loiselle persuasively argues of Quebecois satanic horror films of the seventies such as *Le Diable parmi nous* (1971, Jean Beaudin) and *The Pyx* (1973, Harvey Hart), 'While normal characters are made to appear commonplace in keeping with cultural standards of realism, the monster is performed and filmed to stress its deviant behaviour through the interruption of realism.'[58] Loiselle's choice of both francophone and anglophone films for analysis stresses the degree to which genre cuts across the often artificial linguistic and cultural divisions between the two solitudes, even as the shared Montreal setting of the two films stresses their shared Canadian identity. Moreover, Loiselle logically but also polemically includes Montreal-set and filmed *Shivers* and *Rabid* among his corpus of 'Québécois horror.'[59] And while Cronenberg's films do not fall within the subgenre of Satanism, their contrast of location shooting and blandly realistic drama with wildly fantastic sex-and-violence set pieces strikes a similar effect to the one Loiselle describes, using realist conventions to challenge the ideological assumptions on which they are based. This effect is clear already in the opening to *Shivers*, where, without warning, we watch Dr Emil Hobbes, a respectable-looking middle-aged man, bind, strip, and slit open the belly of Annabelle, a teenager dressed as a schoolgirl, before slitting his own throat. Cross-cut with banal scenes of a young professional couple being toured around the apartment complex by its agent, the sequence shocks not only through its juxtaposition of the normal with the deviant but also through the unannounced sexual violence of the sequence. The evisceration of the young girl's body suggests a wholly different relationship between interior and exterior than the Cartesian coordinates of realism, without having given us the slightest clue as to why it is occurring. Now, the exploitation viewer accepts the fact of the sexual violence as

6.2 The high-concept teaser credit-sequence of *Ginger Snaps* (2000): high school misfits as performance artists.

the conventional teaser for what is to come, but formally the very nature of that convention disrupts the deliberate unfolding of a realist narrative.

We see a similar gambit in the opening minutes of *Ginger Snaps* (2000), director John Fawcett and scenarist Karen Walton's clever and influential update on the werewolf genre via Cronenberg's body horror. After a teaser homage to the suburban garden accident and severed-ear opener of David Lynch's *Blue Velvet* – a child in a suburban sandbox discovers the severed paw of the family dog – the credit sequence plays over a series of perfectly staged and lurid scenes of Ginger's (Katharine Isabelle) and Brigitte's (Emily Perkins) gruesome suicides: impaled on a picket fence, run over by a car, frozen in a freezer, stabbed with a pitchfork, run over by a lawnmower, drinking hydrogen peroxide together (figure 6.2).

The sequence is highly intertextual, referencing not only the eponymous hero's hobby in the cult black comedy of adolescent alienation *Harold and Maude* (1971, Hal Ashby) but also the *Untitled Film Stills* of contemporary artist Cindy Sherman. It is highly self-conscious about the exploitation connotations of the convention of the teaser: several of the shots are sexually suggestive, taking full advantage of Isabelle's looks and figure (a fact knowingly accentuated by a classmate's wolf-whistling crack about wanting to see the slides with Ginger again). At the same time as the sequence fulfils its genre task of titillation, it theatricalizes the task by showing us the process whereby the teenage sisters Ginger and younger Brigitte are stag-ing the shots with all of the skill and dedication of the special effects crew of the film itself. Moreover, at the end of the extended sequence of suicides, the camera pulls back to show us a movie screen, an appreciative audience of teenagers at their classroom desks, and a male teacher, aghast at the result of the sisters' social studies project. In the place of the earnest NFB-style documentary he presumably had in mind, they have proposed genre horror, in full and gleeful awareness of the reception they will receive. What is fascinating about the scene, as about the entire film, is not just its considerable cleverness and its black humour; it is the degree to which the self-consciousness is not external but intrinsic to the film's meaning and its development of character. First, we recognize the suicide pact as an expres-sion of the girls' adolescent alienation; it enunciates simultaneously their misery and their superiority to the world around them. But we also recognize, as they do not, the difference between their aesthetic mobilization of horror tropes as a sign of subversion and the fact that when death actually comes upon them, as it must in a horror movie, it will be neither aesthetic nor a release. Because their student film is a statement of their refusal to accept the gender constraints that accompany the transformation into mature women – at ages sixteen and fifteen neither has yet had her period – it consciously plays on the difference between displaying their bodies in a fiction on screen and hiding them, along with their sexuality, in 'real life.'

The dramatic tension between their intellectual ability to control this distinction and their bodies' betrayal is at the heart of the film's emotional power, as it is in Cronenberg's oeuvre. When Ginger gets her period on the same night she is bit-ten by a werewolf ('the curse,' she calls it, echoing the film's tagline, 'They don't call it the curse for nothing'), she is, like any good Cronenberg protagonist, highly ambivalent about its effects: she grows hair and a tail, becomes excitedly sexually predatory, and develops an insatiable taste for blood even as she equally recog-nizes these symptoms as a betrayal of everything she and her sister continue to believe in. She embodies within the film, in other words, the simultaneous pleas-ure and disavowal of pleasure Paul Coates has identified as the position in which viewers tend to consume exploitation cinema.[60] Isabelle brilliantly captures Gin-ger's ambivalent transformation, all the more uncanny in that it mimics exactly the sexual display her culture expects of a sixteen-year-old girl. Just as Seth Brundle's transformation initially manifests itself as a hyper-masculinity before he is able to recognize the urges as the early symptoms of 'Brundlefly,' so the 'ache' that Ginger at first thinks is sexual desire turns out really to be the desire 'for tearing everything to pieces.' But it is not as if this 'ache' is all that different from the girls' extreme misanthropy at the start of the film; the difference is that previously it was a performance – if a deeply felt performance as only adolescent acting out can be – whereas now it is an uncontrollable 'disease.' And, just as in *The Fly*, the disease is driving a rift between the monster and its only human attachment in the film. Ginger and Brigitte cannot experience the transformation together, and even as Ginger tries to describe its pleasures, the audience knows where those pleasures will take her. As in Cronenberg's films, however, we must determine for ourselves whether it is worth it. 'It feels so good, Brigitte. It's like touching yourself. You know every move. Right on the fucking dot. And after, you see fucking fireworks, supernovas. I'm a goddamn force o' nature. I feel like I could just do anything.' She is describing murder, not sex, but as in Cronenberg's films, the equation of the two suggests the simultaneously transgressive and untenable quality of untrammelled desire within human society.

As Molloy suggests of the film, lycanthropy as disease is 'not a metaphor for AIDS, it is an STD.'[61] Because it is not metaphorical, there is no distance between the thing and its representation; as in *Shivers*, the situation is existential rather than allegorical. This effect is reinforced by the film's refusal to conform to the 'magical' explanations of the Hollywood werewolf: there are no silver bullets, no full moon needed for transformation – the disease is biological. As April Miller observes, the refusal of Ginger's disease to conform to mythology and to Hollywood leads her initially to reject Brigitte's explanation of what has happened to her. Ginger asks, 'Did I change last night, howl at the moon and kill shit and change back this morning? Huh? No. Did it take a silver bullet to stop that thing? No. It [the thing that bit her] got killed by a fucking truck.'[62] The events in the narrative within the film conform perfectly to the film's own revisionary take on the genre. This revisionism is first and foremost a woman-centred one (when Fawcett approached the reluctant Walton about writing the film, he persuaded her by suggesting she 'make the type of horror film that she would like to see.')[63] The result, as Miller argues, 'uses the werewolf as a metaphor not just for the horrors of puberty but also for the limits placed on female sexual subjectivity.'[64] For Aviva Briefel, the film is a key example of the 'menstrual plot' characteristic of female monsters 'that both critiques and enacts our comfort with the familiarity of female monsters by presenting us with a story that can be mapped over twenty-eight days.'[65] Molloy, Miller, and Briefel reach different conclusions about *Ginger Snaps*, dependent on their different attitudes towards genre and popular culture; what this weight of critical attention to a genre film suggests is that the film touched a nerve with a specific audience.

The revisionism of the film is not solely thematic, however; while they may comment on the incongruity of werewolves in a 'normal' suburban environment, the sisters' realistic response to Ginger's plight resonates strongly with the Canadian tradition of realism as well as the Canadian capacity to see all sides of the equation. As critics noted of the film, its characters talk and act like actual teenagers; the werewolf plot brings extreme consequences, but the lead-up to those consequences, and even the events within which they occur, are a high-stakes version of typical teenage life instead of anything extraordinary: the male lead is the local pot grower, Ginger passes on the disease in the back seat of the local boy's car, the climax begins at a raucous party, the parents are well-meaning but clueless. Similarly, rather than a singular phenomenon, lycanthropy in this film and in its two sequels, *Ginger Snaps: Unleashed* (2004, written by Megan Martin and directed by the original film's editor Brett Sullivan) and *Ginger Snaps Back: The Beginning* (2004, written by Christina Ray and Stephen Massicotte and directed by Grant Harvey), exists on a continuum with other phenomena: menstruation and 'female sexual subjectivity' in the first film; drug addiction in the second (Brigitte mainlines wolf's bane to keep her lycanthropy at bay); the Native American monster the Windigo and the forces of colonization in the third, which takes place in 1815 in the Canadian wilderness. The low-key intensity of all three films suggests a Canadian subtext to the revisionism; the films internalize their difference from the Hollywood version of the genre as a Canadian difference: smart-ass, alienated, and ironic. The explicitly Canadian content comes out more strongly in the later films: Brigitte kills a werewolf in *Unleashed* with a curling stone; *Snaps Back* takes place entirely in the wilderness in the dead of winter (it was filmed in Alberta) and involves colonial traders and Native Americans. Nevertheless, the integrated Canadianism of genre revision is strongest in the first film; the explicit Canadianisms in the other two feel more like campy playing to the perceived desire of the first film's audience for 'Canuck-o-vision.'[66] Nevertheless, the idea of rehearsing the sisters' tragedy as the originary moment of Canadian colonial oppression – faced with the choice of killing her sister or cursing the Native people, Brigitte chooses the latter – is a flight of fancy worthy of Canadian horror, suggesting nothing less than the rewriting of Canadian history as the hopeless, atemporal, and savagely contrarian odyssey of a pair of nonconformist sisters.

Science Fiction and Canadian Paranoia

It's a market-driven call. One, if you look at that last 15 years, there's been a wave of erotic thrillers, there's been a wave of mob films, but science fiction is the only genre that has remained absolutely consistent as a reliable performer within the world of B-movie production – the films that go directly to video, with perhaps a symbolic theatrical release before going to cable. And now, as the market faces a higher state of chaos than there's ever been, sci-fi is about the only thing that will make the distributors feel confident. And two, foreign markets are claiming a bigger and bigger role in the ability to finance these pictures.

Daniel D'or (Canadian film producer)

I like science fiction, personally. There's an opportunity to challenge conventional thoughts, to come up with the great 'What if?' scenarios. These are the qualities that give you an opportunity to have real fun. But the fundamental parameters can't change. There has to be action, there has to be guns, there has to be explosions, and there has to be a strong, American lead.

Philip Jackson (Canadian film producer)

Paul Lynch's *Prom Night* launched the first Canadian genre franchise; the *Ginger Snaps* trilogy is probably the most accomplished of them. Before *Ginger Snaps*, however, Cronenberg's sci-fi hit *Scanners* had birthed its own Canadian series – *Scanners II: The New Order* (1991, Christian Duguay), *Scanners III: The Takeover* (1992, Duguay), *Scanner Cop* (1994, Pierre David), and *Scanners: The Showdown* aka *Scanner Cop II* (1995, Steve Barnett). Like *The Fly II* (produced stateside but filmed in Vancouver), the *Scanners* series is a pale imitation of the original with little direct connection beyond the concept and backstory of the scanners and the special effects set piece of the exploding head. Meanwhile, Vincenzo Natali's surprise international sci-fi horror hit *Cube* (1997) would eventually spawn its own trilogy (*Cube²: Hypercube* [2002, Andrzej Sekula] and *Cube Zero* [2004, Ernie Barbarash]); like the *Ginger Snaps* trilogy, the sequels (and prequels) are conceptually intriguing and professionally executed but do not approach the high bar set by the original. The existence of these series testifies to the maturity of the genre industry in Canada, and the success of *Ginger Snaps* and *Cube* suggests a real Canadian affinity to the genres. Science fiction is a newer fixture in Canadian cinema than horror and a less common one, partly due to the budgetary restrictions of the genre. What there is of it is nearly always highly conceptual and, like Canadian sex comedy and Canadian horror, characterized by a concern with the body and identity, mediated here through the theme of technology. Since its beginnings, basically with Cronenberg's *Scanners* and *Videodrome*, unless we include his earlier experimental features *Stereo* and *Crimes of the Future*, Canadian sci-fi has always been strongly imbued with horror. This is equally true of *Cube*, the most successful non-Cronenberg sci-fi film in Canada, as it is of action-sci-fi such as Christian Duguay's *Scanners* sequels and *Screamers* (1995) and its direct-to-video sequel *Screamers: The Hunting* (2008). The consistent thread of nearly all Canadian science fiction is the Philip Dick/William Gibson cyberpunk theme of the human/machine interface.

Where the cult appeal of extreme sex and violence drives the horror genre, science fiction is primarily speculative; its spectacular appeal lies in its representation of technology, the gadgets dear to the space opera that has always dominated the form. Stanley Kubrick's influential epic *2001: A Space Odyssey* (1969) and Andrei Tarkovsky's lyrically allegorical *Solaris* (1972) and *Stalker* (1979) epitomize the cerebral side of the genre, while George Lucas's *Star Wars* (1977) renovated the effects-laden G-rated space opera for a new generation. Canadian sci-fi has had little to do with either of these subgenres; its purview derives from the success of *Scanners*, one of the only Canadian films to debut at #1 in the *Variety* list of box office hits and certainly the first Canadian sci-fi film to do so, and the media theory of Torontonian Marshall McLuhan and cyberpunk guru Gibson (who emigrated to Canada from the United States in 1968, settling in Vancouver). *Scanners* infused science fiction with a strong horror component – indeed, Cronenberg refers to it generically as horror in discussing its popular success[67] – which increased its viability in the new VHS market, while the future noir and dystopian view of technology of Gibson's writing produced a new visual aesthetic better suited for the budget restrictions and scenic interests of Canadian film-makers. The *Alien* and *Terminator* series, which began in 1979 and 1984, respectively, with Canadian transplant James Cameron intimately connected to both, were highly influential in the subgenres of horror-sci-fi and future noir. Both series project dark and dystopian attitudes not only towards authority but also towards historical progress, the *Alien* series working through these themes organically, climaxing in Ripley's impregnation with an alien fetus in *Alien Resurrection* (1997, Jean-Pierre Jeunet), and the *Terminator* series ringing changes on the cyborg premise via its time-travel paradox.

Cronenberg's attitude towards the more spectacular aspects of the genre is evident in his description of his involvement during the eighties in the De Laurentiis production of Ron Shusset and Dan O'Bannon's adaptation of a Dick story as *Total Recall*, which would eventually be directed by Paul Verhoeven with Arnold Schwarzenegger and Sharon Stone in 1990. Cronenberg sharply distinguishes between what he terms the 'silly stuff' in the script and the 'stunning premise … about memory and identity and madness.'[68] In contrast to Shusset's conception of 'Raiders of the Lost Ark Go to Mars,' Cronenberg 'wasn't excited by the gimmicks, the vehicles and the glass city. It was the human element that excited [him].'[69] After a year's work and twelve drafts of the script, Cronenberg and De Laurentiis called it quits; he would make *The Fly* instead, another hybrid of science fiction and horror, high-tech in its premise but focused on the 'human element' and conceived through the body. Cronenberg has never quite adopted Philip Jackson's 'fundamental parameters' of science fiction: 'There has to be action, there has to be guns, there has to be explosions, and there has to be a strong, American lead.'[70] Nevertheless, it is true that *Scanners* is the closest to a mainstream sci-fi picture Cronenberg has made – there is action, even a car chase, and there are guns and explosions – and that his other most strongly sci-fi films, *Videodrome* and *eXistenZ*, also feature action, guns, and explosions, although the gun as anatomical appendage or mutant-creature-bones construction is not exactly the conventional genre usage. Moreover, the latter films feature American lead James Woods and English star Jude Law, respectively. Nevertheless, their action, such as it is, remains subordinated to the high concept.

Following closer to Jackson's dictum is the prolific Quebecois director Christian Duguay (b. 1957). A graduate of Montreal's Concordia Film School, Duguay apprenticed making rock-music videos and as a cinematographer before he was hired by original *Scanners* (and *Videodrome* and numerous further Canuxploitation films) producer Pierre David to direct back-to-back sequels to the film in response to a request from the film's rabid Swedish fan base.[71] A loyal Montrealer, Duguay brought a highly local visual sensibility to *Scanners II* and *Scanners III*, both in identifiably genuine, if generically darkened and noir-styled, Montreal exteriors, and especially in *II*, an increasingly wintry, snow-covered landscape.[72] Moreover, *Scanners II* includes *Déclin* star Dorothée Berryman in a cameo as the unnamed city's well-meaning but inconsequential mayor, assassinated by the plotting villain Commander John Forrester (Yvan Ponton) as part of his plan to turn the city into a police state ruled by a force of drugged scanners. Playing her role with a pronounced accent, in contrast to Quebecois veteran Ponton's 'neutral' English, Berryman lightly suggests a Franco-Anglo tension in the power struggle between the forces of corporate conspiracy and everyday people. This tension is clearest in the scene midpoint in the film where hero David Kellum (British-born Canadian-based actor David Hewlett) travels deep into the snowy country to seek clues about his identity from his parents, played by veteran character actors Murray Westgate and Doris Petrie as quintessentially simple, pragmatic, good farmers. Naturally, Kellum turns out to be the adopted son of Cameron Vale and Kim Obrist (the heroes of *Scanners*, and the film's only nod to its point of origin), and naturally, the corrupt police lieutenant Gelson (Vlasta Vrana) and the rogue scanner Peter Drak (Raoul Trujillo) track Kellum to the farm and kill his parents. Kellum's odyssey takes him further north to 'Lake Washimeska,' where his birth sister Julie Vale

(Deborah Raffin) has been living in seclusion since a run-in with Forrester (their parents' murderer) eight years earlier. Further exposition follows, with the upshot being that David and Julie besiege the headquarters of the evil doctor Morse (Tom Butler), free the scanners, defeat and physically maim Forrester, and restore order to the city. Visually, Duguay traces their ascendancy via the weather; essentially, Julie brings the snow with her into the alien city, and the final shot of the film finds the pair outside the futuristically modernist Morse Institute, now blanketed in snow, as if Canadian wholesomeness has retaken a city besieged by anonymously global interests.

It's a plausible subtext for a director making an English-language movie while professing a deep affinity for Montreal and an inferiority complex vis-à-vis the local Quebecois film culture.[73] And, certainly, thematically there is almost nothing left of Cronenberg's conception of the ambivalent experience of a mutated body; Duguay and scenarist B.J. Nelson pick up on the action potential of telekinesis and mind-reading, transforming it into an enhanced combat skill more than a sci-fi concept. What they primarily retain from Cronenberg, naturally, is the exploding head and some other less interesting 'kills' for the film's cult audience. Although it too features Montreal locations and a beautiful riverside home drenched in autumn foliage (filmed in exclusive Senneville, on Montreal Island), *Scanners III* moves further down the road towards an anonymously global action scenario and shifts gears towards camp, complete with a long and tedious section in Thailand, where Alex Monet (Steve Parrish), traumatized by accidentally sending his best friend flying out of a window high above the downtown mall Les Cours Mont-Royal, tries to find his way and hone his mind-blasting skills in a Buddhist monastery. Along with this venture into scanner kung fu, including a marketplace fight scene homage to Hong Kong martial arts (fairly cutting-edge hip back in 1989, when the film was shot), Duguay also includes a segment of scanner comedy, when Alex's sister Helena (Liliana Komoroska), peeved at being dissed by her corporate boss, mind-forces him into a disco dance and striptease among the tables of a swanky restaurant and in front of some top clients. The Polish-born Komoroska, who would marry Duguay after meeting him on the set of the film, turns in a highly entertaining scenery-chewing performance as the meek and neurotic survivor of abuse at the scanner clinic who is transformed by the experimental drug EPH-3 into an ice-queen bitch, plotting a scanner takeover of the world, and so evil she mind-blasts a pigeon that defecates on her. Her discovery that she can mind-control through video permits an amusing homage to the Deborah Harry cigarette burning and generally mediated thematics of *Videodrome*, but it is used purely for show and for fun. Rather than thematizing the effect of a drug that eliminates the negative symptoms suffered by scanners (the constant psychic chatter) while eliminating inhibitions and moral scruples, Duguay and Nelson play it as straightforward villainy, replete with further exploding heads, hypodermic needles, and other creative violence effects. Both films are competent and engaging genre performances, far superior to the final entries in the series.

Already established in American television, Duguay caught the attention of Hollywood in 1995, the year, according to a cover story in *Take One*, that 'Canadian science fiction came of age,' with the release of two big-budget features, Duguay's $14-million *Screamers* and New York artist-turned-director Robert Longo's $26-million *Johnny Mnemonic*.[74] Although both films received mixed reviews, and neither was a massive hit, they did eventually turn a profit, mostly in the global market, a testimony to the international popularity of the genre, as well as to the drawing power of Hollywood Canadian Keanu Reeves, star of *Johnny Mnemonic*. As Canadian producers Philip Jackson and Daniel D'or note, science fiction is huge around the Pacific Rim.[75] *Screamers* was written by *Alien* and *Total Recall*'s Don O'Bannon and Miguel Tejada-Flores from a short story by Dick; *Johnny Mnemonic* boasted a script by Gibson himself. Although *Johnny Mnemonic* is conceptually the more interesting of the two, it is almost unwatchably bad as a film. The story of a data trafficker (Reeves) who has a brain implant allowing him to carry enormous amounts of sensitive information as a courier, the film takes place in a typical cyberpunk future. The world is controlled by nebulous multinationals, the environment is composed of degraded urban slums, and a disease known as Nerve Attenuation Syndrome is ravaging the population. The plot concerns a battle between the rebel Lo-Teks, who live in a makeshift structure built in an abandoned Newark, NJ, bridge and assassins hired to kill Johnny before he can download the information out of his brain. In typical future noir fashion, Johnny is a loner outsider who eventually and reluctantly sides with the Lo-Teks. Gibson blamed the film's fiasco with the critics on Tri-Star, the American distributor (Robert Lantos and Alliance had produced the film): 'Basically what happened was it was taken away and re-cut by the American distributor in the last month of its pre-release life, and it went from being a very funny, very alternative piece of work to being something that had been very unsuccessfully chopped and cut into something more mainstream.'[76] It is a plausible explanation; one of the hazards of the science fiction genre is that its greater budget requirements lead to loss of artistic control, and certainly the film has a liberal, multi-ethnic, underground vibe somewhat at odds with the mainstream target audience, especially as comedy is an unconventional element of future noir and cyberpunk. Nevertheless, the film also shows undeniable evidence of inexperience in its erratic tone and pacing as well as highly derivative sets, visuals, and, pace Gibson, script. It's an acceptable genre ride, which is why it did well overseas and on video, and it is recognizably Canadian in its anti-authoritarian thematics and multicultural liberalism, which mostly goes to demonstrate the degree to which Gibson's concerns coincide with those of his adopted country. On the other hand, the easy polarity between good and evil, the standard noir dynamics, and Montreal and Toronto's masquerading as Newark and Beijing tend towards making the film more of an exercise in the erasure of the local on the order of Reeves, the invisible Canadian at its head.

Although superficially more like Hollywood in its focus on action and its quest structure, *Screamers* works better as a lean, well-paced genre movie, its Canadian-ness wrought into its dramatic structure and characters as much as its ideas. Just enough of Dick's concept remains to thematize the boundaries of identity, while the initial set-up is strongly redolent of Quebecois history. Against a complicated backdrop of interstellar rebellion and political machinations, all that remains of a distant planet settled as a mining colony is a pocket of Alliance troops led by Colonel Joseph Hendricksson (Peter Weller) holed up in a bunker facility and the nearby stronghold of its enemy, the NEB. The desolate landscape outside is patrolled by 'screamers,' cat-sized machines that burrow through the earth and track and kill NEB soldiers with circular saw appendages. Designed to reproduce independently, the screamers have become sentient, developing sophisticated models of killing machines so closely mimicking the appearance and actions of human beings that by the end of the film, as in *Blade Runner*, it is impossible to distinguish one from the other. The main plot of the film has Hendricksson trekking across the frozen desolation (scenes were shot in nearby quarries at night in the dead of winter) to parlay with the NEB. On the way, he encounters a small group of outsiders camping in underground ruins, including the love interest Jessica (Jennifer Rubin), and a couple of hick soldiers, including Becker (Roy Dupuis). They soon discover that new-model screamers have wiped out what was left of the NEB; next they discover the Alliance bunker has been infiltrated. First Becker and then Jessica reveal themselves to be screamers. Jessica, however, saves Hendricksson as they try to escape the planet on an emergency escape ship, but a screamer herself, she refuses to leave, sacrificing herself. As in moments of the *Scanners* films, Duguay includes signature Quebecois melodramatic emotion, especially at the end. Dupuis's hair-trigger tough guy provides an early English-language sci-fi preparation for his long-running role in *Nikita*. Weller plays his role in businesslike, grizzled, cynical veteran style, and the philosophical speculation is well buried by the fast-moving action. The visuals are an impressive amalgam of realistic Canadian landscape with the urban industrial wasteland architecture typical of future noir, constructed in the genuine wasteland of Montreal's domed Olympic Stadium, abandoned during the baseball strike.[77] Duguay's action-oriented direction turns out good product, but it downplays the subversive elements of the genre to the degree that *Take One* writer Noah Cowan detected a 'pronounced retro-Republican streak' in its depiction of a failed revolution, creating a device that would be its own demise.[78] And while Cowan's analysis downplays both the noir roots lurking beneath a fairly superficial political plot and a greater Quebecois tolerance for macho posturing, there is certainly a distance between Duguay's scanners – gentle and decent David and the empowered Helena – and Weller's world-weary American soldier pose.

   Screamers would get a direct-to-video sequel in 2008 (*Screamers: The Hunting*, Sheldon Wilson), this time shot in Newfoundland; Duguay, meanwhile, continued to hone his reputation as a Hollywood-style action helmer while working out of his Montreal base. He won a Genie award for the English-language CBC docudrama *Million Dollar Babies* (1994), his first work with Roy Dupuis, and the $20-million Alliance Atlantis/CBC/CBS biopic *Joan of Arc* (1999) received twelve Emmy nominations. Nevertheless, he is still primarily regarded as an action director, making Canadian films that hew closely to American conventions, such as the Wesley Snipes global intrigue thriller *The Art of War* (2000), the top-grossing 'Canadian' film of that year, the global prostitution-kidnapping expose *Human Trafficking* (2005), and the crime drama *Lies My Mother Told Me* (2005).[79] Duguay's genre films raise a quandary. He uses a predominantly Canadian cast and crew, thus providing valuable work and industry experience to local talent; indeed, he has used his industry clout to lure expensive productions, like *The Art of War*, to Montreal.

Moreover, unlike many of the tax-shelter movies that were made for the write-off without an intention of being released, Duguay's films tend actually to recoup their investment. Given the degree to which film-makers claim there is not enough work in Canada, it is hard to disparage Duguay's model, even if his recent production serves mainly to demonstrate the degree to which the action-thriller is the most anonymously international genre around. Perhaps we could imagine its very anonymity to make an argument about Canadian identity, and about a particular mode of inhabiting global society. Certainly, the UN versus U.S. set-up of *The Art of War* had the potential for a strong Canadian point of view (as in the Roy Dupuis biopic *Shake Hands with the Devil*), just as *Human Trafficking* raises important ethical issues about the fate of individuals within the system of global commerce. While his industrial contributions to Canadian cinema should be noted, in other respects Duguay seems little different from his invisible colleagues in Hollywood, articulating their identity for themselves and their fellow citizens as an absence rather than as a presence.

Duguay's career makes an interesting comparison with Torontonian Vincenzo Natali (b. 1969), who has made anonymity and invisibility a key thematic component of his films rather than a structuring absence. After working for a number of years as a storyboard artist for Toronto's Nelvana animation studio (he would also do the storyboards for *Johnny Mnemonic*, *Blood and Donuts*, Fawcett's first film *The Boys Club*, and *Ginger Snaps*), Natali parlayed a budget of $1 million from Norman Jewison's Feature Film Project into his first feature *Cube* (1997), a smash theatrical hit in France and Japan and on video in the United States. He has gone on to create the most extensive and original Canadian sci-fi oeuvre since Cronenberg's, including the futuristic corporate espionage caper *Cypher* (2002), the existential fantasy *Nothing* (2003), the genetic engineering thriller *Splice* (2009), and as this book went to press he was associated with a forthcoming adaptation of J.G. Ballard's *Shivers*-style novel of an apartment complex gone out of control, *High Rise*, and with an adaptation of Gibson's cyberpunk classic, *Neuromancer*. A mathematical thriller laced with wicked violence, *Cube* presents a philosophical dialogue in the guise of a suspense movie, with a strong resemblance to Kafka's parables of incomprehensible authority, Luigi Pirandello's *Six Characters in Search of a Play*, and Jean-Paul Sartre's *No Exit*: characters trying to understand a situation about which they don't know why they are there, who put them there, or how they can get out. Like Cronenberg's films, *Cube* is a philosophical rather than a psychological drama, but it expresses its philosophy through the language and imagery of body horror. Its existentialism is highly physical; indeed, you could say that it maps an existential crisis onto space.

The six characters to whom we are introduced are trapped in a seemingly infinite three-dimensional collection of interconnected room-sized cubes. Each represents a different approach to life: the spoiled Leaven (Nicole de Boer) relies on systems and order to care for her; the cynical and ironic Worth (*Scanners II*'s David Hewlitt) is an architect who turns out to have been involved in the cube's design; the autistic Kazan (Andrew Miller) is childlike but possesses an intuitive genius for mathematical calculations; the policeman Quentin (Maurice Dean Wint) believes in the survival of the fittest and taking a straight line out; the paranoid

6.3 The minimalist and elegantly versatile one-and-a-half-cube set of *Cube* (1997). Trimark
Pictures/The Feature Film Project.

liberal Holloway (Nicky Guadagni) rants, perhaps justifiably, about the military-
industrial complex; the hardened prison escapee Rennes (Wayne Robson) is in his
milieu, which doesn't prevent him from being the first to die, with the exception
of teaser victim Alderson (Julian Richings). The subtlety of the scenario (written by
Natali with Andre Bijelic and Graeme Manson) is that it undercuts each character
in turn, showing us, in good Canadian style, the pros and cons of each approach to
the situation. Unfortunately, Natali does overly defer to genre convention near the
end, when Quentin not only goes psycho on the surviving characters, but then gets
resurrected for a Grand Guignol finale. This predictably unpredictable plot turn
underscores *Cube*'s debt to horror tropes to enliven its relatively dry mathematical
premises: each kill is depicted imaginatively, graphically, and with persuasively
realistic full-shot special effects.

But the crowning achievement of *Cube* is its properly sci-fi spatial imagination,
which plays simultaneously on fears of confinement (the enclosed space of each
individual cube) and of agoraphobic infinity – the 17,576-room cube (a number we
eventually discover), twenty-six to a side, constantly in motion. The fact that Natali's scheme ingeniously suited his budget, since he was able to use a single one-
and-a-half-cube set to stand in for each of the fifty rooms visited by the characters
during the course of the film, only better mirrors the existential theme (figure 6.3).
While there is a colour variation (Natali had originally wanted the cubes to be uni-

formly white),[80] each room is structurally identical to the other; the only difference is their constantly changing relationship to one another, and of course, the fact that a certain number contain fatal booby traps. While the blasted winter landscapes of *Screamers* befit a particularly Quebecois sensibility, the geometrical abstraction of *Cube* is eminently Anglo-Canadian. It is a spatial crystallization of alienation, the utter refinement of the modernist anonymity of the institutional architecture of Cronenberg's early films. Precisely because Natali refuses to provide any history or context to the situation of his characters, he avoids pinning down any facile allegories of oppression in the way that *Johnny Mnemonic* does. This decision cleaves the film closely to the ontological effect of horror, but its refusal of any of horror's conventional spaces of familiar domesticity or even corporate villainy keeps the sci-fi speculation in order. Like *Ginger Snaps*, *Cube* is a minor gem, a pure exercise in Canadian genre cinema.

While critics complained about the emptiness of the film – that it was purely an exercise in genre, in other words, without any explanations – it became clear with *Nothing* that Natali is fascinated by emptiness not for its own sake, but as a philosophical concept. The wisdom of his refusal to explain his cube became eminently apparent with the release of two further films in the *Cube* trilogy (produced, like the *Ginger Snaps* sequels, by Lions Gate), with neither of which Natali had any official connection. In *Cube²* a new set of characters finds itself trapped in a tesseract containing alternate dimensions of the same space and characters. It's a neat horror conceit, as characters can die and return and encounter themselves in different incarnations. But the conceit also eliminates all narrative tension, making *Cube²* feel more like a video game than a conventional movie. The fantastical CGI special effects reinforce this feeling, in contrast to the visceral physicality of the digital and prosthetic effects of the original. Of necessity, the sequel also opens up the narrative, adding the predictable backstory of a future police state cum underground rebellion led by a hacker genius, with a secret agent among the prisoners, and so forth into genre banality. *Cube Zero* sensibly returns to the original three-dimensional colour-coded cube, again with a new set of characters and a new set of booby traps. This time, the innovation is to introduce a surveillance system of slacker underlings whose job is to watch the prisoners on closed-circuit televisions. There is a mild self-referentiality to the viewing position of the trilogy's audience, which filters into the film via the split between the underling with a conscience and the conformist company man. The futuristic totalitarian plot is developed further, as is a complicated but closed circuit of steps between outside and inside. In Kafkaesque fashion, most of the prisoners inside seem at some point to have been involved in the design and maintenance of the cube. Like the first film but to a more detrimental degree, *Cube Zero* also introduces a clichéd psychotic authority figure, the next level up from the underlings, heavily overplayed by Michael Riley. While the *Ginger Snaps* sequels were structurally coterminous with the original, the no-exit structure of *Cube* left no real space for expansion, and it shows.

Natali worked on sci-fi television (*Psi Factor* and *Earth: Final Conflict*) before making *Cypher* in Toronto for Miramax. Starring Jeremy Northam and Lucy Liu, *Cypher* is an elaborately plotted corporate espionage thriller about brainwashing and multiple identities. Northam is marvellous from the start with a weird take on the loser hero tradition as Morgan Sullivan, a geeky accountant who signs on to be a corporate spy. Natali gives the technological spaces a cold steely distanced look, which *Variety* reviewer Derek Elley rightly compared to 'classic David Cronenberg.'[81] The mystery is intriguing for much of the film, and Natali pulls off a bravura scene in a huge subterranean data vault deep in the country from which Sullivan must escape after delivering his information. The sequence opens with Sullivan being dropped off by taxi in a flat field in the middle of nowhere straight out of *North by Northwest*. Rather than trapped in the open plain, however, the ground drops out from under him as he descends into the vault, where his duplicity is detected by Virgil Dunn (David Hewlett, in excellent form). Following this high point, the film degenerates into a hokey pyrotechnic finale with a twist which, as reviewer Richard Falcon noted, 'seems to invalidate any promise of complexity or depth.'[82] Where the tunnel vision of *Cube* worked in its favour, the elimination of depth from the intricate plottings of *Cypher*'s multiple identities belies the promise of the thematic space opening up beneath its surface events.

Cypher is reminiscent of Robert Lepage's *Possible Worlds* (2000) and Allan Moyle's *Xchange* (2000), where instead of identities, different lives and different bodies (respectively) are exchanged. In Lepage's elegant adaptation of John Mighton's philosophical play cum love story, George Barber (Tom McManus) pursues Joyce (Tilda Swinton) across multiple lives, in each of which their relationship is different. Simultaneously, police are searching for a murderer who steals the brains of his victims. The perpetrator turns out to be a mad scientist (Gabriel Gascon) who has learned how to keep brains alive separately from their bodies with electrical stimuli. Rather than dwell on the ideas behind the story, Lepage tries to summon them up through associated images, especially of blood and water, just as he links episodes associatively rather than causally, providing clues to different lives through costume and acting rather than by events and dialogue. In place of a genre film, Lepage includes genre markers – the mad scientist from science fiction, the detectives from the policier – among his associative images. Like the character of George, the movie seeks its meanings through myriad, only tangentially connected worlds. The more conventional *Xchange* offers instead the scenario of possible *bodies*. In the future world of Canuck veteran Moyle's sci-fi thriller about corporate terrorism, CEOs and other VIPs possess the privilege of 'floating,' or using another person's body. At the other end of the spectrum are JEFFS, clones with a shelf life of three days. Inevitably, the hero Toffler (played earlier by Kim Coates and Kyle MacLachlan) gets trapped in a clone (Stephen Baldwin), from which he must escape before its expiry date. The high concept permits fairly low-tech visuals, and the film's set-up rings some nice changes on the familiar cyberpunk thematic of media/technology/ corporate world. The plot takes over in the second half to the detriment of the film (as occurred ten years earlier in Moyle's promising teen rebellion drama *Pump up the Volume*) as Toffler in Baldwin's clone body, with love interest reporter Madeleine Renard (Pascale Bussières), races against the clock. Although Moyle and screenwriter Christopher Pelham do not open up the identity issue any more than Natali does in *Cypher*, they do have a fascinatingly ambivalent moment when it sinks in that Toffler is not in his own body and can do what he will with it as long as he can stand the pain. We are made abruptly conscious of what we normally take for granted in action heroes as we watch the ordeal Toffler forces himself through – getting drenched in acid, losing a finger, and so forth – with wanton disregard for the consequences. It's a clever existentialist twist on the unreality of action drama, making realism out of convention, and it's the best part of the film.

Following the trauma of *Cypher*, which Miramax sat on for years before sending it straight to video despite a number of fantasy festival prizes, Natali returned to the minimalist aesthetic of *Cube*. Co-written with his high school buddies and frequent collaborators David Hewlett and Andrew Miller, and partially financed by the TFC and Ontario tax credits, *Nothing* is a high-concept update of the loser tradition, heavily leavened with the influence of Californian stoners Bill and Ted. Faced with an escalating litany of real-life worries, from bill collectors to girl-friends leaving ('You're a loser, Dave. I never even liked you,' snaps Marie-Josée Croze in a brief cameo) to a demolition notice on their house, Andrew and Dave wish it all away and receive the slacker's dream: nothing. They and their house are alone in a white void. As they adapt to their surroundings, they discover they can 'hate' away anything they don't want, but it won't come back. Inevitably, they quarrel, wishing everything they own away, then parts of each other until all that is left is two bouncing, biting heads. Finally, they hate away their hate, reconcile, and live happily ever after with nothing. Natali's visuals are as stylish as ever, mixing animation and Canadian realism with a healthy dollop of Monty Python-esque humour. The original concept is visually compelling, although Natali does have difficulty sustaining a fairly non-existent story for the full length of a feature. As in *Cube*, the style mirrors the concept, as the reduction ad absurdum of a slacker lifestyle is rendered visually. At the same time, Natali and his co-writers do not relent in the purity of their concept – a coda after the credits shows the friends ten years later, their hair grown long, still doing nothing. It took Natali seven years after *Nothing* to get another chance at the full-fledged genre feature *Cypher* certainly was not, and the 2009 *Splice* was a fair go at the synthesis of the English-Canadian art film with high-concept science fiction he had outlined earlier. A Canada/France co-production, *Splice* received a broad commercial release on the strength of its stars Adrien Brody and Sarah Polley. Channelling vintage Cronenberg, *Splice* tells the story of two scientists who secretly blend animal and human DNA to create a hybrid creature that will, naturally, wreak bloody havoc. Much about the film resonates strongly with Canadian cinema. The first half takes place in the sterile metallic bowels of a high-tech research lab, the second half in the wintry grounds of the couple's rural farmhouse. While the film mostly ignores the ethics of genetics, it delves deeply into the moral compromises made by Clive and Elsa as they raise their 'child' Dren, including two perverse sexual encounters, the first when Clive seduces Dren, the second when Dren rapes Elsa. While the film doesn't manage to match the consistency of Cronenberg's chilly tone, its cynically downbeat ending is faithful to its 1970s origins. Along with *Pontypool* and Egoyan's erotic thriller *Chloe*, *Splice* makes a strong argument that genre cinema may prove a viable path forward for English-Canadian auteurs in addition to its long-time status as downmarket moneymaker.

Genre has been intimately bound with Canadian cinema as conventionally defined since that conventionally defined cinema first emerged in the mid-sixties. But since the eighties, it has inched ever more closely to the centre of that cinema, and not only for economic reasons, although the rise of video has created a demand for low-budget product that is not likely to disappear soon. While its economic importance is reason enough to study popular genres within the context of Canadian cinema, there are two further reasons. The first is that the film-makers themselves work in popular genres in order to make a living between more personal films, incorporate popular tropes and motifs into their more personal films, and frequently, make innovative genre films that function simultaneously as auteur cinema. Second, genre films are central to the cinema culture of Canadian viewers. As Taylor persuasively argues against a Canadian critical fear of genre as American assimilation, 'Conceiving of the suspense or horror film as definitively American genres establishes a fixity in our ideas of what constitutes both genre and (by extension) nationhood itself. Accepting genres as stable also discounts the audience's ability to resist accepting standard generic product at face value.'[83] The training in such a viewing practice, Taylor suggests, may derive precisely from the 'extremely *hybridized*' and 'uncertain' national identity that matches the fragmented and contradictory workings of popular genres, leading 'Canadian audiences simultaneously [to] receive *and* disavow the pleasures of genre.'[84] In this sense, the more innovative exercises in Canadian genre, in particular the films of Cronenberg, have provided a supplemental education to an endemic Canadian attitude on how to view popular culture. The heightened realism and focus on the body as site of generic activity, shared by the most common Canadian genres, plot out the lineaments of a specifically Canadian popular cinema while also offering training in the dualistic reading of those local and international products that do not hew so closely to that cinema. It is difficult to know if this, too, is a minority position – Canadians are famously suspicious of their own product – but if it is, it is at least as valid a measurement of cultural identity as the traditional art cinema, and not so distinct a measure from it as we usually think it to be.

Chapter Seven

The Death of the Author? The Case of Atom Egoyan

[Egoyan] has a list of things that attract him to a project: 'Complexity. Conflicting agendas. Different people trying to present a version of reality. A hidden history. How people cope with trauma. The need to create and construct personas.'

Interview in Backstage at the time of the release of Where the Truth Lies (2005)

There is no question that Atom Egoyan regards himself as an auteur in the classic sense of the term, the sense that dominated the burgeoning field of cinema studies during the late seventies and early eighties when he was attending the University of Toronto. Nor is there any question that auteurist approaches have dominated critical writing on his films, be it the journalistic reviews that check off his familiar obsessions, the critical assessments that outline the consistency of his themes from film to film, or the post-structuralist studies that employ his consistent thematization of media technology towards a critique of contemporary culture, representation, and gender.[1] Reviewers and critics, as well as Egoyan himself in pronouncements such as the one cited above, tend to regard his oeuvre as an auteurist continuum, susceptible to value judgments according to the criteria of that continuum; hard-core theorists tend to truncate their analyses with 1989's *Speaking Parts* (in the case of media) or with *Exotica* (1994) and 1997's *The Sweet Hereafter* (in the case of gender), tacitly asserting the lack of interest of the more recent films.[2] Egoyan's international stature has only increased even as scholarly attention to his recent, bigger-budget films pales in comparison to that received by his small-scale productions of the eighties and early nineties. In this chapter, I want to ascertain in a critically satisfying manner exactly what distinguishes the post-*Exotica* works from the prior oeuvre. Not only do I hope thereby to understand better both the films and the film-maker, but also to find a critical vocabulary able to reckon with the fact that Egoyan's turn is by no means unique either in the small world of Canadian cinema, or in the larger, but still small world of what used to be called art-house film-making. Indeed, his turn precisely mirrors the shifting character of Canadian cinema, from the 'golden age' of the last fifteen years of the twentieth century to the changed situation of the new millennium. Close scrutiny of Egoyan's post-new-wave production not only can tell us much about Canadian cinema in the twenty-first century, but also reveals a number of understudied characteristics of the previous fifteen years which tended to be overwhelmed by the force of Egoyan's overtly articulated auteurist themes. Such scrutiny can also help us to delineate the limits of an auteurist approach for making sense of the full range of a particular film-maker's work or of the cultural, economic, and social networks in which that film-making occurred.

Beyond the fact (which I deal with in the conclusion of this chapter) that Egoyan's twelve commercially released feature films (as of 2011) comprise only a part of his cinematic, not to mention his artistic and cultural production, auteurist approaches are unable to account for the dramatic shift in Egoyan's later films in anything other than qualitative terms. In order to distinguish what changed and what did not in the post-*Exotica* period, I divide my analysis into three categories, all of which have regularly been identified with auteurist production, especially in the context of the French cinema and criticism within which the term *auteur* originated: *formal qualities*, those related to narrative structure, theme, and characterization; *stylistic qualities*, those related to the visual and aural aspects of the films; and *qualities of production*, those external to the film itself, such as production and distribution, cast and crew, and the various paratextual elements that compose the discourse of a particular auteur.[3] To be sure, these are heuristic categories as much as anything, and there is much overlap between them. In the space of this chapter I am unable to deal comprehensively with every aspect of Egoyan's authorship. In addition to compensating for the preponderance of formal qualities in the critical analysis of Egoyan's films, this tripartite division has the virtue of bringing sharply into focus the ways in which the later films diverge from the earlier ones, and that Canadian cinema in general in the new millennium diverges from the prior decades.

Formal Qualities

The two primary formal characteristics of Egoyan's oeuvre are the Freudian narrative dynamic he has labelled 'the family romance' and the thematic use of media technology in relation to memory and trauma,[4] or, as Emma Wilson succinctly puts it in her recent monograph, 'traumatic loss, mourning, mania, manipulation, fantasy, and sexuality.'[5] We may add the non-linear presentation of these themes as a collection of fragmented stories that coalesce only in the final reel of the film. It is significant that the media theme dominated early discussion of Egoyan's films, while the 'family romance' began to emerge as a critical rubric in the wake of *Exotica* (1994) and *Sweet Hereafter* (1997), in part to signal a shift in focus away from the problematic of technology within the diegesis of those films. Indeed, it was during the promotion of *Felicia's Journey* (1999) that Egoyan first began discussing publicly a traumatic episode in his own youth – being the passive onlooker of the incestuous abuse of a young woman with whom he was (or wished to be) romantically entangled.[6] This confessionary revelation retrospectively injected a strong autobiographical charge into the family romance dynamic that had punctuated his films from the relationship between the masquerading 'lost son' and his adoptive sister in *Next of Kin* (1984) through to the overtly incestuous relationships at the core of the traumas in *Exotica* and *Sweet Hereafter*, and looked forward to the key relationship between step-siblings in *Ararat* (2002) and the convoluted melodramas of the fractured families in *Adoration* (2008) and *Chloe* (2009).

In the films through to *Exotica*, this narrative dynamic was explicitly mediated by, as well as implicitly subordinated to, the theme of recording technology: Peter records the progress of his infiltration of the adopted Armenian family on tape recorder in *Next of Kin*; Van's father tapes his couplings with a mistress over videos of Van's absent mother in *Family Viewing* (1987); Clara remembers her beloved brother in a video mausoleum in *Speaking Parts* (1989). The celebrated critique of media culture and the substitution of taped for authentic memory is no less foregrounded: the video therapy sessions of the Armenian family and the hand-held camera documenting Peter's surprise party in *Next of Kin*; the battle over the memory of Van's mother conducted through videotape in *Family Viewing*; the climactic daytime talk show dramatization of Clara's trauma in *Speaking Parts*; the censor's clandestine taping of the pornography she reviews in *The Adjuster* (1991); the photographer's obsessive reviewing of the video record of his trip to Armenia in *Calendar* (1993), reliving the loss of his wife while seeking the reasons for it in his memories. The critical reception of this thematic has been heavily one-sided: as a satirical critique of the mediation of memory rather than the equally plausible function of a dialectical analysis of its role in contemporary culture.

In Egoyan's discussion of his films, if not perhaps always in the works themselves, there is in fact a large measure of ambivalence, a desire to have it both ways. On the one hand, there is a thoroughgoing critique of the loss of immediacy, of physical contact, of the deleterious effect of the media and image-making on the human psyche, a critique wholly in keeping with the tradition of Canadian cultural theory and film-making, and a mainstay of Egoyan criticism. On the other hand, there is an inescapable fascination with the potential of new technology, with the ways in which desires and behaviour have been adapted to and transformed by that technology, and the recognition that neither alienation nor experience mediated through technology is a novel experience. Egoyan explains, 'In *Family Viewing*, there's a real ambiguity about the role of technology. It's the means by which the father controls the family, but it's also ultimately the way in which the boy recovers his past. It's very easy to take a moralistic position and condemn these technologies, but the fact is that they are with us. It's a question of educating people how to use the technology, instead of demonizing technology or allowing it to become casual.'[7] Similarly, writing about the concluding sequence in *Speaking Parts*, Egoyan argued that the TV producer's (David Hemblen) structuring of his film within the film as a talk show was actually an innovative, self-conscious approach to dramatizing the issue of organ transplantation.[8] It is difficult, however, fully to reconcile this assertion with the dramatic structure of *Speaking Parts* itself, which so strongly demonized the producer's character as the worst kind of manipulator of people and images. Likewise, the schematic dialectic Egoyan employed for *Family Viewing* emphasized rather than mitigated the facile sentimentality of the boy's escape from his neurotic family and attempt to establish an alternative community.

Put another way, in order for these films to realize the sort of ambiguity attributed to them by Egoyan's paratextual remarks, there would have to be a total lack of identification with the characters as characters, an 'elimination of subjectivity' that many critics and reviewers indeed saw in the films, either for good or for ill.[9] At the same time, for the films to be more than 'cold and unfeeling' dissections of postmodern anomie, there needed also to be a deep emotional investment in the characters, as Egoyan quite well recognized: 'To me, the films are almost operatic. They're almost embarrassingly emotional. To me, there's nothing more vulnerable than showing people who are obviously trying to hold back an emotional agenda ... I thought the other films are pretty obvious in their representation of people incapable of dealing with what's on their emotional plate. But I guess not.'[10] The diegetic relationship to technology was both the vehicle for expressing the fraught tension between the desire for distanced critique and the need for emotional identification with alien emotional practices, and the cinematographic means whereby Egoyan attempted to produce that tension. Of the handheld camera in *Next of Kin*, for example, Egoyan confessed that he was intending 'to pull the audience back but in fact sucked the audience right in': 'what I didn't understand was, the moment you have a shaky camera you say, "Hey this is really happening! Get right in there!"'[11] A mode of representation automatically identified with documentary tilted what had been intended as an interplay between a formal scheme and an emotional identification into a rejection of the film as a realistic portrayal of damaged goods. The effect was heightened by the stereotypically ethnic qualities of the Armenian family, meant probably to be as exaggeratedly animated and emotive as the Wasp family was impossibly cold and distant, but rendered by the same representational codes as if a faithful depiction. The film's evident humour was taken as reflective of ethnic *joie de vivre* rather than the sign of an absurdist fable. Furthermore, Egoyan soon realized that on videocassette, which turned out to be the primary viewing mode of *Family Viewing*'s early audience, the visual tension between film stock and videotape on which the formal scheme of the film depended was lost. It only worked, if at all, when screened in the cinema.[12]

Within the feature films, the thematic presence of media technology recedes to the background from *Exotica* onward, accompanied by what most critics – Egoyan included – have identified as an increased range and depth of emotion and compassion for the characters.[13] Indeed, his two most recent feature films, *Adoration* and *Chloe*, have pushed emotional identification quite deeply into the generic territory of melodrama with, in *Chloe* at least, little discernible accompanying distance or irony. To be sure, Egoyan also maintains that his earlier films had attempted to take the same attitude towards their characters, but that he had not managed successfully to impart that attitude to his audience.[14] This seems like special pleading; whatever the reason for it, there is no question that a shift occurred in the portrayal of character, nor that the shift coincided with a marked widening of budget, audience, and reputation. While Egoyan has remained remarkably consistent in his themes despite the shift in his means of presenting them, it is important to note the increased self-consciousness with which those themes are presented in the post-*Exotica* films, a self-consciousness in which the above claim to continuity participates. With *Sweet Hereafter*, for the first time, Egoyan began to 'cite' his own auteurist themes, explicitly deploying them rather than implicitly reproducing them. This is consonant with the increased openness with which he discussed their origins in interviews and articles. I do not mean by this that Egoyan's earlier films were at all un-self-conscious – they are, in fact, noticeably self-reflective in their intellectual underpinnings – but that it is their meaning that was self-conscious rather than their status as emblems of his identity as auteur.

The ways in which the incest and the media themes are cited changes steadily from *Exotica* onward, but the inversion of thematic prominence is consistent. Whereas in the early films the incest theme provided a subtext through which to enunciate the critique of media, in the later films media technology was subordinated to the task of enunciating the theme of incest, or more generally, the conflicted relation between fathers and daughters – and later, mothers and sons. Video makes a single albeit significant appearance in *Exotica*, providing the audience with a poignant video glimpse of the daughter and wife doubly lost by Francis (Bruce Greenwood) through the actual act of abuse and murder and the false accusations of guilt that followed (see figure 7.1). While doubtless partaking of the same analysis of mediated memory and trauma as the video sequences in the earlier films, the central scenario with Francis's former babysitter (and, the audience suspects, child abuse survivor) Christina (Mia Kirshner) in the Exotica club presents the performative ritual in the more traditionally mediated form of a face-to-face encounter, just as Mitchell Stephens's (Ian Holm) memories of his daughter as an innocent baby are presented to us in the form of a series of first-person anecdotes recounted by Stephens to a childhood friend of Zoe during the course of a long airplane journey. Consequently, neither of these formative episodes is visually mediated through the framework of video.

The invasive quality of Stephens's lawsuit in *Sweet Hereafter*, however, is demonstrated sharply through his relationship to technology. A key confrontation with bereaved parent Billy Ansel (Bruce Greenwood again) occurs while Stephens is videotaping the wrecked school bus. It is interrupted by a cell phone call from Stephens's estranged daughter, which he immediately (and unsuccessfully) appropriates as an anguished remark about how 'we have all lost our daughters,' an ironized rehearsal of the one-sided critique of postmodernity so common to earlier Egoyan criticism that feels singularly crass in the face of an irredeemably real loss of children to a bus crash that had nothing whatsoever to do with the ills of contemporary society. The single manifestation of Stephens's promise of wealth to the townspeople is the computer he donates to the new bedroom of his star witness, the wheelchair-bound Nicole (Sarah Polley). In a supremely and self-consciously ironic remark, the counterpoint of Stephens's above, Nicole's only comment on the devastating effects of her perjured deposition is the faux-innocent question to her abusive father as he sinks dejectedly into the driver's seat of the family station wagon, 'Do you think he'll let us keep the computer?'

In *Sweet Hereafter*, Egoyan reduced Russell Banks's source novel's explicit discussion of Sam's sexual abuse of his daughter Nicole to a single, romantically rendered seduction scene. In his adaptation of William Trevor's novel *Felicia's Journey*, Egoyan altogether eliminated the incestuous relationship between Joseph Hilditch (Bob Hoskins) and his overbearing mother Gala (Arsinée Khanjian) revealed near the end, dismissively remarking that it would have made the son's character 'thunderingly reductive.'[15] Instead, he focused the theme of incest on the relation-ship between the predatory father-figure Hilditch and the teenaged women to whom he offers assistance and protection. Moreover, rather than Trevor's inter-nal monologue to signal gradually to the reader the sinister results of Hilditch's offer, Egoyan introduced surveillance video, obsessively catalogued by Hilditch in an archive hidden in his otherwise Luddite mansion along with the cooking-show videos of his vanished mother, all that remain of Trevor's scenes of cynical seduction.

In Egoyan's more recent films, the incest theme is subordinated to other con-cerns. The pseudo-incestuous relationship between Raffi (David Alpay) and his step-sister Celia (Josée-Marie Croze) in *Ararat* is presented as a fact in the present; video and mediation are reserved for the more fraught issues of representing the Armenian genocide and untangling their mother Ani's (Arsinée Khanjian) rela-tionship to the siblings' respective fathers. The predatory father-figure is thus absent from the family romance, replaced by the mystery of his death(s); the theme is displaced to the psycho-social level of the film-within-a-film's character of Jev-det Bay, the evil Turk (Elias Koteas). A similar pattern is observable in *Adoration*, where Simon's (Devon Bostick) projection of his family romance onto the histori-cal events of the near hijacking of an El Al flight mediates the loss of his mother and father and the betrayal of his grandfather with something of a token motif of incest in his odd relationship with the French teacher (Khanjian) who turns out to have been the first wife of his father. In *Where the Truth Lies* (2005), Egoyan intro-duced a subtext of the theme of father-daughter abuse to the hard-boiled female reporter in Rupert Holmes's source novel by casting youthful and fragile-looking actress Alison Lohman (to much critical derision) and adding a central backstory in which the young Karen O'Connor, played by the same actress, appeared on TV in the comedy duo's fundraising telethon.[16] The addition of a videotaped memory equally added a muted theme of incest, even as the introduction of the theme, as many critics noted, militated against the film's effectiveness as a thriller. In *Chloe*, the only trace of the concern is in a noticeable stress on intergenerational tension and sexual attraction – at various moments in the film we believe the young pros-titute Chloe (Amanda Seyfried) to be sleeping with the father (Liam Neeson), the mother (Julianne Moore), and the son (Max Thieriot) of the central family in the film. Egoyan has noted that the shift from original to adapted screenplays allowed him to escape from the thematic impasse to which his own obsessions had led him after *Exotica*.[17] At the same time, the changes he made to the works he adapted reveal quite clearly the different ways in which he had come to understand those themes. While often dramatically effective, especially in *Sweet Hereafter*, the fact that the themes were intentionally worked into rather than originated with the source text also emphasizes the sense of citation.

In addition to the changes rung on the incest theme, planting it as the secret foundation of the narrative rather than an overt plot point, Egoyan reworked his source material in *Sweet Hereafter* in other significant ways. He expands the single pair of phone calls to Stephens's motel room that climaxes the central monologue in Banks's novel with the revelation that Zoe has tested HIV-positive into a tragi-comic repetition in which she constantly harasses Stephens through his cell phone at inopportune moments. The cell phone motif simultaneously reminds us of the similarity of Stephens's own tragedy to the townspeople's loss and its distance from that same loss, rooting that comparison in a critique of modernity equally signified by Zoe's visual presence in a phone booth in the midst of an urban waste-land at the other end of the line.[18] Egoyan also added the aforementioned video camera and computer as props in the action. Where Banks broadly contrasted the cynical, self-aware lawyer to the damaged psyches of the small-town inhabitants struggling to make sense of their tragedy, Egoyan rooted that contrast in issues of technology and mediation. The immediacy of our emotional relationship with the townspeople's loss is mirrored by their physical relationship to one another and the world around them. The tactile nature of their small-town occupations – Billy Ansel is a mechanic, Sam Burnell is a plumber, the Ottos make crafts, Dolores Driscoll drives a bus – contrasts sharply with lawyer Stephens's abstract relation to loss. At the same time, the sharply delineated introduction of what previously had been a universal critique of media technology serves to complicate the dichot-omy. The sensual relationship to their surroundings encompasses Sam's abuse of his daughter as well as Billy's ability to reject the lawyer's temptation; Stephens's alienated relationship to the tragedy empowers Nicole to free herself from her father's grip.

Consistent with the emotional immediacy of the later movies, Egoyan intro-duced a thematic register wholly absent from his earlier auteurist repertoire: the fairy tale. Used in different ways in every film from *Exotica* to *Chloe*, the fairy-tale motif offers an internal hermeneutic that for the first time provides a broad social context independent of the media-technology thematic. To be sure, only in retro-spect could one identify the schoolgirl scenario ritualistically re-enacted in *Exotica* in terms of a fairy-tale motif, but already Egoyan had dissociated the scenario from a presentation through the means of technology. As a pre-modern form derived from oral culture, the power of the fairy tale lies in its archetypal depiction of inter-personal relations, a version of the family romance accessible, if you will, even to the child. In this sense, the late-coming revelation that the incestuous striptease ritual is as necessary to Christina as it is to Francis is essential to understanding the shift in focus of the film from Egoyan's earlier films.

Egoyan's introduction of Robert Browning's poetic version of the Pied Piper legend to *Sweet Hereafter* is the most prominent use of the fairy-tale motif, and its hermeneutic role within the film has been amply covered in the criticism.[19] What interests me here about the motif is the way it encourages the viewer to engage with the film from the child's point of view. Egoyan defended himself from criti-cism of the perceived romanticism of the single incest scene he included by stating that he had shot it from the point of view of Nicole's perceptions.[20] The Pied Piper motif similarly retells the meaning of the bus crash from a child's perspective, emphasizing the point by concluding the film with a pre-crash scene of Nicole reading the poem to Billy Ansel's twins overlain with her final voice-over, appro-priated from the novel's Dolores, relating the fairy-tale theme to Banks's title met-aphor of 'Sweet Hereafter.'[21]

Only a minority of reviewers caught the added references in *Felicia's Journey* to 'Bluebeard,' another fairy tale of predatory males, just as only a few saw fit to comment on the scenes of the biblical legend of Salome glimpsed by Hilditch in the form of a Rita Hayworth vehicle on a hospital TV screen that prompts a flash-back to the boy at the opera with his mother which in turn motivates the use of opera glasses during his dining rituals.[22] To Egoyan, who had recently directed Strauss's *Salomé* for Toronto's Canadian Opera Company (1996) and who was no doubt familiar with Bartók's *Bluebeard's Castle* (directed by Robert Lepage for the COC in 1992), not to mention Jane Campion's use of the myth in a similar context in her 1993 film, *The Piano*, these were essential subtexts to the film's meaning, as his repeated mention of them in the DVD commentary makes abundantly clear.[23] In the DVD commentary on Elaine Cassidy's hooded blue duffel coat, especially in the key abortion sequence where she dreams of her lost baby playing with its father in the same colour blue, Egoyan also introduces the more familiar figure of Little Red Riding Hood.[24] Given the currency of that myth in popular culture as an image of child abuse and seduction, however, it is not surprising that Egoyan dis-placed it by altering the colour of the cloak and subordinating it to the less familiar forms available through Bluebeard and Salome.

The Bluebeard motif neatly introduces the concept of seriality to the child's perception of the predatory male, while the locked closet neatly tropes the issues of denial and secrecy that Egoyan has repeatedly cited as central to his under-standing of traumatic memory.[25] The Salome motif, conversely, signals Egoyan's amplification of Felicia's power within the narrative. Although it is the maternity signified by her pregnancy rather than the dancer's mature sexuality that ensures the death of the male protagonist, the image testifies in either case to the power of female corporality to trouble male authority. Moreover, Egoyan links that power to his own refusal to depict on screen the serial killer's violence towards his female victims. As he spells out in the DVD commentary, he found it ironically satisfying that the only physically violent moment in the film comes on a TV screen, in a Technicolor Hollywood film from the fifties world of Hilditch's childhood, and at the hands of a woman.[26] Here, too, Egoyan cites the auteurist thematic of his early films to make a secondary point rather than a thorough-going critique. Eschew-ing Trevor's conventionally Oedipal aetiology, Egoyan grounds the mother's trau-matic effect on Hilditch in a sterile relationship to the budding television culture of the fifties, allying Salomé to the TV-star mother, accessible only through the televi-sion screen. She may remain a castrating monster, but that effect will be blamed on the culture rather than psychologized into the individual.[27]

The budding celebrity culture of the late fifties that produced Gala is also indicted for empowering the hedonistic and predatory lifestyle of Vince and Lanny, the famously successful comedy duo in *Where the Truth Lies*. The novel's Alice-in-Wonderland motif is maintained in the film, where a pageant in the Won-derland children's clinic concludes in a threesome in which a costumed Alice per-forms cunnilingus on Karen. Especially as realized by Egoyan, the motif serves to introduce, if in a heavily displaced form, a familiarly paedophilic subtext to the 'wonderland' image of celebrity.[28] Once seduced by the media trappings of that other world in her childhood, the young reporter, now herself a halfway member of it, offers her body as price of entry into its ugly secrets.

Ararat has a wildly different agenda, but like the later *Adoration*, its formal structure reworks its historical material in quite a similar way to Egoyan's reworking of the novelistic sources of several of the recent films. Although the first version of the screenplay focused exclusively on historical events, Egoyan eventually came to realize that, for both aesthetic and practical reasons, he could only depict the events as a film within a film.[29] By framing a tragedy of epic dimensions with the resolutely childish perceptions and traumas of three young persons – Raffi's and Celia's respective searches for the meaning of their fathers' deaths and the painter Arshile Gorky's search (Simon Abkarian) for that of his mother's – and the emotionally raw and socially immature results of those searches (drug smuggling, vandalism, and suicide, respectively), Egoyan situated the meaning of his film within a child's perspective.[30] The perspective of the young Gorky in Van is seized on by the makers of the film within the film as an emotional conduit to the historical melodrama they envision, while Egoyan's more intellectual approach to that same figure structures the present-day narrative. That Ani's reading of Gorky's painting, *Mother and Son*, is drawn from Egoyan's highly personal portrait of his son and exegesis of the painting, *A Portrait of Arshile* (1995, included on the bonus disk of the *Ararat* DVD) only heightens the sense of the child's perspective, just as the fact that he 'had always wanted to make a film about the Armenian Genocide of 1915' frames his own engagement with the film in terms of a youthful perspective.[31]

Here, too, the motif of media and mediation delineates forms of engagement with the past. Celia's relationship to artistic media is simultaneously direct, adversarial, and misplaced: not only does she physically attack Gorky's portrait because of what it represents to Ani, but she is the only character whose decor includes a computer itself, pasted with clipped artworks.[32] His sole conduit to the past before the tragedy is a photograph of himself as a boy with his mother, and Gorky's relationship to media technology is glossed with the nostalgia we now associate with the still photograph. Similarly, Gorky chooses to understand that relationship through what is to us the even more anachronistic mode of the oil painting. The most powerful image available of the Armenian genocide, and in many ways the only cultural product of it available to the Western world before Egoyan's film, Gorky's painting nevertheless seems truly accessible only to the informed gaze of a highly trained intellectual such as Ani. Raffi's video diary of Mount Ararat, while for the young photographer possessed of a profound meaning he was unable to receive from his mother's cold analysis of Gorky's canvas, is equally compromised by the Satanic bargain he has had to make in order to get the shots he wanted. The cans of celluloid filled either with illicit drugs or with invaluable images are a transparently urgent metaphor for the bargain Egoyan must have felt necessary to make in order to do the film: a bargain with dollars, a bargain with Hollywood genres, a bargain with everything his early films had negated. At the same time, as *Calendar* had made abundantly clear, there was no historical meaning or identity to be found from within the terms of that earlier negation. By recovering the absolute conviction of a child's perspective on his profession and his obsessions, Egoyan argued that he could work his way out of the intellectual and emotional impasse of his early films' inability to confront the denial of his own history and identity. The centripetal force of Egoyan's burgeoning world-class reputation went hand in hand with an outward-reaching trend in the films themselves. No longer inward-looking and retentive, they became ever more expansive in terms of emotion and in terms of ambition.

Stylistic Qualities

While formal qualities garner the lion's share of analysis of Egoyan and other film-makers as auteurs, the stylistic means of realizing those themes is equally essential to their meaning and equally revealing of the changes in that meaning over Egoyan's career. A key but unnoticed shift in style from *Exotica* onward is Egoyan's emergence as a studio director, and in his most recent films, as a consummate creator of period pieces. The distinction in approach emerges in Egoyan's discussion of the making of *Felicia's Journey*, where he found himself with the entire repertoire of London's fabled Shepperton Studios at his disposal: 'It was a great privilege for me to create a set. I had never been able to afford one before. The nature of the films I had done before meant that I had to build rooms in warehouses and wait for trains to stop. You just don't have the control that you do when you're using a huge studio like Shepperton and I took full advantage of that. For instance, when you make a set like that and want to populate it in England, there are prop houses where they've kept everything from every film that's ever been made ... In Canada, we don't have that depth. I needed a mixer from the 1950s and had five choices of models that had been stored; that seemed really remarkable.'[33] In his immersion within the new concerns of *Felicia's Journey*, Egoyan neglects to mention several facts. First of all, this was the first period film he had done; there had been no need for such 'remarkable' props as 1950s mixers in any of his previous films. What he stressed in discussions of those earlier films was his ability to discover the settings he needed within the landscape itself. An important aspect of the critique of post-modernity in his early films was the fact that the issues they discussed actually existed and could be represented *as real*: the video mausoleum had already been built in Japan; the emblematic house of *The Adjuster* was a model home discovered on the edge of a non-existent housing development just in time to be incorporated into the film. The essence of the kind of independent, no-budget films he had been used to shooting was the paradoxical freedom to be gained from making do with what he had.

It is not coincidental that the first film in which Egoyan had a sizeable budget, *Exotica* ($2 million), was also the first film in which, rather than a setting whose reality was demonstrably real, the film's meaning centred around the construction of a plausibly real but imaginary set – the Exotica club. The tension in *Exotica* emerges from the fact that its club makes us accept it as real even as we know that its non-exploitative appropriation of an exploitative institution – the strip club – cannot actually exist.[34] The emotional accessibility of the films from *Exotica* on is inseparable from this fundamental shift in the epistemological status of their settings. Whether using primarily locations (*Sweet Hereafter*, *Adoration*, and *Chloe*) or primarily constructed sets (*Felicia's Journey* and *Where the Truth Lies*), or both in equal measure (*Ararat*), these films all require a suspension of disbelief and an emotional identification diametrically opposed to the acceptance of their account of culture and emotional distance required of the earlier films.

What is fascinating about Egoyan's oeuvre is not so much its consistency as the fact that he has managed to elicit a similar set of critical responses in spite of such a radical shift in emphasis. Now, we could just as well explain this shift in terms of economics as in terms of artistic vision. The increase in budget made newly available to Egoyan techniques and strategies previously unavailable to him, while formally his means of production had not changed as much – after all, he retained the screenwriter credit for every one of his films until *Chloe* (credited to U.S. playwright and scenarist Erin Cressida Wilson). Certainly, Egoyan has put those extra dollars up on the screen: the carefully created atmosphere of the establishing shots of the Exotica club; the brilliantly chilling helicopter shot of the (computer generated) bus sliding off the road and sinking through the ice in *Sweet Hereafter*; the languorous opening stroll through Hilditch's house as if with the eyes of a child, matched with Hitchcockian precision by the man's final stroll to his death in the kitchen in *Felicia's Journey*; the powerfully evocative portrait of Felicia and Hilditch against the massive backdrop of the Birmingham locations, on a scale and with a visual sharpness unseen before *Exotica*; the patently artificial epic settings of director Edward Saroyan's (Charles Aznavour) film within a film '*Ararat*,' simultaneously evidence of Egoyan's inability to make a historical epic and a manifesto of his refusal to do so; the use of CGI effects in the battle scenes of *Ararat*; the big-budget recreations of the fifties and the seventies in *Where the Truth Lies* (and the dismissal of their accuracy by one influential reviewer must have galled Egoyan more than any other of the many facets of the film that were also dismissed).[35] There are signs of retrenchment in the resolutely and overtly Toronto- and Ontario-based locations of *Adoration* and *Chloe*, as if his home city and province had somehow once again caught up with his vision; nevertheless, the picturesque lakeside house in *Adoration* and the local landmark 'Ravine House' in *Chloe* have a flashiness as well – if a local one – that was absent in the early films.

The visual representation of the past and of memory has similarly changed in the later films. While no 'past' as such exists outside of video and tape in the early films, and nothing of aesthetic beauty emerges either – think of the taped memories of Van's mother in *Family Viewing*, of Clara's brother in *Speaking Parts*, or of the photographer's images of Armenia in *Calendar*, their grainy texture the proud badge of their refusal to seduce us – every film from *Exotica* onward presents pristine scenes of aching beauty, always set in the past, but always immediately accessible to at least one of the film's characters along with the members of the audience.[36] Now, in every case these images represent a memory of something irretrievably lost, but the change in the visual representation of that loss mirrors the change in the status of the loss. Rather than the postmodern worlds of infinitely receding representations, as which Egoyan's early films were received, we find a modernist world in which lost innocence remains, at least to all appearances, pure and immediate to memory: the fields through which Christina and Eric make their way searching, it will turn out, for the body of Francis's daughter; the overhead shot of Mitchell, his wife and their baby daughter lying in bed that is intercut with the scene of the bus crash; the overwhelmingly green fields of Felicia's home in County Cork; the stunning landscape of the country home of Simon's grandfather north of Ontario (figures 7.1 and 7.2). Only *Chloe* breaks this pattern, for its ideal

7.1 and 7.2 Two irretrievable moments in the past in *Exotica* (1994): the pixilated video image of the lost wife and child (top) and the achingly beautiful green fields where Eric and Christina will soon discover a body (bottom). Photofest.

past is all verbal, and we mistrust images of it we see, such as the framed magazine profile of the 'perfect' family hanging on the waiting room wall of Catherine's gynaecology practice.

Sweet Hereafter amplifies this relationship into the central problematic of the film, for the entirety of the winter landscape is filmed in terms of its wintry beauty until the climactic scene of the deposition. In the scenes set before the accident, the natural beauty reminds us of what is soon to be lost; in the scene of the accident and the scenes following it, that same beauty persists to haunt us. The motivation for this newly found auteurist visual style should be evident from the formal analysis above: as does the fairy-tale motif, it provides a different reading of the perspective of childhood on the critique of memory, trauma, and postmodern culture. And although he responded with noticeable uneasiness and uncharacteristic uncertainty when the issue was raised to him in interviews, it seems difficult to believe that the shift was unrelated to the birth of Egoyan and Khanjian's own son Arshile in 1993 – after all, one can trace it directly from the central scene in *Exotica* that revolves around Christina, club owner Zoe (she inherited it from her parents), and actor Khanjian's exposed and very pregnant belly.

The different way in which *Ararat* plays on this visual motif befits the film's uneasy relationship between the earlier and the more recent attitudes towards the past. In a key choice made at the editing table, Egoyan excised a scene in which he had explicitly located Gorky's studio on the set of Saroyan's '*Ararat*.' While Egoyan recounts that he cut the scene because the self-consciousness of a conversation between Ani and an explicitly fictionalized 'Gorky' would have overly alienated audiences, the omission has another effect as well: it postpones resolving the ambiguity of the Gorky sequence until the premiere of Saroyan's '*Ararat*' near the end of the film, when we see Simon Abkarian, the actor who plays Gorky, in attendance, and are able to conclude that his scenes, also, were a part of the film.[37] This ambiguity is essential to the meaning of the film, since it postpones a decisive knowledge as to whether we are to interpret the scenes set in New York during the 1930s as identified with Saroyan's film or with Egoyan's. If the former, we must interpret them according to their role within the historical melodrama; if the latter, we must interpret them according to the ostensible 'realism' attributed to the modern-day scenes, and in particular, according to Ani's exegesis of the painting and her explanation of Gorky's erasing of the hands.

Given the ambiguity between portraying the Armenian events as melodramatic spectacle and emphasizing their accuracy according to the historical record, the status of the Gorky story that frames the movie in its final cut bears the weight of the film's meaning all the more. And given that the final shot is an image of young Gorky with his mother in a peaceful Van, an idyllic scene punctured by our knowledge of what is to come but ambiguous in its status vis-à-vis the two films that compose *Ararat*, Egoyan's attitude towards this image seems all the more problematic. And what do we make of the trademark exterior shot of beautiful rolling hills (identified in the shooting script only as 'EXT. VAN. TURKEY. COUNTRY. RIVERBANK – DAY'),[38] used here as the backdrop for the long march, a rape scene witnessed by a terrified young girl, and the context for Gorky's mother's death by starvation? Like so much else in *Ararat*, the semantic confusion of Egoyan's auteurist tropes promises a hermeneutic solution while simultaneously sabotaging that solution. Or, phrased in terms of the analysis above, he radically destabilizes the newly grounded permanence of memory at the same time that he appeals to the innate power of the historicity of that very memory. While, formally, Egoyan introduces a series of motifs to resolve the inability of this contradiction to withstand the scrutiny of his own oeuvre – in particular the film canisters as a metaphor for history that is irredeemably compromised on the one hand but redeemed through individual faith and conviction on the other – stylistically, the visual motifs sabotage the thematic motifs. We may know intellectually that the scenes of naked women doused with kerosene and of mothers being raped have been 'staged' for Saroyan's film, and that they are both more (because visualized) and less horrible than what actually happened, but their iconic power as conventional images so far outweighs the elaborate apparatus around them as to call into question that anything besides a melodrama vastly superior to Saroyan's own could ever represent the truth of what happened and also to preclude the appropriateness of any other form of representation of that truth. What had set Egoyan's previous movies apart from the exploitative potential inherent in their charged material of paedophilia, incest, and serial murder was his ability to invest only a certain set of images with the full power of that material. It is those very images – the fields of lost innocence – that *Ararat* profaned with Hollywood atrocities in a decision that was no less misguided for being both well intentioned and brilliantly rationalized.

In *Ararat*, the video that had framed issues of memory instead was used realistically to simulate the artifice of their truth in Saroyan's film. Unlike the decision to shoot the wrecked bus through Stephens's viewfinder in *Sweet Hereafter*, however, this citation of Egoyan's earlier fascination with media technology within the new context of cinematic realism is accessible only to the viewer of the DVD accompanied by Egoyan's commentary – otherwise, it is displaced onto Raffi's customs dilemma. The interplay is more straightforward in *Sweet Hereafter*, where it not only vividly reproduces the subjective monologue form of the novel but adapts that subjectivity to a broader contrast of country versus city that is equally made through the exaggerated urban grime of Zoe's phone booth. Moreover, the stylistic affinity of Stephens's shots to the look of Egoyan's early films raises a tantalizing possibility for accounting for their equally strong affinity to caricature. Just as Stephens's pronouncement that 'we have all lost our children … narcotized in front of the TV' (borrowed from the novel) reads less as a broad cultural critique than a symptom of his own alienation, so does Zoe's depiction seem to emerge from Stephens's stereotyped vision of the city in which he also lives.[39]

The introduction of video to William Trevor's material does a fine job in unbalancing the periodizing assumptions we would otherwise make about the fifties time-warp feel of Hilditch's house. In what must be an homage to the reel-to-reel-tape-wielding bitter old man in Beckett's *Krapp's Last Tape*, which Egoyan would film for English television the year after *Felicia's Journey*, Hilditch is addicted to the recordings of what had once been a novel form of media but which to us – and to the technicians who digitally altered the film footage to give the effect – appear as quaintly outmoded as the faulty mixers Gala had endorsed at the height of her fame. Unlike Beckett's Krapp, however, Hilditch is equally, if more secretly, at home in the contemporary world of technology, and the shot of Felicia's legs from the sinister point of view of the video camera hidden in Hilditch's car, like the grainy, unbalanced video footage of his prior victims, allows Egoyan subtly to insinuate that being trapped in a private cul-de-sac in the past by no means precludes making use of the trappings of the contemporary world for one's own purposes. There is a dialectic between old and new technology far more complex and ambivalent than the simple replacement of one with the other. In this way, Egoyan's substitution of video interviews for Trevor's device of Hilditch's 'Memory Lane,' a mode of remembrance as anachronistic as the rest of him, successfully complicates the portrait as much as does the elimination of most of the backstory.

In *Where the Truth Lies*, by contrast, the periodic framing of the telethon sequences through the grainy black-and-white of 1950s video technology seems, like the touches of paedophilia, a gesture at Egoyan's auteurist past without any intrinsic relationship to the meaning of the movie or deepening of the novel's slick murder mystery. Rather than related to the privileged moment of the meeting of the 'Miracle Girl' with Lanny or in any way disturbing our expectations and assumptions, the revelation of the truth about Maureen's death the night before that meeting feels like the excuse for the sensational material that has preceded it. Like *Chloe*'s rapid descent into *Fatal Attraction* territory with a razor-sharp hair pin, this is a typical situation for a typical genre movie, but without any of the cross-fertilization that makes *Felicia's Journey* and *Ararat* intellectually (if not dramatically) compelling.

Production Qualities

It is a compelling if historically irresponsible proposition to suggest that *Ararat* constitutes Egoyan's most sustained meditation to date on the problems of fame. And yet, the film, time and again, raises the question of his own ambivalence to the movie he is making. Although auteur theory emerged in the 1950s in France in appreciation of the way in which the trademark vision of an individual talent could illuminate even the most conventional of Hollywood studio material, when those same French critics turned to making movies, they were well aware that the auteurist mode of production is inimical in its definition to that of the studio system, however much it might play with the codes of that system. An intimately familiar stable of actors, technicians, and producers that over the years has come to know each other as only a family can is the mark of celebrated auteurs from Renoir to Bergman to Egoyan's compatriots Arcand, Cronenberg, and Maddin. The *Cahiers du cinéma* critics regarded studio directors like Hitchcock and Hawks as geniuses for their success in spite of, not because of, the studio system, and many of their analyses would read the films themselves as a battleground between an individual vision and the template of a popular genre or a star vehicle.

In his post-*Exotica* films, Egoyan too has managed to play both sides of the fence, maintaining his auteur identity by making films that purport to subvert the generic conventions on which their increased funding increasingly relies. Even the $30-million *Where the Truth Lies* was funded in part by Telefilm Canada.[40] Whereas the microscopic budgets of Egoyan's early films could be covered entirely by public funds from local, provincial, and federal sources, the public-private split from *Exotica* onward, and especially the increased pressure of international co-production – the mode from *Sweet Hereafter* onward – altered the fundamental dynamic of the auteurist vision. Egoyan's work as his own scriptwriter ensured formal consistency even as his formal priorities were shifting and evolving; the continuity of producers and crew ensured stylistic continuity – composer Mychael

Danna (since *Family Viewing*), sound designer Steven Munro (since *Family Viewing*), sound supervising re-recording mixer Daniel Pellerin (since *Family Viewing*, responsible for a stunning number of Canadian films since the mid-eighties, and recipient of a shout-out from 'Atom' in the credits of *Chloe*), cinematographer Paul Sarossy (since *Speaking Parts*), editor Susan Shipman (since *The Adjuster*), production manager and producer Sandra Cunningham (since *The Adjuster*), executive producer Robert Lantos (from *Calendar* through *Adoration*), and two latecomers who have ensured the visual consistency of the recent films, costume designer Beth Pasternak and production designer Phillip Barker (both since *Sweet Hereafter*) – even as stylistic priorities were shifting.

The repeated use of actors has ensured another sort of consistency, but a consistency that has more and more receded to the margins of the films – indeed, *Chloe* was the first Egoyan feature film in which Khanjian did not appear. Just as the formal and stylistic motifs of Egoyan's early films reappear bracketed and contextualized in the later ones, so does the extradiegetic meaning of the actors become part of the films' diegesis rather than their reason for being. We glimpse this relationship in a playfully ironic manner in *Calendar*, which arose from Egoyan's winning a cash prize, the sole requirement of which was that he shoot a movie in Armenia and which so successfully played on Egoyan's image as an auteur and Arsinée Khanjian's image as his fetish actor/muse/wife that the small world that saw the film was convinced it was the factual document of a fractured marriage. We glimpse it the following year in the scene of Khanjian pregnant in *Exotica*, discussed above. But only with *Sweet Hereafter* do auteurist qualities of production begin to be encoded into the texture of the film in a thoroughgoing way. This encoding is especially evident in the casting. Every single actor playing the inhabitants of Sam Dent (with the notable exception of English-Canadian staple Tom McManus, who plays Sam Burnell) had appeared in at least one prior Egoyan film, most had appeared in many of them, and one – Khanjian – had appeared in all of them. This continuity results not simply in the intuitive grasp of the director's vision but in a developing allegory of the relation of each new film to that vision. While no doubt partially motivated by funding considerations, Egoyan brilliantly manipulated the casting of well-known English character actor Ian Holm in the film's leading role in order to emphasize his status as outsider to the Canadian regulars. Egoyan aficionados thus found two forms of familiarity in conflict with one another: the expectations of deadened affect and underplaying associated with the actors of the earlier films and the expectations of quality realism associated with Ian Holm. Rather than standing on its own as postmodern alienation, however, the townspeople's stunted affect is motivated within the film's diegesis, as we come to discover, by the accident itself. The same terms equally motivate Holm's different style in terms of his coming from another world – both in the story of the film and in terms of acting traditions.

The allegory becomes even more intriguing if we notice that the most jarring bit of acting comes from the other outsider to the town and to the cast, Mitchell's daughter Zoe, who is played by avowed film fanatic Russell Banks's daughter, Caerthan (the novelist himself cameos as the doctor treating Nicole). Given Egoyan's decision to relocate the novel's setting from upstate New York to the

Okanagan Valley in British Columbia, the film's central conflict of country versus city subtly stages a conflict between local Canadian production values and those of Hollywood that eventually garnered the film a pair of Academy Award nominations. And while it is a testimony to the film's power that this allegory remains only subtext, it certainly adds a punch to the ambiguous character of Stephens, and makes all the more pointed the call of the Pied Piper, especially as it was in fact Nicole's Sarah Polley whose career most benefited from the film's high profile.

Evidently, Egoyan made a concerted effort to duplicate this interplay in pre-production for *Felicia's Journey*, proposing to William Trevor a shift in setting to the English colonialist time warp of Victoria, British Columbia (Egoyan's home town), and of Felicia to a young Quebecois from somewhere in the north country.[41] Trevor predictably balked at the loss of the inimitable texture of the Easter rebellion, but Egoyan's solution was in fact quite plausible given Quebec's Catholic culture, historical backwardness and history of conflict with its English-based colonial master. And one can readily imagine a richly Canadian allegory of anglophone Egoyan regulars cast against established Quebecois stars in place of the Irish characters, with young Marie-Josée Croze caught in the middle, the only question being on which side to place Arsinée Khanjian. Instead, Egoyan ingeniously inserted his own auteurist past into the film via the video memories of French chef Gala and plunged into the unfamiliar. While amusing for Egoyan, Khanjian, and many long-time fans, the subplot remains wholly extrinsic to the rest of the film, like Gala herself, an exotic import to the drab world of Birmingham. Read in terms of Egoyan's prior formal and stylistic interests, it adds an important subtext to the film, deepening Trevor's novel as it betrays its intent. Read in terms of auteurist production, it feels almost like a cry for help, a lifeline to the world he had left behind for the candy shop of Shepperton and the deep pockets of Mel Gibson's Icon Productions. (*Felicity's Journey* was the only one of his films on which Egoyan did not also act as producer until fellow Canuck Ivan Reitman did the honours on *Chloe*.)

Although *Ararat*'s $15-million budget provides one motivation for the distancing device of the film within a film, the fact that the film was an all-Canadian affair renders a different allegory, as Egoyan negotiated his Armenian heritage and community with an auteurist past in which that heritage and community had played a supporting, if nonetheless significant, role. The casting of cultural icons Charles Aznavour and Eric Bogosian as the director and screenwriter neatly reveals the degree to which outside audiences had always assumed they were 'French' and 'American,' respectively, allowing them proudly to display their Armenian heritage, and demonstrating the invisibility of Armenia as a cultural marker in the same way that Canadians have always complained occurs with their own actors within Hollywood.[42] That same maneuver, however, makes it all the more difficult not to read the rest of the film in the same extradiegetic sense.

Consequently, when we find familiar Egoyan leading men in the two most complex supporting roles – Bruce Greenwood as Martin, the actor who plays Clarence Ussher, the ostensibly neutral eyewitness of the siege of Van, and Elias Koteas as Ali, the gay Turkish-Canadian partner of David's son Philip who in Saroyan's film plays the role of the 'evil Turk' who orchestrates the massacre – we can also read those roles in terms of the auteurist past of Egoyan with which they are so closely identified. Each character is given a key scene questioning the relationship between actor and role, past and present, and fiction and reality. Ali's moment comes in the oft-cited scene where Raffi confronts him about Turkey's role in the genocide, of which Ali had been unaware and about which he concludes, 'This is a new country. So let's just drop the fucking history and get on with it.' Martin's turn comes in the equally pivotal scene in which Ani stumbles upon the set in the midst of filming and he confronts her, in character, with a list of atrocities, only to conclude, 'Who the *fuck* are you?' Beyond the expressive impact of being the only two uses of the F-word in the entire film, the scenes are united as the twin climaxes of Egoyan's need somehow to reconcile the cross-purposes of the film and of the two families – his past and his métier – intersecting within it.

In contrast, the casting of venerable Canadian leading man Christopher Plummer and rising Quebecois star Marie-Josée Croze is unprecedented in Egoyan's oeuvre and inexplicable in terms of its internal auteurist parameters. Rather, they seem motivated by a need or desire to reference every form of Canadian cinematic iconicity. If Greenwood and Koteas personify the English-Canadian, Toronto-based roots of Egoyan's oeuvre, Plummer references the famously invisible Hollywood Canadian, apparently indistinguishable from his American colleagues. To be sure, the Toronto-born Plummer makes a brilliant foil for first-timer (and first in a series of pretty, callow, lightweight male roles) David Alpay's Raffi in the quintessentially Egoyan airport customs scenes; his iconic presence bestows upon these scenes not just the allegorical weight of Armenian Canadian versus English Canadian, but the added burden of Armenia's cinematic invisibility uneasily cross-fertilized with the fraught status of an independent Canadian auteur smuggling his familiar themes into the alien yet intimately known territory of mainstream, big-budget film-making.

Croze's role in the film is both more mysterious and less satisfying than Plummer's. The most irritating and far-fetched bundle of issues and coincidences in a film built around them, Celia's character is a laundry list of new Quebecois film motifs – not surprising given Croze's then-recent Genie- and Jutra-prize winning turn in Denis Villeneuve's *Maelström* (2000) (see chapter 4). From her stylish, sexy wardrobe and designer loft apartment to the subculture markers of psychological instability, casual nudity, drug dealing, and violently antisocial behavior, Celia has nothing to do with Egoyan's prior catalogue of characters and everything to do with the seductive but empty art-house surrealism of new Quebecois directors Villeneuve and Turpin. Add a further subtext somehow displacing the 1985 storming of the Turkish Embassy by three Armenians onto the figure of Raffi's father and into Celia's vandalism and FLQ associations inevitably arising from her identity as the lone (and violent) Quebecois in the film. We are left with a half-baked cluster of associations whose range suggests the ambition of *Ararat* but whose refusal to gel suggests the film's distance from a director's oeuvre characterized by nothing so much as the extraordinary tightness of its multiple levels and fragments.[43]

Here, as in the later *Adoration*, Khanjian is the pivot of the myriad themes, plots, and references. Ani is impossible to accept as a realistic character, but neither does she have the hieratic distance necessary to function as the pure allegory we might find in the films of such European masters as Theo Angelopoulos or Sergei Paradjanov. Egoyan's films have always struck a knife's-edge balance between emotional authenticity and intellectual distance, the non-linear movement of the plot forcing the audience to bridge the gap between the characters' deadened emotions and the trauma behind them. As Egoyan was fully aware, only personal trauma can be transmitted effectively in this way; unfortunately, there is no analogous representational mode for jumbling the trauma of an entire people.[44] The code proper to one mode sabotages the other, and the result is that the more a sequence such as Raffi and David's confrontation in the airport is emotionally and intellectually satisfying in itself, the more inappropriate its application to the greater historical subject becomes. Similarly, the more Egoyan insulates himself from criticism of exploitation with arguments that are compelling in intellectual terms, the more the viewer becomes irritated qua viewer. And here Ani, as the voice of authenticity – she is the one who protests at the film's manipulation of reality in the service of emotional truth; she is the one who refuses to compromise her own fidelity to truthfulness in order to provide Celia or Raffi with the emotionally satisfying answers they crave; she is the one who explains Gorky's erasure of his mother's hands as a gesture to the inability of memory to do justice to the past – becomes ever shriller the more we know she is justified in everything she says.[45] And our knowledge of Khanjian's own background as Egoyan's wife, linchpin of his auteurist vision, and catalyst of the director's own burgeoning awareness of his Armenian past only exacerbates this frustration. The self-consciousness that was a necessary evil of the early films and that was craftily subordinated to the diegetic requirements of *Exotica*, *Sweet Hereafter*, and *Felicia's Journey* rages out of control in the expansive vision of *Ararat*.

No wonder Egoyan chose to turn next to his most anonymous project to date in *Where the Truth Lies*, muting Khanjian, Hemblen, Maury Chaykin, Don McKellar, and Gabrielle Rose to supporting roles to his Hollywood stars, as invisible to the casual viewer as any other auteurist markings in the film, as if in an invisibly Canadian nod to his first full-bore, big-budget, Hollywood-style extravaganza. To be sure, there is a wicked irony only a connoisseur of Canadian cinema could appreciate in seeing Chaykin turn up as a Mafioso apologetically described in Lanny's voice-over as 'straight out of central casting' and Khanjian, McKellar, and Rose as Lohman's deep-pocketed publishers, worried sick that their dirt will be trumped by Lanny's tell-all memoir, the upstarts outdone by the ones who really know how the game is played. True, it is an in-joke auteurist pleasure wholly extrinsic to the film as a whole, but it is also a typically Canadian stance towards American popular culture. The shock is that it's coming from a director who had always apparently held that culture at more than an arm's length away.

Perhaps what is most fascinating about the popular turn in Egoyan's career is that his own discourse about the films has remained as consistent and consistently intelligent as the cast and crew with which he has surrounded himself. The latter appear to have insulated him from a full awareness of the unevenness of the products of the partnership just as the former has insulated him from recognizing the growing inability of his brilliant intentions and exegeses fully to account for what actually shows up on screen. The growing degree to which the auteur Egoyan is bracketed in his films by the greater world – financial, historical, cultural – around him thus mirrors the inevitable loss of control to which the auteur submits when he or she emerges from a cocoon of local independence into the global marketplace of contemporary cinema. It is a testimony to Egoyan's ability as a film-maker that he has managed to preserve his identity as much as he has and has continued to make films of compelling intellectual fascination; however, this should not blind us to the fact that the primary reason we still go to his films and bestow them the critical attention we do is in ritualized compulsion to recover the extraordinary memory of the ones we saw in a now-lost past. But even this may be changing: *Where the Truth Lies* sank almost without a trace, while *Chloe* did quite well at the box office. Judging from the blogosphere, this can be put down to the generous nudity provided by the popular television star in the film's title role (Amanda Seyfried), and the presence of quality film stalwarts Julianne Moore and Liam Neeson as the adults. As soft-core films go, it's not bad, but this is the first time that even an Egoyan-inspired auteurist would be hard-pressed. Hard-pressed, that is, except for its location and crew. Both are unmistakably Canadian, the imported actors disporting themselves all over a Toronto that, in a welcome twist from tax-shelter exploitation, is not in disguise, even if, in a further twist from late-twentieth-century expectations, it is glamorous and seductive rather than cold and anonymous.

The Five Hundred Hats of Atom Egoyan

It is a peculiarity of auteurist studies of Egoyan's oeuvre that they tend simply to elide the presence of apparently non-auteurist works from the very beginning of the director's career: CBC movies such as Paul Gross's *In This Corner* (1985) and *Gross Misconduct* (1993), and episodes of *The Twilight Zone* (1985), *Alfred Hitchcock Presents* (1985), and *Friday the 13th* (1987).[46] The common assumption that this was 'only' work for pay is reinforced by the coincidence of its termination following the mainstream success of *Exotica*; a fitting end point would be the near deal to direct a conventional film noir with Warner Brothers that Egoyan eventually passed up in order to adapt *Sweet Hereafter*. Nevertheless, the early work as director-for-hire must have played a role in preparing Egoyan for his superlative rapport with mainstream actors and facility with popular genres evident in *Felicia's Journey*, *Ararat*, *Where the Truth Lies*, and *Chloe* – a role he tacitly acknowledged in referring to Hitchcock as 'the master of self-consciousness' while discussing the thrill of working with Martin Landau on *Alfred Hitchcock Presents* and hearing the venerable actor's memories of *North by Northwest*.[47]

While Egoyan's recent films have, for better or for worse, somehow synthesized the polar opposites of his early work, a new split has emerged between his big-budget cinematic productions and his ever-diversifying work as an economic, intellectual, and artistic force in Canadian culture at large. Egoyan's work with opera began in 1996 with his staging of *Salomé* for the COC, continuing in 1998 with the world premiere of Gavin Bryar's *Dr. Ox's Experiment* for London's

National Opera and Wagner's *Die Walküre* for the COC in 2004, as well as the premiere of *Elsewhereness*, from his own libretto, in 1998. Along with Rozema, he made an hour-long contribution, 'Bach Cello Suite #4: Sarabande' (1997), to the award-winning TV series *Yo Yo Ma: Inspired by Bach*; like Cronenberg, he made a short contribution to the Cannes-anniversary omnibus film, *Chacun son cinema*: *Artaud Double Bill* (2007). Also, like Rozema, he made a brilliant short-feature-length adaptation of a Samuel Beckett play for the Channel Four series, *Krapp's Last Tape* (2000).[48] His musical collaboration 'Mystery' with The Tragically Hip–frontman Gordon Downie appears in *Ararat* as well as on Downie's 2000 solo album 'Coke Machine Glow.' The depth of Egoyan's engagement with opera, classical music, and popular music has long borne fruit in his collaboration with composer Mychael Danna. It has equally provided an outlet for the experimental and non-narrative impulses that have ceased to play a formative role in the feature films.

Since 1995's *A Portrait of Arshile*, Egoyan has exhibited nearly a dozen short films and installations in gallery settings ranging from the Irish Museum of Modern Art in Dublin to the Venice Biennale to the Power Plant in Toronto, as well as 'Steenbeckett' in the former Museum of Mankind in London and 'Hors d'usage' in the Musée d'Art Contemporain in Montreal, which built site-specific exhibitions around the projection of *Krapp's Last Tape* and the conception of taped memories.[49] As with 'America, America,' a combination of extracts from Elia Kazan's film and personal footage exhibited at the 1997 Venice Biennale, *A Portrait of Arshile* played a formative role in the conception of *Ararat*, its highly personal and fragmented meditation on Gorky's portrait and Egoyan and Khanjian's baby son Arshile transmuted into Ani's strident art history lecturing.[50] Other expositions have worked in the opposite direction, revisioning extracts of feature films such as *Calendar*, *The Adjuster*, and *Felicia's Journey* in the context of the visual arts and the aesthetics of the installation. *Evidence*, a nineteen-minute video compilation of the surveillance shots of Hilditch's victims from *Felicia's Journey*, toured the world as part of the exhibition *Notorious: Alfred Hitchcock and Contemporary Art*, originating at the Oxford Museum of Modern Art in 1999. Extracted from the context of a mainstream narrative thriller, the component of *Felicia's Journey* most indebted to the theoretical concerns that had made Egoyan the darling of media theorists found its way back to that original setting, allowing him to sustain his auteur discourse in spite of the popular turn in his feature film-making.

Subtitles, the collection of essays Egoyan co-edited with Ian Balfour, reads like a who's who of the rarified world of art film and cultural theory at the turn of the millennium, with contributions from Claire Denis, B. Ruby Rich, Trinh T. Minh-ha, Fredric Jameson, and Slavoj Žižek, the latter concluding his essay with a timely homage to *Sweet Hereafter*.[51] While the collection includes a few pieces on the more popular aspects of subtitles and foreignness, its primary concern, reflected in the innovative production design mirroring the dimensions of the 1.66:1 aspect ratio of the widescreen frame, is the intransigent cultural critique of Egoyan's early auteurism. Rather than historicized in terms of their different cultural signifying from their identification with art cinema in the 1960s to their current denotation of foreign, often fake, cultures in popular cinema and television, subtitles appear here for the most part as signs of a global alienation of language and culture, an intellectually fascinating but historically inert phenomenon. In this vision, high art remains wholly distinct from popular culture.

While work in the art and music world has allowed Egoyan to retain the avant-garde auteurist currency in which his films no longer so obviously participate, his new economic clout and cultural profile have opened up different doors for him, from serving on the jury of the Cannes Film Festival in 1996 to serving as executive producer of a half dozen Canadian features since 1996 and providing informal assistance on numerous others. In 2004, he opened Camera, a combination fifty-seat cinema and bar designed by business partner Hussein Amarshi in the trendy Queen West neighbourhood of Toronto. In addition to the high-concept cafe, the screening room is used to show alternative features and experimental shorts, including Egoyan and Khanjian's own video documentary, *Citadel* (2004).[52] Weighing in, as a respected authority on all things Canadian and cinematic, on the commercial thrust of Richard Stursberg's tenure at TFC, Egoyan solidified a position of eminence within the culture in which he had always figured himself as outsider even as his feature film production seemed to be moving him further and further away from that very culture. Or, perhaps, as the strangely globalized local focus of *Adoration* and *Chloe* suggests, is this trend actually indicating precisely the direction towards which that culture is moving?[53]

Along with Cronenberg and Maddin, Egoyan has become a staple presence in the pantheon of world cinema auteurs, regularly tapped for short-film contributions, collection forwards, festival committees, and so forth. Rather than achieving a unified auteurist vision of the new global culture in which his feature films circulate, along the lines of Cronenberg, Lepage, or Maddin, Egoyan has diversified himself, effectively severing his mainstream film-making identity from an avant-garde figure whose cachet he rigorously maintains. This is how he formulated the situation at the time of the release of *Where the Truth Lies*: 'The middle film – something like *The Adjuster*, let's say – is hard to do these days. Once you are involved at a certain budget level you have to perform in a different, perhaps more restrictive way. It seems it's either bigger budget stuff or something totally hand-made, like *Citadel*. That middle film is harder and harder to make ... Of course, it all depends on the story you want to tell.'[54] The replacement of a tension within his films by a dialectic of cultural production outside them accurately character-izes Egoyan's shift to the popular that began following *The Adjuster*. While his big-budget travails in the twenty-first century can furnish an object lesson of the dangers and temptations besetting the independent Canadian film-maker in the global market, the ever-widening split in his oeuvre between the growing con-straints of the big budget and the artistic ambition of the experimental suggests the provisional strategy he adopted to weather the storm. His most recent films suggest that Egoyan has found a way to achieve the synthesis. Both *Adoration* and *Chloe* implicitly claim that Toronto itself has now become a global production network. Consequently, rather than moving away from the local concerns of his 'golden age' work, Egoyan's diversified auteur discourse of the new millennium would simply reflect the new reality of Toronto itself. From the abstract theoreti-cal vantage point of the eighties and early nineties, this would mean the city has capitulated to the mediated reality as Egoyan was predicting it would. From the vantage point of a living, breathing, and productive Torontian film-maker, that mediated reality has become a constraint just like any other, simultaneously stultifying and creative. While Egoyan's feature films since 1997 are no match in absolute terms for his brilliant run of the mid-nineties, a clear-headed assessment from beyond the hardened terms of the enduring auteurist approach could well argue that they are quite comparable in their mixed bag of brilliance and flatness to the work of the eighties. They are neither identical to the past nor wholly severed from it. As in the work of any artist or artisan, there is continuity as well as change, but for both to be visible as such requires a vantage point far broader and more varied than Egoyan, or the national cinema in which he has spent his working life, has generally received.

Chapter Eight

The Canadian Mosaic: Margins and Ethnicities

As a metaphor of national identity, the 'Canadian mosaic' exists on the fault lines of two relationships: between American identity and Canadian identity and between the local ideology of multiculturalism and the local reality of a white elite and foundational mythology. The term was coined by Ceylon-born Scottish Canadian writer John Murray Gibbon (1875–1952) in his 1938 book, *The Canadian Mosaic: The Making of a Northern Nation*, in explicit contrast to the American metaphor of the 'melting pot,' positing the conservation of local identity within the broader umbrella of confederation. Publicity agent and prolific author for the Canadian Pacific Railway (CPR), Gibbon organized music festivals and other events under the corporate sponsorship of the CPR, each around a different regional culture: 'French-Canadian in Quebec ..., "All-European" in Winnipeg, Regina and Calgary, Highland in Banff, Sea Music in Vancouver and Old English in Victoria.'[1] Gibbon's mosaic, unsurprisingly, was a white European one; it meant the expansion beyond English and French to other European communities reflected in the CPR festivals and the ideology of CPR expansion and settlement of the Canadian landscape.[2] When the Royal Commission on Bilingualism and Biculturalism, convened in the 1960s to confront the issue of Quebecois separatism, eventually led instead to Canada becoming the first 'officially multicultural' country, it created a legislative narrative of equality that was simultaneously a denial of the reality of inequality and a foundational mythology that ignored the presence of 'visible minorities' from the very beginning of Canadian history.[3] In both cases, support for cultural activity goes hand in hand with an ideology of multiculturalism.[4] It is a fundamentally unstable model, not only because of the inevitable gap between ideology and reality, but because, as Andrew Higson argues of national cinemas, 'The search for a stable and coherent national identity can only be successful at the expense of repressing internal differences, tensions and contradictions – differences of class, race, gender, region, etc.'[5] This contradiction is exacerbated in the case of cinema because, as Higson continues, 'a cinema can only be national, and command a national-popular audience if it is a mass-production genre cinema, capable of constructing, reproducing, and re-cycling popular myth on a broad scale, with an elaborate, well capitalized and well resourced system of market exploitation,' and yet, for the identity to be viable, it must exist in contradistinction to the international Hollywood model that would subvert that identity. Canada's 'mosaic,' then, as a model of national and cultural identity, explicitly articulates the contradiction that underpins the enunciation of any national identity, arguing, in quintessentially ironic Canadian fashion, that its national identity exists precisely in the ideological repudiation of a national identity. This chapter explores the implications of that broader paradox through the specific paradox of a national cinema that seeks to use the tools of the international culture industry to represent an irreducibly local mosaic of national identity. For a country whose identity is explicitly defined as a collection of parts and which has long been conceived in terms of its frontier and geographical expanse, the road becomes essential as a spatial practice connecting those parts and as a spatial metaphor to map the qualities of their association. We find the road present explicitly within the genre of the road movie and implicitly whenever cinema represents the crossing of borders between parts of the Canadian mosaic, especially in terms of the relationship between margin and centre. Following an investigation of the road, I turn to three categories of film that are explicitly concerned with their place in the mosaic and which have been fundamental elements of Canadian cinema since the eighties: regional cinema, ethnic cinema, and queer cinema.

Roads and Border-Crossing

> The most interesting road movies are those in which the identity crisis of the protagonist mirrors the identity crisis of the culture itself.
>
> Walter Salles, 'Notes for a Theory of the Road Movie' (2007)

According to the terms of Brazilian film-maker Walter Salles, if not according to the criterion of cinematic quality, Mark Griffith's teen sex comedy *Going the Distance* (2004) well qualifies as an 'interesting' road movie. The story of a prospective law student travelling cross-country with two high school buddies – one a sex-obsessed surfer, the other a stoner – and two female hitchhikers in order to propose marriage to his careerist girlfriend in Toronto, *Going the Distance* offers everything a Canadian movie ought to have: location scenery from the west coast village of Tofino, BC, to the eastern tip of Newfoundland; an all-Canadian cast and crew including such veteran actors as Jackie Burroughs, Matt Frewer, and August Schellenburg; a climactic scene in Toronto at a local music awards show featuring Canadian pop music stars. It's no wonder that the Script-to-Screen era, TFC financed *Going the Distance* to the tune of more than $3 million and was rewarded by a rapid return on its investment. But Canadian as it may be, *Going the Distance* is also the vacuous product of a global pop culture, its scenes and gags lifted wholesale from countless other teen road comedies, its locations mere window dressing, its regional inclusivity based on local stereotypes, and its entire plot structured around product placement for MuchMusic (which produced the film) and the media giant CTVglobemedia which owns MuchMusic. In other words, *Going the Distance* was composed entirely of Canadian content, but that very content can be viewed as the product of an international media network with no intrinsic connection whatsoever to 'Canada.' So, what Salles terms 'the identity crisis of the culture itself' is perfectly mirrored in the 'identity crisis' of hero Nick (Christopher Jacot), who travels all the way to Toronto only to realize he really wants nothing to do with anodyne media-hound Trish and is really in love with down-home acoustic-guitar strumming Newfie hitchhiker Sasha. The film's plot line mirrors and subverts its conditions of production, suggesting that a road trip undertaken with the goal of big-time show-business conformity can nevertheless end happily amid icebergs off the Atlantic coast.

Going the Distance certainly pays lip service to the Canadian mosaic, from Nick's hippie parents living on a BC beach to Burroughs's and Frewer's cameos as religious fanatic Alberta farmers to life in capitalism nexus Toronto to a strip club in Montreal to the thick accents and inbred behaviour of the Newfies. We get Schellenburg as an alcoholic half-psycho half-nurturing Native special forces veteran hired to keep the friends from reaching Toronto, performances by the multi-ethnic rappers Swollen Members and the singer Avril Lavigne, and last but not least, a pair of what look like cross-dressing men who promise to introduce Tyler to the pleasures of anal sex. If the mosaic is present only in stereotypes and celebrities, is it still a mosaic? The authentically regional Sasha, too, needs a lot of persuading before she finally decides that Nick is not after her only because he's been dumped by a Toronto music intern more interested in sleazy music producer Lenny Swackhammer (played, naturally, by transplanted Canadian former-heart-throb Jason Priestly). Pascal Gin defines the 'intercultural' road movie as a contemporary form of the genre that exists at the tense intersection between 'an experience attentive to the modalities of the local and the personal' and 'paths of transit' belonging to the anonymous spaces anthropologist Marc Augé terms 'non-lieux' (no-places).[6] While Gin's subject of investigation is the road movie in contemporary art cinema, the spatial tension he describes equally characterizes the cultural conflict dramatized spatially in the popular road genre of *Going the Distance* and epitomized in the spatio-sexual double-entendre of its title.

Simultaneously the province of art cinema and popular comedy, quintessentially Hollywood while also a privileged international mode for critiquing Hollywood, identified as both 'establishment' and 'rebellious,' the road movie has long been a fertile vehicle for articulating the vagaries of Canadian identity and, in particular, its fraught relationship with America. *Going the Distance* gingerly separates itself from the economic necessity that drove Pete and Joey to Toronto in *Goin' Down the Road* (1970, see chapter 1). While the subject of money is always in the air, when push comes to shove it is never actually lacking or a motivating factor in the characters' decisions; they, like their target audience, self-identify as middle class. Even salt-of-the-earth Sasha, who has left home to seek her fortune and is last seen waiting tables at a pirate-themed tourist trap in the Quidi Fidi neighbourhood of St John's, nevertheless is granted the mobility conventionally attributed to attractive young women: having finally landed Nick, she can simply drop everything and follow him into the never-never land after the credits, their happiness guaranteed in advance by a bonding experience on the road. The two films share an understanding of the road as a fundamentally free space, although that freedom is constrained in a number of ways. *Going the Distance* is more interested in what happens when the quintet stops along the way than with the road per se; it builds

8.1 Life on the road: Pipefitter (Bernie Coulson) taking in the aging punk band's 'reunion' tour of Western Canada in *Hard Core Logo* (1996). Photofest.

its narrative on the parallel obstacles towards getting laid and moving along the highway. In contrast, *Goin' Down the Road* is more concerned with the misery that awaits Pete and Joey upon arriving at their destination, suggesting that that misery will have more to tell us about contemporary society than does their transitory happiness while in the liminal state of transit.

The road thus offers an imagined space that is neither wholly of the centre nor wholly of the peripheries, and thus a space of representation for articulating and debating the relationship between them. Similar to the transcontinental railway narrative in *Mouvements du désir* and *Stations* (see chapter 5), the way in which road films represent the relationship between traveller and landscape is crucial for interpreting that relationship. *Going the Distance* posits an unproblematic relationship; at the same time, the jarring contrast between the extreme vulgarity of its sex gags, the essential sweetness of its characters and plot, and the faint but unmistakable recourse to the documentary realism tradition suggest an unconscious tension in its surface resolution of the time-honoured Canadian dichotomy between local cinema and the Hollywood machine. We can constructively compare it to Bruce McDonald's mockumentary *Hard Core Logo* (1996), which recounts the travails of a west-coast punk band on a disastrous reunion tour that takes them across the west, from Vancouver through Calgary, Regina, and Saskatoon before imploding in Edmonton (figure 8.1). Whereas *Going the Distance* presents its mosaic as a user-friendly, generically Canadian tourist backdrop, *Hard Core Logo*'s west is both self-reflexive – a retro-style animated map shows us the itinerary – and so grittily realistic that the film has been mistaken for an actual documentary. McDonald further heightens the self-reflexive quality by casting himself as a documentary film-maker recording the tour for posterity, and much of the drama of the film derives from the band members' constant sense of being under the spotlight. This spotlight is all the more intense for the extraordinarily low stakes involved; McDonald's depiction of the gruelling life of an aging punk band is all the more effective for lacking the distraction of a conventional plot. The reality effect is further augmented by McDonald's trademark affinity for music – both soundtrack and performance – not only as a tonal device but as a vehicle for the development of plot and character.

At the same time, the primary conflict between singer Joe Dick (played by Hugh Dillon, lead singer of Kingston, Ontario, band the Headstones) and guitarist Billy Tallent (Callum Keith Rennie, see chapter 4) equally introduces an allegorical level to the makeshift quality of the tour. Childhood friends with a strong but repressed attraction to each other (at least on Dick's part), the pair is torn between Dick's admirable yet pathetic adherence to the anti-commercial creed of the original punk movement and Tallent's desire for career stability and relative fame with the California 'indie' group jenifur. The music industry subplot subtly introduces the tension within punk music itself between local authenticity and the international system of economics and of genres that underpin it. As Will Straw writes of collecting punk and post-punk singles in the late seventies and early eighties, 'Objects with subcultural aura, like punk or speed garage records ... are brought to Canada by individuals intimately bound up with the circulation of information on an international level; they presume cultural capital of the most basic kind, such as that which tells you where to find British music magazines in Montréal or Toronto, or what an imported record is and where to find it. Their principal audiences, within Canada, are marked by an interest in the cosmopolitan and the scarce.'[7] Straw would not deny the specifically Canadian uses to which these imported subcultures have been appropriated; what he stresses is the cultural anxiety that underpins those appropriations and the vitiation of the original political context in which a subculture like punk emerged in London or New York.[8]

As McDonald demonstrates in all of his movies, but especially in his 'rock 'n' roll road trilogy' of *Roadkill*, *Highway 61*, and *Hard Core Logo*, popular music is simultaneously indigenous and alien to Canadian culture. Moreover, music is simultaneously the motor and the interpretive framework of the road trips that structure his films. *Roadkill* began life as a documentary project following a concert tour by Toronto alternative rock band A Neon Rome before transmuting into the story of Ramona (Valerie Buhagiar), a rock promoter's assistant hired to track down the missing band Children of Paradise in the wilds of northern Ontario. A deadpan, tongue-in-cheek exploration of the English-Canadian hinterlands as if they were the remote jungle of Francis Ford Coppola's *Apocalypse Now* (1979), *Roadkill* documents the vast gap between urban hipsterism and rural hickdom while equally asserting the strange influence of American culture on both the Toronto music scene and characters such as Don McKellar's Sudbury-based would-be serial killer, who aspires to fame by co-opting the 'American thing, traditionally,' of serial killing, hoping to top the home-grown spectacle of the Dionne quintuplets.

Highway 61 broadens the musical and geographical palette of *Roadkill*, picking up where it ended, near Thunder Bay, with McKellar now Pokey Jones, a geeky cornet player in 'Pickerel Falls,' and Buhagiar the cynical, Americanized roadie Jackie Bangs (her name itself most likely a double entendre homage to the late, great American rock critic Lester Bangs). With a loosely noir set-up – she persuades him to transport a coffin containing a drug stash south all the way to New Orleans – underpinned by Jones's obsession with popular music, *Highway 61* undertakes a mythic tour of a Canadian version of the American heartland. As Pokey puts it near the beginning of the journey in reference to Bob Dylan's iconic song and album *Highway 61 Revisited* and the blues original that inspired it, 'Highway 61's a song. When you travel south on Highway 61 what you're really doing is tracing popular music back to its roots. I lived on the northern tip of this highway and I studied and I read. I've never left home, but I know every inch of this highway.'[9] Dylan's song envisions Highway 61 as a space of American myth and folklore, from Genesis to the Third World War, bumbled and jumbled together as only popular culture can do, the metaphor underpinned by the spatial symbolism of a highway winding all the way from his own Duluth in the north (Pokey visits Robert Zimmerman's house there) to the southern border, past both Memphis and New Orleans, and the musical history of a blues touchstone.

McDonald extends both the highway and the metaphor northward into Canada, while also extending Canada south into the United States. The border guard is played by Jello Biafra, iconic frontman of the legendary San Francisco punk band Dead Kennedys, but all of the 'Americans' encountered thereafter by Pokey and Jackie are played by Canadians. As Chris Byford argues, Highway 61 is an imagined place neither wholly American nor wholly Canadian, leading him to conclude that 'American culture is not simply a colonizing force but a force that blends and is transformed by its context of reception.'[10] Moreover, as Simmons notes, the film 'conveys ethnic and geographic diversity in its inclusion of French-Canadian, East Indian, Manitoban, and northern-Ontarian characters. Likewise, its representation of the United States includes African Americans, Southerners, and Mid-Westerners.'[11] McDonald's 'diversity' is no less stereotype-based than the 'diversity' of *Going the Distance*, however; stateside, we get religious fanatics, dirt-poor blacks, and obsessed parents torturing their children into becoming pop stars, while Pokey's French-Canadian friend Claude is a quintessential hoser who plays in a BTO tribute band and agrees to sell his soul to Mr Satan for a six-pack. Here, as in McDonald's other films, it is the self-reflexivity that mitigates the potentially condescending stance of urban cool. So, Claude's character is also a sly swipe at the traditionally inward-looking dynamics of Quebecois film-making versus the outward-looking identity crisis characteristic of English-Canadian film-making. While *Highway 61* is ostensibly concerned with America, its underlying argument is that the road reveals more about Canada and Canadian attitudes than about any American 'reality.' Rather than the structuring lack of identity of the earlier generation of films of English-Canadian films, however, McDonald's outward expansion of the road argues that the 'particularity of the lack of particularity' Kieran Keohane sees as characteristic of Canada as a whole can also be embraced as a positive and generative quality.[12] Hence, the redemptive conclusion of *Highway 61* despite Pokey's demonstrable lack of talent as a musician. In contrast, the Canadian roads of *Roadkill* and *Hard Core Logo* more closely resemble those of the earlier generation of films. They offer less hope for redemptive appropriation than does the American road: Ramona is the only survivor of a massacre at the Apocalypse club, while Joe Dick's suicide brings his band, his life, and McDonald's movie to an abrupt end. It is, McDonald seems to suggest, a generic choice: the Canadian road leads to inward brooding on the dysfunctional family of the Canadian mosaic, while the border-crossing road borrows the romance tropes and optimism of American culture. Like Billy Tallent's fateful career change, the American road leads south to fame, fortune, and fabulation.

We see this contrast play out in a number of Canadian road movies, including *Going the Distance*, which experiments with overlaying the American model onto the Canadian road. Sandy Wilson's influential semi-autobiographical coming-of-age film *My American Cousin* (1985), set in the Okanagan Valley of eastern British Columbia in 1959, explicitly contrasts the two versions, while implicitly stressing her film's distance from the urban centres of eastern Canada. When James Dean–wannabe Butch (John Wildman) arrives in a lipstick-red Cadillac Biarritz convertible at the rural cherry farm that belongs to the parents of his young teenage cousin Sandy (Margaret Langrick) following an unseen road trip from northern California, he embodies a myriad of American desires: modernity, mobility, sex, and autonomy. Wilson simply but effectively subverts those desires, without neglecting to register their power. In this dynamic, Canada is feminized, but American masculinity is undercut in the same motion, as Butch's posing is exposed and his prized car is revealed to belong to his mother. Wilson establishes a polarity between a realistic Canadian road that is scenically beautiful but leads nowhere and an American road that promises freedom and happiness but is based on fantasy. Her west-coast film, an early and influential moment in the development of the Vancouver new wave, gently undercuts the masculinist urban anomie of the earlier Toronto-based film-making of Owen, Shebib, and others (see chapter 1) while equally refusing the empty promises of Hollywood. At the same time, Wilson borrows much of the genre conventions of the fifties nostalgia of *Grease* (Broadway musical, 1972–80; film, 1978), *American Graffiti* (1973, George Lucas), and *Happy Days* (television show, 1974–84) that was so important to the Hollywood box office and the American mediascape during the seventies and early eighties, including an exclusively American soundtrack of oldies (with the exception of Ottawa native Paul Anka) performed by Chicago-born and Canadian-based musician Tom Lavin (presumably to save on permissions). Butch's trip thus materializes the cultural connection: 'When you were a kid growing up in Canada, the States was like the land of milk and honey. All the music, all the movies and all the magazines came from there. And then you realize that you actually have some relation, some blood tie, to that fabulous, faraway land.'[13] Wilson took the reverse trip to the States in her poorly received sequel, *American Boyfriends* (1989), in which Sandy travels with three friends to Santa Cruz to attend Butch's wedding. *American Boyfriends* combines portentous cultural references (it is set in 1965) with real-life tragedy transmuted into symbolic melodrama: like Wilson's actual cousin, Butch dies in a car crash days after he is married.

The kidnapping subgenre has provided the model for a number of Canadian films exploring class and ethnic relations, with mixed results. Vancouver director Mina Shum's second feature, *Drive, She Said* (1997), bravely attempted to move out of the autobiographical Asian-Canadian territory of her debut, *Double Happiness*. The story of a bank teller who takes up with the guard who foils an attempted robbery only to be taken hostage at another robbery five years later, *Drive, She Said* uses traditional film noir tropes to explore alternatives to the banality of a routine job and a routine relationship. Tass (Josh Hamilton) takes Nadine (Moira Kelly) on a road trip south of the border during which, naturally, they fall in love. Tass is either taken captive or (more likely) killed. Nadine, back with her old boyfriend Jonathan, soon takes off again, on her own, with a final voice-over assuring us: 'I know I'll get there.' Shum had wanted Sandra Oh (see chapter 4) for the role of Nadine, which would have added a further twist to the fairly tired gender politics, but might not have been enough to mitigate the flat, generic feeling of Shum's deployment of familiar tropes. The plot of Cassandra Nicolaou's debut feature *Show Me* (2004) also revolves around a kidnapped woman. Sarah (Michelle Nolden), stood up on her anniversary by her careerist husband, is taken hostage in Toronto by two squeegee kids (Kett Turton and Katharine Isabelle) with a mysterious backstory. They drive her out to her lakeside cabin where the film turns into a tense but predictable three-way psychodrama in the woods that concludes when Jackson (Turton) drowns himself in the lake. An odyssey in the woods similarly greets a liberal lawyer in Richard Bugajski's *Clearcut* (1992), an uneasy but powerful combination of ethnic awareness and revenge drama. The first half of the film depicts Peter McGuire's (Ron Lea) unsuccessful fight to prevent clear-cutting of land claimed by a group of Ojibway. As if summoned by Peter's anger, Arthur (Graham Greene) appears to act out his revenge fantasy, behaving (and self-consciously commenting on that behaviour) as a 'savage Indian.' Bringing Peter along, Arthur threatens the hostile reporters and then kidnaps the mill manager Bud Rickets (Michael Hogan), taking him into the wilderness where he proceeds to skin him alive. Peter eventually turns on Arthur, trying to kill him. Arthur responds by drowning himself in the lake, at which point Wilf, the benign tribal elder, appears to lead Peter back to civilization. In all three films, the road trip into the wilderness materializes gender, class, and ethnic divisions that are simultaneously seductive and repellent. In all three films, the catalyst of the conflict does not survive the ordeal; however, the effect on the protagonist varies according to gender. Nadine and Sarah find themselves transformed by their experience and their growing sympathy with their captors and unable to return to their prior life. *Clearcut* is more ambivalent about its male protagonist, who has always been more of a personification than a flesh-and-blood character, choosing to close instead on the surviving Native characters. Bugajski borrows road movie conventions to tell 'not a native story' but 'the story of a white man entering a foreign landscape.'[14] As befits its excursion stateside, *Drive, She Said* maintains a glimmer of hope in its transformation; as is typical of internal travel narratives, *Show Me* and *Clearcut* are tragic stories of the results of social inequality and misunderstanding.

For the longest time solely inward looking, the Quebecois film tended to use the narrative of internal travel, between the country and Montreal, modernity and the past, such as Marie Chapdelaine's (Carole Laure) double travel narrative in *La Mort d'un bûcheron* (1973, Gilles Carle): first from her small home town to Montreal and then from Montreal to an isolated logging camp (see chapter 4). As befits a new generation of film-makers thoroughly conversant and comfortable with the external world, Quebecois film of the nineties began to explore the world south of the border. In George Mihalka's popular comedy *La Florida* (1993), Léo Lespérance (Rémy Girard) retires from his job as a bus driver and moves his family to Florida to run a motel. As Bill Marshall sees it, the film depicts the way Léo 'is sucked into American values (individualism, indifference to a death in the hotel, phoney market-driven smiles) only to resist them in the end.'[15] Rather than the internally allegorized conflict between Anglo and French Canadians typical of the 1960s films, *La Florida* suggests that the test of cultural maturity is its ability to incorporate all things American without sacrificing what is fundamental about one's own identity. As in *Going the Distance*, the comic structure here sees the road as a route towards wish-fulfilling maturity. André Forcier's whimsical, surrealistic comedy *Les Etats-Unis d'Albert* (2005), like *Highway 61*, uses the American landscape, in this case the desert outside Hollywood, as a liminal space where Quebec and America meet. After seducing the great aunt of Mary Pickford (we are in 1923), Albert (Eric Bruneau) heads for Hollywood dressed as the 'Sheik of Montreal.' Even more than in his previous films, *La Comtesse de Baton Rouge* (1998) and *Le vent de Wyoming* (1994), Forcier's America here is composed half of cinematic intertextuality (there are allusions to just about every popular genre, with film noir especially dominant) and half of magic-realist eccentricity closely descended from Monsieur Lange's *feuilleton* dreams of Arizona Jim in Jean Renoir's *Le Crime de Monsieur Lange* (1936). As opposed to Forcier's comic resolution – Albert bags a big reward for apprehending a serial killer – the desert setting in Denis Villeneuve's equally surrealist *Un 32 août sur terre* (1998) is a lighter interlude before a tragic ending back in Montreal. The film's main character, fashion model Simone (Pascale Bussières), finds herself in Utah because it is the condition of her friend Philippe's (Alexis Martin) agreement to help her get pregnant that they do so in a desert.

Darrell Varga writes that globalization is the 'political unconscious' of Villeneuve's films since the 'desire and subjectivity of the main characters' is their primary concern.[16] This seems an overly fine distinction since it is precisely through the desire and subjectivity of the main characters that road movies articulate the relationship between the global and the local. This relationship, naturally, is central to globalization theory and the different experience of space and time created by the global circulation of goods and people. Simone's and Philippe's mobility as members of a 'professional elite' is part of both their ability and their desire to travel to Utah for no particular reason, not even the conventional road movie desire of escape or change. But theirs is not the only reason to travel in a global economy. As Arjun Appadurai argues (according to Varga), 'mobility takes multiple forms, including migration, but also through economic and political channels, media, technology, and in the form of cultural texts. This border traffic flows in multiple directions, some of it is state-sanctioned and some of it exists at the fringes of official culture, some of it involves crossing under cover of night.'[17] In a global era, the transformational narratives and tropes previously associated with the physical border crossing of the road movie manifest themselves everywhere. Whether consciously articulated or simply a structuring force, these contradictions are a fundamental component in particular of those films explicitly concerned with their place in the mosaic: regional cinema, ethnic cinema, and cinema of sexual identities.

Regions: Ten Easy Pieces

> When the editors of this volume invited me to contribute to this new, updated portrait of Canadian narrative cinema, they asked me to cover the development of features on 'the prairies' since Telefilm – a regional *faux pas* almost on par with confusing a Newfie with a Maritimer! I said I'd be willing and able to write about Regina – but Winnipeg, Calgary, and Edmonton? 'They're so far away!' I exclaimed. 'Have you looked at a map lately?' I laughed. 'Have you read a newspaper other than *The Globe & Mail*?' I teased.
>
> Christine Ramsay on the collection *Self Portraits* (2006)

Toronto and Montreal have been the centres of Canadian film production and consumption since the movies began, just as they have long been the economic centres of the nation. At the same time, funding was nearly exclusively distributed on a national level until the eighties, through the National Film Board, the Canadian Council for the Arts (established in 1957), and the Canadian Film Development Corporation. Although the Ontario Motion Picture Bureau was 'the first government-founded film organization in the world' when established in May 1917, local film production was basically privately funded until the sixties. The NFB's 1956 move to Montreal from Ottawa laid the groundwork for the Quebecois film industry, solidified by the establishment of a French-language production unit in 1964. But provincial support for local film-makers did not become a priority until the eighties, when provincial offices established around the country began actively targeting feature film-making.[18] The Ontario Film Development Corporation (1986), for example, was instrumental in the creation of the Ontario new wave.[19] Levels of support and funding vary over space and time, but each of Canada's ten provinces has an Arts Council, and many have dedicated film offices that have been instrumental in the proliferation of regional film-making since the eighties. One of the effects of these offices, along with the industrial scale necessary for most narrative film-making and the site of film schools, is to locate regional Canadian cinema in urban centres (the significant exception would be Igloolik Isuma, discussed below).[20] Thus, as Christine Ramsay writes, despite the mythic image of the vast and empty expanse of the Canadian prairie, 'prairie filmmaking' is in fact constituted almost exclusively by the cosmopolitan urban centres of Regina, Winnipeg, Calgary, and Edmonton. Specific movements or schools have been attributed to Vancouver and Winnipeg, whereas other provinces sport individual talents, such as Calgary's Gary Burns, and others, like those of Atlantic Canada, present a mix of forms and influences; we will examine the Inuit territory of Nunavut in the next section of the chapter. Not all of these film-makers or movements fit into the strict definition of 'regional' cinema as articulated, for example, by David Clandfield: 'A film shot on location with a strong sense of local colour does not constitute regional film-making ... true regional film-making is represented by the work of local companies and directors committed to making films that dwell upon a particular region's pictorial qualities, social problems, and dilemmas.'[21] A similarly programmatic allegiance to a regional variant of the critical notion of documentary realism lingers in many funding organizations, while at the same time public funding sets a contradictory goal: the 'wish to foster both an independent Canadian cinema *and* a commercially successful one ... a dream cinema of impossible regional universalism that would appeal to the generalized many through its representation of the local few.'[22] There is no easy line drawn between local, national, and international film-making, however; just as provincial film-makers generally cobble together local, national, and often international funding, so their films themselves demonstrate the intertwinement of all three influences.

Consequently, there is no easy binary distinction between national and international, nor is there any easy distinction to be made in the relationship between the centre and the peripheries in Canada itself. As Longfellow argues, following Appadurai and Sassen, rather than thinking of globalization as 'a single integrated or unified conceptual scheme,' we must consider 'the specific places where the everyday reality of globalization is performed, felt, and resisted by embodied subjects. Central to this shift in focus is the understanding that while the cultural dominant may have a huge impact, its effects are circumscribed and not monolithic, and the everyday is the site where the contradictions of globalization and the tensions of registering differences or resistances are most apparent.'[23] As the closest Canada possesses to the urban 'nodal points through which international networks of capital are organized,' Toronto and Montreal have a privileged relationship to postmodern economic activities such as 'finance, telecommunications, and cultural production.'[24] The sites of prestigious film festivals, established film industries, and important media outlets, both cities promote themselves as spaces for the production and consumption of images of the new global society. While much of their product represents the local cityscapes as anonymous or in disguise as other, more global, urban centres through generically contemporary storylines and characters, this global character (or loss of character) nevertheless retains local significance for expert viewers able to discern the specificity of certain locations, certain actors, even certain stylistic traits of a local director helming a cable television episode, as in TV work by many figures associated with the Toronto new wave. Moreover, local products out of a city aspiring for global significance will often give a quite different representation of local/global relations, as in the incorporation of video chatting technology into Egoyan's *Adoration* (2008) or the representation of radio as a stubbornly local community network intersecting with the global reach of the British Broadcasting Corporation in McDonald's *Pontypool* (2008).

The operative paradox of Canadian cinema (as of any national cinema) at the turn of the millennium was that the greatest preponderance of national cinema was always coterminous with the greatest preponderance of global interests. That is, the films most closely associated with the definition of an intrinsically

Canadian cinema arose in the most globally networked of Canadian cities. Nor is it surprising that the most commercially and artistically viable movement outside of Toronto and Montreal arose at the same time and in the same place as the third urban Canadian nexus between local and global, Vancouver, where rampant development during the nineties accompanied a boom in its media industries and a massive influx of Pacific dollars and bodies. Hyped as the Pacific new wave, this flurry of independent film-making both emerged from and was defined in contradistinction to British Columbia's growing identity as 'a Hollywood back lot.'[25] For Diane Burgess, the Pacific new wave was 'urban, educated, ensemble-driven, political, local, neo-realist, ambivalent, digital, fragmented, and certainly not commercial,' and featured a core group of film-makers (Bruce Sweeney, Ross Weber, Reg Harkema, Bruce Spanger) and cinematographers, along with actors (Tom Scholte, Nancy Sivak, Babz Chula, Benjamin Ratner, and Vincent Gale).[26] However, as Burgess is well aware, the very mechanism of identification of a 'movement' depends on the national, if not international, attention evident in the 'unprecedented' presence of six BC features at the 1999 Vancouver International Film Festival, the inclusion of five BC features in the 2001 TIFF, and the selection of Bruce Sweeney's bitter anti-marriage comedy, *Last Wedding* (2001), to open TIFF the same year, the first ever such honour for a BC film.[27] Moreover, the very act of definition that branded the movement for export simultaneously excluded other film-makers from that brand; Burgess cites important local director Lynne Stopkewich (*Kissed* and *Suspicious River*) and prominent cinematographer Greg Middleton as 'less specifically local' and possessing a 'more fluid and refined' style.[28] And inexplicably, she omits to mention either veteran Saskatchewan director Anne Wheeler, based in BC since 1990, and whose lesbian-themed comedy-drama *Better Than Chocolate* (1998) was set and shot (by Middleton) on Vancouver's Commercial Drive, or Mina Shum, whose *Double Happiness* (1994) and *Long Life, Happiness, and Prosperity* (2002) are focused on the city's Asian-Canadian community.

Whether grittier or glossier in its depiction of the city, local Vancouver film-making shares a concern with the contemporary urban lifestyle that equally attests to the manifestation of the pressures and contradictions of globalization in everyday life. From Bruce Sweeney's attack on conventional institutions and Stopkewich's subversion of sexual norms to Shum's movie-of-the-week in indie garb *Long Life* and actor Benjamin Ratner's writing/directing debut in the Jewish-sitcom inflected *Moving Malcolm* (2003) to Scott Smith's bleak depiction of adolescent anomie, *Rollercoaster* (1999), Vancouver films are character- and psychology-driven in a way quite different from the earlier Toronto wave. Rather than the high concept premises of Rozema, Egoyan, McDonald, and McKellar, these films are focused on drama in the moment. The realistic acting, well-constructed script, and strong production values in a film like Sweeney's merciless examination of three relationships bear a close relation to the slick episodes of Vancouver-produced television. At the same time, the film's refusal of any narrative closure or reconciliation and its focus on creating maximum discomfort in the audience ('I don't like the way that sex is consumed. I don't like [audiences] to go home and jerk off; I want them to be so troubled that they can't even get an orgasm. I don't want it to look good, I want it to look ugly')[29] repudiate the values of that television. Similarly, the middle-class professions of the characters – a waterproofing firm co-manager, a professor of Canadian literature, a librarian, and a pair of architects – refer obliquely to the international stature of a growing city even as the film takes place almost entirely within the interiors of the characters' homes. The dialectic mirrors what veteran actor Babz Chula sees as the pull of the industry that simultaneously fuels the independent scene while constraining its existence:

> Vancouver actors are often forced to choose between the independent scene and the service industry. 'We tend to think it's our industry and that's the thing that becomes a real danger for the artist because then you figure if you get two days on *Stargate* playing an alien in unrecognizable makeup that you're doing your work. You have to make choices here and if you choose to do independent film, you choose to do original material, and material that's indigenous to Canada, with local people, then you give up money. You're constantly choosing content over money. If I choose to work with Bruce Sweeney I may lose a week on the *X-Files*. You lose a week on the *X-Files* that's going to support you for nine months but you're doing what you love. And it's not to say you can't do work you love when you're working for the Americans or on a television series but you've got to know from the very beginning that you're not featured. I mean, those are lucky breaks and they really live in the realm of economics, you know, they have nothing to do with art.[30]

Just as Vancouver uses its actors in apparently incompatible ways, so does it use its landmarks. As Burgess notes, the downtown Vancouver public library has figured prominently both as spectacular backdrop in Hollywood action films such as *Ballistic: Ecks vs. Sever* (2002) and *The 6th Day* (2000) and as a talking point in local work such as Weber's *No More Monkeys Jumpin' on the Bed* (2000).[31] What Burgess does not elaborate in her comparison is the degree to which the development itself is a contradictory landmark in Vancouver's self-image as a world city. Opened in 1995, the $106.8-million Library Square complex was at the time the largest project ever undertaken by the city, and immediately became a symbol of both its local ambitions, as a public library, and its global ones, as a centrally situated and architecturally iconic showpiece with a monumentally curving exterior frequently compared to the Roman Colosseum and likened by the characters in *No More Monkeys* to a roll of toilet paper. So, both the Hollywood and the indie usage of the site identify it with the spatial qualities of globalization. *No More Monkeys* gives it specific texture while its ironic stance to the library's aspiration nicely captures the uneasy relationship of the local film-makers in general to the new cityscape that is also the subject of their films. As Burgess concluded in 2006, 'it is necessary to locate a framework able to account for the interdependence of divergent sectors of B.C. filmmaking.'[32]

That same uneasiness is explicitly the subject of Calgary's principal film-maker, Gary Burns, who has devoted his career to a savage critique of the soulless spaces of his Albertan home's sprawling suburbs and anonymous downtown. Burns's first two features, *The Suburbanators* (1995) and *Kitchen Party* (1997) targeted the aimless teenage progeny of the white middle class, while the mockumentary *Radiant City* (2006) attacked the suburban cityscape without any narrative interme-

8.2 Playing with the cityscape of Calgary in *waydowntown* (2000): identifiably local and generically postmodern at the same time. Photofest.

diary.[33] His third feature, *waydowntown* (2000), takes place exclusively within the closed environment of the Plus 15, the interconnected office buildings and malls of the compact downtown which, Burns argues, killed Calgary's street life (figure 8.2).[34] Burns uses the narrative conceit of an endurance contest between four twenty-something data entry drones to see who can survive the longest without ever stepping outside to develop a potent (if not overly original) metaphor of the sterile life of white-collar capitalism, dead to human feeling and interaction but stressed and neurotic beyond endurance. As Melnyk argues, Burns's creative isolation influenced the inherent anonymity of the urban spaces favoured by his films; in the director's words, 'My films are anywhere in North America.'[35] And yet, that anonymity manifests itself on various levels of local specificity. The iconic presence of Don McKellar as a grumpy and suicidal forty-something colleague provides a Canada-wide reference, just as the pointed critique of the postmodern space of the Plus 15 inserts itself into a long Canadian tradition of reflection on alienation and the modern world. Burns assayed a similar critique in his slightly futuristic disaster fantasy, *A Problem with Fear* (2003), about a neurotically phobic young man who discovers that his fears are causing actual disasters. Set in an unnamed North American city, *Fear* was shot primarily (and recognizably) in Calgary; however, because its script called for extensive subway scenes (and because the film was a co-production with Montreal's micro_scope), Burns spent a month on location in the Montreal metro.[36] While extending Burns's critique of the technological spaces of the contemporary cityscape, the jarring combination of distinct

Canadian locations, neither wholly anonymous nor of a piece, was one of several elements that threw local reviewers for a loop. Nevertheless, as *Radiant City* clearly demonstrates, Burns is not solely concerned with a theoretical critique of urban sprawl, dying downtowns, and white-collar alienation; he is specifically invested in the changes wrought in his own cityscape of Calgary, one of the reasons he has chosen to base himself there despite the difficulty of making films in the absence of any developed industrial base.[37]

While the primary innovation of Burns's regionalism is a keen eye for the local/global tensions in Calgary's modernizing cityscape, his compatriot Michael Dowse has taken a similar approach to the traditional English-Canadian province of hoser culture. Dowse's headbanger mockumentary *FUBAR* (2002), co-written with the movie's stars Paul Spence and David Lawrence, was shot on location in Calgary and the Albertan woods (for a memorable road trip that results in the accidental death of the 'documentary' director). A bleak update of both the loser drama tradition of *Goin' Down the Road* and the hoser comedy tradition of Doug and Bob McKenzie, *FUBAR* succeeds as both comedy and drama by taking the choices of perpetual adolescents Dean and Terry completely seriously as a lifestyle option while simultaneously showing the misery resulting from that option. The effect is an international depiction of white trash loserdom with a nuanced subversion of its Canadian representation. This is clearest in the central plot event, Dean's operation for testicular cancer. Not only does the illness embody physically the traditional emasculation of the hoser character, but the most visible side effect of the chemotherapy – hair loss – cuts to the heart of headbanger identity, the mullet. Real life both humanizes these caricatures and fundamentally threatens their integrity as characters. As Bart Beaty has demonstrated, the film's critical reception focused on the thematic ties to the loser tradition, celebrating the film's combination of commercial success and Canadian thematics, and even claiming Dowse's film and its headbangers as quintessentially 'Albertan.'[38] The clearest signal of regionalism in the film is its irreverent homage to McDonald's *Hard Core Logo*. The homage is evident not only in its formal resemblance – the presence of the 'documentarist' as a character within the film, Dean's truly frightening musical 'performance,' and the tensely homosocial friendship of the central pair – but also in its contrasts: instead of underground punks we have mainstream but marginal nobodies; instead of the lead singer's suicide, here it is the film-maker who dies in a freak accident; instead of professional and beautiful camerawork and accomplished performance scenes, we get the in-your-face DIY of handheld digital video camera and visible mics. No 'big-city' cool for *FUBAR*, in other words. It is curious, then, that Dowse subsequently took the international co-production plunge with his next film, *It's All Gone, Pete Tong* (2004), shot in Ibiza with British stars; his next film, *Young Americans* (2010), was a U.S./Germany co-production shot in Phoenix, Arizona, with American stars. While raising typical twenty-first-century questions about Canadian comedy, his follow-up films imply that Dowse has chosen to exorcise *FUBAR*'s Calgary regionalism rather than continuing to mine it as a creative vein.

Both Vancouver and Alberta suggest the inapplicability of the conventional understanding of regional Canadian film-making as rural, marginal, and focused on deprivation.[39] At the same time, as *FUBAR* demonstrates, that model remains a powerful, if mythical, image against the backdrop of which much of regional cinema continues to create meaning. We find it in genial but facile 'quirky' comedies such as Paul Gross's small-town Ontario curling movie *Men with Brooms* (2002); Vancouver-based Sturla Gunnarsson's Newfoundland-filmed comedy, *Rare Birds* (2001), about a seaside restaurateur (William Hurt) who invents a bird sighting to save his business; or *La grande seduction* (2003, Jean-François Pouliot), about a Gulf of St Lawrence fishing village that puts on an elaborate masquerade to fool a Montreal doctor so they can get a new factory. We find it contested in nearly every independent feature made by Atlantic-Canadian film-makers since the eighties, whether Ken Pittman's documentary realist dramas, Michael and Andy Jones's landmark phantasmagoria *The Adventure of Faustus Bidgood* (1986), or the art films of William MacGillivray.[40] We equally find it in Atlantic-Canadian dramas that simultaneously question and have recourse to the traditional binaries of centre/periphery and urban/rural. In Thom Fitzgerald's debut feature, *The Hanging Garden* (1997), a gay Irish-Catholic New Yorker's return home to Nova Scotia for his sister's wedding after a ten-year absence raises expectations of the inevitable conflict between rural conservatism and urban cosmopolitanism. Certainly, Fitzgerald plays up the oppressive atmosphere that materializes in recurring images of his overweight teenage persona's body hanging by the neck in the garden. But he also roots Sweet William's sexual experience in his seduction by local macho Fletcher (now marrying Sweet William's sister), creating a complex and ambiguous set of characters and relationships. Moreover, he uses the overarching metaphor of the passing down of botanical nomenclature and knowledge to demonstrate subtly the simultaneously oppressive and soothing function of oral tradition, and rejects the genre's predictably tragic ending in favour of an almost conciliatory and happy conclusion. Allan Moyle's more straightforward Cape Breton–set comedy-drama *New Waterford Girl* (1998) skilfully interweaves and contrasts two coming-of-age stories: the local girl Moonie (Liane Balaban), a misfit in dark baggy clothes who wants at all costs to escape from her dead-end town, and Bronx native Lou (Tara Spencer-Nairn), desperate to fit in, who finds the small-town drop-dead gorgeous. When Moonie wins a scholarship to New York but is too young (fifteen) to go, she deviously pretends to conform to local norms; faking an accidental pregnancy, she hopes to be sent away to have the baby. As in *The Hanging Garden*, the characters mature rather than are merely punished, learn how to take control of their lives, and are not constrained into closure-providing relationships. The regional setting enables small, intimate character-driven stories that emerge from conventional expectations without being determined by them.

At the same time, regional films like *The Hanging Garden, New Waterford Girl*, or the historical drama of Cape Breton mining *Margaret's Museum* (Mort Ransen, 1995) place their subjects in a transnational context rather than exploring the isolated traditions of specific regions as a previous generation had required of the genre. It is not accidental that these films explore the intersection of alternative, transnational identities such as queer sexuality or feminism with traditional religious and cultural conventions, just as the comedies play on regional variations as comic eccentricities. This dual perspective is reinforced by the local film industry – Nova Scotia has a vibrant film production facility – that makes awareness of broader film-making trends inevitable for even the most local of film-makers.[41] In 2001, Salter Street Films, Halifax's biggest studio, beat out the national production companies for licensing rights to the new cable TV service, IFC; the studio was subsequently bought by Alliance Atlantis, which closed it two years later, although the co-founders Michael Donovan and Charles Bishop took many of Salter's employees with them to their new company, Halifax Film.[42] Local production and the accompanying tax breaks are, of course, a mixed blessing. On the one hand, we find the rural and seaside equivalent of, rather than counterpart to, anonymously urban Toronto and Vancouver.[43] On the other hand, there are employment opportunities and the industrial base needed for training local film-makers. While a traditionally regionalist vantage point would make a strong distinction between the 'stereotypical representations' found in 'films from central Canada' with Maritime settings, I suggest we view regional productions as a spectrum of representational and production strategies and priorities working with different choices and trade-offs that produce different enunciations of the relationship between the local, the national, and the global.[44] Even the resolutely regional and independent Newfoundland native William MacGillivray found himself in the mid-nineties working in television, making the St John's taxi-company comedy *Gullage's* (1996–7) for the CBC. For MacGillivray, probably Canada's least-known 'great' director, who only a few years before had acidly commented, 'Money can be made in Canada through movies or television, but not with *Canadian* movies or television,' *Gullage's* marked a significant turn towards the popular and national articulation of a set of concerns he had previously voiced as an independent and local art-film director.[45]

MacGillivray's critical reputation rests especially on his second feature film, *Life Classes* (1986), a prime example of the way regional film-making can simultaneously preserve and question its own traditions. The story of a Cape Breton woman who leaves behind her past to make a new life in Halifax, *Life Classes* places the marginalized histories of the region – of Gaels and blacks, in particular – in dialogue with the new energies of feminism and contemporary art. Although at times strident in its satire of the pretensions of the art world (an easy target), earnest in its inclusivity (the history of the century-old community of Africville, destroyed in the 1960s for highway and bridge construction, that we see characters watching on television), and unrealistic in its suggestion that rural Cape Bretonians would bother to watch avant-garde art on television, *Life Classes* is highly innovative in the way it unpatronizingly and self-reflexively combines rural working-class characters with urban intellectual discourses. Needing to support her young daughter, Mary Cameron (Newfoundland singer Jacinta Cormier) begins working as a nude model. At first highly uncomfortable, her posing eventually causes her to see herself and her calling as an artist in a different and highly satisfying way, while MacGillivray makes his audience keenly aware of the complex dynamics of gender, sexuality, and vision involved in his filming of her posing. Mary progresses from embarrassment to simple habit to drawing herself nude at home to forcing her baby's father, Earl, to come visit her in Halifax to pose nude for her to draw. 'Well, I did, for our daughter,' she tells him. Her self-confidence as an individual mirrors her maturity as an artist (from paint-by-number beginnings), as her drawings of Earl earn her a one-woman show, entitled, simply, 'A One Man Show.'

Particularly distinctive in the film is MacGillivray's unambivalent attitude towards television and visual media. Early on, we see Earl setting up a satellite dish on a pristinely beautiful hillside in order to bring cable television to his small town. Rather than a commentary on the colonization of regional Canada's unconscious, however, his effort becomes, as Robin Wood argues, an image of the uneven power relations of capitalism when Earl is taken to court by American power stations for his satellite.[46] Wood's assessment that MacGillivray 'respects' Earl's enterprise is reinforced by the fact that the satellite allows him, in Cape Breton, to pick up a video art exhibition from Halifax which includes Mary among a collection of nude models in tubes. Similarly, television is the medium used by MacGillivray to introduce the African presence on the island into the diegesis of the film. MacGillivray's use of video as a means of self-expression and self-reflexivity, as well as his association of it with the gendered dynamics of looking and contemporary art, relates the film closely to Rozema's contemporaneous *I've Heard the Mermaids Singing* (1987). Where Rozema's film is wholly urban and contemporary, MacGillivray uses his cutting-edge discourse as a way to meditate on and mediate the past. Television both links its viewers to the globalized world of media – in another scene we see Earl and his friends watching porn and drinking – and, potentially, connects them to one another and to their past. The leitmotif of the film is 'Mary's Lament,' a Gaelic song sung by Mary's grandmother whose refrain embodies the movie's duality of past and future: 'My child is my mother returning.' The transnational discourses and technologies of the contemporary world, MacGillivray argues, can be appropriated in order to retain local traditions while also transforming those traditions into something worth retaining.[47]

The cinema of Winnipeg, Manitoba, has had the greatest international impact of any regional Canadian film-making; paradoxically, it has also been the most programmatically local and artisanal of them all. Both the success and the fiercely local quality of the cinema can be put down to the Winnipeg Film Group (WFG), which was founded as a film-making cooperative in 1974, as well as to the support of the NFB's Cultural Industries Development Office, 'a federal-provincial partnership designed to promote the growth of the film industry in Manitoba,' which used matching grants to provide substantial funding for feature film-making in the late eighties.[48] But it was the WFG that provided the equally important culture of support. As Jeff Erbach, director of the queer coming-of-age feature, *The Nature of Nicholas* (2002), and curator of a DVD of WFG shorts, described the experience, 'These small art collectives, where filmmakers can learn the craft in a nurturing, supportive environment, free to explore their own personal stories, might not make anyone much money, but contribute to cinema and society in ways that transcend economic indicators. I've spoken with many European filmmakers who are nothing but jealous of the collectives in our country, a point that should be celebrated, and funded better!'[49] A key element of the WFG, and an important factor in the international profile of its film-makers, is a dedicated distribution arm, including a local cinema (the downtown Cinematheque theatre), submissions to international festivals, and retrospectives such as the one in Paris in 2000 to celebrate the WFG's twenty-fifth anniversary.[50] What is formally distinctive about the WFG films is what is commonly, if reductively, called 'prairie postmodernism,' a way of grounding a contemporary transnational concern with history, ethnicity, and identity in the unique texture of Winnipeg and the province that surrounds it.[51] Thus, Erbach's familiar tale of mid-century sexual repression gains resonance from its prairie locations and its horror-genre trope that doubles Nicholas's friend Bobby into a ghoul he must care for.[52] The three Winnipeggers who have had the greatest international success – Noam Gonick, Guy Maddin, and John Paizs – have all innovated within popular genre structures by injecting them with local concerns. Maddin's transmutation of Winnipeg's political and ethnic past has been the most sustained, encompassing the national hockey team, the Icelandic settlement of Gimli, the legacy of communist radicalism, and the city's geographical situation within lo-fi, handcrafted recreations of forgotten film genres (see chapter 9). The film-makers of the WFG were also the first in Canada to incorporate the tropes of American popular culture into their works as creative if ambivalent appropriations rather than irredeemably evil forces. In their simultaneous immersion in and distance from American culture, Maddin, Paizs, Gonick, and others epitomize José Arroyo's argument that 'Canadians looking at American films see them both differently and the same as Americans.'[53] Paizs's films, credited by Pevere with developing a 'WFG style,' were initially received as a camp critique of 'America's cultural colonialism of Canada,' a marginal sensibility that enjoys the artifice of popular culture while refusing emotional identification with it.[54] There is certainly a camp sensibility at work in the genre appropriations at the heart of Paizs's six half-hour films of the early eighties and his three features: the cult comedy *Crime Wave* (1985), based, according to the director, on 'fast and fantastic' fifties B-movie trailers, which also resulted in Paizs getting hired for five episodes of the comedy series *Kids in the Hall*; the Toronto-filmed 'for hire' riff on fifties alien invasion movies *Top of the Food Chain* (1998, released on U.S. DVD as *Invasion!*), distributed by Lions Gate; and the television movie *Marker* (2005), a coming-of-age and sci-fi-disease hybrid.[55] The same can be said of Gonick's exuberantly hallucinatory and over-the-top first feature *Hey Happy!* (2001), in which a Winnipeg DJ attempts to trigger a biblical apocalypse by having sex with 2000 men. Like Maddin's films, Gonick's second feature, *Stryker* (2004), suggested either that camp could not be reduced to an ironic appropriation of popular culture or that the movies of the WFG could not be so easily reduced to the category of camp. Not only is *Stryker* visually stunning – it was envisioned by cinematographer Ed Lachman as '*City of God* in the snow' – but its collaboratively written story of gang warfare among the ethnic communities of Winnipeg's North End, scored with the music of local Native rapper group HellNBack and MC Karmen, argues for an emotionally intense appropriation of American gang and rapper culture that is none the less conscious of the contradictions of its Canadian context.[56] Similarly, Gonick's inclusion of 'native trannie hookers' both recognizes a transnational subculture and attempts to grant visibility to 'the most fundamentally unique thing about Winnipeg.'[57] Like other WFG film-makers, Gonick finds, celebrates, and exposes in Winnipeg the consequences of life in innumerable and interweaving margins. 'For me,' he comments, 'this film is all about border crossings. As a gay

Jewish filmmaker, I'm not supposed to be on that side of the tracks, and trannies aren't supposed to hang out with thugs, but the reality is that all these people do hang out together. I mean, I have cousins who are fully Jewish, who are very native gang-affiliated. Winnipeg is such a small place, you can't really have those borders if you want to have an interesting life.'[58] When camp gets appropriated to a particular local space, it neither loses its transnational character nor remains exclusively transnational. The 'smallness' characteristic of the marginality of both Canada and its provincial regionalisms nurtures a border-crossing attitude fundamentally different from its rootless identity within a global culture, simultaneously hybrid and rooted.

Ethnicities: Uneasy Pieces

> There are no Europeans in it. It's all Inuit. It's fabulous because Inuit have always been put in the background as extra actors. And if they speak Inuktitut, it didn't mean anything, it was just a part of the show. Seal oil lamps – how they burn, nobody cared. They could be touching the Olympic torch and nobody would care. I was noticing a lot of this when I saw films about the North. We're just background – who cares? We do.
>
> Zacharias Kunuk (Inuit film-maker)

As John Murray Gibbons's original definition of the Canadian mosaic made clear, and as NFB practice ratified (in policy if not in practice) up to the long-delayed promotion of First Nations film-making in the nineties, the documentary realist tradition of Canadian cinema long remained the province of white diversity. As film-maker and writer Dionne Brand asserts, 'Inclusion in or access to Canadian identity, nationality, and citizenship (de facto) depended and depends on one's relationship to this "whiteness."'[59] As Christopher Gittings exhaustively demonstrates, despite the Multicultural Act of 1988, multiculturalism itself is a construct that casts people of colour as 'other' while it 'continues to privilege whiteness as a universal signifier of belonging' both legally and culturally.[60] However valid this analysis may be as an analysis of any colonial culture – and I think it is valid in that sense – when invoked unambiguously and undialectically it risks underestimating the intrinsic value of inclusive ideologies as well as the ability of people of colour themselves to negotiate multiple and hybrid identities. Like the image of the Canadian mosaic, the formal and generic hybridity characteristic of much of Canadian cinema in the decades since the mid-eighties has demonstrated – if not always actually realized – a potential to move past the polarities and dichotomies of a more divisive ideology and the documentary realist aesthetic that underpinned it. Used to explore Scots and Irish-Catholic minorities in Atlantic Canada and the French-Canadian heritage in Quebec, the realist tradition has been highly effective in exposing the economic inequality at the foundation of the ethnic relationship between the centre and the peripheries of white Canadian culture. As the film-making practices of aboriginal peoples and what are known in Canada as the 'visible minorities' emerged in the nineties, they made it clear that formal hybridity and experimentation were the most effective mode for questioning past representations, generating new ones, and defining the place of non-whites in the Canadian mosaic.

Because of the way their place within the mosaic was defined in terms of otherness, visible minorities as well as aboriginal film-makers were restricted by funding structures 'to document, not fictionalize, their experiences.'[61] For example, in order to make the first feature-length film in Inuktitut, Zacharias Kunuk, Paul Apak Angilirq, and Norman Cohn had to form their own production company, Igloolik Isuma, and battle five years with federal funding agencies.[62] Moreover, when finally managing to obtain funding to make fictional features, aboriginal and visible minority film-makers are expected to make those narrative films within a framework of documentary realism concerned exclusively with their own ethnic and Canadian identity, analogous to the way Clandfield has defined regional film-making.[63] As Cecil Foster put it regarding the variety of black Canadian backgrounds and identities, 'we are *blacked* out in a common community ... That is how we are forced to relate to the wider society, as a community, even if members are from different backgrounds and circumstances.'[64] While an institutionalized multiculturalism provides the wherewithal for aboriginal and visible minority Canadians to produce images of themselves, it equally constrains them to a predetermined set of thematic and formal structures as well as to a fixed identity having little if anything to do with a lived reality.

There is no question that government funding on the heels of the Multicultural Act of 1988 enabled the emergence of visible-minority film-making in Canada, even if that film-making emerged in the midst of a full-fledged 'culture war.' Certainly, the 'first' films are highly didactic in their narrative strategies, dramatizing both for their own and for the wider Canadian community the contradictions of ethnic Canadian identity. Hence, Mina Shum's *Double Happiness* (1994), the 'first Chinese Canadian feature film,' borrows American sitcom tropes to establish both the similarity of Jade Li's (played by Korean-Canadian actor Sandra Oh, see chapter 4) family to idealized units such as *The Brady Bunch* and their essential difference. Crucially, Shum represents the comparison as a both/and rather than an either/or proposition: Jade and her family face the pressure of living up to the unreal expectations of two different family structures in which one set of expectations frequently contradicts the other. Shum's film uses the stand-up comedy motif of Jade on a stool in a bare soundstage addressing the audience in comically self-reflexive terms, inviting us both to laugh at her predicament and to identify with it. While the performance invites admiration at Jade's (and Oh's) skill at code-switching between different identities, it also, as Jacqueline Levitin suggests, served as a defensive reaction to rampant late-eighties xenophobia over the Pacific Asian migration into Vancouver, striving with comedy to put local audiences at ease, 'We Chinese are harmless and essentially like you.'[65] Like Shum's debut, Clement Virgo's *Rude* was proposed and marketed as a 'first': 'the first Canadian 35-mm dramatic feature written, directed and produced by a Black team.'[66] Adapting the tropes of American 'hood films to a Toronto housing project to provide audience accessibility and guarantee funding, *Rude* places 'the 'hood, guns, a little bit of drugs' in the context of a self-consciously art-film milieu: disparate story lines united by pirate radio DJ Rude (Sharon Lewis), who functions as a hip, radical, urban update on the traditional African griot figure.[67] This figure, too, is adapted from American film-making, this time from the independent New York City milieu of Spike Lee's *Do the Right Thing* (1989), where Samuel Jackson's Mister Señor Love Daddy provides a calming community voice to the Bed-Stuy street in which the film's overheated events takes place, and of Lizzie Borden's experimental dystopia of racism and feminism, *Born in Flames* (1983), where contrasting pirate radio DJs voice the concerns of white lesbian and African-American feminists. While Virgo's location shooting grounds the film in Toronto, the film's stylistic experimentation and intertextuality assert its place within a transnational discourse of underground film-making and diverse black identities. Like *Double Happiness*, *Rude* is a small film overburdened by the weight of expectations, and like Shum, Virgo has had difficulty living up to the promise of his debut. Nevertheless, he has produced a respectable oeuvre of genre films, including an adaptation of an American novel about an overweight musical prodigy, *The Planet of Junior Brown* (aka *Junior's Groove*, 1997); the drama of white and black brothers (a comic and a boxer), with American actor Lorenz Tate, *Love Come Down* (2000); the twenty-something sex drama *Lie with Me* (2005); and the Halifax-set prison-boxing drama *Poor Boy's Game* (2007). Modest as it may appear, this oeuvre constitutes no mean feat in a national cinema that, as Winnipeg film-maker Jeff Erbach comments, requires so much effort, stubbornness, and talent that 'so many Canadian filmmakers simply melt back into society after one or two films.'[68]

While Virgo has found something of a niche transnational market for his middle-of-the-road black Canadian films (or the other niche of the more experimental style and explicit sexuality of the white characters in *Lie with Me*), Indo-Canadian directors Srinivas Krishna and Ian Iqbal Rashid have struggled to follow up promising first features *Masala* (1991) and *A Touch of Pink* (2004, discussed below), respectively. Both films use comic conventions to situate their theme of ethnic identity within broader contexts of representation and genre. Although *Masala* suffers from uneven acting and a poorly judged conclusion, its iconoclastic imagination and fearless satire brilliantly dismantle the earnestness of both official Canadian multiculturalism and the 'cinema of duty' demanded of ethnic film-makers. As Cameron Bailey observed, '*Masala* is Canada's first feature film to work fully outside' the 'responsible' models of a social-issue content and a documentary-realist style.[69] *Masala* borrows from the American rebel convention for its leather-clad, angry young man protagonist Krishna (played by the director) and from the Bollywood mythological for the character of Lord Krishna (played by Indian actor and British independent cinema icon Saeed Jaffrey), who appears to the family grandmother on television and tries to answer her prayers according to Canadian conventions. The film irreverently mocks not only Canadian institutions (the postal service, Mounties, hockey) but also the Indo-Canadian community. As Krishna put it, 'The whole film deals with stereotypes, and those stereotypes are the way we would like to stereotype ourselves, the way others stereotype, and the way we can assume stereotypes to manoeuvre in society.'[70] Consequently, rather than provide a unified and conventionally realistic depiction of the Indo-Canadian community, Krishna stresses the contradictions within it, the partial way in which different characters adapt to Toronto while also preserving their prior identifications. It is difficult to identify directly with any of the characters, who are both familiar (they crave appliances, watch workout videos, have offensive sexual fantasies, dream of conforming) and alien (they talk to strange gods on television, observe strange customs, and eat exotic food). Krishna similarly mixes up genre expectations, borrowing from Bollywood the formal practice of switching rapidly and without warning between different genres, from comedy to melodrama to fantasy musical sequences. Predictably, there was much debate within the Indo-Canadian and global Indian community as to *Masala*'s 'internalized racism' and its objectification of women. Both issues, as Gittings correctly argues, come down to the conflation of Krishna the film-maker with Krishna the character and a more general flattening out of the satirical structure.[71] Because Krishna refuses to provide an outside context from which to evaluate his characters beyond the distancing devices of his formal structure and genre mixing, it was easy for critics to confuse an ironic representation of stereotypes for a straightforward dissemination of them. To be sure, Krishna seems to have welcomed the confusion; like Deepa Mehta's feminist recasting of Indian conventions or John Greyson's queer activism (see below), part of his goal is to expose hypocrisy and institutional oppression in the role of an *agent provocateur*. The rebel director may be smarter and more nuanced than the rebel anti-hero, but it is not at all clear where to draw the line between them. This attitude places *Masala* firmly within the ranks of popular Canadian comedy, which plays on Canadian stereotypes equally, and the presumption of such a move perfectly echoes the film's many other appropriations of symbols of Canadian whiteness. While the film is highly aware of the difficult position it occupies – hence the abrupt murder of the protagonist at its conclusion – it also argues that this position is an accurate assessment as well as a creatively fruitful place from which to make a film. As Indian critic Sanjay Khanna argued, the film's very individuality and accessibility complicated its reception by negating its validity as a traditional statement of ethnic identity: 'It is not the film of a single community: such a film would be impossible to develop and write because Indians in Canada come from multifarious backgrounds. This is why I doubt the claim that it is the filmmaker's responsibility to take on the role of pleasing everyone "Indian" in Canada when India itself is divided, fractured, and erupting in violence.'[72] *Masala*, in other words, declared its independence from the 'cinema of duty,' calling instead for a new cinema that would, like its title, mix 'purity and impurity, authenticity and inauthenticity.' Rather than reject the cinema of duty and its documentary realism and embrace the pastiche of pure postmodernism, this new mode would combine them in new ways.

Masala was released at the vanguard of the mainstream visibility of Bollywood culture in Western film. In its concern with border crossings and cultural migrations, it echoes both the themes and the controversy of Salman Rushdie's satirical novel *The Satanic Verses* (1988), whose opening plane crash *Masala*'s first scene explicitly echoes. Replacing the 'mosaic' as national metaphor with the culinary image of 'masala' also signalled that ethnic film-making and immigrant populations could offer alternative representational models for multiculturalism along with their tales of identity. When Deepa Mehta, an Indian-born adult immigrant to Canada, made *Bollywood/Hollywood* (2002), the conventions of Mumbai cinema were well enough established to provide a selling point in the title. A Toronto-set comedy based on the themes of masquerade, drag, and multiple identities, *Bollywood/Hollywood* uses the conventions of Indian popular cinema as a metaphor for Canadian and Hollywood assumptions about Indian identity. The protagonist Sue (Indo-Canadian Lisa Ray) is picked up at a bar by Rahul Seth (Bollywood star Rahul Channa) as a 'Latina' whom he hires, *Pretty Woman*–style, to pretend to be his fiancée. Like the actor who plays her, Sue turns out to be both Indian *and* Canadian and a big fan of Atom Egoyan, whose film *Exotica* and its theme of false expectations play a major intertextual role in *Bollywood/Hollywood*. The tone is unsure and the acting uneven, but Mehta's film nevertheless effectively demonstrates the degree to which ethnicity, just like any other form of identity is, as cultural theorist Stuart Hall reminds us, fluid and changeable rather than fixed.[73] Moreover, as the use of Egoyan implies, the function of cinema is not to stabilize but to explore the complex interplay of identity and representation. After all, like the Jewish Canadian David Cronenberg, who made his first self-ethnography film only thirty years into his career (see chapter 2), the Egypt-born Armenian Canadian Egoyan has had the luxury (passing for 'white' all these years) of having his films analysed on their own terms to the degree of passing over their consistent engagement with issues of ethnic identity long before he 'came out' with *Ararat* (2002, see chapter 7).[74]

As Zacharias Kunuk suggests in the quote that opened this section, the aboriginal people of Canada were long as invisible to the camera as they were to the government. Moreover, while the inevitably dual identity of visible minorities led to a natural split between a new local identity and a transnational 'immigrant' identity, the aboriginal status of being strangers in their own land led to a different attitude towards national identity. As the Native actor, producer, and director Gary Farmer puts it, 'Colonisation didn't just happen in the USA. It happened in Canada. It was the same interests, hand in hand, the same people who exploited us. When it comes to indigenous people, there's no difference between Canada and the US. And there's no border for me – not as Gary or as an actor. I'm a North American.'[75] On the one hand, the 'Canadian' identity of Gary Farmer is enough to warrant the inclusion of an essay on American indie director Jim Jarmusch's revisionist western *Dead Man* (1995) in *The Cinema of Canada*. On the other hand, Farmer asserts the irrelevance of that identity to him and to the film, which would instead form part of the transnational canon of motion pictures in which Native Americans produce their own images. The identity of visible minorities in Canada is primarily legal and tied to the free-floating signifiers of ethnic identity – language, clothing, food, custom – while that of the First Nations, as Bill Marshall notes, is tied both legally and symbolically to the land, in terms of the long history of dispossession and confinement and in terms of the metaphorical identification of the Indian with an image of unspoiled nature.[76] The sometimes violent confrontations between Native people and provincial and federal authorities during the nineties were all about disagreements over the possession and use of land. As Alanis Obomsawin implies in the title and the substance of *Kanehsatake: 270 ans de résistance* (1993), her documentary on the Oka conflict of 1990, when self-titled Mohawk 'warriors' blockaded roads and bridges in protest over the extension of a municipal golf course onto burial sites, the conflict derived from a two-hundred-and-seventy-year history of land disputes.

Obomsawin is a long-time employee of the NFB, and the propagandistic intent of *Kanehsatake* places it firmly, as Jerry White argues, in the Griersonian tradition of engaged documentary.[77] While Obomsawin's multi-voiced, bare-bones, and grounded documentary style effectively presents her view on Native issues, realism has been less well served in feature film-making aimed at providing a fictional framework to counter the popular culture depiction of aboriginal people. As Kunuk puts it about the arrival of television to Nunavut, 'After we brought in television and cable, now everybody's glued to the tube. And that's where we wanted to be, so our little company started to bring back the storytelling. And there are a lot of other Inuit trying to get back our culture too, in different ways. We're just doing our portion in video.'[78] To deny Native consumers of mass media the choice of multiple viewing positions is as patronizing as presuming their essential oneness with a 'nature' unsullied by 'civilization.' Indeed, Marshall tacitly corrects Obomsawin's polemical depiction of Quebecois racism, not by denying its existence, but by contextualizing its contours. He cites a 1992 report finding that Quebec 'contained "the lowest social distance" of any province between the aboriginal and non-aboriginal populations,' that the percentage of land controlled was higher than any other province, and that the survival of Native languages was supported more than in any other province.[79] The acid response that this just shows how much further behind the rest of Canada is is of course correct. Nevertheless, acknowledging that response should in no way also prevent recognition of the specificity of aboriginal people within Quebec culture, including, as Marshall notes, the estimation that sixty per cent of Quebecois are of mixed blood, and the cultural identity of *métissage* and hybridity embodied in the coureur de bois myth that underpins that statistic.[80] The contradiction between the institutionalized racism exposed by *Kanehsatake* and the cultural valuation of the aboriginal within Quebecois identity is a more extreme version of the simultaneous dismissal and valuation of aboriginal peoples all over North America that manifests itself culturally for the most part as the classic split between the 'good' and the 'bad' Indian.

One of the trends evident, in retrospect, in film-making of the nineties was the search for other ways of representing this tension. So, we find the awkward but well-meaning inclusion of a Native male stripper in Robert Lepage's *Le Confessionnal* (1995), presumably out of the desire to be inclusive and contemporary without falling back on cinematic stereotype. Gittings dismissively analyses the construction of 'spectacle Indigenes' in erstwhile nineties revisionist depictions of Native Americans by white directors working in Canada: the drama of Jesuit contact in *Black Robe* (Australian Bruce Beresford, 1991), the transnational Inuit epic *Map of the Human Heart* (New Zealander Vincent Ward, 1992), the primal revenge drama *Clearcut* (Polish-born Canadian Richard Bugajski, 1993), the retelling of the Oka conflict as a Quebecois version of *Heart of Darkness* in *Windigo* (Quebecois Robert Morin, 1994), and the rock-music inflected reservation comedy-drama *Dance Me Outside* (Ontarian Bruce McDonald, 1995).[81] While Gittings is mixed in the degree of his disapprobation, his guiding critical privileging of integral meaning to a text presumes the possibility of a 'correct' representation, denies the possibility of ideological and representational ambiguity, and ignores the potential for alternative receptions by either Native or non-Native audiences. The first issue is historical: all of these films were made at a moment in which revisionist representations were both commercially attractive and ideologically compelling for liberal film-makers (as which all of these film-makers would identify themselves). Like the ethnic films discussed above, these films all suffer in varying degrees from the effects of novelty and experimentation. This is perhaps less the case in *Black Robe*, with its larger budget and conventional aesthetics of spectacle, but even here we find a savagery in the interaction between aboriginals and colonizers hitherto unseen. While we may regret, as Gittings does, that the savagery is all on the side of the Natives, this should not mitigate the overall effect of brutality, nor lead us to assume that film viewers remain so naive as not to be able to fill in the brutal history of 'European savagery.'[82] Similarly, while we may regret the heterosexual pairing of Frenchman Daniel (Aden Young) and Algonquin Annuka (Sandrine Holt) as 'hybrid, mobile, sexually glamorous, at ease with "nature,"'[83] we should also be wary of the critical framework that takes an anglophone Torontonian and a London-born Chinese-French model as anything most viewers would actually mistake for a seventeenth-century reality. It is equally, if not more, plausible to argue that the patent disjunction between a de rigueur love interest and sex scene amidst the stark realism of the Jesuit Laforgue's (Lothaire Bluteau) celibate drama disrupts the mimetic spell of the material, revealing it as the multi-national co-production it most patently is. This is not to defend the manifold shortcomings of *Black Robe*, but only to suggest that it, like the other films Gittings discusses, can be productive of diverse and quite useful meanings if we regard them in terms of their generic conventions and economic constraints rather than solely as records of some hypostatized reality.

In the idealistic world of extreme cultural critique, even as subversive and funny a vision of Native life as McDonald's *Dance Me Outside* is, it does not pass the muster, condemned as full of negative stereotypes and as 'anti-racist one-dimensionality.'[84] Terry Lusty's demand to see 'something positive to project about the social and cultural fabric of Indian country' instead of 'drinking, cheating, poverty-stricken, pool-playing racist[s]' mistakes a fabricated narrative for documentary realism.[85] McDonald quite consciously set out not only to avoid 'appropriating non-white stories,' but to make a film that would connect to the young actors who were playing its main characters, 'Having these eighteen-nineteen year-old actors around was great. They were very excited about the fact they were making this movie and because they were making a movie where they didn't have to wear a loincloth, they didn't have to shoot a bow and arrow, and they didn't have to paddle a canoe. They were playing characters, and they thought that was fantastic. They loved the fact that they could wear Metallica T-shirts and they could drive a car and kiss girls.'[86] The way McDonald connected to his actors was through pop music, which he uses with savvy and humour throughout, as when he drops Redbone's 'Come and Get Your Love' over the film's central love scene; it plays like an anodyne seventies background love song unless you know they were one of the first Native American rock groups – it's an inside joke for the Native audience. The love scene is intercut with Silas (Ryan Black) and Frank (Adam Beach) keeping white liberal city lawyer McVey busy while his Native wife's old flame works on getting her pregnant. They stage a 'naming ceremony' that concludes with McVey becoming 'the wolverine' and running wild through the woods, while Silas announces, stone-faced, 'I am the walrus.' It is an extremely funny scene that plays like straight mockery until the coda, when Silas, afterwards, admits to Frank, 'He was pretty cool.' In that moment, McDonald humanizes McVey *and* Silas, breaking through the stereotypes that have accumulated around both of them. The pop culture that creates Indian stereotypes and Beatles songs equally, McDonald argues, also creates common ground that can break through those stereotypes and clichés. It is by no means a perfect film – the narrative has far too conventional a structure for the pop culture veneer that interests McDonald and his young cast – but it's an innovative strategy that resonated, for one, with Adam Beach, who commented of the characters, 'There's no problem here at all, unless it's with a very, very strict traditionalist.'[87] Beach's comment closely resembles John Paizs's remark about the response to his first film, 'I remember the violence in *Crime Wave* rubbed a few old-guard Film Groupers the wrong way, who probably considered it too American.'[88] Both films were part of a sea change in Canadian cinema beyond the antinomies that structured not only the artificial divide between Canadian realism and Hollywood artifice, but between worthy 'cinema of duty' and stories establishing a different relationship with identity and the world.

The new attitude is nothing as simple as a rejection of the past. Just as the 'I am the Walrus' sequence turns the performance of a white man's fantasy of Native culture into a hybrid but effective bonding ritual in spite of itself, so does the appropriation of a transnational culture provide a different mode of representing the past. This strategy was especially effective in Kunuk, Apak Angilirq, and Cohn's *Atanarjuat: The Fast Runner* (2001), made, according to Kunuk, to provide images to the stories told by the local elders but which went on to become a critical and popular success around the world.[89] Based on an ancient Inuit legend set in the area around the filming location of Igloolik, *Atanarjuat* tells the story of the entry of strife into a community, its effects, and its eventual eradication, focusing on the relationship between two brothers, Atanarjuat and Amaqjuaq, and their rivalry with camp leader Oki. Simultaneously narrative and ethnographic, the film aimed to revive and record skills and customs as well as ancient oral tales that had vanished. But it is nothing so simple as a documentary record of the past. According to Kunuk, everything in the film, from clothes to kayaks to the oil lamps, was based on records kept by an early nineteenth-century arctic expedition; the kayak was modelled on a two-hundred-year-old kayak collected during that expedition and studied by the film-makers in the British Museum.[90] The very documents and explorers that disrupted the circular temporality of pre-contact Inuit culture were essential to the process of recreating that culture. Hence, the patient, long-take recording of everyday activity is simultaneously an aesthetic strategy to place the viewer in the mindset of the characters and a self-ethnography, a dramatic recreation by the Inuit cast and crew of its own past. As Kunuk put it, 'We put the whole community to work ... All the ladies work sewing up the caribou clothes and all the men make the props, the harpoons, the bows and arrows and anything you want, [the community makes.] We're becoming the same [as] people who lived on the land.'[91] The artificial recreation of the past becomes, through the specific process of recreation, something more than artifice.

The complex relationship to the past is also reflected in the story itself, since it is centrally concerned with how to reconcile community survival with individual desire and misfeasance. As Darrell Varga notes, Atanarjuat, although the film's hero and a victim of circumstances beyond his control, also performs two selfish and damaging acts during the course of the film: seducing away Oki's betrothed Atuat and sleeping with Oki's sister Puja.[92] While on the one hand the film powerfully inserts the viewer into the pre-contact world of Inuit life, on the other hand, it foregrounds its own post-contact status through its very existence. The widescreen high-definition digital video camera, necessitated by the harsh filming conditions, while beautifully capturing both the impossibly wide horizons and the intense close-ups of characters' faces, also is just grainy enough in comparison to celluloid as to remind us always of the image we are watching. The end-credit images of actors in modern dress equally recall the temporal gap spanned by the film, with the violence of the forced settlement, education, and conversion of the Inuit hovering, unspoken, in that gap (figure 8.3). As Kunuk succinctly puts it, 'Four thousand years of oral history silenced by fifty years of priests, schools and cable TV.'[93] The violence of that gap thus echoes the destructive violence within the narrative, and the film-makers' reaction to one form of violence changes the resolution of the other. In other versions of the legend, Atanarjuat takes the bloody revenge we might expect from an oral epic; in the contemporary retelling, he chooses instead to put an end to the cycle of violence and allow his community to heal.[94] In interviews conducted in 2002, Cohn and Kunuk made explicit the function they saw the film as having taken on in response to 'the bloodiest century in history.' But the local effect of the film was paramount in their minds. As Kerstin Knopf sums it up, the film, far from exploiting Inuit legends for global dollars, gave back to the community precisely as a result of its capacity as a hybrid:

> The filmmakers open up this oral legend, an Inuit intellectual property, to a global market; but with their community approach to filmmaking, they also give something back: the film, national and international attention, jobs, money, and cultural pride. Financial means acquired for the film are returned to at least one Inuit community. The appropriation of this cultural knowledge for a market outside of the Inuit community is 'compensated' through finances that come from the outside community. The Inuit legend is processed by Inuit artists (the filmmaking team), and in this way, it is turned into a modernized Inuit intellectual property. It may be accessed by the Western world, but even more so will be 'used' by the Inuit community and returned as 'their intellectual property.'[95]

Rather than a static conception of identity and of cinema, *Atanarjuat* enacts a hybrid and dynamic model of simultaneously being in the world and being in the local present that is not Luddite, idealistic, or exploitative. Nor was it a simple task either to find funding or to make a film north of the Arctic Circle. But the local and global success of the film suggests the efficacy of this new model for ethnic film-making, a model which, as Jennifer Gauthier suggests, can also revitalize conceptions of national cinema, 'one that can stand up to the homogenizing powers

atanarjuat
Natar Ungalaaq

atuat
Sylvia Ivalu

8.3. Time lapse photography: Peter-Henry Arnatsiaq, who plays the villainous Oki in *Atan-arjuat: The Fast Runner* (2001), shown in modern dress during the film's end credits. Permission of Igloolik Isuma Productions Inc. www.isuma.ca. Distributed by vtape.org.

of globalization. While they attract global audiences, they remain firmly rooted in a specific local culture and place. They not only entertain diverse viewers, but they also empower the colonized other within the postcolonial nation. What more could national cinemas hope for?'[96] Kunuk's own description of the satisfaction he felt in the film finds the same intersection of local and global around him at Igloolik, 'Children right now are very interested in our movie, because for the first time, it's in their language. It's not Arnold Schwarzenegger, blowing people's heads away. Now it's Atanarjuat. It's a story that kids are even playing, like playing some scenes out. I even get feedback from parents. One time a parent told me that he had been looking for his kids and he couldn't find them. When he found them outside, they were playing tent and he could hear they were playing "Atanarjuat." That's cool.'[97]

Genders and Sexualities: Missing Pieces

I feel like Canadians are sort of the gay community of the world. Especially in the North American context, we can go anywhere, do anything and no one will know we're Canadian unless we announce it. We believe in equal rights for all, but struggle with our own identity. Like gays, Canadians wonder how we are all different when we're exactly the same. We're one-tenth of the population of America, just as gays are purportedly 10 per cent of the population.

Brad Fraser (playwright)

He may have expressed it tongue-in-cheek as part of the promotion for the (then) new cable television series *Queer as Folk*, produced in Toronto between 2000 and 2005 for the U.S. channel Showtime and Canada's Showcase.[98] Nevertheless, the irreverent yet pointed quip by playwright Brad Fraser, who was writer and executive story editor for the series, is itself symptomatic of the appropriation of social and sexual norms characteristic of the practice of *queering*. Queer Canadian film scholar Thomas Waugh defines the term as 'a continuum, a spectrum encompassing both a fixed sense of queerness as a grid – a network of discrete sexual identities, social constituencies, and strategic political agendas with a cultural canon belonging to them through historical accident and active construction – and a fluid sense of queerness as a "zone of possibilities" troubling the traditional configuration of gender and sexual identities.'[99] While the first set of meanings is operative within and around the production of *Queer as Folk* – its frank, explicit, and unapologetic depiction of male-on-male sex within the conventional parameters of a serial dramatic structure and the high production values of twenty-first-century cable television – the latter set of meanings, like Fraser's comment above, expands the ramifications of that production beyond the confines of its niche audience and into the broader discourse of Canadian identity. There is an economic ground here, since gay- and lesbian-themed cinema has been an important growth area of Canadian cinema since the mid-eighties, but there is equally a critical sense, as Waugh puts it, that 'a book about Canadian queer moving images [is] by definition about *all* Canadian moving images across the board.'[100] There is also a potential slippage here, since Waugh's capacious language implies that the same claim could be made about *any* national cinema, including Hollywood, while at the same time making a narrower argument for a specifically *Canadian* queerness. Similar to the claims made by Robert Cagle regarding the Canadian affinity for the originally gay-specific attitude of camp, Waugh's definition implicitly argues that while any culture is susceptible to queering, in Canada, it is much closer to a central than to a marginal strategy.

We may legitimately ask what is to be gained by queering Canada instead of merely treating its difference in the more conventionally analytical language employed, for example, by MacGillivray when he argues that English-Canadian cinema's traditional lack of commercial viability 'has attracted filmmakers and television producers both in fiction and non-fiction whose world view has quite often tended to be somewhat more complex than Hollywood's. The movies they have created have been compassionate and less interested in plots that turn on action and reaction.'[101] First, there is the fact that money is to be made in queer cinema, and that Canada's diversified production facilities and long experience with alternative, small-scale, and niche-oriented film-making is eminently suited to the specs of the gay, lesbian, and queer genres. More centrally, though, is the fact that Canadian cinema since the eighties has been characterized by a 'somewhat more complex' attitude towards sexuality than Hollywood's, to the degree that, for example, Vancouver film critic Katherine Monk chose to name her 2001 popularizing book on the subject *Weird Sex & Snowshoes and Other Canadian Film Phenomena*.[102] While the title is unfortunately sensationalizing, its combination of old (snowshoes) and new (weird sex) clichés of Canadian culture reflects a popular perception as well as the grain of truth that nearly all of the canonical films of the late eighties and nineties were centrally concerned with queer sexuality in the broad sense of Waugh's definition: Yves Jacques's cruising art historian and the relative inversion of gender stereotypes in *Déclin*, speculative bodily perversions in nearly the entirety of Cronenberg's oeuvre, the constellation of mediated sexualities in Egoyan's oeuvre, the masquerade of gender roles in David Wellington's *I Love a Man in a Uniform* (1993) and elsewhere, the overheated sexualities of Maddin's confections, the explosion of male sexual fantasy in Krishna's *Masala*, the closeted boxer in Virgo's *Rude*, female necrophilia in Stopkewich's *Kissed*, the homosexual underworld in Lepage's *Le Confessionnal*, polymorphous perversity in Lauzon's *Léolo*, and feral female sexuality in Fawcett's *Ginger Snaps*. And then there are the pointedly queer narratives in the films of Deepa Mehta, Léa Pool, Patricia Rozema, and many others that led Melnyk to the flat but accurate observation that 'the prevalence of lesbian subject matter is a distinct characteristic of Canadian feminist film-makers.'[103] And while Melnyk argues that this is less the case with gay material, Waugh's compendious volume conclusively demonstrates otherwise, both in terms of avant-garde and experimental work and in the more or less narrative films of Bruce LaBruce, Thom Fitzgerald, Noam Gonick, John Greyson, Jeremy Podeswa, and others, as well as individual films such as Scott Smith's *rollercoaster* and Jean Beaudin's *Being at Home with Claude*.[104] That the two television series that most defined queer sexuality in the North American mediascape in the first decade of the twenty-first century were Canadian-produced – *The L Word* in Vancouver and *Queer as Folk* in Toronto – is scarcely accidental. As Fraser suggests, 'I think the Canadian writers are more ready to examine sexual issues from a non-judgmental perspective. We just tend to write about it, not to suggest whether it's good or bad. There seems to be a more open sense of morality ... Americans tend to be either pro or con rather than somewhere in the middle. That's us, the Canadians.'[105] Nor should we underestimate the effect of the predominantly Canadian directors involved in the series themselves – Mary Harron, Bronwen Hughes, Podeswa, Kari Skogland, Stopkewich, and Virgo on *The L Word*; Thom Best, Fawcett, Greyson, John L'Ecuyer, Laurie Lynd, Kelly Makin, Bruce McDonald, Ron Oliver, Podeswa, Skogland, and Wellington on *Queer as Folk* – or the effect of the series on the directors. And this is without considering the Canadian writers, actors, technicians, and others who also worked on the two series. It is not much of a stretch to argue that recent English-Canadian cinema at least has been defined by queerness or to argue that queerness has defined recent English-Canadian cinema.

The English-Canadian and Quebecois films of the late sixties and early seventies formulated political issues as crises of identity and vice versa; with the important exception of Claude Jutra's debut film, David Cronenberg's early experiments, and David Secter's *Winter Kept Us Warm*, this circuit bypassed questions of alternate sexual identities. Less overtly political than the sixties and seventies, the cinema of the late eighties and nineties was more inclined to express questions of identity through sexual categories, and to express these questions in terms of critical ambiguities rather than critical verities. While these questions tended to be obscured at the time by critics' focus on questions of form – the use of video in Egoyan and Rozema, the use of music in McDonald, and the use of dialogue in

Arcand, the hybrid documentary form of Peter Mettler's essay-films and Girard and McKellar's *Thirty Two Short Films about Glenn Gould*, the metatextual mirror-ings of Pool's early films and Cronenberg's *Videodrome* and *Naked Lunch* – they are spelled out and explicitly politicized in Greyson's films. Indeed, because of their aggressive foregrounding of gay sexuality, the many stylistic affinities of *Urinal* (1988), *The Making of 'Monsters'* (1991), *Zero Patience* (1993), *Lilies* (1996), and *Uncut* (1997) with other Canadian films of this period have mostly gone uncommented, the films analysed solely in relation to gay cinema. Like the films of Egoyan and Rozema, *Zero Patience* foregrounds 'technologies of vision' and 'how historical narratives are told, how they are framed, and how they affect our lives'; indeed, Rozema appears in the film in one scene among the 'AIDS demonstrators.'[106] Like Arcand's and Pool's films of the late nineties, *Lilies* moves between French and English, English Canada and Quebec – borrowing, for example, Arcand's fetish actor, Rémy Girard, along with the composer Mychael Danna, who started his career with Egoyan and has scored every one of his films – and like Lepage's *Le Confessionnal*, it employs a formally complex time scheme linking two periods in Quebecois history to tell a tragic story of troubled sexuality.

Greyson's film-making falls into two fairly distinct groups, unified primarily by their gay-themed subject matter: the more formally and narratively unified adap-tations (*Lilies*, the later *Law of Enclosures* [2000], and *Proteus* [2003], as well as his work for television, including *Queer as Folk* [2000] and *Paradise Falls* [2004]) and the agit-prop essay-films deriving from his long-time experience in experimental video art (everything else in the oeuvre, both feature-length films and numerous shorts, many shot on video). His two most widely distributed films, *Zero Patience* and *Lilies*, can serve as examples for each tendency. 'Overloaded' (as Greyson commented on *Urinal*) with everything but 'the kitchen sink,' *Zero Patience* is an irreverent and absurdist attack on the 'culture of repression and blame' surround-ing the AIDS epidemic framed as a cross between the Hollywood musical and Brecht/Weill-inspired cabaret theatre.[107] The film is loosely structured around the 'opposite attracts' romance between the ghost of 'Patient Zero,' the gay French-Canadian flight attendant blamed for bringing AIDS to North America in Randy Shilt's bestselling history of the epidemic, *And the Band Played On* (1987), and the apparently immortal Victorian explorer, translator, and self-styled sex expert Richard Burton, now chief taxidermist at the Toronto Natural History Museum (a lightly disguised Royal Ontario Museum). The film is punctuated by didactic but catchy pop songs modelled by lyricist Greyson and composer Glenn Schel-lenberg on 'gayish bands of the time – The Smiths, Pet Shop Boys, and Erasure' and addressed material (bathhouse ethics, anal sex, various aspects of the politics of AIDS) that Greyson found to be unpalatable to many viewers when presented straight up.[108] Both elements contribute to making the film sublimely entertaining despite (or perhaps because of) the patchy acting, kitchen-sink production val-ues, and incoherent narrative causality similar to the work of Guy Maddin and other Winnipeg practitioners of the cinema of deprivation (see above and chapter 9), as well as to that of outlying members of the new German cinema, especially queer film-makers Rosa von Praunheim and Ulrike Ottinger. The success or failure of the formal qualities matters little to critics who read the film primarily for its (admittedly highly persuasive) theory and who view its formal strategies solely in theoretical terms of its 'wide-ranging critique of the spectacle of AIDS through the conventions of popular narrative filmmaking' or its 'dismantling of the spectral gay other constructed by a white, male heteronormative and homophobic camera eye.'[109] However, if we ignore the humour and humanity through which this critique and this dismantling are presented, we ignore the very problems of form *Zero Patience* so cogently deconstructs in conventional cinema.

That is, we must take the frivolity of the gesture of making 'the world's first gay sci-fi Aids musical' (as the film was advertised) as seriously as we take its political message. While I by no means want to discount the political reading of the film or deny its presence within its discursive strategies, I do think an exclusive focus on that reading risks ignoring the impact of the very dynamics of emotional identification endemic to the genres from which Greyson borrows. Rather than repudiating either the melodrama of the AIDS victim (the scene where the Arab schoolboy bonds with the blind and dying teacher George over a paper airplane he had made in George's class) or the 'monstrous mutability of the retrovirus' (the animals 'come to life' as dancers; Zero himself as a vampire, the 'monstrous' HIV in his blood), Greyson incorporates them into a broader narrative featuring sympathetic characters full of recognizable emotions.[110] Indeed, they are far more emotionally familiar than Egoyan's dysfunctional straights. Similarly, Greyson appears to have aimed for a far more 'realistic' set of production values than the end result, 'But to be fair, a lot of the critique was also about the craft. People wanted properly staged musical numbers and a level of craft that I could not pull off personally as an artist. There are lots of ways to make really cheap indie films, but you can't do it with musicals.'[111] Working with a professional crew and a respectable budget ($1.2 million) for the first time, Greyson had clearly aspired to something different than his earlier, artisanal films. That audiences managed to connect with the film in spite of its technical flaws is a testament to the fecundity of its conception rather than testimony to the necessity of those flaws.

The film is less allegory than phantasmagoria, for its parts inevitably exceed their place in an illustrated lecture about how the world has dealt with AIDS and why. It is impossible for the talking rectums in the 'Butthole Duet' to be reduced to the savvy deconstruction of anality staged by the lyrics, borrowing, for example, from literary theorist Leo Bersani to assert that 'The rectum ain't a grave.' Like Greyson's insistence on full male nudity in all of his films, the visual impact of the actors' singing mouths, full of teeth inside their specially made 'butt puppets,' imprints the viewer with a visceral awareness of the transgressive nature of the image, while the narrative context (this is a love scene, after all) keeps that same viewer locked into the event at hand.[112] It's not so different from the effect Cronenberg achieves with his prosthetics, making visible for us physicalities that we had never imagined could exist. Greyson himself playfully drew the connection, suggesting that Cronenberg's excessive imagery had in fact made it possible for *Zero Patience* to avoid censorship: 'We assumed that there would be demands to cut that scene, but then David Cronenberg's *Naked Lunch* came out and suddenly there was this aesthetic of talking sphincters.'[113] The difference between Greyson and Cronenberg is that the latter uses his excess to imagine where the mind and the body might be heading, whereas the former uses it to let his audience see what is already there but hidden. Cronenberg's films are profoundly speculative, while Greyson's films are profoundly historical; for all their play and imagination, they are always about the world as it is, has been, and will continue to be unless we do something about it.

Like *Zero Patience*, *Lilies* is based on history; however, its history is doubly displaced into the past rather than rendered in the present. Based on a play rehearsed but never performed in the isolated resort town of Robeval on Lac Saint-Jean in the hinterland of 1912 Quebec, *Lilies* turns on the restaging of the events around that play by one of the surviving principals in a men's prison in 1952 for the benefit of a bishop who was also involved in them. Unlike *Zero Patience*, *Lilies* is done in sumptuous period style, with numerous outdoor scenes in ravishing colours, highly verisimilar acting by a number of established English-Canadian and Quebecois actors, seamless continuity editing, and a highly literate script adapted and translated from Michel Marc Boulard's successful stage play *Les Feluettes*. The melodramatic plot is tightly constructed (at least for a Greyson film) around a familiar love triangle composed of three young men and a lot of repression and class resentment. Greyson made several decisions that somewhat distinguish the film from the venerable tradition of Quebecois historical melodrama in which it otherwise participates. In consultation with Boulard, he moved the original setting of released prisoners in a warehouse back to the prison itself, and added the confessional into which Bilodeau is locked while forced to watch the drama of his own past. And, again with the playwright's blessing, Greyson fought to retain the play's casting of men in all the roles in the flashback. Although the casting decision was criticized by a number of reviewers, who felt that it vitiated the credibility of the villagers' repression, Boulard was so invested in it that he turned down a competing offer that would have shot the film in French and with a much larger budget because the Quebecois producer insisted on casting women.[114]

Marshall argues that the use of English 'evacuated ... the specificity of the Quebec context,' but this seems an overly parochial judgment of the bounds of Quebecois cinema.[115] Instead, I see it as a rare example of a truly Anglo-Quebecois collaboration: in addition to the screenplay credit by Bouchard, funding was contributed by TFC, the OFDC (just before their funding was axed by the Harris government), SODEC (see note 18), and the Quebec government, and the film won the Genie award for Best Picture (receiving fourteen nominations in all) as well as the Best Canadian Film award at the Montreal Film Festival. As Greyson puts it, 'The fact that this was an acclaimed Quebec play that could be taken up by Ontario and made into an English film and yet returned to Quebec for the kind of acclaim it has received (winning an audience prize at Montreal film fest) is pretty cool ... In a sense, this is a rejection of the parochial.'[116] Greyson has argued against either a rigid definition of national cinema or a rigidly exclusive definition of 'the equivalent queer nationalism. I have much more of a sense of solidarity with something like *Vaseline* which is just like this very punk, mixed, once-a-month queer night where everybody goes, straights, gays, queers you know, every age.'[117] The melodramatic 1912 segments of *Lilies* play on all manner of hoary clichés of closeted desire, repressed priests, and upstairs/downstairs intrigues. Indeed, if you switch the DVD to the French-language option, or if you watched the French-language version that opened at the Berri Cinema the same day as the English-language premiere at Le Faubourg, you could have been excused for mistaking the Lac Saint-Jean scenes for one of Charles Binamé's big-budget extravaganzas.

Many reviewers certainly would have preferred to have seen the latter film, and Greyson's editing strategies are subtle enough to mess with the minds of those who did, since the film slips back and forth in time with even less warning than in Lepage's *Confessionnal*, subtly altering interior set details to confuse further the space of the past with the space of the prison. Here, too, the decision to cast the actors playing the prisoners as the characters in 1912, with the exception of the aged Bilodeau and Simon, exacerbates the confusion, which creates a cognitive dissonance between the reality effect of the 1912 scenes, shot on location with all of the production values of a typical heritage film, and the jarring recognition of Brent Carver and Rémy Girard as prisoners in the film's present but women in its past. Girard gets little screen time, and plays his character in the conventional drag of popular Quebecois comedy; in contrast, Carver turns in a highly naturalistic performance as Vallier's mother, the Comtesse de Tilly. Meanwhile, Alexander Chapman as the visiting aristocrat Lydie-Anne, whose engagement to Simon precipitates the film's climax, plays both Lydie-Anne and the prisoner playing her in flamboyantly queer fashion. The effect is double, because our expectation of aristocratic behaviour is fairly indistinguishable from our expectation of drag queens. So what is queered in the film is less the events themselves than our experience of them. As Howe argues, the film 'expands the scope' of the play's critique of homophobia beyond the immediate historical context of events.[118] That is, we take the existence of same-sex desire in 1912 (and in 1952) as a given rather than something the film is required to establish for us, and the absence of 'real' women only augments this effect. Consequently, what we are led to question is more a general socio-sexual repression that manifests itself around any open expression of desire rather than the sexual identity within a particular set of historical events. Desire is queered while also being shown to be incompatible to the society as it exists. The repression of desire is driven home by the cold, hard clarity of the prison scenes, ending with Simon's response to Bilodeau's request to be killed with what looks like a kiss but that we presume is a vicious bite, drawing blood and grimaces from both parties. Like *Zero Patience*, *Lilies* is by no means a perfect film, yet this imperfection, which Greyson seems the first to admit, is consistent with the formal refusal of closed meaning or fixed identity. Just as, in the production, the film straddles the great divide of the two solitudes and in its diegesis it confuses the historical gap of its time frame, so it refuses to fix its form. Among the 'blips' noticed by the reviewer for *Variety* was the fact that Aubert Pallascio, the blue-eyed and drawn actor who played the adult Simon, not only looks nothing like the much darker and thick-lipped young Jason Cadieux, but 'has gained a French accent.'[119] Yes, it is completely jarring in terms of verisimilitude, but it is a brilliantly perverse demonstration of the impossibility of predicting the future from a youthful past.

In its insistence on the radical lack of continuity of individual identity, *Lilies* makes a singular contribution to the coming-of-age genre, a genre which, especially in its coming-out variant, predominates in Canadian art cinema. This dominance suggests a metaphorical equivalency of the nation's coming-of-age and reckoning with its queer identity with the crisis of the individuals within the narrative. Because sexuality is nearly always central to the coming-of-age narrative, queerness, again, easily places itself at the centre of the agenda. Rather than the traditional reading of Canadian identity solely in terms of what Waugh dismisses as the 'heterocentric canon of straight male crisis' – the 'loser male' tradition of Canadian film criticism (see the introduction and chapter 1) – the prevalence of the coming-of-age narrative suggests a broader queer context for the crisis of identity analogous to a more capacious and fluid sense of national identity.[120] So, we can find the open questioning of conventional assumptions regarding masculinity and femininity characteristic of earlier coming-of-age films such as *Nobody Waved Goodbye*, *Mon oncle Antoine*, and *My American Cousin* to register an uneasiness with traditional gender roles that also allegorizes an uneasiness with traditional categories of national identity. That uneasiness is more explicitly queer in the 'weird' heterosexuality of the youthful protagonists of *Kissed*, *Léolo*, *Ginger Snaps*, Egoyan's early films, and the entirety of Maddin's oeuvre. The coming-out film became almost a cliché of Canadian cinema during the nineties, especially with Fitzgerald's *The Hanging Garden*, Greyson's *Lilies*, Mehta's *Fire*, Rozema's *Night Is Falling*, Wheeler's *Better Than Chocolate*, and Pool's *Emporte-moi* and *Lost and Delirious*; indeed, Waugh posits the related 'return-of-the-native' scenario of 'adult queers returning to the scene of rural or hinterland childhood socialization' as 'a kind of regional subgenre' of Atlantic Canada.[121] While this frequency is partly a result of funding and market pressures, it also derives, I think, from the aptness of the subgenre for addressing issues of Canadian and transnational identity of the time, especially given the superior quality of many of the films. The frequent journeys between urban centre and rural periphery and between past and present explicitly thematize issues of regional identity, while the focus on national/transnational issues draws attention to choices of cinematic representation between the local tradition of documentary realism and various transnational modes. The queer perspective denoted by the coming-out tale is personal on the part of self-identified gay and lesbian directors such as Fitzgerald and Pool (and, to a more ambiguous degree, Rozema), but it also denotes a fluid if not directly subversive attitude towards the generic and national conventions being deployed. As Marshall and others have argued, queerness similarly manifested itself as a category of national identity in Quebecois cinema of the late eighties and nineties, if frequently in a homophobic context, conceived as a threat to authentic Quebecois masculinity – and by extension, Quebecois identity tout court.[122]

We can usefully compare the queerness of these films to the regional 'eccentricity' of mainstream heterosexual comedies such as *La grande séduction* and *Rare Birds*, which depict regional queerness as harmless difference rather than destabilizing otherness. Not surprisingly, the sexuality, and consequently the identity, of the border-crossing characters – Montreal doctor Christopher Lewis (David Boutin); restaurateur Dave (William Hurt), estranged from his urban wife; erstwhile local Alice (Molly Parker), returned from studying architecture in Montreal – is never troubled except by the generic conflict determined by external events. But then, the same could be said of the more recent and pop-culture-oriented coming-out films *Mambo Italiano* (2003, Emile Gaudreault) and *A Touch of Pink*, both of which treat homosexuality more as a generic conflict than as the identity-shattering event it had been in the Canadian films of the nineties. A crowd-pleasing northern translation of the Italian-American conventions of Hollywood comedies like Norman Jewison's *Moonstruck* (1987), *Mambo Italiano* has the virtue of combining Anglo, Italian, and French Canadian within its sanitized Montreal, but it submerges them all in an overplayed, transnational Italian-American soup. Twenty-first-century self-reflexivity about exploiting stereotypes (protagonist Angelo makes it big by writing a soap opera exaggerating his own family drama, and knowingly references the 'slap' that ends the Italian melodrama as it does the family showdown in the film) isn't enough to distract us from the simple script resolutions and the easy characterizations. Nevertheless, the script is smart enough not to punish recidivist gay Nino or his odious mother beyond consigning them to live with the consequences of their own decisions. All of which is to say that, despite its Italian-accented English, *Mambo Italiano* is typical of Quebecois comedy in subordinating transnational standards of aesthetics and decorum in favour of its own cultural idiosyncrasies. If in the eighties and nineties homosexuality represented a threat to conventional Quebecois identity that needed to be defused and incorporated, by the new millennium it had become simply another trope of minority acceptance. But if *Mambo Italiano* suggests that being gay is no longer more than a generic issue, what do we make of the runaway popular success of Jean-Claude Vallée's *C.R.A.Z.Y.* (2005), a classically tormented coming-of-age/coming-out film if ever there was one? While *Mambo* displaced its crisis onto the non-Quebecois, transnational site of an immigrant Italian community, *C.R.A.Z.Y.* places young Zachary Beaulieu firmly within the style and iconography of Quebecois cinema. Given the local star status of comedian Michel Côté, his turn as the traditional father draws a clear generational allegory which Vallée sketches musically in the contrast between the fifties and sixties culture of Charles Aznavour and Patsy Cline and Zac's love for the British glam and progressive rock of the early seventies. Indeed, it is a testimony to the idiosyncratic temporality of Quebec popular culture that it did not make its first truly mainstream coming-out movie until 2005.

Like Pool's *Emporte-moi*, however, *C.R.A.Z.Y.* eschews the facile narrative of self-discovery in terms of a far more fluid sense of sexual identity – all that is clear is that Zac is incapable of following his father's strict definition of heteronormative identity, however much he might try. As Matthew Decker argues, the 'jumble of sexual situations' in which Zac finds himself ('masturbating to straight porn, spying on his brother have sex with multiple girls, masturbating in a car with another guy, straight sex with his best female friend, and sex with another man') 'makes it rather difficult to identify Zac as definitively gay or straight.'[123] This same fluidity manifests itself in the film's musical program, which not only marks a generational divide but queers the terms of that divide. Zac's father Gervais's firm control of the meanings of Aznavour's 'Emmenez-moi' and Cline's 'Crazy' neatly mirrors not only the rigid confines of conservative post-war Quebec, but Gervais's own rigidly defined desire to escape from those confines. This music also provides the foundation of the son's early, positive identification of his father as different from the others: to his young son, Gervais is, quite simply, 'le meilleur au monde.' As the boy explains to his classmates, his father owns all the records of Patsy Cline, Buddy Rich, and Aznavour, and 'he fired a machine gun in the army.' When, grown older, Zac 'declares war' on his father by breaking an imported Cline LP, the music he chooses as soundtrack to his rebellion is equally coded in terms of escape and difference – 'Shine On You Crazy Diamond,' 'Space Oddity,' 'Sympathy for the Devil' – and equally transnational, although British rather than the father's French and American choices. Moreover, the escape offered by Zac's music is a rejection of fixed identity as such: the fluid gender identity of David Bowie's androgynous and alien Ziggy Stardust, the romanticized insanity of early Pink Floyd guitarist Syd Barrett, and the Rolling Stones' leeringly ironic Satanism. In the context of Val-lée's twenty-first-century Quebec, the film proposes the subject position of a camp enjoyment of the father's fifties pop in the same breath as a contemporary aware-ness of just how much queerness was embedded within a rock music disseminated the world over in the seventies as the epitome of straightness. *C.R.A.Z.Y.* thus pos-ited queerness as a revisionary narrative of the subjectivity of the Quebecois; we may take its extraordinary popular success as testimony either to the province's essential embrace of its queer identity or to the film's successfully having depo-liticized Quebec's queerness to the point of broad acceptability. I'd say that it's a worthy successor to *Mon oncle Antoine*, which perfectly straddled a similar divide thirty-five years earlier.

A Touch of Pink is as much Toronto as *Mambo Italiano* and *C.R.A.Z.Y.* are Montreal, an uneven but gratifyingly weird refraction of the iconicity of Cary Grant and Hol-lywood romance to the same degree that *Mambo* appropriated and localized the tropes of Italian-American comedy. Like *Mambo*, *Touch of Pink* combines gay and immigrant culture, this time Indian. Rather than filtering the former through the latter, however, it queers both, starting with the title play on the Cary Grant and Doris Day comedy *A Touch of Mink* (1962). The dual identity is clearest in the scene where Alim's (Jimi Mistry) romance-movie-obsessed mother Nuru (Suleka Mat-thew) and his English lover Giles (Kristen Holden-Ried) spend a romantic day in London, replete with every tourism/movie cliché from a Doris Day–style suit to a champagne dance on a river boat. 'Pink' is simultaneously a signifier of the vis-ible minority's desire for Giles's 'peaches-and-cream' colouring and the financial success referenced in the original title, and a signifier for homosexuality. The joke, and the conflict, in the film comes in Toronto, which is antipathetic to both com-ponents of romance. The director Rashid expresses this antipathy through Alim's conversations with a phantom and mostly out-of-the-closet Cary Grant (Kyle MacLachlan), which make it clear that neither romance nor Hollywood's closeted sexuality can exist in Toronto. 'Is it always so uneventful?' Grant queries before Alim banishes him for good, choosing the 'documentary approach' against his idol's more duplicitous advice. Like Greyson's *Zero Patience* and Krishna's *Masala*, Rashid queers his genres by mixing them; unlike the radical exuberance of *Zero Patience* and the dissonance of *Masala*, the choice of romance (and the passage of more than a decade since those two films) allows a straightforwardly positive resolution. Because the critiques of *Zero Patience* and *Masala* were structural, they could only diagnose but not resolve. In contrast, *Touch of Pink* regards identity as a subjective choice, a performance rather than an embodied person, and thus belonging to the province of images. Still, we remain uneasy over the implication that the final solution *is* real and embodied (no Cary Grant, no camera, only 'realism') as we do over the almost vicious rejection of the choice of Alim's cousin Khaled to remain in the closet, despite his mother's awareness.

Female identity raises different issues regarding queerness: it is skewed by definition in that it has traditionally been defined in relation to the plenitude of masculinity. So, while Jean Bruce can define 'the lesbian postmodern' in terms directly echoing those of queerness ('She [the lesbian spectator] is constrained by cultural exclusion, but can take pleasure in the willful act of reworking scenarios to include her. Films about sexuality and gender – in other words most, if not all, films, are thus susceptible to unruly lesbian readings'),[124] we can equally argue for a fluid spectrum from straightforwardly lesbian stories to conventional-looking but perfectly queer women's films like, say, *My American Cousin*. The oeuvre of Indo-Canadian film-maker Deepa Mehta is a case in point. Best-known for her Elements trilogy (*Fire* [1996], *Earth* [1998], *Water* [2005]), but equally the author of a number of films set in Canada (*Sam and Me* [1991], *Camilla* [1994], *Bollywood/Hollywood* [2002], *The Republic of Love* [2003], *Heaven on Earth* [2008]), Mehta has made only one explicitly lesbian film within a staunchly woman-centred body of work. Moreover, the lesbian relationship in *Fire*, born of the attraction between the older, long-married Radha (Shabana Azmi) and her young daughter-in-law Sita (Nandita Das), is one element in a broader thematic of tradition versus change rather than an exclusively 'coming-out' narrative. Mehta deploys the highly charged relationship (all three films in the trilogy were controversial in India) as a provocative insertion into what could otherwise be a reasonably conventional Indian melodrama and a traditionally Indian image-cluster of fire. Mehta queers, in this sense, the myth of Rama and Sita that she explicitly references, in which Sita's loyalty to her husband is tested and proven pure when, after he has won her back from Ravana, her kidnapper, he rejects her as impure.[125] She builds a funeral pyre and steps into the flames, which do not touch her, proving her purity. Just as the film proposes a hybrid aesthetic for a transnational audience, it blasts open the purity of the fire imagery, using production design and its narrative arc to call attention to the role of desire in all of the characters' lives and decisions. Moreover, this desire is invariably mediated by movie culture: Radha first encounters Sita in private when she finds the latter in her husband Jatan's clothes, miming to a playback performance; Sita's husband keeps kung fu movie posters in his room, rides a motorcycle, and has an East Asian mistress, Julie (Alice Poon), who dreams of being a Hong Kong actress; mute grandmother Biji spends her days watching 'mythologicals' (popular serial films about the lives of the Hindu gods) when servant Mundu is not replacing her videos with his porno tapes; finally, Radha's husband Ashok, a traditionalist who has taken it upon himself to repudiate both desire and movie culture, views the story of Sita in a live performance with his swami. Like the setting of the religious college where Camille teaches classical mythology in *When Night Is Falling*, *Fire*, along with *Earth* and *Water*, asks us to consider the role of desire within a traditional culture. And, like Rozema's film, Mehta's trilogy concludes that there is none, at least not for women – *Fire* ends with Radha and Sita fleeing after Ashok has left his wife to burn; *Earth* ends with personal tragedy echoing the 1947 partition of India; *Water* ends on a devastating close-up of Shakuntala (Seema Biswas) as she watches the girl Chuyia departing on the train with Gandhi, bound for an uncertain future of which Shakuntala will never be a part.

While not explicitly present as setting or reference within the Elements trilogy, Canada is implicitly present as the external point of view necessary for Mehta to make the films, the diegetic correlative of her own emigration in 1973 at the age of twenty-three. It is there in the choice to film *Fire* primarily in English and in the attitude that film takes towards contemporary culture. It is there, in other words, in the queering of a particular tradition of Indian conservatism and oppression of women. Mehta's films are generically hybrid as well, combining the art-movie conventions of serious, inflammatory subject matter and dense, highly expressive imagery and design with the melodrama and popular sensibility of Bollywood cinema. While *Earth* sags under the weight of its historical backdrop, the intimate settings of *Fire*'s family home and *Water*'s house for widows highlight the personal drama and nuanced interaction between the female characters. Like *Fire*, *Water*, too, is highly intertextual even as superficially it plays out as a straight historical melodrama (it is set near the end of the British Raj in 1938). Forbidden to remarry or to act on their physical desires, the widows are confined like slaves and have their heads shaved. The visual impact of the cropped heads is in itself an effective counterpoint to the Bollywood conventions of long, flowing hair, especially when we realize that Kalyani (Lisa Ray) has retained her hair not only in deference to those extra-diegetic pressures (Mehta's film-making has always had a pragmatic commercialism about it) but also to retain her market value as a prostitute. Mehta thus effectively queers the very commercial convention she is also following. In her slow-burning central role as the older Shakuntala, Seema Biswas, whose awakening to her predicament forms the dramatic backbone of the film, draws extra power from the resonance of her iconic debut role as the abused woman turned eponymous feminist outlaw in the equally controversial art-exploitation classic *Phoolan Devi* (1994). Mehta's Canadian-set work has been lower-key and less distinctive. Levitin observes that each of her films, 'attacks prejudice and injustice, defending the "other" and letting no one off the hook.'[126] This certainly characterizes the bitter report on prejudice of her first film, *Sam and Me*, the Elements trilogy, and her ironically titled Toronto/Punjab arranged-marriage drama *Heaven on Earth*. Yet it seems less applicable to the lighter touch of *Bollywood/Hollywood* or the gentle romance of *Republic of Love*. What is unique about Mehta's filmography in Canadian cinema is not only her broad commercial success, but also her continued ability to bring her dual perspective to bear on both of her home countries, to continue making movies in India despite intense and sometimes violent protests, and to continue making movies in Canada despite ongoing funding battles. While *Fire* stands as her signature piece, the heat of its queering influence spreads itself throughout her work, as Mehta's presence within Canadian cinema exemplifies the profound queerness of the Canadian mosaic in all of its incarnations.

Chapter Nine

Film-Making at the Heart of the World: Guy Maddin

I do feel a bit like Dracula in Winnipeg. I'm safe, but can travel abroad and suck up all sorts of ideas from other filmmakers – both dead and undead. Then I can come back here and hoard these tropes and cinematic devices ... And I sit here in almost eternal darkness all winter long and try to make these dead things live.

Guy Maddin (2004)

Wrapping up the fraught production of his fourth feature, *Twilight of the Ice Nymphs* (1997), Guy Maddin confessed: 'I'm sick of the twenties. I've hung around in the twenties longer than the twenties hung around in the twenties.'[1] Indeed, Maddin's habitation of the seminal decade of modernism could be said to date as far back as his formative undergraduate friendship with fellow Winnipegger John Boles Harvie, who not only shared with Maddin his encyclopedic knowledge and cinephiliac obsession with the silent cinema, but immersed himself in the role: speaking, dressing, and acting like a twenties dandy.[2] While Maddin's persona is resolutely contemporary, his cinematic twenties are the navel of an idiosyncratic but highly original and increasingly influential engagement with the phenomenon of modernism in its myriad facets, a phenomenon that can be said to have stretched from the Romantics through to the end of the Second World War. Consequently, when he accepted the Canadian Broadcasting Corporation's offer that his next feature after *Twilight* be a film of the Royal Winnipeg Ballet's adaptation of Bram Stoker's 1897 novel, *Dracula*, he was not in fact escaping from his twenties aesthetic, but stretching its centripetal force into an earlier thread of modernism. In this chapter, I will discuss the many strands of Maddin's modernism, from the historical aspects of a Manitoban chronology extending from the autonomous Icelandic republic of Gimli in the 1870s to the glory days of Winnipeg in the middle of the twentieth century, to the primitivist credo of one's life as a performance, one's art as a melodramatic refraction of one's life, and one's life and art as wholly at odds with the establishment conventions of professionalism, to the birth of the cinema itself in 1895 and the fecund decades of its childhood search for its most effective identity, to the modernist obsession with memory, nostalgia, the past, and buried truth. Moreover, I will argue that it is through Maddin's peculiar engagement with the era of modernism that we can best distinguish his work from the labels of postmodernism, camp, or pastiche to which it has so often been reduced. For Maddin's oeuvre can be identified neither with the ironic pop culture homages of American directors as diverse as Quentin Tarantino and Todd Haynes, nor with the resolutely highbrow and anti-Hollywood productions with which much of Anglo-Canadian and Quebecois film-making has generally been identified; instead, he suggests a wholly different relationship between Hollywood and the traditions of Canadian cinema – a relationship that is at the heart of what we may call Canadian cinema, wholly unique yet also absolutely exemplary.

The Garage Modernist

> It's sort of like the Ramones. I just refuse to learn how to play my instrument. The Ramones will never go away, as far as I'm concerned. I work more slowly than they did, but I hope that by the time I go away I'll have a nice body of work.
>
> Guy Maddin (2004)

Central to Maddin's image as a film-maker is an insistence on his status as an amateur, auto-didactic dilettante, an insistence customarily framed in terms of laziness and neurosis. In interview after interview, he has honed the slacker image of the aimless twenty-something who got into films because he couldn't be bothered to do anything else. Indeed, in the enticingly narrow but nevertheless essential gap between the slacker persona and the intense labour that has produced the oeuvre that established the persona, Maddin has generated a compelling sociological explanation for the twenty- and thirty-something males who dominated early twentieth-century modernism to at least the same degree as they today dominate independent film-making. Still, unlike the style of what we could perhaps call the mainstream American slackers, the video store, computer game, and Internet addicts that followed Tarantino's inspirational lead, Maddin's style of slacking taps into the modernist lode of self-mortification rather than the late twentieth-century focus on self-promotion. Commenting on his decision to publish the film diaries from the production of *The Saddest Music in the World* (2003) – his most mainstream movie to date – in the *Village Voice*, Maddin sounds genuinely tormented by the embarrassment their exposure will cause him. 'My feelings aren't even mixed; it's almost complete regret. Like many things I've done, it was a snap decision and probably a foolish one. Someone just said to me, "Do you want to publish these diaries?" So I handed them to him and he published them. That was a mistake.'[3] Deadpan episodes like the opening inability to plant a tree from a sapling in his backyard to commemorate the start of the production read like the absurdist failure of a character out of Dostoyevsky or Kafka: frozen ground, skyrocketing overtime rates, and irreparable damage to the garden of his beloved and deceased Aunt Lil echo classic motifs of loser modernism.[4] The details of Maddin's crush on his female stars Isabella Rossellini and Maria Medeiros, however, tap a contemporary vein of pure lust that would not be out of place in a Farrelly Brothers comedy: mentioning that he feels he has long known Medeiros because of the nude shots he has downloaded off the Internet, or penning a delirious paean to the intimate joys of

ADR (Automatic Dialogue Replacement), which concludes, 'At bedtime I let spit-lubricated Isabella slide out of my cramped and throbbing embrace, and dismount tremblingly from her lips.'[5]

Such moments form a major leitmotif of the journals published in 2003 in *From the Atelier Tovar*, which provide both an overview and a context for Maddin's career up to that point.[6] From the way Maddin also brings them up in the more public forum of the interview, they would seem to be motivated by an idiosyncratic twist on the persona of the director as fan that has dominated non-studio film-making since the days of the French new wave. It is less frequently observed that the nouvelle vague itself borrowed the idea of the artist as fan and the slumming populism implied by it from a strand of modernism that originated in Romantic poets such as Baudelaire and his fellow *flâneurs* in the nineteenth-century Paris of Louis-Philippe. It reached its apogee in the Surrealists, the first true cinephiles, who championed the violent blockbuster serial thrillers of Louis Feuillade, the continuous programming of neighbourhood theatres, and the unashamed pursuit of sexual obsession even as their own writing, art, and film-making remained avant-garde in the extreme. In a review of a program at New York City's most punishingly old-school house of experimental film, the Anthology Film Archives, a program that paired Z-movie schlock (*East of Borneo*, *Road to Salina*, *The Entity*) with found-footage films inspired by three artists' obsession with actresses who appeared in them, Maddin alternates his self-consciously adjective-laden and over-excited prose with just enough crit-speak to maintain his bona fides and a fine instinct for the 'boner quotient' that, for him, appears to lie at the core of all cinephilia. He concludes by inserting himself into the genealogy of underground obsessives from Joseph Cornell to Peter Tscherkassky, fantasizing about his own future homage to the reigning queen of 'Cinema Rejecta,' Denise Richards, with a found-footage remix of *Undercover Brother* (2002).[7]

It is precisely the 'boner quotient,' the translation of the classic feminist critique of cinema's voyeuristic foundation into the sophomoric lexicon of the contemporary teen movie, the late-night channel surfer, and the freeze-framing, video-grabbing couch potato that distinguishes Maddin's persona from the realm of camp, a label the director himself resists, preferring, as Steven Shaviro has noted, the term 'decadent.'[8] Shaviro, however, likens Maddin's stance to Oscar Wilde's, arguing that 'Camp ... is a shortcut to radical aestheticism.'[9] Maddin's camp side certainly exists; it is perhaps most in evidence in *Sissy-Boy Slap-Party* (1995), which appears to have been strongly influenced by his friend, fellow film-maker (and actor in the film) Noam Gonick, whose flamboyantly gay and unapologetically camp persona punctuates Maddin's recent oeuvre as an untroubled beacon from an agit-prop and sexually liberated present day to a neurotically heterosexual fellow traveller still working through the repressions of an earlier epoch. While Gonick happily imagines his marginalized films bypassing conventional distribution routes to reach a subculture of 'clandestine basement circle jerks around DVD players,' Maddin's sex-saturated films have always been erotic rather than pornographic in tone, and have treated their material as explicitly perverse rather than straightforwardly natural.[10] As Maddin comments on what he learned from the films of Luis Buñuel, a key figure in the early eighties 'film club' in a Winnipeg living room where he learned to make movies, 'He almost never allows people to consummate.'[11] Until

Cowards Bend the Knee (2003), Maddin's 'rules for nudity,' as he put it, 'ha[d] always been the same as the Hays Office limply enforced in pre-code pictures … a little bit of nudity as long as it's a long shot, smudged out or over-exposed.'[12] Paradoxically, the tone of the films' repressed and tortured context (think of Johann staring at his mother bathing through a mirror attached to a stick while hanging by his knees in a stone-lined air shaft in *Careful* [1992]) seems closer to the closeted fifties; there is none of the sophisticated naughtiness characteristic of the pre-code thirties: until Melissa Dionisio in *Cowards* and the two starlets of *Saddest Music*, Maddin's actors were generally filmed in as unflattering a light as possible, erotic only, perhaps, in the same fetishistic mode that led many young men in the fifties to prefer Doris Day to Marilyn Monroe – indeed, in *Twilight* he even managed to dampen the appeal of the Quebecois icon and art-house favourite, Pascale Bussières (see chapter 4).

In *Cowards*, it is as if the challenge of an alien forum – the cool and haughty confines of the high-art world represented by the Power Plant Gallery in Toronto's Harbourfront Centre, which commissioned the piece – pushed (or perhaps empowered) Maddin to take control of his images in a different way than he had previously done, bringing his sexualized melodrama out of the closet, so to speak, and embracing the mantle of hipness being thrust upon him. Now publishing in the *Village Voice* and *Film Comment*, feted with retrospectives in Rotterdam, New York, and elsewhere, and granted the big-budget, bona fide stars, and commercial distribution of *Saddest Music*: all these factors contributed to push Maddin beyond the brink of cultdom to the status of a legitimate international auteur. This status was solidified by a new image of himself as 'showman' in the most recent features, especially *Brand upon the Brain!* (2006), which he toured stateside with a live orchestra, foley crew, and rotating cast of all-star narrators; for *My Winnipeg*, too, Maddin provided live narration for a screening at Toronto's Winter Garden Theatre.[13] In critical terms, it is legitimated by the publication in 2010 of no less than four full-length books.[14] This places Maddin in the rarefied Anglo-Canadian league of David Cronenberg and Atom Egoyan.

The paradox is that Maddin has never had anything like the commercial success of Egoyan, much less like that of Cronenberg; indeed, his auteurist persona is built on an eccentric avoidance of the mainstream. As Geoff Pevere writes, the cornerstone of the early myth was the rejection of Maddin's debut feature *Tales from the Gimli Hospital* (1988) by the Toronto Festival of Festivals, only to have it become a cult hit as a midnight movie in Manhattan.[15] Despite regular (although not constant) support by federal and provincial sources and frequent appearances at TIFF (*Gimli* notwithstanding), Maddin's reputation, like Cronenberg's and Egoyan's, has an international rather than a national base. Still, it takes only a quick glance over at Egoyan's ticket to global renown, *Exotica* (1994, see chapter 7), to register the fact that Maddin is likely not to stray too far from his provincial slacker roots. Both *Exotica* and *Cowards* revolve around the dynamics of the sex show; both weave their melodramatic narratives out of their sexual theme; and both were received by critics primarily as commentaries on the complicity of the spectator's act of viewing them, a reception that permitted the ambivalently exploitative quality of that theme to be left unexamined within its safe theoretical container while audiences left no doubt what had brought many of them to the gallery, theatre, or later, rental venue.

Exotica used its slick, soft-core derived visuals and detached characters to uncover an emotional core of humanity out of the audience's thwarted expectations of perversion. *Cowards* counters Egoyan's nurturing and spatially anonymous strip club – it could be anywhere – with the equally male and equally eroticized setting of the Winnipeg Arena, insisting on a powerfully localized context for its adaptation of the Electra myth. And while Egoyan's film strongly demarcates its heterosexual main plot from the gay subplot in which Don McKellar's pet-shop owner picks up men at the opera, in Maddin's film, the homoerotic milieu of the hockey rink and dressing rooms insinuates itself outward through the entire action, however straight its primary actors may play their roles.

Rather than an ironic nod at a supremely subtext-aware contemporary audience, however, the steaming bodies of the Maroons' shower scenes seem to have been reproduced directly from Maddin's childhood memories. In interviews and in his unfilmed autobiographical treatment, *The Child without Qualities*, as well as in a brief elegy to the closed-down arena, Maddin repeatedly returns to the memory of himself as a child lathering up the naked players' backs and a primal scene combining a brush with celebrity in the form of an eye-level gape at future Hall-of-Famer Gump Worsely's 'makeshift fig-leaf contrived out of suds.'[16] Because it is rooted so firmly in Maddin's own childhood, this image seems in his oeuvre less a repressed observation of latent homosexuality than a simple fact of his, and perhaps of any, life: the child's free-floating, sense-based sexuality. In 'The Womb Is Barren,' he pairs the memory with that of the adjacent room of the players' wives: 'I loved the olfactory shock of passing from this chamber redolent of wet diapers and breasts swollen with milk into a room of damp men, the dubious smell of athletic supporters, unlaced skates and drenched jerseys.'[17] The bowels of the stadium are a Proustian *lieu de mémoire*, evoking an irreducibly, viscerally personal blast from the past whose intimate meaning the artist tries his best to translate into a common language: 'In the Winnipeg Arena, my inner and outer landscapes were one and the same thing.'[18]

It is a past, moreover, that can no longer directly be accessed: the arena was, as Maddin put it, 'remodelled, modernized, stupid' in 1979, with the same process occurring to those who had grown up with it (it had opened in 1955, a year before Maddin was born); it was finally demolished in 2006, an event poignantly recorded in *My Winnipeg*.[19] At the same time, and in good modernist fashion, the artist's representation of his self is meant to provide an emblem, a rebus for all who follow him. When Egoyan filmed Mia Kirshner caressing his wife Arsinée Khanjian's naked and very pregnant belly in the office of the Exotica Club it certainly carried an extra-diegetic frisson of exposure and voyeurism, but the meaning of that exposure remained enigmatic and the act could only be interpreted within the thematic web of the diegesis, the complex play of parents and children, protection and vulnerability. Maddin's autobiography is both more and less immediately present in his films. It is less so because there is in fact nothing of his current life as such in the film. Even the scene where his mother, Herdis Maddin, playing 'Guy Maddin's' blind grandmother, presides over Meta and 'Guy' rolling around at her feet, a scene Maddin reports will prevent him from ever showing his prudish mother the completed film and that her black-painted glasses prevented her from witnessing during the shooting, plays on a long-ago-endured (if perhaps never overcome) adolescent embarrassment of exposure in front of one's parents.[20] His life is more immediately present because everything in the film, as Maddin has insisted over and over, is wholly autobiographical and true. And we should take him at his word, because the truth he is insisting upon is not the truth of reality television and afternoon talk shows – performative as their ostensible naturalism may also in the end be – but the truth of modernists such as Kafka, Proust, Beckett, or Bruno Schulz, autobiography as a mode for revealing the hidden layers of the self and the society from which that self emerged, not the superficies treated by the conventions of realism. Thus, for all of his perverse contrariness in being 'a resolute fabulist' in a 'largely … documentary or at least realist' cinema, Maddin's modernism suggests yet another permutation of the non-documentary facet of the Canadian approach to the real.[21] The localized insistence on emotionally faithful truth-telling that is characteristic of Maddin's refracted life story in his films, more than various thematic resonances, is what connects his work to Canada.[22]

Proust was a lazy, asthmatic gadfly who nevertheless managed to complete a three-thousand-page novel on top of a lifetime of occasional writing. Maddin certainly does not aspire to such length, but his résumé of nine features and thirty-odd shorts over twenty-five years is more than respectable for someone working as far from the mainstream of movie financing as he has done. Granted, he has succeeded reasonably well in regularly winning state funding, and has made a virtue of working on a shoestring budget, but laziness must still be set down as a facet of rather than a hindrance to his creative personality. But then, isn't such laziness itself also a contemporary take on the hoary old modernist *Sprachkriese*, the ability to write thousands of words on the impossibility of writing any words at all? Nevertheless, while his themes more closely resemble the literary, so-called high modernists such as Proust and Kafka, Maddin's modus operandi as a self-declared primitivist is closer to the avant-gardes whose styles permeate his film-making: the Dadaists, the Surrealists, the Constructivists, and other Soviet artists who saw their art if not as demolishing, than as wholly remaking the world that had gone before them, dissolving the distinction between art and life entirely. Theirs was a garage-band aesthetic *avant la lettre*, celebrating the fact that anyone at all could be an artist in the very moment that their own genius gave the lie to the dictum they were celebrating. After all, however hard we may try to commemorate the truly garage-band bands, the bands that couldn't play their instruments, couldn't write songs, couldn't sing, and were lousy performers, what we return to and what we enjoy most are not such failed extremes but the brilliant compromises of trash with art. Moreover, the very act of commemoration transforms incompetence into genius in the process: you can't even listen to the Ramones today as a tabula rasa, and if Guy Maddin has his way, Alyssa Milano and Denise Richards will be elevated to the camp heaven of Doris Day and Rose Hobart, enshrined as divine apparitions in a garage filmography filled to the ceiling with eroticized dreck.

Speaking about how he stumbled into the role of film-maker, Maddin explains that, 'to be a great author you need to be a genius and need to have been well read for your entire life, but to be a great pop star you just need to pick up a guitar, and maybe to be a film-maker of some impact it's more like being a pop star. You just pick up a camera, seize a garage band aesthetic, and go out there.'[23] It was during the first decades of the twentieth century that the ethos of the garage band became viable, that artistic creation was ideologically severed from classical technique by movements such as Dada or the Surrealist practice of the exquisite corpse. The motion pictures had a different problem, for they were still seeking to be regarded as an art; the primitivist aesthetic did not hit the mainstream in cinema until the break-up of the studios, the rise of exploitation cinema, and the emergence of the French new wave and other new waves in the fifties and sixties. But film-makers still needed money, either from the guaranteed audience of the genre movie or from their families (Truffaut used his wife's money, for example, to make *The 400 Blows*), or as happened in Canada and a few other places, from the government. With the digital video revolution, cinema finally reached the turning point popular music achieved in the sixties. There is a tacit but seldom enunciated class distinction here, for it is from the lower middle-class suburban and provincial kids that most garage bands and most indie film-makers have emerged, while authors (not to mention most mainstream film-makers), to paraphrase Maddin, generally need a nurturing milieu and a lot more connections. Maddin's stubborn faithfulness to Winnipeg, where he still lives and works (the sets for nearly all of his features have been built in different derelict local buildings, relics of better times), to the memories of the hockey arena and his aunt Lil's hair salon, to the cabin on the lake at Gimli, to the slacker ambitions of his gang of Drones, and to the flamboyant antics that could shock and be tolerated in such equal measure only in an isolated town like Winnipeg: they are all imbued with the demographics of the garage band. Now, you can of course parlay garage-band status into superstardom – witness Nirvana in music or Tarantino as the cinematic equivalent – but then you risk being labelled a sell-out, surely another reason Maddin has stuck so resolutely to his home-town roots.

Indeed, this seems to be a bit what R. George Godwin had in mind when he complained in his recent history of the Winnipeg Film Group that it shouldn't be considered a virtue to do something (1920s films) that used to be really easy and has since become incredibly difficult.[24] This seems to me to miss the point, which is first of all that Maddin, like most innovators, maintains that he started making films this way because he was ill-trained and incompetent (famously, Godard always claimed he invented the jump cut because it was the quickest way to shorten the overlong first cut of *Breathless*) and that he continues to make howling mistakes in each film and desperately try to cover them up – he maintains that the six-minute *Heart of the World* is 'the only movie I've made which looked and felt exactly as I hoped it would.'[25] He is equally claiming that he couldn't really make them any other way – just look at the trouble he got into with *Twilight of the Ice Nymphs*, where all the mistakes were in trying to make the film look pristine rather than to distress it into the other films' resemblance of battered relics of an earlier day. To view Maddin's twenties aesthetics as merely a formal gesture of nostalgia or a collector's preciosity is to ignore the crucial ways in which the period of the twenties was responsible for shaping our own understanding of these very terms.

It is the range and depth of his immersion in the twenties that has enabled Maddin to export his own marginality out of garage-band cultism and into urban hip. Paradoxically, the hipper he has become, the more he has revealed the complex underpinnings of what had been taken by many as a simple pose. The more his movies delve into twenties culture and aesthetics, the more they prove to be immersed in the simultaneously sordid and tragic detritus of the director's own life. What at first looked like spot-on absurdist inventions – the father in *Careful* losing his eye to his mother's brooch; the epidemic of suicides; the whole saga of Gimli – turn out to be factual episodes in Maddin's life, which is common knowledge to just about any Winnipegger with an ear for oral history. Maddin takes this mythologizing to a new level with *My Winnipeg*, which mixes fantastic fact and deadpan fiction in a bid both to reimagine the city in his own image and to rewrite its history for the outside world: 'My dream is to show this film at the Berlin Film Festival and have hundreds of Germans watching it as a travelogue of Winnipeg.'[26] The film is both carefully documented (the 1919 General Strike; a centre for early twentieth-century spiritualism) and wildly inventive (the 'Forks beneath the Forks'; the high rate of sleepwalking). Moviemakers worked like this back in the new wave, but they don't work this way anymore – they make movies that have nothing to do with their lives, or they transmute their obsessions into fiction (think Egoyan and Cronenberg, or Lynne Stopkewich and Gary Burns), or they documentarize them pure and simple (*Tarnation* and *Super Size Me*, or anything by Michael Moore). The vertiginous interplay between family history and Maddin's aesthetic is best elucidated through two categories dear to the practitioners of modernism: the child and the city.

Child's Play

> Canada's Centennial splashed a brief Kodachrome illumination into the musty basements, closets and garages of our nascence. But the illumination was for us children alone, the hyper-sensitive brown studies and centennial projects within our cubbyholes remained guardedly private ... We inscribed the choreographies of our revolutionary pleasures behind our bedroom headboards, interrupted regularly from without by terrors so sudden and vehement as to flatten our lungs.
>
> Guy Maddin, *The Child without Qualities*

It is a commonplace of the history of modernism that it was a phenomenon of cities: London, Paris, Berlin, St Petersburg, Moscow, Barcelona, Rome, New York. In Maddin's recreation of the period, Winnipeg takes its proud place among those more celebrated urban centres. The city emerged in the late nineteenth century, and its heyday lasted from the 1920s through to 1950.[27] While, as he put it, 'I had to build a Winnipeg because you still don't want to see the real Winnipeg,' Maddin has remained faithful to its industrial past in a poetic fashion, creating his fantastic sets in disused industrial buildings around the city (*Ice Nymphs* in the former Vulcan Iron Works, *Heart of the World* in the former Dominion Bridge Works, *Saddest Music* in an abandoned steel mill), or in the case of *Gimli*, in the hair salon of his recently retired Aunt Lil; he immortalizes the city with found and also fabricated footage in *My Winnipeg*.[28] Modernism was concentrated in urban centres due both to industrialization and to the unprecedented scale of migrations across Europe and over to North America. In Winnipeg, the original First Nations inhabitants and Métis descended from Quebecois fur traders, and local wives were joined by German-speaking Mennonite immigrants from the Russian Empire in 1874; the autonomous Republic of Iceland was established in 1876 (whence the Maddin family came); Poles, Ukrainians, and Jews later settled in Winnipeg's North End.[29] *Gimli* darkly mocks while commemorating the tragic history of a smallpox epidemic in the Republic of Iceland that killed some of Maddin's own ancestors; *Archangel* recalls the Ukrainian population, not to mention the local soldiers that fought in the Great War, more of whom were killed than from any other part of the country; even the Germanic *Bergfilm* heritage of *Careful* has an ethnic toehold in the flattest region of Canada. Melnyk complains with some justification that this heritage has generally been ignored in the reception of Maddin's work, as it had been in the reception of earlier experimental film-makers such as Michael Snow in favour of the critical terms of a context-free avant-garde.[30] It appears that *My Winnipeg* has somewhat redressed this reception – it is especially rich in mythologized detail of the early twentieth century – but such oversight has long also been a part of scholarship on modernism, which has tended to regard the avant-garde as functioning in a purely formal register, while personal history and specificity of place and time fade before the demands of a universal and universalizing aesthetics.

To recover the specificities of alternative modernisms is complicated because one of the primary goals of the epoch was to subvert traditional patterns of meaning based on the realist notions of self and society that had dominated the nineteenth century. Most if not all modernist artists and writers would have resisted the reduction of their production to the data of their own life and times; nevertheless, most if not all of them addressed their subversions at targets derived precisely out of those data. As much as it sought to make itself wholly new, modernism was parasitic to a degree matched by few other periods. Think of the fondness for allusion, allegory, rewriting – Joyce's *Ulysses*, Kafka's parables, Borges's tales – not to mention the incorporation of the material world into art via collage, assemblages, performances. Moreover, the motion picture, which loomed as an éminence grise over the entire period, was fundamentally parasitic. The early 'cinema of attractions' (in silent cinema scholar Tom Gunning's well-known formulation) imported scenes from every aspect of life to the screen in one-reel snippets. Little if any distinction was made between what we would now call newsreel footage and the common practice of Georges Méliès and others who recreated current events and disasters in their new studios. The earliest cinematic aspirations to legitimacy as an art form consisted of filmed adaptations of plays. These stilted dramas have received short shrift in the history books, but one has to wonder how many audience members may have found pleasure in the unforeseen combination of the artificiality of production and the shocking reality effect of the mechanical reproduction of the image. It is a combination eminently familiar to viewers of Maddin's films, which betray a soft spot for the dated pretensions of middle-brow achievements of the past, pretensions whose intonations and sleepwalking declamations are pointedly reproduced in George Toles's dialogue for the early features.[31]

But in the end, Maddin's heart, like that of most modernists, is always with the trash of the period. The surrealists loved the random and shocking violence of the

9.1 Guy Maddin's 1920s as the gateway to historical memory and a new aesthetic: Weimar animation pioneer Lotte Reiniger as the source for re-envisioning the Winnipeg revolutionary strike in *My Winnipeg* (2007). Animation shot by Andy Smetanka. Permission of Buffalo Gal Pictures.

early serials, their oneiric combination of narrative preposterousness and visual realism. *My Winnipeg* captures this energy in its tale of the General Strike eroticized by the fears of the girls in a local Catholic school rendered (as is the Whittier Park fire of 1926 and the bison stampede that purportedly flattened the Happyland amusement park in 1922) in coloured silhouette animation in homage to silent pioneer Lotte Reiniger; in its fascination with ectoplasm; and in its detailing of subterranean secrets of the cityscape, such as the 1931 bathhouse that extends several stories into the earth (figure 9.1). The motion picture promised a new combination of fidelity to its subject matter and access to truth that was able to bypass the bankrupt aesthetic and political ideologies of realism. Movies only began to become respectable in the twenties, and that cusp between the vulgar energy of their slumming past and the regularized and regulated craft of sound and the studio decades is a crucial factor in Maddin's fascination with the period. Like the characters of most of his films, the motion picture as an art and as a business was in its late adolescence, wildly and uneasily wielding a potent cocktail of naive motivations and adult desires. It was those nascent desires that had caused the traumas and created the joys of childhood, but it was the ensuing adulthood that caused them to be repressed, distorted, and forgotten amid the swirl of sanctioned forms and conventions. This was the modernist narrative of childhood and memory as the path to its hidden truths. It was formulated most famously by Freud and Proust, but as a trope it was everywhere in the early decades of the century, and the cinema, the youngest of the arts, was the ideal place to project the anthropomorphic potential of childhood development (or the lack thereof) as a theory of history. The early cinema was regarded as appealing to the 'childish' portions of the population, but there were many who turned that pejorative appellation on its head, celebrating the childlike wonders of Keaton, Chaplin, Laurel and Hardy, early Disney, Max Fleischer, and Lotte Reiniger as gateways into an aesthetic place unapproachable through the stodgy rigidities of the venerable arts.

In the treatment for perhaps his most self-consciously modernist short, *The Eye, Like a Strange Balloon, Mounts towards Infinity* (1995), Maddin's wish list of influences conjures an unlikely but symptomatic merging of a symbolist modernism (Edgar Allan Poe, Odilon Redon, Abel Gance) with early cartoons, a dead seriousness of formal and thematic intent joined to an iconoclastic, popular playfulness: 'I would like to make a mini-melodrama, very music driven – like a Fleischer Brothers cartoon ... Music will be inexorably linked to the visuals: it should drive the visuals like a Silly Symphony, but with a more Poe-like dead weight.'[32] One of the opening shots introduces the synaesthesia that seems to bind these opposing influences formally: a clam shell opens and closes, shooting out steam and blowing like a train whistle, heralding the train wreck and tragic love triangle that are to come. Melodrama is, of course, a time-honoured component of the genre of children's literature that was invented by the Victorians, but with the exception of *The Night of the Hunter* (1955, Charles Laughton) and various animal-in-danger scenarios, it has seldom received its full due in the movies, and has nearly always been played for laughs, as in Disney's *101 Dalmatians* (1961, 1996). Nor does Maddin deflate the high seriousness of a Poe, a Redon, or a Gance – whose *La Roue* (1923) supplies the narrative and visual backbone of *The Eye* – at least not in the manner of a camp revision. Rather, he brings to them the child's point of view, the 'mini-melodrama': the child that was cinema in the twenties and the child that knows how to view that cinema for what was most important about it. The same attitude is evident in an anecdote Maddin relates in an interview, 'I once watched a Buster Keaton movie shown at eighteen frames per second [silent speed], and the gags took forever to unfold, like *Ordet*. Maybe if we watched them at nine frames per second, they'd be funny again.'[33] The ideal Maddin film would be the film able to maintain comedy and melodrama in perfect, mutually illuminating counterpoise, and he appears to be coming closer to this combination with each new feature.

The first movies that had a lasting impact on Maddin were his family's forgotten treasure trove of silent 16 mm films that he discovered one day hidden away in the house (and which perhaps included the Keaton reel mentioned above).[34] The twenties are not just the historical period of modernism for those artists now in or approaching their middle age (Maddin was born in 1956); they are the decade when their parents were children. Our own childhood is full of available and buried memories both comforting and horrible; our parents' early years are something far more mysterious, glimpsed only at second- or third-hand, through stories, photographs, mementoes, rumours, and fantasies. Since he grew up with three teenage siblings, the displacement of Maddin's memories of the past would have been even more intense. In *The Child without Qualities*, Maddin writes that not just the toys and dolls 'knew a better quality of play' because of the many hands they had passed through and been subjected to before he came along, but 'a residue of better quality seemed to sit on everything in the deserted house. The house held a dormancy, a potential to divulge what it held for his family before.'[35] His play, he suggests, was aimed at enacting this potential. 'Sometimes he intentionally separated himself from his favorite toys, and played with memories of them. And then played with the memories of the memories.'[36] It would not be a stretch to regard Maddin's films as memories of memories of something from which one has wilfully separated oneself; this would account not only for the many strategies of distancing them from the viewer with the celluloid equivalent of the teeth marks, spit-stains, and near-dismemberments that bestowed the 'residue of better quality' onto the family toys, but also for the undeniable desire for the emotional connection intimated by them, a connection that lies, as the introductory title to *Careful* would have it, 'lost behind the Ranges Lost and waiting for you: Go!'

Depravation, even for the most privileged of children, is the essence of childhood, and it is important to recognize the inseparability of the pleasure derived out of that deprivation from the pain caused by it. Like many modernists, Maddin has cultivated that childhood insight (or insight about childhood) into his mature aesthetics, privileging the insights of the local, the marginal, the forgotten, the fragmentary, over the easy allure of the clean, new, and polished. As the concluding line of Bruno Schulz's 'Street of Crocodiles' reads (a line placed by the Quay Brothers at the conclusion of their 1986 film adaptation), 'Obviously, we were unable to afford anything better than a paper imitation, a montage of illustrations cut out from last year's mouldering newspapers.' Maddin once sent a film critic a tape of *Gimli* caught straight from CBC television, complete with commercials. Rather than apologetic, he was pleased with the idea, comparing it to his encounter with *Vertigo*, 'the very first movie I memorized off TV … A friend of mine caught it on TV, but this was pre-video, so he just made an audio tape of it. And I listened to it, maybe about a hundred times before ever seeing it including the commercials. They placed one unfortunate commercial right in the middle of the revelation that Judy is Madeleine … and it was tremendous. So that gave me a thrill. And so I was hoping for some similarly unfortunate mutilations to my movie. And I got some.'[37] It is easy to shrug the story off as postmodern archness and self-protection, just as the analogous stance of Maddin's films is so frequently accounted for in the same terms, or as just plain weird. And, sure, Maddin doesn't mind coming off as weird, he even likes it at times – that is, after all, part of the *épater la bourgeoisie* mentality of modernism that is still able to thrive today in isolated enclaves such as Winnipeg. But on its own, intentional weirdness is unable to account for the undeniable power of Maddin's films, the sheer pleasure and dread of watching them. It can only be hoped that today's kids have access to some analogous deprivation amid the sensory overload of their current existence, but no one who grew up with black-and-white television, portable cassette recorders, and scratchy LPs can fail to recall a moment such as the one elevated by Maddin into an artistic credo.[38]

There was no irony (in the contemporary, Alanis Morissette sense of the word) in modernism, only the biting, tragic variety that dates back to the ancient Greeks, the kind that makes you want to forget what you had tried so hard for so long to remember. Like old tragedies, Maddin's films are replete with ghosts – the Hamlet's-father variety in *The Dead Father* (1986), *Careful*, and *Cowards*; the lost loved one in *Gimli*, *Archangel*, and *Cowards*; a whole host of them in *Brand* and *My Winnipeg* – not to mention spectral presences such as the attic-bound brother Franz in *Careful* or the eponymous vampire Dracula. Not frightening in the strict sense of the word, their presence is a driving force in the narrative action; like childhood memories, they are both impotent and overwhelmingly powerful. Similarly, the films are replete with images of bodies resurrected, or at least brought out into the open from their resting places, whether figuratively, as in Einar's story of the violation of Snjófridur's body in *Gimli*, the wax figures in the Hall of the All-Time Maroons in *Cowards*, or the Black Tuesdays hockey team in *My Winnipeg*, or literally, as in the buried bodies unearthed to the horror of the townsfolk in *Careful* and the apocalyptic emergence of the dead from their graves in *Heart of the World*.[39] We may take pleasure in watching them, and Maddin may take pleasure in manipulating them, but the characters are not granted the same distance. Immersed in the melodrama, they would all be better off remembering nothing. Unfortunately, like the amnesiac soldiers fighting a war that has already ended in *Archangel*, they remember just enough to suffer from and be haunted by it, but not enough to find their way out before it is too late. 'Amnesia,' according to Maddin, 'is a timeless storytelling device. Forgetfulness is a kind of anesthetic for the painful life we all live. We're forced constantly to think about the shameful things we've done, the painful things that have happened to us. We owe most of the feelings we have, as sensate beings, to shoddy memories. The sheer erratic nature of memory keeps life a Luna Park.'[40] Childhood is a lifetime of boredom, suffering and shame; it is also the source of a large part of our happiness, and the surest link we have to the world that came before us. Only children are so constituted as truly to enjoy life as pure sensation, screaming the whole way out of terror and exhilaration inextricably combined. Grown-ups on the roller coaster are usually either bored out of their skull or having a heart attack.

It could be argued that Maddin's oeuvre constitutes one long refutation of the postmodern argument that we have no feeling left and a demonstration of the fact that there is still a difference between false memories and shoddy ones. This is one reason he has engaged with Hollywood more and in a more intricate manner than perhaps any other Canadian film-maker with the possible exception of David Cronenberg. Hollywood – and, as always by metonymy, the United States – is the Luna Park of Maddin's adult mind, of someone who only encountered film as such when he was already in college. While his childhood experience of bursts of America through radio static and television test patterns was an inevitable consequence of life in the hinterlands, the mature form he has given to that experience is anything but. The references with which he dots his interviews demonstrate an ecumenical range still all too rare in the anti-Hollywood discourse of Canadian cinema – everything from Matthew Barney's avant-garde *Cremaster* trilogy to teenage sexpot Alyssa Milano – although they are, it should be noted, bereft of any current blockbusters; clearly, for Maddin the only recent movies worth doing anything with are the termite art, already shot through with the holes of niche marketing and on-the-cheap (relatively speaking) production values, but still retaining traces of the effortless glamour and seduction that only Hollywood can do (you won't find any straight-to-cable Canadian fare showing up in Maddin's discourse). Witness the 'Dreyer and Joan [Crawford]' course he has taught at the local university, or the list of 'Guilty Pleasures' he submitted to *Film Comment*, which roams from a 'naval musical,' obscure Howard Hawks and Howard Hughes war movies, and a Charlton Heston jungle melodrama to the works of cult experimentalist George Kuchar and Oskar Feininger's three-minute modernist city-poem, *From Munich to Berlin*.[41] In his brief comments, Maddin appears to eschew the 'guilty' part in favour of the 'pleasures,' implicitly refusing the high/low distinction of the category itself. If you put enough memories between yourself and Hollywood, he suggests, the themed Disney World rides on which they intend to take you start to break down into something more nebulous and passé – after all, what could be more outdated, more urban and modernist than a Luna Park, a word coined in the twenties from the eponymous Coney Island amusement park to describe those of Europe? These days, we only see them in old movies, or in Maddin's films – Happyland, 'our own Luna Park,' plays a central metaphorical role in the dreamscape of *My Winnipeg*.

Hollywood was young once, too, and it lived its youth during that same magic period that produced everything meant to eliminate what Hollywood would soon come to stand for the world over. A legacy of the First World War, the hegemony was brand new back in the twenties, even in Canada, and the shopworn products of the time no longer carry the patina of market domination that continues to radiate from today's blockbusters, the only lure the audience seems to need. And, as much as Maddin's films are overtly indebted to the great European classics, we shouldn't forget (and he certainly hasn't forgotten) how many of the Europeans were also making movies in Hollywood and how weird the backlot stuff of the twenties and thirties could sometimes get. After all, this was the period when Douglas Fairbanks and David Selznick brought Eisenstein to Hollywood on the success of *Potemkin*. Maddin's approach can be distinguished both from the respectful recreation of European cinema (as, for example, in *Shadow of the Vampire* [2000], E. Elias Merhige's wonderfully strange take on Murnau's *Nosferatu*) and from the American independent revision of Hollywood, which seldom delves further back into cinema history than film noir. Both strategies tend to take the older film syntax at face value, recreating it with the obsessive fidelity of the connoisseur (consider the production design and cinematography of *Far from Heaven* [2002] or *L.A. Confidential* [1997]), often tweaking the themes to bring out their resemblance to current mores or updating the syntax to create an ironic counterpoint to the original (classic examples are Robert Altman's *The Long Goodbye* [1973] in comparison to classic noir adaptations of Raymond Chandler, or Philip Kaufman's 1978 remake of Don Siegel's original *Invasion of the Body Snatchers* [1956]; more recently one could cite Jonathan Demme's *The Manchurian Candidate* [2004]). And then there is the current vogue for the remake as hollow exercise in spectacle and marketing, which is perhaps not without interest for the cultural historian, especially when one sees what gets done to Hollywood blockbusters when transmuted in the powerhouse cruci-bles of the Bollywood and Hong Kong movie industries.

In his fascination with the tropes of vanished genres of commercial film-making and with great films of the past, Maddin's production is closer in spirit to the latter sort of borrowing.[42] Not only in his ongoing fixation on melodrama but in the tech-nologies he resurrects and the genres he adapts (war movies in *Archangel*; mountain films in *Careful*; fairy tales in *Twilight of the Ice Nymphs*; the musical in the unfilmed *Dykemaster's Daughter* and *Saddest Music*; noir and hockey films in *Cowards*; the city film in *My Winnipeg*), Maddin remains intensely engaged in an unholy matrimony between the avant-garde and the popular, a wedding from a surrealist's dream. It is not as if Maddin wishes he could actually have made movies in the twenties: 'I never claimed that living in the past would be better than living now.'[43] The verti-cal integration of the studios' heyday militated against any leeway in the sphere of production, distribution, and exhibition at least as much as the multinational media conglomerates do today. Life is arguably better today for a marginal film-maker working on microscopic budgets as Maddin does; in the twenties he would have had to rely on rich patrons. Where there was play in the cinema then and still is today is overwhelmingly in the reception, which cannot ever be wholly control-led, and where viewers are free to find in a film whatever they want – certainly Maddin could not have predicted the year-long run of *Gimli* in New York, nor was whatever cult vibe the audience was picking up on likely to have been among the ones he had planned for. Freed of preconceptions of quality and integrity, Maddin's voracious and omnivorous consumption of the cinematic past has the potential to liberate his viewers from time-worn categories of cinematic quality without releas-ing them into a void of ironic slumming.

As he puts it in what unintentionally reads like a manifesto for a new conception of cinematic history,

Because film is both a business and an art form, it always struck me that business needs to be fed by technology, and it's so fast that it moves along to the next techno-logical advance before all the artistic potential has even begun to be wrung out of any particular era. So I always see myself as going back along the road of film history and picking up all these great and completely abandoned technologies and film vocabular-ies, which I pick up and try on and learn to speak. For instance, the most salient one would be when sound came in. It's not just a technological thing; it was an economic thing. The technology to make sound movies was there from about 1895, actually. It was just a matter of economically converting all the theaters didn't seem worthwhile to distributors until around 1928, but the silent film era wasn't even close to peaking in its artistic potential then, so mime was quickly abandoned. It was cut down in its prime, cut down in its youth even, so mime and mime comedy and mime melodrama were all euthanized and replaced with a new breed of film that had its own charms, and then the evolution really started fast and musicals came in as a new form and they were quickly deemed cloying and abandoned, even though they hadn't achieved their potential. And the most extreme and manqué forms are 3-D and Odorama and Surround-o-vision. When a painter makes a painting, he or she can use any color or any kind of pigment, doesn't even have to use paint. When a poet makes a poem, they can use any word from any language or even make one up, so it seems to me a film-maker should have the same freedom to use whatever is out there to make movies: old, new vocabularies, humble technologies, sophisticated ones.[44]

Outmoded technologies, 'abandoned' film vocabularies, and failed gimmicks are not simply novelties to be resurrected as historical curiosities or for a quick laugh; they are untapped potentialities for new modes of film-making, available to any-one able to break free of the sealed-off meaning given to them by the march of history. To defuse the ideology of progress is a quintessentially modernist idea, and although Maddin gives no sign of having read its chief proponent, Walter Benjamin, there is no doubt that he has assimilated its lessons. After all, what child ever truly wants to grow up?

In many ways, Maddin's acclaimed short, *The Heart of the World* (2000), is an object lesson in the aesthetic practice defended in the quotation above. The redemptive ending – having refused her two original suitors, Anna kills Akmatov the Indus-trialist after sleeping with him, and selflessly takes the place of the flawed heart at the heart of the world – is pure Hollywood, but everything in the plot derives from the tropes of Soviet anti-capitalism. But while Anna as state scientist is pure modernization propaganda (she would return as 'Citizen Girl' in *My Winnipeg*), the two brothers that love her play atavistic roles: Osip, the undertaker, deals in mortality, and Nikolai the actor plays Jesus in the Passion play. And although in the script Maddin cites the obvious Soviet prototypes – Eisenstein, Pudovkin, Ver-tov – the influence of German expressionism is striking as well: Lang's *Metropolis* and its crowd scenes and dualistic heroine/villainess Maria, and Murnau's *Nos-feratu* in the scene of consummation and murder.[45] What should have been a hom-age to technocratic rationalism owes a greater debt to two films dealing with the resurgence of occult forces into the modern world. Moreover, the rapid-fire editing style owes more to the rhythmic crescendos of Abel Gance than to the dialectical montage of Eisenstein.[46] Less than their cinematic innovations, Maddin takes from the Soviet film-makers the dated iconography of utopia, the constructivist faith in machines and in technological progress. As the flimsy sets are shaken by the earthquake caused by the earth's fatal heart attack, one cannot but recall Maddin's oft-told story of melting and setting fire to action figures of the astronaut Ed White, timed, according to *The Child without Qualities*, to coincide with the patriotic fer-vour of Canada's Centennial.[47] Children are enthralled to an equal degree by the clean, smooth surfaces of the new and by the potential for disrupting those same surfaces. So, *Heart of the World* invokes both the astounding promise of the Soviet twenties and the ominous undercurrents of the Weimar Republic. And while the final transformation of Anna's telescope into a movie projector from the earth's core recalls Leni Riefenstahl in its martial and athletic display of flags and bodies, and Vertov's *kino-eye* in its repetition of 'Kino' as the new mantra of the reprieved world, the stirring image is the director's own, a world made new by Maddin's modernist magic.

Herein lies his riposte at Hollywood, for as Quandt observes, the Sviridov com-position that propels the film forward also makes it feel like a music video.[48] The driving energy and extraordinary synchronization of image and sound primarily account for the film's seductive power (as opposed to Maddin's feature films, I have never received a negative response from students viewing *The Heart of the World*). The movie is simultaneously nostalgic for modernism – the apparently boundless potential of a new medium and a revolution, an apparatus apparently capable of changing the world just as aesthetics made equally heady claims to relevance in the making of history, a time of genuine emotion and sincerity – and eager to appropriate the most marginalized artefacts and credos for its own minor art.[49] Maddin's retro-modernist art would not simply create a counter-cinema to Hollywood, but in the manner of the old avant-gardes, would melt down Hollywood and counter-Hollywood together in a crucible of melodrama to mould them into something entirely new. Given that the globalization of the film industry has for all practical purposes accomplished the same recasting on its own terms, Maddin's quixotic but strangely plausible quest to explain why Winnipeg may lie at the heart of the world (or, as he reformulated it in *My Winnipeg*, 'the heart of the heart of the world') is a timely reminder of the many different ways in which it is possible to march forward while keeping one's eyes fixed on the riveting detritus piling up in the past, the raw material of some unforeseen future *kino*. And while Maddin's version of this reminder is perhaps the most brilliant north of the 49th parallel, it also suggests that much of recent Canadian cinema may be doing something quite similar.

Conclusion

Actually, it was just an excuse for a new creation myth of cinema.

Guy Maddin on *The Heart of the World*

The Heart of the World made a number of ten-best lists for 2001, including those of J. Hoberman at the *Village Voice* and A.O. Scott of the *New York Times*, certainly an unusual accomplishment for a six-minute film. It is always arbitrary to mark historical change with a specific moment or artefact, but there is a powerful heuristic value in finding in the extraordinary critical and popular success of *The Heart of the World* a watershed moment for Canadian cinema. On the one hand, the fifteen-year 'golden age' since the mid-eighties was definitively waning in the new millennium. There was no longer the local funding or the global support for the kind of mid-range art film that the new Canadian auteurs had made their own. The film-makers themselves, for better or worse, had moved on. Canadian cinema in the twenty-first century has been characterized by high-profile genre exercises with clear national markers but of questionable artistry and, for the most part, limited commercial potential. Even Paul Gross's old-fashioned First World War epic *Passchendaele* (2009), which practically swept the Genie awards (only Gross himself lost out for best actor) and was quite successful at the local box office, recouped only 25 per cent of its $20-million budget in its North American theatrical release (nearly all of it in English Canada). It was also the most expensive 100 per cent Canadian-financed film ever made and received at best mediocre reviews. Nevertheless, it reached number two at the box office in its initial weekend, won the Golden Reel Award for the highest grossing Canadian film of the year, and went on record as 'one of the five biggest English-language Canadian films of all time.'[1] And there was something to the fact that the film did as well as it did, and *only* in English Canada. It was a national occasion, if not quite on the par with the francophone historical epics that reigned in Quebec during the 2000s. With his curling comedy *Men with Brooms* (2002) having grossed more than half its $7.4-million budget in its theatrical release, Paul Gross probably ranks as English Canada's most commercially successful director locally, and certainly the closest Canada has to a traditional national popular film-maker in the twenty-first century. Other recent local successes include teen road-movie comedy *Going the Distance* (2004, see chapter 8) and TV-show spin-offs *Trailer Park Boys: The Movie* (2006, Mike Clattenburg) and Red Green's *Duct Tape Forever* (2002, Eric Till). English Canada is not yet competing with Quebec, which regularly wins eight or nine out of every ten Golden Reels, but there is certainly a local market for low-budget, low- to middle-brow Canadian-themed comedies, as there was back during the tax-shelter years, when *Meatballs* (1979, Ivan Reitman), *Porky's* (1982, Bob Clark), and *Strange Brew* (1983, Rick Moranis and Dave Thomas) set box office records. Of those films, of course, only *Strange Brew* is easily recognizable as Canadian. On the evidence, however, Richard Stursberg's four-year tenure at TFC helped to create a climate for a successful indigenous popular cinema, regardless of questions of 'quality,' an important part of the conventional equation for demonstrating the existence of a 'national cinema.'

The same cannot be said unequivocally for the films that made the international reputation of Canadian cinema between 1984 and 2000, which took a turn towards the popular as well. Denys Arcand and Léa Pool have had popular hits (*Invasions barbares*, *Maman est chez le coiffeur*) and misses (*L'Age des ténèbres*, *The Blue Butterfly*). After lying low for most of the decade, Denis Villeneuve and Bruce McDonald both emerged with new genre movies (docudrama *Polytechnique* [2009], political melodrama *Incendies* [2010], zombie movie *Pontypool* [2008], and rock 'n' rollers *Trigger* [2010], *Hard Core Logo 2* [2010]), and *This Movie Is Broken* [2010]). Robert Lepage continued to follow his own path; still, the movie adaptation of his one-man show, *La face cachée de la lune* (2003), was his most emotionally accessible film yet. David Cronenberg, Atom Egoyan, Patricia Rozema, Vincenzo Natali, and others ply the commercial path, with varying degrees of success. And dozens more, actors and directors, tool away in television at home and abroad. As the core group has reached middle age, so their films have settled into familiar patterns, some good work, some mediocre, and some bad, but without the spark of inspiration we saw at the end of the last century.

As the authors collected in *Self Portraits* (2006) recognized, we are now in a position to take stock of what transpired in the heady days of Canadian cinema at the end of the century. There is no question that the new Canadian cinema not only changed the landscape of local film-making, but compelled a re-evaluation of an entire set of critical assumptions about what that landscape had been. In particular, they have broken the hold of an abstract conception of what Canadian cinema *should be*. Gone is the cinema of duty, the doctrine of documentary realism, the judgment of films according to their adherence to a particular set of fixed criteria. Doubtless, something was lost in the process – the sense of unity, the political purpose, the fantasy of cohesion. And it was a fantasy, albeit a powerful and utopian one, for what more than anything the new Canadian cinema has allowed cinema studies since 2000 to see is the degree to which there never had been anything like the consensus of Canadian cinema there had seemed to be for so long. At the same time, we can now recognize the great works of the sixties and early seventies for what they were: the efflorescence of a nation suddenly finding itself, or at least trying to find itself, in the world.

Certain constants remain, for Canadian cinema since the eighties no more escaped the influence of the sixties and seventies than it did the tax-shelter years.

As I have argued throughout this book, Canadian cinema from the beginning has been characterized by an unusually strong insistence on the bond between the cinematic image and material reality. Naturally, there are exceptions, and the variety of expressions of this bond are myriad, but acknowledging this quality simultaneously removes documentary realism from its long central position and provides a way to grasp its relationship to the great variety of Canadian cinema. The cinema of the sixties and seventies was profoundly inward-looking in the relationship it posited to the outside world, almost as if to insulate itself from the stimuli bombarding it from all sides. In contrast, the tax-shelter years went to the opposite extreme, opening up the culture to a network of forces over which it basically eschewed all control. The new Canadian cinema found its creative spark in the fault line where these extremes met, and in doing so, it not only was able to articulate a polyvalent argument that this was in fact the true locus of Canadian identity, but also to suggest that, no matter appearances, the rest of the world would soon be following suit. That moment, both locally and globally, has now passed, a contingent new world order has stabilized itself, the fault line has been smoothed over, and the inevitable new cracks in the global network of capital are surely manifesting themselves, but just not here. What this process left behind is a national cinema that is as contradictory and paradoxical as ever, but that is also healthier and better established than ever, and a far more accurate reflection of the contradictory identity of Canada than either of the extremes of the discourse of the documentary realist years or the tax-shelter years made it out to be.

Which brings me back to *The Heart of the World*, not so much as an answer but as a question. Why, beyond the ever-reliable and inimitable Cronenberg, are the only Canadian film-makers whose work is as consistently original, innovative, and exciting as during the receding 'golden age' and who are also maintaining an international profile the few film-makers who have located the popular somewhere at the margins rather than in the off-centre? Like Maddin's *Heart of the World*, *Atanarjuat* parlayed its very marginality into a significant and unique, if transitory, niche in world cinema. Both Maddin and his entourage in Winnipeg and the Isuma collective in Nunavut have maintained a strong global presence within proto-commercial and alternative distribution networks. Maddin supports his quirky auteur brand with a steady stream of pop-auteur journalism that most closely resembles the brilliantly rigorous fever dream rants of seventies underground music critic Lester Bangs (1948–82).[2] In addition to highly limited commercial releases, the Isuma collective distributes its films digitally through its own webpage. Meanwhile, a healthy chunk of the cinematic history of the NFB is available globally as streaming video on their webpage, NFB.ca. Digital technology is the perfect format for producing, distributing, and exhibiting the diverse, challenging, and geographically dispersed cinema of a generation of film-makers hopefully now emerging and able to seek inspiration in these models.

Like its predecessors, this generation will be immersed in popular culture both at home and abroad. It will take an ironic stance to the culture to its south and a guilty pleasure in its own. It will be ever more ready to incorporate outside influences from wherever they may come, appropriating them as it sees fit for its own concerns. It will maintain a characteristic but well-nigh undefinable relationship

to the 'real' world around it. It will have a vexed relationship to its funding institutions and to the boosterish critical establishment, both of which will no doubt continue to constrain its possibilities according to ideal models of 'Canadian cinema'
– although hopefully new and improved models. But things will have changed,
too. Unlike the film-makers of the first wave in the sixties and early seventies,
this generation will have a diverse array of positive examples – even unvarnished
success stories – to build upon and compete against. It will have mentors with the
cultural capital and economic clout to help them along their way. It will have a
myriad of choices rather than a single beaten path in which to work. It will have
infinite potential and, finally, the means to believe it can realize that potential.

That, at least, is how I like to read the image at the heart of *The Heart of the World*:
when Anna makes the world new with her *kino*, this, for me, is the utopian dream
to which she has given herself. And it's the same message I hear from Isuma as the
end credits roll in *Atanarjuat*: well, if we can do it, why can't you?

Notes

Introduction. What Is Canadian Cinema and What Happened to It at the End of the Twentieth Century?

1 Staines, 'Frye: Canadian Critic/Writer,' 257; Atwood, *Survival*, 32–3.

2 Fothergill, 'Coward, Bully, or Clown.'

3 Although he has never theorized its grounds, the argument has long been made by Pevere in the context of the need for a more capacious definition of Canadian cinema. See particularly 'Ghostbusting'; and Pevere and Dymond, *Mondo Canuck*, 195 (for Lorne Michaels and *Saturday Night Live*).

4 For the sake of simplicity, I refer to the festival in both incarnations with the abbreviation 'TIFF.' For an anecdote-laden chronicle of TIFF through 1999, see Johnson, *Brave Films, Wild Nights*.

5 *Telefilm Canada*, 'History.'

6 D. McIntosh, 'Vanishing Point,' 71.

7 Longfellow follows this trajectory closely in 'Surfing.' However, her exclusively local and economic focus here seems to me to restrict the otherwise international and broad perspective of her analysis.

8 As film critic Sterritt presciently wrote from Telluride in 1987, '*I've Heard the Mermaids Singing* belongs to the new breed of nonstudio independent production that has been attracting much attention – and a growing audience – in the past couple of years.'

9 Mottram, *Sundance Kids*, xvii.

10 King, *American Independent Cinema*. Andrew draws the same distinction in *Stranger than Paradise*; see also Mottram, *Sundance Kids*.

11 In contrast to Merritt, *Celluloid Mavericks*. See King, *American Independent Cinema*, 9.

12 King, *American Independent Cinema*, 9.

13 Ibid., 16–23.

14 Ibid., 41–4.

15 For example, in the introduction to her case studies of 1990s 'mavericks,' the only non-American directors among Waxman's sixteen-odd names of 'new rebel auteurs' are Atom Egoyan (*The Sweet Hereafter*) and Australian Baz Luhrmann (*Moulin Rouge*) (*Rebels on the Backlot*, x–xi).

16 Arcand's next film, *Jésus de Montréal*, won two minor awards at Cannes and was beaten out for the Palme d'Or by Soderbergh's debut, a moment the latter recalled in a recent

interview: 'I know that I was taken and put on live French television immediately afterwards, next to Denys Arcand and Bertrand Blier, neither of whom looked very happy, and I gave this interview' (Soderbergh, 'Steven Soderbergh').

17 Mottram, *Sundance Kids*, 12.
18 Longfellow, 'Surfing,' 115.
19 The latter film would later be made into the syndicated Canadian television series *Nikita* (*La Femme Nikita* in the United States; ninety-six episodes, 1997–2001), the lion's share written by Besson, and starring Australian actress Peta Wilson and Quebecer Roy Dupuis, to this day the role for which he is best known in the United States (see chapter 4).
20 Leach, *Film in Canada*, 114.
21 Frye, 'Conclusion,' 346; Pevere, 'Middle of Nowhere,' 13.
22 Hutcheon, *Canadian Postmodern*, 4.
23 Keohane, 'Symptoms of Canada,' 30.
24 Hutcheon, *Canadian Postmodern*, 1.
25 H. Lefebvre, *Production of Space*.
26 In Klein, *No Logo*, 267.
27 Arroyo, 'Bordwell Considered,' 77.
28 Jameson, 'Third-World Literature.' The current paradigm shift has not substantially altered the heuristic utility of Jameson's argument. On branding and globalization, see especially Klein, *No Logo*.

1. Canadian Cinema 1896–1986: Invisibility and Difference

1 Marshall, *Quebec National Cinema*, 18.
2 Foster, *Once Upon a Time in Paradise* and *Stardust and Shadows*.
3 For more on Reeves's only Canadian feature, *Johnny Mnemonic*, see chapter 6.
4 See, for example, Pevere and Dymond's characterization of 'bland authority figures' as a key category of Hollywood Canadians (*Mondo Canuck*, 92, 153).
5 Berton, *Hollywood's Canada*, 153.
6 For the sake of efficiency and space, I refer to the NFB throughout this monograph by its English acronym rather than by its official double title, the NFB/ONF.
7 Lacasse, 'Cultural Amnesia,' 6–7; Morris, *Embattled Shadows*, 1.
8 Melnyk, *One Hundred Years*, 16; Gittings, *Canadian National Cinema*, 8.
9 Melnyk, *One Hundred Years*, 18–19; Morris, *Embattled Shadows*, 10, 88.
10 Melnyk, *One Hundred Years*, 19; Morris, *Embattled Shadows*, 22.
11 Melnyk, *One Hundred Years*, 21; Morris, *Embattled Shadows*, 26.
12 The quote is from Morris, *Embattled Shadows*, 45. On *Evangeline*, see McSorley, 'Centre,' 271–2.
13 Morris, *Embattled Shadows*, ix.
14 Gittings, *Canadian National Cinema*, 9.
15 Ibid., 15–32.
16 Melnyk, *One Hundred Years*, 38.
17 Armatage, *Girl*; see also Armatage's chapter on Shipman in *Gendering the Nation*.
18 Armatage, *Girl*, 104.
19 Ibid., 78–120.

20 Ibid. Shipman projected a multi-volume autobiography, but was able only to complete the first: *Silent Screen*.
21 Armatage, *Girl*, 118.
22 Ibid., 110–18.
23 Morris makes this point as a broad argument regarding a 'documentary approach to drama' in early Canadian cinema (*Embattled Shadows*, 93).
24 Melnyk, *One Hundred Years*, 89.
25 Qtd. in McGreal, 'Canadian Cinema,' 731.
26 Melnyk, *One Hundred Years*, 67.
27 Benjamin, *Origin*; Deleuze and Guattari, *Kafka*.
28 MacKenzie, *Screening Quebec*, 171.
29 Gittings, *Canadian National Cinema*, 78.
30 Melnyk, *One Hundred Years*, 48.
31 Melnyk, *One Hundred Years*, 49; Gittings, *Canadian National Cinema*, 95.
32 Morris, *Embattled Shadows*, 181.
33 Melnyk, *One Hundred Years*, 51; Gittings, *Canadian National Cinema*, 78; Magder, *Canada's Hollywood*; Pendakur, *Canadian Dreams*.
34 Spaner, *Dreaming in the Rain*, 23–5.
35 Gittings, *Canadian National Cinema*, 54–69, 56 for the quote.
36 Ibid.
37 Melnyk, *One Hundred Years*, 51.
38 Dorland, *So Close*, 15.
39 Ibid., 80.
40 Tousignant, 'Séraphin,' 9.
41 Véronneau, 'Quebec Feature Films,' 46; see also Weinmann, *Cinéma de l'imaginaire québécois*, 91–105; Lever, *Histoire*, 109–17. For an alternative reading of the phenomenon in terms of popular morality, see Gossage, 'La marâtre.'
42 Le Blanc, 'Aurore.'
43 Lever, *Histoire*, 114.
44 Gittings, *Canadian National Cinema*, 93.
45 Melnyk, *One Hundred Years*, 62–4.
46 Aitken, *Film and Reform*, 4; qtd. in Melnyk, *One Hundred Years*, 67.
47 Grierson, 'Film,' 64; qtd. in Gittings, *Canadian National Cinema*, 80.
48 Gittings, *Canadian National Cinema*, 81–6.
49 Ibid., 83, Gittings's emphasis.
50 Jones, *Movies and Memoranda*, 57–8.
51 Waugh, 'Cinemas, Nations, Masculinities,' 36.
52 Druick, *Projecting Canada*, 74.
53 Waugh, 'Cinemas, Nations, Masculinities,' 36.
54 G. Evans, *In the National Interest*, 68.
55 Ibid., 70–5.
56 Ibid., 75.
57 Leach, *Film in Canada*, 13.
58 Melnyk, *One Hundred Years*, 75.
59 Leach, *Film in Canada*, 12.
60 Ibid.

61 Marshall, *Quebec National Cinema*, 20.
62 Ibid.
63 Dick, 'Regionalization,' 110; qtd. in Gittings, *Canadian National Cinema*, 89.
64 Gittings, *Canadian National Cinema*, 90.
65 Ibid., 215.
66 Melnyk, *One Hundred Years*, 101.
67 Marshall, *Quebec National Cinema*, 21.
68 Ibid., 23.
69 Ibid., 27.
70 Koc, 'I'm Just a Simple Filmmaker.'
71 Leach, *Claude Jutra*, 134.
72 As Marshall notes, Jos's rebellious attitude inevitably recalls the 1949 miners' strike at nearby Asbestos, Quebec (*Quebec National Cinema*, 141).
73 Ibid., 142.
74 Leach, *Claude Jutra*, 139.
75 Leach, *Claude Jutra*, 138; Marshall, *Quebec National Cinema*, 142.
76 Melnyk, *One Hundred Years*, 119.
77 Cronenberg, *Cronenberg on Cronenberg*, 36.
78 In an essay published on the occasion of a retrospective of Owen's work at TIFF, Gravestock makes the case for a re-evaluation of the director's oeuvre, blaming the critical community on being unable to see him as anything other than a one-shot 'anomaly, before the real history of Canadian cinema began' ('An Excerpt').
79 Melnyk, *One Hundred Years*, 103–4.
80 Feldman, 'Married Couple.'
81 Feldman, 'Allan King.' The quote is from Leach, *Film in Canada*, 19.
82 Spaner, *Dreaming in the Rain*, 35–46.
83 Ibid.; CFE, 'Larry Kent.'
84 CFE, 'Larry Kent.'
85 Melnyk, *One Hundred Years*, 109.
86 Byford, 'Highway 61,' 12.
87 Ramsay, 'Canadian Narrative,' 38.
88 Melnyk, *One Hundred Years*, 111.
89 Pittman, 'Shebib,' 110.
90 Dorland, *So Close*, 6–7.
91 Schwartz, 'Enchanted & Ominous.'
92 Urquhart, 'You Should Know,' 66–7.
93 Ibid., 65. For a brief account, see Morris and McIntosh, 'Capital Cost Allowance.'
94 Wise, 'Up from the Underground,' 102–3. The entire archive of *Cinema Canada* has been digitized, and is available at the Athabasca University Library Digitization Portal: http://cinemacanada.athabascau.ca/index.php/cinema/index.
95 Vatnsdal, *They Came*, 12, 14.
96 Urquhart, 'You Should Know,' 71–7; and 'Film History/Film Policy,' 29–54.
97 Vatnsdal, *They Came*, 147–50, 164–5, 229–31.
98 I address further arguments regarding genre and national cinema in chapter 6.
99 Vatnsdal, *They Came*, 12.
100 According to Urquhart, there is also a plausible economic argument to be made that

the increase in privately invested funds prompted by the CCA actually freed up CFDC money for investment in films with '100 percent Canadian entrepreneurial, creative, and technical content' – that is, the type of film that TFC would soon be promoting ('Film History/Film Policy,' 37–8).

2. The Anxiety of Influence: David Cronenberg and the Canadian Imagination

1 Cronenberg, Interview, 179.
2 Lowry, 'Biography.'
3 Mathijs, *Cronenberg*.
4 Mathijs, *Cronenberg*; Beard, *Artist as Monster*; M. Browning, *David Cronenberg*.
5 I address these issues in chapter 4 and in 'Across the Great Divide.'
6 I borrow the term from Beard, 'Canadianness.'
7 Morris, *David Cronenberg*, 13–14.
8 Cronenberg, *Cronenberg on Cronenberg*, 2–3.
9 Ibid., 3.
10 Ibid.
11 Mathijs, *Cronenberg*, 135.
12 Cronenberg, *Cronenberg on Cronenberg*, 145; Mathijs, *Cronenberg*, 135.
13 Cronenberg, *Cronenberg on Cronenberg*, 138–9.
14 Ibid., 144.
15 This formulation of the apparent contradiction comes from Mathijs, *Cronenberg*, 5.
16 Cronenberg, *Cronenberg on Cronenberg*, 139, 143.
17 Beard, *Artist as Monster*, 234–76.
18 Cronenberg, *Cronenberg on Cronenberg*, 144.
19 Morris, *David Cronenberg*, 24, 26.
20 Cronenberg, *Cronenberg on Cronenberg*, 10. For an account of these years in Toronto, see Wise, 'Up from the Underground.'
21 Cronenberg, *Cronenberg on Cronenberg*, 27.
22 Ibid., 26.
23 Beard, *Artist as Monster*, 515n24.
24 Consequently, while I agree with Sanjek that the shift in visual style 'compromises [Cronenberg's] distance from the material,' I do not read that compromise wholly negatively, nor do I believe the aquatic setting is solely to be 'parodying "free love" or equating 'unrestrained human sexuality in general with disease and female sexuality in particular with predatory violence' ('Dr. Hobbes's Parasites,' 66–7). Precisely in the shift to a different, less distanced aesthetic mode, we find an investment in the material far more complex and ambiguous than can be encompassed by these polarized terms.
25 Mathijs, *Cronenberg*, 23.
26 Morris, *David Cronenberg*, 54.
27 Cronenberg, *Cronenberg on Cronenberg*, 35.
28 Mathijs, *Cronenberg*, 45, 49, 54.
29 Handling first broached the subject and noted the resemblance of Cronenberg's protagonists to the Canadian model of the loser hero in 'Canadian Cronenberg,' 105.
30 Morris, *David Cronenberg*, 12.

31 McGregor, 'Grounding the Countertext'; Beard, 'Canadianness'; Testa, 'Technology's Body.'.
32 Testa, 'Technology's Body,' 50; Beard, 'Canadianness.'
33 Testa, 'Technology's Body,' 39. For a more extended discussion of popular Canadian genres, see chapter 6.
34 Morris, *David Cronenberg*, 73. See also Mathijs's thorough account of the controversy (*Cronenberg*, 44–8).
35 Beard, 'Canadianness.'
36 Ibid.
37 Lowenstein also takes issue with Beard's 'artificially separating one element from the other, [or] of dividing them neatly into "Canadian" or "American" components, [or] of determining one's ultimate domination of the other' ('Canadian Horror,' 42).
38 Cronenberg, *Cronenberg on Cronenberg*, 36.
39 Ibid.
40 Ibid., 35–6.
41 Ibid., 37.
42 Mathijs, *Cronenberg*, 42.
43 Morris, *David Cronenberg*, 106–7.
44 McKellar, 'Children of Canada,' 58.
45 Cronenberg, 'Existential Deal,' 47.
46 Anderson, 'Comedy of Terror,' 15; qtd. in Mathijs, *Cronenberg*, 250.
47 Cronenberg, *Cronenberg on Cronenberg*, 41.
48 This last phrase, somewhat reductively rendered here, is the central thesis of Beard's *Artist as Monster*.
49 Qtd. in Morris, *Cronenberg*, 106.
50 Mathijs, *Cronenberg*, 57; the words are cinematographer Mark Irwin's from an interview in the extras of the DVD of the film.
51 Ibid., 58.
52 See Mathijs's discussion of the curious fate of this scene (Ibid., 59).
53 Ibid., 67.
54 Dee, 'David Cronenberg's Body Language,' 79.
55 Morris, *David Cronenberg*, 85.
56 Govier, 'Middle-class shivers'; qtd. in Morris, *David Cronenberg*, 84; and Mathijs, *Cronenberg*, 63.
57 Morris, *David Cronenberg*, 84.
58 Cronenberg, 'Film Director as Philosopher,' 8.
59 The quote is from Cronenberg, *Cronenberg on Cronenberg*, 84.
60 Vatnsdal, *They Came*, 122.
61 Cronenberg, *Cronenberg on Cronenberg*, 85.
62 Dee, 'David Cronenberg's Body Language,' 79.
63 Martin Scorsese called this 'last scene, with the cast going out to infect the entire world with sexual dementia' something he's 'never been able to shake. It's an ending that is genuinely shocking, subversive, surrealistic, and probably something we all deserve.' (Qtd. in Jaehne, 'Double Trouble,' 20.)
64 Mathijs, *Cronenberg*, 141.

65 McKellar, 'Children of Canada,' 59.
66 The term 'hyper-realism' comes from Cronenberg, 'The Existential Deal,' 51.
67 Mathijs, *Cronenberg*, 69.
68 Ibid.
69 'I wanted them to be fast, brutal and over before you knew it. There's not one foot of slow motion. No repeated shots. I wanted to make them realistic in a cinematic way, because it's the aftermath that is delicious: that can be savoured and apprehended by the senses. What happens during a crash itself is too fast to feel without slow-motion replay. Most of us don't get replays on our car crashes' (Cronenberg, 'David Cronenberg Talks').
70 Mathijs, *Cronenberg*, 69.
71 Jaehne, 'Double Trouble,' 22.
72 Morris, *David Cronenberg*, 107.
73 Dompierre, *Prent/Cronenberg*, 107.
74 Morris, *David Cronenberg*, 107.
75 Hantke, 'Spectacular Optics,' 46.
76 Ibid., 47.
77 Ibid.
78 Ibid., 48.
79 Shaviro, *Cinematic Body*, 151.
80 Although disputed, this modelling is a commonplace of film theory on spectatorship and viewing position. See in particular Heath, 'Notes on Suture.'
81 Shaviro, *Cinematic Body*, 151.
82 This doubleness ought to stand Mortensen in good stead in his star turn as Sigmund Freud in Cronenberg's next film, *A Dangerous Method* (2011), an adaptation of Christopher Hampton's drama about the birth of psychoanalysis out of Freud's tempestuous relationship with Carl Jung. (Unfortunately, this book went to press before the release of the film allowed me to verify this supposition.)
83 Cronenberg, 'David Cronenberg Talks.'
84 For a full account, see Barker, Arthurs, and Harindranath, *The Crash Controversy*.
85 Mathijs, *Cronenberg*, 188.
86 Cronenberg, 'Logic, Creativity,' 180.
87 Cronenberg, 'David Cronenberg Talks.'
88 Ballard, 'Introduction,' 6.
89 Sinclair, *Crash*, 105.
90 Cronenberg, *Interviews with Serge Grünberg*, 31–2; qtd. in M. Browning, *David Cronenberg*, 151.
91 Cronenberg, 'David Cronenberg Talks.'
92 Ibid.
93 Dillon, 'Existence or *eXistenZ*,' 56–7.
94 *A Dangerous Method* follows the pattern of *Eastern Promises* by shooting in Germany, Austria, Switzerland, with studio work in Westphalia and in the venerable Babelsberg studios outside Berlin.
95 Cronenberg, 'Existential Deal,' 39–40. Cronenberg would have been eleven years old.
96 Taubin, 'Foreign Affairs,' 55.

3. Time Capsules: The Eighties Worlds of Denys Arcand and Patricia Rozema

1 Rozema, Interview by Wyndham Wise, 12.
2 See, for example, ibid., 26.
3 Sterritt, 'Review.'
4 Rozema, 'Commentary.'
5 Of *Missing Mother*, Rozema says that there was money on the table to make it after *When Night Is Falling*, but that she 'backed out': 'The script just wasn't there. I just didn't have faith in the material and I couldn't go through with it' (Interview by Wyndham Wise, 30).
6 For a detailed account of the making and marketing of the film, see Posner, *Canadian Dreams*, 1–21.
7 *Rozema, 'I've Heard the Mermaids Singing,'* 22–3.
8 For a discussion of the 1980s context of video 'as a theme in narrative film' (although one that curiously omits *Mermaids*), see Romney, *Atom Egoyan*, 3–4.
9 Cagle, 'Minority,' 183.
10 Lavoie, *'I've Heard the Mermaids Singing,'* 141.
11 Rozema, 'Commentary.'
12 Rozema, 'Interview.'
13 Rozema, Interview by Wyndham Wise, 15.
14 Rozema, 'I've Heard the Mermaids Singing,' 22; Rozema, Interview by Wyndham Wise, 24.
15 Rozema, 'I've Heard the Mermaids Singing,' 22–3.
16 Parpart nicely summarizes the stakes of these feminist arguments and their context in the mid-eighties in 'Political Alignments.'
17 Qtd. in Cagle, 'Minority,' 185.
18 Parpart, 'Political Alignments,' 296.
19 Although this may not be an especially grand claim, *Gina* was, according to Arcand, his 'biggest financial success of the 70s' (Arcand, 'I Only Know,' 145).
20 Coulombe, *Denys Arcand*, 39.
21 Ibid., 40.
22 Arcand, 'Le Documentaire.'
23 Dorland, 'Denys Arcand's *Déclin de l'empire américain*,' 20.
24 Arcand, 'Le Documentaire.'
25 Coulombe, *Denys Arcand*, 27.
26 Ibid., 27–8.
27 Marshall, *Quebec National Cinema*, 153–4.
28 Ibid., 155.
29 La Rochelle, *Denys Arcand*, 138.
30 Coulombe, *Denys Arcand*, 89.
31 Arcand, 'Filmmakers and Advertising,' 335.
32 Ibid., 333.
33 Ibid.
34 Jean-Claude Lauzon supported himself with work in commercials in the late eighties and early nineties (see chapter 5). It would become common by the nineties for film-

makers such as André Turpin and Denis Villeneuve to move openly back and forth between commercials and feature film-making, although it continued to be viewed as an aesthetic choice. According to veteran Montreal producer Bob Presner, the unspoken practice dates back to the early seventies: 'During that time, the people who were directing these things included Francis Mankiewicz and Gilles Carle. All of the directors who were making movies or who wanted to make movies would moonlight on TV commercials because it paid very well, and there was no other way to earn a living' ('Interview').

35 Posner, *Canadian Dreams*, 222.
36 Marshall, *Quebec National Cinema*, 285–312.
37 Coulombe, *Denys Arcand*, 118-19.
38 La Rochelle, *Denys Arcand*, 223.
39 According to Loiselle and McSorley, this decision was the result of the Alberta Motion Picture Development Corporation's refusal to fund the production due to an excessively Quebecois 'orientation' (*Self Portraits*, 17).
40 La Rochelle, *Denys Arcand*, 199.
41 Ibid., 208, 221–2.
42 Coulombe, *Denys Arcand*, 95. The article was by Richard Martineau, editor-in-chief of *Voir*, an alternative Montreal weekly newspaper.

4. Crossover Icons: The Faces of Canadian Cinema

1 Dyer, *Heavenly Bodies*, ix.
2 Ibid., 2.
3 Hayward, *French National Cinema*, 12.
4 Ibid., 8.
5 Ibid., 12.
6 Mlynek and Pulfer, 'Power Players'; *Canadian Business*, 'Canada's Fourth Annual.' See also Moffitt's half-serious, half tongue-in-cheek checklist of Canadian content on top-rated TV shows on his Buzz Canuck blog ('TV Buzz').
7 Howell, 'Stars Share.' I explore this question in more detail in 'Across the Great Divide.'
8 Marshall, *Quebec National Cinema*, 197.
9 Ibid., 197–8.
10 Ibid., 198.
11 Melnyk, *One Hundred Years*, 95.
12 A. McIntosh, 'Geneviève Bujold.'
13 To be fair, according to Leach, 'Quebec critics were generally more sympathetic to the trilogy … than their English-Canadian counterparts' (*Film in Canada*, 164n1).
14 Almond, 'Paul Almond.'
15 French, 'In the Sun,' 35.
16 Bujold, qtd. in Arnold, 'Banking On Bujold.'
17 A. McIntosh, 'Geneviève Bujold.'
18 The epithet comes from Canadian critic Robert Martin's review of the film 'Dr. Bujold's Skill.'

19 Arnold, '*Coma*.'

20 Martin, 'Dr. Bujold's Skill.'

21 Ibid.

22 Jeremy Irons would win the Genie award as best actor; Bujold was nominated, but lost out in the film's near sweep of the awards to Jackie Burroughs's controversial performance in *A Winter Tan*.

23 Smith, 'Alan Rudolph,' 61.

24 Knelman, 'Mature Bujold.'

25 McKellar and Rennie would in fact both have been in high school at the time *Coma* was released.

26 Taubin, 'Death Be Not Proud,' 140.

27 Gerard Peary, 'Babes in Bovland,' *Take One* 8 (Summer 1995); qtd. in Alioff, 'Healing Beauty.'

28 Conlogue, 'Unquenchable Sizzle.'

29 The words are Alioff's in 'Healing Beauty.'

30 Marshall, *Quebec National Cinema*, 100.

31 The quote is from Leach, *Film in Canada*, 63–5; on these issues, see also Handling, 'Gilles Carle.'

32 Leach, *Film in Canada*, 66–7.

33 Laure denies the rumours about her quarrels with the director, claiming she went to court 'to get the producers to stop saying I was against the film and Dusan' (Scott, 'Ooh That Is Wonderful'). Elsewhere, however, she says that she quit the film before it was finished (Godfrey, 'I Wanted to Be a Singer'). On the ban, see Privett, 'Country of Movies.' The 2007 Criterion Collection DVD release somewhat mitigates the ban.

34 A. McIntosh, 'Carole Laure.'

35 See, for instance, the way Quebecois blogger Marc-André Lussier refers back to *La Mort d'un bûcheron* to discuss his sense that Laure has regained a place in the 'collective French imaginary' ('Carole Laure').

36 Scott, 'Ooh That Is Wonderful.'

37 Kelly, 'Actress Laure.'

38 Dickinson, 'Being at Home.'

39 Bawden, 'Translating Success.'

40 Hays, 'Two Solitudes.'

41 Dickinson, 'Being at Home.'

42 Ibid.

43 Adilman, 'Director's Reputation.'

44 Marshall, *Quebec National Cinema*, 202.

45 Ibid., 203.

46 Dickinson, 'Being at Home.'

47 Roy Dupuis Online, '*Montreal Mirror*.'

48 The quarrel is recorded on *Roy Dupuis Online*: http://www.roydupuis-online.com/library/f_magazines/24images01.htm (accessed 13 July 2009).

49 Provencher, 'Marie-Josée Croze.'

50 Helm, 'Actor Rennie.'

51 Bawden, 'Late Bloomer.'

52 Helm, 'Actor Rennie.'
53 Posner, 'Get This Man a Script.'
54 Ibid.
55 'Callum Heads South,' *Bath Chronicle*, 30 May 1998: 5 (LexisNexis Academic); quote from Kirkland, 'You Can Just Call.'
56 Kirkland, 'You Can Just Call.'
57 Digital Chosunilbo, 'Sandra Oh.'
58 Kirkland, 'It's the Work.'
59 Cuthbert, 'Living in the Moment.'
60 Ibid.
61 Digital Chosunilbo, 'Sandra Oh.'
62 Elber, 'Actress'; Cunningham, 'Sandra Oh's Cutting Edge.'
63 Kirkland, 'Glad To Be'; Cunningham, 'Sandra Oh's Cutting Edge.'
64 Page, 'Oh La La'; Digital Chosunilbo, 'Sandra Oh.'
65 Adilman, 'A Career Comes Alive.'
66 George, 'Hollywood/Mollywood.'
67 Braun, 'T&A Takes Over'; S. Smith, '24.'
68 The label comes from the plot summary at IMDB.com (accessed 16 July 2009).
69 DeMara, 'One Woman's Literary Mission.'
70 Torregrosa, '*L Word* Star.'
71 Onstad, 'An Actress.'
72 Conant, 'No Hype, Please.' For a broader analysis of the culturally flattening effect of Disney on the show's production, see Kotsopoulos, 'L.M. Montgomery,' 277–81.
73 Conant, 'No Hype, Please.'
74 C. Taylor, 'Paradoxes.'
75 Johnson, 'Living Dead.'
76 Ibid.
77 Conant, 'No Hype, Please.'
78 For this quote, and on Disney's influence in general, see B. Lefebvre, '*Road to Avonlea*,' 175; for an argument on the complexity of the cultural reception of the show, see Kotsopoulos, 'L.M. Montgomery,' 281.
79 Onstad, 'An Actress.'
80 Polley, 'The New Catchers in the Rye.'
81 Ibid.
82 B. Kelly, 'Featured Player.'
83 Dillon, 'An Elegy,' 68.
84 R. Kelly, 'Last Night.'
85 McKellar, 'Canadian Style.'
86 Varga, 'Locating the Artist,' 102. The second quotation is from Rosadiuk, 'Thirty Two Short Films,' 164.
87 Varga, 'Locating the Artist,' 104.
88 Ibid, 105.
89 Trelkubrations, 'Les meilleurs films québécois.'
90 B. Kelly, 'Small Screen.'
91 Varga, 'Locating the Artist,' 107.
92 Longfellow, '*The Red Violin*,' 12.

5. Quebecois Auteurs: The New Internationalism of Jean-Claude Lauzon, Léa Pool, and Robert Lepage

1 MacKenzie, *Screening Quebec*, 172.
2 Wise, 'Robert Lantos.'
3 Ibid.
4 Adilman, 'Quebec director Lauzon.'
5 Gerstel, 'Quebec.'
6 Ibid.
7 Lauzon, 'It Is an Image,' 125–6.
8 Melnyk, *One Hundred Years*, 201.
9 Canuel et al., 'Table ronde,' 16.
10 Scott, 'Canada's *Zoo*.'
11 Marshall, *Quebec National Cinema*, 113.
12 Ibid.
13 Ibid., 114.
14 Scott, 'Canada's *Zoo*.'
15 Scott, '*Un zoo la nuit*.'
16 Marshall, *Quebec National Cinema*, 115.
17 Ibid.
18 Leach, 'It Takes Monsters,' 55.
19 Lauzon, 'It Is an Image,' 118.
20 Ibid., 127.
21 Leach rightly observes that the translation of *Dompteur des vers*, rendered in the English version of the film and by most critics as 'Word Tamer' is, strictly speaking, 'Worm Tamer' ('It Takes Monsters,' 57). Larrivée also notes the distinction, noting also the French homonym of *worm/verses* that presumably led to the translation as 'words' ('Identities and Oppressions,' 91). As in the poetry of one of Lauzon's literary models, Charles Baudelaire, the wordplay of worms/verses emphasizes the tension between the materiality of waste and decomposing bodies and the abstract textuality of verse. On Baudelaire's use of the wordplay, see Pike, *Metropolis*, 130–1.
22 For more on the iconic status of this pair, see Larrivée, 'Identities and Oppressions,' 87.
23 Melnyk, *One Hundred Years*, 204.
24 Lauzon, 'It Is an Image,' 121.
25 Ramsay, 'Léo Who?,' 35.
26 Marshall, *Quebec National Cinema*, 117.
27 Leach, 'It Takes Monsters,' 60.
28 Toles, 'Drowning for Love,' 287.
29 Leach, 'It Takes Monsters,' 57. See also Garrity, who emphasizes the temporal disjunction between the image and the voice-over track ('True Lies,' 82).
30 For a discussion of the film's use of the novel and a comparison of the depiction of dysfunctional families in each, see W. Browning, 'Chilling Childhoods.'
31 Corbeil plausibly suggests that we assume Léo was born, like Lauzon, in 1953, which would place the scenes when he is six in the late fifties and those when he is twelve in 1962 ('Indiscreet Charm'; Leach, 'It Takes Monsters,' 56).
32 Leach, 'It Takes Monsters,' 56.

33 Lauzon, 'It Is an Image,' 123.
34 T. Simons gives a complete inventory of the soundtrack in 'Tout le monde croit,' 119–22.
35 Ibid., 122.
36 Ibid., 121.
37 Lauzon, 'It Is an Image,' 122.
38 Toles, 'Drowning for Love,' 299–300.
39 This may partly account for the film's presence at the centre of Loiselle's polemic against the selective reception of Quebecois cinema by anglophone critics, 'The Decline.' While Loiselle is certainly correct regarding the very different reception of Lauzon and other Quebecois art-film directors at home and 'abroad,' a plausible explanation he ignores is that these films interpellate an international rather than solely a local audience.
40 Nadeau notes the 'close association' of feminist criticism with Pool's early films to the point of not even mentioning the later ones ('Représentation,' 87).
41 T. Simons stresses the issue of gender and the refusal of fixed categories in Pool's move beyond 'the purely Quebec context' ('Anne Trister,' 232).
42 On the 'urban coldness' of Pool's vision of women and its 'transformation' of familiar Montreal into a 'foreign milieu,' see Green, 'Léa Pool's,' 57–8.
43 Marshall, Quebec National Cinema, 234.
44 Ibid. For the figure of the wandering Jew, see also Nadeau, 'Représentation,' 88.
45 Gauthier, 'Living In/Between,' 228, 232.
46 Melnyk, One Hundred Years, 177.
47 Gauthier, 'Living In/Between,' 245.
48 For an astute analysis of the situation of women's film-making within Quebec, see Marshall, Quebec National Cinema, 208–31; on Pool's early features in terms of the documentary mode, formal avant-gardism, and the constraints of commercial distribution, see Green, 'Léa Pool's.'
49 Marshall, Quebec National Cinema, 235–6.
50 Green calls attention to the modernist trope of mise en abyme in the film within a film device used in La Femme de l'hôtel ('Léa Pool's,' 54).
51 Kehr, 'Finding Succor.'
52 Longfellow, 'Gender, Landscape,' 176–81.
53 Kaprisky's stateside fame from playing opposite Richard Gere in Jim McBride's steamy Godard remake Breathless (1983) was duly noted by reviewers, as was surprise at the 'unexpected depths' coaxed by Pool out of an actor whose star discourse had not up to that point articulated the necessity of such skills (Harris, 'Film Review').
54 Longfellow, 'Gender, Landscape,' 177.
55 Dunphy, 'Lea Pool.'
56 McSorley, 'Centre,' 284.
57 Kehr, 'Finding Succor.'
58 Dunphy, 'Lea Pool.'
59 W. Browning sees in this lack of identity an 'unspoken homage' to the young Jewish protagonist Berenice in L'avalée des avalés ('Chilling Childhoods,' 565); the allusion is likely filtered through Léolo as well, a restoration of the gender and ethnic identity within Lauzon's Montreal stomping ground.

60 Kelleher, 'Coming of Age,' 30, 40.
61 Scott, *Anne Trister*.'
62 Stone, 'Quebec Director.'
63 Hays, 'Art in the Danger Zone.'
64 Lepage, 'Appendix,' 13.
65 Hays, 'Art in the Danger Zone.'
66 Dundjerovic, *Cinema of Robert Lepage*, 22–4.
67 Ibid., 24.
68 O'Mahony, 'Aerial Views.'
69 Harvie, 'Robert Lepage,' 224–5.
70 O'Mahony, 'Aerial Views.'
71 Ibid.
72 B. Kelly, 'Anything's Possible.'
73 Wolf, 'Robert Lepage'; Napoleon, '*ED* Problem/Solution.'
74 Armistead, 'Pursuit of the Trivial.'
75 Romney, 'In a World or Two.'
76 Ibid.
77 Dickinson accurately summarizes the standard approach as based theoretically on the writings of Gilles Deleuze with recourse to the cinematic influence of Resnais and Hitchcock ('Space, Time,' 133).
78 Dundjerovic, *Cinema of Robert Lepage*, 101–2.
79 Ibid., 128.
80 Donnelly, 'Expanding World.'
81 Ibid.
82 Ibid.
83 Harvie and Hurley, 'States of Play,' 308.
84 Owen, 'Turn Over a New Lepage.'
85 O'Mahony, 'Aerial Views.'
86 Dault, '*Le confessionnal* & *Le polygraphe*,' 19.
87 Cornelius, 'Boxes and Bridges,' 119.
88 P. Clandfield, 'Bridgespotting.'
89 Lepage, 'Appendix,' 153.
90 M. Lefebvre, 'Sense of Time,' 92; qtd. in Dundjerovic, *Cinema of Robert Lepage*, 59. On the specifically Quebecois reception of the 1902 French stage play, see Dickinson, 'Double Take,' 180.
91 Tschofen, '*Le Confessionnal*,' 205.
92 L'Hébreux, *Le Pont de Québec*, 29.
93 P. Clandfield, 'Bridgespotting.'
94 Lepage remarked on the screening at Cannes, 'I thought that for everyone it would be a metaphor for vertigo, an image evoking the danger of living … One day, someone asked, why is someone killing themselves at the end? At Cannes and at Toronto [Film Festival], it was really split 50-50' (qtd. in P. Clandfield, 'Bridgespotting').
95 On the notion of haunting, see Manning, 'Haunted Home,' 49–50; and P. Clandfield, 'Bridgespotting.'
96 The term is from Dundjerovic, *Cinema of Robert Lepage*, 142.

6. Cronenberg's Mutant Progeny: Genre Film-making around the Turn of the Millennium

1 Vatnsdal, *They Came*, provides a comprehensive survey of the horror genre, while touching on other popular forms; Paul Corupe's Canuxploitation.com provides informative, if not always wholly reliable, capsule histories of key genres, a generous sampling of reviews, and a number of informative interviews with Canadian genre film-makers.

2 The films are: *Avatar* (2009, #1), *Titanic* (1997, #2), *Shrek 2* (2004, #5), *Shrek* (2001, #45), *How the Grinch Stole Christmas* (2000, #48), *Bruce Almighty* (2003, #60), *My Big Fat Greek Wedding* (2002, #63), *Ghostbusters* (1984, #64), *Austin Powers in Goldmember* (2002, #87), *Austin Powers: The Spy Who Shagged Me* (1999, #94), and *Terminator 2: Judgment Day* (1991, #96) (IMDB, 'All-Time USA Box Office').

3 See Canada's Awards Database at the Academy of Canadian Cinema and Television (http://www.academy.ca/hist/history.cfm).

4 Pevere and Dymond, *Mondo Canuck*, 112–15, x. For an exaggeratedly polemical but broadly correct elaboration of this position, see Loiselle, 'The Decline.'

5 Marshall, *Quebec National Cinema*, 175.

6 Ibid., 296.

7 Marshall astutely analyses the latter in a separate chapter on 'Popular Cinema' (*Quebec National Cinema*, 172).

8 Ibid., 128–30.

9 Ibid., 296–7. For example, Leach's *Film in Canada*, which devotes three of its scant 160 pages to the use of American genres in *Pouvoir Intime* (52–4), does not mention *Dragon*. This is not meant as a critique, only as symptomatic evidence of the way critical rubrics pre-select canons.

10 Véronneau, 'Genres and Variations,' 96.

11 The earliest systematic analysis of art cinema as a distinct set of conventions and practices, Bordwell's 'Art Cinema,' eschewed the term 'genre' in favour of the vaguer 'mode.' Similarly, Neale took a broader, contextualized approach in terms of public policy in his study of 'Art Cinema as Institution,' although he noted how by 1980 art cinema had begun to gravitate towards specific genres (33). Still, at that point, art cinema could appear to retain some manner of independence or distinction from mainstream commercial film-making. Elsaesser's clear-sighted revisionary reading of Ingmar Bergman's career is able to be far more sanguine about the multiple pressures within art cinema production that in hindsight clearly resemble those inhering in any type of genre production ('Putting on a Show').

12 Elsaesser, 'Putting on a Show,' 23.

13 Altman, *Film/Genre* (London: British Film Institute, 1999), 161–2; qtd. in Grant, 'National Cinema.'

14 For a survey of the different Canadian production companies involved in exploitation, see Canuxploitation, 'From Cinépix to Cineplex.'

15 On the formative role played by sex in the global marketability of the classic art film, see Bordwell, 'Art Cinema,' 57; Elsaesser, 'Putting on a Show,' 25; Neale, 'Art Cinema,' 33.

16 Canuxploitation, 'Back to God's Country.'
17 Ignoring this common ground is a weakness of film critic Katherine Monk's effort to analyse the sex in Canadian cinema, leading her to view it solely in terms of repression and solely in terms of art and independent film (*Weird Sex & Snowshoes*, 119–54).
18 Corupe, 'Sin and Sovereignty.'
19 Cronenberg, *Cronenberg on Cronenberg*, 37. The film would be directed by John Sole and released in 1971. It would gross half a million dollars in its first six months (Cinema Canada, 'Canadian Film News,' 5).
20 Corupe, 'Sin and Sovereignty.'
21 Cronenberg, *Cronenberg on Cronenberg*, 50.
22 Shaviro, *Cinematic Body*, 127, 129, 132.
23 Loiselle, 'Subtly Subversive,' 80; see also Lever, *Histoire*, 305–10.
24 Loiselle, 'Subtly Subversive,' 78.
25 Ibid., 76.
26 Ibid.
27 Ibid.
28 Ibid., 77.
29 Shaviro, *Cinematic Body*, 54.
30 Ibid., 236.
31 Mihalka, 'Interview.'
32 Ibid.
33 Clark, 'Interview.'
34 Ibid.
35 For more on what Corupe terms the 'screwball' comedies of the early eighties, see Canuxploitation, 'Primer.'
36 Thiessen, 'Deconstructing,' 67.
37 Ibid., 71, 73.
38 Ibid., 73.
39 Canuxploitation, 'Primer.'
40 Ibid.
41 Clark, 'Interview.'
42 The partial exception to this rule would be Greyson, whose film-making has alternated between serious but self-reflexive dramas and no-holds-barred carnivalesque genre hybrids (see chapter 8).
43 Loiselle, 'Quebecus Horribilis.'
44 Straw, 'Thingishness of Things.'
45 A. Taylor, 'Blood in the Maple Syrup,' 18–20.
46 Loiselle, 'Quebecus Horribilis.'
47 Vatnsdal, *They Came*, 13.
48 Ibid., 14.
49 A. Taylor, 'Blood in the Maple Syrup,' 22.
50 Vatnsdal, *They Came*, 13.
51 Presner, 'Interview.'
52 Vatnsdal, *They Came*, 148.
53 On *Goin' Down the Road*, see Ramsay, 'Canadian Narrative Cinema'; Melnyk, *One Hundred Years*, 111–12; and the discussion in chapter 1 above.

54 Mihalka, 'Interview.'
55 Ibid.
56 Ibid.
57 Badley, *Film, Horror*, 21; qtd. in Molloy, 'Perpetual Flight.'
58 Loiselle, 'Quebecus Horribilis,' 7.
59 Ibid., 2n1.
60 Coates, *Film*, 176; qtd. in Taylor, 'Blood in the Maple Syrup,' 27.
61 Molloy, 'Perpetual Flight.'
62 Miller, 'The Hair,' 286.
63 Karen Walton, *Ginger Snaps*, DVD Commentary; qtd. in Molloy, 'Perpetual Flight.'
64 Miller, 'The Hair,' 281.
65 Briefel, 'Monster Pains,' 25.
66 Molloy's reading of the trilogy as an integrated allegory of biopolitics in 'Perpetual Flight,' while persuasive at moments, fails to account for the multiple pressures and origins of genre films, and the consequently fragmentary meanings.
67 Cronenberg, *Cronenberg on Cronenberg*, 92.
68 Ibid., 120.
69 Ibid.
70 Jackson and D'or, 'Science Fiction,' 14.
71 According to both David and Cronenberg, the former offered the films to the latter; they differ on the details, but the upshot is that the director declined the offer (A. Jones, *Inside Scan*; Cronenberg, *Cronenberg on Cronenberg*, 92).
72 David Hewlett commented of the night-time winter shoot that the temperature hit as low as –30°C (Warren, 'Typecast at 21').
73 B. Kelly, 'Next Action Hero.'
74 Cowan, 'Canadian Science Fiction.'
75 Jackson and D'or, 'Science Fiction,' 14.
76 Lincoln, 'Cyberpunk on Screen.'
77 Brownstein, 'Ex-Robocop.'
78 Cowan, 'Canadian Science Fiction,' 12.
79 On the situation, the fluently bilingual Montreal native Duguay commented in 1994, 'I have been regularly trashed by much of the press here … They said I was only good for music clips – and much worse. It hurts because I'm a Montrealer – and because I'm treated so well everywhere else' (Brownstein, 'Man behind Dionne Series').
80 Dillon, 'Production Slate,' 16.
81 Elley, 'Film Reviews.'
82 Falcon, 'Reviews.'
83 Taylor, 'Blood in the Maple Syrup,' 26.
84 Ibid., 27.

7. The Death of the Author? The Case of Atom Egoyan

1 The benchmark critical monograph is English critic Romney's thoughtful, exhaustively researched, and conventionally auteurist film-by-film survey (through *Ararat*) *Atom Egoyan*, published in the BFI World Directors series; see also Wilson's briefer *Atom Egoyan*. Kraus's *Bild* uses an equally auteurist but far more theoretically inclined

approach, as does the French essay collection, Desbarats et al., *Atom Egoyan*. Kass Banning's entry in the *CFE* accounts for Egoyan's entire career in plausible, if relentlessly positive, auteurist terms. Along with Romney, R. Masterson's straightforwardly thematic analysis, 'Family Romances,' is the only detailed approach to the mid-career films as a group. The essays collected in Tschofen and Burwell's *Image + Territory* together provide a fairly comprehensive account of the disparate components of Egoyan's career through *Ararat*. Pevere's 'No Place like Home' provides an excellent overview of Egoyan's early career; Tschofen's 'Repetition, Compulsion' is one of the best of many thematic studies.

2 As Romney tactfully but unmistakably calls into question, 'Egoyan's increasing visibility has entailed a change of perception in terms of his authorial voice, which has inevitably come to represent a certain auteur mastery, as opposed to the productively neurotic outsider vulnerability of the early work. It remains to be seen how this will affect Egoyan's future freedom to operate relative to the pressures of audience demand and public image' (*Atom Egoyan*, 13). The determining word here is the adverb 'productively.'

3 The classic collection on auteur theory in its cinephilic and structuralist manifestations, as well as reactions against it, is Caughie, *Theories of Authorship*; for a sanguine approach to auteurism in terms of contemporary cinema and its relation to Hollywood film-making, see Lavery, 'The Movie Artist.' I use the term to describe the mostly unarticulated tendency to use auteurist principles to examine and evaluate Egoyan's film-making as a coherent oeuvre rather than as a strictly delineated theory of cinema.

4 Egoyan labels the dynamic in 'Family Romances,' 9; this theme forms the basis of R. Masterson's analysis (881). On media, see especially Lageira, *Atom Egoyan*; Kraus, *Bild*; Romney, *Atom Egoyan*, 3–6 and 94 (where he even manages to find the theme in Egoyan's hockey biopic *Gross Misconduct* [1992]); and Del Rio, 'The Body.'

5 Wilson, *Atom Egoyan*, ix.

6 Johnson, 'Atom's Journey.' R. Masterson singles out the 'darkest mystery' of incest as the central component of what he sees as the growing emotional maturity and accessibility of the family romance theme in *Exotica* and especially *Sweet Hereafter* ('Family Romances,' 883–8).

7 Egoyan, 'Family Romances,' 12.

8 Egoyan, 'Surface Tension,' 34–5.

9 Burnett, 'Introduction,' 18.

10 Egoyan, 'Difficult to Say,' 60. The need for emotional involvement is much less clear in a 1988 interview made after the release of *Family Viewing*. While it is evident that Egoyan was deeply invested in the film ('the film is very personal'), he seems more concerned with the audience responding to the challenge of the film's aesthetics (Egoyan, 'Atom Egoyan').

11 Egoyan, 'Difficult to Say,' 60.

12 Egoyan, 'Emotional Logic,' 42.

13 As Egoyan put it in interview with film critic Brian Johnson about *Sweet Hereafter*, 'In all my other films, the characters have been fragments or aspects of my own personality. They were people looking for their own identity through rituals or gestures. But they were just shells' ('How Sweet It Is'). See also R. Masterson's discussion of Egoyan's shift away from 'stylization' ('Family Romances,' 884).

14 Egoyan, 'Difficult to Say,' 60.

15 Egoyan, qtd. in Howe, 'Film Notes.'

16 Egoyan's shooting script further developed Karen's relationship to her father (also a reporter) through a reel-to-reel tape player he used at the telethon and which she continued to use in her own reporting as an adult ('Deleted Scenes from *Where the Truth Lies*'). Some early examples of discussion of Lohman's performance in what became a leitmotif of reviews: McCarthy, '*Where the Truth Lies*'; James, 'Right Stuff'; Howell, 'Souls for Sale.'

17 Johnson, 'How Sweet'; evidently, it was Khanjian who initially persuaded Egoyan to consider adapting Banks's novel (Howell, 'Egoyan's Muse').

18 Egoyan has increasingly incorporated the cell phone, along with the laptop, as a contemporary mode of mediated communication, into his films. Wireless communication plays a central role in *Adoration*, where it documents the viral spread of Simon's performance piece; in *Chloe*, where a text message initiates the wife's suspicion of her husband's infidelity and she is able to overhear (and be spotted overhearing) her son's cell phone and video conversations; and most strikingly in *Artaud Double Bill*, the short metacinematic piece Egoyan contributed to the Cannes Film Festival commemorative omnibus film, *Chacun son cinema* (2007), in which two women text each other from adjacent screenings of Godard's *Vivre sa vie* (1962) and Egoyan's own *The Adjuster* – in the contest for the women's attention, the former (and its embedded footage of Dreyer's *La Passion de Jeanne d'Arc* [1928]) wins out over the latter.

19 See Beavis, '*Sweet Hereafter*'; S. Dillon, 'Lyricism and Accident,' 228; Weese, 'Family Stories'; Romney, *Atom Egoyan*, 135–7.

20 Johnson 'How Sweet'; Egoyan, 'Family Romances,' 10. See also Egoyan's discussion of the ambiguity of 'the most controversial scene in the film' in the audio commentary to the DVD.

21 Banks, *Sweet Hereafter*, 254.

22 Hunter, '*Felicia's Journey*'; Egoyan says that the only scene in which he thought of Hitchcock explicitly was the one of *Salome* (qtd. in Schaefer, 'Egoyan Embarks'). Egoyan pays a great deal of attention to both myths in his audio commentary to the DVD of the film; in interviews (*Toronto Star*, 'Applause') and on the audio commentary, he has also mentioned the influence of Jean Cocteau's *Beauty and the Beast* (1946), in particular on the dreamlike scene where Felicia wanders the hallways of Hilditch's house while he is at work.

23 On Egoyan's production of *Salomé*, see Armatage and Clark, 'Seeing and Hearing.'

24 Egoyan, 'Politics of Denial,' 39–41. Schaefer also lightly touches on the allusion ('Egoyan Embarks'), as does Rosen, 'Hoskins, Egoyan.'

25 Denial figures most prominently in Egoyan's myriad comments to journalists regarding the impact of historical events on personal lives in *Ararat*; see also his detailed discussion of the issues in 'In Other Words.' In his audio commentary on *Felicia's Journey*, Egoyan discusses the secrecy as part of Hilditch's lack of awareness of his own actions (Egoyan, 'Politics of Denial').

26 Egoyan, 'Politics of Denial'; Egoyan makes a similar comment in Schaefer, 'Egoyan Embarks.'

27 As Egoyan put it in a widely quoted, if disturbingly reductive, comment, Hilditch 'may be the first monster that television created' (qtd. in *Toronto Star*, 'Applause').

Howell quotes the comment somewhat dubiously in his review of the film, 'Modern Horror Story.'

28 As one unconvinced reviewer put it, Lohman's character 'reads as so naïve, there is something pedophilic about the sex scenes' (Levine, 'Strange Brew'). Nevertheless, the overlay of drug anthem 'White Rabbit' onto the sequence ensures that the dominant note is hallucinatory hedonism.

29 Since Egoyan has suggested both reasons, although never at the same time, I am assuming that, as with many such decisions, they had equal weight notwithstanding the radically different spheres in which the weight of each reason would have asserted itself. For the artistic version, see Stone, 'Egoyan'; Gabereau, 'Portrait'; Egoyan says something similar in *Making of Ararat* (2003). For the lack of budget version, see McKay, 'Already Hot.'

30 Indeed, in the shooting script, the perspective of a fourth child, David's grandson Tony, equally structured perception of that family romance around the story of Noah's ark (Egoyan, *Ararat*, 6–7, 15–17, 76–8). Egoyan shot all of the scenes from this thread of the narrative, and speaks wistfully of the need to cut them ('Audio Commentary to Deleted Scenes'). Only the middle of these scenes survived in the final cut, along with a related scene where Ali's excitement at hearing about getting the part of Jevdet Bey is played out in the museum in front of a school group of kids for whom Ali immediately puts on his stage villainy act.

31 On Egoyan's long-time desire to make the film, see 'In Other Words,' 887.

32 Here, too, material excised in the final cut amplifies this relationship. The encounter with Raffi that concludes in the scene in which Celia urges him, in her only seemingly unselfish moment, to travel to the land around Ararat to find meaning begins with her ignoring her lover's dilemma by typing away at her keyboard. Another scene had her visiting the site of her father's death, simulating the plummeting height through a vertiginously held video camera.

33 Egoyan, 'Politics of Denial,' 41. In addition to location work in Los Angeles and Toronto (masquerading as New York City), *Where the Truth Lies* was also shot at Shepperton.

34 Nowhere has that difference been made more evident to me than in a question Egoyan received at the screening of the film during the New York Film Festival asking him the address of the club in Toronto. The director's understandably nonplussed and dismissive response to the question nevertheless ignored its emergence out of the success of the film's fundamental premise.

35 *Variety* reviewer Todd McCarthy (somewhat unfairly) called the attempt to recreate the ambiance of the duo's act 'half-hearted' and deemed the period detail 'uneven.'

36 To be sure, one could argue that the origin of these images lies in the 16 mm shots of Armenia that represent the experience of the photographer's wife and the guide beyond the viewfinder that traps the photographer. But precisely to the extent that our perceptions are limited to those of the photographer, the only thing the beauty of those rural images can be said to represent is what the photographer is unable to experience.

37 The excised scene and Egoyan's commentary are included on the bonus disk to the *Ararat* DVD.

38 Egoyan, *Ararat*, 83. According to Egoyan's audio commentary on the DVD, the background setting was shot in Alberta and the extras were digitally added later; Gabereau

adds the detail that it was Drumheller, Alberta, matched to surreptitiously shot DV camera footage of Armenian hills.

39 Banks, *Sweet Hereafter*, 99. In the novel, Stephens's pronouncement comes near the beginning of his central monologue, in a general, private meditation of the fate of the people of Sam Dent, rather than in the conversational interchange in which Egoyan resituated it.

40 Indeed, writing from Cannes after Cronenberg's *History of Violence* and Egoyan's *Where the Truth Lies* were shut out of prizes because of their perceived commercialism, the *Toronto Star* directly ascribed the shift in direction of this pair of films to the directors' frustration at Telefilm Canada's recently departed director Richard Stursberg's push to link film funding to commercial viability (*Toronto Star*, 'Lessons Can Be Found').

41 Finlay, 'Atom Egoyan on Set'; Dwyer, 'Atomic Power'; Johnson, 'Atom's Journey'; Klawans, 'Getting inside.'

42 As quoted by David Spaner in the *Vancouver Province* on the occasion of the film's premiere in Egoyan's home town, the director had the '"romantic idea" to assemble for Ararat as many accomplished actors with Armenian backgrounds as possible' ('Egoyan Returns to His Roots').

43 Egoyan and Khanjian discussed the importance of this 1985 episode in their own lives, and implicitly, in *Ararat*, in a three-way phone conversation with Richard Ouzonian on the occasion of the gala opening-night screening of the film at the Toronto International Film Festival ('Dealing with the Ghosts').

44 As *New Yorker* reviewer Anthony Lane brutally but aptly summarized the dilemma: 'This was new to me: the emotionally useful genocide' ('Worlds Apart').

45 Characteristically, the irritation is an intentional effect on Egoyan's part: '"Of all people, Ani is someone who should understand what the effects of denial are," Mr. Egoyan said. "And yet, she's in a very privileged position where she refuses to acknowledge another woman's history. And that privilege takes a huge emotional toll on someone."' (Whyte, 'Facing the Pain'). The problem is, this typical Egoyan manoeuvre functions far differently in the vast canvas of *Ararat* than in the intimate milieus of his previous films.

46 The notable exception is the completist Romney, who instead manages to find the auteurist stamp on everything Egoyan has ever done. Wilson notes that the complete Egoyan retrospective at the Centre Pompidou in Paris included his work for television (*Atom Egoyan*, x).

47 Egoyan, 'Spellbound.' Note, however, how the issue never arose (from either party) in the detailed discussion of Hitchcock in the intellectual, left-leaning film journal *Cineaste* (Egoyan, 'Politics of Denial,').

48 For more on *Krapp's Last Tape*, see Pike, 'The Passing of Celluloid'; and Romney, *Atom Egoyan*, 158–70.

49 The Médiathèque of the Musée d'art contemporain in Montreal provides a complete list up to 2002.

50 Egoyan and cinematographer Paul Sarossy screened Kazan's 1963 turn-of-the-century story of a Greek boy escaping Turkish oppression in considering the visual look of the film within a film (Dillon, 'Egoyan').

51 Egoyan and Balfour, *Subtitles*.

52 Stoffman, 'A Film'; Ellis, 'Ready for Its Closeup'; Davidson, 'Lights, Camera, Drinks.'

53 For more on these two films and their paradoxically local and global concerns, see Pike, Review of *Adoration* and Review of *Chloe*.
54 McSorley, 'How Do We Know,' 24.

8. The Canadian Mosaic: Margins and Ethnicities

1 Bassin, 'John Murray Gibbon'; B., 'John Murray Gibbon.'
2 Milroy, 'Sound of a Canadian Identity.'
3 Cecil Foster, 'Jan Carew,' 3–5.
4 Foster notes that the Massey Commission, instrumental in establishing modern governmental support for cultural activity (including cinema), along with the Royal Commission on Bilingualism and Biculturalism, 'gave shape to the modern Canadian nation' (Ibid., 5).
5 Higson, 'Concept of National Cinema,' 43.
6 Gin, 'Les bifurcations culturelles,' 32–3.
7 Straw, 'Thingishness of Things.'
8 Ibid.
9 Qtd. in Simmons, 'Border Crossings,' 58.
10 Byford, 'Highway 61,' 16.
11 Simmons, 'Border Crossings,' 58.
12 Keohane, 'Symptoms of Canada,' 32.
13 Wilson, 'You Can Go Home Again.'
14 Cinexus Productions Press Kit 1993, 8; qtd. in Gittings, *Canadian National Cinema*, 208.
15 Marshall, *Quebec National Cinema*, 192–3.
16 Varga, 'The Local and the Global,' 34.
17 Ibid., 33–4.
18 Quebec's funding agency, now known as SODEC (Société de développement des entreprises culturelles), was established in 1977; the AMPDC (Alberta Motion Picture Development Corporation, now Alberta Film Development Program) in 1981; the OFDC (now Ontario Media Development Corporation) in 1986; the Film Development Society of British Columbia, or BC Film, in 1987; CIDO (the Manitoba Cultural Industries Development Office, now Manitoba Film and Sound) in 1987; the Saskatchewan Film Development Corporation in 1989; and film development corporations in Nova Scotia, and Newfoundland and Labrador in the 1990s (Loiselle and McSorley, 'Introduction,' 16).
19 Bailey, 'Standing in the Kitchen'; Glassman, 'Toronto New Wave.'
20 Ramsay, 'Made in Saskatchewan!' 220–2.
21 D. Clandfield, *Canadian Film*, 105; qtd. in Austin-Smith, 'Strange Frontiers,' 255.
22 Austin-Smith, 'Strange Frontiers,' 238.
23 Longfellow, 'Counter-Narratives,' 70.
24 Varga, 'The Local and the Global Revisited,' 30.
25 Anderlini, 'West Coast Nouvelle Vague,' 1; qtd. in Burgess, 'Charting the Course,' 29. In 'Air Bud,' Burgess attributes the coining to journalist Cori Howard (150).
26 Burgess, 'Charting the Course,' 31.
27 Ibid., 30.
28 Ibid., 31.

29 Peranson, 'Riding the Pacific New Wave.'
30 In Spaner, *Dreaming in the Rain*, 211; also in Burgess, 'Air Bud,' 129.
31 Burgess, 'Charting the Course,' 32.
32 Burgess, 'Air Bud,' 159.
33 Note, however, the irony reported by Jerry White: as a result of funding cuts to the Alberta Motion Picture Development Corporation, Burns was compelled to shift production of *Kitchen Party* to British Columbia, resulting in production decisions rendering its world 'literally ... a faceless suburb' rather than a continuing 'meditation' on the 'impossibly sprawling suburbs' of Calgary in particular ('Typically Canadian,' 309).
34 Grady, 'Mining the Urban Core.'
35 In Melnyk, *One Hundred Years*, 220.
36 B. Kelly, 'Urban Paranoia Runs Deep.'
37 For details on the vagaries of support for film-making in Alberta, see White, 'Typically Canadian.'
38 Beaty, 'Coward, Bully, and Clown,' 322.
39 Golfman, 'Imagining Region,' 47.
40 McSorley, 'Centre,' 274–6.
41 For studies of the region's film-making, see Golfman, 'Imagining Region'; and McSorley, 'Centre.'
42 Macdonald, 'East Coast Update'; Cox, 'Salter Street Films to Close.'
43 Golfman, 'Imagining Region,' 54.
44 The quote is from McSorley, 'Centre,' 289; see also 272.
45 The quote is from MacGillivray, 'Sitting in the Dark,' 18.
46 Wood, 'On William D. MacGillivray,' 30.
47 Although he agrees that MacGillivray develops this appropriation, McSorley takes a more traditionally dubious overall stance towards the 'processes of cultural imperialism' ('Centre,' 287–8).
48 Austin-Smith, 'Strange Frontiers,' 246–7.
49 Erbach, 'From an Interview.' On the importance of the support of the co-op system, see White, 'Typically Canadian,' 304.
50 Binning, 'Prairie Populism.'
51 The term was coined by Pevere in 'Prairie Postmodern.'
52 Lesk, 'Caress, Denial, Decay.'
53 Arroyo, 'Bordwell Considered,' 77.
54 Pevere, 'Greenland Revisited'; Pevere, 'Prairie Postmodern'; Cagle, 'Persistence of Vision.'
55 For Paizs on *Crime Wave*, see Cagle, 'Persistence of Vision,' 49; on *Kids in the Hall*, see Paizs 'Interview'; on *Top of the Food Chain*, see Paizs, Interview with Jason Anderson.
56 Gonick, 'Fires Were Started.'
57 Ibid.
58 Ibid.
59 Brand, 'Notes,' 173–4, qtd. in Gittings, *Canadian National Cinema*, 231.
60 Gittings, *Canadian National Cinema*, 232.
61 Lee, 'Coming Attractions,' 8; qtd. in Gittings, *Canadian National Cinema*, 255.
62 Kunuk, 'Interview.'
63 Clandfield, *Canadian Film*, 105.

64 Foster, *A Place Called Heaven*, 25; qtd. in Gittings, *Canadian National Cinema*, 256.

65 Levitin, 'Mina Shum,' 274.

66 Gittings, *Canadian National Cinema*, 255.

67 Virgo, 'Interview'; qtd. in Gittings, *Canadian National Cinema*, 259.

68 Erbach, 'From an Interview,' 28.

69 Krishna, 'What the Story Is.'

70 Ibid., 42.

71 Gittings, *Canadian National Cinema*, 252–3.

72 Khanna, 'Masala Take Two,' 16; qtd. in Gittings, *Canadian National Cinema*, 255.

73 Hall, *Questions of Cultural Identity*, 1–17.

74 For a study of Armenian identity within Egoyan's work in the light of *Ararat*, see Siraganian, 'Telling a Horror Story.'

75 Qtd. in Silverman, '*Dead Man*,' 184.

76 Marshall, *Quebec National Cinema*, 240–1.

77 White, 'Alanis Obomsawin,' 364.

78 Kunuk, 'Interview.'

79 Marshall, *Quebec National Cinema*, 239.

80 Ibid., 240, 244.

81 Gittings, *Canadian National Cinema*, 198–215.

82 Ibid., 20

83 Marshall, *Quebec National Cinema*, 248.

84 Pevere, 'Dances with Natives,' 214.

85 Lusty, '*Dance Me Outside*,' 18; qtd. in Pevere, 'Dances with Natives'; Gittings, *Canadian National Cinema*, 214.

86 Baldessare, *Reel Canadians*, 79.

87 Kirkland, 'Digging Fencepost.'

88 Paizs, 'Interview.'

89 *Atanarjuat* grossed $3,789,952 in North America and $5,188,289 worldwide (boxoffice-mojo.com, accessed 6 May 2010), well over double its production cost.

90 On the film's production, see M.R. Evans, *Fast Runner*.

91 Kunuk, 'Interview.'

92 Varga, '*Atanarjuat*,' 226.

93 Qtd. in Varga, '*Atanarjuat*,' 231.

94 Ibid., 232. For three variants of the legend 'in circulation in the Igloolik area' and a discussion of their relation to the screenplay, see M.R. Evans, *Isuma*, 76–100, and *Fast Runner*, 63–85.

95 Knopf, *Decolonizing*, 318–19.

96 Gauthier, 'Indigenous Feature Films.'

97 Kunuk, 'Interview.'

98 Hays, 'Canadians in the Closet.'

99 Waugh, *Romance of Transgression*, 8. Waugh draws his definition primarily from Jagose, *Queer Theory*, and Sedgwick, *Epistemology of the Closet*.

100 Waugh, *Romance of Transgression*, 8.

101 MacGillivray, 'Sitting in the Dark,' 18.

102 Monk, *Weird Sex & Snowshoes*.

103 Melnyk, *One Hundred Years*, 182.

104 Perhaps we should not be surprised, then, that not a single one of these film-makers is mentioned by name in Melnyk's *One Hundred Years*.

105 Hays, 'Canadians in the Closet.'

106 The language comes from Hallas, 'The Genealogical Pedagogy,' 23. Hallas does not mention the context of Greyson's fellow Torontonians.

107 Greyson, 'Interview.'

108 The quote about music is from Greyson, 'Interview,' 109; the final clause is from Greyson qtd. in Johnston, 'Going for a Burton.'

109 Hallas, 'Genealogical Pedagogy,' 17; Gittings, '*Zero Patience*,' 28.

110 The terms in quotes are borrowed from Hallas, 'Genealogical Pedagogy,' 17.

111 Greyson, 'Interview,' 110.

112 Greyson, 'Movie Masterclass.'

113 Greyson in Johnston, 'Going for a Burton.'

114 Greyson, 'Interview,' 112.

115 Marshall, *Quebec National Cinema*, 124.

116 Kirkland, '*Lilies*' Blooming Genius.'

117 In Gittings, 'Activism and Aesthetics,' 131.

118 L. Howe, 'Epistemology of Adaptation,' 45.

119 *Variety*, 'Rev. of *Lilies*.'

120 Waugh, 'Cinemas, Nations, Masculinities,' 18–22.

121 Waugh, *Romance of Transgression*, 100–1.

122 Marshall, *Quebec National Cinema*, 119–32.

123 Decker, 'Masculinity.'

124 Bruce, 'Querying/Queering,' 276.

125 See Gairola's fine reading of the film as it both appropriates 'the mythological ideals of Hinduism' and 'narratively counters those ideals' through the imagery of fire ('Burning with Shame,' 316–20).

126 Levitin, 'Deepa Mehta,' 284.

9. Film-Making at the Heart of the World: Guy Maddin

1 Maddin speaking in *Waiting for Twilight* (1997, Noam Gonick); qtd. in Vatnsdal, *Kino Delirium*, 123.

2 On Harvie, see in particular *Waiting for Twilight* and Maddin's nomination of this 'perfervid anachronist, fixated on all things 1920s' as 'a great genius we've never heard of' in an interview with Scott Shrake in *Used Wigs*.

3 Maddin, 'Pleasures of Melancholy,' 23.

4 Maddin, 'Sad Songs Say So Much.'

5 Maddin, 'Twilight of the Ice Nymphs'; 'Wait until Dark.' See also the account of the ADR work for *Twilight* with Alice Krige and Pascale Bussières (Vatnsdal, *Kino Delirium*, 119).

6 Maddin, *From the Atelier Tovar*, 15–64, 115–61, 209–28. The journals span fifteen years, but are concentrated in 1996, 1998–2000, and 2002. According to McBride's account of editing the journals for publication, Maddin's self-exposure was originally more extensive ('Secret Sharer').

7 Maddin, 'You Give Me Fever,' 86. See also 'Pleasures of Melancholy,' 24.

8 Shaviro, 'Fire and Ice,' 217.

9 Ibid.

10 For Gonick's comment, see his interview with Maddin, 'Happy Ever After.'

11 Snyder, 'Sexuality and Self,' 119. The living-room in question was Snyder's.

12 Maddin, 'Chicken Soup,' 145.

13 For Maddin as showman, see Halfyard, 'Guy Maddin Talks.'

14 Beard, *Into the Past*; Church, *Playing with Memories*; Holms, *Guy Maddin: Interviews*; Wershler, *My Winnipeg*. The only prior book-length study was Vatnsdal's essential albeit slim and non-scholarly *Kino Delirium*.

15 Pevere, 'Guy Maddin,' 48–9.

16 Maddin, 'Womb Is Barren,' 90.

17 Ibid. Maddin repeats these polymorphically perverse memories of the arena's eroticized childhood spaces in *My Winnipeg*, while also documenting a final use of the arena's urinals as a last act of farewell nostalgia before its demolition.

18 Ibid. 87.

19 Maddin, *Child without Qualities*, 177.

20 Maddin, 'Chicken Soup,' 136–7. Maddin plays further on the same embarrassment in *My Winnipeg*, where his narrating voice assures us his mother is playing herself in the film, including scenes with actors hired to re-enact childhood traumas involving her and his siblings; in fact, the mother is played by cult actress Ann Savage, best remembered for her unforgiving role as a femme fatale in Edgar Ulmer's poverty-row noir, *Detour* (1944).

21 Pevere, 'Foreword,' xii.

22 For more on Maddin's working methods in relation to his own past, see D. Masterson, 'My Brother's Keeper.' For an argument that Maddin's films engage directly with issues of Canadian identity, see Semley, 'Big snow.'

23 Vatnsdal, *Kino Delirium*, 30.

24 Godwin, 'Far from the Maddin Crowd,' 17.

25 Maddin, 'Pleasures of Melancholy,' 21. He would later add *Brand upon the Brain!* to this list (D. Masterson, 'My Brother's Keeper,' 27).

26 Qtd. in Gilmour, 'Home Truths.'

27 Melnyk, *One Hundred Years*, 199.

28 For the quotation, see Maddin, 'Pleasures of Melancholy,' 22. For the production locations, see Vatnsdal, *Kino Delirium*, 7, 50; Maddin, 'Twilight.'

29 Artibise, 'Divided City.'

30 Melnyk, *One Hundred Years*, 195.

31 For a sustained examination of Toles's essential work as Maddin's long-time collaborator, see D. Masterson, 'My Brother's Keeper.'

32 Maddin, *The Eye*, 164.

33 Maddin, 'Purple Majesty.'

34 Ibid.

35 Maddin, *Child without Qualities*, 187.

36 Ibid., 188.

37 Maddin, qtd. in John Anderson, 'Guy Maddin,' 67.

38 It wasn't until I was in college, for example, that I discovered that *The Wizard of Oz* switched to colour when Dorothy left Kansas – my myriad viewings had only ever

been its annual network television screening on our family's old black-and-white television.

39 See also Quandt and Maddin's discussion of the theme of resurrection in Maddin, 'Purple Majesty.'

40 Ibid.

41 Maddin, 'Guilty Pleasures.'

42 Indeed, even Maddin's sense of Canadian cinema combines the local with the Hollywood. 'I earned a painful but desperately needed $750,' his journal reads, 'for a one-hour lecture on Canada's cinema century – showing clips from the two great Canadians: Lipsett and Lauzon. Then, clips from *Leave Her to Heaven*, *Written on the Wind*, *Strange Illusion* and *Dishonoured*. Canadian cinema has been a history of absence. This is what we missed!' ('Journal Two, 1998–1999,' 158).

43 Maddin, 'Pleasures of Melancholy,' 21.

44 Maddin and Rossellini, 'Melodrama.'

45 Maddin's script for *Heart of the World* is reproduced in Vatnsdal, *Kino Delirium*, 146–54, the reference is to 146.

46 Maddin, 'Pleasures of Melancholy,' 24.

47 Maddin, *Child without Qualities*, 194; see also Vatnsdal, *Kino Delirium*, 28.

48 Maddin, 'Purple Majesty.'

49 On Maddin's interest in minor movements and their relation to his own Winnipeg aesthetic in *Careful*, see Varga, 'Desire in Bondage,' 66–8; and Straw, 'Reinhabiting Lost Languages.' Although I disagree with Varga's and Straw's underestimation of the role of Hollywood in Maddin's film-making, I agree with their distinction of Maddin's use of cinematic history from the strategies of camp.

Conclusion

1 Howell, 'Gross finds *Passchendaele*.'

2 A selection of Bangs's reviews and unpublished writings was collected in *Psychotic Reactions and Carburetor Dung*.

Works Cited

Adilman, Sid. 'A Career Comes Alive: Molly Parker Catches Directors' Attention as Necro-philiac in *Kissed*.' *Toronto Star*, 4 Apr. 1997. LexisNexis Academic.

– 'Director's Reputation Spreads across Quebec's Borders.' *Toronto Star*, 7 Nov. 1992. Lexis-Nexis Academic.

– 'Quebec Director Lauzon Considers Offer from Disney.' *Toronto Star*, 29 Sept. 1992: D5. LexisNexis Academic.

Aitken, Ian. *Film and Reform: John Grierson and the Documentary Film Movement*. London: Routledge, 1990.

Alioff, Maury. 'Healing Beauty: Carole Laure's *CQ2*.' *Take One* (Dec. 2004). http://www.highbeam.com/doc/1G1-126683511.html.

Almond, Paul. 'Paul Almond: Talks about His Marriage to Genevieve Bujold, the Creation of Telefilm Canada and the Beginnings of Feature Filmmaking in Canada.' By Wyndham Wise. *Take One* (Sept.–Dec. 2003). http://www.highbeam.com/doc/1G1-109568321.html.

Altman, Rick. *Film/Genre*. London: British Film Institute, 1999.

Amsden, Cynthia. 'The Tao of Callum Keith Rennie.' *Take One* 35 (Dec. 2001–Feb. 2002): 16–19.

Anderlini, Ken. 'A West Coast Nouvelle Vague.' *Film Festival Fresh Sheet* 2 (Oct. 1999): 1.

Anderson, Jason. 'A Comedy of Terror.' *Eye* 22 (Sept. 2005): 15.

Anderson, John. 'Guy Maddin.' *Film Comment* 34.2 (Mar./Apr. 1998): 63–7.

Andrew, Geoff. *Stranger than Paradise: Maverick Film-Makers in Recent American Cinema*. London: Prion, 1998.

Arcand, Denys. 'Le Documentaire selon Denys Arcand.' Disc 4. *Denys Arcand L'Oeuvre Documentaire Intégrale 1962–1981*. DVD. ONF/NFB, 2004.

– 'Filmmakers and Advertising.' Dec. 1987. In La Rochelle, *Denys Arcand*, 332–6.

– '"I Only Know Where I Come From, Not Where I Am Going": A Conversation with Denys Arcand.' By André Loiselle. In *Auteur/Provocateur: The Films of Denys Arcand*, edited by Loiselle and Brian McIlroy, 136–61. Westport, CT: Praeger, 1995.

Armatage, Kay. *The Girl from God's Country: Nell Shipman and the Silent Cinema*. Toronto: Univ. of Toronto Pr., 2003.

Armatage, Kay, Kass Banning, Brenda Longfellow, and Janine Marchessault, eds. *Gendering the Nation: Canadian Women's Cinema*. Toronto: Univ. of Toronto Pr., 1999.

Armatage, Kay, and Caryl Clark. 'Seeing and Hearing Salome.' In Tschofen and Burwell, *Image+ Territory*, 307–29.

Armistead, Claire. 'Pursuit of the Trivial: Play Is the Key to the Drama of Director Robert Lepage, the Wunderkind of Quebec. But Can the Eternal Child Survive the Growing

Demands of an International Reputation?' *Guardian* (London), 5 Oct. 1994. LexisNexis Academic.

Arnold, Gary. 'Banking On Bujold.' *Washington Post*, 2 Feb. 1978. LexisNexis Academic.

– '*Coma*: A Scary Whodunit at the Hospital.' *Washington Post*, 8 Feb. 1978. LexisNexis Academic.

Arroyo, José. 'Bordwell Considered: Cognitivism, Colonialism, and Canadian Cinematic Culture.' *CineAction* 28 (1992): 74–88.

Artibise, Alan F. J. 'Divided City: The Immigrant in Winnipeg Society, 1874–1921.' In *The Canadian City: Essays in Urban and Social History*, edited by Gilbert A. Stelter and A.F.J. Artibise, 360–91. Montreal: McGill-Queen's Univ. Pr., 1984.

Atwood, Margaret. *Survival: A Thematic Guide to Canadian Literature*. Toronto: Anansi, 1972.

Austin-Smith, Brenda. 'Strange Frontiers: Twenty Years of Manitoba Feature Film.' In Loiselle and McSorley, *Self Portraits*, 237–70.

B., R.E. 'John Murray Gibbon.' *Journal of the English Folk Dance and Song Society* 7.1 (Dec. 1952): 55. JSTOR.

Badley, Linda. *Film, Horror, and the Body Fantastic*. Westport, CT: Greenwood, 1995.

Bailey, Cameron. 'Scanning Egoyan.' *CineAction* 16 (Spring 1989): 45–51.

– 'Standing in the Kitchen All Night: A Secret History of the Toronto New Wave.' *Take One* (Summer 2000). http://www.highbeam.com/doc/1G1-30574556.html.

Baldessare, Angela. *Reel Canadians: Interviews from the Canadian Film World*. Toronto: Guernica, 2003.

Ballard, J.G. *Crash*. New York: Vintage, 1974.

– 'Introduction.' In Ballard, *Crash*, 1–6.

Bangs, Lester. *Psychotic Reactions and Carburetor Dung: The Work of a Legendary Critic*. Edited by Greil Marcus. New York: Anchor, 1988.

Banks, Russell. *The Sweet Hereafter*. New York: HarperCollins, 1991.

Banning, Kass. 'Atom Egoyan.' *CFE* (last updated 2002).

Barker, Martin, Jane Arthurs, and Ramaswami Harindranath. *The Crash Controversy: Censorship and Film Reception*. London: Wallflower, 2001.

Bassin, Ethel. 'John Murray Gibbon.' *Journal of the International Folk Music Council* 5 (1953): 67. JSTOR.

Bawden, Jim. 'Late Bloomer: A Rising Star Callum Keith Rennie Sobered Up and Found the Road to Stardom.' *Toronto Star*, 15 Dec. 1996. LexisNexis Academic.

– 'Translating Success.' *Toronto Star*, 31 Oct. 1992. LexisNexis Academic.

Beard, William. *The Artist as Monster: The Cinema of David Cronenberg*. Toronto: Univ. of Toronto Pr., 2006.

– 'The Canadianness of David Cronenberg.' *Mosaic* 27.2 (June 1994): 113–33. ProQuest Research Library (accessed 1 July 2009).

– *Into the Past: The Cinema of Guy Maddin*. Toronto: Univ. of Toronto Pr., 2010.

Beard, William, and Gerald White, eds. *North of Everything: English-Canadian Cinema: 1980 to 2000*. Edmonton: Univ. of Alberta Pr., 2002.

Beaty, Bart. 'Coward, Bully, and Clown: The Dream-life of Michael Dowse.' In Melnyk, *Great Canadian Film Directors*, 313–28.

Beavis, Mary Ann. 'The Sweet Hereafter: Law, Wisdom, and Family Revisited.' *Journal of Film and Religion* 5.1 (Apr. 2001): 22–3. http://www.unomaha.edu/jrf/sweether.htm.

Benjamin, Walter. *The Origin of German Tragic Drama*. Translated by John Osborne. London: Verso, 1998.

Berton, Pierre. *Hollywood's Canada: The Americanization of Our National Image.* Toronto: McClelland and Stewart, 1975.

Binning, Cheryl. 'Prairie Populism: The Winnipeg Film Group's 25th Anniversary.' *Take One* (Spring 2000). http://www.highbeam.com/doc/1G1-30385901.html.

Bordwell, David. 'The Art Cinema as a Mode of Film Practice.' *Film Criticism* 4.1 (1979): 56–64.

Brand, Dionne. 'Notes for Writing thru Race.' In *Bread out of Stone: Recollections on Sex, Recognitions, Race, Dreaming, and Politics,* by Dionne Brand, 173–83. Toronto: Coach House, 1994.

Braun, Liz. 'T&A Takes Over; New Best Friend Could Have Been So Much More.' *Toronto Sun,* 12 Apr. 2002. LexisNexis Academic.

Briefel, Aviva. 'Monster Pains: Masochism, Menstruation, and Identification in the Horror Film.' *Film Quarterly* 58.3 (Spring 2005): 16–27.

Browning, Mark. *David Cronenberg: Author or Film-maker?* Bristol: Intellect Books, 2007.

Browning, Will. 'Chilling Childhoods in Quebec: *Léolo* and *L'avalée des avalés.*' *French Review* 79.3 (2006): 561–9.

Brownstein, Bill. 'Ex-Robocop Has Big Co-star in Screamers; Olympic Stadium Plays Desolate Planet in New Peter Weller Film.' *Montreal Gazette,* 26 Dec. 1994. LexisNexis Academic.

– 'Man behind Dionne Series Overlooked; Director Duguay Just Can't Shake Scanners Reputation.' *Montreal Gazette,* 28 Nov. 1994. LexisNexis Academic.

Bruce, Jean. 'Querying/Queering the Nation.' In Armatage et al., *Gendering the Nation,* 274–90.

Burgess, Diane. 'Air Bud and Stickgirl Share Leaky Condo: The Changing Landscape of B.C. Cinema since the 1980s.' In Loiselle and McSorley, *Self Portraits,* 129–65.

– 'Charting the Course of the Pacific New Wave.' *CineAction* 61 (Feb. 2003): 29–33.

Burnett, Ron. 'Introduction.' In Egoyan, *Speaking Parts,* 9–22.

Byford, Chris. 'Highway 61 Revisited.' *CineAction* 45 (1998): 10–17.

Cagle, Robert. 'A Minority on Someone Else's Continent: Identity, Difference, and the Media in the Films of Patricia Rozema.' In Armatage et al., *Gendering the Nation,* 183–96.

– 'Persistence of Vision: The Wonderful World of John Paizs.' *CineAction* 57 (March 2002): 42–9.

Canadian Business Online. 'Canada's Fourth Annual Celebrity Power List Unveiled.' 25 Sept. 2008. http://www.canadianbusiness.com/article.jsp?content=20080925_102016_8800.

Canuel, Érik, Philippe Falardeau, and Jean-François Pouliot. 'Table ronde avec Érik Canuel, Philippe Falardeau et Jean-François Pouliot – Voix et vues du cinéma populaire (2ème partie): Le financement, la distribution, la commercialization,' *Nouvelles ‹‹vues›› sur le cinéma québécois* (Winter 2008–9): 1–20. http://www.cinema-quebecois.net/index.php/articles/10/.

Caughie, John, ed. *Theories of Authorship: A Reader.* New York: Routledge, 1981.

Canuxploitation. 'Back to God's Country.' http://www.canuxploitation.com/review/backtogods.html (accessed 10 July 2010).

– 'Canuxploitation Primer.' http://www.canuxploitation.com/article/primer.html (accessed 10 July 2010).

– 'From Cinépix to Cineplex: The Studios That Dripped Maple Syrup.' http://www.canuxploitation.com/article/studio.html (accessed 10 July 2010).

CFE. 'Larry Kent.' (Last updated Mar. 2006.)

Church, David, ed. *Playing with Memories: Essays on Guy* Maddin. Winnipeg: Univ. of Manitoba Pr., 2009.

Cineac. 'Top 100 Québec (Films québécois).' http://www.cineac.ca/Top%20100%20 Qu%E9bec.pdf.

Cinema Canada. 'Canadian Film News.' *Cinema Canada* 1 (Mar. 1972): 5–6.

Clandfield, David. *Canadian Film.* Toronto: Oxford Univ. Pr., 1987.

Clandfield, Peter. 'Bridgespotting: Lepage, Hitchcock, and Landmarks in Canadian Film.' *CJFS* 12.1 (Spring 2003): 2–15.

Clark, Bob. 'Interview: Bob Clark.' Canuxploitation, 29 July 2005 and 23 Oct. 2006. http:// www.canuxploitation.com/interview/clark.html.

Coates, Paul. *Film at the Intersection of High and Mass Culture.* Cambridge: Cambridge Univ. Pr., 1994.

Conant, Jennet. 'No Hype, Please: This Star Is Serious.' *New York Times,* 26 Sept. 1999. LexisNexis Academic.

Conlogue, Ray. 'The Unquenchable Sizzle of Carole Laure.' *Globe and Mail,* 16 Oct. 2000. LexisNexis Academic.

Corbeil, Carole. 'The Indiscreet Charm of Jean-Claude Lauzon.' *Saturday Night* 107 (Dec. 1992): 89.

Cornelius, Nathalie. 'Boxes and Bridges: Robert Lepage's *Le Confessionnal* and *La face cachée de la lune.*' *French Review* 82.1 (Oct. 2008): 118–28.

Corupe, Paul. 'Sin and Sovereignty: The Curious Rise of Cinépix Inc.' *Take One* (1 Mar. 2005). http://www.highbeam.com/doc/1G1-131050380.html.

Coulombe, Michel. *Denys Arcand: La Vraie Nature du Cinéaste.* Montreal: Boréal, 1993.

Cowan, Noah. 'Canadian Science Fiction Comes of Age.' *Take One* 4.11 (Spring 1996): 8–13.

Cox, Kevin. 'Salter Street Films to Close.' *Globe and Mail,* 17 Dec. 2003. LexisNexis Academic.

Cronenberg, David. *Cronenberg on Cronenberg.* By Chris Rodley. London: Faber, 1992.

– *David Cronenberg: Interviews with Serge Grünberg.* By Serge Grünberg. London: Plexus, 2006.

– 'David Cronenberg Talks about His New Film *Crash.*' By Chris Rodley. *Sight & Sound* 6.6 (June 1996): 7–11. IIPA.

– 'The Existential Deal: An Interview with David Cronenberg.' By Adam Simon. *Critical Quarterly* 43.3 (Autumn 2001): 34–56.

– 'The Film Director as Philosopher: An Interview with David Cronenberg.' By Richard Porton. *Cineaste* 24.4 (Sept. 1999): 4–9.

– Interview with Piers Handling and William Beard. In Handling, *Shape of Rage,* 158–98.

– 'Logic, Creativity and (Critical) Misinterpretations: An Interview with David Cronenberg.' By Xavier Mendik. In *The Modern Fantastic: The Films of David Cronenberg,* edited by Michael Grant, 168–85. Westport, CT: Praeger, 2000.

Cunningham, Alison. 'Sandra Oh's Cutting Edge: Grey's Anatomy Star Does Not Mince Words.' *National Post,* 30 July 2005. LexisNexis Academic.

Cuthbert, Pamela. 'Living in the Moment with Sandra Oh.' *Globe and Mail,* 18 Oct. 1997. LexisNexis Academic.

Dault, Gary Michael. '*Le confessionnal* & *Le polygraphe*: A Rumination.' *Take One* 5.15 (Spring 1997): 17–21.

Davidson, Sean. 'Lights, Camera, Drinks.' *Playback*, 11 Oct. 2004. LexisNexis Academic.

Decker, Matthew. 'Masculinity and the Threat of the Queer Body: Disfiguring Perceptions of Homosexuality in the Works of Queer Cinema.' Working paper, Dept. of Literature, American Univ., 2010.

Dee, Jonathan. 'David Cronenberg's Body Language.' *New York Times Magazine*, 18 Sept. 2005: 74–9.

Deleuze, Gilles and Félix Guattari. *Kafka: Toward a Minor Literature*. Translated by Dana Polan. Minneapolis: Univ. of Minnesota Pr., 1986.

Del Rio, Elena. 'The Body as Foundation of the Screen: Allegories of Technology in Atom Egoyan's *Speaking Parts*.' *Camera Obscura* 38 (May 1996): 92–115.

DeMara, Bruce. 'One Woman's Literary Mission; Why One Rising Star Turned Her Attention away from Hollywood to Focus on the Plight of the World's Oppressed.' *Toronto Star*, 23 Oct. 2008. LexisNexis Academic.

Desbarats, Carole, Jacinto Lageira, Danièle Rivière, and Paul Virilio. *Atom Egoyan*. Paris: Editions Dis Voir, 1994.

Dick, Ronald. 'Regionalization of a Federal Cultural Institution: The Experience of the National Film Board of Canada 1965–1979.' In *Flashback: People and Institutions in Canadian Film History*, edited by Gene Walz, 107–33. Montreal: Mediatexte, 1986.

Dickinson, Peter. 'Being at Home with Roy Dupuis and Pascale Bussières: Or, Stargazing in and out of Quebec.' *CineAction* (Summer 2007). http://www.highbeam.com/doc/1G1-178268105.html.

– 'Double Take: Adaptation, Remediation, and Doubleness in the Films of Robert Lepage.' In Melnyk, *Great Canadian Film Directors*, 175–97.

– 'Space, Time, Auteur-ity and the Queer Male Body: The Film Adaptations of Robert Lepage.' *Screen* 46.2 (Summer 2005): 133–53.

Digital Chosunilbo. 'Sandra Oh on the Challenge of Being Korean in Hollywood.' *Digital Chosunilbo*, 13 Apr. 2007. http://english.chosun.com/site/data/html_dir/2007/04/13/2007041361012.html.

Dillon, Mark. 'Egoyan, Sarossy Think Bigger on *Ararat*.' *Playback* (16 Sept. 2002): 43. LexisNexis Academic.

– 'An Elegy for the Earth: In *Last Night*, Canadian Writer/Director Don McKellar and Cinematographer Douglas Koch, CSC Take a Low-Key Look at Armageddon.' *American Cinematographer* 80.3 (Mar. 1999): 66–8, 70–1.

– 'Existence or *eXistenZ*?: Toybox Uses Digital Wizardry to Enhance Cronenberg's Imaginative Fantasy.' *American Cinematographer* 80.5 (May 1999): 56–7.

– 'Production Slate: Gleaming the Cube.' *American Cinematographer* 79.3 (Mar. 1998): 16, 18, 20.

Dillon, Steven. 'Lyricism and Accident in *The Sweet Hereafter*.' *Literature/Film Quarterly* 31.3 (2003): 228.

Dompierre, Louise. *Prent/Cronenberg: Crimes against Nature*. Toronto: Power Plant, 1987.

Donnelly, Pat. 'The Expanding World of Robert Lepage.' *Montreal Gazette*, 1 Apr. 1995. LexisNexis Academic.

Dorland, Michael. 'Denys Arcand's *Déclin de l'empire américain*.' *Cinema Canada* (Oct. 1986): 20.

– *So Close to the State(s): The Emergence of Canadian Feature Film Policy*. Toronto: Univ. of Toronto Pr., 1998.

Druick, Zoë. *Projecting Canada: Government Policy and Documentary Film at the National Film Board of Canada*. Montreal: McGill-Queen's Univ. Pr., 2007.

Dundjerovic, Aleksandar. *The Cinema of Robert Lepage: The Poetics of Memory*. London: Wallflower, 2003.

Dunphy, Catherine. 'Lea Pool: Veteran at 41.' *Toronto Star*, 28 Feb. 1992. LexisNexis Academic.

Dwyer, Michael. 'Atomic Power.' *Irish Times*, 21 Aug. 1999. LexisNexis Academic.

Dyer, Richard. *Heavenly Bodies: Film Stars and Society*. 2nd ed. London: Routledge, 2004.

Egoyan, Atom. *Ararat: The Shooting Script*. New York: Newmarket, 2002.

– 'Atom Egoyan: An Interview.' By Ron Burnett. *CineAction* 16 (Spring 1989): 41–4.

– 'Audio Commentary to Deleted Scenes from *Ararat*.' *Ararat*. Directed by Egoyan. DVD. Miramax Home Entertainment, 2003.

– 'Audio Commentary.' *Felicia's Journey*. Directed by Egoyan. DVD. Artisan Entertainment, 1999.

– 'Deleted Scenes from *Where the Truth Lies*.' *Where the Truth Lies*. Directed by Egoyan. DVD. Sony, 2006.

– 'Difficult to Say: An Interview with Atom Egoyan.' By Geoff Pevere. In *Exotica: The Screenplay*, edited by Atom Egoyan, 43–67. Toronto: Coach House, 1995.

– '"Emotional Logic": Marc Glassman Interviews Atom Egoyan.' In Egoyan, *Speaking Parts*, 41–57.

– 'Family Romances: An Interview with Atom Egoyan.' By Richard Porton. *Cineaste* 23.2 (1997): 8–15.

– 'In Other Words: Poetic License and the Incarnation of History.' *University of Toronto Quarterly* 73.3 (Summer 2004): 886–905.

– 'The Politics of Denial: An Interview with Atom Egoyan.' By Richard Porton. *Cineaste* 25.1 (Dec. 1999), 39–41.

– *Speaking Parts*. Edited by Marc Glassman. Toronto: Coach House, 1993.

– 'Spellbound: From a Filmmaking Fan, an Appreciation of the Master of Suspense's Show Business.' *Village Voice*, 6 Dec. 2005. http://www.villagevoice.com/film/0549,egoyan,70702,20.html.

– 'Surface Tension.' In Egoyan, *Speaking Parts*, 25–38.

Egoyan, Atom, and Ian Balfour, eds. *Subtitles: On the Foreignness of Film*. Cambridge, MA: MIT Pr., 2004.

Egoyan, Atom, and Russell Banks. 'Audio Commentary.' *The Sweet Hereafter*. Directed by Egoyan. DVD. New Line Home Video, 1998.

Elber, Lynn. 'Actress Finds Comedy Success in a Raunchy, Greedy World.' *Toronto Star*, 6 July 1997. LexisNexis Academic.

Elder, Bruce. 'The Cinema We Need.' In *Documents in Canadian Film*, edited by Douglas Fetherling, 260–71. Peterborough, ON: Broadview, 1988.

Elley, Derek. 'Film Reviews: PiFan; *Cypher*.' *Variety* 391.10 (28 July–3 Aug. 2003): 30. IIPA.

Ellis, Don. 'Ready for Its Closeup: Film Fans Create a Haven on Queen West.' *National Post*, 9 Oct. 2004. LexisNexis Academic.

Elsaesser, Thomas. 'Putting on a Show: The European Art Movie.' *Sight & Sound* 4.4 (Apr. 1994): 22–7.

Erbach, Jeff. 'From an Interview with Jeff Erbach.' By Andrew Lesk. *CineAction* 65 (Jan. 2005): 28–9.

Evans, Gary. *In the National Interest: A Chronicle of the National Film Board of Canada from 1949 to 1989*. Toronto: Univ. of Toronto Pr., 1991.

Evans, Michael Robert. *The Fast Runner: Filming the Legend of Atanarjuat*. Lincoln: Univ. of Nebraska Pr., 2010.

– *Isuma: Inuit Video Art*. Montreal: McGill-Queen's Univ. Pr., 2008.

Falcon, Richard. 'Reviews: *Cypher*.' *Sight & Sound* 13.10 (Oct. 2003): 46–7. IIPA.

Feldman, Seth. 'Allan King.' *CFE* (last updated July 2006).

– 'A Married Couple.' *CFE* (accessed 19 July 2010).

Finlay, Marion. 'Atom Egoyan on Set with Challenging British Tale.' *Toronto Star*, 11 Dec. 1998. LexisNexis Academic.

Foster, Cecil. 'Jan Carew and the Reconstruction of the Canadian Mosaic.' *Race & Class* 43.3 (2002): 3–17.

– *A Place Called Heaven: The Meaning of Being Black in Canada*. Toronto: HarperCollins, 1996.

Foster, Charles. *Once Upon a Time in Paradise: Canadians in the Golden Age of Hollywood*. Toronto: Dundurn Pr., 2003.

– *Stardust and Shadows: Canadians in Early Hollywood*. Toronto: Dundurn Pr., 2000.

Fothergill, Robert. 'Coward, Bully, or Clown: The Dream-Life of a Younger Brother.' In *Canadian Film Reader*, edited by Seth Feldman and Joyce Nelson, 234–50. Toronto: Peter Martin, 1977.

French, Tony. '"In the Sun It All Looks So Nice": A Note on Paul Almond's *Isabel*.' *CineAction* 57 (Mar. 2002): 35–41.

Frye, Northrop. 'Conclusion to the First Edition of *Literary History of Canada* (1965).' In *Collected Works of Northrop Frye*, vol. 12 of 29, edited by Jean O'Grady and David Staines, 339–72. Toronto: Univ. of Toronto Pr., 1996.

Gabereau, Eve. 'Portrait of a Genocide.' *The Independent* (London), 15 Nov. 2002. LexisNexis Academic.

Gairola, Rahul. 'Burning with Shame: Desire and South Asian Patriarchy, from Gayatri Spivak's "Can the Subaltern Speak?" to Deepa Mehta's *Fire*.' *Comparative Literature* 54.5 (Fall 2002): 307–24.

Garrity, Henry. 'True Lies: Autobiography, Fiction and Politics in Jean-Claude Lauzon's *Léolo*.' *Quebec Studies* 20 (1995): 80–5.

Gauthier, Jennifer L. 'Indigenous Feature Films: A New Hope for National Cinemas.' *CineAction* (Spring 2004). http://www.highbeam.com/doc/1G1-123468067.html.

– 'Living In/Between: The Cinema of Lea Pool.' In Melnyk, *Great Canadian Film Directors*, 227–50.

George, Lianne. 'Hollywood/Mollywood: In Three Festival Films: Good Parts Interest Actress More Than Blockbusters.' *National Post*, 13 Sept. 2002. LexisNexis Academic.

Gerstel, Judy. 'Quebec Filmmaker Was "Eager to Live Fully": Lauzon Suffered through Movie-Making Process.' *Toronto Star*, 12 Aug.1997. LexisNexis Academic.

Gilmour, Alison. 'Home Truths: Guy Maddin Takes a Dream-like Tour of Winnipeg.' *CBC News*, 7 Sept. 2007. http://www.cbc.ca/arts/tiff/features/tiffmaddin.html.

Gin, Pascal. 'Les bifurcations culturelles du road movie contemporain.' *CiNéMAS* 18.2–3 (Spring 2008): 31–45.

Gittings, Christopher. 'Activism and Aesthetics: The Work of John Greyson.' In Melnyk, *Great Canadian Film Directors*, 125–47.

– *Canadian National Cinema: Ideology, Difference and Representation*. London: Routledge, 2002.

– 'Zero Patience, Genre, Difference, and Ideology: Singing and Dancing Queer Nation.' Cinema Journal 41.1 (Fall 2001): 28–39.

Glassman, Marc. 'The Toronto New Wave.' Take One (Summer 1996). http://www.high-beam.com/doc/1G1-30528863.html.

Godfrey, Stephen.'"I Wanted to Be a Singer, Rather Than an Actress Who Sings": Carole Laure Avoids Mixed Media.' Globe and Mail, 14 May 1990. LexisNexis Academic.

Godwin, R. George. 'Far from the Maddin Crowd: Thirty Years of the Winnipeg Film Group.' Cinemascope 20 (Fall 2004): 14–18.

Golfman, Noreen. 'Imagining Region: A Survey of Newfoundland Film.' In Beard and White, North of Everything, 46–59.

Gonick, Noam. 'Fires Were Started: An Interview with Noam Gonick.' By Ioannis Mookas. Senses of Cinema. http://archive.sensesofcinema.com/contents/05/36/noam_gonick.html.

– 'Happy Ever After.' The Village Voice, 23–9 Jan. 2002. In Maddin, From the Atelier Tovar, 80–3.

Gossage, Peter. 'La marâtre: Marie-Anne Houde and the Myth of the Wicked Stepmother in Quebec.' In Histories of Canadian Children and Youth, edited by Nancy Janovicek and Joy Parr, 146–66. Don Mills, ON: Oxford Univ. Pr., 2003.

Govier, Katherine. 'Middle-class Shivers.' Toronto Life (July 1979): 50–62.

Grady, Pam. 'Mining the Urban Core: Filmmaker Gary Burns and actor Don McKellar hit the satirical mother lode with waydowntown.' http://www.reel.com/reel.asp?node=features/interviews/-waydowntown (accessed 2 Aug. 2009).

Grant, Barry Keith. 'National Cinema and Genre.' Film Reference. http://www.filmreference.com/encyclopedia/Criticism-Ideology/Genre-NATIONAL-CINEMA-AND-GENRE.html (accessed 15 June 2008).

Gravestock, Steve. 'An Excerpt from Don Owen: Notes on a Filmmaker and His Culture.' CFE, 2005.

Gravestock, Steve, and Kate Lawrie Van de Ven, eds. Toronto on Film. Toronto: TIFF, 2009.

Green, Mary Jane. 'Léa Pool's La Femme de l'hôtel and Women's Film in Quebec.' Quebec Studies 9 (1989): 48–62.

Greyson, John. 'Interview with Wyndham Wise.' Special edition, Take One (Sept.–Nov. 2004): 95–120.

– 'Movie Masterclass: John Greyson on Zero Patience.' The Guardian (London), 4 Aug. 1994: T6. LexisNexis Academic.

Grierson, John. 'A Film Policy for Canada.' In Documents in Canadian Film, edited by Douglas Fetherling, 51–81. Peterborough, ON: Broadview, 1988.

Halfyard, Kurt. 'Guy Maddin Talks My Winnipeg, Self-mythologizing, Psychological Honesty, and Even The Host.' Twitch, 2 Oct. 2007. http://twitchfilm.net/site/view/guy-maddin-talks-up-my-winnipeg-self-mythologizing-pyschological-honesty-an/.

Hall, Stuart. Questions of Cultural Identity. Edited by Stuart Hall and Paul du Gay. London: Sage, 1996.

Hallas, Roger. 'The Genealogical Pedagogy of Zero Patience.' CJFS 12.1 (Spring 2003): 16–37.

Hammond, Wally. 'Cold Comfort: Lynne Stopkewich on Sex with the Dead.' Time Out 1429 (1998): 73.

Handling, Piers. 'A Canadian Cronenberg.' In Handling, Shape of Rage, 98–114.

– 'Gilles Carle.' CFE (last updated Jan. 2003).

– ed. The Shape of Rage: The Films of David Cronenberg. Toronto: General Publishing, 1983.

Hantke, Stefan. 'Spectacular Optics: The Deployment of Special Effects in David Cronenberg's Films.' *Film Criticism* 29.2 (Winter 2004/2005): 34–52.

Harcourt, Peter. 'A Conversation with Atom Egoyan.' *Post Script* 15.1 (Fall 1995): 68–74.

– 'Imaginary Images: An Examination of Atom Egoyan's Films.' *Film Quarterly* 48.3 (Spring 1995): 2–14.

Harris, Christopher. 'Film Review: *Mouvements du désir*.' *Globe and Mail*, 24 June 1994. LexisNexis Academic.

Harvie, Jennifer. 'Robert Lepage.' In *Postmodernism: the Key Figures*, edited by Hans Bertens and Joseph Natoli, 224–30. Malden, MA: Blackwell, 2002.

Harvie, Jennifer, and Erin Hurley. 'States of Play: Locating Québec in the Performances of Robert Lepage, Ex Machina, and the Cirque du Soleil.' *Theatre Journal* 51.3 (1999): 299–315.

Hays, Matthew. 'Art in the Danger Zone: Creativity Is All About Risk-taking, Robert Lepage Tells Matthew Hays. As His Own Life Shows, Nothing Inspires Like Fear.' *Globe and Mail*, 11 Oct. 2001. LexisNexis Academic.

– 'Canadians in the Closet; Hit Series Queer as Folk Prides Itself on Being Ultra-forthright on Gay Issues. What It Hasn't Come Out about Are Certain Hints of Geographical Orientation.' *Globe and Mail*, 5 Apr. 2003. LexisNexis Academic.

– 'Two Solitudes, One Busy Lady: Rendez-vous with Pascale Bussières.' *Globe and Mail*, 17 Feb. 2000. LexisNexis Academic.

– 'Where Is Here? Here Is Queer: Four Defining Bent Moments in Canadian Film.' In Gravestock and Van de Ven, *Toronto on Film*, 139–48.

Hayward, Susan. *French National Cinema*. London: Routledge, 1993.

Heath, Stephen. 'Notes on Suture.' *Screen* 18 (Winter 1978). http://www.lacan.com/symptom8_articles/heath8.html.

Helm, Richard. 'Actor Rennie Speaks His Mind – Bluntly.' *Montreal Gazette*, 21 Dec. 1996. LexisNexis Academic.

Higson, Andrew. 'The Concept of National Cinema.' *Screen* 30.4 (1989): 36–46.

Holms, D.K., ed. *Guy Maddin: Interviews*. Jackson: Univ. Pr. of Mississippi, 2010.

Howe, Desson. 'Film Notes; After *The Sweet Hereafter*.' *Washington Post*, 19 Nov. 1999. LexisNexis Academic.

Howe, Lawrence. 'The Epistemology of Adaptation in John Greyson's *Lilies*.' *CJFS* 15.2 (Autumn 2006): 44–61.

Howell, Peter. 'Egoyan's Muse.' *Toronto Star*, 27 Aug. 1999. LexisNexis Academic.

– 'Gross Finds *Passchendaele* Unites Generations.' *Toronto Star*, 14 Nov. 2008. LexisNexis Academic.

– 'Modern Horror Story.' *Toronto Star*, 12 Nov. 1999. LexisNexis Academic.

– 'Souls for Sale in Tales of Intrigue.' *Toronto Star*, 7 Oct. 2005. LexisNexis Academic.

– 'Stars Share Inside Jokes.' *Toronto Star*, 4 Aug. 2006. LexisNexis Academic.

Hunter, Stephen. '*Felicia's Journey*: Soup to Nut.' *Washington Post*, 19 Nov. 1999. LexisNexis Academic.

Hutcheon, Linda. *The Canadian Postmodern: A Study of Contemporary English-Canadian Fiction*. Toronto: Oxford Univ. Pr., 1988.

IMDB. 'All-Time USA Box Office.' http://www.imdb.com/boxoffice/alltimegross (accessed 2 May 2010).

Jackson, Philip, and Daniel D'or. '"Science Fiction on a Shoestring," Philip Jackson and Daniel D'or interviewed by Angela Baldassarre.' *Take One* 4.11 (Spring 1996): 14–17.

Jaehne, Karen. 'Double Trouble: Cronenberg's Chronic Case.' *Film Comment* 24.5 (Oct. 1988): 20–5.

– 'I've Heard the Mermaids Singing: Interview With Patricia Rozema.' *Cineaste* 16.3 (1988): 22–3.

Jagose, Annamarie. *Queer Theory: An Introduction.* New York: New York Univ. Pr., 1996.

James, Nick. 'The Right Stuff.' *Sight & Sound* 15.7 (July 2005): 12, 14, 16–17. IIPA.

Jameson, Fredric. 'Third-World Literature in the Era of Multinational Capitalism.' *Social Text* 15 (Fall 1986): 65–88.

Jean, Marcel. *Le Cinéma québécois.* New edition. Montreal: Boréal, 2005.

Johnson, Brian D. 'Atom's Journey.' *Maclean's*, 13 Sept. 1999. LexisNexis Academic.

– *Brave Films, Wild Nights: 25 Years of Festival Fever.* Toronto: Random House Canada, 2000.

– 'How Sweet It Is.' *Maclean's*, 8 Sept. 1997. LexisNexis Academic.

– 'Living Dead, Losing Luck.' *Maclean's*, 29 Mar. 2004.

Johnston, Sheila. 'Going for a Burton.' *The Independent* (London), 12 Aug. 1994: Film Page 20. LexisNexis Academic.

Jones, Alan. 'Narration to *Inside Scan: The New Order.*' Featurette extra on *Scanners II: The New Order.* DVD. Anchor Bay, 2005.

Jones, D.B. *Movies and Memoranda: An Interpretative History of the National Film Board of Canada.* Ottawa: Canadian Film Institute, 1981.

Kehr, Dave. 'Finding Succor at the Cinema.' *New York Times*, 21 Apr. 2000. LexisNexis Academic.

Kelleher, Ed. 'Coming of Age in Montreal: Quebecois Filmmaker Lea Pool Offers a Bracing Family Drama.' *Film Journal International* 103 (Apr. 2000): 30, 40.

Kelly, Brendan. 'Actress Laure Loves New Life as Singer; "Music Brings You Toward Your Secrets."' *Montreal Gazette*, 5 Dec. 1991. LexisNexis Academic.

– 'Anything's Possible: Robert Lepage Switches to English for His Newest Movie.' *Montreal Gazette*, 15 Nov. 1999. LexisNexis Academic.

– 'Featured Player: Canuck Film Finds Homegrown Hero.' *Variety* 407.8 (16 July–22 July 2007): 14. IIPA.

– 'The Next Action Hero: Montreal Director Christian Duguay Is Just What Hollywood Is Looking For.' *Montreal Gazette* 13 Aug. 2000. LexisNexis Academic.

– 'Small Screen Is Big Business.' *Montreal Gazette*, 20 Apr. 1998. LexisNexis Academic.

– 'Urban Paranoia Runs Deep: Montreal Metro Trains Racing along with All Doors Wide Open Make for Memorable Scene in *A Problem With Fear*.' *Montreal Gazette*, 27 Oct. 2003. LexisNexis Academic.

Kelly, Richard. 'Last Night.' *Sight & Sound* 9.7 (July 1999): 44.

Keohane, Kieran. 'Symptoms of Canada: National Identity and the Theft of National Enjoyment.' *CineAction* 28 (1992): 20–33.

Khanna, Sanjay. 'Masala Take Two: Cutting Your Own Deals.' *Rungh* 1.3 (1992): 14–16.

King, Geoff. *American Independent Cinema.* Bloomington: Indiana Univ. Pr., 2005.

Kirkland, Bruce. 'Digging Fencepost.' *Toronto Sun*, 9 Mar. 1995. LexisNexis Academic.

– 'Glad to Be Oh So Canadian.' *Toronto Sun*, 19 Oct. 1998. LexisNexis Academic.

– 'It's the Work: For Callum Keith Rennie, the Only Business of Films Is Acting.' *Toronto Sun*, 14 Nov. 2003. LexisNexis Academic.

– '*Lilies*' Blooming Genius: Director John Greyson Can Hardly Believe His Success.' *Toronto Sun*, 26 Oct. 1996: 35. LexisNexis Academic.

– 'You Can Just Call Callum Charismatic.' *Toronto Sun*, 22 Oct. 1998. LexisNexis Academic.

Klawans, Stuart. 'Getting Inside the Head for a Portrait of Evil.' *New York Times*, 21 Nov. 1999. LexisNexis Academic.

Klein, Naomi. *No Logo*. London: Flamingo, 2000.

Knelman, Martin. 'Mature Bujold.' *Financial Post*, 29 Oct. 1990. LexisNexis Academic.

Knopf, Kerstin. *Decolonizing the Lens of Power: Indigenous Films in North America*. Amsterdam: Rodopi, 2008.

Koc, Aysegul. 'I'm Just a Simple Filmmaker: An Interview with Michel Brault.' *CineAction* 73–4 (Sept. 2007). http://www.thefreelibrary.com/-I'm+just+a+simple+filmmaker%3A+an+interview+with+Michel+Brault-a0178268103.

Kotsopoulos, Patsy Aspasia. 'L.M. Montgomery on Television: The Romance and Industry of the Adaptation Process.' In *Canadian Cultural Poesis: Essays on Canadian Culture*, edited by Sheila Petty, Garry Sherbert, and Annie Gérin, 271–88. Waterloo, ON: Wilfrid Laurier Univ. Pr., 2005.

Kraus, Matthias. *Bild – Erinnerung – Identität. Die Filme des Kanadiers Atom Egoyan*. Marburg: Schüren, 2000.

Krishna, Srinivas. 'What the Story Is: An Interview with Srinivas Krishna.' By Cameron Bailey. *CineAction* 28 (1992): 38–47.

Kunuk, Zacharias. 'Zacharias Kunuk Interview.' By Michelle Svenson. *Native Networks*, 1 Apr. 2002. http://www.nativenetworks.si.edu/eng/rose/kunuk_z_interview.htm.

Lacasse, Germain. 'Cultural Amnesia and the Birth of the Cinema in Canada.' *Cinema Canada* 108 (June 1984): 6–7.

Lane, Anthony. 'Worlds Apart: *Far from Heaven* and *Ararat*.' *New Yorker* 78.35 (18 Nov. 2002): 104–5. IIPA.

La Rochelle, Réal. *Denys Arcand: A Life in Film*. Translated by Alison Strayer. Toronto: McArthur, 2005.

Larrivée, Pierre. 'Identities and Oppressions: Jean-Claude Lauzon's *Léolo* (1992).' *New Cinemas* 6.2 (2008): 85–96.

Lauzon, Jean-Claude. '"It Is an Image That I Have Retained from Infancy": Jean-Claude Lauzon.' By Claude Racine. Translated by Jim Leach. In *The Young, the Restless, and the Dead: Interviews with Canadian Filmmakers*, edited by George Melnyk, 117–29. Waterloo, ON: Wilfrid Laurier Univ. Pr., 2008.

Lavery, David. 'The Movie Artist.' http://davidlavery.net/Courses/3870/Extras/Auteur_Theory.htm (accessed 5 Jan. 2006).

Lavoie, André. '*I've Heard the Mermaids Singing*,' In White, *Cinema of Canada*, 136–43.

Leach, Jim. *Claude Jutra: Filmmaker*. Montreal: McGill-Queen's Univ. Pr., 1999.

– *Film in Canada*. Don Mills, ON: Oxford Univ. Pr., 2006.

– '"It Takes Monsters To Do Things Like That": The Films of Jean-Claude Lauzon.' In Melnyk, *Great Canadian Film Directors*, 49–63.

Le Blanc, Alonzo. 'Aurore, L'Enfant Martyre.' In *Dictionnaire des oeuvres littéraires du Québec*, vol. 2, edited by Maurice Lemire et al, 97–100. Montreal: FIDES, 1980.

Lee, Helen. 'Coming Attractions: A Brief History of Canada's Nether-Cinema.' *Take One* 5 (Summer 1994): 4–11.

Lefebvre, Benjamin. '*Road to Avonlea*: A Co-production of the Disney Corporation.' In *Making Avonlea: L.M. Montgomery and Popular Culture*, edited by Irene Gammel, 174–85. Toronto: Univ. of Toronto Pr., 2002.

Lefebvre, Henri. *The Production of Space*. Translated by Donald Nicholson Smith. Oxford: Blackwell, 1991.

Lefebvre, Martin. 'Sense of Time and Place: The Chronotope in *I Confess* and *Le Confessionnal*.' *Quebec Studies* 26 (Fall 1998/Winter 1999): 88–98.

Lepage, Robert. 'Appendix: Interview with Robert Lepage.' By Aleksandr Dundjerovic. In Dundjerovic, *Cinema of Robert Lepage*, 147–57.

Lesk, Andrew. 'Caress, Denial, Decay: Queer Desire in *The Nature of Nicholas*.' *CineAction* 65 (Jan. 2005): 25–8.

Lever, Yves. *Histoire générale du cinéma au Québec*. 2nd edition. Montreal: Boréal, 1995.

Levine, Melissa. 'Strange Brew: The Truth is, Egoyan's Latest Is B-movie Noir, with Killer Performances.' *SF Weekly*, 19 Oct. 2005. LexisNexis Academic.

Levitin, Jacqueline. 'Deepa Mehta as Transnational Filmmaker, or You Can't Go Home Again.' In Beard and White, *North of Everything*, 270–93.

– 'Mina Shum: The 'Chinese Films' and Identities.' In Melnyk, *Great Canadian Film Directors*, 271–91.

L'Hébreux, Michel. *Le Pont de Québec*. Sillery, QC: Septentrion, 2001.

Lincoln, Ben. 'Cyberpunk on Screen: William Gibson Speaks.' *The Peak* 7.100 (19 Oct. 1998). http://www.peak.sfu.ca/the-peak/98-3/issue7/gibson.html.

Loiselle, André. '*The Decline* … and the Rise of English Canada's Quebec Cinema.' In Loiselle and McSorley, *Self Portraits*, 55–91.

– 'Quebecus Horribilis: Theatricality, the "Moment of Horror" and Quebec's "Satanist" Cinema.' *Nouvelles 'vues' sur le cinéma québécois* 8 (Winter 2008): 1–23. http://cinema-quebecois.net/index.php.

– 'Subtly Subversive or Simply Stupid: Notes on Popular Quebec Cinema.' *Post Script* 18.2 (Winter/Spring 1999): 75–84.

Loiselle, André, and Tom McSorley, eds. *Self Portraits: The Cinemas of Canada since Telefilm*. Ottawa: Canadian Film Institute/Institut canadien du film, 2006.

Longfellow, Brenda. 'Counter-Narratives, Class Politics and Metropolitan Dystopia: Representations of Globalizaton in *Maelström*, *waydowntown*, and *La Moitié gauche du frigo*.' *CJFS* 13.1 (Spring 2004): 69–83.

– 'Gender, Landscape, and Colonial Allegories in *The Far Shore*, *Loyalties*, and *Mouvements du désir*.' In Armatage et al., *Gendering the Nation*, 165–82.

– '*The Red Violin*, Commodity Fetishism and Globalization.' *CJFS* 10.2 (2001): 6–20.

– 'Surfing the Toronto New Wave: Policy, Paradigm Shifts and Post-Nationalism.' In Gravestock and Van de Ven, *Toronto on Film*, 109–34.

Lowenstein, Adam. 'Canadian Horror Made Flesh: Contextualizing David Cronenberg.' *Post Script* 18.2 (Winter 1998–Spring 1999): 37–51.

Lowry, Lynn. 'Biography.' Lynnlowry.com, 2009.

Lussier, Marc-André. 'Carole Laure serait-elle devenue une icône?' http://blogues.cyberpresse.ca/moncinema/lussier/2008/06/18/carole-laure-serait-elle-devenue-une-icone/ (accessed July 13. 2009).

Lusty, Terry. '*Dance Me Outside* Maintains Stereotypes.' *Windspeaker* (Apr. 1995): 18.

Macdonald, Ron Foley. 'East Coast Update.' *Take One* 32 (May 2001): 53.

MacGillivray, William D. 'Sitting in the Dark.' *CineAction* 28 (Spring 1992): 16–19.

MacKenzie, Scott. 'National Identity, Canadian Cinema, and Multiculturalism.' *Æ Canadian Aesthetics Journal* 4 (Summer 1999). http://www.uqtr.ca/AE/vol_4/scott.htm.

– *Screening Quebec: Québécois Moving Images, National Identity, and the Public Sphere.* Manchester: Manchester Univ. Pr., 2004.

Maddin, Guy. 'Chicken Soup for the Stone Baby: *Interrogations for an Autobiography*.' By Robert Enright. In *Cowards Bend the Knee*, by Guy Maddin, 129–51. Toronto: The Power Plant, 2003.

– 'The Child without Qualities.' In Maddin, *From the Atelier Tovar*, 176–208.

– 'The Eye, Like a Strange Balloon, Mounts towards Infinity.' In Maddin, *From the Atelier Tovar*, 164–8.

– *From the Atelier Tovar: Selected Writings.* Toronto: Coach House Books, 2003.

– 'Guilty Pleasures' *Film Comment* (Jan./Feb. 2003). In Maddin, *From the Atelier Tovar*, 96–8.

– 'Interview: Guy Maddin.' By Scott Shrake. *Used Wigs.* http://www.usedwigs.com/interview_maddin.html (accessed Sept. 2004).

– 'Journal Two, 1998–1999.' In Maddin, *From the Atelier Tovar*, 115–61.

– 'The Pleasures of Melancholy: An Interview with Guy Maddin.' By Marie Losier and Richard Porton. *Cineaste* (Summer 2004): 18–25.

– 'Purple Majesty: Guy Maddin talks with James Quandt.' *Artforum* (June 2003). http://www.findarticles.com/p/-articles/mi_m0268/is_10_41/ai_103989792/pg_2.

– 'Sad Songs Say So Much.' *The Village Voice*, 7–13 May 2003. http://www.villagevoice.com/issues/0319/maddin.php.

– 'Twilight of the Ice Nymphs.' *The Village Voice*, 3–9 Mar. 2004. http://www.villagevoice.com/issues/0409/maddin.php.

– 'Wait until Dark.' *The Village Voice*, 5 Apr. 2004. http://www.villagevoice.com/issues/0414/maddin.php.

– 'The Womb Is Barren.' *Montage* (Winter 2001). In Maddin, *From the Atelier Tovar*, 87–90.

– 'You Give Me Fever.' *The Village Voice* (12–18 June 2002). In Maddin, *From the Atelier Tovar*, 84–6.

Maddin, Guy, and Isabella Rossellini. 'Melodrama as a Way of Life: Guy Maddin and Isabella Rossellini Talk about *Saddest Song*.' By Andrea Meyer. *indieWIRE*, 3 May 2004. http://www.indiewire.com/people/people_040503maddin.html.

Magder, Ted. *Canada's Hollywood: The Canadian State and Feature Film.* Toronto: Univ. of Toronto Pr., 1993.

The Making of Ararat. Directed by Michele Francis. Featurette on bonus disk of *Ararat*. Directed by Egoyan. DVD. Miramax Home Entertainment, 2003.

Manning, Erin. 'The Haunted Home: Colour Spectrums in Robert Lepage's *Le Confessionnal*.' *CJFS* 7.2 (Fall 1998): 49–65.

Marshall, Bill. *Quebec National Cinema.* Montreal: McGill-Queen's Univ. Pr., 2001.

Martin, Robert. 'Dr. Bujold's Skill Saves *Coma*.' *Globe and Mail*, 14 Feb. 1978. LexisNexis Academic.

Masterson, Donald. 'My Brother's Keeper: Fraternal Relations in the Films of Guy Maddin and George Toles.' In Church, *Playing with Memories*, 26–47.

Masterson, Richard. 'Family Romances: Memory, Obsession, Loss, and Redemption in the Films of Atom Egoyan.' *University of Toronto Quarterly* 71.4 (Fall 2002): 881–91.

Mathijs, Ernest. *The Cinema of David Cronenberg: From Baron of Blood to Cultural Hero.* London: Wallflower, 2008.

McBride, Jason. 'The Secret Sharer: Guy Maddin's *My Winnipeg*.' *Cinemascope* 32. http://www.cinema-scope.com/cs32/feat_mcbride_winnipeg.html.

McCarthy, Todd. '*Where the Truth Lies.*' *Daily Variety*, 16 May 2005. LexisNexis Academic.

McDonald, Bruce. '*Highway 61.*' *CineAction* 61 (Feb. 2003): 58–61.

McGreal, Jill. 'Canadian Cinema/Cinéma Canadien.' In *The Oxford History of World Cinema*, edited by Geoffrey Nowell-Smith, 731–40. New York: Oxford Univ. Pr., 1996.

McGregor, Gaile. 'Grounding the Countertext: David Cronenberg and the Ethnospecificity of Horror.' *CJFS* 2.1 (1992): 43–62.

McIntosh, Andrew. 'Carole Laure.' *CFE* (last updated Nov. 2007).

– 'Geneviève Bujold.' *CFE* (last updated Nov. 2007).

McIntosh, David. 'Vanishing Point: Proliferations, Purifications and the Convergence of Canadian and Mexican National Cinema.' *CJFS* 10.2 (Fall 2001): 59–79.

McKay, John. 'Already Hot, *Ararat* Skips Spotlight: Atom Egoyan's Controversial Film on Armenian Genocide Will Be Hors-Concours at Cannes.' *Montreal Gazette*, 25 Apr. 2002. LexisNexis Academic.

McKellar, Don. 'Canadian Style: Don McKellar Talks about *Childstar*, Hollywood and Fame.' By Wyndham Wise. *Take One* 47 (Sept. 2004). http://www.highbeam.com/doc/1G1-122765021.html.

– 'Children of Canada.' *Sight & Sound* 9.7 (July 1999): 58–9.

McSorley, Tom. 'The Centre Cannot Hold: The Cinema of Atlantic Canada.' In Loiselle and McSorley, *Self Portraits*, 271–96.

– 'How Do We Know What We Know? Atom Egoyan's *Where the Truth Lies*.' *Take One* 14.51 (Sept.–Dec. 2005): 24.

Melnyk, George. *One Hundred Years of Canadian Cinema*. Toronto: Univ. of Toronto Pr., 2004.

Melnyk, George, ed. *Great Canadian Film Directors*. Edmonton: Univ. of Alberta Pr., 2007.

Merritt, Greg. *Celluloid Mavericks: A History of American Independent Film*. New York: Thunder's Mouth, 2000.

Mihalka, George. 'Interview: George Mihalka.' Canuxploitation, 9 May 2009. http://www.canuxploitation.com/interview/mihalka.

Miller, April. '"The Hair That Wasn't There Before": Demystifying Monstrosity and Menstruation in *Ginger Snaps* and *Ginger Snaps Unleashed*.' *Western Folklore* 64.3/4 (Summer 2005): 281–303.

Milroy, Sarah. 'The Sound of a Canadian Identity: Two Exhibits Set Out to Document the Relationship between Music and Art in Canada, but End Up Doing Much More.' *Globe Review*, 30 Sept. 2003. LexisNexis Academic.

Mlynek, Alex, and Rachel Pulfer. 'Power Players: Canada's Top Actors.' *Canadian Business*, 14 Aug. 2006. http://www.canadianbusiness.com/after_hours/lifestyle_activities/article.jsp?content=20060814_79827_79827&page=3.

Moffitt, Sean. 'TV Buzz – Canada's 43 Most Buzz-able TV Programs.' *Buzz Canuck*, 17 Feb. 2006. http://buzzcanuck.typepad.com/agentwildfire/2006/02/index.html.

Molloy, Patricia. 'Perpetual Flight: The Terror of Biology and Biology of Terror in the *Ginger Snaps* Trilogy.' *Jump Cut* 49 (Spring 2007). http://www.ejumpcut.org/archive/jc49.2007/GingerSnaps/index.html.

Monk, Katherine. *Weird Sex & Snowshoes and Other Canadian Film Phenomena*. Vancouver: Raincoast, 2001.

Morris, Peter. *David Cronenberg: A Delicate Balance*. Toronto: ECW, 1994.

– *Embattled Shadows: A History of Canadian Cinema 1895–1939*. Montreal: McGill-Queen's Univ. Pr., 1978.

Morris, Peter, and Andrew McIntosh. 'Capital Cost Allowance/The Tax Shelter Years: 1975 to 1982.' *CFE* (accessed Jan. 2007).

Mottram, James. *The Sundance Kids: How the Mavericks Took Back Hollywood*. New York: Faber, 2006.

Nadeau, Chantal. 'La Représentation de la femme comme autre: L'Ambiguïté du cinéma de Léa Pool.' *Quebec Studies* 17 (1993): 83–96.

Napoleon, Davi. '*ED* Problem/Solution: The Far Side of The Imagination.' *Entertainment Design* 39.6 (June 2005): 30. IIPA.

Neale, Steve. 'Art Cinema as Institution.' *Screen* 22.1 (1981): 11–39.

O'Mahony, John. 'Aerial Views: In Quebec, He Was a French-Speaking Child with English-Speaking Siblings. Bullied at School, He Had a Breakdown after an Early Experiment with Drugs. Then He Discovered Theatre and Went On to Become One of Its Most Daring Exponents.' *Guardian* (Manchester), 23 June 2001. LexisNexis Academic.

Onstad, Katrina. 'An Actress with Doubts, But Not about Directing.' *New York Times*, 29 Apr. 2007. LexisNexis Academic.

Ouzonian, Richard. 'Dealing with the Ghosts of Genocide.' *Toronto Star*, 5 Sept. 2002. LexisNexis Academic.

Owen, Michael. 'Turn Over a New Lepage: Michael Owen Meets a Theatrical Wunderkind Who Confesses He's Ready for the Movies.' *Evening Standard* (London). 26 Oct. 1995. LexisNexis Academic.

Page, Shelley. 'Oh La La: She Doesn't Go Looking for Them, but Unsettling Roles Just Find Sandra Oh.' *Ottawa Citizen*, 8 Dec. 2001. LexisNexis Academic.

Paizs, John. 'Interview: John Paizs.' Canuxploitation, 20 Jan. 2007. http://www.canuxploitation.com/interview/paizs.html.

– Interview with Jason Anderson. *Eye Weekly.com* (9 Apr. 2008). http://www.eyeweekly.com/film/interview/article/23758.

Parpart, Lee. 'Political Alignments and the Lure of "More Existential Questions" in the Films of Patricia Rozema.' In Beard and White, *North of Everything*, 296–302.

Pendakur, Manjunath. *Canadian Dreams and American Control: The Political Economy of the Canadian Film Industry*. Detroit: Wayne State Univ. Pr., 1990.

Peranson, Mark. 'Riding the Pacific New Wave: Bruce Sweeney Wants His New Movie to Make You Uncomfortable. What Better Choice, Then, to Open the Toronto International Film Festival.' *Globe Review*, 3 Sept. 2001. LexisNexis Academic.

Pevere, Geoff. 'Dances with Natives.' *Globe and Mail*, 10 Mar. 1995. LexisNexis Academic.

– 'Foreword.' In Church, *Playing with Memories*, xi–xiii.

– 'Ghostbusting: 100 Years of Canadian Cinema, or Why My Canada Includes *The Terminator*.' *Take One* 5.12 (Summer 1996): 6–13.

– 'Greenland Revisited: The Winnipeg Film Group during the 1980s.' In *Dislocations*, edited by Gilles Hébert, 37–52. Winnipeg: City Press, 1995.

– 'Guy Maddin: True to Form.' *Take One* (Fall 1992): 4–11. In Church, *Playing with Memories*, 48–57.

– '"Middle of Nowhere" Ontario Movies after 1980.' *Post Script* 15.1 (Fall 1995): 9–22.

– 'No Place like Home: The Films of Atom Egoyan.' In *Exotica: The Screenplay*, edited by Atom Egoyan, 9–42. Toronto: Coach House, 1995.

– 'On the Brink.' *CineAction* 28 (1992): 34–7.

– 'Prairie Postmodern: An Introduction to the Mind and Films of John Paizs.' *Cinema Canada* (Apr. 1985): 11–13.

Pevere, Geoff, and Greig Dymond. *Mondo Canuck: A Canadian Pop Culture Odyssey*. Scarborough: Prentice-Hall, 1996.

Pike, David L. 'Across the Great Divide: Canadian Popular Cinema in the Twenty-First Century.' *Bright Lights Film Journal* 56 (May 2007). http://www.brightlightsfilm.com/56/canada.php.

– 'Canadian Cinema in the Age of Globalization.' *CineAction* 57 (March 2002): 2–10.

– 'Four Films in Search of an Author: Reflections on Egoyan since *Exotica*.' *Bright Lights Film Journal* 52 (May 2006). http://brightlightsfilm.com/52/egoyan.htm.

– *Metropolis on the Styx: The Underworlds of Modern Urban Culture, 1800–2001*. Ithaca: Cornell Univ. Pr., 2007.

– 'The Passing of Celluloid, the Endurance of the Image: Egoyan, "Steenbeckett" and *Krapp's Last Tape*.' In Tschofen and Burwell, *Image + Territory*, 101–22.

– Review of *Adoration*. *Bright Lights Film Journal* 61 (Aug. 2008). http://www.brightlightsfilm.com/61/61adoration_pike.php.

– Review of *Chloe*. *Bright Lights Film Journal* 69 (Aug. 2010). http://www.brightlightsfilm.com/69/69chloe_pike.php.

– 'Thoroughly Modern Maddin.' *CineAction* 65 (November 2004): 6–16.

Pittman, Bruce. 'Shebib Exposes Himself.' *Cinema Canada* 81 (Feb. 1982): 18–21.

Polley, Sarah. 'The New Catchers in the Rye: The Interviews; Sarah Polley.' By Mark Ruffalo. *Interview* 33.1 (Feb. 2003): 137. IIPA.

Posner, Michael. *Canadian Dreams: The Making and Marketing of Independent Films*. Vancouver: Douglas & McIntyre, 1993.

– 'Get This Man a Script, Okay?' *Globe and Mail*, 25 Sept. 1997: C1. LexisNexis Academic.

Presner, Bob. 'Interview with Bob Presner.' Canuxploitation, 19 Oct. 2004. http://www.canuxploitation.com/interview/presner.html.

Privett, Ray. 'The Country of Movies: An Interview with Dusan Makavejev.' *Senses of Cinema* (Dec. 2000). http://archive.sensesofcinema.com/contents/00/11/makavejev.html.

Provencher, Normand. 'Marie-Josée Croze: La quête du talent.' *Le Soleil (Québec)*, 12 July 2008. http://www.cyberPe.ca/le-soleil/200809/08/01-666375-marie-josee-croze-la-quete-du-talent.php.

Ramsay, Christine. 'Canadian Narrative Cinema from the Margins: "The Nation" and Masculinity in *Goin' Down the Road*.' *CJFS* 2.2–3 (1993): 27–49.

– 'Léo Who? Questions of Identity and Culture in Jean-Claude Lauzon's *Léolo*.' *Post Script* 15.1 (1995): 23–37.

– 'Made in Saskatchewan!' In Loiselle and McSorley, *Self Portraits*, 203–35.

Robinson, Marcus. 'Box Office Just Average in '06.' *Playback*, 18 Dec. 2006.

Romney, Jonathan. *Atom Egoyan*. Berkeley: Univ. of California Pr., 2003.

– 'In a World or Two of His Own.' *Independent*, 15 July 2001. LexisNexis Academic.

Rosadiuk, Adam. 'Thirty Two Short Films about Glenn Gould.' In White, *Cinema of Canada*, 162–71.

Rosen, Steven. 'Hoskins, Egoyan, make *Journey* important.' *Denver Post*, 19 Nov. 1999. LexisNexis Academic.

Roy Dupuis Online. '*Montreal Mirror* Best of Montreal Poll.' http://www.roydupuis-online.com/library/others/Best_of_Montreal.htm (accessed 10 Nov. 2010).

Rozema, Patricia. 'Commentary.' *I've Heard the Mermaids Singing*. Directed by Rozema. DVD. Miramax Home Entertainment, 2004.

– 'Interview with Patricia Rozema.' *Yo Yo Ma Inspired by Bach: Six Gestures*. DVD. Rhombus Media/Sony Classical, 2000.

– Interview. By Wyndham Wise. Special edition, *Take One* (Sept.–Nov. 2004): 9–33.

– 'I've Heard the Mermaids Singing: Interview With *Patricia Rozema*.' By Karen Jaehne. *Cineaste* 16.3 (1988): 22–3.

Salles, Walter. 'Notes for a Theory of the Road Movie.' *New York Times Magazine*, 11 Nov. 2007: 66–70.

Sanjek, David. 'Dr. Hobbes's Parasites: Victims, Victimization, and Gender in David Cronenberg's *Shivers*.' *Cinema Journal* 36.1 (Fall 1996): 55–74.

Schaefer, Stephen. 'Egoyan Embarks on Dangerous, Adolescent *Journey*.' *Boston Herald*, 21 Nov. 1999. LexisNexis Academic.

Schwartz, Sanford. 'Enchanted & Ominous.' *New York Review of Books*, 17 July 2008. http://www.nybooks.com/articles/archives/2008/jul/17/enchanted-ominous/.

Scott, Jay. '*Anne Trister*: A Miniature Mosaic on Film.' *Globe and Mail*, 27 Mar. 1987. LexisNexis Academic.

– 'Canada's *Zoo* Causes Sensation at Cannes.' *Globe and Mail*, 11 May 1987. LexisNexis Academic.

– 'Ooh That Is Wonderful, Yes.' *Globe and Mail*, 17 May 1985. LexisNexis Academic.

– '*Un zoo la nuit* Balances Just above the Gutter.' *Globe and Mail*, 16 Apr. 1987. LexisNexis Academic.

Sedgwick, Eve Kosofsky. *Epistemology of the Closet*. Berkeley: Univ. of California Pr., 1990.

Seguin, Denis. 'A *C.R.A.Z.Y.* Situation.' *Canadian Business*, 21 Nov. 2005. LexisNexis Academic.

Semley, John. 'From Big Snow to Big Sadness: The Repatriation of Canadian Cultural Identity in the Films of Guy Maddin.' *CineAction* (Summer 2007). http://www.highbeam.com/doc/1G1-178268104.html.

Shaviro, Steven. *The Cinematic Body*. Minneapolis: Univ. of Minnesota Pr., 1993.

– 'Fire and Ice: The Films of Guy Maddin.' In Beard and White, *North of Everything*, 216–21.

Shipman, Nell. *The Silent Screen & My Talking Heart*. Boise: Boise State Univ. Pr., 1987.

Silverman, Jason. '*Dead Man*.' In White, *Cinema of Canada*, 183–94.

Simmons, Rochelle. 'Border Crossings: Representations of North American Culture in Bruce McDonald's *Highway 61*.' *CineAction* 61 (Feb. 2003): 58–61.

Simons, Tony. '*Anne Trister*.' In *Where Are the Voices Coming From? Canadian Culture and the Legacies of History*, edited by Coral Ann Howells, 231–46. Amsterdam: Rodopi, 2004.

– '"Tout le monde croit que je suis un Canadien français. Parce que moi je rêve, je ne le suis pas." Les conflits identitaires dans *Léolo* de Jean-Claude Lauzon.' *Globe: revue internationale d'études québécoises* 6.1 (2003): 107–23.

Sinclair, Iain. *Crash*. BFI Modern Classics. London: BFI, 2008.

Siraganian, Lisa. 'Telling a Horror Story, Conscientiously: Representing the Armenian Genocide from *Open House* to *Ararat*.' In Tschofen and Burwell, *Image + Territory*, 133–56.

Smith, Gavin. 'Alan Rudolph: I Don't Have a Career, I Have a Careen.' *Film Comment* 29.3 (May 1993): 59–71.

Smith, Scott. '24 and the Rules of Death.' *The TOC Blog*, 19 Sept. 2007. http://timeoutchicago.com/things-to-do/out-about-blog/135455/24-and-the-rules-of-death.

Snyder, Stephen. 'Sexuality and Self in the Guy Maddin Vision.' In Church, *Playing with Memories*, 119–32.

Soderbergh, Steven. 'Steven Soderbergh: Hiding in Plain Sight.' By Alex Simon. *The Hollywood Interview*, 21 Mar. 2008. http://thehollywoodinterview.blogspot.com/2008/03/steven-soderbergh-hollywood-interview.html.

Spaner, David. *Dreaming in the Rain: How Vancouver Became Hollywood North by Northwest*. Vancouver: Arsenal Pulp, 2003.

– 'Egoyan Returns to His Roots: His Drama of Armenian Genocide Is the Big Canadian Film of Christmas Season.' *Vancouver Province*, 10 Nov. 2002. LexisNexis Academic.

Staines, David. 'Frye: Canadian Critic/Writer.' In *Northrop Frye's Canadian Literary Criticism and Its Influence*, edited by Branko Gorjup, 251–9. Toronto: Univ. of Toronto Pr., 2009.

Sterritt, David. 'Review of *I've Heard the Mermaids Singing*.' *Christian Science Monitor*, 23 Sept. 1987. LexisNexis Academic.

Stoffman, Judy. 'A Film, Cup of Joe, Some Chat; Screening Room Has 50 Seats.' *Toronto Star*, 29 Sept. 2004. LexisNexis Academic.

Stone, Jay. 'Egoyan and the Urge to Forget: Memory, Resolution Are Director's Themes in Film, *Ararat*.' *Ottawa Citizen*, 6 Sept. 2002. LexisNexis Academic.

– 'Quebec Director Takes the "Slow" Path: After Six French Films, Lea Pool Enters the English Market with *Lost and Delirious*.' *Ottawa Citizen*, 21 July 2001. LexisNexis Academic.

Straw, Will. 'Reinhabiting Lost Languages: Guy Maddin's *Careful*.' In Walz, *Canada's Best Features*, 304–17.

– 'The Thingishness of Things.' *Invisible Culture* 2 (1999). http://www.rochester.edu/in_visible_culture/issue2/straw.htm.

Taubin, Amy. 'Death Be Not Proud.' *Village Voice* 44.44 (9 Nov. 1999): 140.

– 'Foreign Affairs: David Cronenberg Talks about His Strangely Intimate New Russian Mafia.' *Film Comment* 43.5 (Sept./Oct. 2007): 52–5.

Taylor, Aaron. 'Blood in the Maple Syrup: Canon, Popular Genre and the Canuxploitation of Julian Roffman.' *CineAction* 61 (Feb. 2003): 18–28.

Taylor, Craig. 'Paradoxes of a Beautiful Life.' *Guardian* (Manchester), 25 Oct. 2003. LexisNexis Academic.

Telefilm Canada. 'History.' http://www.telefilm.gc.ca/en/telefilm/telefilm/history (accessed 10 July 2009).

Testa, Bart. 'Technology's Body: Cronenberg, Genre, and the Canadian Ethos.' *Post Script* 15.1 (Fall 1995): 38–56.

Thiessen, Randy. 'Deconstructing Masculinity in *Porky's*.' *Post Script* 18.2 (Winter/Spring 1999): 64–74.

Toles, George. 'Drowning for Love: Jean-Claude Lauzon's *Léolo*.' In Walz, *Canada's Best Features*, 275–303.

Toronto Star. 'Applause Greets Egoyan's New Movie.' 19 May 1999. LexisNexis Academic.

– 'Lessons can be found in Canadian loss.' 22 May 2005. LexisNexis Academic.

Torregrosa, Luisita Lopez. '*L Word* Star Basks in an Erotic Mystery.' *New York Times*, 5 Apr. 2004. LexisNexis Academic.

Tousignant, Isa. '*Séraphin*: Charles Binamé Talks about the Enduring Appeal of a Classic Tale from Quebec.' *Take One* 11.41 (Mar.–May 2003): 8–13.

Trelkubrations. 'Les meilleurs films québécois.' 11 Feb. 2007. http://trelkubrations.canalblog.com/archives/2007/02/11/3973489.html.

Tschofen, Monique. '*Le Confessionnal*,' In White, *Cinema of Canada*, 204–13.

– 'Repetition, Compulsion, and Representation in Atom Egoyan's Films.' In Beard and White, *North of Everything*, 166–83.

Tschofen, Monique, and Jennifer Burwell, eds. *Image + Territory: Essays on Atom Egoyan*, Waterloo, ON: Wilfrid Laurier Univ. Pr., 2006.

Urquhart, Peter. 'Film History/Film Policy: From the Canadian Film Development Corporation to Telefilm Canada.' In Loiselle and McSorley, *Self Portraits*, 29–54.

– 'You Should Know Something – *Anything* – about this Movie. You Paid For It.' *CJFS* 12.2 (Fall 2003): 64–80.

VanderBurgh, Jennifer. 'Ghostbusted! Popular Perceptions of Canadian Cinema.' *CJFS* 12.2 (Fall 2003): 81–98.

Varga, Darrell. '*Atanarjuat: The Fast Runner*.' In White, *Cinema of Canada*, 225–33.

– 'Desire in Bondage: Maddin's *Careful*.' *CJFS* 8.2 (Fall 1999): 56–70.

– 'The Local and the Global Revisited: *Un 32 août sur terre*.' *CineAction* 65 (Jan. 2005): 30.

– 'Locating the Artist in *Thirty Two Short Films about Glenn Gould*.' *CJFS* 12.2 (Fall 2003): 99–120.

Variety. 'Rev. of *Lilies*.' 9–15 Sept. 1996: 121. IIPA.

Vatnsdal, Caelum. *Kino Delirium: The Films of Guy Maddin*. Winnipeg: Arbeiter Ring, 2000.

– *They Came from Within: A History of Canadian Horror Cinema*. Winnipeg: Arbeiter Ring, 2004.

Véronneau, Pierre. 'Genres and Variations: The Audiences of Quebec Cinema.' In Loiselle and McSorley, *Self Portraits*, 93–127.

– 'Quebec Feature Films: The First Wave; 1944–53.' *Cinema Canada* 56 (June–July 1979): 42–6.

Virgo, Clement. 'Interview with Clement Virgo.' Conquering Lions Productions Inc. *Rude* Press Kit, 1995. Film file held at the Toronto Film Reference Library.

Walz, Gene, ed. *Canada's Best Features: Critical Essays on 15 Canadian Films*. Amsterdam: Rodopi, 2002.

Warren, Ina. 'Typecast at 21? Psycho Roles Started to Worry David Hewlett.' *Globe and Mail*, 29 Dec. 1989. LexisNexis Academic (accessed 26 July 2009).

Waugh, Thomas. 'Cinemas, Nations, Masculinities: The Martin Walsh Memorial Lecture (1998).' *CJFS* 8.1 (Spring 1999): 8–44.

– *The Romance of Transgression in Canada: Queering Sexualities, Nations, Cinemas*. Montreal: McGill-Queen's Univ. Pr., 2006.

Waxman, Sharon. *Rebels on the Backlot: Six Maverick Directors and How They Conquered the Hollywood Studio System*. New York: Harper, 2005.

Weese, Katherine. 'Family Stories: Gender and Discourse in Atom Egoyan's *The Sweet Hereafter*.' *Narrative* 10.1 (Jan. 2002): 76–80.

Weinmann, Heinz. *Cinéma de l'imaginaire québécois: De 'La Petite Aurore' à 'Jésus de Montréal*.' Montreal: L'Hexagone, 1990.

Wershler, Darren. *My Winnipeg*. Toronto: Univ. of Toronto Pr., 2010.

White, Jerry. 'Alanis Obomsawin, Documentary Form, and the Canadian Nation(s).' In Beard and White, *North of Everything*, 364–75.

– ed. *The Cinema of Canada*. London: Wallflower, 2006.

– 'A Typically Canadian Cinema: Filmmaking in Alberta, Its Institutions and Authors.' In Loiselle and McSorley, *Self Portraits*, 297–317.

Whyte, Murray. 'Facing the Pain of a Past Long Hidden.' *New York Times*, 17 Nov. 2002. LexisNexis Academic.

Wilson, Emma. *Atom Egoyan*. Urbana: Univ. of Illinois Pr., 2009.

Wilson, Sandy. 'You Can Go Home Again.' By John Lekich. *Globe and Mail*, 24 Nov. 1984. LexisNexis Academic (accessed 5 Aug. 2009).

Wise, Wyndham. 'Robert Lantos.' *CFE* (last updated Sept. 2004).

– 'Up from the Underground: Filmmaking in Toronto from *Winter Kept Us Warm* to *Shivers*.' In Gravestock and Van den Ven, *Toronto on Film*, 87–107.

Wolf, Matt. 'Robert Lepage: Multicultural and Multifaceted.' *New York Times*, 6 Dec. 1992. LexisNexis Academic.

Wood, Robin. 'On William D. MacGillivray.' *CineAction* 69 (Spring 2006): 24–33.

Index

Page numbers in italics refer to figures

Abitibi, Quebec, 119
Abkarian, Simon, 212, 216
Aboriginal Canadian, 4, 10, 275; actors, 5, 114, 117, 132, 229, 234, 245–6, 250, 252–3; film-makers, 5–6, 114, 146, 250–5, 286–7; representations, 5, 20, 34, 35, 117, 128, 132, 191–2, 229, 234, 245–6, 251–5. *See also names of tribes and indigenous peoples*
A bout de souffle (Godard), 273
Academy Awards. *See under* awards
Ackroyd, Dan, xii, 101, 172, 175
A corps perdu (Pool), 155–6, 157
action film, 108, 192–8, 202, 239
Act of the Heart (Almond), 39, 111
Adjuster, The (Egoyan), x, 100, 139, 183, 206, 213, 219, 224, 225, 307n18
Adoration (Egoyan), 78, 206, 207, 209, 211, 213, 214, 219, 221, 225, 237, 307n18
Adventure of Faustus Bidgood, The (Jones), 242
Adventures of Baron Munchausen, The (Gilliam), 134
advertising, 92, 97, 145, 146, 278, 296n34
Aeneid (Virgil), 3
L'Age des ténèbres (Arcand), 105, 285
Africville, Halifax, 243
AIDS. *See* cinema, HIV / AIDS in
Air Bud (Smith), 172
Airplane!, 18
Alberta: persons from, 97, 125, 239; film-making, 192, 239–41, 297n39, 311n37; setting, 185, 192, 229, 241; as stand-in location, 308n38. *See also names of cities and sites*
Alberta Motion Picture Development Corporation, 297n39, 310n18, 311n33
Alfred Hitchcock Presents (Egoyan), 223
Alice in Wonderland, 211, 308n28

Alien (Scott), 196
Alien Resurrection (Jeunet), 193
Alien series, 193
allegory: of the artist, 71; biopolitical, 305n66; of film-making, 12, 104, 219–21; generational, 103–4, 263; historical, 196; modernist, 275; national, 88, 149–50, 182, 220–2, 235, 262; political, 31, 37–8, 111, 142, 148; religious, 87, 97, 99; in science fiction, 193, 200
Allen, Jay and Jules, 19
Allen, Jeremy Peter: *Manners of Dying*, 122, 123
Alliance, 101, 126, 142, 144, 196
Alliance Atlantis, 144, 197, 243
Almodóvar, Pedro, x, 161, 162
Almond, Paul, 39, 63, 111; *Act of the Heart*, 39, 111; *Isabel*, 39, 111; *Journey*, 39
Almost Famous (Crowe), 135
Alpay, David, 209, 221
Alphaville (Godard), 60
Altman, Rick, 174
Altman, Robert, 59; *Long Goodbye*, 280
Amanita Pestilens (Bonnière), 111
'America, America' (Egoyan), 224
America, America (Kazan), 224, 309n50
American Boyfriends (Wilson), 233
American Graffiti (Lucas), 233
Amores Perros (Iñárritu), 169
Anderson, Pamela, 109
And the Band Played On (Shilt), 258
Ange de goudron, L' (Chouinard), 167
Ange et la femme, L' (Carle), 116
Animal House (Reitman), 182
Animation: Canadian, 13; effects, 202, 230, 276; Nelvana, 198; NFB, 19, 23, 27, 29–31; 1920s, 276–7

Anka, Paul, 233

Anna Karenina (Rose), 132

année dernière à Marienbad, L' (Resnais), 165

Anne of the Thousand Days (Jarrott), 111

Anne Trister (Pool), 154

Apaq Angilirk, Paul: *Atanarjuat*, xi, 5–6, 246, 247, 253–5, 286–7, 312n89, 312n94

Apatow, Judd, 123

Apocalypse Now (Coppola), 231

Appadurai, Arjun, 235, 237

Apprenticeship of Duddy Kravitz, The (Kotcheff), 13, 39–40, 43, 58, 104, 158

Ararat, Mount, Armenia, 212

Ararat (Egoyan), 124, 206, 209, 211–12, 213, 214, 216–17, 220–2, 223, 224, 250, 305n1, 307n25, 308nn29–32, 308nn37–8, 309nn42–5, 309n50, 312n74

Arcand, Denys, 89–106; actor, 79, 81, 98, 104; advertising, 92, 146; auteur, 123, 218; career trajectory, xiii, 14, 36, 79, 89, 144, 285; in English, xii–xiii, 14, 79, 93, 97, 99–101, 131, 162, 165, 183, 258; and genre cinema, 89–92, 96; and Hollywood, xii, 98, 174; philosophy of history of, 23, 89, 93–6, 105; reception, 91, 93; and religion, 79, 96–9, 105–6; satirist, 89, 92, 97, 102, 165; scriptwriter, 36, 89, 91, 258; television, 89, 91, 99

Arcand, Denys, works of: *Age des ténèbres*, 105, 285; *Confort et l'indifférence*, 90, 92, 96; *Crime d'Ovide Plouffe*, 89; *Déclin de l'empire américain*, ix–x, xii, 9, 14, 23, 79, 81, 89, 90–1, 92–7, 99, 100, 102, 105, 155, 172, 179, 194, 257; *Duplessis*, 89; *Empire, Inc.*, 89, 91; *Gina*, 89, 90–3, 117, 296n19; *Invasions barbares*, 14, 79, 89, 102–5, 122, 124, 285; *Jésus de Montréal*, x, 14, 79, 89, 91, 96–9, 100, 102, 105, 146, 147, 165, 172, 289n16; *Joyeux Calvaire*, 99; *Love & Human Remains*, 79, 97, 99–101, 131, 165, 183, 297n39; *Maudite Galette*, 89, 90; *On est au coton*, 89–90, 91, 93; *Québec*, 90, 91; *Réjeanne Padovani*, 89, 90, 91; *Seul ou avec des autres*, 36; *Stardom*, xii–xiii, 79, 93, 97, 99, 100–1, 165

Arcand, Gabriel, 91, 92

Archangel (Maddin), 275, 279, 281

Argent de poche, L' (Truffaut), 43

Arletty, 19, 109

Arli$$, 129

Armatage, Kay, 20, 22

Armenia, 206, 214, 216, 219

Armenian Canadian, 153, 206, 207, 220–2, 250, 309n42, 312n74

Arnatsiaq, Peter-Henry, *255*

Arquette, Rosanna, 72

Arroyo, José, 11, 245

Artaud Double Bill (Egoyan), 224, 307n18

art: avant-garde, 275, 280, 281, 283; drawing, 243–4; eighties scene, x, 84, 196; gallery, 84, 87, 224, 270; and globalization, 142; modernist, 269; painting, 44–5, 85, 154, 212; performance, 82, 101, *189*; photography, 82, 84, 93, 154, 156, 157, 189–90; post-colonial, 36; postmodern, 87, 101; symbolist, 277; video, 84, 97, 224, 244. *See also* cinema, art; *names of artists and movements*

art cinemas. *See names of cinemas*

Art of War, The (Duguay), 197–8

Ashby, Hal: *Harold and Maude*, ix, 189

Asian Canadian, 28, 163; actors, 128, 129–30, 234, 247, 248, 250, 264–6; film-makers, 142, 234, 238, 247, 248–50, 264–6; representations, 24, 75–6, 95, 232, 238, 247, 248–50, 264–6

Asselin, Emile, 26

Astral, 176

Atanarjuat: The Fast Runner (Kunuk, Apak Angilirk, and Cohn), xi, 5–6, 246, 247, 253–5, 286–7, 312n89, 312n94

Atlantic Canada, 236, 246, 262; film-makers, 242

Atlantis, 142, 144

A tout prendre (Jutra), 35, 36, 178, 257

At the Suicide of the Last Jew in the World at the Last Cinema in the World (Cronenberg), 78, 250

Atwood, Margaret, 3

Augé, Marc, 229

Aurore (Dionne), 27

Austin Powers movies, 5

auteurism: limits of, 12–13, 43, 83, 204–5; 'professional families' and, 62, 110, 214, 218–19, 220–2; theory of, 12–13, 218, 306n3. *See also names of film-makers; and under* cinema, art; cinema, French; cinema, genre; cinema, independent; cinema, world

authenticity: documentary, 38, 41, 61, 138, 158, 181, 253; emotional, 222, 272, 278; ethnographic, 5, 20, 34–5, 249; local, 5, 34–5, 39, 59, 229, 231; of memory, 206; professional, 59, 111, 125, 174

Avatar (Cameron), 303n2

awards: Academy, xii, 18, 27, 101, 111, *112*, 117, 220; Emmy, 197; festival, 124, 154, 260, 309n40; Gemini, 128, 129; Genie, 110, 113, *120*, 128, 129, 130, 145, 150, 172, 197, 221, 260, 284, 298n22; Golden Reel, 172, 284, 285; Jutra, 110, *120*, 122, 221; music, 228

Away from Her (Polley), 32, 137, 138, 143

Azmi, Shabana, 265

Aznavour, Charles: actor, 214, 220; 'Emmenez-moi,' 153, 263; as musician, 152–3, 263–4

'Bach Cello Suite #4: Sarabande' (Egoyan), 224

Back to God's Country, 20–2, 32, 176

Badley, Linda, 188

Bailey, Cameron, 248

Baillargeon, Paule, 79, 84, 154

Balaban, Liane, 242

Baldwin, Stephen, 107, 201

Balfour, Ian: *Subtitles*, 224–5

Ballard, J. G.: *Crash*, 73; *High Rise*, 198

Ballistic: Ecks vs. Sever, 239

Banff, Alberta, 227

Bangs, Lester, 232, 286

Bankolé, Isaach de, 98

Banks, Caerthan, 219

Banks, Russell, 219; *Sweet Hereafter*, xi, 208, 217, 307n17, 309n39

Banning, Kass, 305n1

Barbarash, Ernie: *Cube Zero*, 193, 200

Bardem, Javier, 108

Bardot, Brigitte, 109

Barker, Philip, 219

Barnet, Steve: *Scanner Cop II*, 192

Barney, Matthew: *Cremaster*, 279

Barrett, Syd, 264

Bartók, Béla: *Bluebeard's Castle*, 211

Baruchel, Jay, 123, 175

Barzman, Paolo: *Emotional Arithmetic*, 122

Bas-Saint-Laurent, Quebec, 105

Bates, Alan, 111

Battlefield Earth, 124

Battleship Potemkin (Eisenstein), 280

Baudelaire, Charles, 269, 300n21

Bazin, André, 146

Beach, Adam, 252, 253

Bean, 129

Beard, William, 50, 54, 55, 56, 57, 60–1, 70–1, 72, 294n37, 294n48

Beatles, The, 253

Beaty, Bart, 241

Beaudin, Jean: *Being at Home with Claude*, 121, 257; *Diable parmi nous*, 188; *Filles de Caleb*, 119, 121

Beauté de Pandore, La (Binamé), 121

Beckett, Samuel, 224, 272; *Happy Days*, 80, 81, 83, 86, 224; *Krapp's Last Tape*, 217, 224

Behrman, Keith: *Flower & Garnet*, 128

Beineix, Jean-Jacques: *Diva*, ix, 9, 147, 148

Being at Home with Claude (Beaudin), 121, 257

Bélanger, Louis, xiii

Belle-Baie, 121

Belle et la bête, La (Cocteau), 307n22

Bell Lightbox, Toronto, 110

Belmondo, Jean-Paul, 109, 111

Benjamin, Walter, 23, 282

Benner, Richard: *Outrageous!*, 45

Benoit, Jacques: *Comment faire l'amour avec un nègre*, 98

Benton, Robert: *Kramer vs. Kramer*, 64

Beresford, Bruce: *Black Robe*, 251

Bergman, Ingmar, ix, 39, 62, 80, 218, 303n11

Bergman, Ingrid, 19

Berling, Charles, xiii, 101

Bernal, Gael García, 108

Berri Cinema, Montreal, 261

Berryman, Dorothée, 194

Bersani, Leo, 259

Bertolucci, Bernardo, 145, 147

Berton, Pierre, 19, 25, 31

Bessai, Carl: *Unnatural & Accidental*, 128

Besson, Luc, 9, 290n19; *Nikita*, 9, 290n19; *Subway*, 147

Best, Thom: *Queer as Folk*, 257

Better Than Chocolate (Wheeler), 238, 262

Between Friends (Shebib), 43

Biafra, Jello, 232

Big Heat, The (Lang), 1

Bigras, Jean-Yves, 26; *La petite Aurore*, 25, 26, 32

Bijelic, Andre, 199

Bill and Ted, 202

Billson, Anne, 61

Binamé, Charles, xiii, 26, 27, 261; *Beauté de Pandore*, 121; *Blanche*, 119, 121, 124; *C'était le 12 du 12*, 121; *Eldorado*, 121, 167; *Marguerite Volant*, 121; *Maurice Richard*, 119; *Séraphin*, 26, 124, 173

biopic: Quebecois, 121, 123, 124

Birmingham, England, 214, 220

Birth of a Nation, The (Griffith), 3

Bishop, Charles, 243

Bishop, Kenneth, 24; *Secrets of Chinatown*, 24

Biswas, Seema, 266

Bitter Ash, The (Kent), 41

Black, Ryan, 252

Black Canadians, 28, 98, 100, 243, 244, 247–8

Black Christmas (Clark), 45, 185, 187

Black Dahlia, The (De Palma), 132

Black Lake, Quebec, 37, 176

Black Robe (Beresford), 251

Blade Runner (Scott), 174, 197

Blanche (Binamé), 119, 121, 124
Bleeders (Svatek), 185
Blier, Bertrand: *Préparez vos mouchoirs*, 117
Blindness (McKellar and Meirelles), 143
Blood and Donuts (Dale), 184, 198
Bloody Brood, The (Roffman), 185
'Bluebeard,' 210–11
Bluebeard's Castle (Bartók and Lepage), 211
Blue Butterfly, The (Pool), 122, 160, 285
Blue Monkey (Fruet), 185
Blue Velvet (Lynch), x, 189
Bluteau, Lothaire, 97, 165, 252
body: dead, 37, 45, 77, 148, 166, 188, 214, *215*, 242,
     279; existential, 64, 73, 77, 150, 160, 201–2, 203;
     language, 85–6, 122; Quebecois cinema, 178,
     242; spectacular, 70, 77, 114–17, 121, 138, 164,
     178, 180–1, 211; and technology, 62, 183, 194.
     See also under Cronenberg, David; horror, body
Bogosian, Eric, 220
Bollywood cinema. *See* cinema, Bollywood
Bollywood/Hollywood (Mehta), 249–50, 265, 266
Bon Cop Bad Cop (Canuel), 123, 147, 173
Bonnière, René: *Amanita Pestilens*, 111
bons debarras, Les (Mankiewicz), 36
Borden, Lizzie: *Born in Flames*, 248
Bordwell, David, 303n11
Borges, Jorge Luis, 275
Born in Flames (Borden), 248
Borsos, Philip: *One Magic Christmas*, 134
Bostick, Devon, 209
Boulard, Michel Marc: *Les Feluettes*, 260
Bourgault, Pierre, 149, 150
Boutin, David, 262
Bowie, David, 264; 'Space Oddity,' 152, 264
boxing, 248.
Boys Club, The (Fawcett), 198
Boys franchise, *Les* (Saïa), 123, 178
Boyz n the Hood (Singleton), 8
Brady Bunch, The, 247
Brand, Dionne, 246
Brand upon the Brain! (Maddin), 270, 279, 314n25
Brault, Michel, 33, 34, 36; cinematographer, 31,
     34, 36, 148; *Entre la mer et l'eau douce*, 35, 36, 111;
     noces de papier, 36, 113; *Les Ordres*, 36; *Pour la
     suite du monde*, 34, 38; *Raquetteurs*, 34, 38
Brel, Jacques, 152
Briand, Manon, xiii, 164; *Turbulence des fluides*,
     113–14
Briefel, Aviva, 191
British Broadcasting Corporation (BBC), 237

British Columbia: setting, 135, 220; film-making,
     24, 238
British Museum, London, 253
Brody, Adrien, 202
Brood, The (Cronenberg), 51, 59, 60, 61, 62, 63,
     64–6, 68
Brooklyn, New York, 101, 248
Broue, 178
Browning, Robert: 'Pied Piper,' 210
Browning, Will, 301n59
Bruce, Jean, 265
Bruneau, Eric, 235
Bryar, Gavin: *Dr. Ox's Experiment*, 223–4
Bugajski, Richard: *Clearcut*, 234, 251
Buhagiar, Valerie, 231, 232
Bujold, Geneviève, 110–14, 124, 131; American
     indie, ix, 110, 113; English-Canadian, 39, 72,
     110–11, 113–14, 139, 298n22; French art cinema,
     110–11, 118; Hollywood, 108, 110, 111–13;
     international star, 107, 110–14, 118, 119, 142;
     Quebecois, 14, 110–11, 113–14, 116
Buñuel, Luis, 269
Burgess, Diane, 238
Burns, Gary, xiii, 236, 239–41, 274; *Kitchen Party*,
     239, 311n33; *Problem with Fear*, 240; *Radiant
     City*, 239, 241; *Suburbanators*, 239, *waydown-
     town*, 240
Burroughs, Jackie, 298n22; actor, 185, 228, 229,
     298n22; *Winter Tan*, 298n22
Burroughs, William S., 53, 63, 71
Burton, Richard, 111
Burwell, Jennifer, 305n1
Bussières, Pascale, 118–25; child actor, xii, 122;
     English-Canadian, 79, 107, 119, 121, 122, 201,
     270, 313n5; French art cinema, 119, 122; Que-
     becois star, 14, 27, 79, 107, 119–25, 158, 235, 270;
     queer icon, 122
Butler, Tom, 195
Byford, Chris, 232

Cadavres (Canuel), 147
Cadieux, Jason, 261
Cagle, Robert, 85, 256
Cahiers du cinéma, 44, 218
Calendar (Egoyan), 206, 212, 214, 219, 224, 308n36
Calgary, Alberta, 227, 230, 236, 239–41; film-
     makers and actors, 236, 239–41
California, 43, 163, 202, 231, 233, 235. *See also*
     cinema, Hollywood
Californication, 128–9

Camera Bar, Toronto, 225

Cameron, James, 19, 50, 172, 193; *Avatar*, 303n2; *Terminator 2*, 303n2; *Titanic*, 173, 303n2

Camilla (Mehta), 265

camp, 245–6, 256, 264, 268, 269, 272, 315n49

Campion, Jane: *The Piano*, 88, 211

Canada: conservatism, 7, 26, 27, 56, 90, 134–5, 242, 263; dual perspective, 5–6, 23, 61, 242–3, 266; mosaic, 15, 88, 172, 227–66; relationship to United States, 11, 61; transcontinental railway, 156–7, 227, 230; visible minorities, 28, 167, 227, 246–50, 264–6; wilderness, 19–20, 65, 234. *See also names of specific ethnic groups*; cinema, Canadian; cinema, English-Canadian; cinema, Quebecois; English Canadian; identity: Canadian; Quebec

Canadian Broadcasting Corporation (CBC): movies, 41, 111, 125, 129, 197, 223, 267, 278; in Quebec, 26; television series, 83, 89, 91, 128, 134, 140, 142, 243. *See also* Radio-Canada

Canadian cinema. *See* cinema, Canadian

Canadian Council for the Arts, 236

Canadian Film Development Corporation. *See under* Telefilm Canada

Canadian Motion Picture Distributors Association, 172

Canadian Opera Company (COC), 211, 223–4

Canadian Pacific railway, 19, 227

Canby, Vincent, 147

Candid Eye, 31

Candy, John, 175

Cannes Film Festival. *See under* film festivals; awards

Cannibal Girls (Reitman), 177

Canuel, Erik, 146–7, 171, 185; *Bon Cop Bad Cop*, 123, 147, 173; *Cadavres*, 147; *dernier tunnel*, 147; *Flashpoint*, 147; *Loi du cochon*, 147

Canuxploitation (Corupe), 171, 303n1

CanWest Global Communications, 144

Cape Breton Island, Nova Scotia, 41, 130, 242–4

Capital Cost Allowance. *See* cinema, Canadian: tax shelter years

Capture, La (Laure), 118

Care Bears Movie, The (Selznick), 172, 185

Careful (Maddin), x, 45, 270, 274, 275, 278, 279

Carle, Gilles, 27, 33, 36, 41, 114, 116–17, 118; and advertising, 296n34; *L'Ange et la femme*, 116; *Corps Célestes*, 116; *Les Mâles*, 116; and maple syrup porno, 91, 131, 178, 180; *Maria Chapdelaine*, 27, 116; *Mort d'un bûcheron*, 116, 117, 235, 298n35; *Les Plouffe*, 27; *Red*, 116; *Tête de Normande St.-Onge*, 116; *Viol d'une jeune fille douce*, 116; *vraie nature de Bernadette*, 116

Carmody, Don: *Surrogate*, 118

Carpenter, John, 59; *Halloween*, 181

Carrey, Jim, 5, 50, 109, 172, 175

Carrière, Marcel, 31

Cartier-Bresson, Henri, 31

Carver, Brent, 261

Case of the Missing Mother, The (Rozema), 83, 296n5

Caserne Dalhousie, La, Quebec City, 166

Cassavetes, John, 8

Cassidy, Elaine, 211

CBS-television, 130, 197

celebrity: Canadian, 105, 109, 110, 125, 135, 271; culture, 83, 97, 99, 100, 104, 211

Center of the World, The (Wang), 130

Century Hotel (Weaver), 132

C'était le 12 du 12 et Chili avait les blues (Binamé), 121

Chacun son cinéma, 78, 224, 307n18

Chairy Tale, A (McLaren), 30–1

Chambers, Marilyn, 56

Channa, Rahul, 250

Channel Four, 8, 80, 224

Chapman, Alexander, 261

Chartrand, Alain: *Ding et Dong*, 172, 178

chat dans le sac, Le (Groulx), 35

Château Frontenac, Quebec City, 167, 168

Chaykin, Maury, 222

Chicago, Illinois, xi, 12, 172

children. *See* coming-of-age film; cinema, Hollywood: children; English Canadian: childhood; Inuit: children; Quebec: childhood. *See also under* cinema, Canadian

Children of Men (Cuarón), 169

Childstar (McKellar), 139, 140, 142, 146

Child without Qualities, The (Maddin), 271, 278, 282

Chinese Canadian: actors, 265; film-makers, 234, 238, 247, 248; representations, 24, 75–6, 129, 163, 238, 247, 248

Chloe (Egoyan), 202, 206, 207, 209, 210, 213, 214–15, 218, 219, 220, 223, 225, 307n18

Choose Me (Rudolph), 113

Chouinard, Dénis: *Ange de goudron*, 167; *Délivrez-moi*, 114

Christiansen, Hayden, 18

Christie, Julie, 135, 138

Christmas Story, A (Clark), 185

Chronique d'un été (Rouch), 34

Chula, Babz, 238, 239

Cinar, 142

Cineaste, 309n47

Cinecity, Toronto, 55

cinema, art: and auteurism, 79, 91, 111, 123, 169, 174, 180, 183; Canadian, xiii, 14, 31, 44, 45, 46, 47, 79, 106, 138, 185, 187; career, xiii, 140; coming-of-age in, 261–2; contemporary, 121, 148, 229; eighties, ix, 174; English, xiii, 111; English-Canadian, xi, 7, 15, 45, 63, 80, 119, 134, 138, 182–3, 202, 203, 204–26, 242, 243, 247, 266; European, 39, 55, 108, 114, 116, 155, 222, 280; French, 110, 111; as genre, 27, 144, 160, 174; 303n11; icons, xiii, 107, 123, 138, 147; and popular genres, 13, 15, 57, 60, 105, 123, 160, 180, 187; Quebecois, 4, 27, 93, 110, 121, 123, 124, 144–70, 147, 148, 170, 172, 173, 175, 178, 301n39; seventies, 110, 155; sex in, 9, 108, 131, 176, 178, 270, 303n15; sixties, xiii, 39, 110, 224; transnational, 12, 23, 147, 165. *See also under* cinema, exploitation

cinema, Bollywood, x, 175, 248–50, 265–6, 281. *See also under* musical

cinema, Canadian: before 1939, 17–24, 32, 236; critical discourse on, xii, 3–5, 10, 12–13, 20, 24, 33, 43–4, 46–7, 50, 56–7, 84, 142, 185, 187–8, 203, 204, 249, 252, 255–6, 262, 285, 287; distinctive qualities of, 10–12, 16, 23, 285–7; and Holly-wood, 23–5, 40, 57, 61, 109, 125, 128, 138, 140, 171–3, 181, 183, 192, 264, 267, 279; as 'minor' cinema, 16, 23, 46, 232, 283, 286–7, 315n49; provincial funding of, xiii, 7, 15, 166, 236–7, 244, 260, 272, 284, 310n18; 'quota quickies,' 22–4, 46; sixties and early seventies, xiii, 33–44, 53–6, 89–91, 110–13, 116–17, 233, 285–6, 287; stars in, 107–43; tax-shelter years, xiii, 6, 44–7, 58, 59, 61–3, 110, 118, 144, 171, 172, 176, 198, 223, 285–6, 292n100; twenty-first century, 76–8, 102–5, 138, 142–3, 169–70, 204, 205, 225–6, 228–30, 284–7; 'two solitudes' in, 10, 13, 39, 123, 188, 260–1; and the United States, ix–xiii, 11–12, 94, 104, 125–43, 167–8, 232–6, 279–81; and urban centres, 6, 9, 35–6, 233, 236–8, 240–1, 243, 274. *See also* Canadian Broadcasting Cor-poration; cinema, English-Canadian; cinema, Quebecois; National Film Board of Canada; Radio-Canada; Telefilm Canada; *under specific genres and topics*

cinema, English-Canadian, xiii, 48–78, 80–8, 125–43, 204–26, 228–34, 238–46, 256–62, 267–83, 284; eighties new wave, xii, 9, 10, 45, 88, 100, 134, 142, 204, 236, 238; lack of specific identity of, 11–12, 17, 40, 43, 173; until 1939, 20–5; pes-simism of, 81, 200; post-war, 29–31; provincial support of, 7, 218, 236, 284; Quebecois actors in, 107, 114, 118, 119, 121, 122, 124, 201, 202, 209, 220, 221; and Quebecois cinema, 13, 17, 79, 100, 142, 176, 177, 232; and queer television, 257; sixties, 39–44; tax-shelter years, 44–7. *See also under* cinema, art; comedy; *specific topics*

cinema, exploitation: and art cinema, 57, 132, 222–3, 266; genre, xi, 7–8, 46, 48–50, 59, 113, 114, 117, 144, 171–8, 182–90, 273; market, 56; producers, 58, 303n14; silent, 20–2; tax-shelter, 9, 62, 223

cinema, experimental: American, 8, 9, 248, 269, 280; Canadian, 9, 13, 31, 125, 139, 257, 275; Cronenberg's, 53, 55, 193; Egoyan's, 224, 225; Greyson's, 258

cinema, feminist: Canadian, 257; English-Canadian, 79, 105, 242, 243, 249–50, 265–6, 296n16; Quebecois, xii, 36, 93, 104, 116, 119, 122, 154–62, 301n48; criticism and theory, 20, 81, 88, 118, 248, 269

cinema, French, ix, 26, 92: alternative to Holly-wood, 9, 43, 173; and auteurism, 9, 44, 205, 218; *cinéma du look*, ix, 9, 144, 147–8, 155, 173; icons of, 19, 109; and national identity, 4, 109; new wave, 14, 35, 37, 111, 144, 155, 158–9, 164–5, 269, 273; Quebecois actors in, 111, 117, 122, 124, 126; silent, 275, 277, 282. *See also* cinema, art: French

cinema, genre, x, 4, 15, 32, 33, 50, 59, 61, 89, 171–203, 227, 248; and auteurism, 15, 59, 90, 171, 202–3, 218; Canadian franchises, 123, 192–3; conventions, 90, 91, 100, 190, 201, 218, 233, 252, 281; critical paradigms of, 174–5; Hollywood, 173, 212, 253, 303n9; hybrid, 31, 91, 142, 145, 147, 173, 175, 194, 246, 248–9, 264, 266, 304n42; local appropriation of, 175, 180–1, 231–3, 284–5; parody, 130, 132, 175; Quebecois, 171, 173–4, 176–81; Winnipeg, 245–6, 267–83. *See also names of individual genres*

cinema, German: *Bergfilm*, 275; expressionism, 282; new, 258; silent, 276, 277, 280

cinema, HIV/AIDS in, ix, 142, 179, 191, 209, 258–9

cinema, Hollywood, xiii; Canadian content in,

109; Canadians in, 4–5, 17–20, 22, 43, 50, 61,
62, 94, 107–43, 172, 195–6, 221, 222, 229, 290n4;
children, 140; closeted sexuality in, 264; conventions, 8, 9, 10, 24, 61, 67, 69–70, 72, 77, 92,
212, 217; eighties, ix; foreign actors, 19, 108–9;
golden age, 280–1; and independent cinema,
8–9, 92, 230, 239; market forces, 22–5, 47, 57, 78,
168, 175, 203, 220, 233, 239, 280–1; and national
identity, 4, 203, 227; new wave, 59; romance,
264; spatio-temporal vagueness, 39, 46; and
star discourses, 109, 264
cinema, Hong Kong, 108, 175, 195, 265, 281
cinema, independent: and auteurism, 9, 160, 221,
243; early, 176; eighties, x, 113, 213, 248, 289n8;
and genre, 91, 280; global, 7–9, 125, 146, 225;
nineties, 92, 126, 129–30, 166, 238–9; queer,
80–1; sixties, 41, 46, 53, 111
cinema, national, 17; and coming-of-age genre,
261–2; and ethnic film-making, 254–5; and
globalization, 237–8; and identity, 3–6, 18–20,
23, 28, 40, 227–8; and popular cinema, 285; and
queer theory, 256, 260; quotas in, 23; stars and,
18–19, 107–43
cinema, Quebecois, 4, 34–40, 89–106, 113–25,
144–70, 172–4, 242, 285; abroad, 121; Duplessis era, 22, 25–8; in English, xii–xiii, 47, 79, 97,
99–101, 162, 195, 197–8, 258, 260–1, 305n79;
English-Canadian characters in, 148; English-
Canadian reception of, 89, 118, 121, 172, 221,
301n39, 303n4; European actors in, xiii, 101,
154, 155, 156, 157, 158; and Hollywood, 173,
179, 235; immigrants in, 95, 98, 153–62; influence of French cinema on, 26–7, 34, 35, 37, 101,
147–8, 155, 157–60; insularity of, 121, 155; masculinity in, 121, 148, 197, 262; new wave, 27,
34–40, 89, 96, 110, 111, 144, 158, 167; nineties,
110, 113–14, 144–70, 221, 235–6; star system in,
109–25, 141, 270. See also under specific genres
and topics; le direct; Duplessis, Maurice
cinema, queer, 16, 29–31, 45, 53, 69–70, 80–8, 97,
153–70, 182, 231, 255–66, 269; icons, 119, 132,
264; new queer cinema, x, 8, 121, 152–3, 154,
177, 183, 242, 244–6, 249. See also gay characters; lesbian characters; under coming-of-age
film; spectatorship; television
cinema, regional, 16, 33, 41, 47, 157, 186, 228,
235–46
cinema, silent, 17–22, 267, 269, 275–7, 281, 282–3
cinema, Soviet, 193, 280, 282
cinema, world, xii, 13, 50, 55, 270; and auteurism,

13, 55, 270; economy of, 23, 108; transnational,
12, 50, 169–70, 250–1, 286. See also globalization; mediascape: global
Cinema Canada, 45–6, 292n94
cinéma direct. See le direct
cinéma du look. See under cinema, French
'cinema of duty,' 249, 253, 285
cinemas, x, 19, 184, 269. See also Bell Lightbox;
Berri Cinema; Camera Bar; Cinecity; Cinematheque; Faubourg; Film Forum; Lincoln
Plaza; Little Theater; Museum of Modern Art;
National Arts Centre; Winter Garden Theatre
Cinematheque, Winnipeg, 44, 244
cinematic image, ontological realism of, 22, 32,
181, 275–6, 286
cinematographers. See Brault, Michel; Cohn,
Norman; Coutard, Raoul; Dufaux, Georges;
Dufaux, Guy; Irwin, Mark; Koch, Douglas;
Lachman, Ed; Lapoirie, Jean; Middleton, Greg;
Sarossy, Paul; Turpin, André
cinéma vérité. See direct cinema
Cinépix, 40, 57–8, 63, 91, 144, 176, 177, 182
Circulations (Lepage), 163
Citadel (Egoyan and Khanjian), 225
city. See names of cities; cinema, Canadian: urban
centres; modernity: urban; postmodern:
urban;
city film, 280, 281. See under cinema, Canadian;
cinema, Quebecois
City of God (Meirelles), 169, 245
City of Gold (Low and Koenig), 31
Claim, The (Winterbottom), 135
Clandfield, David, 237, 247
Clandfield, Peter, 167, 168
Clark, Bob: Black Christmas, 45, 185, 187; Christ-
mas Story, 185; Death Dream, 185; horror films,
59; Murder by Decree, 113; Now & Forever, 128,
132; Porky's, 47, 176, 181–2, 185, 285
Clarke-Williams, Zoe: New Best Friend, 132
Clattenburg, Mike: Trailer Park Boys, 285
Clearcut (Bugajski), 234, 251
Cline, Patsy, 152–3, 263–4; 'Crazy,' 263
Clouse, Robert: Deadly Eyes, 46
CN Tower, Toronto, 185
Coates, Kim, 201
Coates, Paul, 190
Cockburn, Bruce, 41
Cocteau, Jean: Belle et la bête, 307n22
Coeur a ses raisons, Le, 121
Cohen, Leonard, 118

Cohn, Norman, 254; *Atanarjuat*, xi, 5–6, 246, 247, 253–5, 286–7, 312n89, 312n94

Coixet, Isabelle, 138; *Les Filles ne savent pas nager*, 122; *My Life without Me*, 138; *Secret Life of Words*, 138

Coma (Crichton), 113, 298n25

'Come and Get Your Love' (Redbone), 252

comedy: English-Canadian, 57, 128, 130, 140–1, 142, 175, 222, 228–30, 238, 240–2, 243, 245, 248–9, 264, 284–5; English-Canadian in Hollywood, 57, 123, 129; heterosexual, 262; Hollywood, 263, 268; Italian-American, 263; Monty Pythonesque, 202; Quebecois, 46, 57, 121, 122, 123, 124, 147, 172, 173, 175, 176, 178–9, 181, 235, 242, 261, 263, 303n7; sex, 176–81, 193, 268; silent, 277, 281; situation, 140, 142, 238, 247; sketch, 172, 173, 175, 178–9, 303n7; stand-up, 172, 175, 247; tax-shelter, 285; teen-sex, 181–2, 228–30, 304n35

coming-of-age film: coming-out in, 262, 263–5; English-Canadian; 39–41, 181–2, 189–92, 228–30, 233, 242, 244, 245; Quebecois, 36–9, 147, 149–53, 157–60, 169, 263–4; queer, 244, 245, 261–2, 263–4

Comment faire l'amour avec un nègre sans se fatiguer (Benoit), 98

Commercial Drive, Vancouver, 238

Commish, The, 126

Complexe Desjardins, Montreal, 90

Comtesse de Baton Rouge, La (Forcier), 235

Concordia Film School, Montreal, 194

Confessionnal, Le (Lepage), 13, 163, 165, 166–9, 251, 257, 258, 261

Confort et l'indifférence, Le (Arcand), 90, 92, 96

Conlogue, Ray, 114

constructivism, 272, 282

contes pour tous, 150

Coppola, Francis Ford, 59; *Apocalypse Now*, 231

co-production, international: Canadian, xii, xiii, 143, 252; English-Canadian, 7, 118, 143, 202, 218, 240, 241; Quebecois, 144, 155, 157, 165–6, 174, 240

Corbeil, Carole, 300n31

Cormier, Jacinta, 243

Cornelius, Nathalie, 167

Cornell, Joseph, 269

Cornwall, Ontario, 99, 101

Corps Célestes, Les (Carle), 116

Corupe, Paul: Canuxploitation, 171, 182, 303n1, 304n35

Costa-Gavras: *Mad City*, 132

Côté, Michel, 123, 178–9, 181, 263; *Cruising Bar 2*, 178, 179

Coulombe, Michel, 90, 102

Coulter, Allan: *Hollywoodland*, 131

County Cork, Ireland, 214

coureur de bois, 26, 37, 95, 124, 145, 147, 251

Cours Mont-Royal, Les, 195

Cousture, Arlette: *Filles de Caleb*, 119

Coutard, Raoul, 59

Cowan, Noah, 197

Cowards Bend the Knee (Maddin), 270–1, 279, 281

CQ2 (Laure), 118

Crabe dans la tête, Un (Turpin), 146

Crash (Ballard), 73

Crash (Cronenberg), xi, xii, 11, 55, 62, 66–7, 72–5, 131, 172, 177, 183, 295n69

Crawford, Joan, 19, 280

Crawley, Budge, 111

C.R.A.Z.Y. (Vallée), xi, 152–3, 263–4

Cremaster (Barney), 279

Crichton, Michael: *Coma*, 113, 298n25

Crime de Monsieur Lange, Le (Renoir), 235

Crime d'Ovide Plouffe, Le (Arcand), 89

crime drama, 198

Crimes of the Future (Cronenberg), 53–4, 55, 59, 61, 193, 257

Crime Wave (Paizs), 245, 253

Cronenberg, David, 48–78; actor, 114, 139; auteur, 55, 79, 111, 125, 138, 182–3, 174, 218, 225, 259–60, 274, 279; beauty, 48–9, 61, 70, 74; body horror, 32, 40, 57, 60, 171, 178, 181, 187–8, 195; Canadian, 50–2, 55–8, 70, 72, 75, 76, 78, 100, 157, 166, 187–8; at Cannes Film Festival, xii, 7, 55–6, 309n40; career trajectory, 13, 71–2, 177, 285, 286; childhood, 50–1, 78; early films, 53–63, 200, 202; existentialism, 60, 69, 76, 190, 198; family, 51, 63–70, 77; female characters, 71–2, 180; influence, 13–15, 45, 59, 171–203, 259; Jewishness, 50, 78, 250; modernist, 70–2; reception, 56, 63, 72, 83, 100, 178, 187–9, 194, 270; science fiction, 32, 48, 53–4, 57, 181, 192, 193, 194, 198; space and setting, 53–4, 59–60, 61, 64, 65–8, 188, 200, 201; during tax-shelter years, 47, 61–3, 178, 187; technology, 62, 63–6, 68–70, 72–6; vehicles, 62, 66–7, 72–5, 295n69; violence, 48, 60, 63, 77–8, 114, 187–9

Cronenberg, David, films of: *Brood*, 51, 59, 60, 61, 62, 63, 64–6, 68; *Crash*, xi, xii, 11, 55, 62, 66–7,

72–5, 131, 172, 177, 183, 295n69; *Crimes of the Future*, 53–4, 55, 59, 61, 193, 257; *Dangerous Method*, 295n82, 295n94; *Dead Ringers*, 51–2, 59, 62, 63, 65, 68–70, 71, 72, 73, 113, 182, 187, 298n22; *Dead Zone*, 51, 59, 63, 65, 66, 68, 75, 187; *Eastern Promises*, 51, 60, 65, 66, 71–2, 76–8, 295n94; *eXistenZ*, 55, 60, 64, 66, 72, 75–6, 101, 135, 194; *Fast Company*, 55, 60, 61–3, 66–8, 294n52; *The Fly*, 7, 61, 63, 65, 66, 68, 71, 72, 75, 182, 187, 190, 194; *From the Drain*, 53; *History of Violence*, 7, 51, 61, 65, 66, 71–2, 76–7, 309n40; *Lie Chair*, 66; *M. Butterfly*, 63, 66, 183; *Naked Lunch*, xi, 63, 66, 71, 72, 75, 177, 182–3, 258, 259; *Rabid*, 54, 55, 56, 59–60, 61, 63, 65, 66, 67, 68, 188; *Scanners*, x, 32, 60, 63, 66, 68, 192, 193, 194, 305n71; *Shivers*, 48–9, 54, 55, 56, 58, 59, 60, 61, 65, 66, 68, 70, 74, 77, 171, 177–8, 187, 188–9, 191, 198, 294n63; *Spider*, 65, 72, 77; *Stereo*, 53–4, 55, 59, 193, 257; *Suicide of the Last Jew*, 78, 250; *Transfer*, 53; *Videodrome*, x–xi, 54, 62, 63, 65, 66, 68, 71, 75, 77, 78, 187, 193, 194, 195, 258
Cronenberg, Denise, 50
Cronyn, Hume, 18
Crowe, Cameron: *Almost Famous*, 135
Croze, Marie-Josée, 103–4, 107, 118, 119, 124, 126, 132, 202, 209, 220, 221
Cruising Bar (Ménard), 178–80, 181
Cruising Bar 2 (Côté and Ménard), 178, 179
C't'à ton tour, Laura Cadieux (Filiatrault), 124
CTV, 147, 228
Cuarón, Alfonso: *Children of Men*, 169
Cube (Natali), 11, 192–3, 198–200, 201, 202
Cube² (Sekula), 193, 200
Cube Zero (Barbarash), 193, 200
Cunningham, Sandra, 219
Cunningham, Sean: *Friday the 13th*, 45
curling, 192, 242, 284
Currie, Andrew: *Fido*, 184
Curtis's Charm (L'Ecuyer), 126
Curzi, Pierre, 94, 105, 174
cyber-noir. *See* future noir
cyberpunk, 193, 196, 201
Cypher (Natali), 198, 200–1, 202
Czerny, Henry, 82

Dadaism, 272, 273
Dahl, John: *Unforgettable*, 126
Dale, Holly: *Blood and Donuts*, 184, 198
Dallaire, Roméo, 122
Daly, Tom, 31

Dance Me Outside (McDonald), 251, 252–3
Dangerous Method, A (Cronenberg), 295n82, 295n94
Danna, Mychael, 218–19, 224, 258
Dansereau, Mireille, 155
Dans le ventre du dragon (Simoneau), 174, 303n9
Dans une galaxie près de chez vous, 175
Dante, Joe, 59
Dark Summer (Marquette), 132
Das, Nandita, 265
David, Pierre, 194; *Scanner Cop*, 192
Dawn of the Dead (Snyder), 134, 135, *137*, 138
Day, Bryan, 62
Day-Lewis, Daniel, 8
Dead Father, The (Maddin), 279
Dead Kennedys, 232
Deadly Eyes (Clouse), 46
Dead Man (Jarmusch), 250
Dead Ringers (Cronenberg), 51–2, 59, 62, 63, 65, 68–70, 71, 72, 73, 113, 182, 187, 298n22
Deadwood, 131
Dead Zone, The (Cronenberg), 51, 59, 63, 65, 66, 68, 75, 187
Death Dream (Clark), 185
Death Weekend (Fruet), 185
de Boer, Nicole, 198
de Broca, Philippe: *Roi de cœur*, 111
De Carlo, Yvonne, 18
Decker, Matthew, 263
Déclin de l'empire américain, Le (Arcand), ix–x, xii, 9, 14, 23, 79, 81, 89, 90–1, 92–7, 99, 100, 102, 105, 155, 172, 179, 194, 257
De Laurentiis, Dino, 193–4
De Laurentiis, Raffaella, 52
De Lauretis, Teresa, 88
Deleuze, Gilles, 23, 302n77
Délivrez-moi (Chouinard), 114
del Toro, Benicio, 108
del Vecchio, Giudetta, 150, 152
Demers, Rock, 150
Demme, Jonathan, xi, 8, 58, 59; *Manchurian Candidate*, 280; *Married to the Mob*, xi; *Silence of the Lambs*, xi, 8; *Something Wild*, xi
demoiselle sauvage, La (Pool), 155, 157
Denis, Claire, 224
De Palma, Brian, 59; *Black Dahlia*, 132; *Obsession*, 113
Depardieu, Gérard, 108, 109, 117
dernière fugue, La (Pool), 160
dernières fiançailles, Les (Lefebvre), 36

dernier tunnel, Le (Canuel), 147

DeSève, Joseph-Alexandre, 26

Desperanto (Rozema), 79, 81, 82, 87, 89

Detour (Ulmer), 314n20

Deux femmes en or (Fournier), 176, 178

Deux ou trois choses que je sais d'elle (Godard), 95

Dewaere, Patrick, 117

Diable noir, Le (Méliès), 31

Diable parmi nous, Le (Beaudin), 188

Diary of Evelyn Lau, The, 129

DiCaprio, Leonardo, 123, 133

Dick, Philip K., 54, 193, 194, 196

Dickinson, Peter, 119, 121, 302n77

Dieterle, William: *Salome*, 211, 307n22

Dillon, Hugh, 231

Ding et Dong le film (Chartrand), 172, 178

Dion, Céline, 171, 173

Dionne, Luc: *Aurore*, 27

direct-to-video, 8, 46, 131, 142, 171–2, 175, 183, 192, 193, 197, 203

direct, le. See direct cinema: Quebecois

direct cinema, 5, 31, 34, 53, 55, 98; Quebecois, 5, 34–5, 37, 38, 55, 89–90, 117, 176

disaster movie, 139, 240

Dishonored, 315n42

Disney, 8, 134, 135, 145, 172, 277, 299n72

Diva (Beineix), ix, 9, 147, 148

docudrama, 197, 285

documentary: contemporary, 225, 239, 250–1, 274; conventions of, 207; fictionalized, 39, 85, 93, 125–6, 157, 230–1, 239, 241; feature, 5, 34–5, 40, 41, 58, 89–90; genre, 13, 19, 23; Griersonian, 3, 27–8, 30, 31, 32–3, 97, 190, 251; hybrid, 31, 90–1, 97–8, 258, 274; Quebecois, 34–5, 89–92, 104, 177. *See also* authenticity; direct cinema; documentary realism

documentary realism: Canadian, 13, 32, 33, 43–4, 46, 181, 237, 246–9, 262, 285; English–Canadian, 43, 78, 186, 225, 242, 252, 264, 272; European, 43, 55–6; Quebecois, 14, 90–1, 99, 102, 111, 116, 144, 158, 167

Doig, Peter, 44–5

Donovan, Michael, 243

D'or, Daniel, 192, 196

Dorland, Michael, 25, 44

Do the Right Thing (Lee), 248

Double Happiness (Shum), 125, 126, 129, 234, 238, 247

Downie, Gordon, 'Mystery,' 224

Downtown Eastside, Vancouver, 128

Dowse, Michael: *FUBAR*, 240, 241; *It's All Gone, Pete Tong*, 241; *Young Americans*, 241

Dracula (Stoker), 267

Dracula: Pages from a Virgin's Diary (Maddin), 267, 279

Dragons' Trilogy (Lepage), 163

drama, historical. *See* historical drama

dreams and dreamscapes, 38–9, 48, 61, 150

Dressler, Marie, 18

Dreyer, Carl-Theodor, ix, 280; *Ordet*, 277; *Passion de Jeanne d'Arc*, 307n18

Dreyfuss, Richard, 39, 58

Drive, She Said, 129, 234

Dr. Ox's Experiment (Bryar and Egoyan), 223–4

Druick, Zoë, 30

Drylanders, 20, 33–4

Ducharme, Réjean, 99; *L'avalée des avalés*, 151–2

Duchovny, David, 129

Duct Tape Forever (Till), 285

Due South, 126

Dufaux, Georges, 157

Dufaux, Guy, 148

Duguay, Christian, 194–8, 305n79; *Art of War*, 197–8; *Human Trafficking*, 197, 198; *Joan of Arc*, 197; *Lies My Mother Told Me*, 197; *Million Dollar Babies*, 197; *Scanners II*, 32, 192, 193, 194–5, 197, 198, 305n72; *Scanners III*, 192, 193, 194, 195, 197; *Screamers*, 122, 193, 196–7, 200

Duluth, Minnesota, 232

Dumb and Dumber, 5

Dunning, John, 40, 58, 177

Duplessis (Arcand), 89

Duplessis, Maurice, 26, 89. *See also* Quebec: fifties

Dupuis, Roy, 14, 27, 103, 107, 118–23, 125, 141, 197, 198, 290n19

Durban, Deanna, 18

Dyer, Richard, 109

Dyke Master's Daughter (Maddin), 281

Dylan, Bob: *Highway 61 Revisited*, 232

Dymond, Greig: *Mondo Canuck*, 172–3

Earth (Mehta), 265–6

Earth: Final Conflict, 15, 200

Earthquake (Robson), 113

Eastern Promises (Cronenberg), 51, 65, 66, 71–2, 76–8, 295n94

Eastern Townships, Quebec, 37, 94

East of Borneo, 269

Eastwood, Clint: actor, 108, 113; *Tightrope*, 108, 113

Eccleston, Christopher, 76

Eclipse (Podeswa), xi, 100

editing, 36, 69, 89, 164–5, 166, 168, 179, 181, 216, 261, 273, 282

Edmonton, Alberta, 33, 62, 97, 99, 125, 230, 236

Edmonton Motor Speedway, 62

EdTV (Howard), 101

effects, special. *See* special effects

Eggar, Samantha, 64

Egoyan, Arshile, 216

Egoyan, Atom, xiii, 15, 82, 139, 204–26; adapted screenplays of, xi, 208, 209–10, 211, 217–18, 219–20; 307n17, 309n39; auteur, 125, 138, 204–26, 238, 274, 305n1; at Cannes Film Festival, 9, 225, 309n40; cellphone in, 209–10, 307n18; early films of, xii, 13, 100–1, 139, 153, 155, 183, 206–7, 210, 211, 212, 213, 214, 218, 219, 222, 224, 226, 259, 262; fairy tale motif, 210–11, 216, 220; family romance in, 205–6, 208–9, 210, 211, 306n6; fetish actors of, 12, 219, 220–2; identity, 212, 220–3, 250, 312n74; influence of, 100, 223–6, 250; mediation, 84–5, 156, 204, 205, 206, 207, 208, 209, 210, 211, 212, 214, 217–18, 224, 237, 257, 258; at the New York Film Festival, x, 308n34; on his own films, 70, 206, 217, 222–3, 309n45; post-*Exotica*, xi, 204–5, 207–10, 213–14, 218–19, 285; producer, 225; reception of, 83, 204, 214, 225–6, 270; short films of, 224; space and setting, 213–16; studio director, 213, 223, 309n47

Egoyan, Atom, works of: *Adjuster*, x, 100, 139, 183, 206, 213, 219, 224, 225, 307n18; *Adoration*, 78, 206, 207, 209, 211, 213, 214, 219, 221, 225, 237, 307n18; *Alfred Hitchcock Presents*, 223; 'America, America,' 224; *Ararat*, 124, 206, 209, 211–12, 213, 214, 216–17, 220–2, 223, 224, 250, 305n1, 307n25, 308nn29–32, 308nn37–8, 309nn42–5, 309n50, 312n74; *Artaud Double Bill*, 224, 307n18; 'Bach Cello Suite #4: Sarabande,' 224; *Calendar*, 206, 212, 214, 219, 224, 308n36; *Chloe*, 202, 206, 207, 209, 210, 213, 214–15, 218, 219, 220, 223, 225, 307n18; *Citadel*, 225; *Dr. Ox's Experiment*, 223–4; *Elsewhereness*, 224; *Evidence*, 224; *Exotica*, x, 45, 131, 132, 134, 141, 176–7, 183, 185, 187, 204, 205, 208, 210, 213, 214, *215*, 216, 219, 222, 223, 250, 270–1, 306n6; *Family Viewing*, 9, 84, 183, 206, 207, 214, 219, 306n10; *Felicia's Journey*, 7, 205, 208–9, 210–11, 213, 214, 217–18, 220, 222, 223, 224, 307n22, 307n25, 307n27; *Friday the 13th*, 223; *Gross Misconduct*, 223, 306n4; 'Hors d'usage,' 224; *In This Corner*,

223; *Krapp's Last Tape*, 217, 224; 'Mystery,' 224; *Next of Kin*, 6, 205, 206, 207; *Portrait of Arshile*, 212, 224; *Salomé*, 211, 223; *Speaking Parts*, 100, 183, 204, 206, 214, 219; 'Steenbeckett,' 224; *Subtitles*, 224–5; *Sweet Hereafter*, xi, xii, 12, 135, 138, 204, 205, 207–8, 209–10, 213, 214, 215–16, 217, 218, 219–20, 222, 223, 224, 289n15, 306n6, 306n13, 307n17, 307n20, 309n39; *Twilight Zone*, 223; *Walküre*, 224; *Where the Truth Lies*, 204, 209, 211, 213, 214, 218, 222, 223, 225, 307n16, 308n33, 308n35, 309n40

Eisenstein, Sergei, 282; *Battleship Potemkin*, 280

Eldorado (Binamé), 121, 167

Elley, Derek, 201

Elliott, Denholm, 39

Ellroy, James, 132

Elsaesser, Thomas, 174, 303n11

Elsewhereness (Egoyan), 224

Emotional Arithmetic (Barzman), 122

Empire, Inc. (Arcand), 89, 91

Emporte-moi (Pool), xii, 122, 124, 155, 156, 157–60, 169, 262, 263, 301n59

English Canadian: actors, xii, 14, 107, 110, 125–43, 219–20; childhood, 50–2, 134–5, 271, 276–9; film-makers, xiii, 7, 25, 83, 125, 138, 172; minorities, 227, 246; repression, 139, 178, 244. *See also* cinema, Canadian; cinema, English-Canadian; Quebec: anglophones in; Quebec: and English Canada; *under individual cities, names, and topics*

Entity, The, 269

Entre la mer et l'eau douce (Brault), 35, 36, 111

Erasure, 258

Erbach, Jeff, 244, 248; *Nature of Nicholas*, 244, 245

Ernie Game, The (Owen), 41

Etats-Unis d'Albert, Les (Forcier), 122, 235

Evangeline, 20

Event, The (Fitzgerald), 142

Evert, Chris, 104

Evidence (Egoyan), 224

existentialist: film-making, 15, 76; narrative, 69, 154, 190, 198–200, 202; philosophy, 60, 155, 158; style, 90; *See also under* body

eXistenZ (Cronenberg), 55, 60, 64, 66, 72, 75–6, 101, 135, 194

Ex Machina, 166

Exorcist, The (Friedkin), 80

Exotica (Egoyan), x, 45, 131, 132, 134, 141, 176–7, 183, 185, 187, 204, 205, 208, 210, 213, 214, *215*, 216, 219, 222, 223, 250, 270–1, 306n6

exploitation cinema. *See* cinema, exploitation
Eye, Like a Strange Balloon, Mounts towards Infinity, The (Maddin), 277

face cachée de la lune, La (film; Lepage), 163, 166, 167, 285
face cachée de la lune, La (play; Lepage), 163, 167, 285
fairy tale, 30–1, 80, 210–11, 216, 281
Falcon, Richard, 201
Family Viewing (Egoyan), 9, 84, 183, 206, 207, 214, 219, 306n10
Fanon, Frantz, 35
Far from Heaven (Haynes), 280
Farmer, Gary, 250
Fast Company (Cronenberg), 55, 60, 61–3, 66–8, 294n52
Faubourg, Le, Cinema, Montreal, 261
Fawcett, John, xiii, 191; *Boys Club*, 198; *Ginger Snaps*, 32, 189–92, 193, 198, 200, 257, 262, 305n66; *Queer as Folk*, 257
Feature Film Fund, 6
Feature Film Project, 198
Feininger, Oskar: *From Munich to Berlin*, 280
Felicia's Journey (Trevor), 208–9, 211, 217–18
Felicia's Journey (Egoyan), 7, 205, 208–9, 210–11, 213, 214, 217–18, 220, 222, 223, 224, 307n22, 307n25, 307n27
Fellini, Federico: *La Strada*, 78
Feluettes, Les (Boulard), 260
femme de l'hôtel, La (Pool), xii, 154
femme fatale, 49, 107, 314n20
Femme Nikita, La. See *Nikita*
Feore, Colm, 123
Ferguson, Matthew, 100
Fido (Currie), 184
Fiennes, Ralph, 131
Filiatrault, Denise, actor, 116; *C't'à ton tour, Laura Cadieux*, 124; *Laura Cadieux*, 124; *Laura Cadieux … la suite*, 124; *Ma vie en cinemascope*, 119, 122, 124
Filles de Caleb, Les (Beaudin), 119, 121
Filles de Caleb, Les (Cousture), 119
Filles ne savent pas nager, Les (Coixet), 122
Film Comment, 270, 280
Film festivals, xii; Berlin, xii, 274; Cannes, xii, 6, 9, 55–6, 78, *115*, 118, 121, 129, 145, 225, 302n94, 307n18, 309n40; Montreal, 237, 260; New York, x–xi, 308n24; Sundance, 8; Toronto, xii, 6, 9, 45, 56, 110, *126*, 131, 237, 238, 270, 302n94; Vancouver, 238; Venice, xii

Film Forum, New York, 55
film journals and magazines. See *Cahiers du cinéma*; *Cineaste*; *Cinema Canada*; *Film Comment*; *Sight & Sound*; *Take One*; *24 Images*; *Variety*
film noir, 40, 46, 49, 89, 90, 223, 232, 235, 280, 281, 314n20; French, 173, 175; tropes of, 234. *See also* future noir; femme fatale; neo-noir
Fils de Marie, Les (Laure), 118
Fire (Mehta), xi, 262, 265–6
Firm, The (TV), 131
First Nations, 128, 132, 191–2, 229, 234, 245–6, 250–3; in Quebec, 4, 34, 35, 117, 251
Fitzgerald, Thom, xiii, 138, 183, 257, 262; *The Event*, 142; *Hanging Garden*, 242, 262
Five Senses, The (Podeswa), xi, 100, 122, 130
Flaherty, Robert: *Nanook of the North*, 5
Flashpoint (Canuel), 147
Florida, 47, 181–2, 235
Florida, La (Mihalka), 176, 179, 235
Flower & Garnet (Behrman), 128
Fly, The (Cronenberg), 7, 61, 63, 65, 66, 68, 71, 72, 75, 182, 187, 190, 194
Fly II, The, 192
Food of the Gods II, 185
Foolproof (Phillips), 175
Forcier, André, xiii, 235; *Comtesse de Baton Rouge*, 235; *Etats-Unis d'Albert*, 122, 235; *Vent de Wyoming*, 235
Ford, Glenn, 18
Ford, John, 44; *The Searchers*, 18
Forster, E.M., 8
Foster, Cecil, 247, 310n4
Foster, Charles, 18
Fothergill, Robert, 3–4
Foucault, Michel, 80
Fournier, Claude, 91; *Deux femmes en or*, 176, 178; *Hot Dogs*, 46; *J'en suis!*, 123
Four Weddings and a Funeral (Newell), 166
Fox-television, 132
Frank's Cock (Hoolboom), 125
Frappier, Roger, 100
Fraser, Brad, 100, 255–6, 257; *Unidentified Human Remains and the True Nature of Love*, 97, 99, 100, 101
Frears, Stephen: *My Beautiful Laundrette*, 8
Freer, James, 19
French cinema. See cinema, French
Freud, Sigmund, 277, 295n82; 'oceanic' feeling, 55
Frewer, Matt, 228, 229
Friday the 13th (Cunningham), 45

Friday the 13th (Egoyan), 223
Friedkin, William: *Exorcist*, 80
From Munich to Berlin (Feininger), 280
From the Atelier Tovar (Maddin), 269, 313n6
From the Drain (Cronenberg), 53
Front de libération du Québec (FLQ), 164–5, 221
frontier myth: Canadian, 28, 228; Quebecois, 26, 124
Fruet, William, 185; *Blue Monkey*, 185; *Death Weekend*, 185; *Killer Party*, 185; *Spasms*, 185; *Wedding in White*, 185
Frye, Northrop, 3, 55
FUBAR (Dowse), 240, 241
Fulford, Robert, 56
Furey, Lewis, 114, 117–18; *Night Magic*, 118; *Rats and Rabbits*, 114
future noir, 174, 193, 196, 197–9

Gabin, Jean, 19, 109
Gaels, 243, 244
Gagnon, Aurore, 26
Gairola, Rahul, 313n125
Gale, Vincent, 238
Gallen, Joel: *Not Another Teen Movie*, 132
Gance, Abel, 277, 282; *La Roue*, 277
gangster film: French, 90; Hong Kong, 175; Quebecois, 173
Gascon, Gabriel, 201
Gaspé Peninsula, Quebec, 177–8
Gaudreault, Emile: *Mambo Italiano*, 263, 264
Gauthier, Jennifer, 154, 155, 254–5
gay characters: Canadian cinema, 31, 183, 229, 256–62, 271; English-Canadian cinema, 53, 220, 231, 242; European cinema, 8; Quebecois cinema, 9, 93, 121, 123, 148, 152–3, 160, 166, 174, 179–80; television, 256, 257. *See also* cinema, queer
Gemini Awards. *See under* awards
Genie Awards. *See under* awards
genre cinema. *See* cinema, genre
genres. *See* action; animation; biopic; cinema, art; city film; comedy; coming-of-age; crime; disaster; docudrama; documentary; documentary realism; espionage; exploitation; fairy tale; film noir; future noir; gangster; heist; heritage; historical drama; 'hood film; horror; maple syrup porno; martial arts; melodrama; musical; neo-noir; policier; pornography; rape-revenge; road; science fiction; serial killer; sports; thriller; 'troubled youth'; vampire; war; werewolf; western; zombie

Ghostbusters (Reitman), 175
Ghostbusters II (Reitman), 175
ghosts, 183, 258, 264, 279
Gibbon, John Murray, 227, 245
Gibson, Mel, 7, 220
Gibson, Thomas, 97, 100–1
Gibson, William, 193, 196; *Neuromancer*, 198
Gilda, 18
Gilliam, Terry: *Adventures of Baron Munchausen*, 134
Gimli, Manitoba, 245, 267, 273, 274, 275
Gin, Pascal, 229
Gina (Arcand), 89, 90–3, 117, 296n19
Ginger Snaps (Fawcett and Walton), 32, 184, 189–92, 193, 198, 200, 257, 262, 305n66
Ginger Snaps Back (Harvey), 191–2, 200, 305n66
Ginger Snaps: Unleashed (Sullivan), 191–2, 305n66
Girard, François, xiii; *Red Violin*, 130, 143; *Thirty Two Short Films about Glenn Gould*, 141–2, 258
Girard, Rémy, 27, 123, 179, 235, 258, 261
Gittings, Christopher, 20, 23, 24, 28, 30, 246, 249, 251–2
globalization, xiii, 5, 11; double-edged, 143, 237; economic, 108, 286, 290n28; and the local, 167, 169, 254–5, 283; media, 244; and postmodernity, 147–8, 235–6, 237–9
Glover, Guy, 29
Go (Liman), 135
Godard, Jean-Luc, 9, 59, 116, 145, 147, 155, 158; *A bout de souffle*, 273; *Alphaville*, 60; *Deux ou trois choses*, 95; *Vivre sa vie*, 158, 159, 307n18
Godbout, Jacques, 36
Godwin, George, 88, 273
Goin' Down the Road (Shebib), 41–3, 185, 186, 229–30, 241
Going the Distance (Griffiths), 13, 228–30, 232, 233, 235, 284
Goldstone, James: *Swashbuckler*, 113
Gonick, Noam, 185, 245–6, 257; actor, 269; *Hey Happy!*, 245; *Stryker*, 245–6; *Waiting for Twilight*, 313n1
Good Shepherd, The (Webb), 131
Gorky, Arshile, 212, 216; *Mother and Son*, 212, 222, 224
Gosling, Ryan, 18
Gosselin, Bernard, 36
Gould, Glenn, 141–2, 166
Goyette, Patrick, 166, 168
grande seduction, La (Pouliot), 242
Grant, Cary, 19, 264
Grass Harp, The (Matthau), 132

Gravestock, Steve, 41
'Great Gig in the Sky, The' (Pink Floyd), 152
Green Card (Weir), 108
Greene, Graham, 234
Greenwood, Bruce, 208, 220, 221
Grey Gardens (Rozema), 83
Grey's Anatomy, 128, 132
Greyson, John, xiii, 138, 183, 249, 257, 258–61,
    304n42; experimental video, 258; *Law of Enclo-
    sures*, 135, 258; *Lilies*, 258, 260–1, 262; lyricist,
    258; *Making of 'Monsters,'* 258; *Paradise Falls*,
    258; *Proteus*, 258; *Queer as Folk*, 257, 258; *Uncut*,
    258; *Urinal*, 258; *Zero Patience*, 258–60, 261, 264
Grierson, John, 3, 27–9, 31, 32, 33
Griffith, D.W., 18; *Birth of a Nation*, 3
Griffiths, Mark: *Going the Distance*, 13, 228–30,
    232, 233, 235, 284
Grignon, Claude-Henri, 26
Gross, Paul: actor, 126, 284; *Men with Brooms*, 130,
    242, 284; *Passchendaele*, 172, 284; screenwriter,
    223
Gross Misconduct (Egoyan), 223, 306n4
Groulx, Gilles, 33, 34, 36, 40; *chat dans le sac*, 35;
    Raquetteurs, 34, 38
Guadagni, Nicky, 199
Guattari, Félix, 23
Guerre est finie, La (Resnais), 111
Guilhe, Albane, 154
Guinevere (Wells), 135, 137
Gullage's (MacGillivray), 243
Gunnarsson, Sturla: *Rare Birds*, 130, 242
Gunning, Tom, 275
Gury, Paul: *Un homme et son péché*, 26; *Séraphin*,
    26–7

Habich, Matthias, 155, 157
Halifax, Nova Scotia, 109, 243–4, 248
Halifax Film, 243
Hall, Stuart, 250
Hallier, Lori, 186
Halloween (Carpenter), 181
Halprin, Ann, 163
Hamilton, Josh, 234
Hampton, Christopher, 295n82
Hampton, Paul, 48
Handling, Piers, 56, 293n29
Hanging Garden, The (Fitzgerald), 242, 262
Hanson, Curtis: *L.A. Confidential*, 280
Hantke, Stefan, 68
Happy Days (Beckett and Rozema), 80, 81, 83, 86,
    224

Happy Days (TV), 233
Hard Core Logo (McDonald), 7, 85, 125–6, 129,
    230–1, 233, 241
Hard Core Logo 2 (McDonald), 285
Hard Part Begins, The (Lynch), 185
Harkema, Reg, 238
Harold and Maude (Ashby), ix, 189
Harris, Mike, 135, 260
Harrison, Marion, 88
Harron, Mary: *L-Word*, 257
Harry, Deborah, 195
Hart, Harvey: *Pyx*, 188
Hartley, Hal, 138: *No Such Thing*, 135, 138
Harvey, Grant: *Ginger Snaps Back*, 191–2, 305n66
Harvie, Jennifer, 163, 166
Harvie, John Boles, 267, 313n2
Hawks, Howard, 44, 218, 280
Haynes, Todd, 268; *Far from Heaven*, 280
Hayward, Susan, 109, 110
Hayworth, Rita, 19, 211
HBO, 80, 83, 129, 131
Headstones, The, 231
Heartaches (Shebib), 43
Heartbreakers (Roth), 118
Heart of the World, The (Maddin), 16, 273, 274, 279,
    282–4, 286–7, 315n49
Heaven on Earth (Mehta), 265, 266
heist movie: English-Canadian, 43, 175; Quebe-
    cois, 147, 174
Hemblen, David, 206, 222
Henenbert-Faulkner, Carl, 158
heritage film, 8, 80, 110, 111, 261
Héroux, Denis, 36, 91; *L'Initiation*, 36; producer,
    144; *Seul ou avec des autres*, 36; *Valérie*, 36, 58,
    111, 177, 178
Heston, Charlton, 280
Hewlett, David, 194, 198, 201, 202, 305n72
Hey Happy! (Gonick), 245
Hiawatha, the Messiah of the Ojibway, 20
Highlander: The Series, 15
High Park, Toronto, 87
High Rise (Ballard), 198
Highway 61, 232
Highway 61 (McDonald and McKellar), 11, 139,
    231, 232–3, 235
Highway 61 Revisited (Dylan), 232
Higson, Andrew, 227
Hillcoat, John: *The Road*, 131
Hindle, Art, 181
Hiroshima, mon amour (Resnais), 164
historical drama, 118, 174; English-Canadian, 20,

33–4, 172, 216–17, 242, 284; Quebecois, 27, 121, 124, 174, 176

History of Violence, A (Cronenberg), 7, 51, 61, 65, 66, 71–2, 76–7, 309n40

Hitchcock, Alfred, 214, 302n77, 307n22, 309n47; auteur, 44, 218, 223, 224; *I Confess*, 165, 166, 167; *North by Northwest*, 201, 223; *Psycho*, 184; in Quebec, 167–8; *Vertigo*, 113, 278

Hobart, Rose, 272

Hoberman, J., 284

hockey: arena, 271, 273; film, 119, 123, 178, 179, 281; national team, 245; theme, 99, 101, 135, 248, 271, 279

Hoffman, Dustin, 132

Holden-Ried, Kristen, 264

Hollywood cinema. *See* cinema, Hollywood

Hollywoodland (Coulter), 131

Holm, Ian, xi, 12, 135, 208, 219

Holmes, Rupert: *Where the Truth Lies*, 209

Holt, Sandrine, 252

homme et son péché, Un (Gury), 26

'hood film, 8, 247

Hoolboom, Mike: *Frank's Cock*, 125

Hooper, Tobe, 59

horror, 15, 32, 46, 48, 56, 171, 203; actors, 58; animal, 184; body, 32, 40, 57, 60, 171, 178, 181, 184, 188–92, 195, 198; cannibal, 184; conventions of, 60, 64, 69; English-Canadian, 48–50, 58–61, 63–6, 175, 183–92, 245; fifties, 54, 59, 60, 280; monsters, 60, 135; mutant humanoid, 184; and post-structuralism, 183, 188; Quebecois, 188; in the seventies, 59, 68; silent, 280, 282; tax-shelter, 59; women in, 108, 134, 188–92. *See also* Satanism; science fiction; vampire movie; werewolf movie; zombie movie

'Hors d'usage' (Egoyan), 224

hoser, 41–3, 175, 232, 241

Hoskins, Bob, 208

Hot Dogs (Fournier), 46

Houle, Pierre: *Monica la mitraille*, 124

Howard, Ron: *EdTV*, 101

Howe, Lawrence, 261

Huard, Patrick, 123

Hudson, Kate, 135

Hughes, Bronwen: *L-Word*, 257

Hughes, Howard, 280

Hughes, John, ix

Human Trafficking (Duguay), 197, 198

Humongous (Lynch), 195

Hunger, The (Rozema), 83

Hunter, Holly, 72, 88

Hurley, Erin, 166

Hurt, William, 242, 262

Huston, Nancy, 155, 158

Huston, Walter, 18

Hutcheon, Linda, 10

Hyams, Peter: *Time Cop*, 126

hybrid: cinema, 12, 47, 174, 248–50; creation, 202; local/global, 101, 246; music, 152; representation, 11, 252–3; space, 148; spectatorship, 140. *See also under* cinema, genre; documentary; identity; postmodernity (hybridity, 96)

Ibiza, Spain, 241

I Confess (Hitchcock), 165, 166

Icon Productions, 220

identity: artistic, 13, 170; Canadian, 3–6, 18–20, 28, 33, 39, 110, 133, 142–3, 157, 172, 181, 198, 286; cultural, 141–2, 166–7, 203; discontinuous, 260–2; English-Canadian, 40, 43–4, 50–1, 76, 175–6, 232, 314n22; ethnic, 16, 78, 129, 154, 212; female, 20, 265; fragmented, 15, 97, 148, 228–9; and genre, 174, 187–8, 229; hybrid, 4, 107, 158, 163, 203, 246, 251; local, 39, 107, 108, 119, 133, 147, 153, 174–5, 227; masculine, 18, 121, 241; minority, 121–2; national, 3–4, 10, 19–20, 46, 109–10, 148, 227–8; personal, 52, 55, 65, 76–7, 108, 153, 154, 157–60, 165, 184, 193–4, 196, 201; political, 257; professional, 62–3, 76, 108, 208, 218, 223, 225; provisional, 38; Quebecois, 14, 34–6, 110, 116, 121, 124, 145, 147–50, 153–5, 157, 166–7, 174, 246, 262–4; queer, 119, 183, 255, 264; regional, 10, 157, 166, 245, 262–3; sexual, 16, 159, 180, 257; social, 158; transnational, 108, 119, 133, 149, 152–3, 157, 242, 246, 248, 250, 262

Igloolik, Nunavut, 253

Igloolik Isuma, 236, 247, 286

Île aux Coudres, L', Quebec, 34

I Love a Man in a Uniform (Wellington), 257

Iñárritu, Alejandro González: *Amores Perros*, 169

Incendies (Villeneuve), 123, 285

Inception (Nolan), 133

India, 265–6

Indo-Canadian, 248–50, 264–6

Initiation, L' (Héroux), 36

In This Corner (Egoyan), 223

In Treatment (Rozema), 83

Inuit, 5–6, 20, 246, 247, 251, 253–5, 286–7; children, 255

Inuktitut, 246, 247

Invasion!. See *Top of the Food Chain*

Invasions barbares, Les (Arcand), 14, 79, 89, 102–5, 122, 124, 285
Invasion of the Body Snatchers (Kaufman), 280
Invasion of the Body Snatchers (Siegel), 280
Irish Museum of Modern Art, Dublin, 224
Irons, Jeremy, 69, 113, 187, 298n22
Irwin, Mark, 62, 284n50
Isabel (Almond), 39, 111
Isabelle, Katharine, 189, 234
It's All Gone, Pete Tong (Dowse), 241
I've Heard the Mermaids Singing (Rozéma), x, 7, 9, 14, 79, 80, 81, 82, 83–8, 244, 289n8, 296n6

Jackson, Philip, 192, 196
Jackson, Stanley, 31
Jacot, Christopher, 229
Jacques, Yves, 160, 167, 179, 257
Jaffrey, Saeed, 248
Jameson, Fredric, 11, 224
Japan, 17, 162, 198, 213
Jarmusch, Jim: *Dead Man*, 250
Jarrott, Charles: *Anne of the Thousand Days*, 111
J'en suis! (Fournier), 123
Jésus de Montréal (Arcand), x, 14, 79, 89, 91, 96–9, 100, 102, 105, 146, 147, 165, 172, 289n16
Jeunet, Jean-Pierre: *Alien Resurrection*, 193
Jewish Canadian, 275; film-makers and actors, 39–40, 48–78, 153–62, 175, 238, 245–6, 250; Quebecois, 4, 39–40, 43, 58, 153–62, 175; representations, 35, 39–40, 78, 154, 156, 158–60, 238, 301n44
Jewison, Norman, 19, 50, 198; *Moonstruck*, 263
Joan of Arc (Duguay), 197
Johnny Mnemonic (Longo), 172, 196, 198, 200
Johnson, Brian, 135, 306n13
Jones, Michael and Andy: *Adventure of Faustus Bidgood*, 242
Jordan, John, 11
Journey (Almond), 39
Joyeux Calvaire (Arcand), 99
Jung, Carl, 295n82
Junior's Groove. See *Planet of Junior Brown*
Juno, 109, 133
Jutra, Claude, 30–1, 33, 36–9, 47; *A tout prendre*, 35, 36, 178, 257; *Kamouraska*, 36; *Mon oncle Antoine*, 36–9, 96, 149, 168, 172, 176, 262, 264
Jutra Awards. *See under* awards
Kafka, Franz, 198, 200, 268, 272, 275
Kakogiannis, Mihalis: *Sweet Country*, 118
Kamouraska (Jutra), 36
Kanehsatake: 270 ans de résistance (Obomsawin), 250–1

Kaprisky, Valérie, 156, 301n53
Karina, Anna, 158
Kaufman, Philip: *Invasion of the Body Snatchers*, 280
Kazan, Elia: *America, America*, 224, 309n50
Keaton, Buster, 277
Kelly, Brendan, 138
Kelly, Moira, 234
Kensington, Toronto, 140
Kent, Larry, 41, 43; *Bitter Ash*, 41; *Sweet Substitute*, 41; *When Tomorrow Dies*, 41; *Yesterday*, 46
Keohane, Kieran, 10, 232
Khanjian, Arsinée, x, 216, 271; actor, 208, 209, 216, 219, 220, 221–2; *Citadel*, 225; collaborator, 225, 307n17, 309n43
Khanna, Sanjay, 249
Kidder, Margot, 43
Kids in the Hall, The, 140. *See also* de Boer, Nicole; McCullough, Bruce; McKinney, Mark
Kids in the Hall, The (TV), 245
Killer Party (Fruet), 185
King, Allan, 41, 44; *A Married Couple*, 41; *Warrendale*, 41
King, Edward, 89
King, Geoff, 8
Kingston, Ontario, 231
Kirshner, Mia, 107, 125, 126, 129, 135; *I Live Here*, 132, 133; movies, 14, 97, 100, 131–2, 208, 271; television, 14, 132, *133*, 143,
Kissed (Stopkewich), 130, 131, 176–7, 183, 187, 238, 257, 262
Kitchen Party (Burns), 239, 311n33
Kit Kittredge: An American Girl (Rozema), xi, 80, 81, 83, 85
Knelman, Martin, 113
Knopf, Kerstin, 254
Koch, Douglas, 139
Koenig, Wolf, 31, 34; *City of Gold*, 31
Komoroska, Liliana, 195
Korean Canadian: actors, 14, 107, 125, 126, 128, 129–30, 132, 133, 139, 234; film-makers, 142
Koteas, Elias, 72, 209, 220, 221
Kotcheff, Ted, 39; *Apprenticeship of Duddy Kravitz*, 13, 39–40, 43, 104, 158
Kramer vs. Kramer (Benton), 64
Krapp's Last Tape (Beckett and Egoyan), 217, 224
Kraus, Matthias, 305n1
Krige, Alice, 313n5
Krishna, Srinivas, x, 248; *Masala*, 248–9, 257, 264
Kroitor, Roman, 31, 34; *Paul Tomkowicz*, 28; *Universe*, 31

Kubrick, Stanley: *2001*, 193

Kuchar, George, 280

Kunuk, Zacharias, 6, 246, 247, 250, 253–5; *Atan-arjuat*, xi, 5–6, 246, 247, 253–5, 286–7, 312n89, 312n94

Kureishi, Hanif, 8

Kusturica, Emir, 158

Labrèche, Marc, 105

LaBruce, Bruce, 257

LaBute, Neil: *Wicker Man*, 131

Lachapelle, France, 166, 167

Lachman, Ed, 245

L.A. Confidential (Hanson), 280

Laferrière, Dany, 98

Lai, Chatur, 31

L'Allier-Matteau, Jolianne, 156

Lanctôt, Micheline, xii, xiii, 104, 155; actor, 39, 104, 116; *Deux actrices*, 122; *Sonatine*, xii, 122

Landau, Martin, 223

Lane, Anthony, 309n44

Lang, Fritz: *Big Heat*, 1; *Metropolis*, 282

Langella, Frank, 101

L'Anglais, Paul, 26

Langrick, Margaret, 233

Lantos, Robert, 100, 101, 144, 196, 219

Lapoirie, Jean, 157, 158

La Rochelle, Réal, 99

Larrivée, Pierre, 300n21

Last Night (McKellar), 114, 128, 129, 135, 139, 298n25

Last Wedding (Sweeney), 131, 238

Laura Cadieux (TV), 124

Laura Cadieux … la suite (Filiatrault), 124

Laure, Carole, 14, 114–18; *La Capture*, 118; *CQ2*, 118; English Canada, 118; European art cinema, 110, 116–17, 124, 126, 298n33; *Fils de Marie*, 118; international star, 107, 114–18, 119, 142; pop singer, 117–18; Quebecois, 114–18, 124, 131, 178, 180, 235, 298n35

Laurier, Lucie, 154

Lauzon, Jean-Claude, xiii, 4, 14, 145–53, 162, 166, 170, 177, 300n31, 301n39, 315n42; and advertising, 145, 146, 296n34; and Hollywood, 145; *Léolo*, x, 13, 145, 147, 149–53, 157, 158, 169, 177, 183, 257, 262, 300n21, 300n31, 301n39, 301n59; use of music, 149, 152; *Zoo, la nuit*, xii, 100, 145, 147–8, 149, 155, 177

Lavigne, Avril, 229

Lavin, Tom, 233

Lavoie, André, 85

Law, Jude, 72, 75, 194

Law of Enclosures, The (Greyson), 135, 258

Lawrence, David, 241

Lawrence, Florence, 18

Lea, Ron, 234

Leach, Jim, 10, 31–2, 37, 38, 117, 148, 150, 151, 152, 297n13, 300n21, 303n9

Léaud, Jean-Pierre, 159

Leave Her to Heaven, 315n42

L'Ecuyer, John: *Curtis's Charm*, 126; *Queer as Folk*, 257

Lee, Spike, 145, 147; *Do the Right Thing*, 248

Lefebvre, Henri, 11

Lefebvre, Jean-Pierre, 36, 41; *dernières fiançailles*, 36

Lefebvre, Martin, 167

Leigh, Jennifer Jason, 72, 75, 76

Léolo (Lauzon), x, 13, 145, 147, 149–53, 157, 158, 169, 177, 183, 257, 262, 300n21, 300n31, 301n39, 301n59

Lepage, Robert, 162–70; actor, xiii, 79, 93, 97, 101, 147, 167; auteur, 4, 14–15, 147, 149, 225; bilingualism of, 162; dramatist, 145, 162–4; film-maker, 163–4; and Quebec City, 162, 166, 167–8, *169*; and Quebecois history, 164–5; use of autobiography, 166

Lepage, Robert, works of: *Bluebeard's Castle*, 211; *Circulations*, 163; *Le Confessionnal*, 13, 163, 165, 166–9, 251, 257, 258, 261; *Dragons' Trilogy*, 163; *face cachée de la lune* (film), 163, 166, 167, 285; *face cachée de la lune* (play), 163, 167, 285; *Needles and Opium*, 164; *Nô*, 163, 164, 165; *Polygraphe* (film), 163, 166–7; *Polygraphe* (play), 166–7; *Possible Worlds*, xiii, 164, 165, 201; *Ring* cycle, 170; *Seven Streams of the River Ota*, 163, 164

Lepage-Beaulieu, Lynda, 162

lesbian characters: American, 160, 248; Canadian, 122, 183, 257; English-Canadian, xi, 87, 183, 238, 265; Quebecois, xiii; television, 132. *See also under* cinema, queer

Lessard, Jacques, 163

Lesser Slave Lake, Alberta, 20

Lever, Yves, 27

Levitin, Jacqueline, 247, 266

Lewis, Sharon, 247

Lexx, 15

Library Square, Vancouver, 239

Lie Chair, The (Cronenberg), 66

Lies My Mother Told Me (Duguay), 197

Lie with Me (Virgo), 248

Life Classes (MacGillivray), 243–4

Lilies (Greyson), 258, 260–1, 262
Liman, Doug: *Go*, 135
Lincoln Plaza Cinema, New York, x
Link, André, 40, 58, 177
Lions Gate, 176, 200
Lipsett, Arthur, 315n42
Little Theater, Rochester, 9
Liu, Lucy, 200
Lohman, Alison, 209, 222, 307n16, 308n28
Loi du cochon, Le (Canuel), 147
Loiselle, André, 178, 179, 180, 181, 184, 188,
    297n39, 301n39, 303n4; *Self Portraits*, 285
London, England, 65, 77, 103, 231, 264
Lonesome Dove, 126
Longfellow, Brenda, 143, 156, 289n7
Longfellow, Henry Wadsworth, 20
Long Goodbye, The (Altman), 280
Long Life, Happiness and Prosperity (Shum), 128,
    238
Longo, Robert: *Johnny Mnemonic*, 172, 196, 198,
    200
loser hero, 3, 39, 40–3, 141, 185, 202, 241; female,
    87–8; non-, 71; Quebecois, 178–9; queered, 56,
    71, 201, 262
Lost and Delirious (Pool), xiii, 160–2, 262
Louis 19, roi des ondes (Poulette), 101
Love Come Down (Virgo), 135, 248
Love & Human Remains (Arcand), 79, 97, 99–101,
    131, 165, 183, 297n39
Loving and Laughing (Sole), 177, 303n19
Low, Colin, 31; *City of Gold*, 31; *Universe*, 31
Lowenstein, Adam, 294n37
Lowry, Lynn, 48–9, 58
Lucas, George, ix, 59; *American Graffiti*, 233; *Star
    Wars*, 193
Luck (Wellington), 135
Lussier, Marc-André, 298n35
Lussier, Patrick: *My Bloody Valentine*, 186
Lusty, Terry, 252
Luxembourg, 160
L-Word, The, 132, 133, 143, 257. *See also directors of
    individual episodes*
Lynch, David: 145, 147; *Blue Velvet*, x, 189
Lynch, Paul, 185; *Hard Part Begins*, 185; *Humon-
    gous*, 185; *Prom Night*, 185; *Robocop* (TV), 185
Lynd, Laurie: *Queer as Folk*, 257
Lyu, Soo: *Rub & Tug*, 142

Ma, Yo Yo, 86, 87
MacGillivray, William, 157, 242, 243, 256, 311n47;
    Life Classes, 243–4; *Stations*, 157, 230

Machiavelli, Niccolò, 90; *Prince*, 90
MacIvor, Daniel, 141
MacKenzie, Scott, 23, 144
MacKinnon, Gilles: *Pure*, 131
MacLachlan, Kyle, 201, 264
Mad City (Costa-Gavras), 132
Maddin, Guy, xiii, xv, 3, 16, 267–83; aesthetics
    of deprivation, 16, 258, 272, 278; auteur, 125,
    218, 225, 267–83; on Canadian cinema, 315n42;
    career trajectory, 272, 286; childhood, 267, 271,
    276–9, 282; fan, 185, 269, 280; and Hollywood,
    268, 279–80, 282, 315n49; journalist, 268–9, 270,
    286; at the New York Film Festival, x; recep-
    tion, 83, 270, 281, 283, 314n14; sexuality in,
    257, 262, 268–70; showman, 270, 314n13; use
    of autobiography, 271–4, 277–8, 314n22; Win-
    nipegger, 185, 245, 267, 271, 273, 274–8, 315n49
Maddin, Guy, works of: *Archangel*, 275, 279, 281;
    Brand upon the Brain!, 270, 279, 314n25; *Care-
    ful*, x, 45, 270, 274, 275, 278, 279; *Child without
    Qualities*, 271, 278, 282; *Cowards Bend the Knee*,
    270–1, 279, 281; *Dead Father*, 279; *Dracula*, 267,
    279; *Dyke Master's Daughter*, 281; *Eye, Like a
    Strange Balloon*, 277; *From the Atelier Tovar*,
    269, 313n6; *Heart of the World*, 16, 273, 274, 279,
    282–4, 286–7, 315n49; journals, 268–9; *My Win-
    nipeg*, 270, 274, 276, 279, 280, 281, 282, 283, 284,
    314n20; *Saddest Music in the World*, 7, 268, 270,
    274, 281; *Sissy-Boy Slap-Party*, 269; *Tales from
    the Gimli Hospital*, 270, 274, 275, 278, 279, 281;
    Twilight of the Ice Nymphs, 7, 122, 267, 270, 273,
    274, 281, 313n5
Maddin, Herdis, 271, 314n20
Maelström (Villeneuve), 124, 146, 167, 221
Magder, Ted, 24
Makavejev, Dušan, 298n33; *Sweet Movie*, 116, 117,
    298n33
Makin, Kelly: *Queer as Folk*, 257
Making of 'Monsters,' The (Greyson), 258
Mâles, Les (Carle), 116
Malle, Louis: *Le Voleur*, 111
Maman est chez le coiffeur (Pool), 160, 285
Mambo Italiano (Gaudreault), 263, 264
Manchurian Candidate, The (Demme), 280
Manitoba, 232, 267
Mankiewicz, Francis, 296n34; *Les bons debarras*,
    36
Manners of Dying (Allen), 122, 123
Manojlovic, Miki, 158
Mansfield Park (Rozema), xi, 7, 80, 81, 83, 84, 85
Manson, Graeme, 199

maple syrup porno, 36, 40, 46, 57, 58, 91, 95, 111, 173, 177–8, 182; and art film, 114, 131; female protagonists in, 180

Map of the Human Heart (Ward), 251

Margaret's Museum (Ransen), 242

Marguerite Volant (Binamé), 121

Maria Chapdelaine (Carle), 27, 116

Marion Bridge (von Carolsfeld), 109, 130, 131

Maritime provinces, 186, 236, 243

Marker (Paizs), 245

Marleau, Louise, 154

Marquette, Gregory: *Dark Summer*, 132

Married Couple, A (King), 41

Married to the Mob (Demme), xi

Marshall, Bill, 34, 35, 38, 91, 96, 109, 110, 116, 121, 148, 150, 154, 156, 173–4, 235, 251, 262, 292n72, 303n7

martial arts movie, 195, 265

Martin, Alexis, 235

Martin, Megan, 191

Martin, Robert, 113, 297n18

Martineau, Richard, 297n42

Masala (Krishna), 248–9, 257, 264

Mask, The (Roffman), 46, 185

Massey, Raymond, 18

Massey Auditorium, Toronto, 114

Massey Report, 25, 28

Massicotte, Stephen, 191

Masterson, Richard, 305n1

Mathijs, Ernest, 50, 51, 57, 58, 61–2, 63, 66–7, 72, 293n15, 294n34, 294n52

Matrix, The (Wachowski), 18, 101

Matthau, Charles: *Grass Harp*, 132

Matthew, Suleka, 264

Maudite Galette, La (Arcand), 89, 90

Maurice Richard (Binamé), 119

Ma vie en cinémascope (Filiatrault), 119, 122, 124

Max (Meyjes), 131

Mayer, Louis B., 18

M. Butterfly (Cronenberg), 63, 66, 183

McCarthy, Sheila, 81, 82, 84, 87

McCarthy, Todd, 308n35

McCullough, Bruce, 140, 141

McDonald, Ann-Marie, 84

McDonald, Bruce, xiii, 230–3; actor, 231; auteur, 125, 126, 141, 238; *Dance Me Outside*, 251, 252–3; *Hard Core Logo*, 7, 85, 125–6, 129, 230–1, 233, 241; *Hard Core Logo 2*, 285; *Highway 61*, 11, 139, 231, 232–3, 235; *Picture Claire*, 128, 175; *Platinum*, 122; *Pontypool*, 184, 202, 237, 285; *Queer as Folk*, 257; *Roadkill*, 139, 231; *This Movie Is Broken*, 285; *Tracey Fragments*, 109; *Trigger*, 110, 126, 127, 131, 285; *Twitch City*, 128, 131, 139, 140–1; use of music, 231–3, 252–3, 257

McGrath, Doug, 185

McGregor, Gail, 56

McIntosh, David, 6

McKellar, Don, 14, 107, 125, 134, 138–43; actor, 75, 76, 128, 134, 142–3, 222, 231–2, 240, 271; auteur, 138, 140, 141, 238; growing up in Toronto, 59, 65; screenwriter, 134, 139, 143

McKellar, Don, films and screenplays of: *Blindness*, 142; *Childstar*, 139, 140, 142, 146; *Highway 61*, 11, 139, 231, 232–3, 235; *Last Night*, 114, 128, 129, 135, 139, 298n25; *Michael*, 83, 142; *Red Violin*, 130, 143; *Roadkill*, 139, 231; *Thirty Two Short Films about Glenn Gould*, 141–2, 258; *Twitch City*, 128, 131, 139, 140–1

McLaren, Norman, 29–31, 32; *Chairy Tale*, 30–1; *Neighbours*, 29–30, 31

McLuhan, Marshall, 55, 142, 193

McManus, Tom, 201, 219

McSorley, Tom, 297n39, 311n47; *Self Portraits*, 285

Meatballs (Reitman), 175, 285

Medeiros, Maria, 268, 270

mediascape: American, 233; global, 100, 142, 158, 168, 237, 265; North American, 250, 257; Quebecois, 27, 97, 100, 121

mediation, 27, 34, 97, 101, 105, 153, 160, 183, 195, 265. *See also under* Egoyan

Mehta, Deepa, xiii, 249, 257, 265–6; *Bollywood/ Hollywood*, 249–50, 265, 266; *Camilla*, 265; *Earth*, 265–6; *Fire*, xi, 262, 265–6; *Heaven on Earth*, 265, 266; *Republic of Love*, 265, 266; *Sam and Me*, 265, 266; *Water*, 265–6

Meirelles, Fernando: *Blindness*, 142; *City of God*, 169

Méliès, Georges, 30–1, 275; *Diable noir*, 31

Melnyk, George, 20, 22–3, 24, 28, 32, 39, 149, 155, 240, 257, 275, 313n104

melodrama, x, 20, 24, 32, 34, 41, 57, 104, 105, 233; English-Canadian, 207, 212, 216, 259, 266, 277, 279, 281, 283; film noir, 90; for children, 277; historical, 57, 173, 176, 212, 216, 260, 266, 284; Hollywood, 315n42; Italian, 263; jungle, 280, Native, 132; political, 285; Quebecois, 3, 26, 30, 46, 57, 119, 124, 148, 154, 173, 175, 197, 260, 284, 285; sexual, 270–1; silent, 281

Melville, Jean-Pierre, 9

Mémoires affectives, 123

Memphis, Tennessee, 232

Memphremagog, Lake, Quebec, 94

Ménard, Robert: *Cruising Bar*, 178–80, 181; *Cruising Bar 2*, 178, 179
Men with Brooms (Gross), 130, 242, 284
Mercure, Monique, 158, 176, *177*, 183
Merhige, E. Elias: *Shadow of the Vampire*, 280
Mérineau, Alexandre, 159
Métis, 34, 114, 117, 146, 251, 275
Metropolis (Lang), 282
Mettler, Peter, 258
Meyjes, Menno: *Max*, 131
Michael: Tuesdays & Thursdays (McKellar and Rozema), 83, 142
micro_scope, 240
Middleton, Greg, 238
Mighton, Tom: *Possible Worlds*, 201
Mihalka, George, 45, 175, 186–7; *La Florida*, 176, 179, 235; *My Bloody Valentine*, 45, 46, 176, 181, 183, 186–7; *Pinball Summer*, 181
Milano, Alyssa, 272, 279
Mile End, Montreal, 150, 157, 301n59
Miller, Andrew, 198, 202
Miller, April, 191
Millette, Jean-Louis, 168
Million Dollar Babies (Duguay), 197
Minh-Ha, Trinh T., 224
mining, 37–8, 41, 186, 242, 292n72
Minnelli, Vincente, 44
'minor' art forms, 16, 23. *See also under* cinema, Canadian
Miramax, x, 7–8, 84, 200
Mirandola, Pico della, 10
Mistry, Jimi, 264
modernist: alienation, 154, 156; architecture, 65, 73, 195, 200; art, 36, 55; cinema, ix, 36, 70–2, 153, 156, 159–60, 267–83; defiance of convention, 20, 278; loser, 268; memory, 214, 267, 277; theory, 23
modernity, 49; alternative, 275, 282–3; critique of, 210, 233; and music, 153; Quebecois, 116, 167–9, 234–5; and religion, 79; and tradition, 35, 210, 253–5; urban, 24, 35, 59–60, 241, 274–7, 280
Moderns, The (Rudolph), 113
Mohawk, 250
Molloy, Patricia, 191, 305n66
Mondo Canuck (Pevere and Dymond), 172–3
Monica la mitraille (Houle), 124
Monk, Katherine, 256, 304n17
Mon oncle Antoine (Jutra), 36–9, 96, 149, 168, 172, 176, 262, 264

Montand, Yves, 111
Montgomery, L.M., 134
Montmarquette, Yves, 150
Montreal, Quebec, xvi, 26, 34, 101, 164–5, 242, 262; anglophone, 39, 111, 118, 123, 240; demi-monde, 121, 124, 145, 159; film-makers and actors, 14, 39, 41, 79, 104, 110, 146, 154, 175, 194, 305n79; film-making, 19, 33, 57–8, 117, 153, 157, 166, 197–8, 238; homelessness, 99; Jewish, 35, 39–40, 43, 58, 158, 175; media industry, 40, 92, 98–9, 105, 144, 146–7, 176, 236, 237; metro, 97, 99, 122, 240; setting, 35–6, 39, 43, 48, 53, 59–60, 65, 73, 79, 81, 89, 94, 98–9, 150–1, 154, 155, 158, 159, 188, 194–5, 197, 235, 240, 263, 264, 301n42; stand-in location, 196, 237; theatre, 97. *See also names of individual buildings and sites*
Montréal, Université de, 93, 94
Montréal vu par …, 79, 89
Mont-Royal, Parc: cruising, 94; St Joseph's Oratory, 97, 98–9
Moonstruck (Jewison), 263
Moore, Julianne, 209, 223
Moore, Michael, 274
Moranis, Rick, 43, 172, 175; *Strange Brew*, 43, 175, 241, 285
Moreau, Jeanne, 159
Morin, Robert: *Windigo*, 251
Morris, Peter, 20, 24, 56, 59, 61, 63, 291n23
Mort d'un bûcheron, La (Carle), 116, 117, 235, 298n35
Mortensen, Viggo, 71, 295n82
Mother and Son (Gorky), 212, 222, 224
Motion Picture Association of America, 186
Motion Picture Production Code, 26, 270
Mourir à tue-tête (Poirier), 36
Mouvements du désir, 156–7, 230, 301n53
Moving Malcolm (Ratner), 238
Moyle, Allan, 202; *New Waterford Girl*, 242; *Pump up the Volume*, 201; *Xchange*, 107, 122, 201–2
MuchMusic, 228
Multicultural Act, Canadian, 246, 247
Munich (Spielberg), 107
Munro, Alice, 138
Munro, Stephen, 219
Murder by Decree (Clark), 113
Muriel (Resnais), 165
Murnau, F. W.: *Nosferatu*, 280, 282
Musée d'Art Contemporain, Montreal, 224
Museum of Mankind, London, 224
Museum of Modern Art, New York, 55

music, 4, 31, 81, 117–18, 119; business, 228, 231; blues, 232; cartoon, 277; classical and orchestral, 35, 70, 81, 85–6, 218–19, 224, 270, 282; country, 152–3, 263–4; DJ, 245, 247–8; folk, 40, 41, 140, 227, 244; Gaelic, 227, 244; garage band, 272–3; hybrid, 149, 152–3; oldies, 233; opera, 96, 163, 170, 211, 223–4; pop, 69–70, 85, 145, 158, 224, 228–9, 232–3, 252–3, 258, 263–4, 272–3; prodigy, 248; punk, 125–6, 230–1, 232, 241, 268; rap, 229, 245; rock, 58, 152, 166, 224, 231–3, 241, 251, 252, 263–4, 273, 285; video, 9, 85, 146, 147, 194, 282, 305n79; world, 152. *See also names of albums, artists, and songs*

musical: Bollywood, 175, 249, 250, 265; Broadway, 233; Canadian, 118, 258–61, 281; 'gay sci-fi AIDS,' 259; Hollywood, 18, 258, 281; 'naval,' 280

My American Cousin (Wilson), 40, 233, 262, 265

My Beautiful Laundrette (Frears), 8

My Big Fat Greek Wedding (Zwick), xi, 172

My Bloody Valentine (Lussier), 186

My Bloody Valentine (Mihalka), 45, 46, 176, 181, 183, 186–7

Myers, Mike, 5, 17, 50, 109, 172, 175

My Life without Me (Coixet), 138

My Own Private Idaho (Van Sant), 18

'Mystery' (Egoyan and Downie), 224

myth, national, 3; Canadian, 3–5, 19–20, 28, 182, 227, 236, 242; Quebecois, 26–7, 35, 38. *See also under* allegory

My Winnipeg (Maddin), 270, 274, 276, 279, 280, 281, 282, 283, 284, 314n20

Nadeau, Chantal, 301n40

Naked Lunch (Cronenberg), xi, 63, 66, 71, 72, 75, 177, 182–3, 258, 259

Nanook of the North (Flaherty), 5

Natali, Vincenzo, 138, 198–202, 285; storyboard artist, 198; *Cube*, 11, 192–3, 198–200, 201, 202; *Cypher*, 198, 200–1, 202; *Nothing*, 198, 200, 202; *Splice*, 198, 202; work in television, 200

National Arts Centre, Ottawa, 55

national cinema. *See* cinema, national

National Film Board of Canada, 3, 19, 22–3, 24–5, 27–35, 44, 146, 236, 290n6; censorship by, 30, 89, 91; English-Canadian film-makers, 33; l'équipe française, 31, 33–6, 40, 89–91, 146; film production, 20, 40, 41, 58, 93, 177, 236, 250–1; fifties, 5; and First Nations film-making, 33, 246, 250–1; online, 286; parody of, 39, 190; and

regional film-making, 245; Studio D of, 33; Unit B of, 31, 34

Nature of Nicholas (Erbach), 244, 245

Neale, Steve, 303n11

Needles and Opium (Lepage), 164

Neeson, Liam, 209, 223

Neighbours (McLaren), 29–30, 31

Nelson, B.J., 195

Nelvana, 142, 198

neo-noir, 175

Neon Rome, A, 231

Neuromancer (Gibson), 198

Newark, New Jersey, 196

New Best Friend (Clarke-Williams), 132

new Black cinema, 8, 247–8

Newell, Mike: *Four Weddings and a Funeral*, 166

Newfoundland, 197, 229, 236, 242; film-makers and actors, 157, 243; film-making, 310n18; setting, 157, 197, 228, 229, 242

New Line Cinema, 72

New Orleans, Louisiana, 232

New queer cinema. *See under* cinema, queer

New Waterford Girl (Moyle), 242

new wave. *See under* cinema, English-Canadian; cinema, French; cinema, Hollywood; cinema, Quebecois; Vancouver

New World Pictures, 58

New York City, ix–xi, 55, 87, 111, 170, 242; aquarium, 35; film-makers, 196; music, 231; setting, 35, 59, 87, 99, 101, 142, 216

New Yorker Films, ix

New York Film Festival. *See under* film festivals

New York Times, 284

Next of Kin (Egoyan), 6, 205, 206, 207

Niagara Falls, 19

Nicolaou, Cassandra: *Show Me*, 234

Nielsen, Leslie, 18

Night Magic (Furey), 118

Night of the Living Dead, The (Romero), 59

Nikita (Besson), 9, 290n19

Nikita (TV), 15, 107, 119, 121, 197, 290n19

Nô (Lepage), 163, 164, 165

Nobody Waved Goodbye (Owen), 40–1, 42, 262

noces de papier, Les (Brault), 36, 113

Nolan, Christopher: *Inception*, 133

Nolden, Michelle, 234

No More Monkeys Jumpin' on the Bed (Weber), 239

Northam, Jeremy, 200–1

North by Northwest (Hitchcock), 201

North End, Winnipeg, 245, 274

Nosferatu (Murnau), 280, 282

No Such Thing (Hartley), 135, 138

Not Another Teen Movie (Gallen), 132

Nothing (Natali), 198, 200, 202

Nova Scotia, 41–3, 186; film-makers and actors, 41; film-making, 242–3, 310n18; setting, 20, 41, 45, 242–4. *See also names of individual towns and sites*

Now & Forever (Clark), 128, 132

Nunavut, 236, 251, 286

O'Bannon, Don, 196; *Total Recall*, 194, 196

Obomsawin, Alanis, 251; *Kanehsatake*, 250–1

Obsession (De Palma), 113

October Crisis, 36, 60, 164, 165

Oh, Sandra, 14, 107, 125, 126; movies, 128, 129, *130*, 139, 234; television, 128, 129–30, 132; theatre, 133

O'Hara, Catherine, 175

Ojibway, 20, 234

Oka conflict, 250–1

Okanagan Valley, British Columbia, 220, 233

Oliver, Ron: *Queer as Folk*, 257

Olympia (Riefenstahl), 34

Olympic Stadium, Montreal, 81, 82, 105, 197

O'Mahony, John, 163

Omega Man, The (Sagal), 139

101 Dalmations, 277

One Magic Christmas (Borsos), 134

On est au coton (Arcand), 89–90, 91, 93

Ontario, 64, 117, 138, 231–2; northern, 231, 232; setting, 184, 214, 231–3, 242; small-town, 184, 185, 231–2; southern, 175. *See also names of towns and sites*

Ontario Film Development Corporation, 6, 84, 202, 236, 260

Ontario Motion Picture Board, 236

Ordet (Dreyer), 277

Ordres, Les (Brault), 36

Orsini, Inès, 104, 105

Orsini, Marina, 119

Ottawa, Ontario, 19, 33, 55, 83, 111; performers and film-makers, 129, 233

Ottinger, Ulrike, 258

Ouimet, Ernest, 19

Outer Limits, The, 126

Outrageous! (Benner), 45

Owen, Don, 40–1, 44, 233, 292n78; *Ernie Game*, 41; *Nobody Waved Goodbye*, 40–1, 42, 262

Oxford Museum of Modern Art, 224

Pacific new wave. *See* Vancouver: new wave

Page, Ellen, 109, 130, 133

Paizs, John, 185, 245; *Crime Wave*, 245, 253; *Kids in the Hall*, 245; *Marker*, 245; *Top of the Food Chain*, 245

Pallascio, Aubert, 261

Paradise Falls, 258

Paré, Jessica, xiii, 101

Paris, France, xi, 34, 95, 99, 103, 111, 117; architecture of, 59–60; émigré intellectuals in, 155; fashions from, 176; film-making, 166; 19th-century, 269; streets of, 159; underworld, 147, 148

Paris or Somewhere, 126

Parker, Molly, 14, 107, 125, 129; movies, 110, 126, *127*, 130–1, 262; television, 126, 131, 141

Parpart, Lee, 88, 296n16

Parrish, Steve, 195

Parti pris, 36

Parti Québécois. *See* Quebec: separatist

Passchendaele (Gross), 172, 284

Passion – A Letter in 16 mm (Rozema), 84

Passion de Jeanne d'Arc, La (Dreyer), 307n18

Pasternak, Beth, 219

Paul Tomkowicz (Kroitor), 28

Peary, Gerald, 114

Pellerin, Daniel, 219

Pendakur, Manjunath, 24

Peoples of Canada, 28

Perkins, Emily, 189

Perrault, Pierre, 34; *Pour la suite du monde*, 34, 38

Perron, Clément, 36

petite Aurore, La (Bigras), 25, 26, 32

Petrie, Doris, 194

Petrie, Sue Helen, 177

Petrowski, André, 146

Pet Shop Boys, 258

Pevere, Geoff, 57, 245, 289n3, 305n1; *Mondo Canuck*, 172–3

Phillips, William: *Foolproof*, 175

Phoenix, Arizona, 241

Phoolan Devi, 266

photography: commercial, 274; fashion, 97; reality effect of, 31 308n36; snapshot, 212. *See also under* art

Piano, The (Campion), 88, 211

Pichette, Jean-François, 156

Pickford, Mary, 18, 235

Picture Claire (McDonald), 128, 175

Pidgeon, Walter, 18

'Pied Piper of Hamelin, The' (Browning), 210

Pilon, Daniel, 116
Pin (Stern), 184
Pinball Summer (Mihalka), 181
Pink Floyd, 264; 'Great Gig in the Sky,' 152; 'Shine On You Crazy Diamond,' 152, 264
Pinsent, Gordon, 138
Pittman, Ken, 242
Planet of Junior Brown, The, 248
Planet of the Apes, The, 139
Platinum (McDonald), 122
Playboy of the Western World, The (Synge), 126
Plouffe, Les (Carle), 27
Plummer, Christopher, 18, 221
Plus 15, Calgary, 240
Podeswa, Jeremy, xi, 100, 183, 257; *Eclipse*, xi, 100; *Five Senses*, xi, 100, 122, 130; *L-Word*, 257; *Queer as Folk*, 257
Poe, Edgar Allan, 277
Poirier, Anne Claire, 155; *Mourir à tue-tête*, 36
Polanski, Roman: *Rosemary's Baby*, 59
policier, 145, 147, 149, 201
Polley, Sarah, 134–8, 143; actor, 75, 76, 129, 132, 134–8, 139, 141, 185, 202, 208, 220; auteur, 14, 107, 125; *Away from Her*, 32, 135, 138, 143; child actor, 134–5, *136*
Polygraphe, Le (film; Lepage), 163, 166–7
Polygraphe, Le (play; Lepage), 166–7
Polytechnique (Villeneuve), 285
Ponton, Yvan, 194
Pontypool (McDonald), 184, 202, 237, 285
Pool, Léa, xiii, 4, 14, 145, 148, 149, 153–62, 170, 183, 257; and advertising, 146; auteur, 79, 144, 154, 285, 301n48; early films, 153–6, 258; emotional intensity of, 32, 154, 156; in English, xiii, 122, 160–2, 258; exile, 154, 155; Jewish identity, 154, 301n44; lesbian film-maker, 160, 262; scriptwriter, 157; space and setting, 154, 156–7, 301n42; and Switzerland, 155, 157; use of autobiography, 155, 156, 157, 166
Pool, Léa, films of: *A corps perdu*, 155–6, 157; *Anne Trister*, 154; *Blue Butterfly*, 122, 160, 285; *demoiselle sauvage*, 155, 157; *dernière fugue*, 160; *Emporte-moi*, xii, 122, 124, 155, 156, 157–60, 169, 262, 263, 301n59; *La Femme de l'hôtel*, xii, 154; *Lost and Delirious*, xiii, 160–2, 262; *Maman est chez le coiffeur*, 160, 285; *Mouvements du désir*, 156–7, 230, 301n53; *Strass Café*, 154
Poon, Alice, 265
Poor Boy's Game (Virgo), 248
popular culture: American, 140, 155, 158, 203, 222, 232, 245, 268; and Canadians, 4, 11, 12, 105, 134, 138-9, 140–1, 142, 143, 171–203, 222, 228, 231, 243, 286–7; double nature of, 182; global, 6, 174, 228; and Native Canadians, 252–3; Quebecois, 26–7, 32, 46, 57, 91–2, 110–25, 173–4, 176–81, 194–8
Porky's (Clark), 47, 176, 181–2, 185, 285
pornography, 56, 72–3, 78, 97, 206, 244, 265, 269
Portal, Louise, 179
Portrait of Arshile, A (Egoyan), 212, 224
Possible Worlds (Lepage), xiii, 164, 165, 201
Possible Worlds (Mighton), 201
postmodern, 6, 93, 101, 213; allegory, 87; anomie, 207–8, 219, 279; art, 101; Canadian, 10–11, 100, 101; cinema, 145–8; genre blending, 173, 175, 249; 'lesbian,' 265; play, 148, 156, 165, 214, 278; 'prairie,' 245–6, 267–8; urban, *95*, 96–9, 148, 165, 167–9, 237, 239–40; theory, 23
Potts, Annie, 43
Poulette, Michel: *Louis 19, roi des ondes*, 101
Pouliot, Jean-François: *grande seduction*, 242
Pour la suite du monde (Brault and Perrault), 34, 38
Pouvoir intime (Simoneau), 174, 303n9
Power Plant Gallery, Toronto, 224, 270
Préparez vos mouchoirs (Blier), 117
Presner, Bob, 186, 296n34
Priestly, Jason, 229
Prince, The (Machiavelli), 90
Prince Edward Island, 134
Problem with Fear, A (Burns), 240
production and distribution companies, 303n14. *See also* Alliance; Astral; Atlantis; Canadian Broadcasting Company; CBS-television; Channel Four; Cinar; Cinépix; CTV; De Laurentiis; Disney; Feature Film Project; Fox-television; Halifax Film; HBO; Icon; Igloolik Isuma; Lions Gate; micro_scope; Miramax; National Film Board of Canada; Nelvana; New Line Cinema; New World Pictures; New Yorker Films; Rhombus Media; Salter Street; Showcase; Showtime; Telefilm Canada; Tri-Star; Warner Brothers; Winnipeg Film Collective
Prom Night (Lynch), 185, 192
Proteus (Greyson), 258
Proust, Marcel, 271, 272, 276
Psi Factor, 200
Psycho (Hitchcock), 184
Pudovkin, Vsevolod, 282
Pulp Fiction (Tarantino), 8
Pure (MacKinnon), 131

Pump up the Volume (Moyle), 201
Pynchon, Thomas, 54
Pyx, The (Hart), 188

Quandt, James, 282
quatre cents coups, Les (Truffaut), 37, 43, 158, 159, 273
Quay Brothers: 'Street of Crocodiles,' 278
Quebec: anglophones in, 4, 38, 39–40, 89–90, 118, 162; changing demographics of, 95–6, 100; childhood, 25, 26–7, 36–9, 149–53; election of 1970, 90; fifties, 25–8, 34–8, 61, 90, 96, 116, 165, 263; hybrid nature of, 4, 100, 110, 121; labour relations in, 37–8, 89, 90–1, 104; north country of, 26, 37, 116, 119, 145, 166, 220, 235; personifications of, 116–17, 124, 149; post-referendum, 144, 145, 156; separatist, 38, 39, 46, 90, 121, 148, 149, 155, 165, 174, 221, 227. *See also names of cities and sites*; cinema, Quebecois; coureur de bois; Duplessis, Maurice; Front de libération du Québec; mediascape: Quebecois; October Crisis; Quiet Revolution; Radio-Canada; *under specific topics*
Quebec Bridge, 167, 168, *169*
Quebec City, 26, 162; film-making, 166; setting, 167–8, *169*
Québec: Duplessis et après (Arcand), 90, 91
Quebecois cinema. *See* cinema, Quebecois
Queen West, Toronto, 225
Queer as Folk, 256, 257, 258. *See also directors of individual episodes*
queer cinema. *See* cinema, queer
Quidi Fidi, St John's, 229
Quiet Revolution, 10, 35–8, 90, 96, 110, 118, 121, 151, 158, 165, 168, 169, 178; icons of, 158; ideology of, 148, 174
'quota quickies.' *See under* cinema, Canadian

Rabid (Cronenberg), 54, 55, 56, 59–60, 61, 63, 65, 67, 68, 188
Radiant City (Burns), 239, 241
radio, 26, 27, 33, 158, 184, 237, 247–8, 279
Radio-Canada, 26, 119
radio serials. *See under* serials
Radner, Gilda, 175
Raffé, Alexandra, 84
Raffin, Deborah, 195
Ramones, The, 268, 272
Ramsay, Christine, 42, 150, 236
Ransen, Mort: *Margaret's Museum*, 242

rape-revenge drama, 89, 91
Raquetteurs, Les (Brault and Groulx), 34, 38
Rare Birds (Gunnarsson), 130, 242
Rashid, Ian Iqbal, 248; *Touch of Pink*, 248, 263, 264–5
Ratner, Benjamin, 238; *Moving Malcolm*, 238
Rats and Rabbits (Furey), 114
'Ravine House,' Toronto, 214
Ray, Christina, 191
Ray, Lisa, 250, 266
Rea, Stephen, 137
realism, 216; in art cinema, 219; Canadian, 185, 202, 246, 272; conventions of, 29, 272; 248, 252, 262, 264, 285–6; in genre cinema, 181, 188–9, 230; Hollywood, 188; in horror, 59, 183–92; linear structure of, 163; and theatricality, 185. *See also* documentary realism
Red (Carle), 116
Redbone: 'Come and Get Your Love,' 252
Redon, Odilon, 277
Red Riding Hood, 211
Red Violin, The (Girard and McKellar), *130*, 143
Reed, Oliver, 64
Reeves, Keanu, 18, 109, 196
Regina, Saskatchewan, 227, 230, 236
Règle du jeu, La (Renoir), 90
Reiniger, Lotte, 276, 277
Reitman, Ivan, 59, 172; *Animal House*, 182; *Cannibal Girls*, 177; *Ghostbusters*, 175; *Ghostbusters II*, 175; *Meatballs*, 175, 285; producer, 56, 58, 220; *Stripes*, 175
Réjeanne Padovani (Arcand), 89, 90, 91
religion: Calvinism, 79, 81; Catholicism, 27, 79, 97, 98, 158, 167, 220; Hinduism, 265, 313n125; Islam, 178; and postmodernity, 79, 96–9, 105–6
Rendall, Mark, 140
Rennie, Callum Keith, 14, 107, 125–9, 132, 298n25; movies, 75, 110, 114, 125–6, *127*, 128, 129, 130, 139, 231; television, 126, 128–9, 141
Reno, Ginette, 124, 149, 150
Renoir, Jean, ix, 9, 19, 62, 218; *Crime de Monsieur Lange*, 235; *Règle du jeu*, 90
Republic of Love, The (Mehta), 265, 266
Reservoir Dogs, 8
Resnais, Alain, 111, 164–5, 302n77; *L'année dernière à Marienbad*, 165; *La Guerre est finie*, 111; *Hiroshima, mon amour*, 164; *Muriel*, 165
Reynolds, Ryan, 18
Rhombus Media, 142
Rich, B. Ruby, 224

Rich, Buddy, 264

Richard, Maurice, 119

Richards, Denise, 269, 272

Richardson, Miranda, 77

Richings, Julian, 199

Richler, Mordecai, 39

Rideau Vert, 111

Riefenstahl, Leni, 34, 282; *Olympia*, 34

Riley, Michael, 200

Ring cycle (Lepage and Wagner), 170

Rioux, Geneviève, 81, 94, 179

Road, The (Hillcoat), 131

Roadkill (McDonald and McKellar), 139, 231

road movie, 15–16, 41–3, 185, 228–36, 241, 284; kidnapping, 234; Quebecois, 234–5

Road to Avonlea, The, 134, 135, *136*, *137*, 141, 185, 299n72

Road to Salina, 269

Roberge, Guy, 33

Robeval, Quebec, 260

Robi, Alys, 119, 124

Robocop (Lynch), 185

Robson, Mark: *Earthquake*, 113

Robson, Wayne, 199

Rocket, The. See *Maurice Richard*

Rodley, Chris, 56

Roffman, Julian, 184; *Bloody Brood*, 185; *The Mask*, 46, 185

Rogen, Seth, 109, 175

Roi de coeur, Le (de Broca), 111

Rollercoaster (Smith), 238, 257

Rolling Stone, 138

Rolling Stones, The, 264; 'Sympathy for the Devil,' 152, 264; 'You Can't Always Get What You Want,' 152

Romero, George, 59; *Night of the Living Dead*, 59

Romney, Jonathan, 164, 305n1, 306n2, 309n46

Rose, Bernard: *Anna Karenina*, 132

Rose, Gabrielle, 222

Rosemary's Baby (Polanski), 59

Rossellini, Isabella, 268–9, 270

Roth, Bobby: *Heartbreakers*, 118

Rouch, Jean, 34; *Chronique d'un été*, 34

Roue, La (Gance), 277

Rousseau, Stéphane, 103–4

Royal Bank Plaza, Toronto, 82

Royal Ontario Museum, Toronto, 258

Royal Winnipeg Ballet, 267

Rozema, Patricia, xiii, 79–88; allegory, 87; auteur, 14, 83, 100, 125, 174, 238, 258; Calvinism, 81; career trajectory, xi, 89, 100, 105–6, 285; embarrassment, 86–7; emotions in, 80–1, 85; extra, 258; fairy tales, 80; feminist, 79, 81, 88, 105; innocent protagonists, 81; lesbian film-maker, 79, 80, 88, 183, 257, 262; optimism, 81; and postmodernity, 96; and Quebecois cinema, 79; reception, 86, 88; scriptwriter, 83; space and setting, 81–3; use of video, 84, 257

Rozema, Patricia, works of: *Case of the Missing Mother*, 83, 296n5; *Desperanto*, 79, 81, 82, 87, 89; *Grey Gardens*, 83; *Happy Days*, 80, 81, 83, 86, 224; *Hunger*, 83; *In Treatment*, 83; *I've Heard the Mermaids Singing*, x, 7, 9, 14, 79, 80, 81, 82, 83–8, 244, 289n8, 296n6; *Kit Kittredge*, xi, 80, 81, 83, 85; *Mansfield Park*, xi, 7, 80, 81, 83, 84, 85; *Michael*, 83, 142; *Passion*, 84; 'Six Gestures,' 81, 83, 85–6, 87, 224; *Tell Me You Love Me*, 80, 83; *When Night Is Falling*, xi, 79, 80, 81, 82, 83, 85, 119, 121, 122, 139, 262, 265; *White Room*, 81, 82, 83, 84, 85, 87, 183, 185

Rub & Tug (Lyu), 142

Rubin, Jennifer, 197

Rude (Virgo), 247–8, 257

Rudolph, Alan, ix, 110, 113; *Choose Me*, 113; *Trouble in Mind*, 113; *The Moderns*, 113

rural: childhood, 262; conservatism, 22, 26, 242; masculinity, 91, 148; nature, 22, 99, 202, 308n36; sensibility, 114, 243; settings, 59, 65, 233; underclass, 93, 241, 243; /urban binary, 148, 231, 242, 262

Rushdie, Salman, 76; *Satanic Verses*, 249

Rutherford, Camilla, 101

Saddest Music in the World, The (Maddin), 7, 268, 270, 274, 281

Sagal, Boris: *Omega Man*, 139

Saïa, Louis: *Les Boys* franchise, 123, 178

Sainte-Cathérine, rue, Montreal, 94

Saint-Jean, Lac, Quebec, 260, 261

Saint Joan (Schaefer), 111

Salles, Walter, 228–9

Salome, 211, 307n22

Salome (Dieterle), 211, 307n22

Salomé (Strauss and Egoyan), 211, 223

Salter Street Films, 243

Sam and Me (Mehta), 265, 266

Sanders, Ronald, 62

Sandler, Adam, 108, 138

Sanjek, David, 293n24

Santa Cruz, California, 233

Saramago, José, 142

Sarossy, Paul, 92, 100, 219, 309n50

Saskatchewan, 20, 34, 126; film-makers and
	actors, 238; film-making, 128, 132

Saskatoon, Saskatchewan, 230

Sassen, Saskia, 237

Satanic Verses, The (Rushdie), 249

Satanism, 184, 188, 264

Saturday Night Live, 4–5, 175

Savage, Ann, 314n20

Scanner Cop (David), 192

Scanner Cop II (Barnett), 192

Scanners (Cronenberg), x, 32, 60, 63, 66, 68, 192,
	193, 194

Scanners II (Duguay), 32, 192, 193, 194–5, 197,
	198, 305n72

Scanners III (Duguay), 192, 193, 194, 195, 197

Schaefer, George: *Saint Joan*, 111

Scheider, Roy, 177

Schellenberg, Glenn, 258

Schellenburg, August, 228, 229

Scholte, Tom, 238

Schrader, Paul, 113

Schulz, Bruno, 272; 'Street of Crocodiles,' 278

Schwarzenegger, Arnold, 194, 255

science fiction; action, 193; Canadian, 15, 46, 192–
	203; English-Canadian, 53–6, 60, 73–6, 78, 122,
	139–40, 175, 178, 201; fifties, 54, 245; French,
	173; genre conventions, 48, 57, 108; horror,
	192–3, 196–7, 198–200, 280; mad scientist, 48,
	201; Quebecois, 175, 194–8; realism in, 32;
	seventies, 139, 202; silent, 282–3; television, 15,
	126, 175, 185, 200, 239; urban apocalypse,139.
	See also cyberpunk; future noir

Scoop, 119

Scorsese, Martin, 59, 294n63

Scott, A.O., 284

Scott, Jay, 118, 147

Scott, Ridley: *Alien*, 196; *Blade Runner*, 174, 197

Screamers (Duguay), 122, 193, 196–7, 200

Screamers: The Hunting (Wilson), 193, 197

SCTV, 43, 175

Secret Life of Words, The (Coixet), 138

Secrets of Chinatown (Bishop), 24

Secter, David: *Winter Kept Us Warm*, 53, 257

Seeger, Pete, 140

Séguin, Maurice, 96

Seizure (Stone), 59

Sekula, Andrzej: *Cube²*, 193, 200

Self Portraits (Loiselle and McSorley), 285

Selznick, Arna: *Care Bears Movie*, 172, 185

Sennett, Mack, 18

Senneville, Montreal, 195

Séraphin (Binamé), 26, 124, 173

Séraphin (Gury), 26–7

serial killer, 8, 118, 139, 183, 211, 231, 235

serials: movie, 248, 265, 269, 276; printed, 235;
	radio, 26–7; television, 27, 89, 119, 121

Seth, Roshan, 8

Seul ou avec des autres (Arcand and Héroux), 36

Seven Streams of the River Ota (Lepage), 163, 164

Sex, Lies, and Videotape (Soderbergh), 8, 9, 289n16

sexualities: childhood, 51–2, 251–2, 271, 314n17;
	contemporary, 80, 202, 238; eighties, 8–9, 93–5,
	100, 102, 178–82; female, 20–1, 110–18, 124,
	130–2, 153–6, 159, 188–91, 223, 243–4; fifties,
	53, 63; masculine, 121, 123, 126, 128, 147–8, 150,
	182, 228–30, 248, 269–70; mediated, 15, 54–5,
	72–5, 100, 104–5, 176–83, 252, 304n17; queer,
	31, 69–70, 97, 154–5, 256–66, 269; seventies,
	48–9, 91–2, 176–8; sixties, 41, 58.

Seyfried, Amanda, 209, 223

Shadow of the Vampire (Merhige), 280

Shake Hands with the Devil (Spottiswoode), 122,
	198

Shankar, Ravi, 31

Shareshian, Steven, xi

Shatner, William, 18, 123

Shattered, 128, 131

Shaviro, Steven, 69, 178, 180, 269

Shaw, Fiona, 86

Shaw, George Bernard, 111

Shawinigan, Quebec, 114

Shearer, Norma, 18, 19

Shebib, Don, 41–4, 233; *Between Friends*, 43; *Goin'
	Down the Road*, 41–3, 185, 186, 229–30, 241;
	Heartaches, 43

Shepperton Studios, London, 213, 220, 308n33

Sherbrooke, Quebec, 34

Sherman, Cindy: *Untitled Film Stills*, 189

Shilt, Randy: *And the Band Played On*, 258

'Shine On You Crazy Diamond' (Pink Floyd),
	152, 164

Shipman, Ernest, 20, 176

Shipman, Nell, 20–22, 176

Shipman, Susan, 219

Shivers (Cronenberg), 48–9, 54, 55, 56, 58, 59, 60,
	61, 65, 66, 68, 70, 74, 77, 171, 177–8, 187, 188–9,
	191, 198, 294n63

Shore, Howard, 70

Short, Martin, 175

Showcase, 256

Showtime, 128, 132, 256

Shum, Mina, xiii, 234, 238, 248; *Double Happiness*, 125, 126, 129, 234, 238, 247; *Drive, She Said*, 129, 234; *Long Life, Happiness and Prosperity*, 128, 238

Shusset, Ron: *Total Recall*, 194

Sidney Mines, Nova Scotia, 186

Siegel, Don: *Invasion of the Body Snatchers*, 280

Sight & Sound, 140

Signoret, Simone, 109

Silence of the Lambs, The (Demme), xi, 8

silent cinema. *See* cinema, silent

Silverman, Robert, 65, 75

Simmons, Rochelle, 232

Simoneau, Yves, 166; *Dans le ventre du dragon*, 174, 303n9; *Pouvoir intime*, 174, 303n9; *Yeux rouges*, 166, 173–4

Simons, Tony, 152

Sinclair, Iain, 73

Singleton, John: *Boyz n the Hood*, 8

Sirk, Douglas, 162; *Written on the Wind*, 315n42

Sissy-Boy Slap-Party (Maddin), 269

Sivak, Nancy, 238

'Six Gestures' (Rozema), 81, 83, 85–6, 87, 224

6th Day, The, 239

Skogland, Keri: *L-Word*, 257; *Queer as Folk*, 257

Slater, Christian, 131

Slings and Arrows (Wellington), 142

Smetanka, Andy, 276

Smith, Charles Martin: *Air Bud*, 172

Smith, Scott: *Falling Angels*, 128; *Rollercoaster*, 238, 257

Smiths, The, 258

Snider, Norman, 51

Snipes, Wesley, 197

Snow, Michael, 55, 275

Snyder, Zach: *Dawn of the Dead*, 134, 135, 137, 138

SODEC, 260, 310n18

Soderbergh, Steven, 9, 289n16; *Sex, Lies, and Videotape*, 8, 9, 289n16

Solaris (Tarkovsky), 193

Sole, John: *Loving and Laughing*, 177, 303n19

Something Wild (Demme), xi

Sonatine (Lanctôt), xii, 122

space, conceptions of, 11, 67–8

space and setting, 59–60; airport, 221, 222; bridge, 159, 167–9, 196; club, x, 93, 208, 213, 214, 229, 233, 269, 271, 308n34; confessional, 260; convent, 58; desert, 81, 122, 235; factory,

75, 274; house, 37, 59, 65, 77, 81, 83, 85, 90, 93, 94, 104, 140, 143, 151, 168, 202, 213, 214, 217, 232, 266, 277–8; laboratory, 53–4, 65, 67, 202; locker room, 271, 314n17; prison, 148, 198–200, 248, 260–1, 266; river, 34–5, 65, 77, 157, 195, 216, 264; road, 37, 40, 41–2, 65, 185, 228–34; stadium, 81, 82, 105, 197, 271, 273, 314n17; suburbia, 184, 189–91, 239, 311n33; train, 156–7, 230, 266, 277; underground, 147, 196–7, 201, 202, 240, 271, 276, 314n17; wilderness, 19–22, 32, 65, 148, 191–2, 234, 254; winter, 20, 22, 59, 64–5, 138, 192, 194–5, 200, 202, 215–16, 245, 254, 305n72. *See also* under specific cities and locations; Cronenberg, David; Egoyan, Atom; Pool, Léa; Rozema, Patricia

'Space Oddity' (Bowie), 152, 264

Spader, James, 72

Spaner, David, 24

Spanger, Bruce, 238

Spasms (Fruet), 185

Speaking Parts (Egoyan), 100, 183, 204, 206, 214, 219

special effects, 60, 63–4, 68–9, 77; digital, 64, 68–9, 75–6, 199, 200, 214; prosthetic, 60, 64, 68–9, 75–6, 181, 186, 187, 190, 199, 200, 259

spectatorship, 45, 50, 69, 98; alternative modes of, 25, 180–1, 184, 203, 237, 252, 264–5, 281; Canadian, 25, 109, 121, 181, 184, 187, 203, 237, 245; English-Canadian, 25, 118, 181; French, 198; and genre films, 174, 181, 184, 185, 200, 203, 269; Inuit, 251; lesbian, 265; Native, 252; Pacific Rim, 196, 198; Quebecois, 166, 181; queer, 122, 141, 264–5

Speed, 18

Spence, Paul, 241

Spencer-Nairn, Tara, 242

Spider (Cronenberg), 65, 72, 77

Spielberg, Steven, ix, 59; *Munich*, 107

Spier, Carol, 62

Splice (Natali), 198, 202

sports movie. *See* boxing; curling; hockey

Spottiswoode, Roger: *Shake Hands with the Devil*, 122, 198

Spry, Robin: *Suzanne*, 46

Stalker (Tarkovsky), 193

star discourse, 109–10, 117–19, 133, 141, 301n53

Stardom (Arcand), xii–xiii, 79, 93, 97, 99, 100–1, 165

Stargate SG-1, 15, 239

Star Wars (Lucas), 193

Stations (MacGillivray), 157, 230
Steele, Barbara, 58
'Steenbeckett' (Egoyan), 224
Stereo (Cronenberg), 53–4, 55, 59, 193, 257
Stern, Sandor: *Pin*, 184
St John's, Newfoundland, 157, 243
St Joseph's Oratory. *See* Mont-Royal, Parc
St Lawrence River, 34, 36, 242
Stoker, Bram: *Dracula*, 267
Stone, Oliver: *Seizure*, 59
Stopkewich, Lynn, xiii, 22, 238, 274; *Kissed*, 130,
   131, 176–7, 183, 187, 238, 257, 262; *Suspicious
   River*, 126, 128, 238
Strada, La (Fellini), 78
Strange Brew (Moranis and Thomas), 43, 175, 241,
   285
Strange Illusion (Ulmer), 315n42
Strass Café (Pool), 154
Strauss, Richard: *Salomé*, 211, 223
Straw, Will, 184, 231, 315n49
Street of Crocodiles (Quay), 278
'Street of Crocodiles' (Schulz), 278
Stripes (Reitman), 175
Stryker (Gonick), 245–6
Stursberg, Richard, 7, 225, 285, 309n40
Subtitles (Egoyan and Balfour), 224–5
Suburbanators, The (Burns), 239
Subway (Besson), 147
Sudbury, Ontario, 43, 231
Sullivan, Brett: *Ginger Snaps: Unleashed*, 191–2,
   305n66
Sundance Film Festival. *See under* film festivals
Sunshine (Szabo), 130
surrealism, 14, 269, 272, 273, 275, 281
Surrogate, The (Carmody), 118
Suspicious River (Stopkewich), 126, 128, 238
Sutherland, Donald, 18
Sutherland, Kiefer, 109
Suzanne (Spry), 46
Svatek, Peter: *Bleeders*, 185
Sviridov, Gyorgy, 282
Swashbuckler (Goldstone), 113
Sweeney, Bruce, xiii, 131, 238, 239; *Last Wedding*,
   131, 238
Sweet Country (Kakogiannis), 118
Sweet Hereafter, The (Banks), xi, 208, 217, 307n17,
   309n39
Sweet Hereafter, The (Egoyan), xi, xii, 12, 135,
   138, 204, 205, 207–8, 209–10, 213, 214, 215–16,
   217, 218, 219–20, 222, 223, 224, 289n15, 306n6,
   306n13, 307n17, 307n20, 309n39

Sweet Movie (Makavejev), 116, 117, 298n33
Sweet Substitute (Kent), 41
Swingtown, 130
Swinton, Tilda, xiii, 201
Switzerland, 153, 157, 158
Swollen Members, 229
'Sympathy for the Devil' (Rolling Stones), 152,
   264
Synge, J. M.: *Playboy of the Western World*, 126

Take One, 195, 197
Tales from the Gimli Hospital (Maddin), 270, 274,
   275, 278, 279, 281
Tarantino, Quentin, 8, 268, 273; *Pulp Fiction*, 8;
   Reservoir Dogs, 8
Tarkovsky, Andrei: *Solaris*, 193; *Stalker*, 193
Tate, Lorenz, 248
Tati, Jacques, 9
Taubin, Amy, 78, 114
tax-shelter years. *See under* cinema, Canadian
Taylor, Aaron, 185, 203
Tcherkassky, Peter, 269
technology: and the body, 62, 63–6, , 68–70, 72–6,
   183, 193, 201; and change, 281–2; digital, 12,
   68–70, 164, 237, 286; and globalization, 235,
   244; Western, 5. *See also* Egoyan, Atom: mediation; mediation; sexualities: mediated
Tejada-Flores, Miguel, 196
Telefilm Canada, xiii, 44, 46, 84, 134, 175, 202, 260,
   292n100; as Canadian Film Development Corporation, 6, 33, 46, 55, 56, 58, 111, 187, 236; 'The
   Math,' xiii, xvi, 6–7, 138, 225, 228, 285, 309n40
television: American, 14, 111, 125–6, 129, 131,
   140, 146, 147, 195, 197, 223, 247; cable, 8, 9, 11,
   46, 78, 80, 83, 131, 142, 171–2, 243, 254, 256,
   280; Canadian, 14, 15, 31, 39, 41, 43, 89, 107,
   125, 126, 206, 211, 223, 237, 239, 243–4, 257,
   290n18; Canadian cinema on, 278; daytime,
   272; English, 80, 217; English-Canadian, 89, 91,
   122, 128, 134, 140–1, 142, 146, 175, 185, 197, 223,
   243, 245, 256, 267, 285; in the fifties, 211, 218,
   307n27; in Nunavut, 251; Quebecois, 89, 99,
   119, 121, 123, 124, 160, 179; queer, 122, 132, 141,
   256, 257; reality, 272; Vancouver-produced, 15,
   238, 257. *See also names of producers and distributors*; serials, television
Tell Me You Love Me (Rozema), 80, 83
Tenerife, Spain, 81
Terminator series, 193
Terminator 2, 303n2
Testa, Bart, 56

Tête de Normande St.-Onge, La (Carle), 116
Thames River, 65, 77
Thetford Mines, Quebec, 37
Thieriot, Max, 209
Thiessen, Randy, 181, 182
Thirty Two Short Films about Glenn Gould (Girard and McKellar), 141–2, 258
This Movie Is Broken (McDonald), 285
Thomas, Dave, 43, 175; *Strange Brew*, 43, 175, 241, 285
Thomas, Kristin Scott, 165
thriller, 174, 198, 203, 224; action, 197–8; erotic, 202, 218, 223; espionage, 198, 200, 280; science fiction, 201; serial, 173; slasher, 45, 184, 186
Thunder Bay, Ontario, 232
Tightrope (Eastwood), 108, 113
Till, Eric: *Duct Tape Forever*, 285
Time Cop (Hyams), 126
Titanic, 173, 303n2
Tofino, British Columbia, 228
Toles, George, 150, 152, 275, 314n31
Top of the Food Chain (Paizs), 245
Toronto, Ontario: film-makers and actors, x, 18, 40, 41, 50–1, 62, 72, 75, 79, 131, 134, 153, 166, 175, 186, 198, 221, 252, 258; film-making, 33, 53, 55, 131, 198, 200, 225–6, 233, 238, 245; housing project, 247–8; media industry, 99, 142, 144, 147, 174, 225–6, 228–9, 236, 237, 243, 256; multiculturalism, 78; setting, 41–3, 51, 59–60, 64–5, 72–3, 75, 82, 147, 184, 186, 214, 223, 247–8, 250, 264, 266; sexual repression, 58, 264–5; stand-in location, xi, 172, 196, 213, 237. *See also names of individual buildings and sites*
Toronto, University of, 53, 55, 204
Toronto Festival of Festivals. *See* film festivals: Toronto International Film Festival
Toronto International Film Festival. *See under* film festivals
Toronto new wave. *See* cinema, English-Canadian: eighties new wave of
Torvill and Dean, 86
Total Recall (O'Bannon, Shusset, and Verhoeven), 194
Touch of Mink, A, 264
Touch of Pink, A (Rashid), 248, 263, 264–5
Tougas, Marie-Soleil, 145
Tracey Fragments, The (McDonald), 109
Trailer Park Boys: The Movie (Clattenburg), 285
Transfer (Cronenberg), 53
transnational: corporations, 11; culture, 133, 245–6, 248, 253, 264; desire, 156; music, 152,

264. *See also under* cinema, world; identity; technology
Tremblay, Johanne Marie, 105, 155–6
32 août sur terre, Un (Villeneuve), 146, 235
Trevor, William, 220; *Felicia's Journey*, 208–9, 211, 217–18, 220
Trigger (McDonald), 110, 126, *127*, 131, 285
Tri-Star, 196
'troubled youth' films, 40
Trouble in Mind (Rudolph), 113
Trudeau, Pierre, 148
Truffaut, François, 43, 146; *Argent de poche*, 43; *quatre cent coups*, 37, 43, 158, 159, 273
Trujillo, Raoul, 194
Truman Show, The (Weir), 101
Tschofen, Monique, 167, 305n1
Tulasne, Patricia, 157
Turbulence des fluides, La (Briand), 113–14
Turgeon, Marthe, 154
Turpin, André, xi, xiii, 123, 147, 164, 221, 296n34; cinematographer, 142, 146; *Crabe dans la tête*, 146
Turton, Kett, 234
24 (TV), 132
24 Images, 123
Twilight of the Ice Nymphs (Maddin), 7, 122, 267, 270, 273, 274, 281, 313n5
Twilight Zone, The (Egoyan), 223
Twitch City (McDonald and McKellar), 128, 131, 139, 140–1
2001: A Space Odyssey (Kubrick), 193

Ulmer, Edgar: *Detour*, 314n20; *Strange Illusion*, 315n42
Uncut (Greyson), 258
Undercover Brother, 269
Unforgettable (Dahl), 126
Unger, Deborah Kara, 72, 131
Unidentified Human Remains and the True Nature of Love (Fraser), 97, 99, 100, 101
Union Nationale, 26
Universe (Low and Kroitor), 31
Unnatural & Accidental (Bessai), 128
Untitled Film Stills (Sherman), 189
Urinal (Greyson), 258
Urquhart, Peter, 46, 292n100

Valérie (Héroux), 36, 58, 111, 177, 178
Vallée, Jean-Marc: *C.R.A.Z.Y.*, xi, 152–3, 263–4; use of music, 152–3
Vampire Diaries, The, 132

vampire movie, 49, 61, 183, 267, 280, 282
Van, Armenia, 212, 216
Vanasse, Karine, 27, 124, 158
Vancouver, British Columbia, 184, 193, 230;
    Chinatown in, 24; film-makers and actors, 41,
    131, 175, 238, 242; film-making, 233, 236, 238–9,
    311n33; First Nations in, 128; media industry,
    24, 126, 131, 192, 239, 243, 257; music in, 126,
    227; new wave, 233, 236, 238–9; Pacific Asians
    in, 247; setting, 24, 184, 230, 238, 239. *See also*
    names of individual buildings and sites; under
    television
van Palleske, Heidi, 69
Van Sant, Gus: *My Own Private Idaho*, 18
Varda, Agnès, 9
Vardalos, Nia, 172
Varga, Darrell, 141, 235, 254, 315n49
Variety, 138, 178, 193, 201, 261, 308n35
Vaseline, 260
Vatnsdal, Caelum, 46, 47, 56, 64, 171, 185, 186,
    314n14
Vega, Paz, 108
Venice Biennale, 224
Venice Film Festival. *See under* films festivals
Vent de Wyoming, Le (Forcier), 235
Verhoeven, Paul: *Total Recall*, 194
Véronneau, Pierre, 174
Vertigo (Hitchcock), 113, 278
Vertov, Dziga, 282
Victoria, British Columbia, 24, 220, 227
video, 84–5, 97, 156, 172, 195, 244, 251, 254, 296n8.
    See also under Egoyan, Atom
Videodrome (Cronenberg), x–xi, 54, 62, 63, 65, 66,
    68, 71, 75, 77, 78, 187, 193, 194, 195, 258
video games, 75–6, 200
vieux pays où Rimbaud est mort, Le (Lefebvre), 36
Village Voice, 268, 270, 284
Villeneuve, Denis, xi, xiii, 123, 146, 147, 164, 221,
    296n34; *Incendies*, 123, 285; *Maelström*, 124, 146,
    221; *Polytechnique*, 285; *32 août sur terre*, 146,
    235
Viol d'une jeune fille douce, Le (Carle), 116
Virgil, 3
Virgo, Clement, xiii, 138, 247–8; *Lie with Me*, 248;
    Love Come Down, 135, 248; *L-Word*, 257; *Planet
    of Junior Brown*, 248; *Poor Boy's Game*, 248; *Rude*,
    247–8, 257
Viva Communications, 144
Vivre sa vie (Godard), 158, 159, 307n18
Voïta, Michel, 155

Voleur, Le (Malle), 111
von Carolsfeld, Wiebke: *Marion Bridge*, 130, 131
von Praunheim, Rosa, 258
vraie nature de Bernadette, La (Carle), 116
Vrana, Vlasta, 194

Wachowski, Andy and Larry: *Matrix*, 18, 101
Wagner, Richard, 170; *Die Walküre*, 224
Waiting for Twilight (Gonick), 313n1
Waits, Tom, 152
Walküre, Die (Wagner and Egoyan), 224
Walton, Karen, 191; *Ginger Snaps*, 32, 184, 189–92,
    193, 198, 200, 257, 262, 305n66
Wang, Wayne: *Center of the World*, 130
Ward, Vincent: *Map of the Human Heart*, 251
war movie, 172, 275, 279, 280, 281, 284
Warner, Jack, 18
Warner Brothers, 223
Warrendale (King), 41
Water (Mehta), 265–6
Watts, Naomi, 71
Waugh, Thomas, 29, 256–7, 262
waydowntown (Burns), 240
Weaver, David: *Century Hotel*, 132
Webb, Lewis: *Good Shepherd*, 131
Weber, Ross, 238; *No More Monkeys*, 239
Wedding in White (Fruet), 185
Weinstein, Harvey, 7, 84
Weir, Peter: *Green Card*, 108; *Truman Show*, 101
Weller, Peter, 122, 196, 197
Wellington, Peter: *I Love a Man in a Uniform*, 257;
    Luck, 135; *Queer as Folk*, 257; *Slings and Arrows*,
    142
Wells, Audrey: *Guinevere*, 135, 137
Wenders, Wim, 138, 145, 147
werewolf movie, 183, 189–92
western: revisionist, 250; spaghetti, 175
Westgate, Murray, 194
Wheeler, Anne, 238; *Better Than Chocolate*, 238,
    262
When Night Is Falling (Rozema), xi, 79, 80, 81, 82,
    83, 85, 119, 121, 122, 139, 262, 265
When Tomorrow Dies (Kent), 41
Where the Truth Lies (Egoyan), 204, 209, 211, 213,
    214, 218, 222, 223, 225, 307n16, 308n33, 308n35,
    309n40
Where the Truth Lies (Holmes), 209
White, Ed, 282
White, Jerry, 250, 311n33
'White Rabbit,' 308n28

White Room (Rozema), 81, 82, 83, 84, 85, 87, 183, 185

Wicker Man, The (LaBute), 131

Wieland, Joyce, 55

Wilde, Oscar, 269

Wildman, John, 323

Wilkening, Catherine, 146

Williams, Tennessee: *Grass Harp*, 132

Wilson, Emma, 205, 305n1, 309n46

Wilson, Erin Cressida, 214

Wilson, Sandy, 233; *American Boyfriends*, 233; *My American Cousin*, 40, 233, 262, 265

Wilson, Sheldon: *Screamers: The Hunting*, 193, 197

Windigo (Morin), 251

Winnipeg, 16, 28, 236; film club, 269; film-makers, 46, 171, 185, 245–6, 267–83; film-making, 236, 244–6, 248, 267–83; history, 267, 271, 274–5; industrial sites of, 274; in the 1920s, 267, 274; music in, 227; setting, 245–6, 273

Winnipeg Arena, 271

Winnipeg Film Group, 185, 236, 244–6, 253, 258, 273, 286

Wint, Maurice Dean, 198

Winterbottom, Michael, 130, 138; *Claim*, 135; *Wonderland*, 130

Winter Garden Theatre, Toronto, 270

Winter Kept Us Warm (Secter), 53, 257

Winter Tan, A (Burroughs), 298n22

Wise, Wyndham, 293n20

Wonderland (Winterbottom), 130

Woo, John, 175

Wood, Robin, 244

Woods, James, 194

world cinema. *See* cinema, world

Worsely, Gump, 271

Wray, Fay, 18

Wright, Tracy, 141

Written on the Wind (Sirk), 315n42

Xchange (Moyle), 107, 122, 201–2

X-Files, The, 15, 126, 129, 239

Yesterday (Kent), 46

Yeux rouges, Les (Simoneau), 166

'You Can't Always Get What You Want' (Rolling Stones), 152

Young, Aden, 252

Young Americans (Dowse), 241

Yo Yo Ma: Inspired by Bach, 81, 83, 85–6, 87, 224

Zero Patience (Greyson), 258–60, 261, 264

Žižek, Slavoj, 224

zombie movie, 48–9, 59, 60, 65, 138, 183, 285

Zoo, la nuit, Un (Lauzon), xii, 100, 145, 147–8, 149, 155, 177

Zwick, Joel: *My Big Fat Greek Wedding*, xi, 172